DECISION IN
THE UKRAINE

The Stackpole Military History Series

THE AMERICAN CIVIL WAR
Cavalry Raids of the Civil War
Ghost, Thunderbolt, and Wizard
In the Lion's Mouth
Pickett's Charge
Witness to Gettysburg

WORLD WAR I
Doughboy War

WORLD WAR II
After D-Day
Airborne Combat
Armor Battles of the Waffen-SS, 1943–45
Armoured Guardsmen
Army of the West
Arnhem 1944
Australian Commandos
The B-24 in China
Backwater War
The Battle of France
The Battle of Sicily
Battle of the Bulge, Vol. 1
Battle of the Bulge, Vol. 2
Beyond the Beachhead
Beyond Stalingrad
The Black Bull
Blitzkrieg Unleashed
Blossoming Silk against the Rising Sun
Bodenplatte
The Brandenburger Commandos
The Brigade
Bringing the Thunder
The Canadian Army and the Normandy Campaign
Coast Watching in World War II
Colossal Cracks
Condor
A Dangerous Assignment
D-Day Bombers
D-Day Deception
D-Day to Berlin
Decision in the Ukraine
Destination Normandy
Dive Bomber!
A Drop Too Many
Eagles of the Third Reich
The Early Battles of Eighth Army
Eastern Front Combat
Europe in Flames
Exit Rommel
The Face of Courage
Fist from the Sky
Flying American Combat Aircraft of World War II
For Europe
Forging the Thunderbolt
For the Homeland

Fortress France
The German Defeat in the East, 1944–45
German Order of Battle, Vol. 1
German Order of Battle, Vol. 2
German Order of Battle, Vol. 3
The Germans in Normandy
Germany's Panzer Arm in World War II
GI Ingenuity
Goodwood
The Great Ships
Grenadiers
Guns against the Reich
Hitler's Nemesis
Hold the Westwall
Infantry Aces
In the Fire of the Eastern Front
Iron Arm
Iron Knights
Japanese Army Fighter Aces
JG 26 Luftwaffe Fighter Wing War Diary, Vol. 1
JG 26 Luftwaffe Fighter Wing War Diary, Vol. 2
Kampfgruppe Peiper at the Battle of the Bulge
The Key to the Bulge
Knight's Cross Panzers
Kursk
Luftwaffe Aces
Luftwaffe Fighter Ace
Luftwaffe Fighter-Bombers over Britain
Luftwaffe Fighters and Bombers
Massacre at Tobruk
Mechanized Juggernaut or Military Anachronism?
Messerschmitts over Sicily
Michael Wittmann, Vol. 1
Michael Wittmann, Vol. 2
Mission 376
Mountain Warriors
The Nazi Rocketeers
Night Flyer / Mosquito Pathfinder
No Holding Back
On the Canal
Operation Mercury
Packs On!
Panzer Aces
Panzer Aces II
Panzer Aces III
Panzer Commanders of the Western Front
Panzergrenadier Aces
Panzer Gunner
The Panzer Legions
Panzers in Normandy
Panzers in Winter
Panzer Wedge

The Path to Blitzkrieg
Penalty Strike
Poland Betrayed
Red Road from Stalingrad
Red Star under the Baltic
Retreat to the Reich
Rommel's Desert Commanders
Rommel's Desert War
Rommel's Lieutenants
The Savage Sky
Ship-Busters
The Siege of Küstrin
The Siegfried Line
A Soldier in the Cockpit
Soviet Blitzkrieg
Stalin's Keys to Victory
Surviving Bataan and Beyond
T-34 in Action
Tank Tactics
Tigers in the Mud
Triumphant Fox
The 12th SS, Vol. 1
The 12th SS, Vol. 2
Twilight of the Gods
Typhoon Attack
The War against Rommel's Supply Lines
War in the Aegean
War of the White Death
Winter Storm
Wolfpack Warriors
Zhukov at the Oder

THE COLD WAR / VIETNAM
Cyclops in the Jungle
Expendable Warriors
Fighting in Vietnam
Flying American Combat Aircraft: The Cold War
Here There Are Tigers
Land with No Sun
MiGs over North Vietnam
Phantom Reflections
Street without Joy
Through the Valley
Two One Pony

WARS OF AFRICA AND THE MIDDLE EAST
Never-Ending Conflict
The Rhodesian War

GENERAL MILITARY HISTORY
Carriers in Combat
Cavalry from Hoof to Track
Desert Battles
Guerrilla Warfare
Ranger Dawn
Sieges
The Spartan Army

DECISION IN THE UKRAINE

German Panzer Operations
on the Eastern Front, Summer 1943

George M. Nipe Jr.

STACKPOLE
BOOKS

Copyright © 1996 by J. J. Fedorowicz Publishing, Inc.

Published in paperback in 2012 by
STACKPOLE BOOKS
5067 Ritter Road
Mechanicsburg, PA 17055
www.stackpolebooks.com

Originally published by J. J. Fedorowicz Publishing in 1996. This edition published by arrangement with J. J. Fedorowicz Publishing. All rights reserved, including the right to reproduce this book or portions thereof in any form or by any means, electronic or mechanical, including photocopying, recording, or by any information storage and retrieval system, without permission in writing from the publisher. All inquiries should be addressed to J. J. Fedorowicz Publishing, 104 Browning Boulevard, Winnipeg, Manitoba, Canada R3K 0L7.

Cover design by Tracy Patterson

Printed in the United States of America

10 9 8 7 6 5 4 3 2 1

Library of Congress Cataloging-in-Publication Data

Nipe, George M.
  Decision in the Ukraine : German Panzer operations on the Eastern Front, summer 1943 / George M. Nipe, Jr.
     p. cm. — (Stackpole military history series)
  Originally published: Winnipeg, Man., Canada : J.J. Fedorowicz Pub., c1996.
  Includes bibliographical references and index.
  ISBN 978-0-8117-1162-3
  1. World War, 1939–1945—Campaigns—Ukraine. 2. Germany. Heer. Panzer-Korps, III. 3. Waffen-SS. Panzer-Division "Das Reich", 2. I. Title.
  D764.7.U5N57 2012
  940.54'2177—dc23
                                                            2012012222

Contents

	List of Maps vii
	Preface ix
	Introduction xiii
	Terminology and Abbreviations xxv
Chapter 1	Heeresgruppe Süd and Armee-Abteilung Hollidt: Retreat and Recovery in the Ukraine 1
Chapter 2	From Prochorovka to the Mius: III. Panzerkorps and II. SS-Panzerkorps 19
Chapter 3	6. Armee Stands Fast 95
Chapter 4	A Strategy of Deception 169
Chapter 5	6. Armee Strikes Back 183
Chapter 6	The First Day 201
Chapter 7	Deadlock 237
Chapter 8	The Decisive Day: 1 August 267
Chapter 9	The Destruction of the Bridgehead 321
Chapter 10	The Battles for Bogodukhov 337
Chapter 11	The Counterattack of III. Panzerkorps 373
Chapter 12	Aftermath: 6. Armee Retreats from the Mius 441
Chapter 13	Conclusions and Review 473
Appendix I	A Soviet Tank Army as Established during Early 1943 505
Appendix II	Typical Organization of Soviet Tank Corps in the Summer of 1943 507
Appendix III	Tank Strength of II. SS-Panzerkorps during the Battle of Kursk 509
Appendix IV	Order of Battle of III. Panzerkorps, August 1943 . . 511
Appendix V	Organization of 3. SS-Panzer-Division *Totenkopf* in the Summer of 1943 513
Appendix VI	Soviet Order of Battle for Operation "Rumyantsev" 515
Appendix VII	Waffen SS Ranks and U.S. Army Equivalent Ranks 517
	Notes 519
	Bibliography 533
	Acknowledgments 539
	Index 541

List of Maps

Operation "Citadel." 27
II. SS-Panzerkorps, 11 July 1943. 33
Situation on 11 July 1943. 38
6. Armee, July 1943. 97
The counterattack of 16. Panzergrenadier-Division,
  morning of 18 July 1943. 118
The failure of the counterattack of 16. Panzergrenadier-Division. . . 122
The counterattack of XXIV. Panzerkorps, 19 July 1943. 126
The 13th Guards Rifle Corps and the 2nd Guards
  Mechanized Corps, 20 July 1943. 135
6. Armee scores a critical defensive success, 22 July 1943. 144
The situation on the Mius, 29 July 1943. 146
The counterattack of 6. Armee, 30 July 1943. 203
The counterattack of II. SS-Panzerkorps, 31 July 1943. 239
The decisive day, 1 August 1943. 269
The situation in the Kharkov-Belgorod area, 2 August 1943. ... 339
Operation "Rumyantsev," 8 August 1943. 343
Bogodukhov area, 9 August 1943. 349
1st Tank Army advances, 10–11 August 1943. 351
The counterattack of III. Panzerkorps, morning of
  11 August 1943. 368
III. Panzerkorps, afternoon of 11 August 1943. 371
The counterattack of the III. Panzerkorps, morning of
  12 August 1943. 384
1st Tank Army is driven back, 12 August 1943. 388
III. Panzerkorps prepares to attack, 13–14 August 1943. 395
III. Panzerkorps, afternoon of 14 August 1943. 400
III. Panzerkorps, 15 August 1943. 403
Totenkopf, 16 August 1943. 405
Totenkopf and *Das Reich* assault the Merla, 17 August 1943. 421
III. Panzerkorps bridgeheads on the Merla, 18 August 1943. ... 425
Totenkopf crosses the Merla. 432

Preface

There were three great summer offensive campaigns mounted by the Germans during the Russo-German War. The first began in June of 1941 and culminated in the drive to capture Moscow, which came to a halt in December of that year in the face of winter conditions, declining German strength and Soviet counterattacks. In the following year, the 1942 offensive ended in the debacle of Stalingrad. The third and last great German summer offensive was known as Operation "Citadel" and took place in July 1943. After "Citadel" failed, the Russians launched a series of massive counterattacks all along the front, the most important of which were in southern Ukraine. The overwhelming strength of the Russian tank and infantry armies shattered the German lines. Attacks by hundreds of Soviet tanks followed massive artillery preparations and overran and destroyed whole divisions within a matter of days. The initial breakthroughs quickly resulted in the loss of Belgorod, and by the third week of August, after weeks of bitter fighting, the Germans abandoned Kharkov also.

The Germans slowly retreated towards the Dnepr River, no longer strong enough to stop the relentless advance of the Soviet army. The casualties and weapon losses suffered by Heeresgruppe Süd (Army Group South) during and immediately after "Citadel" resulted in the eventual loss of of the entire region of southern and eastern Ukraine, a setback from which the Germans never recovered. The failure of the last great Eastern Front German offensive, during the summer of 1943, meant unavoidable defeat for Germany in World War II. It can be debated as to whether the Germans actually still had any remaining chance of winning the war by July of 1943. Some authors and former German officers alike believe that the war was lost at Stalingrad or even earlier, at Moscow. However, there can no doubt whatsoever that following the conclusion of Operation "Citadel," Germany had absolutely no chance of reversing the Russian tide that eventually swept its shattered armies into the ruins of Germany.

This book was written with three main objectives. The first of these is to study the operations of II. SS-Panzerkorps and III. Panzerkorps during three important battles that took place in southern Ukraine in the Heeresgruppe Süd sector from 5 July 1943 through August of that same year. The three battles are the 12–17 July battles around Prochorovka, the defense of the Mius River by General der Infanterie Karl Hollidt's 6. Armee (formerly Armee-Abteilung Hollidt), and the fighting of III. Panzerkorps in the Bogodukhov sector during the fourth battle for Kharkov. The three battles are closely related events of the summer of 1943, and the relationship between them involves an interlocking mesh of Soviet and German strategic planning, hard-fought, bloody battles, Soviet military deception and decisions made by Adolf Hitler. The Mius battle is largely unknown, and the Bogodukhov fighting is dealt with briefly in most texts. The most famous of the three, Prochorovka, has been extensively mythologized. My second objective is to provide an accurate basic account of the battles around Prochorovka.

I believe that Prochorovka has never been understood properly, first due to the failure to use available primary materials, namely the records of II. SS-Panzerkorps, and second to the acceptance of early, incorrect accounts of the battle. The number of SS panzers involved in the fighting and the tank losses of the three SS divisions that took part in the combat west of Prochorovka have been grossly exaggerated. German records very clearly show the numbers of tanks available to each division, and study of these primary sources result in some interesting conclusions regarding what actually happened in this sector on 12–17 July, 1943.

The defensive fighting of Hollidt's army at the Mius River is the second of the battles studied in this work. It can be considered to be a part of the larger battle of Kursk for several reasons that are not apparent in the study of either battle as essentially unrelated events. It is an almost unknown battle and is only briefly mentioned in many of the comprehensive accounts of the Eastern Front. The battle is closely linked with the outcome of Operation "Citadel" on the southern wing of Heeresgruppe Süd during the summer of 1943. The accounts of 6. Armee's struggles at the Mius River clearly illustrate the problems of the German Army after the losses suffered during the campaigns of 1941–43. It was also the first of the post-Kursk counterattacks which characterized the combat operations of the Waffen SS panzer divi-

Preface

sions during the remaining years of the war. For these reasons, it will be studied in greater detail than the fighting at Prochorovka.

The third battle covered in this book took place immediately after the Mius battle ended, and it involved the combat operations of III. Panzerkorps against elements of five entire Soviet armies west of Kharkov. This complex series of thrusts, river crossings, mobile operations and counterattacks lasted from the first week of August until nearly the end of the month. The III. Panzerkorps was charged with stopping the attack of the Soviet 5th Guards Tank Army, 1st Tank Army, 6th Army, 5th Guards Army, and 27th Army. Led by nearly 1,100 tanks of the two Soviet tank armies, this force tore a huge gap between 4. Panzerarmee and 8. Armee. The 8. Armee defended the northern approaches to the city and the section of front that extended south from the city, while 4. Panzerarmee defended the section of front west of Kharkov.

The tired and weakened German panzer divisions of III. Panzerkorps were thrown into the gap and ordered to bring the massive Soviet offensive west of Kharkov to a halt. For three weeks, III. Panzerkorps, with only weak reinforcements, led by the aggressive attacks of 2. SS-Panzer-Division *Das Reich* and 3. SS-Panzer-Division *Totenkopf*, blunted repeated thrusts by the 1st Tank Army and the 5th Guards Tank Army, which were supported by infantry elements of three other Soviet armies. These battles, which were centered around the Merchik and Merla Rivers south of the town of Bogodukhov, provide interesting studies of the operations of Soviet mobile groups and the desperate actions that characterized the late war operations of German mobile divisions.

Throughout the whole narrative, the hand of Adolf Hitler is evident. He made a series of decisions begining with the conduct of Operation "Citadel" that decisively influenced the conduct of the war in the East. Hitler issued a series of orders affecting the use and positioning of panzer divisions after Prochorovka that were crucial to the outcome of Heeresgruppe Süd's offensive around the Psel-Prochorovka area. These decisions are directly related to the failure of the Kursk offensive on the south flank of the salient and strategic developments that took place as late as August in the Bogodukhov area. The events of this time period and the decisions by Hitler influenced not only the war in the East, but the entire course of World War II.

My third objective is to objectively study combat operations of the Waffen SS panzer divisions that fought in all of the above battles. The participation of *Das Reich* and *Totenkopf* provides one of the common threads that linked all three engagements. Misconceptions about the operations of the units of the Waffen SS, their combat record and their fighting qualities are common in many of the histories of the Eastern Front. Many writers have dismissed the accomplishments of these units and disparaged the military qualities of the SS combat units, either through ignorance or contempt for anything associated with the runic symbols of the SS.

I have attempted to provide an account of the combat operations of a number of those divisions that qualify for elite status by any objective classification. It must be understood that there are literally no common standards or characteristics that can be applied to all Waffen SS divisions. There was an enormous variance in divisional organization, equipment and quality of leadership. While several of the earliest units were made up of truly magnificent human material, many of the later divisions had personnel of dubious or poor quality. By the end of 1943, even the elite divisions were receiving replacements of transferred Luftwaffe personnel with little or no training in ground warfare and Volksdeutsch recruits who did not share the motivation level of the original volunteers. There were SS divisions that never actually fought for any time as organized combat formations. Some were ill-equipped and undisciplined formations with little military value, although others, such as the Baltic divisions, fought fairly well. The last divisions to be established were little more than reinforced regiments made from training school staffs and support units cobbled together from whatever was available. There is almost no common ground between these formations and the panzer divisions of the Waffen SS that fought in southern Ukraine during the summer of 1943.

In order to completely understand the military history of the Eastern Front during the summer of 1943, it is necessary to objectively understand the participation of the elite Waffen SS divisions in battles such as Prochorovka or Bogodukhov. However, these achievements have been ignored or minimized in the writings of former German Army officers and many postwar historians. I have presented the operations of the SS divisions during this period from an objective point of view in the hope that I might correct some of the myths and misconceptions regarding these fighting formations.

Introduction: Germany Invades Russia, 22 June 1941

On 22 June 1941, the German Army swept out of eastern Poland and into the Soviet Union. This was the beginning of Operation "Barbarossa," Hitler's invasion of his arch national enemy, Communist Russia. Three army groups (Heeresgruppen), led by the fast-moving panzer divisions and preceded by bombing and strafing planes of the Luftwaffe, quickly drove deep into Russian territory. In the center, Heeresgruppe Mitte, under command of Feldmarschall Fedor von Bock, pushed ahead rapidly, crossed the Dnepr and reached Smolensk by 16 July. On 5 August, Heeresgruppe Mitte eliminated a huge pocket of Soviet troops, capturing over 300,000 Russian soldiers. On the right flank, in the Ukraine, Feldmarschall Gerd von Rundstedt's Heeresgruppe Süd encountered stubborn resistance that delayed its advance. It was not until mid-July that Feldmarschall Walter von Reichenau's 6. Armee broke through the Russian defenses, advancing to Kiev on 11 July. By early August, Heeresgruppe Süd forces encircled a huge pocket of Soviet troops at Uman, capturing hundreds of thousands of dispirited prisoners. With German armor at Pervomaisk, the Soviet South Front was forced to retreat east, leaving behind a covering force at Odessa. On the north flank, Heeresgruppe Nord, aided by a Finnish offensive that began on 11 July, was only seventy miles from Leningrad. To the left of this attack from the center of Heeresgruppe Nord, 18. Armee drove the Russians out of Estonia. Meanwhile, Generaloberst Ernst Busch's 16. Armee advanced eastward on the left flank of Heeresgruppe Mitte.

At this point in the war, when the Soviets fell back on all fronts, losing men and equipment at a rate that they could not sustain for long, it seemed to the world that Russia was about to fall victim to the German Army just as the western armies had in France. However, when the spearheads of the panzer divisions threatened to split Russia in half, the German armies were given new orders by Adolf Hitler.

These orders changed the course of the war in the East just when it seemed that nothing would stop the Germans from capturing Moscow. In two directives issued in July 1941, Adolf Hitler diverted the panzer divisions of Heeresgruppe Mitte and sent them in attacks toward the flanking army groups on the north and south. With these orders, the dictator did what the Soviets could not do themselves, stop Heeresgruppe Mitte from advancing deeper into the heart of Russia and taking Moscow.

When OKH (Oberkommando des Heeres, or the Army High Command) expressed their objections to weakening what they correctly saw as the decisive effort, a month-long series of arguments and discussions began which resulted in an operational pause in front of the Russian capital. When the advance was resumed, in the area east of Kiev, the Russian Southwest Front was encircled on 11 September, which resulted in the capture of 665,000 prisoners and tore a huge gap in the line. However, this success would not compensate for the loss of the window of opportunity that Heeresgruppe Mitte had in August. The Germans never again threatened Moscow.

Hitler issued his next directive on September 6, detailing plans for the conduct of the war on the Eastern Front for the remainder of the year. This was the order for Operation "Typhoon," Hitler's plan for the resumption of the drive to capture Moscow. Fortunately for the Soviets, they had been given time to gather their strength in front of Moscow, where they now employed three entire fronts (the Russian equivalent of army groups) against Heeresgruppe Mitte. These were the West, Bryansk, and Reserve Fronts, and they now had more than a million and a quarter men to deploy between the Germans and the Russian capital.

When the offensive began again in the center on 2 October, it seemed that the Germans were invincible once more. Bock's panzer groups chopped through the Russian lines, cutting the Bryansk Front to pieces. Within days, the front was penetrated and encircled west of Vyazma, where once again the Russians lost over 600,000 prisoners. Stalin, alarmed at the destruction of his armies, brought General of the Army Georgi Zhukov to Moscow from Leningrad. At Leningrad, Zhukov had stabilized a crisis situation and prevented the capture of the ancient city. He took charge of the West and Reserve Fronts during the second week in October, immediately building up a defensive line around Mozhaiysk, throwing the survivors of the Bryansk Front,

Introduction: Germany Invades Russia, 22 June 1941

civilians and any warm bodies he could find into these positions. The population of Moscow was mobilized to build vast defensive works around the Russian capital while more reserves were brought up from troops stationed in the Russian far east. All efforts were made to gain time, time for the Russian winter to set in, slowing movement to a crawl and disabling men and machines that were not prepared for a Russian winter. Civilian and workers battalions were organized to man combat positions if trained troops were not available for commitment.

On 14 October, the Germans captured Kalinin, lying just northwest of the capital, a victory which caused a frenzied reaction in Moscow and widespread civilian and government panic in the streets. Five days later, the capital was put under martial law and order was harshly re-established, while much of the government infrastructure and vital industry was evacuated to the east. The removal of industrial machinery in order to prevent it from falling into German hands, resulted in a drastic loss of production capacity during the months of September and October while the machinery was being relocated. War production dropped by 60 percent or more.[1] Foreign military attaches in the capital began to prepare for the loss of the city and sent out dispatches reporting that the fall of the capital was imminent. Hitler believed that the war with Russia was all but over and that the Russian army was finished due to "military reasons, from the point of view of personnel and materiel, as well as for organizational reasons" and that Russia "was at the end of its tether."[2] Lend-Lease aid had not started to reach the Soviet Union in any quantities as President Franklin Roosevelt could not persuade the United States Congress that the survival of the Soviet Union was in the best interests of the U.S. It was not until 28 October when Congress decided that shipments of U.S. arms and material would be able to begin. The end appeared near for Stalin. Time appeared to have run out on the Soviets. At this dark hour, a strong traditional ally made its first appearance in support of the Russian army and nation during World War II.

On 6 October, the first snow fell in the Heeresgruppe Mitte sector, signaling the onset of *rasputitsa*, the season of fall rains and mud. By mid-October, the movement of panzer divisions was limited to roads, which quickly turned into quagmires of mobility robbing mud. Supply shortages began to occur more frequently because of difficulty in transporting supplies by truck but also because wartime demands had already gone beyond the capacity of German industry. Not only were raw materials, particularly fuel and rubber, in short supply, but the German factories were further hamstrung by the removal of thousands of young workers conscripted to replace the enormous casualties sustained by the Germans in Russia. The troops began to suffer from exposure to the worsening cold and wet weather because they had not been issued winter uniforms and boots. The 9. Panzer-Division reported on 2 October 1941 that 30 percent of its shoes were unwearable, all socks were issued and there was a shortage of suitable underwear. The men of the Waffen SS divisions suffered less than the army because Himmler had decided to stockpile a supply of winter uniforms and large quantities of furs which were made into coats and vests.

Hitler's response to the reports of lack of proper winter supplies for the troops was to demand that "I do not want to hear another word about the problem of supplying our troops in winter. . . . For there will be no winter campaign. . . . The army need only strike the Russians a few strong blows. . . . I expressly forbid anybody to speak of a winter campaign in my presence."[3] On another disturbing development, the T-34 tank, capable of better cross-country performance than German tanks due to its wide tracks, began to appear in ever increasing numbers. The standard German 37mm antitank gun proved next to useless against the sloped frontal armor of the T-34. German troops were forced to use emergency tactics to destroy this new Russian weapon. The main armament of German tanks, the 37mm gun of the Panzer III and the short-barreled 75mm cannon of the Panzer IV, proved to be ineffective against the frontal armor of the T-34 and the even heavier KV-1 tanks. This deficiency forced the Germans to upgrade the Panzer III main gun to a longer barreled 50mm and to develop a higher velocity 75mm gun for the Panzer IV.

Mired down by the rains, with the number of operational supply and combat vehicles declining at an alarming rate, Heeresgruppe Mitte came to a standstill, separated from the environs of Moscow by little more than thirty miles. It became apparent to the tired German fighting men, if not their supreme commander, that the Russians were not a beaten foe, fleeing in disorder, but were gaining strength each day and fighting with determination from well-prepared positions. Partisan bands created havoc behind the lines with ever increasing raids and supply disruptions. This in turn demanded that more troops

Introduction: Germany Invades Russia, 22 June 1941

be detailed to fighting this new threat, exacerbating the manpower problems of the frontline fighting divisions. The German Army had sustained casualties totalling 686,000 men by 1 November and its 136 divisions were the actual equivalent of only 83 full-strength divisions.

On the Russian side, the view remained far from optimistic, however, in spite of the improving situation. Stalin knew that with the first onset of colder weather, the roads and countryside would be frozen, thus allowing German vehicles to move again for a period of time before the snows began to accumulate. The Stavka (Soviet High Command) had even begun formulating plans for the loss of the capital and the defense of a line east of Moscow. Stalin told the American ambassador that the loss of the Soviet industrial capacity resulting from a retreat to this line meant the destruction of 75 percent of the remaining factories of the Soviet Union.[4]

In spite of this uncertain situation, Stalin was able to dramatically improve the defenses of the capital in the breathing space given him by Hitler. This was aided by the advantage of being able to operate on interior lines, with railroad nets available to supply the front lines and, just as importantly, provide parallel movement, thus facilitating movements of reserves to critical points. Stalin also massed the Soviet air force around Moscow, which was able to operate from a number of well-located air bases and had a strength of over 1,100 planes by 15 November. Siberian troops, well equipped for and experienced in winter fighting, began to arrive in ever increasing numbers. In an ominous development for the Germans, the West Front was ordered by Stalin to begin counterattacks, over Zhukov's objections. Zhukov preferred to remain on the defensive for the time. These attacks resulted in some success for the Russians against XII. and XIII. Armeekorps of 4. Panzerarmee and inflicted serious losses on the Germans; however, the Russian troops suffered severe casualties also.

On 15 November, Heeresgruppe Mitte, prodded by Hitler into action, went over to the attack again and initially proved Stalin's pessimism to have been well founded when LVI. Panzerkorps drove rapidly to the Volga River on the first day. The Russian 3rd Army's front was penetrated by German panzer forces and the 16th Army's front nearly collapsed. Its commander urgently requested to be allowed to retreat to a more defensible line but was personally ordered by Zhukov to stand, fight and die—if necessary, to the last man. The front held.

At other points, the German attacks broke down after hard fighting against the strong Soviet positions and counterattacks from the fresh Siberian divisions. Continuing supply problems and the weakened state of the panzer divisions combined to take the steam out of the renewed attack. The German corps and army commanders, disturbed over their increasing lack of men, vehicles and fuel, began to bicker among themselves over who should take the blame for the lack of success of the attacks. This reflected the tenseness of the situation at the higher levels of command and was a sure sign of the lack of confidence in success and the growing realization that the orders being given from the highest levels did not take into consideration and realities of conditions at the front. In a telephone conversation with the OKH HQ, Bock stated this opinion to OKH commander Brauchitsch: "I no longer have the forces necessary to encircle the enemy. . . . I am continually under the impression that our fighting power is being completely overestimated."[5]

The attack was nevertheless continued and resulted in successes at several points in spite of the fatigue of the troops and additional tank losses. A bridgehead over the Volga Canal at Yakroma caused great concern to Zhukov and the advance of XXIV. Panzerkorps toward Kashira, a key supply center for the defense of Tula, brought a quick reaction. Zhukov personally ordered the commander of the 2nd Cavalry Corps to attack the German spearhead at Kashira and the resulting assault, well supported by Russian planes, forced 17. Panzer-Division, the division leading the attack, to fall back. The advance continued to make progress at other points. All attempts by the Germans to take Tula, however, subsequently failed, in spite of the almost complete envelopment of the town by 3 December. While the German divisions became weaker and weaker, with men and equipment falling to the winter or the harsh fighting, Russian reinforcements were arriving at the front continuously.

In the first week of December 1941, time ran out for the German divisions fighting to gain the outskirts of Moscow. Already Russian counterattacks on a local scale had begun to probe the spearhead units of Heeresgruppe Mitte. On 29 November, Zhukov informed Stalin that the defensive phase of the battle for Moscow was over, with German strength declining to the point where the time had come to use the large reserves that had gathered for just this purpose. When the order to attack was given on 6 December, 41 percent of the entire

Introduction: Germany Invades Russia, 22 June 1941

Soviet army was concentrated in the defense of the capital, along with 40 percent of all the operational tanks then available to Stalin. This force attacked the Germans at an ideal moment. In addition to being exhausted, Heeresgruppe Mitte had vulnerable flanks which were extended and not prepared for defensive positions. This was due to the fact that the German command, out of touch with the conditions at the front, continually pushed Bock to offensive action. Hitler and the OKH did not even consider that the army group was not in any shape to accomplish much more. Any suggestion that the army group should withdraw to winter positions and await the spring met with lectures about the "will" necessary for mastering the situation.

On 6 December, the Soviets launched their main counterattacks against the over-extended German spearheads. These attacks drove the Germans back at all points, with heavy casualties produced by several doomed attempts by the panzer divisions to close gaps they no longer had the strength to close. By 13 December, 6. Panzer-Division had less than 400 panzergrenadiers left and no tanks. Only days later, 7. Panzer-Division, Rommel's once proud unit, had only 200 panzergrenadiers still in action. By the third week in December, the northern flank of Heeresgruppe Mitte had been driven back as much as sixty miles at some points. Kalinin was evacuated on the fourteenth, three days after Stalinogorsk had fallen. As early as 10 December, several units of the Soviet 10th Army had reached the banks of the Don River. Huge gaps in the line formed, sometimes twenty to thirty kilometers in width, which Bock had no divisions to close. Battalions and even companies were marched into the gaps with orders to attack the tide of Soviet troops. These doomed men, along with security detachments and police units, were thrown into the breakthrough areas and promptly disappeared. As the ragged, freezing German soldiers fought hordes of fresh Russian troops and ever increasing numbers of Soviet tanks, their little remaining confidence drained away. It became evident that there were no reserves to come to their rescue, and abandoned and destroyed heavy equipment became a common sight because of lack of fuel or prime movers. Thoughts of the horror of Napoleon's rout and his army's destruction while retreating from Russia were on the mind of many. Men froze to death while proper winter equipment remained at rear-area depots because there were not enough trains to move it forward. There was not sufficient rail capacity for even fuel, ammunition, or food, and so much of the available stocks of overcoats, woolen socks, gloves and blankets remained at the supply centers, far from the front. The rear area noncombatants had warm clothing in abundance, while the men at the front lost their fingers and toes due to frostbite.

Hitler ordered Bock to hold his positions, "to close and . . . hold ground . . . in the gaps by bringing up all the reserves." The fact that he thought there were sufficient reserves remaining to save the situation illustrated how out of touch with reality the high command was. On 15 December, after his own adjutant, Rudolf Schmundt, and Feldmarschall Walther von Brauchitsch personally reported on the desperate circumstances of Bock's troops, Hitler finally took substantive action to help the army group. Several training and replacement divisions were ordered mobilized and sent to Russia, and five other divisions on occupation duty in the west were also moved east. Significantly, he ordered them to be provided with winter equipment before being sent to the front lines. There was still to be no retreat, however, and Hitler explained to Bock that if he retreated and left the heavy weapons behind due to lack of prime movers and fuel, then the army would be in the same situation a few days later, but without its abandoned artillery and equipment. Shortly afterwards, after becoming exasperated with unwanted facts and dismal reports from Bock, Hitler replaced him with Generalfeldmarschall von Kluge. Kluge, however, could not do better given the shortages of men, equipment and supplies.

In the face of continued pressure against his army group, Kluge could not stem the Soviet tide, and Hitler was forced to allow limited withdrawals at one point or another. However, the order to withdraw the whole front to defensible positions was not immediately forthcoming, and the Russians continued to batter the German lines, breaking through at many places. During the last week in December, 9. Armee' s front was penetrated by the freshly committed Soviet 39th Army, and its defenses collapsed. On 31 December, 9. Armee' s VI. Korps was crushed, opening a gap which the Soviets quickly exploited, evidence of improving Soviet flexibility in command and logistics. Only days later, the front of 4. Panzerarmee was also penetrated, a development which prompted its commander, Generalleutnant Erich Hoepner, to withdraw his XX. Armeekorps on his own responsibility, a decision which cost him his command.

It was not until 15 January that Hitler, finally bowing to the inevitable, allowed Kluge freedom to withdraw his battered army group to a defensible line east of Yukhnov-Gzhatsk-Zubtsov. After extraordinary efforts by the men, the new front began to stabilize. A gap west of Rhzev was closed off when the Russians were momentarily short of reserves and could not maintain the penetration. Fighting continued for some time with the Soviets attempting to open the gap again and the Germans, by a superhuman effort, maintaining a cohesive front. On the north flank, a breakthrough between Heeresgruppe Mitte and Heeresgruppe Nord was brought to a halt near Velizh. Events in 4. Armee's sector were also favorable, due primarily to the exhaustion of Russian reserves rather than German strength.

Although the Russian counteroffensive slowed and eventually ground to a halt, the German eastern armies suffered losses that Germany could not entirely replace. The Germans suffered nearly a million casualties by the end of January 1942. The number of destroyed trucks, prime movers and other vehicles created a shortage of transport that would never be completely made good. From that time on, the Germans were faced by a shortage of vehicles which critically restricted the mobility of the infantry divisions, as most of the production of this type of vehicles had to be sent to the mobile divisions. The panzer and panzergrenadier divisions had to be kept operational at all costs. By the spring, the front stabilized in the Heeresgruppe Mitte sector. The Russian counteroffensives could not be sustained after suffering enormous losses of men and equipment at all points. Large numbers of Soviet forces were stalled while involved in siege of the small German pocket at Cholm and the much larger Demyansk encirclement.

With the onset of warm weather, the critical axis of events shifted to the Ukraine, where the German Army once again went over to the offensive in 1942, a drive which culminated in General der Panzertruppen Friedrich von Paulus's 6. Armee assault on Stalingrad. Hitler, who needed the oil of the Caucasus desperately, sent his armies and the armies of his allies, Italy and Rumania, pushing to the east. By 4 October, Panzerarmee units had pushed as far east as Astrakhan, which reconnaissance elements of 16. Panzergrenadier-Division actually reached. This was the farthest east any unit of the German Army penetrated during the war.

In Stalingrad, 6. Armee became embroiled in brutally tough street fighting. The Russians defended each ruined house, each street corner and factory with fanatic determination. Trying to dig the Russians out of their holes cost the Germans dearly, as battalions shrank to company size and regiments could muster only the strength of a weak battalion. By early October, 6. Armee was reporting gains of "two thirds of a block" or "about half" of a worker's settlement. Infantry losses increased, and replacements were not available in sufficient numbers, resulting in the average battalion having about seventy-five to eighty officers and men. On 6 October, the army reported that "The army's attack into Stalingrad had to be temporarily suspended (today) because of the exceptionally low infantry combat strength."[6] While German strength dissipated, the Russian reserve forces were able to supply over 180 rifle divisions and 159 tank brigades to the frontline armies in the southern sector of the front from April to October 1942.

Week after week, Paulus fed infantry and assault troops into the furnace of Stalingrad and saw them consumed without decisive success. Early in November, the fall rains stopped, and below-freezing temperatures were noted for the first time. Equally as ominous, the Russians began to counterattack the stalled German troops in the city with greater numbers of newly identified divisions. On 12 November, the commander of 6. Armee's right flank neighbor, 4. Panzerarmee (General der Panzertruppen Hoth) reported large-scale Russian troop movements opposite his front. On the left flank, the 3rd Rumanian Army had shown such weakness that the Germans were forced to try to scrape together German troops to stiffen their resistance, even at a time of infantry shortage in 6. Armee itself.

Six days later, the Southwest Front launched a counterattack that quickly broke through the 3rd Rumanian Army and drove south toward Kalach, a city about sixty miles west of Stalingrad. Simultaneously, the Stalingrad Front penetrated 4. Panzerarrnee's front at a point defended by the Rumanian VI. Korps and drove north toward Kalach. Hoth soon found his army irrevocably split in half, with part of it pushed into Stalingrad and the remnants outside of the city fighting westward to avoid encirclement.

On 20 November, Hitler created Heeresgruppe Don, placing Feldmarschall Erich von Manstein in command of the new army group that was to be comprised of Paulus's 6. Armee, 4. Panzerarmee and the various Axis commands. This decision unified the command of the endangered armies and was a promising development. However, Hitler then issued orders that doomed Paulus's 6. Armee. He commanded the army to fight for Stalingrad, regardless of the specter of encirclement. On 23 November, east of Kalach, the 4th Mechanized Corps met the 4th Tank Corps and the ring was closed around the Germans.

The following battles, both inside the city and to the west, resulted in the destruction of 6. Armee and enormous losses to the Italian and Rumanian armies in the east. This victory set the stage for another series of Russian counterattacks that pushed the Germans back for hundreds of miles. However, the Russian spearheads, suffering from attrition and support deficiencies, were weakened considerably by this time.

Heeresgruppe Don, now renamed Heeresgruppe Süd, struck back at the Russian advance southwest of Kharkov. In a stunning reversal, Manstein, counterattacking with XXXXVIII. Panzerkorps and II. SS-Panzerkorps, inflicted tremendous losses on the Russians and drove them back to the east, recapturing Kharkov. The familiar pattern of successful warm-weather German offensives seemed about to repeat itself in 1943 with the culmination of the Kharkov campaign's successful end and the dry summer weather ahead. When the spring mud brought an operational pause to the Eastern Front, a huge Russian salient projected to the west from the Kursk area. The opportunities that the Kursk bulge presented to both sides and the subsequent fighting in and around it determined the course of the war in the summer of 1943.

Terminology and Abbreviations

I have kept the use of German terminology to a minimum; however, the following list will help clarify those terms that were used.

Abteilung	unit designation
AOK	army headquarters
Arko	artillery commander, usually numbered
Armee	army
Armee-Abteilung	ad hoc group of divisions
assault gun	nonturreted armored vehicle, used by both the Germans and Russians
Aufklärungs-Abteilung	reconnaissance battalion
Bataillon or Btl.	Battalion
Befehlspanzer	commander's tank
Flak	antiaircraft gun or unit
front	Soviet equivalent to a German army group
Gebirgs-Division	mountain division
Gruppe	combat group of varying size
88	88mm gun
Heeresgruppe	army group
HKL	main defense line
Ia	1st General Staff officer (operations)
Ib	2nd General Staff officer (quartermaster)
Ic	3rd General staff officer (reconnaissance and intelligence)
Kampfgruppe	combat group of flexible size and composition
KTB	unit combat diary/records
kurz	"short," used to differentiate between short- and long-barreled guns of the same caliber
KV-1	heavy Russian tank

lang	"long," see kurz
Mitte	center
MG 42 or MG 34	German machine guns characterized by a high rate of fire
Nebelwerfer	German rocket launcher
Nord	North
Ia	1st General Staff officer, the second in command; the primary assistant to a division or corps commander
OKH	High Command of the German army (*Oberkommando des Heeres*)
OKW	High Command of the German Armed Forces (*Oberkommando der Wehrmacht*)
Pak	antitank gun/unit
Panther	Panzer V medium tank
Panzer I, II, III, etc.	types of German tanks
Panzerfaust	German handheld shaped-charge antitank weapon
Panzer Pioniere	armored division combat engineers
Panzerjäger	antitank unit
Pionier-Abteilung	engineer battalion
Pz.	Panzer
SPW	light armored vehicles
Stalinorgel	"Stalin organ," a Soviet rocket launcher
Sturmgeschütz	assault gun, a limited-traverse cannon fixed to an armored chassis
Süd	South
Tiger	Panzer VI heavy tank
T-34	Russian medium tank (most numerous model used)
Waffen SS	military divisions of the SS

CHAPTER 1

Heeresgruppe Süd and Armee-Abteilung Hollidt: Retreat and Recovery in the Ukraine

After the defeat of Feldmarschall Friedrich Paulus and his 6. Armee at Stalingrad in the winter of 1942–43, the subsequent defensive efforts of Heeresgruppe Don (later Heeresgruppe Süd), commanded by Feldmarschall Erich von Manstein, resulted in the tenuous stabilization of the southern flank of the Eastern Front. In light of the existing conditions, this achievement was remarkable in itself, but Manstein also conducted a simultaneous offensive drive attempting to relieve the Stalingrad garrison. Although the Stalingrad relief effort was unsuccessful, Manstein did manage to patch together a coherent defensive line, thereby avoiding the collapse of the entire southern wing of the Eastern Front in the aftermath of the surrender of Paulus's 6. Armee. That Manstein was able to accomplish this with worn-out divisions, short of both men and machines, attests both to his skill as a commander and the remarkable courage and stamina of the German soldier.[1] Manstein's success was also due in no small part to the over-confidence of both the Soviet High Command (Stavka) and the leader of the Soviet Union, Joseph Stalin. Stalin and his generals incorrectly believed that the Soviet army had sufficiently remedied the problems and many operational shortcomings that were evident in the first major counteroffensive after the German defeat before Moscow in the winter of 1941–42.

The crisis of early 1943 in the south of Russia was a result of the offensive operations that the Soviets launched after Stalingrad. Subsequently, a bad situation was made much worse due to poor decisions made by the highest elements of the German leadership (Hitler). The Soviet counteroffensives penetrated the German lines in several places along Heeresgruppe B's (Army Group B) front, which lay to the north of 1. Panzerarmee, then constituting the left wing of Heeresgruppe Don (soon to be renamed Heeresgruppe Süd). On 1. Panzerarmee's right was Armee-Abteilung Hollidt, named for its commander, General der Infanterie Karl Hollidt. On 30 January 1943, Armee-Abteilung Hollidt manned a defensive line stretching from the Don River northeast to where the Donets intersected the Don and there bent back westward toward Voroshilovgrad.

In order to restore a continuous line of defense, Manstein proposed to withdraw Hollidt's army to more defensible positions on the west bank of the Mius River and there tie in the flanks of the army with 1. Panzerarmee on the north flank and rest the south flank on the coast. These plans were hindered by Hitler's refusal to allow timely withdrawals and by the Russians, who followed up the surrender at Stalingrad with strong attempts to destroy the German troops west of the city.

In the first weeks of 1943, several major Russian spearheads drove westward in both Heeresgruppe B's and Heeresgruppe Don's sectors. On the north flank of Heeresgruppe B's front, the Soviet Voronezh Front, commanded by Lieutenant General F. I. Golikov, strove to encircle Kharkov with the 64th Army and 3rd Tank Army. Meanwhile, the Soviet 6th Army and 1st Guards Army of Lieutenant General N. F. Vatutin's Southwest Front had crossed the Donets on either side of Izyum and then driven into the Dnepropetrovsk area, some 200 miles to the northwest of Armee-Abteilung Hollidt's frontline defenses. To Hollidt's immediate defensive front, his army was penetrated by elements of Mobile Group Popov; which was the operational armored formation of Vatutin's Southwest Front. This armored group of four tank corps, three rifle divisions, two tank brigades, and attached support units was commanded by Lieutenant General M. M. Popov and was given the task of first deeply penetrating the German lines and then driving south to the Sea of Azov. The result was to be the severance of lines of communication and supply in Hollidt's rear areas. This mobile operation and the resulting chaos would precede a general frontal advance by the Southwest Front with the ultimate goal being the destruction of Armee-Abteilung Hollidt.[2]

Vatutin sent Popov's tanks forward on 25 January in a drive toward Slavyansk and Pavlograd, far to the rear of Hollidt's army. Elements of Popov's 4th Tank Corps on the morning of 11 February captured the town of Krasnoarmeiskoye. This was a devastating blow to the Germans because it cut the Dnepropetrovsk–Mariupol railway, which was a critical line of communication for Heeresgruppe Don.[3] Rail traffic could be directed to the south on the Zaporozhye–Stalino route, but that was a more circuitous path and was furthermore necessary for the supply of Heeresgruppe A in the Caucasus. Hoth's 4. Panzerarmee, which was at that time deployed in the Kuban, also depended on this rail line. The capture of the rail line created a situation that could not be tolerated for long due to the overloading of the railroad and the resulting shortages.

The Russian penetrations were also well to the west of the Mius River, which ran from the Gulf of Taganrog near Rostov to the north. There were old fortifications on the Mius's western bank, built the previous winter, and it was to that position that Manstein had hoped to withdraw the right wing of Heeresgruppe Don. However, when Mobile Group Popov sliced deeply through the front and drove to a position well west of Hollidt, the situation threatened to end in another catastrophe. Hollidt's army was threatened by encirclement and destruction before it had even reached the Mius position.

This serious situation was created by Hitler's refusal to allow the timely withdrawal of Manstein's army group. The Führer's order created the potential for a massive encirclement of German forces just weeks after the Stalingrad pocket surrendered. It was very clear to Manstein that the course of the war in the East depended on the prevention of the destruction of Heeresgruppe Süd. If it was allowed to become fragmented and destroyed, it would also doom the divisions of Heeresgruppe A to strangulation and destruction in the Caucasus. According to Manstein,

> The question henceforth was whether that winter would bring the decisive step towards Germany's defeat in the East. Momentous and distressing though the Stalingrad disaster undoubtedly was, it could not, in terms of World War II, effect such a blow on its own, whereas the annihilation of the German Army's entire southern wing might well have paved the way to an early victory over Germany.[4]

Nor was Manstein in any doubt as to why the potentially fatal crisis on the southern wing of the Eastern Front had occurred at this time:

There were two reasons why the Soviet High Command could hope to attain this goal in the south of the Eastern Front. One was the extraordinary numerical superiority of the Russian forces; the second was the favourable position it found itself in operationally as a result of the German errors of leadership associated with the name of Stalingrad.[5]

Manstein was persistent in his efforts to persuade Hitler to allow him to withdraw Hollidt's troops to the Mius line before they were cut off and annihilated. The critical nature of Manstein's demands resulted in a conference with Hitler on 6 February, where, after hours of evasion and procrastination, the Führer finally gave in and allowed him to give the orders for withdrawal to the Mius position. Hollidt began to move his army on 8 February. The withdrawal was very aggressively and closely pursued by the Russians, who did not intend to let the Germans get settled into their old defensive positions unmolested. There was some doubt whether Hollidt could even reach, much less hold, the line because the pursuing Russians were literally on his heels.[6] Manstein commented on this possibility during the meeting with Hitler and voiced the concern he felt at the time that the decision was too late. Hitler even tried to persuade Manstein to wait for the weather to change and bog down the Russians in spring mud, an argument that held no appeal to Manstein. Only after his absolute refusal "to stake the fate of my army group on the hope of a quite unseasonable change of weather" did Hitler finally relent and allow Hollidt to pull back toward the Mius River. Manstein wrote:

> Indeed, it was already doubtful—thanks to the delay in taking a decision—whether Armee-Abteilung Hollidt, now saddled with the defense of the whole front from the coastline to the Middle Donetz, would ever get back to the Mius in time. Consequently, I had to receive permission that very day to give up the eastern part of the Donetz area as far as the Mius.[7]

On 17 February, Armee-Abteilung Hollidt successfully reached its new positions. It had been a near thing for the Germans, and the Soviets prepared to push across the river only a short time after Hollidt's divisions settled into the Mius line. Early on the next day, Russian troops of Malenovsky's Southern Front forced a crossing over the

Mius at several points. The 3rd Guards Mechanized Corps pushed ahead quickly, and its tanks penetrated nearly eighteen miles deep into the depth of the German defenses.[8] There it was halted by hastily organized concentric German counterattacks mounted by battle groups thrown together to meet the emergency situation. In spite of this dangerous development that threatened the integrity of the German defense, Malenovsky was not able to exploit the success of the 3rd Guards Mechanized due to a capricious local turn of the weather. A brief thaw made quick supply and reinforcement of the breakthrough unit temporarily impossible when the countryside turned into a sea of mud. This lucky change of weather allowed the Germans to attack the stalled Soviet tanks and infantrymen when they began to run out of fuel and ammunition. Before the Russians could resupply the spearhead elements, they were isolated, completely surrounded and destroyed.[9] However, even if the weather had not turned against them, the Soviets would have ultimately been hard pressed to follow up the breakthrough of the 3rd Mechanized Corps with decisive reinforcement and supply due to a sudden development on the northern flank of Southern Front's advance.

THE MANSTEIN COUNTERATTACK AT KHARKOV

West of Kharkov, beginning on 21 February, Manstein put into execution a counterattack designed to regain the initiative for the Germans in the Heeresgruppe Süd sector. This was his Kharkov counterstroke, the end result of which was the reversal of the tide of Soviet success following Stalingrad. When the German attack began, due to overconfidence at the higher levels of the Soviet command, it was not immediately apparent to the Soviet commanders that the Germans had launched a large-scale counterattack. Because of this misreading of Manstein's intentions, the situation was made worse for the Soviet units in the field. The Soviet command did not respond quickly or realistically to the beginning of the German counterattack. Intelligence regarding German troop movements and assembly of armor was misinterpreted or disregarded. In spite of the fact that German armor was massed in positions enabling them to cut off large elements of the Soviet spearheads, Russian divisional and corps commanders were urged to push their attacks deeper and faster. This occurred even as they reported that their divisions were depleted and too weakened by their losses to carry on.[10] When Popov, on 21 February, found that his three tank corps had a total of thirty-seven tanks among them, he radioed a message to Vatutin requesting permission to withdraw. Vatutin ordered Popov to continue his mission directive and push on, rebuking him and explaining that a withdrawal "contradicts the group's mission and the existing conditions whereby the enemy at all costs hurries to withdraw his forces from the Donbas across the Dnepr."

Overconfidence and blindness to reality at higher levels of Soviet command contributed significantly to the makings of a critical setback to the Russians in the spring of 1943. At that time, unknown to Vatutin, who habitually was unduly optimistic, disaster was already in the making, in the form of attacking concentrations of German armor.[11] The same combinations of unwarranted Soviet optimism and operational shortcomings had contributed to the spring reversals after the winter of 1941–42. The Russian command was so blinded as to what was actually happening in the field that it refused to believe evidence that should have sent up a red flag of warning. When aerial reconnaissance photos showed large columns of German armor and support units on the move into staging areas for the counterattack, the photos were interpreted as proof that the Germans were retreating out of the Donbas.[12] By the time their mistake was realized, the Soviets could do little but react desperately to escape Manstein's trap. By then, it was too late for the men and machines of the Soviet advance formations.

On the other hand, Manstein astutely launched his counterstroke at the right moment. In a correct assessment of the situation, it was evident to the Heeresgruppe Süd command that the Russian spearheads had run out of steam due to attrition of men and machines and an increasing scarcity of fuel. After the overly ambitious advance across the Donets Basin, the Soviet logistical system failed. Soviet supply columns did not reach the mobile spearheads with fuel or ammunition in sufficient quantities. Tanks and other vehicles that broke down with mechanical problems were left unrepaired due to shortages of parts or lack of forward repair facilities. The advance was littered with a trail of abandoned and destroyed vehicles. Popov's mobile formations were, as a result, running short of tanks. The armor that was still operational became immobilized by periodic shortages of fuel on occasion, which allowed the Germans to easily destroy stranded units.

By 24 February, the Soviets finally began to realize what was about to happen to their advance spearhead formations. Vatutin, commander of the Southwest Front, then frantically canceled all offensive operations of Mobile Group Popov, although by that time the lead formations were too weakened to have driven much farther west in any event.[13] Popov had correctly smelled the danger earlier than those at the top, but his assessment of the situation had been ignored. By 24 February, when Vatutin finally realized his mistake, it was too late to do anything about it, and Popov's stranded units were encircled and annihilated within days by concentric German attacks. The Soviet 6th Army was carved up by the panzer spearheads of II. SS-Panzerkorps and XXXXVIII. Panzerkorps and largely destroyed by the end of the month.

Manstein had engineered a dramatic reversal that set the stage for the recapture of Kharkov and the halt of the Soviet drive to the west after the Stalingrad debacle. The resulting stabilization of the southern wing of the Eastern Front created the Kursk bulge that was so important to the events of the summer of 1943.

ARMEE-ABTEILUNG HOLLIDT PREPARES TO DEFEND THE MIUS

On the Mius front, the elimination of Popov's armor and the earlier destruction of the 3rd Guards Mechanized Corps removed the threat to Armee-Abteilung Hollidt's rear areas and allowed Hollidt's weary troops to settle into their new defensive positions overlooking the Mius River. Soon after, the spring thaw brought large-scale mobile operations to a halt on both sides, as roads became rivers of bottomless black mud and small streams became wide torrents of rushing muddy water. The open steppes were transformed into a sea of sticky muck, which made cross-country movement impossible. The thaw, as well as mutual exhaustion, brought both armies to a halt until the summer sun could dry the countryside out.

During the halt in operations on the Heeresgruppe Süd front, in March 1943, Armee-Abteilung Hollidt was renamed by Hitler as a new 6. Armee. Perhaps it eased the dictator's mind to again see a 6. Armee on the daily situation maps of the Eastern Front. However, the new 6. Armee did not resemble Field Marshall Paulus's destroyed army in either quality or quantity. The hundreds of thousands of German troops from the first 6. Armee, now dead or trudging into a wretched captivity, could not be replaced by the stroke of a grease pen on a map.

In the meantime, Hollidt's army continued to man the defensive line from near Taganrog, on the Azov coast, to the north along the Mius on to the Donets, where it bent back to the west toward Belaya Gora.[14] The weeks of reduced activity were spent upgrading the fortifications and trench lines while recovering from the struggles of the winter. Very few replacements arrived because the first priority for men was given to the buildup of the divisions that were to be involved in the offensive at Kursk. What few men did arrive were mostly those who returned from convalescence from wounds or sickness. There were not enough to bring any of the 6. Armee divisions to even approximate establishment strength, although for the conditions of the Eastern Front in mid-1943, the state of manpower was not unusual.

The ten infantry divisions available to this new 6. Armee were barely sufficient to man the defensive length of frontage that was assigned to the army. The army was made up of three infantry corps that divided the 150-mile front among them. Further complicating the problem of organizing an adequate defense, these units also varied greatly in quality, experience and equipment. This fact caused Hollidt and his staff to devote a great deal of time and effort to preparing the weaker divisions for the coming summer. Reflecting the preparations for "Citadel," which saw the entire Eastern Front stripped of mobile divisions to provide armor for the attack, only one mobile division, the 16. Panzergrenadier, was available in reserve.[15]

On the 6. Armee's left flank, IV. Armeekorps was made up of 304. Infanterie-Division, 3. Gebirgs-Division, and 335. Infanterie-Division. The mountain division was a high-quality fighting unit that had seen combat in Norway and above the Arctic Circle before being sent to Heeresgruppe Süd in late 1942. It was probably the best of all of the infantry divisions assigned to 6. Armee. Both 304. and 335. Infanterie-Divisions were first stationed in the West previous to their arrival on the Eastern Front in 1943. Two years of non-combat, sedentary duty in France and Belgium were a poor preparation for the rigors and horrors of the type of war that they were to experience in Russia. The first combat experienced by 304. Infanterie-Division resulted in unit panic and a very poor combat performance, and it apparently was never a wholly reliable unit. Similarly, 335. Infanterie-Division was stationed in France from mid-1941 until 1943, when it was sent to Russia. While slightly more capable than 304. Infanterie, it never developed into a first-rate fighting unit.

Defending the right flank of the army was XXIX. Armeekorps, consisting of the 17., 111., and 336. Infanterie-Divisions and 15. Luftwaffe-Felddivision. The 17. Infanterie-Division was a good-quality unit that fought in the Moscow campaign after seeing action in the West during 1939–40. After rest and recovery in France during 1942, the division returned to duty in Russia in 1943. 111. Infanterie-Division was a Saxon unit that first saw combat in Russia with Heeresgruppe Süd in the Caucasus and the Kuban. It was a competent infantry formation also, although it suffered severe, largely unreplaced losses of personnel during 1942. 336. Infanterie-Division, also raised in Saxony, also suffered heavy casualties during 1942–43. This was particularly true during the drive to relieve Stalingrad and the subsequent retreat to the Mius. The weakest link of the XXIX. Armeekorps was one of Goering's nearly hapless air force divisions, 15. Luftwaffe Felddivision. In its first combat, earlier in 1943, it quickly fell apart and was taken out of the line for reoganization. It was subsequently combined with survivors from another disentegrated Luftwaffe division and sent back to the front.[16] By the winter of 1943, it would be disbanded, a waste of potentially valuable manpower, as were most of the Luftwaffe ground units. The one exception was the Hermann Goering Panzer-Division, which was a competent formation.

The XVII. Armeekorps, with three divisions, defended the center of the Mius line, holding the Kuibyshevo-Dmitrievka sector. North of the town of Dmitrievka, on the left flank, in the Ivanovka-Krasny Luch area, the trenches were manned by 302. Infanterie-Division, known as the "Dieppe" Division because it had been stationed at Dieppe at the time of the landing there by British and Canadian forces in 1942. The division had been in Russia since early in 1943 and was adequate by the standards of the Russian front in mid-1943.[17]

In the center, from the northern half of Dmitrievka to the village of Novo-Pavlovka, the line was occupied by 306. Infanterie-Division, which had also arrived in the East after occupational duty in Belgium. This unit was an experienced division, having fought in Russia for some months, and had suffered badly during the Stalingrad relief drive, the defense of Taganrog, and the retreat of Armee-Abteilung Hollidt to the Mius. The division was to have such severe losses in the coming months that it would be disbanded by September 1944. In July 1943, it was considered adequate for defensive duties but not sufficiently mobile or strong enough for extended offensive missions. However, in spite of this situation, the division would be called on repeatedly to carry out supporting attacks from 18 July to 3 August.

The 294. Infanterie-Division was on the right flank of XVII. Armeekorps, defending the section of the line from Dmitrievka to south of Kuibyshevo. It had also suffered heavily during the previous winter. After Stalingrad, the division was assigned large numbers of former Luftwaffe personnel to fill the places of the men lost in the retreat after the Taganrog fighting, where the division had been badly mauled. These personnel were not up to the stresses of combat when first assigned to the division, and much time had been devoted since the winter to training them.

Reorganization and training, as well as diligent improvement of the Mius defenses, occupied much of the infantrymen's time during the spring lull. Hollidt made every possible effort to prepare his army for the resumption of combat that was inevitable with the coming of summer. Although the Luftwaffe replacements arrived essentially untrained for ground warfare, at this stage in the war, any replacements were better than none at all. If they lived long enough to gain a modicum of experience, they were adequate. Hollidt utilized all possible methods to improve the fighting capacity of these men, including continued training in combat skills, some of which took place in a large section of trenches constructed for training of the soldiers of 6. Armee. This training area would prove to be of great benefit to the army, albeit in an unintentional role.

The 294., 304., and 335. Infanterie-Divisions were particularly in need of rest and reorganization because of the severe losses sustained during the winter. However, their recovery was hampered by shortages of key personnel such as support troops and those soldiers with special technical training. These men with special skills and knowledge had been forced to serve as replacements in the combat companies during the winter. The result was that most were dead or wounded by summer. The condition of the three units was typical of average German divisions in the summer of 1943 and point up several weaknesses of 6. Armee.

One of the most critical deficiencies was the lack of sufficient noncommissioned officers and company- or battalion-level officers.[18]

Companies were often led by NCOs temporarily due to the alarming death rates for company commanders, and squads often were commanded by ordinary soldiers. The general shortage of the men with the necessary command skills at these grades was a serious hindrance to unit performance in the German Army at this date in the war in the East. From June 1941 until March 1942, there were 15,000 German officer casualties. During this same period, the number of first lieutenants fell from 12,055 to 7,276.[19] The situation was alleviated to some extent by the policy of training every officer to do the job of his superior and the premium placed on developing initiative in leadership at all levels of command, from NCOs on up. However, the campaign in Russia began with a deficiency of officers with the necessary training and experience. In the prewar years, the army discovered that the enormous expansion that began after Hitler came to power created problems due to the limited number of officers that were sufficiently trained for combat as a result of the limitations placed on the German Army after 1919. Studies conducted after the Polish campaign revealed serious shortcomings in command due to this shortage. Intensive training only partially corrected the problem before the launching of "Barbarossa," although, by that time, experience in the West provided necessary seasoning of German officers without serious losses as there were only 1,253 officers lost to death or wounds during the conquest of France, Holland, and Belgium. Thus, in 1943, the enormous officer casualties exacerbated an already serious problem.

A second deficiency was that most infantry divisions were chronically short of men after the first winter due to two factors. First was the population base of Germany. It simply was not sufficient to provide replacements for losses sustained on a scale seen in the fighting in Russia. Almost from the beginning, German casualties on the Eastern Front were from 200,000 to 500,000 per every six-month period.

During World War II, 80 percent of the casualties suffered by the German Army fell on the Eastern Front alone. The remaining 20 percent were lost in the other areas of the war, in Africa and Italy, during the German conquest of France, or in the bitter fighting following the Allied invasion of Europe. During the summer of 1943, Germany's army lost 232,000 men either missing or dead. This is a startling number of casualties when compared with American losses for the entire war, which reached a total of just over 400,000 dead and missing for all services in 1941–45.[20] The Wehrmacht was barely able to provide sufficient manpower for the divisions assigned to Operation "Citadel," and those armies on the periphery made do with scanty replacements.

A third extremely serious deficiency of 6. Armee was its lack of armored divisions. Hollidt's sole mobile reserve consisted of 16. Panzergrenadier-Division. In July 1943, it was stationed west of Chistyakovo, about fifteen miles behind the front lines. The division had only twenty operational tanks (in addition to an assault gun battalion), but it was a tough, combat-proven formation. It had the distinction of making the farthest penetration to the east of any German unit during the war in Russia when elements of its reconnaissance battalion pushed nearly to Astrakhan in 1942.[21] Later in the war, it was converted into 116. Panzer-Division and fought in Normandy and the Ardennes, where it was to give good account of itself. Within a few days of the division's assembly in the Mius sector, it was thrown against an entire Soviet mechanized corps, which was at full strength and equipped with about 200 tanks.

THE MIUS LINE AND TERRAIN
The terrain that 6. Armee defended was not ideal, although it furnished some advantage to the defender. This could not compensate for the manpower shortages and lack of armor. The Mius itself is a small, shallow river averaging only fifty yards in width, presenting no great obstacle to crossing at most points along its meandering course. To the east of its banks lay the featureless plains of the Russian steppe, marked only by low rounded hills or the slight elevation of small, sometimes wooded ridges. There are numerous ravines of varied size, a common characteristic of the Ukraine, ranging from small washed-out stream beds to flat-bottomed valleys. The west bank, like that of many rivers in southern Russia, is higher than the east bank and offers some observation and elevation advantages to a defender.

The river bank immediately opposite Dmitrievka and Kuibyshevo was characterized by low ridges, thinly soiled and rocky. Each was cut by innumerable steep-walled ravines and gullies, often bordered by scruffy vegetation or concealed completely by very large corn or sunflower fields.[22] From the region west and slightly north of Dmitrievka, there were three low ridges that ran roughly parallel to each other to the southeast in the direction of Kuibyshevo. The first ran from just west of the northern half of Dmitrievka to the northwest into the area around the village of Nikitoroff. The second and dominant elevation extended from Point 194.3, just opposite the southern edge of Dmitrievka also in a northwest direction to near the Remvosky Grusse sector. Along the crest of this ridge ran a road from Sneshnoje to the town of Marinovka. On the southern half of this ridge lay a key point—a broad, low and featureless hill identified on German maps as Hill 213.9. Its primary value lay in the fact that it was the highest point in the ridge sector and dominated the ridges to the north and south as well as the valleys that lay between the three ridges.

This tactically important hill and the whole of its surrounding approaches were covered by great fields of corn and sunflowers that were taller than a man. This vast expanse of cultivated fields concealed the multitude of ravines and small stream beds or erosion cuts that offered excellent concealment for a defender. They also furnished good avenues of infiltration for an attacker who was familiar with the terrain.

The Mius line in this sector was largely a forward-slope defensive position due to the alignment of the ridges that ran away to the northwest instead of parallel to the river. In addition, the shallow soil and scarcity of wood caused problems for the Germans in the construction of sufficiently deep bunkers. As a result, many bunkers were unable to withstand heavier artillery fire. In general, there were broad fields of fire, an advantage lessened somewhat by the vegetation and by the presence of numerous ravines of all sizes. Although the Germans had first occupied a defensive position behind the Mius in the fall of 1941 and had then constructed a continuous trench line, the handicap of having to man a forward-slope position was critical. At this stage in the war, the Soviet artillery was growing more numerous, having recovered from the enormous material losses of 1941–42. As a result, the Soviets were able to mass large concentrations of cannon and heavy mortars (120mm and larger). While lack of sophisticated fire control and radio communication meant that the Soviet artillery was nowhere near as flexible or formidable as the German artillery, it was still dangerous when concentrated due to the sheer weight of fire that could be delivered by line of sight fire or on carefully registered targets. After an attack began, the Soviet artillery support was sometimes not as effective when compared with that of the Germans. This was primarily due to a lack of sufficient prime movers for the artillery, which did not allow the Soviet guns to relocate swiftly enough during the penetration phase of an offensive. Radio communication in the Soviet artillery formations of summer 1943 was not always adequate for the demands placed on it by the swiftly changing events of modern battle.

The large amount of artillery that could be deployed by the Soviets and their characteristically plentiful ammo supply forced the Germans to utilize reverse-slope positions when possible. This minimized casualties due to destruction of the frontline trenches.[23] The tremendous firepower that the Russians typically massed in support of an attack guaranteed that forward positions would be completely smashed by preparatory artillery fires with correspondingly high casualties inflicted on the defending troops. Tactically, the Germans also adjusted by changing their defensive principle of deploying two thirds of a force in the front positions and one third in reserve. This principle led to heavy casualties in the forward units and provided an insufficient reserve strength to successfully counterattack Soviet penetrations. As a result, by late 1942, it was common for the Germans to have no more than one third of a force assigned to the first line of trenches and outposts (often much less). The remaining two thirds were stationed in the second or third line of trenches, which, in ideal situations, were positioned on a reverse slope and supplied with abundant strongpoints, alternate firing positions and adequate communication trenches. These measures enabled the Germans to make quick counterattacks on the flanks of a penetration.[24] The reverse-slope entrenchments prevented the Soviet artillery fires from decimating the defenders in the opening phase of the attack. However, in the Mius sector, the Germans were not able to utilize reverse-slope positions as often as in other areas. The alignment of the ridges west of the river was not parallel to the river, and the front line ran through the valleys between the ridges.

Lacking ideal terrain, 6. Armee constructed a continuous first trench line with numerous dug-out shelters placed behind barbed wire and extensive minefields. The minefields were laid along likely routes of advance for tanks and concealed avenues of approach for infantry. Successive defensive positions were built and consisted of fortified strongpoints with concrete bunkers and additional wire and mines.[25]

Early in July, 6. Armee became aware of an impending Soviet attack. The evidence indicated that the main attack was most likely to be expected at Kuibyshevo, although Soviet offensive doctrine typically favored a broad axis of advance. Although air reconnaissance was ineffectual in early July, due to extemely bad weather, ground observation obtained information which confirmed that the Soviets were building up forces for an offensive. On 10 July, 6. Armee was startled by a sudden burst of unusual radio activity in the sectors of XXIX. and XVII. Armeekorps. A great deal of information was gained from long- and short-range signal interception units. This intelligence was combined with the information gathered from vigilant observation from forward positions and patrol activity. Reports from the 623rd and 549th Signal Intelligence Detachments enabled the army to identify the main Soviet assembly area as being east of Kuibyshevo and Dmitrievka.[26] This was directly opposite the corps boundary between XXIX. and XVII. Armeekorps. Large concentrations of Soviet artillery, infantry and motorized formations were detected in and around these two towns.

A large number of Russian artillery and mortar batteries were easily identified by specific location. It was also frequently possible to identify the HQ to which each was attached. The fact that most of these concentrations were located in the same area across from the corps boundary reinforced the evidence that the point of main effort would be there. Attacking at such a boundary was a favored tactic of the Russians (as well as the Germans) because the dual responsibility for these areas often resulted in a less than unified response. There was a tendency for each corps to "let his neighbor" take care of the boundary, especially if the corps involved were already under attack. German Army commanders often countered this tactic by simply shifting a corps boundary using the device of transfering one of the affected divisions to the adjacent corps.

6. Armee intelligence continued to rather easily gather a great deal of information about the Soviet build-up. Groups of Russian officers were observed studying terrain in order to discover avenues of attack and advance. Incredibly, elements of the Soviet 2nd Guards Mechanized Corps arrived at night with all of its vehicles using their headlights. Through what was perceived by the Germans as numerous instances of poor security measures on the part of the Russians from divisional level on down, 6. Armee was able to easily identify

newly arrived units. Large concentrations of mortar regiments were identified and pinpointed. The German intelligence units were even able to discover that mortar units were detached from the Soviet rifle divisions and placed under unified commands in regimental sized concentrations. This was particularly noted in the XVII. Armeekorps area. Russian artillery was observed to fire ranging rounds on likely targets, a practice of the Russians that to veterans of the Eastern Front was sure and ominous evidence of bloody work ahead for the infantry.[27]

By 13 July, 6. Armee command could scarcely have had any more detailed information on Russian preparations and troop dispositions. They knew where the main attack was coming and they knew the exact strength of the Russians that were massed on the other side of the river. In addition, the locations of all the enemy rifle divisions were known. It was certain that the Russians had armor on the eastern bank because the arrival of Soviet mobile units was actually observed, in what seemed to be an incredible breach of security. The weight of information was unmistakable, and 6. Armee prepared itself for the inevitable attack.

Hollidt continued to make visits to the corps and division headquarters of his army, reviewing responsibilities and procedures. He made every effort to prepare the weaker divisions of 6. Armee for the storm that was coming by making sure commanders and men knew what was expected of them. The Luftwaffe division had real deficiencies that could only be corrected over a period of time. Training continued when allowed by the busy schedule of preparing the Mius line for attack by the Soviets. In order to provide further training for the infantry, a large training facility had been built north of Hill 213.9 (which was to be the site of several bloodbaths in the following days), complete with trench system and defensive positions. It was used by the divisional training battalions, where such units still existed, to train the new arrivals in the techniques of fighting on the Eastern Front.

The Russian build-up across from Hollidt's army left no doubt that there would be an attack soon and the intensive training would be valuable. To the north, only days before, the battle of Kursk had reached its climactic moment, but Hollidt had more immediate worries to concern him, and he was unaware of events in the Kursk salient that would directly affect his army and the course of events on the Eastern Front in the decisive summer of 1943. On 14 July, the

Soviet activity on the eastern bank of the Mius River subsided, with radio transmission interceptions almost nonexistent and very little troop movement observed by the Germans. An ominous quiet descended upon the Mius River. Within days, 6. Armee would begin a battle for its very survival that had an importance far beyond the existence of Hollidt's army and, in fact, played a key role in the failure of Operation "Citadel," the last great German offensive in the East. Thus, the events that occurred during July and August 1943 along the Mius had an extremely influential role on the outcome of the entire war on the Eastern Front.

CHAPTER 2

From Prochorovka to the Mius: III. Panzerkorps and II. SS-Panzerkorps

OPERATION "CITADEL"

In the first week of July 1943, shortly before 6. Armee first began to receive indications that the Russians were preparing to attack across the Mius River, the Eastern Front stood ready to experience the largest tank battle that the world had yet seen. In a theater of the Second World War that was characterized by battles on a scale that dwarfed many Western Front operations, a massive German attack was about to be launched. This was Operation "Citadel," which would be the last great summer offensive by the Germans in Russia. The attack would be the final chance Germany had to influence the course of the war on the Eastern Front before the Allied invasion of Europe, which was expected in 1944. Although many in the highest levels of command were confident of success, the attack was a huge gamble, and many of those involved in its planning, including Hitler himself, knew it. Failure of Operation "Citadel" would see an already depleted German Army exhausted even further just before the winter months and the inevitable Soviet winter attacks.

Germany could not produce enough guns, tanks, trucks and other vehicles to keep pace with the destruction resulting from the great battles in Russia. This became evident as early as winter of 1941. There was another, more critical shortage as well. Because of the heavy casualties suffered in the period from June 1941 to summer 1943, there were fewer German soldiers in the East than had entered Russia in 1941. The Axis allies of Germany had been largely knocked out of the war as a result of the slaughter seen in the Stalingrad campaign, during which the Italian, Hungarian and Rumanian armies were decimated and lost tens of thousands of men. A series of emergency measures instituted by the Wehrmacht to find warm bodies to replace the dead and wounded were stopgap measures at best and could not remedy the core problem, which was a shortage in Germany of personnel fit for active military service. While Russian losses were many times higher than those of Germany, the seemingly inexhaustible manpower of the Soviet Union could provide replacements, while the Reich, with its smaller population, could not.

German industry proved incapable of turning out tanks and other heavy equipment at a rate equal to that of the Soviet Union. The twenty-four-hour-a-day Soviet factories, working on a permanent war footing, were producing more than 20,000 tanks a year in late 1943. By the end of the war, the Soviets produced more than 50,000 of its main battle tank, the T-34. In fact, one factory alone, Zavod #183, turned out more than 35,000 T-34s of all variants by 1945. In contrast, the total production of German tanks for the entire war was just over 30,000 vehicles. Only 1,834 Tiger tanks were produced during 1941–45 and only 5,508 Panthers, a very small number when compared to T-34 production. In addition, the Russians also produced tens of thousands of other tank types during the war.

In order to provide the divisions assigned to carry out Operation "Citadel" with motor vehicles, artillery, and tanks, the Germans were forced to strip equipment from the armies manning other areas of the Eastern Front. The divisions of Heeresgruppe Süd and Heeresgruppe Mitte were given priority in receiving replacements for the winter casualties. On the extreme north and south sectors of the front, divisions received few new replacements and were often given only those men who returned to duty after recovery from wounds. Panzer divisions were taken from both the north and south flank armies, which left only the barest amount of armor available to those sectors of the front. It was for this reason that Hollidt's 6. Armee had only the 16. Panzergrenadier-Division. Tank production was almost exclusively utilized to build up the panzer divisions that were massed on the flanks of the Kursk salient, as was the production of heavy weapons and various motor vehicles. There was also a shortage of trucks, prime movers and other types of necessary support and transport vehicles. In order to equip the panzer and panzergrenadier divisions in the mobile units of the two attack groups, thousands of these types of motor vehicles were taken from the divisions on the flanks. They were replaced with horses, small horse-drawn carts known as *panje* wagons and even bicycles.

By the day for the launching of Operation "Citadel," 900,000 men and thousands of tanks were poised to begin the attack. The plan called for Heeresgruppe Süd (Army Group South) and Heeresgruppe Mitte (Army Group Center) to chop off a huge hundred-mile-wide bulge in the front lines between Orel in the north and Belgorod in the south. This large salient protruded to the west for approximately seventy miles and added greatly to the length of the front, forcing the German infantry divisions to spread their already thin ranks for many additional miles. In the approximate center of the bulge lay the city of Kursk. While the city was an important railway hub, it had no great intrinsic value other than its location. It was there that the Germans planned for the two armored pincers to meet, resulting in the encirclement of the seven Russian armies that held the perimeter of the salient. The attacks, led by the panzer divisions, were to drive from both the north and south shoulders of the salient and meet in the Kursk area. If a link-up could be made there, the Russian armies west of Kursk would be cut off and destroyed. These Soviet forces consisted of five infantry armies and the 1st and 2nd Tank Armies. Destruction of the bulk of these formations would result in losses that even the Russian army could not make good without an extended period of recovery.

It is without a doubt that had the Germans succeeded in encircling and destroying the Soviet armies in the Kursk bulge, the history of the war in the East would have been altered significantly. It is extremely doubtful, however, that the Russians would have lost the war even in the event of a German victory at Kursk. Without the strength to make major attacks at multiple locations along the massive length of the front, the Germans had little chance to defeat the Russians militarily. By July 1943, the Russians had already recovered from the spring losses at Kharkov and had massed seven fronts (roughly equal to an army group) from north of Orel to the Gulf of Taganrog, positioned operational reserves at intervals in the tactical depth of the Kursk salient, and concentrated enormous strategic reserves on both the northern and southern flanks where the main German efforts were expected. While Hitler's armies had difficulties even finding enough mobile divisions to constitute reserves at points outside of the "Citadel" operational sectors, Stalin could raise and equip whole armies of operational and strategic reserves.

The Soviet 3rd and 4th Tank Armies, for example, were aligned in a position of strategic reserve opposite Kluge's 2. Panzerarmee and 9. Armee. The largest of the Russian mobile strategic reserves, 5th Guards Tank Army, was positioned in the key southern sector by July 1943. Commanded by one of the Soviet Union's better armor commanders, General P. A. Rotmistrov, its primary purpose was to carry out the main counterattack in the south after the German onslaught was brought to a halt. This operation was known as "Rumyantsev" and was the linchpin of a series of major counterattacks planned for 1943. Rotmistrov's secondary role was to serve as the last line of defense should the Germans break through the belts of fortifications in the south. On 12 July, the 5th Guards Tank Army would face the challenge of stopping German panzer forces in the south before they penetrated into the strategic depths of the Russian defenses. In spite of the handicaps imposed by the losses of the previous years of the war and the superior strength of the Soviets, the German Army would find itself with the opportunity to achieve partial success in the south on that date.

HITLER AND THE LAUNCHING OF "CITADEL"
Many German officers, who, as veterans of the Eastern Front, had experienced the Russian method of waging war, correctly realized the relative German weakness when compared with the vast resources of the Soviet Union. Due to their evaluation of the strategic situation, some of these officers proposed alternative courses of action. The most influential of these German officers was the inspector general of the panzer divisions, Generaloberst Heinz Guderian, who favored a defensive strategy. However, Hitler rejected all alternative plans of a mobile defense put forth by Guderian and decided to continue to prepare for a great summer offensive.

This decision was not made without qualms by some of those in charge of its planning and execution, although Guderian was evidently the most vocal during the early stages of planning. Model and Manstein voiced some degree of caution, particularly after the spring passed and the Russians were given too much time to prepare. Even Hitler himself, desperate as he was for a victory in the summer of 1943, had grave anxieties about throwing his armies against the massively fortified salient. Although he needed a great triumph to stand as "a beacon seen round the world," he confessed to Guderian on 10 May 1943, that the very thought of the attack caused his "stomach to turn over."[1] Since being appointed inspector general early in 1943, Guderian had directed a rebuilding of the panzer divisions which were severely weakened during the winter of 1942–43. Guderian expressed his vehement opposition to "Citadel," recognizing that even a victory would result in high armor losses for the panzer divisions, so painstakingly reconstituted during the winter and spring. In Guderian's opinion, the failure of "Citadel" would result in the loss of the war.

In his judgment, the more realistic course of action was to position the German panzer and panzergrenadier divisions as a powerful strategic reserve and then wait until the Russians attacked. This would present the opportunity to destroy significant Soviet strength after their initial penetrations were halted and the momentum of attack slowed. The panzer divisions would then be able to launch counterattacks and destroy the Soviet attacking forces. There were convincing precedents to support Guderian's argument. The Russian army had not yet perfected an operational force structure that allowed it to conduct and sustain large offensive penetrations in great depth. There were still organizational deficiencies in the Russian mobile forces and more importantly, a tactical inferiority when compared to the Germans panzer divisions. Due to these shortcomings, major Soviet attacks, although always strongly begun, tended to run out of fuel, tanks and ammunition after initial breakthroughs. Because of the priority given tank production, the Soviet army sometimes suffered from a shortage of vehicles to transport infantry and artillery, which affected its ability to sustain deep penetrations. Given the tactical superiority of the German panzer forces and their relatively strong condition at this point in the war, Guderian wanted to employ them in counterattacks after the Soviet offensive ran out of steam. In the spring–summer of both 1942 and 1943, following massive Soviet winter counteroffensives, the Germans skilfully chopped up overextended Russians spearheads, enveloped whole armies, regaining large amounts of territory. Huge losses of manpower and vehicles were suffered by the Russian army in both instances.

However, Guderian's opinion was disregarded by Hitler, who could never bring himself to wholeheartedlly endorse the concept of mobile defense. He knew only one defensive tactic and that was to hold ground stubbornly until the end, regardless of the long-term consequences. Guderian continued to plead his case, however, determined to persuade Hitler that his plan would be best for German forces. After being informed by Feldmarschall Wilhelm Keitel, Chief of the German Armed Forces High Command (Oberkommando der Wehrmacht, or OKW), that Germany had to attack in the East for political reasons, Guderian again pressed Hitler to abandon the plan to attack.

"How many people do you think even know where Kursk is?" asked Guderian. "It's a matter of profound indifference to the world whether we hold Kursk or not . . ."[2] Others opposed to "Citadel" included Generaloberst Walter Model, 9. Armee commander, who presented his views in the form of a position paper given at a conference during which Kluge; Generaloberst Kurt Zeitzler, Chief of Staff of the Army High Command (Oberkommando des Heeres, or OKH); Manstein; and Guderian were all present. Model, after studying detailed air reconnaissance photos of the Russian defenses, quite correctly concluded that the whole salient was a vast killing ground prepared for the express purpose of bleeding a German offensive of its men and machines.[3]

Zeitzler and Kluge, however, were ardent supporters of the plan, Zeitzler somewhat more enthusiastically, as he was one of the authors of a preliminary plan of attack on the salient. Zeitzler's enthusiasm was absolutely unaffected by experience in combat in Russia as he had remained far removed from the realities of the Eastern Front, unlike Model or Manstein. Manstein was also less than optimistic and expressed the opinion that while the plan was good in essence, delays had hurt the chances of its success because too much time had been given to the Russians to prepare their defenses. He knew the consequences of allowing the Soviets time to prepare a defensive position for an expected attack. Manstein believed that the opportunity for victory had been excellent in April, but chances were less certain in the summer. However, he evidently voiced no more strongly worded disapprovals of the plan of attack.[4]

In any event, plans to launch the summer offensive went forward, and Hitler finally gave the formal order to attack on 1 July 1943. On that date, in the Führer bunker complex at Rastenburg, Hitler announced his decision to the assembly of the officers who would carry out "Citadel." Hitler began his speech to the officers with the words. "I have decided to fix the starting date of 'Citadel' for 5 July."[5] Hitler thus gave the official approval of Operational Order no. 6, first signed on 15 April, which had formally notified OKH of the Führer's intention to attack in the summer of 1943. Hitler's decision to launch "Citadel" set the stage for the battle of Kursk, the enormous gamble that so turned the dictator's stomach when he and Guderian had earlier discussed the plan. Arguments for the conduct of a mobile defense were to no avail. In Hitler's opinion, where the German soldier had set his foot, there he should remain by the order of the Führer, and over a million were condemned to do just that, buried by their comrades, frozen in deep snow and ice or rotting in the baking heat of the Russian summer.

On 5 July, led by swarms of Stukas and bombers, the panzer commanders signalled their tanks to move forward and the infantry advanced behind massive artillery and air cover. The last chance of the German Army to gain a strategically significant victory on the Eastern Front rested on the shoulders of the nearly one million German soldiers who marched or rode into the maelstrom. Preceded by waves of Stukas and fighter bomber attacks, following heavy artillery barrages, the attacking divisions began their drives into the Russian defensive system.

"CITADEL"

On the north shoulder, Generaloberst Walter Model's 9. Armee was led by XXXXVII. Panzerkorps, which was equipped with more than 250 Panzer IVs and IIs. In corps reserve was 4. Panzer-Division with 92 tanks. XXXXVII. Panzerkorps was by far the strongest of Model's three panzer corps and it was expected to make the decisive breakthroughs. A second panzer corps, XXXXVI. Panzerkorps, actually had no armor and consisted of four infantry divisions. Model's third panzer corps, XXXXI. Panzerkorps, had only one panzer division, 18. Panzer, which was the weakest of any of the 9. Armee panzer divisions, having only 32 Panzer IVs and IIIs. In reserve was 10. Panzergrenadier-Division and an additional panzer unit, 12. Panzer-Division, which had 55 Panzer III/IVs and at least 30 older tanks.

Model's army was reinforced by several attached armored formations. These included 21. Panzer-Brigade, which was equipped with 66 of the new Brummbär assault guns mounting a 150mm heavy howitzer and schwere-Panzer-Abteilung 505 with 45 Tiger tanks. It is interesting to note that there were more Tigers in this brigade alone, than were given to the entire II. SS-Panzerkorps. There were also seven assault gun battalions fielding a total of 250 Sturmgeschütz IIIs attached to 9. Armee and a regiment that consisted of 90 Elephants, a monstrous assault gun mounting an 88mm gun and heavy armor.

In Heeresgruppe Süd's area, Feldmarschall Erich von Manstein commanded the forces of the southern attack group made up of Colonel General Hermann Hoth's 4. Panzerarmee and General der Panzertruppen Werner Kempf's Armee-Abteilung Kempf. This powerful mass of army and Waffen SS panzer divisions, even stronger than Model's, was given the mission of penetrating the Russian defenses from the south and driving north to Kursk. Hoth's 4. Panzerarmee was made up of two panzer corps, the XXXXVIII. Panzerkorps and II. SS-Panzerkorps.

General der Panzertruppen Otto von Knobelsdorff's XXXXVIII. Panzerkorps had 460 tanks, mostly Panzer IVs and IIIs, in addition to 58 assault guns, 22 flamethrower tanks, and an attached panzer brigade of Panther tanks. The strongest division of the corps was the elite army panzergrenadier division, *Grossdeutschland*, with 120 Panzer III/IVs, a Tiger battalion, and 10. Panzer-Brigade.[6] This brigade consisted of the 51. and 52. Panzer-Bataillons, each of which was equipped with 100 of the new Panther tanks.[7] Although *Grossdeutschland* was the most powerful division in the German Army on paper, the Panther had been rushed into operation without sufficient time to work out design flaws, at least partially as a result of Hitler's insistence on using the new design. As a result, many of these powerful tanks were soon disabled with mechanical problems as well as combat damage, and 75 percent were out of action within days. The other divisions of the corps were 3. Panzer-Division, 11. Panzer-Division, and 167. Infanterie-Division.

The second panzer corps of 4. Panzerarmee, II. SS-Panzerkorps, reported a strength of 327 operational tanks ready on 4 July (not including 25 Befehlpanzers or command tanks) and 95 assault guns.[8] It was ably commanded by a former army Generalleutnant, SS-Obergruppenführer Paul Hausser, the senior officer of the Waffen SS and the officer who organized the SS officer schools. It consisted of 1. SS-Panzergrenadier-Division *Leibstandarte Adolf Hitler*, 2. SS-Panzergrenadier-Division *Das Reich*, and 3. SS-Panzergrenadier-Division

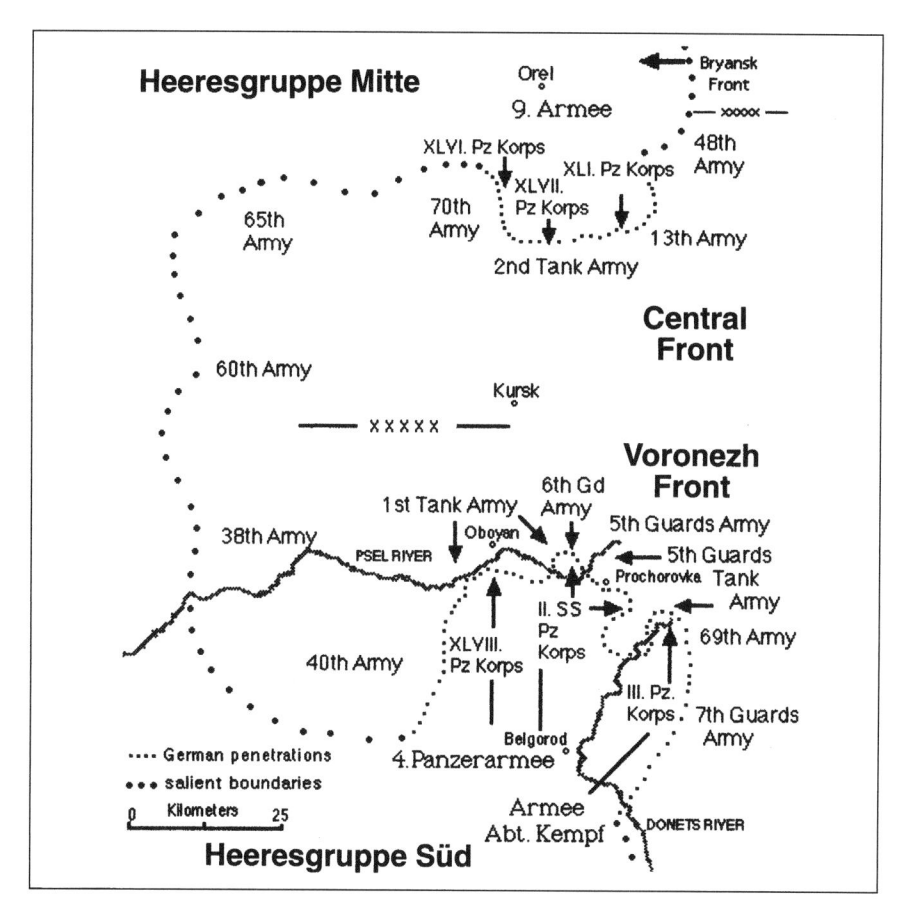

Operation "Citadel."

Totenkopf. Attached to the army were 31 assault guns of 911. Sturmgeschütz-Abteilung. In all, 4. Panzerarmee had an armored strength of about 900 main battle tanks of all types and nearly 180 assault guns for a total of over a thousand armored vehicles.

Armee-Abteilung Kempf's III. Panzerkorps, commanded by General der Panzertruppen Hermann Breith, was made up of several veteran units and included 6. Panzer-Division, 7. Panzer-Division, and 19. Panzer-Division, with a total of 243 Panzer IVs and IIIs between them. Kempf also had some 50 obsolete tanks and 13 flamethrower tanks, altogether over 300 tanks of all types. In addition, he was assigned schwere-Panzer-Abteilung 503 (Heavy Tank Battalion 503) with about 45 Tigers and three additional assault gun battalions with

75 Sturmgeschütz IIIs. This vas a total of about 350 tanks and 75 assault guns for a total of nearly 430 armored vehicles of all types. In reserve was XXIV. Panzerkorps, made up of three veteran divisions, including 17. Panzer-Division, 23. Panzer-Division, and 5. SS-Panzergrenadier-Division *Wiking*.[9] Of the three divisions, 23. Panzer-Division was probably the strongest as XXIV. Panzerkorps records listed it as having 30 Panzer IVs and 26 Panzer IIIs on 13 July, while *Wiking* had 41 tanks on the same date, all of which were Panzer III/IVs.[10] Other sources state that 17. Panzer-Division had 31 Panzer IVs and 25 Panzer IIIs at this date. In total, XXIV. Panzerkorps thus had about 150 tanks on 13 July, not including 40 odd obsolete tanks and a number of assault guns.

The two German armies fielded a total of about 1,650 armored vehicles of all types, a massive amount of armor. However, Manstein's divisions had a formidable task ahead of them, for between the attack start positions and Kursk lay about fifty-five miles. The Soviets had constructed three main lines of defense, characterized by enormous minefields, concealed trenches and antitank strongpoints. Just north of the third line of fortifications, twenty-five miles from Belgorod, was the southernmost bend of the Psel River, the last natural defensive barrier south of the immediate area of Kursk. Beyond the Psel was a great featureless expanse of grassy steppe, perfect tank country for the panzer divisions if they could reach it.

The Soviet formations aligned against Manstein's attack force included six infantry armies in the bulge itself: the 40th, 60th, 65th, 38th, 70th, and 6th Guards Armies. Each army was assigned a large number of subordinate formations, ranging from corps to battalion size, of additional engineer, artillery, antitank, and mortar units. There were numerous heavy assault gun battalions assigned to army and corps commanders to stiffen their antitank defenses. North of the Psel, the 1st Tank Army, the operational armored reserve, deployed the 31st Tank Corps, 3rd Mechanized Corps, and 6th Tank Corps with about 600 to 650 tanks. East of Belgorod, the Soviet Steppe Front constituted the strategic reserve in the south and consisted of several infantry armies and the 5th Guards Tank Army with about 650 tanks. These two Soviet tank armies, the 1st Tank and 5th Guards Tank, opposite Heeresgruppe Süd totaled about 1,250 to 1,300 tanks. There were several additional tank corps available in the south also. The 2nd and 2nd Guards Tank Corps were in position west of a Belgorod-Kharkov line. The 10th Tank Corps was located at Stary Oskol, and the 9th Tank Corps was positioned south of Kursk. Each of these tank corps possessed about 200 tanks. In addition, there were a number of tank or tank destroyer regiments and brigades assigned to the infantry armies. Thus, the Soviets possessed well over 2,000 tanks and other armored vehicles in the south. Given the large operational and strategic mobile reserves possessed by the Soviets, Hitler had more to make him nervous than he was aware of.

9. ARMEE FOUGHT TO A STANDSTILL

On 5 July, the last major German offensive in Russia began. The armored spearheads began their drive to meet in the Kursk area and lop off the salient. The fighting quickly reached a ferocious intensity everywhere, with great phalanxes of tanks and whole divisions of infantry locked in deadly combat. Overhead, great numbers of fighters swirled in dogfights while bombers and ground-attack planes swept in over the battlefield to bomb and strafe targets on the ground.

In the north, Model attacked with his infantry divisions first in order to create breakthoughs for the panzer divisions. This was a major failure of his plan of attack, which failed to utilize manuever and caused 9. Armee's advance to slow quickly. During the initial fighting, the German infantry divisions suffered severe losses without creating sufficient gaps for the armor to exploit successfully. Model's advance ran out of steam, the infantry hopelessly entangled in deep Soviet defenses constructed along lines of fortified villages and hilltops. At three villages, Terploye, Olkhovatka, and Ponyri, the German lead divisions found themselves involved in vicious fighting against Russians entrenched in fortifications behind huge belts of minefields and barbed wire. Although Model's heavy-handed attacks succeeded in bloodily grinding through about ten miles of the Soviet lines against extremely determined resistance, it was halted at these three strongpoints. Instead of utilizing the most important weapon of his armor, its mobility, Model then fed the panzer divisions tanks into frontal assaults on Russian fortifications. Tank losses mounted quickly and German infantry divisions were gutted in bitter combat.

The sacrificial initial gains of the German infantry in the early fighting forced the opposing commander of the Soviet Central Front, General of the Army K. K. Rokossovsky, to commit a significant proportion of his operational reserves to prevent a German breakthrough.

Beyond the fortified line of hills and villages lay open steppe, flat, rolling countryside and ideal terrain for Model's panzers if they could penetrate the Russian line and reach it.[11] However, the German attack struck unyielding Soviet resistance at three fortified towns. Each of these points was a fortress studded with antitank gun positions, machine guns and hidden strongpoints. In front of them were extensive minefields and great tangles of barbed wire, and the fighting there came to resemble the slaughters of World War I in which the fathers and grandfathers of Model's men had fought and died twenty-five years earlier in France. Just as in that war, whole divisions were essentially destroyed fighting in desperate, brutal battles of attrition as both the Germans and Russian fed men into the storm of battle.

One by one, 9. Armee's spearheads exhausted themselves, tantalizingly close to the open ground beyond the range of hills and villages. In the end, both sides fought to a standstill, but the Russians held on to their battered hills and devastated towns while Model's divisions were ruined after suffering thousands of dead and losing hundreds of panzers. Model's pre-"Citadel" fears about the strength of the Russian defenses were correct, as the condition of his infantry divisions and weakened panzer divisions proved. The Russian strategy succeeded, although narrowly, in exhausting the German forces upon deep, well-prepared concentric lines of fortifications situated behind large minefields. The most decisive factor in this sector, however, was that the Soviet command was able to utilize its operational reserves in an absolutely ruthless and successful commitment of men and machines against the German attacks at critical points. After the Germans had used their last mobile reserves in the north, the Soviets still had the 3rd and 4th Tank Armies, their strategic armored reserve, ready for employment when the German attack petered out.

On 11 July, when it became evident that 9. Armee was exhausted, a formidable diversionary counterattack by the Soviet Bryansk and West Fronts was launched north of 9. Armee's left flank, above Orel. By 12 July, in the north, Model's 9. Armee suspended offensive operations, having penetrated a distance of only ten miles from their start position. His exhausted infantry and the decimated panzer divisions had spent their strength after seven days of battering the Soviet defenses. By the above date, Model was now becoming aware of the strength of the counterattack from the Soviet Bryansk and West Fronts which had been launched from north and south of Orel.

This counterattack fell upon 9. Armee's northern neighbor, 2. Panzerarmee, and succeeded in driving deep into the German rear areas. The Soviet penetrations threatened the flank and rear of 9. Armee and forced Kluge to divert forces that otherwise would have been available to 9. Armee. They succeeded in compelling him to commit the few reserves available to Heeresgruppe Mitte against the Orel attacks in order to keep them from cutting off Model's divisions in the south. With this development, there remained no chance that the attack in the north would break through the Russian positions. The strength of the Russian forces left no doubt in Model's mind as to their objective when he reported on 13 July that "Already today it can be concluded from the scale of the offensive against 2. Panzerarmee that the enemy has set as his aim the complete conquest of the Orel Salient . . . radical changes have taken place during the last forty-eight hours. . . . The center of gravity of all operations has shifted to the panzer army. Here the crisis has continued to develop at unprecedented speed."[12] Kluge's army group was so hard pressed that he saw no possible hope for a renewal of his offensive with the forces he had at hand. In fact, by 13 July, Kluge was already in the process of pulling divisions out of the attack area in the southern sector of 9. Armee's front, in order to hurriedly send them north to Orel for commitment against the Soviet penetrations there. He stated that there "could be no question of continuing with Citadel or of resuming the operation at a later date."[13] With the Russians pushing hard for Orel in 2. Panzerarmee's area, there was some doubt in his mind whether 9. Armee would survive the Soviet onslaught, which was entirely unexpected in both timing and strength.

The Germans did not detect the massive Soviet reserves in the north previous to the launching of the attack, and the sudden appearance of such strength unnerved them. Also becoming known was the presence in the north of two entire Soviet tank armies, the 3rd and 4th Tank, which on 12 July had yet to be utilitized by the Russians. Model and Kluge could not know that they would not be committed against Heeresgruppe Mitte until the night of 18–19 July, after the situation in the south stabilized. Until then, the Soviet command may have still cast an uneasy eye to the south, where the battle had not gone as well as in the north. Manstein's 4. Panzerarmee and Armee-Abteilung Kempf had smashed through the 7th Guards Army, 6th Guards Army, and 1st Tank Army as well as elements of the strategic reserve from the Steppe Front. By 12 July, the Soviet strategic armored reserve in the south was in battle. Although Soviet attacks against Heeresgruppe Mitte began to slow down due to German resistance and bad weather, the two Soviet tank armies remained inactive until after Hitler pulled II. SS-Panzerkorps back across the Psel River, abandoning a bridgehead on the northern bank.

MANSTEIN'S 4. PANZERARMEE AND ARMEE-ABTEILUNG KEMPF: THE SOUTHERN WING OF "CITADEL"

The attack began well for 4. Panzerarmee as Hoth's army blasted its way through the first Soviet line of fortifications by nightfall of the first day. In contrast, Armee-Abteilung Kempf pushed forward more slowly, suffering serious losses of men and tanks. The fighting was marked by ferocity and great determination on both sides. Although the Germans made little progress after the first few days in the north, the situation was different in the south. There it quickly became apparent to the Soviet command that the most dangerous German threat of "Citadel" was from Heeresgruppe Süd, led by the armor of XXXXVIII. Panzerkorps and II. SS-Panzerkorps of 4. Panzerarmee. To the east of Hoth's army, III. Panzerkorps of Armee-Abteilung Kempf struggled northward, with difficulty, in an advance parallel to 4. Panzerarmee. Hoth's two panzer corps, in conjunction with III. Panzerkorps, thus threatened to create an extremely dangerous predicament for the Russians south of the Psel River. On 8 July, the situation was so critical that 5th Guards Army was removed from the command of the Steppe Front's strategic reserve and ordered to concentrate north of the Psel River. South of the river, the 6th Guards Army, commanded by Colonel General I. M. Chistyakov, was forced back by 4. Panzerarmee's attack. Vatutin began to hurriedly move all available reinforcements to the critical Psel-Prochorovka area. The operational armored reserve, 1st Tank Army, commanded by Colonel General M. E. Katukov deployed its 31st Tank Corps, 6th Tank Corps and 3rd Mechanized Corps behind 6th Guards Army and attacked through the infantry divisions.

On 9 July, the Russians transfered elements of their 40th Army to 6th Guards Army in the area south of Oboyan after the left flank of Hoth's attack deeply penetrated the 6th Guards Army defenses, forcing its commander to hurriedly move his HQ behind the advance of tanks from Katukov's 1st Tank Army. 1st Tank Army attacked with its

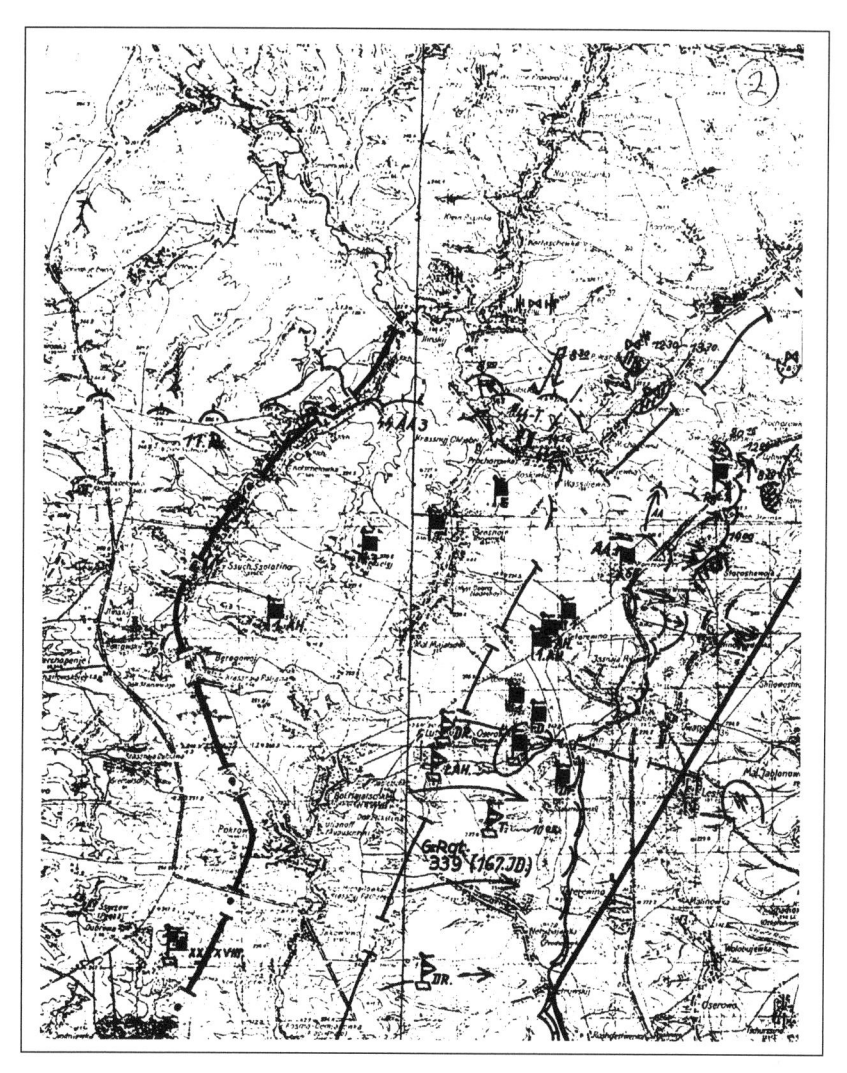

II. SS-Panzerkorps, 11 July 1943.

three corps in order to halt the advance of XXXXVIII. Panzerkorps toward Oboyan and II. SS-Panzerkorps on the Psel River. The 10th Tank Corps was brought up from reserve and also committed to the battle south of the Psel River against Knobelsdorff's panzer corps. Two other Soviet armored units, the 2nd Tank Corps and 2nd Guards Tank Corps concentrated in the sector due south of the town of Prochorovka, on the right flank of II. SS-Panzerkorps and north of III. Panzerkorps. By the afternoon of 10 July, 4. Panzerarmee had succeeded in penetrating about twenty-five miles northward toward the Psel, and XXXXVIII. Panzerkorps split the junction between 1st Tank Army's 3rd Mechanized Corps and 31st Tank Corps.

The Russian 6th Guards Army and 1st Tank Army threw every man and tank they had against the armored spearheads of 4. Panzerarmee in fanatical attempts to prevent a German breakthrough. Tanks were dug in with orders to fight to the death. Infantry made suicidal assaults into the teeth of German panzer attacks and Russian tank crews fought with such determination that on occasion dying drivers rammed German tanks in attempts to destroy them. However, Hoth's panzer divisions continued to grind inexorably through the Soviet defenses. The fact that the Germans were quickly approaching the Psel River resulted in additional decisions by the Soviet command. The strategic armored reserve in the south, Rotmistrov's 5th Guards Tank Army, was also removed from the command of the Steppe Front and by 10 July was well on its way toward the crucial Psel River area and the town of Prochorovka.

Under close scrutiny by Nikita Khrushchev, Stalin's political officer in charge of the southern sector, the Russians utilized all forces necessary against Hoth's panzer divisions in order to stop the Germans before they broke out across the river through the operational depth of the Russian defenses. Even if it meant the use and subsequent destruction of the Steppe Front's reserve armies, the Soviets realized the importance of preventing the Germans from crossing the river in force. It became apparent that Manstein's panzer divisions threatened to do just that after elements of 3. SS-Panzergrenadier-Division *Totenkopf* established a small bridgehead on the north bank.

Totenkopf's river assault began on 10 July, with attacks by Panzergrenadier-Regiment *Totenkopf*, commanded by SS-Obersturmbannführer Otto Baum and Regiment *Eicke*, led by SS-Standartenführer Hellmuth Becker. Soviet infantry of the 33rd Rifle Corps, reinforced by the 11th Mechanized Brigade counterattacked with support of artillery and mortar fire. SS assault elements forced a crossing of the Psel near the village of Kljutschki at 1100 hours when II./*Totenkopf* established a small bridgehead across the river after several earlier, unsuccessful attempts. At 1515 hours, I./*Eicke* also fought its way over the river in spite of heavy Soviet defensive fire. Close behind came the SS engineers with their bridging equipment. After the divisional artillery regrouped to support the crossings, the first panzers moved up and prepared to cross the river while Stukas continued to pound Russian positions. At 1800 hours, III./*Totenkopf*, under command of SS-Sturmbannführer Karl Ullrich, crossed the river north of Krassny Oktjabr.[14] Torrential rain and the resulting mud delayed the arrival of bridging equipment and heavy weapons.

The Russians tried to throw the Germans out of their bridgehead and force them back across the river, but the SS infantry fought back savagely. The 1st Tank Army's 31st Tank Corps reinforced the 33rd Guards Rifle Corps with its remaining tanks and continued the assaults, but the Germans held their ground. On 11 July, at 1125 hours, *Totenkopf* engineers erected a bridge over the river and continued work on a sixty-ton-capacity bridge, which could support the division's Tiger tanks. By that date, the north bank of the river was full of destroyed Russian tanks amid piles of dead Soviet infantry. On 11 July alone, twenty-seven Soviet tanks were knocked out of action. The *Totenkopf* bridgehead marked the northernmost penetration by Heeresgruppe Süd during Operation "Citadel." The tough, battle-hardened SS soldiers resolutely held their ground against major elements of two entire Soviet corps while *Das Reich* and *Leibstandarte* prepared to advance on the following day. *Totenkopf* firmly anchored the left flank of II. SS-Panzerkorps and prepared to attack out of the bridgehead and push its armor across the river for an attack to the north.

On the eve of the fighting of 12 July, *Totenkopf* was in better shape in regard to tank strength than the other two divisions of the corps. It reported to 4. Panzerarmee that it had 54 Panzer IIIs, 30 Panzer IVs, and 10 Tigers, for a total of 94 tanks.[15] This was a net change of 23 tanks since the beginning of the fighting on 5 July, at which time the division had 117 panzers. *Totenkopf* had by that date returned a number of damaged vehicles to action or received a few replacement panzers (possibly both) because the division had been reduced to 78 tanks on 10 July.

Realizing the threat posed by Hoth's two panzer corps, the Soviets transferred all of the artillery from their 38th and 40th Armies to the defense of the Psel.[16] Rotmistrov's 5th Guards Tank Army was ordered to concentrate in the section of land between the end of the Psel and the northern branch of the Donets. Nearly in the center of this sector, between the two rivers, lay the town of Prochorovka.

There Rotmistrov's army arrived on 11 July, assembling where Hoth had correctly anticipated that he could expect an armored attack on his flank. Hoth was almost certainly aware of the advance of the 5th Guards Tank Army due to aerial reconnaissance because the Russians did not use the *maskirovka* measures that would have normally been used to cover an advance of this nature, due to the urgent need of armor in the Psel-Prochorovka area.

Because of the critical nature of the situation on the Psel, Rotmistrov moved his army by day and night, at maximum speed from its assembly areas just west of the Don River, which was approximately 200 miles from Prochorovka. The army had to cover so much a distance in the short time allotted to Rotmistrov that he could not take the normal precaution of travelling only at night. Since it moved on an axis that was twenty-five to thirty kilometers wide, it was impossible to hide the advance from the German reconnanissance planes. The Soviet command realized that the Germany would detect the army and provided additional air support to counter expected air attacks. Evidently, this measure was successful because Rotmistrov was able to cover the distance without significant losses in vehicles. It is possible that due to the demands on the Luftwaffe in the combat areas on the north and south flanks of the salient, there were few planes to spare that could be used to attack the 5th Guards Tank Army route of travel.

The 5th Guards Army and the 5th Guards Tank Army were the forces that Vatutin planned to use to lead the most important Soviet counterattack in the Kharkov-Belgorod area after "Citadel" was defeated in the south. However, when the armies that originally faced Hoth and Kempf were not sufficient to stop the march of the panzer divisions, even after the use of the operational armored reserve, Katukov's 1st Tank Army, extraordinary measures were called for. The Soviets were also forced, as has been noted previously, to use armor, artillery and infantry strength transferred from inactive armies on the flanks of the German attack. This was in direct contrast to the situation in the north, where the Russians were able to stop 9. Armee with their operational reserves. In the Orel sector, neither the 3rd Guards Tank Army nor the 4th Tank Army were needed to halt Model's advance. However, in the south, the Soviet strategic reserve shrank steadily, as one army followed another into action and was consumed. The Russian command had little choice, as it would have been useless to save their strength and lose the Kursk salient with the resultant encirclement of five or more Soviet armies. Vatutin sent Rotmistrov's tank army forward with orders to stop the SS panzers from crossing the Psel at all costs. German and Russian armor met all around Prochorovka on 12 July.

THE BATTLE OF PROCHOROVKA, 12 JULY 1943

By 10 July, as the main body of 5th Guards Tank Army approached Prochorovka from the east, some elements of the 2nd Tank Corps and 2nd Guards Tank Corps were already involved in fighting against Kempf's III. Panzerkorps. The remaining formations of these two tank corps, including the majority of the 2nd Guards Tank Corps, concentrated south of Prochorovka. The Russian tank commanders were given orders to drive the panzers of III. Panzerkorps back, regardless of losses. If Kempf's armor was allowed to break through Soviet defenses south of Prochorovka, the Germans would be in position to attack the left flank of the 5th Guards Tank Army while it was engaged with the SS panzer divisions to its front.

The Soviet command realized early in the fighting that they had to keep the Germans from crossing the Psel in strength or risk defeat in the south. Rotmistrov's army was the last hope of the Soviets to stop the German advance south of the river. The Soviet defensive efforts were aided by torrential downpours of rain that made the terrain difficult to traverse and which helped slow down the Germans enough for the main element of 5th Guards Tank Army to narrowly win the race to Prochorovka. In the days immediately before 12 July, the 1st Tank Army and 5th Guards Army had defended the approaches to the river with suicidal fervor but could not stop the armored spearheads of 4. Panzerarmee. South of the town, however, Kempf's III. Panzerkorps was slowed dramatically.

PROCHOROVKA: 12 JULY 1943

On the morning of 12 July, the climactic day began, with *Das Reich* deployed southwest of Prochorovka on the right, *Leibstandarte* in the center (slightly southwest of the town), and *Totenkopf* on the left, holding the Psel bridgehead and defending the south bank, east of its two bridges over the river. The battle of Prochorovka is one of the most misunderstood major battles of the Eastern Front. The strength of German forces, the course of the fighting and the losses of each protagonist have been incorrectly reported. Of significance are the inflated reports of tank losses by Hausser's II. SS-Panzerkorps and the enormous (factual) losses of Rotmistrov's tank army.

Early on 11 July, Rotmistrov was in Prochorovka, personally directing and concentrating his forces in the area around the town. The 5th Guards Tank Army was made up of the 18th and 29th Tank Corps and 5th Guards Mechanized Corps (see appendix I for order of battle of a typical Soviet tank army). In addition, the 2nd Tank Corps and 2nd

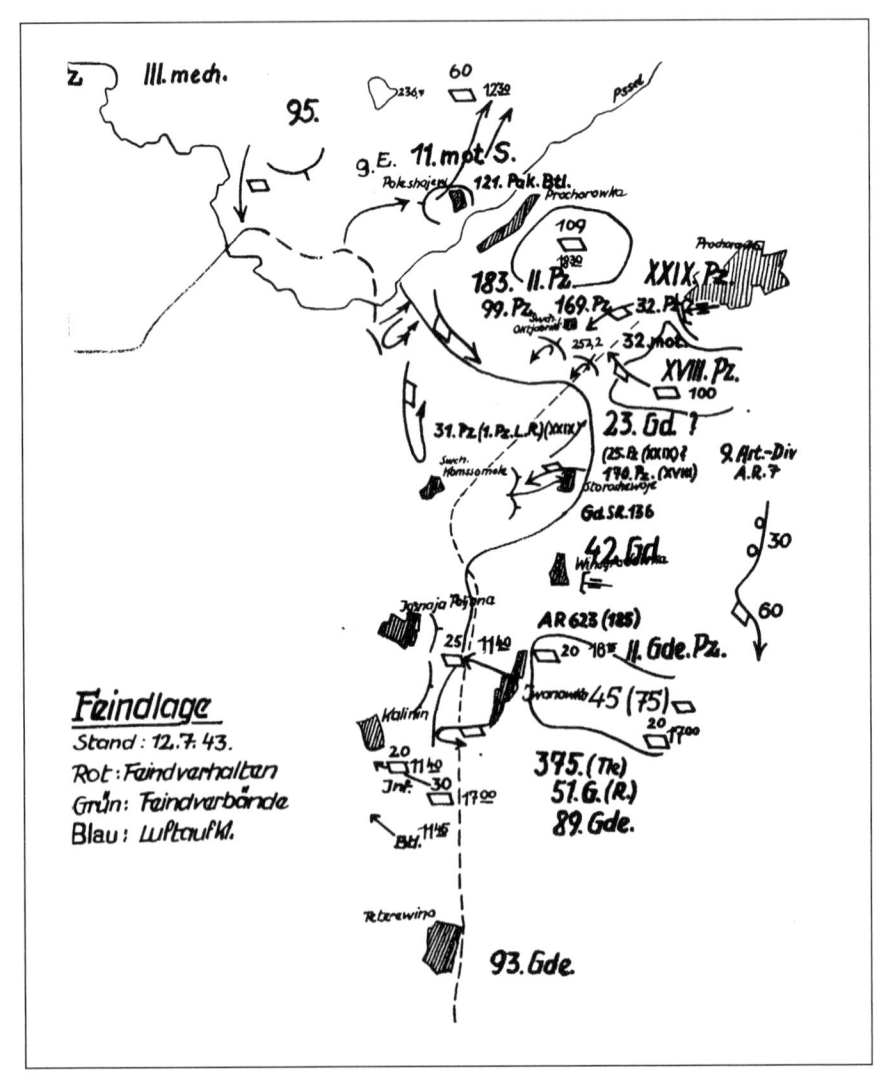

Situation on 11 July 1943.

Guards Tank Corps were attached to Rotmistrov's army by 11 July (see appendix II). Most authorities agree that the 5th Guards Tank Army, including the two attached tank corps, probably had 850 tanks, of which 500 were T-34s. The rest were lighter T-70s and a few Lend-Lease Churchill tanks. The Soviet tanks had barely arrived in time to prevent the capture of the town by the Germans. When he first reached Prochorovka early on 11 July, the Russian commander drove a light vehicle to the outskirts of the town, intending to conduct a preliminary reconnaissance of the terrain beyond the town. He was unpleasantly surprised to see German tanks already assembling in the distance to the west. He hurriedly returned to prepare for his attack, which was to be launched on the following morning.

Prochorovka itself was of no great importance, but it lay square in the middle of the open ground between the Psel and the origin of the Donets River. Since this land bridge was the most likely route of advance for a Russian armored counterattack on the SS-Panzerkorp's right flank, Hoth planned to take the town with II. SS-Panzerkorps in order to secure his right flank prior to the advance north of the Psel. He did not want to continue an advance to the north across the Psel and thereby leave his right flank open to this attack. When his panzer spearheads approached the Psel west of Prochorovka, Hoth ordered II. SS-Panzerkorps to turn to the northeast and deploy for the expected attack. After defeating the Soviet reserves at Prochorovka, he planned to resume his advance north of the Psel and drive on to Kursk with III. Panzerkorps on the right of the SS panzer corps and XXXXVIII. Panzerkorps on the left. North of the river, the terrain was a sea of flat steppe, very favorable for tanks, with no significant natural barriers between the Psel and the Kursk area. In the meantime, while Hausser's divisions prepared to take Prochorovka, XXXXVIII. Panzerkorps continued to push toward Oboyan.

The right flank of the attack by II. SS-Panzerkorps was to be protected by Armee-Abteilung Kempf's III. Panzerkorps' parallel advance east of the line of advance of the SS-Panzerkorps. On 12 July, however, Breith's panzers were twenty-five kilometers south of Prochorovka. This delay, combined with the reports of stalemate in the north, was discussed in a conference between Manstein, Hoth, and Kempf that took place on 11 July during which preparations for the continuation of the attack were discussed. Kempf, his opinion obviously influenced by the heavy losses of tanks that III. Panzerkorps had suffered, favored the ending of the offensive. Hoth, whose two panzer corps were steadily advancing, was of the opinion that the attack should continue. Manstein, after further study of the situation, realized the opportunity presented him by the presence of the 5th Guards Tank Army and agreed with Hoth. Breith's III. Panzerkorps was to resume its attack toward Prochorovka and hit the 5th Guards Tank Army on its southern flank while the Russians were heavily involved fighting II. SS-Panzerkorps. Manstein's intention was to fix the Soviets with a frontal attack by Hausser and cut into the flank and rear of the Soviet tank army with III. Panzerkorps and, if necessary, use XXIV. Panzerkorps, Heeresgruppe Süd's panzer reserve, to finish off the Russians. However, on the following morning, the Soviets beat the Germans to the punch, launching a massive attack all along the front of II. SS-Panzerkorps, while continuing to delay Breith's advance.

Rotmistrov's army deployed on a fifteen-kilometer-wide front of advance, with the 18th Tank Corps on the Soviet right, west of the town; 29th Tank Corps deploying forward southwest of Prochorovka along both sides of the railroad leading out of the town and on the left; the 2nd Guards Tank Corps and 2nd Tank Corps attacking from staging areas to the south. The 5th Mechanized Corps was held in reserve. The action began very early in the morning with sporadic attacks at several points. *Totenkopf* reported a battalion-strength Soviet attack by infantry on the west edge of the bridgehead at 0315 hours, moving south from the village of Wess'elyj. This attack was not supported by tanks. On the southern bank, Soviet armor and infantry were observed assembling near Michailovka.

Leibstandarte reported its first contact with Soviet armor northwest of Prochorovka, after a few Russian tanks made contact with SS panzers at first light. Shortly thereafter, ominously, the dull roar of large numbers of tank motors was reported from the vicinity of the town. With the arrival of daylight, numerous squadrons of Soviet planes swooped in over the battlefield to bomb and strafe forward positions. Reports of heavy artillery fire confirmed the growing sense that this was something more than normal activity.

Totenkopf also noted heavy enemy activity in the air and Russian artillery grew steadily stronger all along its front. *Totenkopf* reported the beginning of an attack by two regiments of infantry with tanks at

0745 hours. This attack was on the south bank of the Psel and advanced to the southwest from the village of Michailovka, which was several kilometers due west of Prochorovka. Its objective was probably the bridges crossing the river, defended by Regiment *Eicke* and some of the division's assault guns.

Southwest of Prochorovka, while *Totenkopf* fought to defend the bridgehead and the vital bridges, *Leibstandarte* and *Das Reich* prepared to attack. *Leibstandarte*, commanded by SS-Brigadeführer Theodor Wisch, was to attack Prochorovka on a narrow three- or four-kilometer front between the Psel and the Prochorovka–Belgorod railroad line. *Das Reich*, commanded by SS-Gruppenführer Walter Kruger, was assembled on its right, on a five-kilometer front, ready to advance east toward Belenichirici and Storoshewoje. Records of 4. Panzerarmee show that *Leibstandarte* had a strength of 56 tanks late on the evening of 11 July, and *Das Reich* had 61, including 8 captured T-34s. This was a total of 117 operational combat tanks, not counting command tanks of which each division had 7. According to 4. Panzerarmee and II. SS-Panzerkorps records, *Leibstandarte* had just 4 Tigers still in action by that date, while *Das Reich* had only 1 Tiger still operational.

Soon after the first scattered fighting of the morning was reported, hundreds of T-34s and T-70s emerged from Prochorovka and advanced in waves all along the front. The loud motor noises heard from the vicinity of Prochorovka had been these tanks assembling for the attack. Rotmistrov observed his army's attack from a nearby hill as the Soviet tanks rolled out of Prochorovka and its environs toward *Leibstandarte*. The 18th and 29th Tank Corps moved quickly to the attack, some of this armor assaulting the base of the bridgehead, defended by Regiment *Eicke*. However, the main body hit the positions of *Leibstandarte*, whose own armor was assembled southwest of the town. By 1000 hours, the SS division reported massive tank attacks at several points. In groups of 30 to as many as 100 tanks, the Soviet armor rolled forward, preceded by heavy artillery support. Soviet infantry clung to the tanks as they careened wildly over the ground between the Germans and the town.

From his hilltop observation post, Rotmistrov had a perfect vantage point to watch his tanks charge headlong toward the Germans. In order to negate the advantage the Germans had in long-range optics and main gun range, particularly the 88s of the Tiger, the

Soviet tank corps was ordered to charge at high speed and close with the Germans quickly. The Russians greatly outnumbered the SS tanks, as a Soviet tank corps normally had about 200 tanks when at established strength, and Rotmistrov believed he could overwhelm the SS panzers if his tanks could close with them. Judging from the direction of attack and the map positions of the forces involved, almost all of the more than 400 T-34s and T-70s of the two Soviet tank corps were headed toward the 56 tanks of 1. SS-Panzergrenadier-Division in the center of the battlefield between the railroad line and the Psel River. About 40 Soviet tanks were reported in action against Regiment *Eicke*, east of the bridges. Some of the 18th and 29th Tank Corps may have contacted the left flank of *Das Reich*'s advance, but the majority assaulted *Leibstandarte*. *Leibstandarte* grenadiers and tank crews watched in amazement as hundreds of tanks emerged from positions of assembly west and south of the town and continued to advance at full speed toward the Germans. The German tanks, assault guns, and antitank guns began to fire at the oncoming Russian tanks at ranges of 1,800 meters or more.

Rotmistrov held the 5th Guards Mechanized Corps in reserve, although one brigade of this corps was already in action against III. Panzerkorps south of Prochorovka. While the 18th and 29th Tank Corps roared toward the panzers of *Leibstandarte*, the rest of the armor of Rotmistrov's army, 2nd Guards and 2nd Tank Corps, moved to the attack against *Das Reich*, advancing in groups of from twenty to forty-five tanks in the first wave.[17]

South of Prochorovka, *Das Reich*, on a line of Storoshevoje-Belenichino-Pravorot, became increasingly involved in repelling these attacks. On the right flank of II. SS-Panzerkorps, from the Storoshevoje area, the main elements of 2nd Guards Tank Corps attacked *Das Reich* throughout the day, supported by armor from 2nd Tank Corps. The intense fighting, with Soviet armored battlegroups continually pressuring the SS and being forced back by repeated German counterthrusts, was a series of ripostes, each side attacking or defending in efforts to destroy the other. During the course of the early part of the day, *Das Reich* was attacked by tanks and infantry from north and south of the Belenichino area.[18]

Totenkopf deployed its panzer regiment, commanded by SS-Sturmbannführer Georg Bochman, across the Psel in attempts to enlarge the bridgehead to the north and the Karteschevka-Prochorovka road. The panzer group of the division apparently included all ten of the heavy Tigers.[19] The *Totenkopf* panzers faced armor of the Soviet 1st Tank Army's 31st Tank Corps, a force much reduced from an original strength of about 200 tanks. How many Soviet tanks were still in action on this date is not precisely known. While 31st Tank Corps, supported by a rifle corps, fought to destroy the SS battle group on the north bank of the Psel, two entire tank corps with a strong infantry support assaulted *Leibstandarte*, and one and a half tank corps attacked *Das Reich*.

The resulting thunderous collision, with a total of about 1,000 tanks in action, was a day-long, chaotic, swirling tank battle. The German tanks, with superior sight optics and better crew training, held a decided advantage over the Russian tankmen when combat took place at long range on open ground. In addition, the Soviet tanks were at a disadvantage because their cannons could not penetrate the frontal armor of the German Tiger tank at even moderate range, while the 88mm gun of the Tiger could penetrate the glacis armor of the T-34 at ranges out to 1,500 to 2,000 yards. However, the relatively small number of Tigers that were left in action with the three SS panzer divisions meant that the bulk of the fighting was carried out by Panzer IIIs and Panzer IVs, even though the small number of remaining Tigers proved to be dangerous opponents, as always. An example of the deadly effect of their 88mm guns occurred during the afternoon.

Untersturmführer Michael Wittmann, the famed SS tank commander, took part in the fighting at Prochorovka, his detachment protecting the left flank of the main afternoon attack by *Leibstandarte*. Wittmann's tank was one of a group of Tigers from 13./SS-Panzer-Regiment 1 (the heavy company) during this engagement. The detachment met main elements of the 18th Tank Corps when the entire 181st Tank Brigade deployed in an attack along the southern edge of the Psel, just as the German advance began. The Soviet brigade advanced to meet the German attack just south of the river.[20] It was during this encounter that a celebrated incident took place that is often given as an example of the intensity of the fighting at Prochorovka. In the Soviet version, which is most often reported, the command tank of the Soviet force, manned only by a wounded driver after the rest of the crew was wounded and abandoned the tank, rammed an SS Tiger and destroyed it in the resulting explosion. This incident is described below, as witnessed by Wittmann:

> The three Tigers rumbled forward in line astern, their turrets trained to two o'clock, until they reached a position at the head of the German armoured force. Then they set out again, keeping pace with the main body. Some time later, they rolled through a corn field and then along an extended balka. The tanks halted on a low rise. The silver band of a stream appeared through Wittmann's vision slit.
>
> Prochorovka already lay behind them. Wittmann hoped to veer towards the village, which was still shrouded in the smoke and flames of battle, and hurry to the aid of his comrades. If they could attack the enemy from behind, they would turn the tide of battle in their favor. But then he heard a warning call from his company commander, followed soon after by the voice of Hauptsturmführer Kling: "Achtung! Strong force of enemy tanks approaching from ahead! Many tanks!"
>
> Moments later, Wittmann, too, saw them. There were at least a hundred enemy tanks of all types, and they were approaching quickly.
>
> "Fire from the halt! Begin firing at 1,800 meters!"
>
> Each gunner selected a target. The mass of Soviet tanks rushed toward the Germans, disappeared into a depression and reappeared again a good 1,000 meters away.
>
> "Aim well, Woll!" gasped Wittmann.
>
> The long-ranging guns of the Tigers opened fire. The first gaps were smashed in the advancing phalanx of enemy tanks. There were explosions and fires. Pillars of smoke rose into the sky. But the main body of enemy tanks—the 181st Brigade of the Soviet 18th Tank Corps—continued to come.
>
> The Soviets were trying to close the range as quickly as possible, because they knew that they had to get to within 800 meters to pose a threat to the heavily-armoured Tigers.
>
> . . . His crew, and those of Lotzsch and Hoflinger, maintained a high rate of fire. By the time the Soviet tanks were within 1,000 meters, every shot was a direct hit. The enemy now began to reply.

They fired on the move and were therefore unable to aim precisely. . . . One group of about fifteen tanks rushed in from the flank. They rolled directly towards Wittmann's three Tigers. . . . "The lead tank, Woll!" shouted Wittmann.

Gunner Woll aimed and fired. They all saw how the shell pierced the side of the T-34. . . . Another hit. The T-34 halted again. . . . As Wittmann watched, the burning T-34 suddenly began to move towards Lotzsch's Tiger. He called a warning!

"Look out! He's coming!"

The blazing ball of fire rolled onwards. Seconds later, the T-34 rammed the Tiger. Flames covered the German tank. It seemed as if the Tiger crew had lost its nerve.

"Lotzsch, back up! Back up!" implored Wittmann.

Suddenly, the Tiger began to back up, separating itself from the ball of fire; one meter, two meters, five meters! At that moment, the T-34's reserve ammunition exploded. After the dust settled, the Tiger backed up to its original position.

The Soviet armored phalanx had been halted. The battlefield was saturated with burning and disabled tanks. Some of stricken tanks continued to fire on the Tigers, until they too were hit again and destroyed.[21]

Throughout the morning and early afternoon, groups of Russian tanks tried to break through *Leibstandarte* in the center of the German attack while other Soviet battle groups jabbed repeatedly at *Das Reich*. Rotmistrov sent the armor of four entire tank corps against the Germans in successive waves. The main elements of the 5th Guards Mechanized Corps remained in reserve during the morning and early afternoon.

Both sides claimed destruction of large numbers of tanks. The tank losses that the 1st Tank Army's three armored corps suffered against XXXXVIII. Panzerkorps and *Totenkopf* are not known, but Katukov's 6th Tank Corps had only 50 tanks left two days earlier, on 10 July and two additional days of hard fighting would only have reduced its strength and that of the army in general.[22] However, the severity of the damage done to the Soviets by the German panzer divisions can be roughly estimated from the following information. Colonel David Glantz, who utilized Russian sources, reports that the 1st Tank Army received 200 new tanks by 3 August, repaired all of its vehicles that could be put back in action and still was 20 percent under strength in tanks by that date. Thus, it would be safe to assume that Katukov's army probably was reduced to between 100 and 150 tanks on 13 July. German losses on 12 July were moderate although *Totenkopf* had only 49 operational panzers left on 13 July, from a total of 94 on 11 July. On that same date, the division's Tiger tanks were all out of commission, although most were back in action within days. These figures and estimates provide stark testimony to the intensity of the fighting across the river in the bridgehead. The panzer losses of *Leibstandarte* and *Das Reich* were much lighter, contrary to popular conception.

Past histories dealing with the battle of Prochorovka have given inaccurate figures in regard to the number of SS tanks that took part in the fighting around the town, leading to misconceptions about the facts of the battle and resulting in incorrect conclusions. Various sources give totals of SS tank strength before the battle of Prochorovka, ranging from 300 to 600 tanks. These numbers are inaccurate, as can be seen from study of the records of II. SS-Panzerkorps, which are available at the National Archives (see appendix III). These records show that the corps had 327 combat tanks on the day before the battle of Kursk began. After seven days of hard fighting, late on 11 July, II. SS-Panzerkorps reported a total of 211 operational tanks. Of these, only 117 were in action against the 5th Guards Tank Army south of he river. As we have seen, most, if not all, of *Totenkopf*'s armor was across the Psel, in the bridgehead. Nor were there large numbers of Tigers in action. Of the tanks of the two SS divisions south of the river, the majority were Panzer IIIs, by that time equipped with a long-barreled 5cm gun or Panzer IVs, which were upgraded with a 7.5cm high-velocity gun. SS battle records give daily tank strength reports, carefully listing each type of tank, even down to barrel length, and list the numbers of each type in operation on that day.

The fighting in which Wittmann took part resulted in the destruction of the 181st Tank Brigade and was the last gasp of 18th Tank Corps. Evidently, by late in the day, the 18th and 29th Tank Corps were both substantially reduced in strength or destroyed because Rotmistrov believed that they had failed to stop the SS tanks, and as a result, he committed his last reserve, the 10th Guards Mechanized Brigade and 24th Guards Tank Brigade of 5th Guards Mechanized Corps. At this point in the battle, hundreds of Soviet tanks were already out of action. Exact figures on the losses of the individual Soviet formations are not usually available; however, the numbers of German tanks that were lost in the fighting can be more accurately determined.

It is difficult to pinpoint exactly how many tanks were actually operational with combat divisions in action at any given time. However, as a general indication of how many total tanks a division had, the daily reports from II. SS-Panzerkorps are enlightening, particularly in regard to the numbers of Tigers that actually took part in the battle on 12 July and the total number of German tanks that were on hand. As an example, II. SS-Panzerkorps records for 11 July report four *Leibstandarte* Tigers still operational. However, in the account of the fighting of Wittmann's group, there were only three Tigers left in action, one evidently having been knocked out earlier in the day. From this example, it can be seen that divisional tank strengths change by the hour during combat and corps-level reports reflect only the number of tanks in operation at a given time on a certain day.

As a second example concerning the heavy tanks, the battle report of *Totenkopf* for 11 July lists ten operational Tigers, while, on 13 July, the division reported none of the huge panzers as available for action, all ten having been damaged or knocked out in the fighting in the bridgehead.[23] On the evening before the battle, *Leibstandarte* listed five Panzer IIIs and forty-seven Panzer IVs, while having just four Tigers and seven command tanks. *Das Reich* on 11 July had thirty-four Panzer III (5cm long-barreled), eighteen Panzer IVs (7.5cm long-barreled), and only one Tiger, in addition to eight captured T-34s and seven command tanks. Not including command vehicles, this is a total of 117 SS tanks in action west or south of Prochorovka. They were opposed by five tank or mechanized corps of the 5th Guards Tank Army with 850 tanks.

However, in warfare, numbers alone do not always mean superiority on any given battlefield. In spite of the mediocre armor and less than dominating main armament of the Panzer IIIs and IVs, the Germans remained tactically superior to the Russians due to flexible, aggressive command, better crew training, superior optics and a crucial advantage in communication capability. All German tanks had radios and thus could instantly adjust to changes in battle conditions and react accordingly. On the other hand, Russian tank formations were, until later in the war, not equipped with radios except in the company commander's tank. This meant that not only were individual tanks unable to communicate with each other, but unit commanders could not give orders to their tanks by radio. This deficiency resulted in delayed or nonexistent response to the changing events of battle, a shortcoming that was exacerbated by tactics often characterized by rigid adherence to orders regardless of losses and conditions. The Russian tank units were led by officers who were trained to follow orders, not operate with personal initiative, because orders could not be easily transmitted to individual tanks or small units. As a result, time after time on the Eastern Front, particularly in the first years of the war, Soviet armor losses were often catastrophic when confronted with good-quality German panzer units. On 12 July, these deficiencies, combined with a disastrous tactical decision by Rotmistrov, contributed to the virtual destruction of the 5th Guards Tank Army.

The Russians, by order of Rotmistrov, who was concerned about the 88mm cannon and heavy frontal armor of the Tigers, closed at high speed with the SS divisions in order to negate the deadly main armament of these tanks This tactic was particularly evident in *Leibstandarte*'s battle sector in the narrow strip between the Psel and the railroad west of Prochorovka. The decision was disastrous and resulted in the destruction of scores of Soviet tanks due to accurate long-range German fire. German losses were light because the Russian tanks fired while running at high speed and the result was inaccurate fire. Neither Russian nor German tanks of the period were equipped with gun stabilizers, and accurate fire was only possible when stationary. Although at point-blank range, the T-34 cannons could destroy even the heavy Tiger tanks, particularly when directed against side or rear armor, it would have been impossible to fire with accuracy while moving fast.

As the Russian onslaught roared across the battlefield toward them, German tanks scored many kills in the first moments of battle. Reacting quickly, the panzers moved and fired, covered by their comrades, working in practiced teamwork. Antitank projectiles slammed around inside T-34s and T-70s, killing or mangling crews and detonating ammunition. Thunderous explosions blew turrets weighing thousands of pounds completely off turret mounting rings and blazing wrecks belched columns of oily black smoke into the sky. When surviving Soviet tanks reached the forward SS defensive positions, the conditions became more chaotic as they passed through the positions of the German armor. Confusion reigned in the fluid situation, with individual German tanks firing at the Russian tanks as they raced past. The Soviet tanks continued moving forward, through the ranks of the panzers, moving with single-minded purpose.

Clouds of choking dust and smoke swallowed up vehicles and made identification of units and tanks difficult. The veteran SS tank commanders were instantly forced to rely on their experience and instincts in that situation. They kept on the move, firing at the Russian tanks frantically, stopping to utilize whatever cover was available. The Russian infantry had leapt off their tanks once they came under fire, were left behind and became scattered, forced to fend for themselves when the tanks rushed on.

As they continued their charge forward, Russian tanks continued to fall victim to the experienced SS tank commanders, who turned around, moved in behind the Soviets and picked off the T-34s from the rear, one after the other. One of the German tank commanders who experienced the massed armor attack of the Soviets at Prochorovka was Obersturmführer Rudolf von Ribbentrop, a panzer company commander serving with *Leibstandarte* at the time of the battle at Prochorovka. His account gives a vivid picture of the confusion that reigned when the Soviet tanks made their wild attack:

> As we waited to see if further enemy tanks were going to appear, I looked all around, as was my habit. What I saw left me speechless. From beyond the shallow rise about 150 to 200 meters in front of me appeared fifteen, then thirty, then forty tanks. Finally, there were too many to count. The T-34s were rolling toward us at high speed, carrying mounted infantry. . . . Soon the first shell was on the way and with the impact a T-34 began to burn. It was only fifty to seventy meters from us. . . . The avalanche of enemy tanks rolled straight towards us: tank after tank!
>
> We had only one slim chance: we must remain constantly in motion. A stationary tank would be immediately recognised by the foe as an enemy and fired upon, because all the Russian tanks were rolling at high speed across the terrain. . . .

> At the repaired bridge over the antitank ditch our tanks and antitank guns fired at the onrushing enemy. I had managed to roll into cover behind a knocked out T-34. From there we took part in the battle against the enemy tanks. . . . Burning T-34s drove into and over one another. It was a total inferno of fire and smoke. . . . The entire slope was soon littered with burning enemy tanks.[24]

After the confusion and carnage of the battle, during which he was credited with the destruction of fourteen enemy tanks, Ribbentrop was surprised to find that most of his company had survived unscathed in spite of the masses of Soviet tanks that had overrun the German position. When the commander of II. SS-Panzerkorps, SS-Obergruppenführer Paul Hausser, visited the scene of this battle later in the day, he marked the destroyed Soviet tanks with chalk in order to count them accurately. There were over a hundred knocked-out Soviet T-34s at one point alone. Ribbentrop's account supports the conclusion that II. SS-Panzerkorps did not lose a catastrophic number of tanks during combat on 12 July 1943 and instead inflicted enormous tank losses on the Russians during the battle of Prochorovka.

> The losses suffered by my company were astonishingly low. The only two total losses were those I witnessed at the. Beginning of the attack. The other two companies had suffered no total losses. . . . Within our main line of resistance, there were over one hundred knocked-out Russian tanks.

Meanwhile, the fighting went on at other points near Prochorovka. From the north and northeast, the divisions of 5th Guards Army (commanded by General A. S. Zhadov and not to be confused with 5th Guards Tank Army) attacked *Totenkopf* with strong air support throughout the day, supported by the surviving tanks of 31st Tank Corps.[25] In this sector, the German and Soviet air forces were constantly in the air over the battleground. Waves of German planes supported *Totenkopf,* making a number of attacks on Soviet artillery positions and assembly areas. Swarms of low-flying Soviet Ilyushin 2s roared through the clouds of smoke and dust searching for German targets. Stukas screamed down to attack Russian tanks with bombs or specially mounted 37mm cannon that could penetrate thin armor on hull tops or engine covers. The advance of *Totenkopf* was led by nearly continuous Stuka support, the dive-bombers destroying one Soviet strongpoint after another. Fighters fought duels high above the battlefield, the losers crashing to earth trailing smoke and flame, adding their wreckage to the blasted terrain.

On the north bank of the Psel, the stubborn SS grenadiers of *Totenkopf* held their ground against assaults by tanks supported by the infantry of the 33rd Guards Rifle Gorps, air attacks and rocket barrages. Regiment *Eicke*, reinforced with some assault guns, successfully defended the base of the bridgehead south of the river by counterattacking the Soviet force that had threatened the bridges earlier in the day. During the course of the day, the Soviets kept continuous pressure on the small bridgehead with a series of strong attacks all along the frontline positions of *Totenkopf*. The fighting was bitter at all points. On 12 July, the SS division reported that it knocked out twenty-seven Russian tanks in the fighting north of the river and had taken 238 prisoners.

In spite of difficulties in getting heavy weapons over the river due to mud and poor roads, the SS engineers kept the bridges in operation, funneling weapons and supplies into the bridgehead. On the afternoon of 12 July, while the chaotic battle west of Prochorovka was in progress, the *Totenkopf* panzer group pushed to the northwest of the village of Poleshajev, battling Soviet tanks as barrages of *Stalinorgel* (rockets) impacted all over the attack sector. By 2245 hours, the panzer group reached and cut an east-west road northwest of Poleshajev, the Kartaschevka-Prochorovaka road. Poleshajev was situated just across the Psel, lying a few kilometers to the northwest of Prochorovka.[26] However, *Totenkopf* found that it was unable to further enlarge its bridgehead perimeter due to constant Russian counterattacks. Nevertheless, on 12 July, the left flank of II. SS-Panzerkorps remained secure, as the division turned back all Soviet attempts to crush the toehold on the north bank of the Psel.

In the meantime, on *Leibstandarte*'s front, the Russian tanks that survived their charge past the guns of the SS tanks continued to push blindly into the rear areas of the division. The sudden appearance of Soviet armor resulted in frantic small-unit battles when packets of T-34s or single tanks appeared unexpectedly. Without infantry or artillery support following their headlong rush through the German armor, the Soviet tanks were vulnerable to close assault or heavy weapons. Some were destroyed by direct fire from artillery. Others were destroyed by antitank guns or *Leibstandarte* infantry and assault guns when they blundered into German strongpoints.

The tactical deficiencies of the Russian tank units, the decision to close at speed and the superiority of the German tank crews at this point in the war combined to produce a slaughter of Soviet armor. The SS divisions destroyed hundreds of Soviet tanks, decimating Rotmistrov's army. Besides the various factors previously mentioned above, there may have been other dynamics at work that contributed to their peculiar behavior and heavy tank losses of the magnitude suffered by Rotmistrov's army. Recognizing an inevitable degree of bias in German accounts that mention situations where Soviet tank formations were awkwardly commanded or tactically inflexible when compared to German tank formations, there may be a very logical reason for instances of clear lack of tactical skill in Soviet armor actions during this period of the war.

In June 1941, the Soviet Union possessed more armored vehicles than any other nation in the world, with more than 22,000 tanks alone. Within six months, there were fewer than 2,500 left in action and nearly all of the prewar Soviet tank corps were destroyed, most so completely that they had to be totally rebuilt, having lost their vehicles, equipment and command structure. Losses of trained officers, tank commanders and crews were catastrophic. After the winter of 1941, the Soviets rebuilt their armored force, organizing regiment- and battalion-size units instead of the more unwieldy prewar tank corps.

Beginning in early 1942, these units helped drive the Germans back from Moscow. In doing so, however, the Russians once again endured high losses of vehicles and a corresponding percentage of tank crews, an assumption based on the loss of 1,386 additional tanks, during the fighting around the Soviet capital between December 1941 and the spring.[27] The warm weather of 1942 brought German attacks that regained the lost territory of the winter. Again large numbers of shattered Russian tanks and dead crews littered the battlefields behind the inexorable advance of the German panzers during spring and summer of 1942.

The enormous losses of personnel that occurred in the first two years of the war resulted in shortages both of trained officers, crews and the ability to provide adequate training instructors. The Soviet army was forced to employ emergency tactics to provide crews for the thousands of tanks that their enormous factories were producing every month. An example of the measures that the Soviet were forced to utilize in order to man their tanks was evident as late as the end of 1942. The Russians were so desperate for tank crews at Stalingrad that they manned newly produced tanks with the factory workers who built them. The workers finished a tank and drove it from the factory to the battlefield, untrained in even the rudiments of armored warfare. The results were predictable. This is not to say that all or even most of the Soviet tank crews were untrained because there was a growing number of trained and experienced tank soldiers commanded by equally experienced and skilled Soviet commanders forged by the experiences of 1941 and 1942. However, after losses on the scale endured by the Soviet armored forces during these two years, the percentage of inadequately trained and less experienced tank crews must sometimes have been high.

This situation continued later in the war as well. Mellenthin, in *Panzer Battles*, mentions an interrogation of a captured Russian tank commander in mid-1943 during which the Germans learned some startling information. This man had been a farm tractor driver and was conscripted into service as a tank commander solely on the basis of his ability to drive a tracked vehicle. Inevitably, most of such tank crews must have been slaughtered very quickly. However, this Soviet practice, although costly, kept tanks in the field and allowed the quick rebuilding of shattered Soviet armored units. This became a singular characteristic of the Soviet tank force during the Second World War. The Germans were often startled when a division, corps or even an army that had been destroyed in battle only weeks or months before suddenly appeared again on the battlefield, miraculously reborn and fully equipped.

There were instances when a Russian tank army suffered heavy losses in armor and was reduced to a hundred tanks or less, but was back in action within weeks equipped with hundreds of new tanks. It is simply not possible to train replacement tank crews adequately in two or three weeks. The only explanation was the use of significant numbers of very quickly trained tank crews. When they had to utilize such troops, the pragmatic Soviets may very well have realized that to attempt to employ complex armored tactics would certainly confuse novice crews and commanders. Only the simplest orders could be expected to be understood and obeyed. It may also explain why the Soviets did not bother to install radios in their tanks in the first years of the war. The confusion of battle may have caused hesitation and weakening of the attack and so the Russians accepted the lesser of two evils.

Rather than try to utilize more complex offensive tactics and communication capabilities, the Russian stressed a rigid conduct of battle according to simple and specific orders (accepting the resulting losses) that characterized Soviet armored operations in the years from 1941 to 1943. By later in the war, toward the end of 1943, there began to be enough survivors to provide a growing nucleus of experienced tank commanders and crews. Just as the rank and file gained experience, the brigade and battalion commanders who survived the first two years of the war, such as Rotmistrov, Katukov, Rybalko, and others, became first corps and then army commanders. The Soviet tank arm, under the leadership of officers such as these, gradually developed into a formidable weapon of war.

However, in the summer of 1943, although improving steadily, the Soviet tank formations were no match for the well-trained German tank units. There is no way to measure the number of sufficiently trained crews that made up the 5th Guards Tank Army in July 1943. However, the attack of the 5th Guards Tank Army was characterized by inflexible adherence to orders regardless of the fluid, changing nature of armored warfare.

Whatever the state of training in Rotmistrov's army, it was decimated by the Germans west of Prochorovka and dug its surviving tanks into positions along the front during the night of 12 July. Having gone over to defensive operations, giving up its mobility, it was in a position to be destroyed by the end of the day. Combined with a successful advance from the south by Breith's III. Panzerkorps, Manstein's panzer divisions could have cut off and isolated 5th Guards Tank Army as well as 1st Tank Army. Hoth's decision to turn east was the correct operational move. Combined with a successful advance from the south by Kempf's III. Panzerkorps, it could have resulted in the utter destruction of Rotmistrov's army. But the Soviet 69th and 7th Guards Armies, supported by elements of 2nd Tank Corps and detached elements of Rotmistrov's 5th Mechanized Corps, successfully delayed the advance of III. Panzerkorps. As a result, the right flank of the SS panzer corps' attack was exposed to the attacks of Soviet armor on 12 July.

The failure of III. Panzerkorps to keep pace with the attack of Hausser's divisions was a serious setback for the Germans because it resulted in the weakening of II. SS-Panzerkorps main effort directed at Prochorovka. The initial attack on the town was made without the full strength of the corps because *Totenkopf* was fighting for its life in the Psel bridgehead and on the south bank of the river where it defended the bridges that it had thrown over the river. As a result, *Totenkopf* was not able to add much weight to the attack on the town itself. During the day, *Das Reich* was forced to increasingly turn its attention to the repeated counterattacks of 2nd and 2nd Guards Tank Corps on its front and right flank. The Soviets did not advance in reckless waves against *Das Reich,* instead choosing to attack with tank and infantry columns that probed for gaps in the division's front. These lead elements struck SS defenses or advancing elements of the division at numerous points, and ferocious fighting broke out at each spot of contact.

Leibstandarte became essentially isolated in the center, taking most of the full impact of the attack of 18th and 29th Tank Corps and later elements of the 5th Guards Mechanized Corps. It is not surprising that a single division, under this type of pressure, could not take Prochorovka. The division was faced with an aggressive attack by overwhelming numbers of Soviet tanks before it could get its own assault underway. While *Totenkopf* fought on the Psel and *Das Reich* fought off the attacks from the south and held firm, *Leibstandarte* initially recoiled from the shock of the ferocious Soviet tank attacks. It was able to regroup later in the day. By that time, the division was exhausted from non-stop fighting against a seemingly unending supply of 5th Guards Tank Army tanks and infantry. Rotmistrov could devote nearly his entire strength to the attacks on *Das Reich* and *Leibstandarte* because his southern flank was secured by the blocking action of the Soviet troops fighting against Breith's III. Panzerkorps. The inability of III. Panzerkorps to keep up with the attack of Hausser's divisions was thus a major factor in the failure to capture the town on 12 July.

Almost from the first day of "Citadel," General der Panzertruppen Herman Breith's III. Panzerkorps, the armored element of Armee-Abteilung Kempf, had difficulties fighting its way north. It was only after great difficulties that Breith's three panzer divisions and the infantry of 168., 106., and 320. Infanterie-Divisions advanced to the east from their starting positions south of Belgorod and reached the west bank of the Donets. They successfully crossed the section of the river that ran due south through the area east of Belgorod, throwing small detachments of infantry across the river in rubber boats. However, the Soviets shelled the crossing sites heavily, and this caused delays in constructing bridges across the river and supply interruption. The tanks of 19. Panzer-Division and reinforcements of 168. Infanterie-Division were held up and were not able to cross the river on the first day. Only 7. Panzer-Division was able to quickly establish a large bridgehead on the east bank and support it with armor and heavy weapons. It was decided to exploit this success by the use of 6. Panzer-Division. That division was switched from its route of advance and brought up through the positions of 7. Panzer-Division. On the second day, the two panzer divisions pushed east of the river, encountering strong Soviet resistance in the form of well-entrenched infantry supported by antitank guns and smothering artillery.

On 6 July, the two panzer divisions encountered further difficulties. The Germans were surprised by the appearance of a new Soviet weapon and reported this to army headquarters. A heavy Soviet assault gun, the SU-152, which was a T-34 tank chassis equipped with a 152mm howitzer as its main armament, appeared in the sector of 7. Panzer-Division. The German tankers found that this new Soviet weapon, firing a 100-pound shell, was a deadly opponent.

In the area of 6. Panzer's attack, the terrain was difficult and poorly suited for tanks. The Russian defenses were anchored on wooded high ground which hampered the movements of armor. In the first days of the fighting, the panzer divisions of III. Panzerkorps had already lost large numbers of tanks. Stubbornly fighting on, enduring continued losses of armor and infantry, Armee-Abteilung Kempf finally forced its way through the Soviet positions.

Penetrations by 19. and 7. Panzer were reinforced and broke the defensive line of the Soviet 7th Army at several points, forcing it to retire from its positions along the Donets. The army withdrew to the east, across a smaller parallel river, the Koren. It was at this point, after III. Panzerkorps penetrated the 7th Guards Army's lines and shattered its front, that the Soviet command ordered elements of 5th Guards Tank Army to turn to the south and protect the southern flank of the army at any cost. A tank brigade of Rotmistrov's 5th Guards Mechanized Corps and the 92nd Guards Rifle Division moved to support the 69th Army along the section of the Donets River that bent to the east from a point several kilometers north of Belgorod. Elements of the 2nd Tank Corps were already fighting against Kempf's armor. The reinforced 69th Army bore the brunt of Kempf s attack toward II. SS-Panzerkorps and Prochorovka. The 7th Guards Army had retreated in some disorder to the east over the Koren and was attempting to regroup.

On that day, 19. Panzer-Division and 6. Panzer-Division turned north and broke out of the area east of Belgorod. The attack of 19. Panzer-Division successfully pushed north, toward the town of Sabynino, which resulted in the creation of a narrow salient west of the division's path of attack. This developement threatened to trap elements of two Russian rifle divisions between the panzer division on the east, 168. Infanterie-Division on the south and 167. Infanterie-Division on the west edge of the ten-kilometer-long salient which ran from south to north. The Soviet forces that could not escape were destroyed by concentric attacks of the infantry divisions and elements of 19. Panzer-Division. In a parallel attack on the right of 19. Panzer-Division, 6. Panzer-Division drove several kilometers forward and took the village of Melikhovo, which lay more than fifteen kilometers northeast of Belgorod. However, 19. Panzer-Division's attack fell behind its neighbor because it remained involved in attacks on the salient.

On the right flank, 7. Panzer-Division occupied defensive positions on the east flank of the corps, facing 7th Guards Army. It held those positions until replaced late on 10 July by infantry of 168. Infanterie-Division. During the night of 10 July, the three divisions of the panzer corps regrouped and prepared for renewed fighting on the following day. After being replaced, 7. Panzer-Division moved up to the south of Melikhovo, in order to support the attack of 6. Panzer-Division on 11 July. The attack was renewed late on that day, and in subsequent advances, the eastern spearhead of 6. Panzer Division reached the Kazachye area, where it was counterattacked by strong Soviet tank forces from the north. On its left, 19. Panzer-Division reached the southern edge of the town of Sabynino. North of Kazachye, the Donets River veered eastward, and the 69th Army defended the approaches to the river on the southern bank, fighting to hold bridges at several points along the river. By that time, the Soviet 7th Guards Army had recovered and was able to exert some pressure on the right flank of III. Panzerkorps by 9 July, attacking with infantry and a few tanks in small attacks on the eastern front of 168. Infanterie-Division and 7. Panzer-Division.

By early on 11 July, his army debilitated by very serious infantry and armor losses, Kempf believed that it would be wise to cancel the offensive. He did not believe that his army had the armored strength to reach its objectives and tried to persuade Manstein to call off the attack during a meeting that was also attended by Hoth, whose army had smashed through to the Psel but had also suffered less serious tank losses. Hoth and Manstein believed the attack should be continued, and so III. Panzerkorps continued to slog forward, now turning to the northwest, toward Prochorovka. Kempf's panzer divisions, having less than a total of 100 tanks on that date, succeeded in crossing the Donets using deception, after forcing a crossing with brute force had failed.

Under cover of darkness on the night of 11 July, III. Panzerkorps seized a small bridge crossing the Donets River near Rzhavets. Led by a captured T-34 acting as a Trojan horse, an audacious attempt to capture the main bridge across the river narrowly failed when elements of 6. Panzer-Division's 11. Panzer-Regiment, under command of Major Franz Bäke, surprised the Russian troops guarding the bridge. The daring Bäke penetrated the town defenses without firing a shot or alarming the occupying troops until they reached the main bridge. However, Bäke's men were not able to eliminate the bridge's defenders quickly enough, and it was blown up by demolition charges at the last instant. Although the main bridge was destroyed before it could be captured, a smaller bridge was found intact and was quickly seized. German infantry and support weapons were thrown across the river as quickly as they arrived and dug in on the opposite bank.

By morning, a German bridgehead was firmly established on the northwest bank of the Donets. This development caused a panic at Steppe Front headquarters because a III. Panzerkorps attack on the left flank of the 5th Guards Tank Army while it was fully engaged to its front with II. SS-Panzerkorps would spell disaster for Rotmistrov. The Russians tried desperately to maintain a solid front south of the Donets, throwing elements of armor, infantry and antitank units against Kempf's panzers. Russian air attacks were heavy, and with few

German fighters to provide air cover or tactical support, III. Panzerkorps operated at a distinct disadvantage. The German advance did not stop, but continued slowly.

Stubbornly fighting from successive defensive positions and counterattacking ferociously with armor and infantry, the Russians had inflicted losses of nearly 200 tanks on III. Panzerkorps by 12 July. It was only through the boldness of the attack by Bäke and a generous helping of luck that it got across the Donets. In spite of this success, counterattacks against III. Panzerkorps on 11–12 July prevented it from supporting the attack by the SS panzer divisions against Prochorovka. As a result, major elements of two Soviet tank corps were free to attack *Das Reich* along the entire axis of advance of the SS unit. The southern flank of 5th Guards Tank Army was secured by the sacrifices of the Soviet forces south of Prochorovka. By late morning on 12 July, *Das Reich* was fully engaged with attacks from the south by 2nd and 2nd Guards Tank Corps.

At 1140 hours, a strong Russian infantry attack, supported by tanks, struck II./Regiment *Deutschland* a few kilometers southwest of Prochorovka when the battalion advanced toward the village of Storoshevoje. The grenadiers destroyed nine Soviet tanks and turned back the infantry, after which the attack foundered. The loss of armor forced the Russians to retreat and their infantry units regrouped in a nearby wooded area. The SS battalion pressed on with its attack towards Storoshevoje, which was strongly held by the Russians, assaulting and breaking into the defensive perimeter on the southern edge. After bitter house-to-house fighting, the southern half of the village was reported captured at 1340 hours. Soon afterward, contact with elements of *Leibstandarte* was established near the village. At 1600 hours, the regiment's comannder, SS-Standartenführer Heinz Harmel, reported that II./*Deutschland* was attacking the northern section of Storoshewoje.

Shortly before noon, other Soviet armor/infantry battle groups attacked lead units of *Das Reich.* One such assault hit I./Regiment *Der Führer* near the village of Jasnaja Poljana with a strong force of seventy tanks supported by infantry. Only after intense fighting lasting over an hour was the Soviet armor repulsed. At 1205 hours, II./*Der Führer* was assaulted on both flanks by a series of attacks involving a total of about fifty tanks that advanced westward from Belenichino. The left flank of the battalion endured the strongest Soviet attack when about forty tanks and large numbers of infantry hit the SS positions at that point. On the right flank of the battalion, a smaller force of ten tanks was turned back. A detachment of Soviet infantry, with several T-34s, was able to break through the forward perimeter of the battalion, but this penetration was sealed off and destroyed by counterattack.

While *Der Führer*, led by SS-Obersturmbannführer Sylvester Stadler, fought off Soviet armor around Belenichino, SS-Panzer-Regiment 2, commanded by SS-Obersturmbannführer Hans-Albin von Reitzenstein, was involved in a meeting engagement with about forty Soviet tanks. The Russians used large numbers of fighter-bombers to support their attack, some of which were American. One Martin plane was reported shot down by antiaircraft units. After a short fight during which the panzer regiment repelled two attacks, the Russians withdrew, leaving twenty-one destroyed or disabled tanks behind.[28] Despite these setbacks, the Soviets continued to aggressively pressure *Das Reich* from the east and south with continued attacks. The numbers of Russian tanks seemed to be without end, and although Soviet armor losses were high, more tanks continued to arrive. Late in the afternoon, German air reconnaissance reported a large Soviet column of sixty tanks and twenty-five to thirty other vehicles moving to the south from a point near Pravorot. These were probably the tanks of the 5th Guards Mechanized Corps sent south to join the fight against either *Das Reich* or possibly III. Panzerkorps.

LEIBSTANDARTE ATTACKS PROCHOROVKA

With *Das Reich* heavily involved in fighting on the right flank of the attack by the SS panzer corps and with Breith's III. Panzerkorps unable to break through in the south, it was left to *Leibstandarte* to renew the attack on Prochorovka. Although the division inflicted enormous losses on the Soviets during the first battle, it was temporarily halted in the open ground between the village of Bogoroditskoye and the Belgorod–Kursk railroad by the vigor of the armored assaults of the Soviet tank corps. The first assaults of the 5th Guards Tank Army had stunned the veteran division, but it recovered after repelling the massed tank attacks and attempted to advance on Prochorovka once again. The panzer regiment moved to the attack, supported by the division's few remaining Tiger tanks.

Rotmistrov watched the attack of the 18th and 29th Tank Corps from his hilltop position, observing his tanks rush toward the German tanks and disappear into the maelstorm. The smoke, confusing nature of the battle and huge clouds of dust made observation difficult, and it was not until the afternoon that it became clear to Rotmistrov that *Leibstandarte* was advancing past the wreckage of his initial assaults. The attack of 18th and 29th Tank Corps had spent its power. Soviet tanks had been destroyed by the hundreds, and when the SS panzers emerged out of the smoke and fire, Rotmistrov was forced to throw more tanks into the battle. Late in the day, the last reserves of the 5th Guards Mechanized Corps, which consisted of the 24th Guards Tank Brigade and the 10th Guards Mechanized Brigade, were committed against Hausser's panzers. These were the last reserves of 5th Guards Tank Army, and their counterattacks blunted *Leibstandarte*'s final thrusts toward the town as night fell over the battlefield.[29] In the darkness, lit by burning tanks and distant explosions, Russian tanks battled the SS panzers to a standstill while heavy rain poured down and thunderstorms erupted overhead. The crash of thunder and lightning added to the din of battle to create a surreal atmosphere of smoke, fire and torrents of rain. Late in the evening, the fighting began to die down, as both sides were exhausted.

Although the Soviet tank corps of Rotmistrov's army were decimated, Hausser's SS panzer corps was halted by late 12 July. Because of the endless hours of continuous combat, during which there seemed to be a limitless supply of Russian tanks, the Germans were spent temporarily. After seven straight days of hard fighting and the resulting mental and physical strains that its men had endured, II. SS-Panzerkorps could not take Prochorovka. The fighting gradually came to a halt after dark. Lightning flashes lit up the battlefield sporadically above the hulks of burnt-out tanks and thunder rolled through the skies. Columns of black, oily smoke rose to the sky, marking where tanks burned. Driving rain storms pelted the soldiers and flooded low spots, turning them into morasses. Death, destruction and exhaustion ended the combat in the night of 12–13 July. The *Leibstandarte*, although it destroyed the main Soviet tank force of 5th Guards Tank Army in the center, did not have enough strength to take the town alone.

When the fighting wound down in the blasted fields surrounding Prochorovka, Armee-Abteilung Kempf's tanks were also at a standstill, with 6. and 7. Panzer-Divisions still some ten to twelve kilometers to the south, fighting to break out of the Donets bridgehead.

The sacrificial efforts of Rotmistrov's 5th Guards Tank Army and the armor and infantry of Zhadov's 5th Guards Army and the attached reinforcements had halted the Germans by sheer weight of numbers and determination. According to Soviet accounts, the 29th Tank Corps lost 60 percent of its armor, approximately 125 tanks. The 18th Tank Corps reported the destruction of over 30 percent of its armor. Several Soviet tank brigades were essentially destroyed, notably the 181st Tank Brigade, whose mix of T-34s and T-70s ran into the *Leibstandarte*'s Tiger tanks and were annihilated by the 88mm guns of the heavy panzers. Taken as a whole, the 5th Guards Tank Army suffered the destruction of a major portion of its tanks, having only 150 to 200 operational vehicles left after its collision with the SS panzer divisions.[30] This figure is supported by Rotmistrov's own account of the battle in his 1984 book, *Stal'naya gvardiya*, in which he states that by 13 July, he had 400 tanks out of action with battle damage that could be repaired, not counting those that were total losses or unrecoverable at that time. The SS panzer divisions met most of a full-strength, reinforced Soviet tank army and elements of an infantry army in battle and had held their ground, while sustaining only moderate losses of their own armor. The three SS panzer divisions still had a total of 163 operational tanks on the following day, 13 July, having destroyed several times their number of Soviet tanks.[31] The XXXXVIII. Panzerkorps, on the left of Hausser's corps, had a few more tanks, listing 173 operational panzers on the same date. Thus, Hoth's 4. Panzerarmee still had 336 operational tanks, and III. Panzerkorps still had an additional 83 tanks. The Germans tanks thus outnumbered the remnants of 5th Guards Tank Army by approximately two to one after the fighting halted for the day. Hoth and Kempf planned to resume the attack on the following day, reporting to the OKH that massive Soviet forces had been committed against them.

The HQ of 4. Panzerarmee commented in the daily combat report that it had been counterattacked along its whole front during the course of the day. The army stated that it had been attacked near Prochorovka by two tank corps, in the north by several rifle divisons supported by armor from two tank corps and on its western flank by two armored corps and a mechanized corps.[32] The successful capture of the hill to the northwest of Michailovka (by the panzer group in the *Totenkopf* bridgehead) was mentioned. The divisions of both German armies prepared for another hard day of fighting, unaware that while they planned for 13 July, Manstein would be in a meeting with Adolf Hitler and Kluge on that day. During that conference, decisions were made, in the opinion of Manstein, that "threw away a victory."

THE EFFECTS OF THE FAILURE OF III. PANZERKORPS' ATTACK

The inability of III. Panzerkorps to secure the flank of Hoth's attack was a critical failure, and the result was that Hausser's II. SS-Panzerkorps, although it severely damaged elements of five Russian tank corps and decimated the infantry of the supporting rifle divisions, was not able to achieve its objective. That Hausser could not advance with at least *Das Reich* and *Leibstandarte* attacking side by side was a direct result of the attacks made by 2nd Tank Corps and 2nd Guards Tank Corps on *Das Reich*. The failure of III. Panzerkorp's attack from the south thus had serious consequences for the attack on Prochorovka on 12–13 July and subsequently to 4. Panzerarmee's attempts to secure a second bridgehead over the Psel. If III. Panzerkorps had broken through the Soviet counterattacks and advanced to Prochorovka, it would have penetrated the southern flank of 5th Guards Tank Army. At the very least, the success of Breith's attack could have freed *Das Reich* to deal with only those forces advancing from Prochorovka itself, the 18th and 29th Tank Corps. Since these two tank corps were destroyed in fighting against *Leibstandarte* panzers early in the day, the two SS divisions may have been able to destroy the last elements of Rotmistrov's army, the 5th Guards Mechanized Corps. This formation was already at reduced strength, having only two brigades at that time since one brigade of its tanks had earlier been sent to join the fight against III. Panzerkorps. Since one SS division destroyed two tank corps in the early fighting on 12 July, it is likely that two entire SS divisions could have annihilated Rotmistrov's two remaining brigades and retained sufficient strength to advance on the town itself. This would have essentially meant the destruction of the 5th Guards Tank Army and probably would have resulted in the capture of Prochorovka.

Had Hoth taken the town, the consequences for the Soviets in the Psel area could have been catastrophic, given the losses inflicted on 5th Guards Tank Army. The Soviet command correctly understood the danger to Rotmistrov's army presented by the approach of III. Panzerkorps and took appropriate steps to keep the two panzer spearheads from crushing Rotmistrov's army between them. The united advance of two panzer corps may have been enough to force their way past Prochorovka and push across the Psel at a second point. If *Das Reich* had penetrated Russian lines southeast of the town and united with III. Panzerkorps elements, the opportunity would have been available to turn north and cut the supply lines of the 5th Guards Tank Army. This would have resulted in a crisis situation for the Russian command because it had no more available armor reserves in the Psel-Prochorovka area. The II. SS-Panzerkorps would have been in position to throw a second bridgehead over the Psel east of *Totenkopf* while protected by III. Panzerkorps' presence on its right. This would have put the Germans in the ideal position to use Heeresgruppe Süd's panzer reserves, XXIV. Panzerkorps. A German advance north of the Psel would have cut 1st Tank Army's lines of supply and communication to the east. Thus, it would have been forced to either withdraw or be destroyed. Either choice would have resulted in relief of the pressure against *Totenkopf*'s bridgehead across the Psel.

The annihilation of the command and organizational structure of the 1st Tank Army and Rotmistrov's 5th Guards Tank Army, beyond the ability of the Soviets to defeat a resumption of the German attack across the Psel on 13 July, would have critically affected the Soviet plans for the summer of 1943 in south Ukraine. The consequences of the destruction of Russian armored reserves in the south and the effect on Soviet objectives in south Ukraine and their relationship to Prochorovka will be examined in greater detail in later chapters. However, the 69th, 5th Guards and attached armor were able to sufficiently delay III. Panzerkorps' advance and prevented the link-up with II. SS-Panzerkorps on 12 July. It was not until 14 July that III. Panzerkorps elements made contact with *Das Reich*. Although this belated success encircled and destroyed Soviet forces south of Prochorovka, it was a hollow victory. By that date, it was too late to affect the battle for Prochorovka, due to events on the extreme right wing of Heeresgruppe Süd and decisions made by Hitler in response to those situations. When Hausser's II. SS-Panzerkorps was stalemated on 12 July by the sacrifice of Rotmistrov's army and Breith was unable to attack the southern flank of the 5th Guards Tank Army, Manstein lost the best chance that the Germans had of breaking into the tank country north of the Psel.

II. SS-PANZERKORPS FIGHTS ON: 13 JULY TO 17 JULY

Hausser continued to probe for a weakness in the Soviet defenses on the following day, although the attacks were again hampered by violent rain storms and mud. While *Leibstandarte* regrouped from the bloodletting of 12 July, *Das Reich* worked at the flank of the Russian defenses south and east of Prochorovka. Battered Soviet units were observed withdrawing along the division's front, pulling back toward Prochorovka from out of the Pravorot area, which lay just to the south of the town.[33] In *Leibstandarte*'s sector, it became evident that Rotmistrov was content to dig in his surviving tanks and wait. It was obviously to the Soviets' advantage to force the Germans to attack them as opposed to resuming their own offensive operations when the German armor was still relatively strong.

The Russians began to conduct an aggressive defense west of the town with the coming of first light. On the morning of 13 July, a Soviet reconnaissance force of about two companies pushed down the road from Prochorovka. This was a prelude to a larger, regiment-size attack just after noon. The attack was supported by heavy artillery fire, rocket barrages and swarms of Soviet fighter-bombers but only a handful of tanks. The guns of *Leibstandarte*'s artillery regiment and heavy infantry weapons broke up the attack. The surviving Soviet infantry withdrew without penetrating the frontline positions of the division. Small groups of tanks had cautiously supported the Soviet infantry but made no aggressive advances. Under the cover of this and other strong probing attacks, the Soviets remained dug in along a broad defensive line opposite *Leibstandarte*'s front. The Russian attacks were effective harrassing attempts designed to keep the Germans busy and off balance. In the meantime, the Soviets continued to strengthen their defenses with emplaced tanks, antitank guns and automatic weapons.[34]

Totenkopf managed to hold on against the counterattacks of the Soviet 31st Tanks Corps and the 33rd Guards Rifle Corps. It became clear that the main effort of the Russians for 13 July was directed against the SS positions on the north bank of the Psel. The German bridgehead was under constant pressure by Russian infantry and tanks during the entire day. In the air, Russian attack planes were overhead constantly. Although the Soviet air force was able to operate over the entire area of the bridgehead throughout the day, the Luftwaffe found its operations considerably restricted by difficulties with muddy airfields, which prevented Germans planes from taking off. The bridgehead defenders, with the aid of the *Totenkopf* panzers, fought off all Soviet attacks, which were supported by artillery and fearful barrages of rockets. Sturmbannführer Karl Ullrich, commander of III./*Totenkopf*, personally exhibited such courage and leadership in turning back the Russian efforts that he was described by the divisional commander, Priess, as the "soul of the resistance," in Ullrich's recommendation for the Oak Leaves to the Knight's Cross.[35]

The *Totenkopf* panzer group remained in action near Hill 226.6. During the fighting on the previous day, the division had lost all ten of its Tiger tanks to battle damage and reported no operational Tigers on 13 July. Late in the morning, from the northwest corner of the bridgehead, the Russians launched a tank and infantry attack from the town of Vesselyj at 1000 hours. Heavy artillery and rocket fire supported the attack, which was followed by a second that originated from east of the same village.[36] A third Russian attack, in regimental strength, advanced out of Vessely at 1545 hours and pushed toward Hill 226.6. This attack resulted in a dangerous local penetration of the defensive line and the bridgehead forces urgently requested air support. Three hours after this request was made, German planes had not appeared, and the grenadiers and panzers of *Totenkopf* cleaned up the Soviet breakthrough without the support of the Luftwaffe.

On the southern bank of the river, elements of *Totenkopf* were under attack also. Regiment *Eicke* turned back an attack at 0945 hours by eight to ten tanks and infantry, which was followed by an infantry assault in battalion strength. Soviet fighter-bombers were in action in this sector as well, with several Russian planes being shot down by the divisional flak detachments. Although *Totenkopf* could not enlarge its bridgehead, the Russians could not destroy it and continued to suffer heavy losses. The Soviet tank losses during the attacks on 13 and 14 July further reduced the strength of 1st Tank Army. Two companies of SS-Panzerjäger-Abteilung 3 were credited with destroying thirty-eight Russian tanks in less than twenty minutes during an attack on 13 July.[37] Since 31st Tank Corps had been reduced to fifty tanks by 10 July, these losses must have resulted in almost total destruction of the corps.

A further indication of how the Russian tank losses continued to mount before and after Prochorovka can be derived from the daily reports of II. SS-Panzerkorps. On 13 July, a single Tiger tank commander, SS-Untersturmführer Hans Mennel of 6./SS-Panzer-Regiment 2, was cited for his destruction of six Russian tanks. These victories were in addition to his being credited with the destruction of eight Soviet tanks on the second day of the offensive and ten more on 10 July.[38] In a span of six days, this one panzer destroyed twenty-four enemy tanks. This type of performance, while not the rule, was not unique, as can be seen from Ribbentrop's total of fourteen destroyed Russian tanks on 12 July.

While the other two divisions of II. SS-Panzerkorps were fully occupied with Russian counterattacks on 13 July, *Das Reich*, after it repulsed 2nd Guards Tank Corp on 12 July, continued to push to the east in an attempt to get around Prochorovka. At 2100 hours on 13 July, the division received its orders for the next day from 4. Panzer-armee. While *Leibstandarte* and *Totenkopf* maintained their positions, *Das Reich* was to push first to the east, take Belenichino and from there advance farther east before turning northwest to attack the rear of the Russian defenses at Prochorovka. The right flank of the division was to be protected by the 167. Infanterie-Division, which was to close to the Ivanovka area. *Das Reich* was ordered to capture Belenichino, located just to the southwest of Prochorovka, as its initial objective in preparation for the subsequent drive past the town.[39]

After a short artillery preparation by divisional artillery and attached Nebelwerfer detachments, early on the morning of 14 July, I./ and III./*Der Führer* attacked Belenichino at 0400 hours, securing a base to push from there on to Pravorot, which was due south of Prochorovka. In furious house-to-house fighting, the *Das Reich* grenadiers destroyed twelve Russian tanks in close assault and turned back several infantry counterattacks, before finally gaining the upper hand and driving the Russians out of the town for the first time. Almost immediately, Russian infantry counterattacked and pushed back into the town aggressively, only to be driven out again. After fierce see-saw fighting in which some portions of the village changed hands repeatedly, *Der Führer* took the town for the last time at 1130 hours.

Again the Russians regrouped and made a determined effort to throw the Germans out of Belenichino by assaults of infantry and tanks, strongly supported by artillery and air attacks. However, all attempts to fight through the German perimeter and recapture the town were unsuccessful. The arrival of SS armor settled the issue, and the last Russian attackers withdrew under machine-gun and cannon fire from the panzers. After *Das Reich* tanks moved to the east edge of the town, the division prepared to push farther to the east, intending to gain ground south of Prochorovka before turning back north. In this manner, Hausser meant to skirt the strong Soviet defenses in front of the town and find less formidable Russian forces on the southeast edge of the area. If a breakthrough could have been made east of Prochorovka, the Russian troops facing *Leibstandarte* would have been in danger of being cutoff.

At 1715 hours, *Das Reich*, continuing its advance to the east, captured Ivanovka after battling Russian tanks near Hill 234.9. The Ia of the division, SS-Sturmbannführer Georg Maier, was forward with the two battalions of *Der Führer* and the supporting divisional armor, personally directing the attacks on both Belenichino and Ivanovka. Following the capture of Ivanovka, *Das Reich* advanced to the northeast along both sides of the Leski–Pravorot road. As darkness settled over the battlefield, *Das Reich* spearhead elements pushed Russian defenders out of a small wooded area 1.5 kilometers north of Ivanovka. After this last action of the night, a halt was called to further advances, *Das Reich* remaining just short of its final objective of the day, Pravorot.

During the night of 14–15 July, a heavy downpour of rain once more turned the battle area into a quagmire, with the dirt roads of the Russian countryside becoming almost impassable. Resupply of fuel and ammunition was extremely difficult and was accomplished only with the greatest difficulties.

While *Das Reich* struggled to advance through the mire on 15 July, the other two divisions of II. SS-Panzerkorps were fighting to keep their gains. *Leibstandarte* and *Totenkopf* were again probed strongly during the hours of darkness by aggressive and increasingly more powerful reconnaissance forces, while Russian artillery, rocket and mortar units delivered constant heavy barrage and harrassing fire on the frontline positions, communication trenches and supply routes.

In spite of the difficulties presented by the mud, *Das Reich* slogged to the attack once again on the next day, somehow managing to move its vehicles through the muck on the morning of 15 July. At 0605 hours, the division received a radio transmission from 7. Panzer-Division, indicating that it had reached Malo Jablonovo, which was just a few kilometers south of Pravorot. Spurred to the attack once more by this knowledge, *Das Reich* pushed forward with renewed effort. By early afternoon, the two divisions established communications at Malo Jablonovo. Leski, just to the southwest of that point, was reported clear of Russians by reconnaissance units of Regiment *Der Führer*. The SS grenadiers received a welcome surprise when they cautiously reconnoitered the village. Instead of Russian infantry, the SS men found men of 167. Infanterie-Divison occupying the town. From there, the troops of that division advanced to Hill 234.9, near Ivanovka, establishing a solid link with *Das Reich* units west of Pravorot.

As the day passed, *Das Reich* continued to push all the way to the outskirts of Pravorot. The attack was hampered by minefields and antitank ditches in addition to horrendous difficulties presented by the mud. The combination of the elements and strong Soviet defensive positions in and around Pravorot proved too much for one tired division to overcome, particularly one that had been in combat continuously since 5 July. This was the obvious time to commit the army group's reserve panzer force, the XXIV. Panzerkorps, which was then located at Belgorod, only twenty-five to thirty kilometers from Prochorovka. However, as later chapters will show, other events determined the use of the three panzer divisions of XXIV. Panzerkorps and its 150 tanks. Without commitment of reserves, the last offensive action of II. SS-Panzerkorps in the Prochorovka area gradually slowed. When orders were received to prepare for withdrawal from the area by 17 July, any further attempts to take Prochorovka were pointless. Hausser's men, by this time, were close to exhaustion, although tank strength had steadily increased from the 13 July total of 163 machines, due to the return to action of repaired panzers. In the evening report to 4. Panzerarmee on 16 July, II. SS-Panzerkorps reported that it had a total of 197 operational combat tanks.[40]

On the other two SS divisional fronts, while *Das Reich* slogged steadily to the east, the Russians maintained heavy artillery and mortar fire on the *Leibstandarte* and *Totenkopf* positions. In *Leibstandarte*'s sector, the Soviets mounted company- to battalion-size attacks on the German front lines, feeling for a weakness or gap. Sometimes the Soviet attacks were accompanied by a few tanks, but each was supported by artillery, mortar and rocket fire as well as fighter-bombers. Behind this screen of small-unit activity, which kept the division fully occupied, the Russians continued to strengthen their defenses around Prochorovka. They avoided large-scale offensive action with armor, which invariably drew quick, destructive reaction by the Germans. The Russians dug in most of their surviving tanks and conducted an aggressive defense, primarily with infantry. Fighting in the bridgehead across the Psel remained almost continuous.

Essentially, the front stabilized after 15 July, with both of the opponents too worn out by the fighting to do anything decisive. Late in the night of 15–16 July, the divisions of II. SS-Panzerkorps received orders from Hausser that effectively meant the end of Operation "Citadel" in the south. *Das Reich* and *Leibstandarte* were given defensive assignments, and *Totenkopf* was ordered to prepare to withdraw its troops from the bridgehead over the Psel on the night of 17–18 July.

The fighting had gone on after 12 July, all around Prochorovka, with *Das Reich* doggedly trying to outflank the defenses of the town while *Totenkopf* repulsed Russian tank and infantry attacks on the north bank of the Psel and *Leibstandarte* held on to the ground west of the town. But the German leadership at the highest level had lost its enthusiasm for the attack. The men at the front still fought and died, but Hitler's attention had already turned to other matters just at the critical stage of the battle for Prochorovka. The inability of 4. Panzerarmee and Armee-Abteilung Kempf to capture Prochorovka on 12 July resulted in an obvious slowdown of the advance. Had the town been taken and a second penetration over the Psel taken place, possibly in conjunction with a successful use of the panzer reserves, arguments that Manstein put forth to Hitler on 13 July in regard to continuance of the Heeresgruppe Süd attack may have carried more weight. However, frustrated by the obvious slowing of the "Citadel" offensive and distracted by other events, Hitler had already abandoned hope of success.

HITLER MEETS WITH MANSTEIN AND KLUGE: "CITADEL" CANCELLED

Although the German troops continued to fight and made modest offensive gains after Prochorovka, their sacrifice was for nothing. Unknown to the officers and men in the field, on 13 July, Hitler had told Manstein and Kluge that he intended to pull II. SS-Panzerkorps out of the Eastern Front in order to send it to Italy and that he wanted to utilize XXIV. Panzerkorps at Izyum and the Mius River. Manstein, in his remembrances of this meeting, reported that Hitler was very concerned with events in Italy because of the Allied invasion of Sicily. Agitated that the Italians were not making much of an effort to fight back, he intended to transfer the three SS divisions to the West, thereby adding some additional strength to the German forces there. Hitler explained that Operation "Citadel" was to be cancelled due to the events in the West, the stalemate on the Heeresgruppe Mitte front and the slowed pace of the offensive in the sector of Heeresgruppe Süd. Kluge was in total agreement, as Model's 9. Armee was then completely on the defensive, drastically short of armor and hard pressed to fight off the Russian counterattack at Orel. He adamantly requested that several panzer divisions from Heeresgruppe Süd be released to him. Over Manstein's objections, Hitler ordered that *Grossdeutschland* was to be sent north to Model, resulting in a further weakening of 4. Panzerarmee south of the Psel River.[41]

When Hitler announced that he was going to cancel "Citadel," Manstein argued for more time to develop the situation; however, it became clear that the Führer's attention was not on the the Psel-Prochorovka area, the critical arena of the war on that date. Mussolini had been deposed shortly after the invasion, which also concerned Hitler. The dictator told the two officers that he needed divisions with the "political" character of the SS divisions. The importance that Hitler placed on the assumption of political conviction and the corresponding will to fight in a fascist cause gives a clue as to why the panzer divisions of the Waffen SS became so important in the last two years of the war. His comments illustrate the detachment from reality that often influenced his commands and the concern with matters of secondary importance while critical decisions were avoided: "The point is, I can't just take units from anywhere. I have to take politically reliable units. . . . Down there, I can only accomplish something with elite formations that are politically close to fascism."[42] Due in large part to their perceived "political" reliability, the SS panzer and panzergrenadier divisions continued to be shuffled from one crisis to the next, without rest, for the remaining months of the war.

Hitler had already written off "Citadel" at this date, and he had Kluge's clear endorsement, although Manstein saw the situation differently. Essentially, however, the last great German summer offensive of the war was all but finished. Operation "Citadel," the attack that was to have restored German dominance on the Eastern Front—and in Hitler's own words, to "dispel the gloom of our Allies and crush any silent hopes still lingering within our subjugated people"—was ended, at least in his mind. After 12 July, all the sacrifices made by the men of the army and SS divisions were in vain. Soon the divisions of II. SS-Panzerkorps were dispersed to various hot spots on the Eastern Front, while shortly afterward *Leibstandarte* entrained for the journey to Italy. The foremost proponent of the importance of "will," Adolf Hitler, had himself lost the will to continue Operation "Citadel" at the very moment when he had a chance of achieving at least some measure of victory in the south.

In Manstein's opinion, the decisive moment had only then arrived, and he argued that to disengage now while he had uncommitted panzer reserves (XXIV. Panzerkorps) would be a disastrous mistake.[43] The Soviet armored operational reserve in the south, the 1st Tank Army, had already suffered tank losses of catastrophic proportions. When it had failed to stop the German advance, the armies of Steppe Front, the strategic reserve in the south, were fed piecemeal into the battle. The battlefields of Prochorovka and the *Totenkopf* bridgehead were littered with hundreds of destroyed Russian tanks. The premature use of these armored reserves was detrimental to the most important purpose assigned to the front, which was to offensively exploit the situation after the defeat of the German attack on the Belgorod-Kharkov axis. This premature commitment greatly disturbed the commander of Steppe Front, Lieutenant General I. S. Koniev. He protested strongly, though futilely, when he saw 27th Army taken away from him very early in the battle, on 6 July. Later, he could only watch as, one by one, the armies under his command were thrown into the battle and dismantled. The 5th Guards Army was ordered to the Psel also and endured heavy losses of infantry and equipment fighting II. SS-Panzerkorps as well as elements of III. Panzerkorps. Steppe Front's strategic armored reserve, Rotmistrov's 5th Guards Tank Army, joined the battle on 12 July and had lost about 650 tanks, reporting only 150 to 200 operational tanks in action on 13 July.[44] Rotmistrov was ordered to move his army toward Prochorovka only days after the beginning of "Citadel." It was a measure of the seriousness of the situation as early as 8–9 July that the Soviet leadership ordered Rotmistrov's army into action so much earlier than was planned.

Manstein thus had good reason to believe that some degree of success was still possible on the southern wing. He held a rare temporary superiority in local tank strength in the Psel-Prochorovka sector on 13 July. His reserve, XXIV. Panzerkorps, with three panzer divisions, including 5. SS-Panzergrenadier-Division, was concentrated in the Belgorod area, barely thirty kilometers from the battlefield at Prochorovka. The veteran 23. Panzer-Division had 61 tanks, all Panzer IIIs and IVs, while 17. Panzer and 5. SS-Panzergrenadier-Division had 56 and 31 tanks, respectively. In addition, the corps had thirty to forty obsolete tanks and a few assault guns.[45] That was a considerable weight of armor considering the damage done to 5th Guards Tank Army on 12 July. On 13 July, 4. Panzerarmee still had about 330 panzers, which, combined with the armor of XXIV. Panzerkorps and Kempf s divisions, would have totaled nearly 600 German tanks in addition to the assault guns and self-propelled antitank guns of each division. Manstein and Hoth were dumbstruck when they weren't allowed to continue the attack: "To Fourth Panzer Army and Armee-Abteilung Kempf, convinced that victory lay in their grasp, the order to stop 'Citadel' came as a shock. Manstein and the commanding generals of the armies at first still hoped to be able to mop up south of the Psel River, but even that satifaction was denied them."[46] Manstein's further comments regarding his reaction to Hitler's decisions are given in *Lost Victories*: "Speaking for my own army group, I pointed out that the battle was now at its culminating point, and that to break it off at this moment would be tantamount to throwing a victory away. On no account should we let go of the enemy until the mobile reserves he had committed were completely beaten."

Because of the losses inflicted upon Soviet armor, the battle of Prochorovka resulted in local numerical tank superiority of at least two to one in favor of the Germans south of the Psel on 13 July. Considering that SS panzers of *Das Reich* and *Leibstandarte* and the attacks of III. Panzerkorps inflicted losses on the magnitude that 5th Guards Tanks Army suffered in one day of fighting at Prochorovka, this situation clearly presented an opportunity for the Germans. The nearest significant uncommitted Soviet armor was located near Kursk and consisted of the 4th Guards Tank Corps and elements of the 4th Mechanized Corps. Less than two armored corps would have been hard pressed to stop the full panzer strength of Manstein's two armies in an all-out attack on Kursk. It is evident by Khrushchev's comments regarding the importance of stopping the Germans south of the Psel that the Stavka did not have confidence in their ability to prevent the loss of the city if Manstein wasn't stopped at the river.

The losses of 1st Tank Army early in the fighting and III. Panzerkorps' approach toward Prochorovka had alarmed the Soviet leadership sufficiently to force them to commit Rotmistrov's tank army, their strategic reserve. Since the primary task of this army was offensive in nature, the gravity of the situation is evident. Following the destruction of two thirds of the 5th Guards Tank Army, the opportunity was then at hand on the day after Prochorovka to push fresh troops up to the front and break out into the flat land north of the Psel. It was clear to Manstein that this was the time to commit the panzer divisions of XXIV. Panzerkorps, Heeresgruppe Süd's reserve. These fresh German panzer divisions, attacking over the open steppe south of Kursk, would have been in their element and the Soviets were obviously not yet capable of defeating the Germans in a mobile battle of this type. In spite of marked improvement in the organization, command and logistical support of the Soviet armor formations, they remained inferior to the German panzer troops.

Support of this statement can be seen from the events of 12 July, when two divisions of II. SS-Panzerkorps engaged the main part of 5th Guards Tanks Army, in addition to elements of 5th Guards Army and two attached corps of tanks. Major elements of 18th and 29th Tank Corps assaulted a single SS division, *Leibstandarte*, during the morning and early afternoon, supported by infantry and attack planes, and were essentially destroyed. Elements of two Soviet tank corps, the 2nd and 2nd Guards, hit *Das Reich* during the day but failed to stop the division, which resumed its advance on the following day. In spite of all efforts by two corps of armor and infantry, *Totenkopf* maintained firm control of the bridgehead on the Psel.

The bridgehead provided a secure jumping off point for further offensive action by German armored reserves. In addition, the Soviet forces assaulting the bridgehead were not in a defensive organization as they were attacking almost continually rather than preparing for holding a line; thus, a fresh German panzer corps, able to safely assemble south of the Psel and attacking through the *Totenkopf* positions, may have wreaked havoc in this situation. This is particularly likely given the heavy losses of 31st Tank Corps and 33rd Rifle Corps and the lack of Russian armored reserves in the sector.

Thus, the use of Manstein's armored reserve may have supplied sufficient impetus to break the stalemate and could have allowed both XXXXVIII. Panzerkorps and II. SS-Panzerkorps to recover. By 16 July, a significant number of damaged SS tanks were back in action, the three divisions reporting a total of 197 operational panzers and 75 assault guns.[47]

By contrast, the Russians temporarily had no other significant armored reserves to commit in the immediate Prochorovka-Psel sector. That situation would be remedied within weeks, a remarkably short time, but on 13 July, a German breakthrough north of the Psel would have had little but open country between it and Kursk. The only Russian tank reserves of any size were 4th Tank Army and 3rd Guards Tank Army in the area north of Orel, but these forces were scheduled to be committed against Heeresgruppe Mitte. The nearest of the two, 3rd Guards Tank Army, was nearly 100 miles away and was thus in no position to furnish immediate help on that date. A successful breakout over the Psel by 4. Panzerarmee and Armee-Abteilung Kempf toward Kursk thus would have been unopposed by a Soviet strategic armored reserve. Such a German advance would have cut off the Russian armies in the western section of the bulge, which included the remnants of 1st Tank Army and 6th Guards, 40th, 60th, 65th, and 38th Armies.

More importantly, an advance to Kursk would have put the Germans in a position to strike the rear of the Bryansk and Central Fronts at Orel, which were at that time fully occupied with attacking Kluge's Heeresgruppe Mitte. Had the two Soviet fronts been threatened from the rear or flank while facing Kluge, it would have presented great difficulties for the Russians. At the very least, it would have meant that a major realignment of forces would have been necessary by the Soviet armies on the Heeresgruppe Mitte front. The use of 4th Tank Army and/or 3rd Tank Army to counter Manstein's attack would have resulted in a great weakening of the forces attacking Kluge and invites speculation regarding renewed offensive actions by Heeresgruppe Mitte if these two Soviet tank armies had not been committed against Kluge's 2. Panzerarmee and 9. Armee on 18–19 July.

Of course, all this remains just speculation because it did not occur. Even if the Germans had broken through to Kursk in the south, it is problematic whether they could have prevented the breakout or the filtering through of significant numbers of Russian troops trapped in the western area of the Kursk bulge. This was due to the manpower limitations of the German infantry divisions, a situation that had worsened considerably due to the casualties inflicted on the infantry during "Citadel." In all likelihood, the majority of the Soviet manpower would have been able to escape encirclement although heavy equipment losses are impossible to estimate. Undoubtedly, they would have been serious. Nor should the ability of the Russians to survive catastrophe be underestimated. Stalin would have reacted with the familiar draconian measures and sacrificed whatever men and equipment necessary to master the crisis, knowing that more tanks were pouring out of his factories by the hundreds every week. Finding trained tank soldiers would have been another matter although hurriedly gathered and quickly trained crews would have been found. Without sufficient training, these crews often did not last long against the Germans, but Stalin knew that even such men as these take time to kill and time was on his side. Those who lived long enough were battle hardened in this harsh school of combat and survived to pass on their hard-earned experiences.

In any event, had Manstein been allowed to commit fresh panzer divisions on 4. Panzerarmee's front, the course of events on the Eastern Front in the summer of 1943 could have been significantly altered. At the very least, the use of the Soviet 3rd and 4th Tank Armies may well have been different and the August counteroffensive at Belgorod-Kharkov could possibly have been delayed significantly as well. This operation, called "Rumyantsev," was launched on 3 August and was spearheaded by 1st Tank Army and 5th Guards Tank Army, the armored reserves that Manstein had the opportunity to trap and annihilate on 13 July. If these two tank armies had been destroyed and major portions of the staff and organizational component personnel captured or killed, the Soviets would not have had the framework with which to rebuild these two armies in time for the summer offensive at Belgorod-Kharkov. Hitler's decisions allowed these two tank armies to withdraw and reorganize, and the Soviets were able to refit the armies with tanks in a matter of weeks. Infantry manpower was another matter. The rifle divisions had lost so many men that even the Soviets could not replace their catastrophic casualties in time to bring their rifle divisions back to strength before "Rumyantsev" was launched.

However, in spite of these losses, both 1st Tank Army and 5th Guards Tank Army had over 500 tanks each by 3 August, and as a result, the SS divisions of II. SS-Panzerkorps were to face their familiar opponents once again in the battles of August west of Kharkov. This is the important link between the events at Prochorovka and the conduct of operations in south Ukraine during the second half of the summer of 1943. Not only was the outcome of the battle on the Psel affected by Hitler's loss of will, but the opportunity to destroy the two Soviet tank armies was lost due to Hitler's interference in affairs on the front that was contrary to the more astute evaluation of the situation by Manstein and Hoth.

PROCHOROVKA: FICTION AND FACT

In the postwar years, the important studies of the history of the Eastern Front during World War II describe the battle of Prochorovka as being a bloody defeat for Hausser's II. SS-Panzerkorps, with heavy tank losses and huge personnel casualties that resulted in the near destruction of the three SS divisions. Most accounts of the battle paint a picture leading one to believe that the armored strength of II. SS-Panzerkorps was essentially annihilated in the fighting on 12 July. The acceptance of high SS tank losses led to the conclusion that these divisions were destroyed as effective combat formations at Prochorovka and were thus unable to continue to operate effectively. This has been given as the reason for the loss of the battle at Prochorovka and, by extension, seemed to be the fatal blow to "Citadel." The German defeat at Prochorovka has been cited as providing evidence that the Russian tank arm had come of age and by the summer of 1943 could defeat German armor in a head-to-head battle. These beliefs are some of the great myths of the Second World War. They appear to have resulted from acceptance of the Soviet version of the battle and its aftermath. In the absence of any research utilizing the primary materials available, there seemed little evidence to refute these conclusions. A factor that contributed to this oversight is that captured Waffen SS records in the United States dealing with the Eastern Front operations of II. SS-Panzerkorps inexplicably remained classified for some time after the war and were not available for study. The finding guides for Eastern Front records of SS units preserved on microfilm at the National Archives were not published until 1978–81. By that date, a number of major works about the Eastern

Front were already published and subsequent authors accepted as fact the accounts of the battle in these books. Study of the microfilmed records of II. SS-Panzerkorps provides information that calls into question accepted historical notions regarding both the number of German tanks in action at the battle of Prochorovka as well as the tank losses suffered by German panzer divisions, particularly the SS divisions. These records reveal a meticulous accounting for the numbers of panzers in action daily, even listing the type and gun size of the tanks that were operational with each division. For instance, on 13 July, the report from the *Totenkopf* Ia (chief operations officer) shows that the division had seventeen Panzer IVs available and further breaks this number down to fourteen L46-barreled high-velocity 7.5cm gun types and three equipped with the short-barreled 7.5cm gun.

The Soviets stated that they removed 400 destroyed German tanks from the Prochorovka battlefield after the fighting was over, and this figure appears in print frequently.[48] They also claimed to have destroyed 70 to 100 SS Tiger tanks and dozens of Panther tanks and to have driven the SS panzer corps from the field by using the daring tactics of closing with the German panzers to nullify the advantage of the 88mm guns of the Tiger. Since it was without doubt that the Germans did not take Prochorovka, these assertions seemingly provided conclusive reasons for German defeat. With the mistaken assumption of massive panzer losses by II. SS-Panzerkorps, a number of incorrect beliefs or conclusions emerged in literature published during the years after the war. The nature and conduct of the battle itself is not well understood, and these incorrect beliefs led to faulty assumptions and skepticism regarding statements of some German officers, notably Manstein himself, in his wartime memoirs, *Lost Victories*.

The postwar statements made by Manstein in regard to the continued possibility of success in the south after 12 July did not ring true if one accepted the notion that Hausser's SS panzer corps was essentially annihilated on 12 July, because it was assumed that the Germans had little armored strength with which to continue the battle. The possible commitment of XXIV. Panzerkorps was not taken into account, when it was considered at all, probably because it was only one panzer corps and could not have been expected to make a decisive difference. However, as we have seen, a single German panzer corps annihilated the armor of 5th Guards Tank Army on

12 July. This fact is particularly ironic because the battle of Prochorovka has often been described as the first victory of a resurgent, well-trained Soviet tank arm exhibiting a sudden superiority in armored tactics. The German tank losses at Prochorovka and the failure to capture the town supposedly resulted, at least in part, from the use of these daring tactics by the Russian tank corps.

The decision made by Rotmistrov, ordering his tankers to close with the SS panzers by driving straight into their guns, in fact, led to the destruction of hundreds of his tanks, with the result being that his army had to halt offensive operations for the remainder of the fighting around the town. Soviet and other accepted versions of the battle claimed the destruction of hundreds of German tanks while admitting less than heavy losses of their own. In the years following the first major histories of the Eastern Front, most subsequent accounts of the battle repeated incorrect information from the earliest works. Thus, few writers have previously given any credence to Manstein's accurate estimation of the situation.

A notable exception is the two-volume history of the war on the Eastern Front that Earl F. Ziemke and Magda Bauer produced for the U.S. Army Center of Military History. In volume two, *Stalingrad to Berlin*, the authors acknowledged the Soviets had used their available reserves while the Germans had yet to commit XXIV. Panzerkorps. It is not coincidence that this study relied heavily on documentary evidence rather than on rehashing previous works. Other works acknowledge this possibility although in most cases do not exhibit a correct understanding of the complex events of the battle of Kursk. Colonel Albert Seaton, in *The Russo-German War*, recognized that Manstein was closer to "tactical success than the Soviet accounts will allow" although incorrectly stated that the battle of Prochorovka was fought in the narrow section of terrain between the Psel and the Prochorovka railroad line.[49] In his classic book on the Eastern Front, *Scorched Earth*, Paul Carell also gives a basically correct assessment of the situation in the south and recognizes the possibility of a limited success for Manstein's attack although he accepted the Soviet account of the heavy tank losses supposedly suffered by Hausser's II. SS-Panzerkorps.

In other works, incorrect information and beliefs abound in regard to the battle of Prochorovka, most of which center on the SS divisions or the numbers and types of armor used in the battle. The number of tanks that II. SS-Panzerkorps had in action on 12 July—and more importantly on the following day—as well as the numbers of Tiger and Panthers possessed by II. SS-Panzerkorps and the actual identity of the 400 destroyed tanks supposedly removed from the field after the battle, have been incorrectly reported. The conduct of the battle, in regard to where each of the three SS divisions actually fought in relation to the town of Prochorovka, is not accurately reported in most studies of the battle, which assume that the three divisions fought west of Prochorovka. These myths are addressed below, using primary evidence to correct popularly held but mistaken conclusions.

THE TANK STRENGTH OF II. SS-PANZERKORPS

The number of SS tanks that were actually in combat with Hausser's panzer divisions has been variously reported as being from 300 to 700. Jukes, in *Kursk: The Clash of Armour*, states that II. SS-Panzerkorps had 700 tanks in action on 12 July, including 100 Tigers.[50] Erickson gives the figure as 600 and also stated that there were 100 SS Tigers in action at Prochorovka. He further stated that on the day following the battle, there were 300 destroyed SS tanks, including 70 Tigers, scattered over the Prochorovka battlefield, and also mentions 400 German tanks found in the entire battle area.[51]

However, according to the daily report of II. SS-Panzerkorps to 4. Panzerarmee on 4 July 1943 (the day before the launching of "Citadel"), the three SS divisions had a total of 327 tanks ready for action, including 35 Tigers, but not including 25 to 30 command tanks.[52] The records of 4. Panzerarmee show that by 11 July, II. SS-Panzerkorps had lost 116 tanks due to enemy action or mechanical breakdown when it reported that the three divisions had a total of 211 running vehicles on the eve of the battle for Prochorovka. *Totenkopf* had 94 operational tanks, *Leibstandarte* 56 and *Das Reich* 61, including 7 captured T-34s. There were only 15 SS Tigers still combat ready and available for action on that date, 10 of which belonged to *Totenkopf*.[53]

On the day after the battle of Prochorovka, 4. Panzerarmee reports list the II. SS-Panzerkorps as having 163 operational tanks and 65 assault guns, a total of 228 armored vehicles. The net loss from the number of operational tanks reported on 11 July was thus a total of 48 tanks. The SS tank losses at Prochorovka were, however, somewhat heavier than 48, the discrepancy almost surely resulting from the continual return of tanks to operational status after having been repaired from earlier damage. The return to action of repaired tanks is a variable that makes reporting exact numbers difficult, if not impossible. However, the meticulous records kept by the Germans make a reasonably accurate accounting possible. In any event, accounts of the battle that claim 300 to 400 German tanks destroyed at Prochorovka are clearly mistaken, most obviously because Hausser's divisions began the battle on 12 July with just over 210 tanks, as shown by the 11 July report to 4. Panzerarmee. At no time did the II. SS-Panzerkorps have 600, much less 700 panzers. Accounts that give the numbers of Tigers in action as 70 to 100 are also completely inaccurate, as the SS divisions never had more than a total of 35 Tigers and that number was operational only on the first day.

It is impossible to say exactly how many German tanks were lost just by simple subtraction due to the previously mentioned variable factors related to a divisional tank strength on any given day. Using 4. Panzerarmee records, it can be seen that *Totenkopf*, on 11 July, had 54 Panzer IIIs, 30 Panzer IVs, and 10 Tigers, for a total of 94 vehicles. On 13 July, it had 32 Panzer IIIs, 17 Panzer IVs and no Tigers, a total of 49 tanks. This is a loss of 45 vehicles. *Leibstandarte* had 5 Panzer IIIs, 47 Panzer IVs, and 4 Tigers on 11 July, for a total of 56 tanks, while on the day after Prochorovka, it had 5 Panzer IIIs, 31 Panzer IVs, and 4 Tigers, a total of 39. This is a loss of 17 tanks. The tank losses for these two divisions can thus be fairly accurately determined. However, in the case of *Das Reich*, we see a peculiar difference in numbers of tanks for these two days, which illustrates the imprecise nature of coming up with exact numbers of losses during a battle even with the carefully kept records of II. SS-Panzerkorps.

On 11 July, this division had 34 Panzer IIIs, 18 Panzer IVs, 8 T-34s, and only one Tiger, a total of 61 tanks. However, on 13 July, the day after Prochorovka, it had 43 Panzer IIIs, 20 Panzer IVs, a single Tiger, and 11 T-34s. This is an *increase* of 14 panzers. It is most likely that this can be accounted for by the return to action of repaired tanks that were damaged in the earlier fighting or the transfer of a few tanks from either *Leibstandarte* or *Totenkopf*. The transfer of tanks may have been due to the planned attack by *Das Reich* south of Prochorovka.

The increased numbers of T-34s could have resulted from capture of additional Russian tanks or repaired enemy vehicles. While waiting for the return of its I./Panzer-Regiment 2, which was detached at this time and in Germany while receiving the new Panther tanks, *Das Reich* used captured tanks for some time. In fact, its most successful tank ace, Emil Seibold, fought at Kursk as commander of one of the captured T-34s, and a number of the first of Seibold's sixty-nine confirmed tank kills were made while using one of these vehicles.

Disregarding the unknown number of damaged or destroyed tanks belonging to *Das Reich*, we can see that between *Leibstandarte* and *Totenkopf*, these two divisions lost 62 tanks on 12 July. *Das Reich* obviously suffered combat losses in the fighting against 2nd and 2nd Guards Tank Corps, but exact figures cannot be known due to the increase in numbers of operational tanks. It can probably be assumed that this division's losses were not very severe on 12 July because heavy losses would have cancelled out the number of tanks returning to action or the number of transferred or new tanks. In this event, an increase in operational vehicles would not have been in evidence on 13 July. If we arbitrarily assume that 20 to 25 *Das Reich* tanks were lost in action on 12 July, a rough estimate can be made that about 70 to 80 tanks were lost for the day by II. SS-Panzerkorps. Since *Leibstandarte* lost less than 20 tanks during fighting in which its 56 tanks were faced by 300 to 400 Soviet tanks, this figure is probably high. The 2nd and 2nd Guards Tank Corps were weaker than Rotmistrov's 18th and 29th Tank Corps because they had been involved in fighting before 12 July. However, a loss of 70 to 80 tanks, even given the inherent problems in figuring exact tank losses, is obviously more accurate than the 400 destroyed SS panzers claimed by the Soviets or various other numbers that are available as given by other authors.

SS TIGERS AND PANTHERS

Various previous studies of the Eastern Front state that 70 or even 100 SS Tiger tanks were destroyed by the Russians and left on the battlefield to be captured after the battle at Prochorovka. Since the SS-Panzerkorps possessed only thirty-five Tigers on the day *before* "Citadel" was launched and only fifteen were still in operation on 11 July, it is clear that these figures cannot be accurate. It was impossible for the SS divisions to have lost more than seventy Tigers on 12 July, most obviously because they had only half that number before the battle even began. Moreover, only about five were still in action with *Leibstandarte* and *Das Reich*, the two divisions actually in combat in the immediate Prochorovka area. The other ten heavy tanks were fighting with *Totenkopf*'s panzer group in the bridgehead across the river and not directly involved in the fighting west of the town. Statements that the field was left to the Russians, who claimed the capture of the tank repair shops of the SS and the damaged vehicles in them, are also incorrect. The combat records of 4. Panzerarmee and II. SS-Panzerkorps show that the SS divisions were, in fact, not driven from the battlefield by the Russians on 12 July. *Das Reich* continued to attack in the next days, gaining ground to the south and east from attack positions south of Prochorovka. *Leibstandarte* did not advance in the days following the first day of the fighting for Prochorovka, but it was able to hold on to its former frontline positions. *Totenkopf* was never driven out of its bridgehead, giving it up only on receiving the order to withdraw, which came days after the initial battle of Prochorovka. That order did not come until 15 July, when the headquarters of II. SS-Panzerkorps received orders to prepare to withdraw from the sector for transfer to other areas. The actual movement was not executed until the night of 17–18 July. At that time, the divisions of II. SS Panzerkorps began a phased, deliberate withdrawal. It was not driven back by Soviet attacks but was assembled for commitment elsewhere as ordered.

In five days between the first battle around Prochorovka and the withdrawal, the divisions would have been able to salvage any tanks that could be repaired. It is unlikely that any tank repair shops were captured by the Russians because the divisions made an orderly withdrawal from the sector, which would have provided ample time for these vital service units to move to the rear. There is substantial evidence that the tank repair units of each division remained in action until the withdrawal. Again, the records of II. SS-Panzerkorps provide this evidence.

On 14 July, II. SS-Panzerkorps had 179 tanks back in action, a number that included 14 Tigers. On the following day, Hausser's divisions had 197 tanks in action in addition to 22 command tanks, including 23 Tigers.[54] Most of the Tigers and other tanks returning to actions were probably repaired vehicles, which provides evidence that the repair shops were at work. Track and running gear damage could be repaired within hours and other minor repairs could be completed over night, and it is very probable that most of the Tigers returned to action had suffered light damage. It is not likely that all or even most of the 23 heavy tanks operational on 16 July were new vehicles if for no other reason than Tiger production in 1943 was only about 25 to 50 vehicles per month. Since new SS divisions with Tiger battalions were being worked up and equipped and there were both SS and army heavy battalions that were also supplied with the huge tanks, it is unlikely that nearly a whole month's production would have been sent to an area where Hitler had already given up hope of success. It can thus be reasonably assumed that only a few Tiger tanks were captured or destroyed by the Soviets at Prochorovka.

Another German tank, the Panzer V or Panther, has been said to be in use by the SS divisions at Prochorovka. This is also a misconception, in spite of Soviet pictures that purportedly show SS Panthers destroyed at Prochorovka. A number of accounts describe the use of this tank by II. SS-Panzerkorps during "Citadel." However, there were no Panthers issued to any of the SS divisions until later in the summer. The records of *Das Reich* do not show any Panthers assigned to the division until 22 August, when it received its battalion of these superb tanks, which had been training and organizing in Germany during the battle of Kursk. *Totenkopf* did not get its Panthers until late 1943 or early 1944, when it also received a battalion equipped with this tank. The records of 4. Panzerarmee do show Panthers in action with the elite army division, *Grossdeutschland*, but it served under the command of XXXXVIII. Panzerkorps during the battle of Kursk and was not in action at Prochorovka. The SS divisions had to be content with the older-model panzers and a few Tigers until later in the war. It is interesting to note how many Panzer IIIs were still in service with the three SS divisions in 1943, particularly in regard to those who believe that the Waffen SS divisions were always given preference over the army in receiving the most modern equipment.

In fact, the army divisions received all of the newly arrived Panther tanks as well as all of the huge Elephant assault guns and the heavy 150mm assault gun named Brummbär. The panzer divisions of the SS continued to use the Panzer III and Panzer IV as their main battle tanks late into 1943, although the Panzer III was essentially obsolete after the first appearance of the T-34, which was more heavily armored, possessed a better-designed front glacis plate and had a superior gun of 76mm when compared to the 50mm cannon of the Panzer III

THE 400 DESTROYED TANKS OF PROCHOROVKA

After a study of the records of the SS divisions, which clearly show that II. SS-Panzerkorps did not suffer the tank losses that have been previously reported, the identity of the 400 destroyed hulks that the Russians claimed to have been removed from the battlefield becomes clear. Undoubtedly, there were hundreds of knocked-out tanks all over the area when Hausser's divisions withdrew from the Psel. However, the vast majority recovered from the Prochorovka battlefield could not have been German tanks since the losses of Hausser's divisions were a total of approximately 70 to 80 tanks, most of which were probably recovered and returned to action. However, Rotmistrov's army lost approximately 600 to 650 tanks on 12 July in actions against II. SS-Panzerkorps as well as Breith's divisions, and it is thus clear that if 400 tanks were actually removed from the battlefield, the overwhelming majority of these destroyed vehicles were Russian.

Given the nature of the political situation in the Soviet Union in the immediate postwar years and into the 1960s, it was obviously not possible for the Russians to state that most of the armored wrecks removed from the battlefield were the remains of Soviet tanks that sacrificed themselves running headlong into SS panzer division guns. This becomes particularly apparent given that Nikita Khrushchev was premier of the Soviet Union from 1958 to 1964 and much of the history of the war was written to emphasize his wartime achievements (and diminish the influence of Stalin). As he was the ranking political officer in south Ukraine during this period and played a role in the fighting in the south during "Citadel," it would not have been appropriate for the Soviets to reveal that under Khrushchev's "guidance," the tank crews of 5th Guards Tank Army essentially were sacrificed in a suicidal charge straight into the guns of Hausser's II. SS-Panzerkorps.

THE COURSE OF THE BATTLE

Even the basic facts of the conduct of the battles around Prochorovka have been distorted, incorrectly understood or ignored. The impression one receives from most accounts is that the SS divisions attacked the town abreast, with the entire armored strength of the II. SS-Panzerkorps arrayed shoulder to shoulder, all three divisions colliding with the Soviet tanks west of the town in an enormous collision of armor. In fact, only *Das Reich* and *Leibstandarte* actually attacked on line and only *Leibstandarte* advanced on the town itself. As we have seen, *Das Reich* was engaged on a line south of the town and soon became fully involved fighting Soviet infantry and armor attacking from the southeast. The majority, if not all, of *Totenkopf*'s tanks, were fighting north of the Psel and remained there until ordered to abandon the bridgehead on the night of 17–18 July.

It is clear that the notion of large numbers of SS Tiger and Panther tanks rolling to their destruction against Rotmistrov's 5th Guards Tank Army is false. Nor was the battle for Prochorovka concluded on 12 July, as some authors have incorrectly stated.

Alan Clark, in *Barbarossa*, wrote that "by evening the Russians were in possession of the battlefield, with its valuable number of disabled hulks and wounded crews" and that "by evening the Germans began slowly to withdraw to their starting line."[55]

In actuality, *Das Reich* and *Totenkopf* continued to slowly gain ground in attacks during the following days, both across the Psel and south of Prochorovka. *Leibstandarte*, in actuality, held its positions until the withdrawal date. The small expansion of the Psel bridgehead by *Totenkopf* and the advances of *Das Reich* around the southern edges of Prochorovka were tactical victories at best and not decisive by any definition. However, the importance of these events lies in the fact that they contribute to the better understanding of what actually took place in the Psel-Prochorovka area from 12 to 18 July. There are other events that have been ignored or not evaluated properly that affected the battle of Prochorovka and the southern wing of "Citadel."

The role of III. Panzerkorps and the importance of its failure to attack 5th Guards Tank Army on its southern flank is generally ignored or almost treated as an unrelated event. When it is discussed at all, the importance of this failure in relation to the attack of II. SS-Panzerkorps is not understood. The availability of German panzer reserves is forgotten or dismissed as insignificant. After all, what difference could one SS panzer corps have made? However, two divisions of a single German panzer corps, in one day of fighting, knocked out 600 to 650 Soviet tanks in the Prochorovka sector, essentially eliminating major elements of the Soviet strategic armored reserve in the south. In that context, the use of the more than 150 panzers of XXIV. Panzerkorps may have been extremely crucial.

THE DESTRUCTION OF THE FIGHTING POWER OF II. SS-PANZERKORPS

Prochorovka was not the death blow to the fighting power of the SS divisions as has generally been believed. This fact can be demonstrated by further study of the combat operations of these units for the remaining months of the summer. The SS divisions were by no means rendered incapable of further action due to their losses at Prochorovka. In fact, *Das Reich* and *Totenkopf* continued fighting nearly without pause for the next month and a half. After being withdrawn from the Kursk sector, these two SS divisions were transferred to the 6. Armee's sector, where they conducted a counterattack that eliminated a strong Soviet bridgehead at the Mius River during fighting from 30 July to 3 August. During this fighting, these two SS divisions, with 3. Panzer-Division replacing *Leibstandarte*, knocked out the better part of two Soviet armored formations, 2nd Guards Mechanized Corps and 4th Guards Mechanized Corps.

Subsequently, without any time to rest and recover, the divisions were transferred to the Bogodukhov sector, west of Kharkov in August 1943. There they were joined by another SS unit, 5. SS-Panzergrenadier-Division *Wiking*. In three weeks of constant combat, beginning on 6 August, 1943, the SS divisions played a key role in the combat around Bogodukhov and Kharkov. In fighting west of Kharkov, they fought a rebuilt 5th Guards Tank Army (503 tanks) and elements of 1st Tank Army (542 tanks) to a standstill under command of III. Panzerkorps. *Das Reich*, *Totenkopf*, 3. Panzer-Division, and *Wiking* destroyed a major percentage of the 450 tanks that 5th Guards Tank Army lost during the fighting west of Kharkov. By 25 August, Rotmistrov's army had but 50 tanks still running. Katukov's 1st Tank Army was all but decimated also, listing only 120 operational tanks on the same date.

A LOST VICTORY?

The battle at Prochorovka was a microcosm of the war on the Eastern Front. It was characterized by tactical German superiority faced with massive Russian superiority in numbers. Strategically, the Russians once again demonstrated their superiority and were victorious in the final analysis, defeating the German attack through superior intelligence, enormous sacrifice and single-minded determination to achieve their strategic objectives by whatever means necessary. In contrast to the Soviet dedication to their plans and objectives, decisions made by Adolf Hitler were in the end decisive to the German defeat in the south.

Hitler lost the will to press on with "Citadel" at the critical moment of the fighting in the Psel-Prochorovka area and turned his attention to events in the West and on the southern wing of Heeresgruppe Süd. South of the Kursk battlefield, Hitler became concerned with Soviet build-ups at Izyum and the Mius River that were obviously preliminary preparations for attacks. Both of these operations were carefully planned diversionary efforts that were integral parts of the Soviet strategical plan for the crucial summer of 1943. At both sectors, the Soviets operated with a clear lack of any intention to conceal their preparations, violating nearly every principle of *maskirovka*, the normally strictly observed guidelines for concealment, camouflage and communications security that characterized virtually every other major Soviet operation from the winter of 1942–43 until the end of the war.

At the critical moment, these secondary attacks, one at Izyum against 1. Panzerarmee and another at Dmitrievka on the Mius, resulted in just the weakening of the Kursk offensive that the Soviets had hoped for. Taken as *isolated events* on the Eastern Front, the Soviet attacks in these areas were not greatly significant in regard to the course of the war in Russia. However, Hitler ignored the advice of his generals to finish the battle in the south and chose instead to disperse the panzer divisions of 4. Panzerarmee and III. Panzerkorps to areas of much less importance. His decision to withdraw from the Psel-Prochorovka area when his armies held a distinct advantage in armor was decisive not only in regard to the failure of "Citadel" in the south but had far reaching strategic consequences for the remaining months of 1943.

These two battles, when recognized as key parts of the Russian strategy, illustrate the strategic superiority of the Soviet Union, both in planning and execution. The Soviets influenced the course of "Citadel" by the use of military deception, *maskirovka*—or in this case, the absence of *maskirovka*. Exactly how these diversionary attacks were executed and how well they succeeded is a fascinating story involving Soviet deception, Hitler's influence on the conduct of the war and in no little part, German arrogance. This subject will be dealt with in more detail in later chapters.

Hitler sent four panzer divisions to rectify the situation on the Mius River. It was there that Hitler ordered Manstein to send two divisions of II. SS-Panzerkorps plus an army unit, 3. Panzer-Division, on 17 July. The XXIV. Panzerkorps, Manstein's panzer reserve, was split up, and its 23. Panzer-Division was also sent to the Mius. In spite of Manstein's protestations that Hausser's II. SS-Panzerkorps and XXIV. Panzerkorps should be combined in order to continue the attack of Heeresgruppe Süd toward Oboyan-Kursk, Hitler split up the German armor and dispersed it to various points in the East rather than concentrating it at a critical time. Ultimately, his orders resulted in the redeployment of eight Heeresgruppe Süd panzer divisions. This spelled the end of the battle of Kursk on the southern flank. Although the attack in the north was already halted, Hitler, had he listened to the counsel of his generals, in particular Manstein, could have still snatched some measure of victory from the battle in the south. However, trusting his own intuition, not guided by a workable strategy that could have reasonably led to victory, he did not heed the advice of Manstein.

There were other factors and events that exerted a negative influence on the 1943 German summer offensive, some of which took place before the battle even began. Of significant importance was intelligence information made available to the Russians in the spring of the year. It is almost certain that the Russians had excellent intelligence regarding the German plans for the Kursk salient from Ultra and, according to some authors, notably Paul Carell, a spy close to Hitler. Whatever their means of obtaining information, the Soviets expected the Germans to attack just where the attacks actually came. Certain knowledge of the location, forces involved, and plan of attack allowed the Russians to prepare their defenses accordingly and place their forces correctly.

The second factor that was of vital importance to the Soviet victory at Kursk was their ability to build up large operational and strategic reserves. This was in contrast to the German Army, which had to overcome the problems of a constantly shrinking number of soldiers available for service on the Eastern Front. Germany also had difficulty providing enough vehicles to keep its panzer divisions up to strength. The Soviet population and its industrial power, mobilized effectively by a strongly centralized national power structure, at the top of which sat Stalin, became the decisive weapon of the war against the Germans. In direct contrast, these resources provided the constantly evolving and improving Soviet army with the men and equipment necessary to build the massive reserves that allowed them to seize the initiative on the Eastern Front in 1943. These reserves, utilized ruthlessly and at great cost, furnished the time necessary for the Soviet army to convert itself into the powerful weapon it became by the last two years of the war.

By 1944, not only did the Soviets retain an enormous numerical superiority, but the quality of their tank units had been significantly upgraded by a methodical, systematic process of training and force-structure improvement. The Soviet army, perhaps more than any other of the major participants of the war, exhibited a dynamic ability to change and adapt to the requirements of war. No other army made fundamental changes in force structure, command or doctrine to the degree that the Soviet army achieved during the Second World War.

Considering the course of events, however, the essential element of victory for the Soviets on the southern wing may have been the use of deception as an influence on the German command and Hitler. These measures succeeded in influencing decisions that Hitler made in regard to the continuation of the decisive battle of Kursk and to the commitment of German armored reserves to counter Soviet diversionary operations. In this context, contrary to generally accepted accounts of Operation "Citadel," it can be seen that the Germans were probably closer to a significant victory in the south than is generally believed. The comparison of tank numbers in the vital Psel-Prochorovka area is the single most important factor that forces at least a reevaluation of the situation after the first day at Prochorovka, beyond German command decisions. It is in situations like that which developed on 13 July—when spearhead troops created the chance for victory, but are temporarily in need of rest—that reserves are to be committed in decisive action. Manstein had such reserves; the Russians did not, at least in the immediate area.

Primarily because of the mistaken belief that the SS divisions were essentially destroyed as effective fighting formations on 12 July, the possibility of a renewed push across the Psel or a breakout from the existing bridgehead has not been addressed. It has been assumed that Hausser's divisions were too weakened to have made further gains. However, it is without question that the SS divisions would have been capable of further effective offensive action after the benefit of a little recovery time. It is without question because this is what happened during the rest of the summer of 1943, at least in the case of *Das Reich* and *Totenkopf*. These units, as well as 3. Panzer-Division, fought first at the Mius River at the end of July and then, without rest, were immediately transferred to Bogodukhov, where they blunted a dangerous major Soviet offensive west of Kharkov. Their opponents during these battles, which took place south of the town of Bogodukhov, were 1st Tank Army and 5th Guards Tank Army, the very formations that Manstein wanted to finish off on 13 July. In this fighting, the two Soviet tank armies were again essentially destroyed fighting against a small number of German panzer divisions. This fact again effectively demonstrates that far from being destroyed and incapable of combat, *Das Reich*, *Totenkopf*, and, to a lesser extent, 3. Panzer-Division and 5. SS-Panzer-Division *Wiking* remained fully capable of fighting and defeating entire Soviet tank armies.

However, interesting speculation aside, one fact is beyond any question, regardless of tanks possessed by either side and discussions over what might have been. Because of the suicidal actions of the Soviet tank corps on 12 July, the momentum of 4. Panzerarmee was slowed dramatically when II. SS-Panzerkorps failed to take Prochorovka on that date and III. Panzerkorps did not reach the battlefield on schedule. This lack of success indirectly contributed to the defeat of the southern flank of Operation "Citadel." But it remained for Hitler himself to strike the last blow and guarantee that "Citadel" would fail. Distracted by obvious Soviet build-ups at Izyum and the Mius River, Hitler abandoned "Citadel" in the south, reacting to Russian attempts to divert German attention from the critical events on the Psel River–Prochorovka sector. At that point, "Citadel" was truly finished. The last opportunity for the Germans to influence events on the strategic level in the East was ended.

II. SS-PANZERKORPS MOVES TO THE MIUS

The first post-Kursk operation of the Waffen SS divisions in which they were employed as one of Hitler's "fire brigades" was the counterattack of Hausser's panzer corps at the Mius River. Among the troops that Hitler used most in the counterattack role during these final months of the war were the elite SS panzer divisions. *Leibstandarte, Das Reich* and *Totenkopf* thus became increasingly employed in these types of operations for the remainder of the war, not only on the Eastern Front but in the West as well. Much of the superb human material that characterized the elite divisions of the Waffen SS in the first years of the war was lost in these battles. Thousands of the cream of the Waffen SS personnel were killed in Russia in 1943 and the three divisions were never the same again. Trained officers and men from these divisions were also detached to help train and command new SS divisions, and in late 1943 and early 1944, the Germans were forced to transfer hundreds of Luftwaffe personnel and men from other sources in order to fill out the depleted ranks of the divisions. This was a necessary expedient, but it did not maintain the level of training and dash that was so evident in the operations of the elite Waffen SS formations during 1941 and 1943. By the end of 1943, these divisions, while remaining dangerous opponents until the end, were not the same units that had destroyed 5th Guards Tanks Army and 1st Tank Army twice in a matter of two months on the Eastern Front.

The battles of the last years, however, were in the future during late July 1943. *Das Reich* and *Totenkopf* were withdrawn from the Prochorovka area, and after some indecision as to the exact disposition of the divisions of the II. SS-Panzerkorps, they prepared for commitment at the Mius River, where they were ordered to throw the Russians of Colonel General Fedor Tolbukhin's Southern Front back across the river. *Leibstandarte* departed for Italy, leaving some of its tanks behind to replace the losses of the remaining two SS divisions.

The subsequent battle in 6. Armee's area was the first major counterattack by the SS panzer divisions after Kursk. This was a role that they would become familiar with after the summer of 1943. The battle at the Mius River perfectly exemplifies the role of the panzer divisions of the Waffen SS for the next twenty-two months of World War II in Europe. Other divisions became so worn down by the incessant fighting and heavy casualties that they were fit only for defensive duties and in some case were even disbanded, but the elite Waffen SS panzer divisions, along with the better army panzer divisions remained combat effective long after Kursk. They were thrown into one hot spot after another by Hitler, until even the panzer divisions were worn out remnants of what they once had been. In the next chapter, the crisis of 17–30 July in the 6. Armee sector along the Mius River and the operations of II. SS-Panzerkorps are studied in detail.

CHAPTER 3

6. Armee Stands Fast

OMINOUS QUIET ON THE 6. ARMEE'S FRONT
While the fighting raged to the north of the Mius River, as Operation "Citadel" reached its critical stage, intense Russian activity continued on the eastern bank of the river all along the front of Hollidt's 6. Armee. Suddenly, it became apparent that the Russian preparations were at an end. On 14 July, there was an abrupt, dramatic lack of activity on the east bank of the river. German observation posts reported an absence of observable Russian activity in the front lines opposite their own positions. The Soviet 2nd Guards Mechanized Corps was known to have concentrated its units closer to the western edge of the town of Dmitrievka during the day, but other large-scale mobile formation movement was absent.[1] The 6. Armee correctly assessed this development as meaning that the Soviets had finished their concentration of forces and attack preparations and that the attack across the Mius could come at any time. In attempts to disrupt the Soviet attack as much as possible, 6. Armee artillery shelled known Soviet troop concentrations, fired interdiction fire on roads and bridges, while air strikes were directed at targets east of XVII. Armeekorps' defensive positions.

Previously, during the days following the detection of first signs of a Soviet build-up, Hollidt prepared his army for the coming attack as much as possible, given the shortcomings of some of its divisions and lack of armor. He took several measures as a result of a correct anticipation that the coming attack was most likely to occur in XVII. Armeekorps' sector in the Dmitrievka-Kuibyshevo area. Hollidt made special efforts in the case of his single mobile division, 16. Panzergrenadier-Division, a veteran, hard-fighting division. He carefully stressed the importance of its role as his only armored reserve. The division was moved closer toward the front into assembly areas near Chistyakovo, which lay a few kilometers west of the river, during the night of 15–16 July. The XVII. Armeekorps was reinforced with several heavy antitank gun units. Assault guns batteries were also detached from other corps of 6. Armee and concentrated in the area across from Kuibyshevo. The neighboring corps, XXIX. and IV. Armeekorps, were directed to form mobile Kampfgruppen (battle groups) that consisted of an artillery battalion and antitank and engineer elements. Corps-level artillery and antitank batteries were prepared for possible use in the threatened sector, and 23. Panzer-Division was issued a warning order by Heeresgruppe Süd in order for the division to move at short notice toward the Mius. At this time, it was still in the Belgorod area with XXIV. Panzerkorps, along with 5. SS-Panzergrenadier-Division *Wiking* and 17. Panzer-Division.

On 15 July, Hollidt met with officers of 294. Infanterie-Division and XVII. Armeekorps in order to make clear the expectations of the army because it seemed likely from all indications that the main blow would fall in this sector of the front.[2] By this date, Hollidt had prepared his army for the expected attack about as well as he was able to, given the constraints of time and men. Two days later, in the hot and humid early-morning hours of 17 July 1943, a thunderous Soviet artillery preparation signalled the beginning of the attack.

THE ATTACKS ON THE FLANKS

As the Russian divisions crossed the Mius behind their artillery fires, it became apparent that the main attack was, as expected, in the center. This was opposite Dmitrievka and fell primarily against the right flank of 294. Infanterie-Division. Three smaller attacks were mounted on the frontage of the army at other points on the first day. Two of these efforts were north of Kuibyshevo-Dmitrievka, and one was to the south.

A strong Russian diversionary attack was made on the north flank of XVII. Armeekorps' sector. The Soviet attack force consisted of a tank brigade and three rifle divisions.[3] It was directed at the divisional boundary between 302. Infanterie-Division of IV. Armeekorps and 304. Infanterie-Division of XVII. Armeekorps and originated from the area near the town of Malaya Nikolayevka. From the direction of the attack, its apparent objective was the larger town of Krassny Luch, which lay southwest of where the river crossing was made. The Soviets succeeded in making some headway at first when a force of about forty tanks followed attacking infantry out of a large

6. Armee Stands Fast

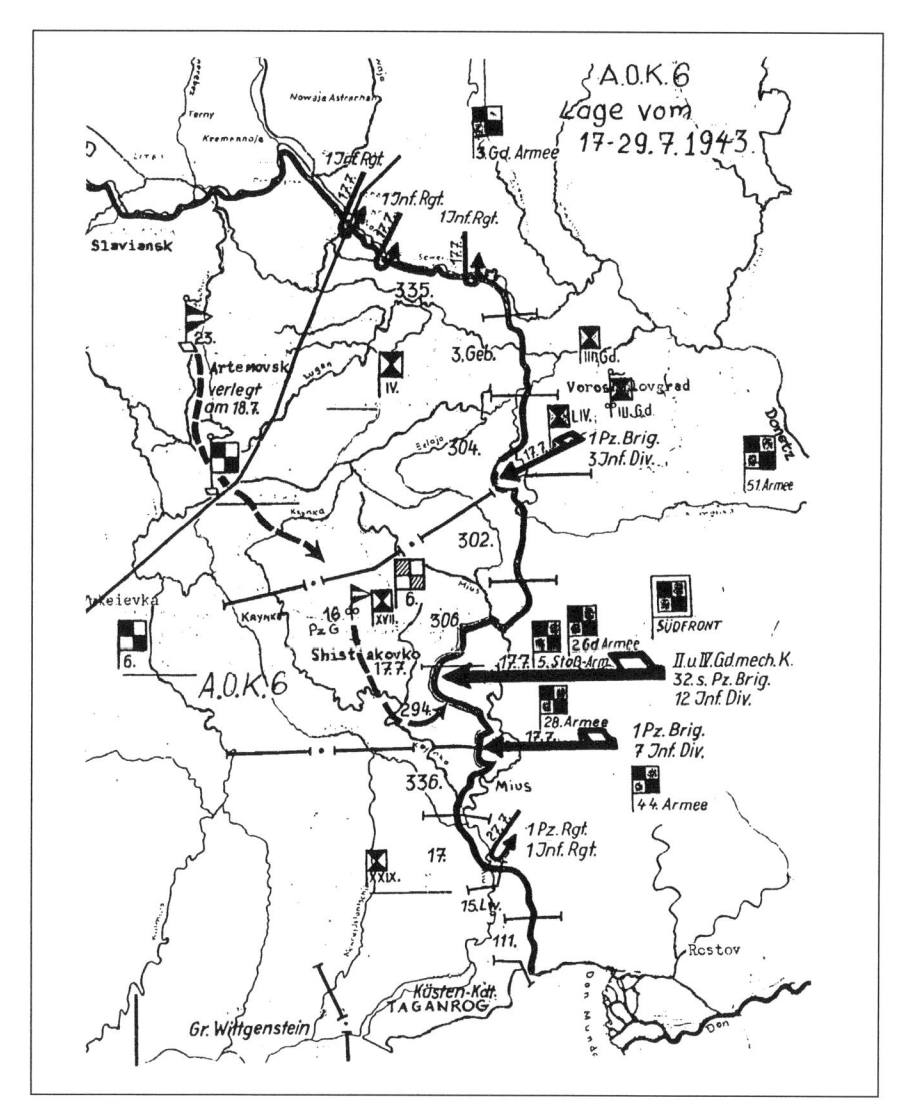

6. Armee, July 1943.

balka (flat-bottomed valley characteristic of the terrain in southern Russia) and pushed toward the small town of Ivanovka. A German minefield at the eastern end of the *balka* initially delayed this attack and resulted in the immobilization of a number of tanks. Artillery fire and heavy small-arms fire forced the Russian infantry to withdraw. However, the Russians soon regrouped and pushed forward again in spite of additional delays caused by the mines. The renewed

Soviet assaults subsequently captured several key German frontline positions, forcing the defenders to withdraw. After this breach of the German defenses was made by the Soviet infantry, the attack gathered strength and rolled over the next line of trenches, resulting in a four-kilometer penetration in the German lines at the boundary between the two divisions. However, the Germans quickly mounted well-organized counterthrusts against the Russians, using small assault groups made up of a few assault guns and infantry to attack the flanks of the penetration.

In addition to destruction of several tanks in the minefield earlier in the day, the counterattacks against the Soviet force destroyed or crippled eight more. After these losses, aggressive thrusts by German infantry were able to contain the Soviets, infiltrating into gaps between the Russian formations and working at the flanks. Effective artillery fire forced the Russian infantry to halt its advance and quickly mounted German counterattacks at several points kept the Russians occupied in defending their gains. Later in the day, 571. Grenadier-Regiment (302. Infanterie-Division) mounted a stronger assault against the now stalled Russian units. This attack, supported by artillery and assault guns, penetrated the northern flank of the bulge and drove to the south, where it made contact with other German troops. It effectively ended further Russian offensive action on 17 July in this sector of the front. The penetration was sealed off at the river, trapping Russian troops and a few surviving tanks on the west bank.

On 18 July, the Russians lost more tanks and hundreds of prisoners when the Germans pressed home their counterattacks. Assault detachments split the Soviet force into fragments which were then destroyed piecemeal by artillery, mortar fire and close assault. A strong infantry attack made by II./571. Grenadier-Regiment, supported by assault guns of 209. Sturmgeschütz-Abteilung, pushed into a large ravine known as the Redkina Balka. A large number of Soviet infantry was concentrated there, having dug in during the night of 17 July. Unable to withdraw, they fought back tenaciously. After dark on 18 July, a battalion of 304. Infanterie-Division, sent to the sector by 6. Armee, recaptured Hill 207.0, a key position near the river. This hill was of tactical importance because it commanded the terrain at the river crossing site. With the Germans in possession of key high ground, which cut off lines of retreat and supply, the Russian advance

6. Armee Stands Fast

on Ivanovka completely collapsed.[4] By the end of the day, the Germans began to mop up the trapped Russian infantry in spite of a number of weak attempts by the Soviets to get reinforcements across the river in order to reach the trapped attacking force. The Russians attempted to get the attack moving again by sending small numbers of troops across the river at other crossings, but these men failed to provide any relief when German artillery fire prevented the reinforcement of the encircled troops.

The second attack in the northern part of the front occurred opposite 335. Infanterie-Division, which held the extreme left of 6. Armee's front. In this sector, on the left flank of 6. Armee, the front bent to the west, away from the Mius. The trench line followed the south bank of the Donets River before reaching the boundary units of 1. Panzerarmee which defended the sector north of 6. Armee. The Russians crossed the river in regimental strength at three separate points and utilized heavy artillery support but did not supply accompanying armor. None of these regiment-size attacks were made with any determination, and counterattacks by 335. Infanterie-Division crushed them. The division encircled and destroyed the entire 1001st Rifle Regiment near the village of Belaya Gora, taking 300 prisoners. The other Donets bridgeheads were also eliminated and hundreds of other prisoners were taken. After the destfuction of these small bridgeheads, the remaining Russian infantry were driven back over the river, pursued by German infantry. As the Russians tried to escape by boat or swimming, the Germans closed to the bank and slaughtered the helpless Soviet infantry with machine-gun and rifle fire. By 20 July, XVII. Armeekorps was able to regain its old main defense line at all points.

In an attack below Kuibyshevo, several kilometers south of the main attack, a much stronger Russian force made up of elements of several rifle divisions, supported by a number of tanks, crossed the river behind artillery fire from forty batteries and rolling salvoes of rocket fire. This attack hit the corps boundary betweem XXIX. and XVII. Armeekorps, with the main blow against the right flank of 294. Infanterie-Division. Huge clouds of dust and smoke from the heavy Soviet artillery fires obscured the advance of the Soviet troops. From out of this cover emerged masses of Soviet infantry, either on foot or clinging to hand holds welded to the engine decks of tanks. The Soviet armor was not committed in sufficient strength to force a breakout at this point. It consisted of primarily light T-70 tanks and was utilized only in close support of the infantry. This weakness of the northern attack and the absence of large numbers of tanks in the south further confirmed the opinion of 6. Armee that the main assault would be at Kuibyshevo-Dmitrievka.

At many points of the Russian attack, massive numbers of Soviet infantry attacked in human waves, nearly shoulder to shoulder, while smaller groups crept up the deep, wooded gullies and attempted to infiltrate through gaps in the line. Elements of seven rifle divisions attacked the German lines (151st, 347th, 320th, 271st, 118th, 127th, and 387th Rifle Divisions) on a ten-kilometer frontage. This large concentration of force advanced against a German front manned by just two regiments, the 686. Grenadier-Regiment (336. Infanterie-Division) and the 515. Grenadier-Regiment (294. Infanterie-Divison). Faced with this unnerving superiority in numbers, some of the defenders gave way, creating gaps in the line which were soon exploited by the Russians. When the following waves of Soviet soldiers streamed through the gaps, the Germans on either side were forced to give ground in order to prevent becoming encircled. When the gaps were secured and enlarged, the Soviets threw more tanks and men into them.

XXIX. Armeekorps reported at 0645 hours that the Russians had successfully made an initial penetration of its defensive line in the strength of 250 men supported by tanks. This attack broke through on both sides of the village of Petropolye, with the main effort 1.5 kilometers to the east of the village of Gustafeld.[5] The direction of the spearhead of the Russian attack was to the west, and thirty to forty tanks were observed to move through the gap in support of the Soviet infantry. Immediately, XXIX. Armeekorps ordered the neighboring 17. Infanterie-Division to stand ready to commit its reserve group at any moment. This battle group consisted of a regimental command HQ, one mortar company, one infantry battalion, a light field howitzer battery and one Panzerjäger company. An assault gun unit, 243. Sturmgeschütz-Abteilung, was alerted to stand by for employment by XXIX. Armeekorps in support of the counterattack by the Kampgruppe of 17. Infanterie-Division. The XXIX. Armeekorps also ordered a battalion of infantry from 336. Infanterie-Division to be ready to support the counterattack if necessary.

6. Armee Stands Fast 101

By 0755 hours, XXIX. Armeekorps reported to 6. Armee that the Russians had overrun the front lines at several other spots and pushed to the west past Gustafeld. At all points Soviet armor accompanied the advance of the Russian infantry, eliminating German strongpoints and providing close-quarter fire support. The quick, multiple Soviet breakthroughs threatened to overwhelm the two German regiments before counterattacks could be successfully organized and the penetrations attacked. The German reaction was hindered by 6. Armee's lack of sufficient numbers of mobile reserves. The mobile reserve, 16. Panzergrenadier-Division, was stationed opposite the center, where Hollidt expected the major Soviet effort, and thus could not be spared. The situation had to be remedied with the forces at hand. From east of Gustafeld, after receiving the first alarming reports of the now critical situation, XXIX. Armeekorps ordered 336. Infanterie-Division to move against the advance of the Soviet tanks and infantry. Its reconnaissance battalion (Aufklärungs-Abteilung) was used in this attack in an attempt to rescue German troops encircled at the village of Petropolye. At 0935 hours, the division reported that although it momentarily expected a renewed strong infantry and tank attack, Petropolye remained in German hands. Although the Russians made several strong attempts to capture Petropolye during the morning, the defenders fought back skilfully and refused to give up the village. The Petropolye garrison, if 686. Grenadier-Regiment, held out in spite of this heavy pressure until relief arrived. The reinforced reconnaissance battalion of the division broke through to the village with a fast-moving attack which surprised and disorganized Russian forces. The Soviet troops recoiled from this unexpected assault, lost their composure and streamed in disorder back to the east. Meeting fresh reserves which were advancing toward Petropolye, the retreating Russian troops soon rallied however. The situation stabilized temporarily due to the attack of the reconnaissance unit, but Russian pressure resumed soon after the attack. The Russian advance continued at all points along the line.

Throughout the early morning, XXIX. Armeekorps fought to hold the Russians in front of a line of fortified hills and village strongpoints on either side of Gustafeld, while the Russians streamed through undefended gaps between these positions by the hundreds. By late morning, the corps had moved up its reserve battalions, various reconnaissance detachments and assault gun batteries in order to stem the Russian tide. A few 88mm guns were also positioned to give their support, primarily in an antitank role although Soviet aircraft remained thick in the skies over the battlefield. Wave after wave of hundreds of Soviet infantry attacked German positions, hoping to overwhelm the defenders by sheer weight of numbers. Only resolute efforts by the German infantry and accurate artillery support prevented a major collapse in the first hours. However, the overwhelming numbers of Soviet infantry began to wear down German resistance.

In the late afternoon, Russian numerical superiority prevailed and German units began to give way. A situation report of XXIX. Armeekorps to 6. Armee stated that both I./ and II./686. Grenadier-Regiment were overrun and disorganized by relentless Russian infantry attacks and the use of substantial numbers of tanks. However, in the center of the regimental sector, III./686. Grenadier-Regiment held firm and stopped the Russian advance east of Petropolye. Reserve elements of XXIX. Armeekorps made a timely appearance and reinforced that regiment's right flank defensive positions which were located on several hills. Slowed due to the stubborn resistance of the battalion holding firm in the center, the Russian attack lost its momentum. The Germans began to stabilize the penetrations of the front on either side of the center, and the two battalions of 686. Grenadier-Regiment that had given way were able to rally and hold new defensive positions. Counterattacks mounted on the flanks of the Russian penetrations sealed off the gaps which remained local in scale due to III./686. Grenadier-Regiment's refusal to yield to enormously superior numbers of Russian infantry. The stand of this battalion on the first day prevented the Russians from rolling back the entire regimental front and channeled the attack into two narrow breakthroughs which were dealt with by the forces at hand.

On the left flank of the division, in the sector dominated by the hill position known as the "3 Sternhöhe," the Russians were stopped also—at this point halted by quick counterattacks and flexible reaction by various elements of XXIX. Armeekorps. Hollidt's careful preparations and organizational effort during the previous days, thus bore fruit early in the battle. This was in contrast to the situation regarding air support by the Luftwaffe.

The Germans were less well prepared in regard to the battle in the air. Luftwaffe support was nonexistent in the sector defended by

XXIX. Armeekorps. There were no German planes available for support of the infantry and Soviet planes were able to operate essentially unhindered. This deficiency significantly contributed to the partial collapse of the German defenses on either side of Gustafeld. Both of the two battalions of 686. Grenadier-Regiment that were overrun were particularly hard hit by Soviet fighter-bombers during the first hours of the attack. Their frontline positions were bombed and strafed repeatedly by groups of as many as eighty Russian ground attack aircraft. This demoralizing development resulted in initial disorder and panic and the eventual loss of the positions. Heavy losses from the Russian air attacks, combined with the stress of massed Soviet infantry assaults, resulted in the disintegration of organized defense by the two battalions. The German infantry abandoned their trenches in retreat, and once in the open, the Soviet planes pounced on them and inflicted additional casualties. German planes were completely absent on the first day of fighting in the sector and the Soviet planes remained unopposed in the air.

In the sector of 336. Infanterie-Division, the Russians were limited to a two-kilometer advance thanks to firm defensive efforts at several key areas which slowed down the advance. Strongpoints in the second line of trenches held firm, and although the Soviet attack flowed around the first-line islands of resistance, the end result was a loss of offensive momentum. Counterattacks by XXIX. Armeekorps reserve elements disrupted Soviet efforts to reinforce their penetrations later in the day. The Soviets were also hampered by minefields, which crippled significant numbers of their infantry support tanks. In several areas, well-defended minefields were instrumental in causing delays and vehicle damage that contributed to the lack of decisive success by the Soviets. When a number of Russian tanks became immobilized in minefields at one point, German artillery drove off their supporting infantry and tank destroyer teams crept stealthily out of their trenches and destroyed six of the tanks.

German artillery played a major part in offsetting the large Soviet numerical advantage by breaking up attacks with high explosive, dropping a storm of shells on top of massed Soviet infantry attacks with deadly effect. In several instances, the artillery stopped several such attacks in their tracks. When the Russian infantry halted, artillery and heavy mortars zeroed in and pounded them, forcing them to keep their heads down while small groups of German infantry, supported by assault guns, organized counterattacks.

The skilful defensive reaction and flexible artillery response limited the breakthrough in this sector. Soviet armor was not introduced into the battle in sufficient strength to break into the depths of XXIX. Armeekorps' defenses. As a result, German resistance remained firm and able to deal with the situation with local reserves. The German artillery and antitank positions in the depth of the defenses remained intact because the Soviets were not able to penetrate deep enough to force any relocation of the guns. In many situations, if German artillery support remained organized and shells were in sufficient supply, it was difficult and costly for the Soviets to make infantry attacks. The skilled German artillery batteries decimated the Russian infantry when it advanced over open ground.

Early on 18 July, the Soviets tried again to break through south of Kuibyshevo but had little success. After the losses of the previous day, the Soviet infantry had become noticeably less aggressive and uncharacteristically hesitant in their attacks. It became apparent that the Russian effort south of Kuibyshevo had weakened. Later in the day, radio intercepts by 294. Infanterie-Division indicated that the Russians had begun to pull their remaining armor out of the secondary penetration areas and moved it toward Kuibyshevo-Dmitrievka. These forces were observed regrouping toward these two towns, and it was obvious that they were to be used to reinforce the main attack there.

Evidently, Tolbukhin was determined to create operating room for his main armored formations in the center and attempted to ensure the success of the infantry attack by providing the strongest armor support in that area. Soviet doctrine dictated that only after an infantry and artillery attack punched a hole in the defenses or gained enough ground to give room to manuever, should the main armored force be committed. Since 4th Guards Mechanized Corps had not yet reached the battle area, the tanks in operation around Kuibyshevo were probably from 32nd Tank Brigade, which was equipped mainly with the lighter T-70 tank. Normally, Soviet rifle divisions were reinforced with attached units of infantry support tanks in the initial phase of attack that were separate from the offensive tank formations. However, lack of sufficient armor forced Tolbukhin to use tanks from his main armored units, 32nd Tank

Brigade and 2nd Mechanized Corps. The subsequent losses of tanks suffered by these units in the diversionary attacks on either flank resulted in a weakening of the subsequent main effort in the center.

At this point in the war, Russian infantry support tanks were not the formidable T-34s but often were instead slow, clumsy KVs or light T-70s and T-60s. The lighter tanks were considerably more vulnerable to antitank gun fire and close assault infantry weapons than the heavier armored T-34. Later in the war, after Soviet production went into high gear and churned out thousands of T-34s every month, the T-70s were gradually replaced with heavier tanks or assault guns. Large numbers of assault guns mounting heavy guns up to 12.2cm and 15.2cm were eventually produced and utilized in the infantry support role. 6. Armee's report on the Mius battle, translated into English by the U.S. Army after the war in the Foreign Military Studies program, commented specifically on the Russian principle of creating breakthroughs with infantry attacks:

> Mobile units were committed by the Russian only after their infantry had penetrated deep into the German defensive system and had thus gained sufficient room for the tanks to deploy, or else after a breakthrough had been achieved. That was the moment for the tank units to advance and complete the breakthrough.[6]

However, Tolbukhin's front did not have the typical large amount of armor on hand at the beginning of the attack when compared to the normal massing of Soviet armored strength before an offensive was launched. The strongest tank unit assigned to South Front was not even in the area on the first day of the attack. When the attack began, Tolbukhin had only 32nd Tank Brigade, with a strength of 40 to 50 T-70s, and 2nd Guards Mechanized Corps, with about 100 to 120 T-34s and approximately 80 T-70s. The 4th Guard Mechanized Corps had about 200 tanks, which were primarily T-34s, but on 17 July, this formation was not yet available.[7] Tolbukhin's lack of sufficient armor became even more critical after the Russians squandered their tank strength all along the front during the first day without producing a decisive penetration at any point. Even if a breakthrough had occurred during the subsequent days of fighting, there was a steadily diminishing amount of Soviet armor on hand to exploit any favorable situation. This lack of sufficient armor was not only uncharacteristic, but was against Russian general practice—normally attacks were not launched until all forces were at hand. However, this was not a blunder on Tolbukhin's part. This situation could not be avoided given the specific role his attack played in the Soviet operational scheme for the summer of 1943, which will be studied in more detail in a following chapter. Time was of the essence and he could not wait for the arrival of all of his armor. The timing of his attack had to take precedence over the lives of his infantry and even the success of the attack itself in order to carry out his mission.

SOVIET AIR POWER AND THE ABSENCE OF THE LUFTWAFFE
Overhead, in all sectors of the battlefield, large numbers of low-flying Soviet Ilyushin-2 and other ground-attack planes supported the advance, strafing and bombing targets of opportunity or attacking designated German strongpoints. Many phosphorus bombs were dropped and a large number of small ground fires flared to life in the tinder dry brush covering the ridges and ravines of the Mius River valleys. The resulting thick clouds of smoke, acrid and heavy, obscured the vision of the German defenders and furnished cover for the Russian attack. German planes were not in evidence on the first day, and as a result, the Soviet planes roamed the air above the battlefield without fear of interception from enemy fighters. Without any Luftwaffe to hinder their operations, swarms of Russian planes attacked targets at will, opposed only by Flak units or ground fire from small arms. Small arms, however, posed little threat to the Soviet fighter-bombers.

The Ilyushin-2, or "Sturmovik," was a formidable weapon, and the Germans never developed anything like it. The plane was equipped with twelve-millimeter armor surrounding the cockpit, engine, and fuel tanks, which made it resistant to small-arms fire and light antiaircraft guns. The IL-2s were able to carry rockets and/or bombs and were armed with 20mm or 37mm cannons. In the absence of German planes, only antiaircraft weapons of 20mm or larger were consistently effective against these heavily armored fighter-bombers. Throughout the battle, whether attacking or on the defensive, the Soviets employed large numbers of the IL-2s on the Mius, sending

6. Armee Stands Fast

them against the Germans in groups of fifty or more. The Sturmovik was not an agile plane and was at a disadvantage when faced by Me-109s or other more maneuverable planes such as the Focke-Wulf 190. Without German fighter cover, however, the Soviet planes could operate with impunity. Many German individual and unit records of the battle mention the Soviet air strength although it is interesting to note that at no time were attacks by the Germans stopped by Soviet air operations. It appears that the Russian planes were most effective when attacking stationary targets. It may be that the Soviet attack planes, like Russian tanks, were hampered by poor communications capabilities and may not have been equipped with radios. This deficiency could also have caused poor coordination with ground observers, or it is possible that the Russians did not have an effective system for coordinating air support with ground operations. The Western Allies struggled with the proper organization of support aircraft also in this respect, although the tactical air war in the West was different due to several factors. The relatively small size of the theater of war in the West allowed the numerous aircraft of the British and Americans to be dominant in multiple areas. In the East, the enormous size of Russia prevented either opponent from being dominant along the entire length of the front. Of course, it is also possible that the Russian air arm was hampered by characteristic rigid following of orders, which limited the ability of Soviet air support to react to the swiftly changing events of battle.

The absence of the Luftwaffe fighters was due to the concentration of the majority of planes then available to the Germans on the Eastern Front in the Kursk sector. Fighter support remained scanty during the course of the battle and the most apparent German air effort was Stuka operations.

THE RUSSIAN ADVANCE ON THE SECOND DAY

On 18 July, with massive Soviet artillery fires, rocket barrages and air attacks suppressing German defensive fire, the Russians resumed their attack and crept up the small hills and ridges and made great use of many small ravines to infiltrate past strongpoints using gaps in the wire and minefields created by the preparatory bombardment. The Russian infantry had few, if any, peers when it came to infiltration skills. Many times Russian soldiers were able to pass through German lines in incredible numbers without being detected by the

Germans until suddenly they appeared behind the front lines. A veteran of the Eastern Front, Generalmajor F. W. von Mellenthin, made the below observations about the Russians skilful use of infiltration:

> In this kind of warfare, the Russians have not yet found their masters. However much the outlying areas were kept under observation, the Russian was suddenly there, in the very midst of our own positions and nobody had seen him come, nor did anybody know whence he had come. In the least likely places, where the going was incredibly difficult, there he was, dug in . . . and in considerable strength.

Mellenthin further described the difficulties that the Soviet tactics presented for the Germans: "But the amazing fact was that in spite of everybody being alert and wide awake during the whole night, the next morning entire Russian units were sure to be found far behind our front line, complete with equipment and ammunition, and well dug in."[8]

On the second day after the Russian attack came to a temporary halt in the south, the Germans launched a series of local attacks south of Kuibyshevo in attempts to regain their front line and to eliminate troublesome Russian positions. At all points, the Germans had been able to inflict very high losses on the Soviet infantry, with the result that the attackers appeared to be regrouping on the following day and only weak attacks were reported early on 18 July in the attack sector south of Kuibyshevo. By 0940 hours on that day, all of the local penetrations except one had been cleared out by counterattacks of the reserve detachments.

When the initial impetus of the Russian attack was halted, the follow-up counterattacks launched on 19 July at several points by XXIX. Armeekorps were able to stabilize the situation somewhat without having to call on reinforcements from outside the corps. Troops from 111. Infanterie-Division were shifted from the right flank of XXIX. Armeekorps and employed as a corps reserve. A Kampfgruppe (battle group) named after its commanding officer, Oberst Recknagel, prepared to counterattack on the morning of 19 July in order to erase the Russian penetration south of Kuibyshevo. Continued high tank losses must have been a serious concern to Tolbukhin as he was forced to continue to supply their rifle divisions with support tanks

6. Armee Stands Fast

from 2nd Guards Mechanized Corps. An additional ten Soviet infantry tanks had been destroyed on 18 July.

The morning of 19 July began well for the Germans. In a particularly determined counterattack by Kampfgruppe Recknagel, which was reinforced by elements of 294. Infanterie-Division, the Russians were pushed back so quickly that hopes were high after the first reports that the old frontline trenches could be regained. Kampfgruppe Recknagel pushed quickly to the east, toward the old main line of trenches, but a Russian infantry and armor assault, supported by the ever-present Soviet air force, materialized suddenly with such strength that the Germans were halted in their tracks and overrun.[9] Most of the ground that had been recaptured was lost, and Recknagel's group was scattered and had difficulty disengaging from the Russians and withdrawing to the west. The Russian thrust continued to gain ground before it was stopped near a deep ravine. There the survivors of Kampfgruppe Recknagel regrouped, quickly entrenched and held firm in spite of all attempts by the Russians to overrun the ravine. After several hours of fighting, the situation stabilized temporarily.

The counterattack by Kampfgruppe Recknagel, although ultimately driven back, discouraged the Russians sufficiently that there was little subsequent action south of Kuibyshevo during the next few days. Russian casualties were very heavy judging from German estimates that reported hundreds of Soviet dead in the sector, a byproduct of massed infantry attacks that advanced into a storm of German artillery and machine-gun fire. German casualties were relatively light after two days of fighting, considering the violence of the attack: 125 dead, 651 wounded, and 78 missing in action. The failure to achieve a major breakthrough and the substantial casualties suffered by the Russian rifle divisions were severe enough that the attack in this sector was not pressed further by Tolbukhin. Their inability to make sufficient progress to warrant subsequent offensive action was clear to the Russian command even as early as 18 July because on that date large numbers of Soviet troops were observed moving out of the southern bridgehead and marching to the north toward Dmitrievka. This was a visual confirmation of information that had been intercepted by the radio intelligence detachments of 6. Armee. Although elements of five Soviet rifle divisions remained in the area, there was no renewal of combat of any significance other than patrol activity. These divisions were either not fit for further offensive action or it is possible that Tolbukhin never intended to make anything other than a brief diversionary attack south of Kuibyshevo.

The important factor for 6. Armee after the first two days was that on the northern flank of the army front, at Belaya Gora and to the south of Kuibyshevo, the first Soviet assaults were quickly broken and did not succeed in forcing the Germans to commit reserves from out of the corps sector. On both flanks of 6. Armee, the attacking forces were halted without being able to make penetrations to a dangerous depth. As a result, the artillery positions and reserve assembly areas remained undisturbed, allowing the XXIX. and XVII. Armeekorps to counterattack the Russian attack elements supported by well-directed artillery fire. This was a key factor in the German success, because they were outnumbered by a factor of six to one or more in manpower. Firepower and aggressive defense had to make up for lack of numbers. In all of the penetration sectors, the Soviets were significantly delayed by mines and wire that channeled their attacks into fields of fire covered by entrenched antitank guns or assault guns. The Russian infantry support tanks were crippled or diverted by mines, and a number were then destroyed by German tank killer teams or assault guns (Sturmgeschütze). As a result, the Soviet advances on the flanks bogged down after making some initial headway, leaving the infantry spearheads either pinned down in front of strongpoints along the second line of fortifications or cut off and isolated.

Once forced to stop and dig in, the Russian infantry became vulnerable to the aggressive counterattacks that were standard German doctrine. On the Eastern Front, the lightning-quick counterattack was literally a matter of survival for the Germans. In Russia, they learned that to allow small Soviet penetrations to remain unmolested for even a short time was a fatal mistake that would inevitably be paid for in blood at a later date. Again it is instructive to study the opinion of Generalmajor Mellenthin, who wrote emphatically about the necessity of responding with instant reaction to Soviet attacks and the subsequent attempts to build bridgeheads:

> There is again only one sure remedy which must become a principle: If a bridgehead is forming or an advanced position is being established by the Russians, attack, attack at once, attack strongly. Hesitation will always be fatal . . .

Even if there is no more than one infantry platoon and one single tank available, attack. Attack while the Russians are still above ground . . .[10]

German combat experience showed that counterattacks were particularly effective when launched against a flank or from the rear, while the Russians were not yet organized for defense. Another veteran officer with extensive combat experience on the Eastern Front as a regiment and division commander, Generalleutnant der Waffen SS Max Simon, described the effectiveness of counterattacks on Soviet troops, particularly when mounted from unexpected directions:

> Attacks against the enemy's flank or rear nearly always led to success within a surprisingly short time. Whenever an attack was launched from an unexpected direction, the Russian system failed . . .
>
> If the Russians succeeded in penetrating our position, it was of the utmost importance to launch an immediate counterthrust.
>
> A small force of determined infantrymen, accompanied by panzers and supported by heavy arms was usually sufficient to annihilate the force who had affected the penetration before they had time to enlarge it.[11]

By 20 July, German counterattacks eliminated the last stubborn Soviet resistance at the corps boundaries at Belaya Gora and south of Kuibyshevo. The deeper penetrations were sealed off, and German artillery, along with assault gun detachments, destroyed trapped pockets of Russian infantry. Although Soviet infantry elements remained in the area south of Kuibyshevo and the main defensive line was not recovered, the Russian armor and major infantry elements were withdrawn to reinforce the main attack which had come in the center, at Dmitrievka.

THE ATTACK AT DMITRIEVKA

In the center, the fighting had not gone as well for the Germans. Elements of 2nd Guards Army and 5th Shock Army attacked on a thirteen-kilometer-wide front into which they packed eight rifle divisions and strong elements of 2nd Guards Mechanized Corps. At full strength, the mechanized corps had about 185 to 200 tanks, most of which were T-34s. In addition, 32nd Tank Brigade became available for service after it was withdrawn from the corps boundary attack. However, many of the tanks of each of these units had been doled out to support infantry assaults and neither were at full strength by 18 July. It is likely that Tolbukhin would have preferred to wait for the arrival of the tanks of this force, but given the diversionary nature of the Mius operation, time was of the essence and delay not possible.

The Germans had a great deal less armor on hand at the beginning of the battle even given the tank losses suffered by the Russians in the first two days. On 17 July, the total tank strength available to 6. Armee was twenty-nine Panzer IIIs and seven Panzer IVs, all belonging to 16. Panzergrenadier-Division.[12] Hollidt had several batteries of assault guns attached to either corps- or army-level headquarters, which were switched from one hotspot to another as needed, but his army possessed no other tanks.

In the center, as on the flanks, the attack began with a tremendous volume of artillery and rocket fire concentrated on the left flank positions of 294. Infanterie-Division. The Soviet artillery was supplemented by very heavy mortar fire from at least three mortar regiments. Soviet mortar regiments contained generous numbers of tubes much heavier than the 8cm weapons common to the German mortar units. They commonly employed 12cm and even larger mortars in great quantities, which were heavier than the mortars used by the Germans during the first years of the war in the East. In 1939–40, the Germans used a 5cm mortar at company level, but this weapon was quickly found to be inadequate, using only a 0.89-kilogram bomb and having only 500 meters' effective range. By 1941, it had been essentially phased out and replaced by the 8cm GrW 34, which fired a 3.4-kilogram bomb and had a range of 2,400 meters. This weapon was an improvement, but heavier mortars were found to be necessary. The Germans eventually produced 12cm tubes copied directly from the Soviet model, but before these weapons became plentiful, captured Soviet mortars were often used by German troops against their former owners. By deploying these weapons and mortars of 160mm or larger in battalion- or regiment-size formations, the Russians were able to powerfully augment their already large amount of artillery. Extensive use was also made of the rockets of the *Stalinorgel*, which could lay down tremendous fields of fire although with less accuracy than artillery or mortars. Mortars and rocket launchers had an added advantage: they were relatively cheap and simpler to manufacture than artillery pieces. When the attack began west of Dmitrievka on 17 July, hundreds of these weapons added the weight of their projectiles to the high-explosive shells of the conventional Russian artillery batteries.

The central sector of the front, where this storm of fire descended on the frontline positions, was defended by two German infantry regiments, 581. Grenadier-Regiment (306. Infanterie-Division) and 513. Grenadier-Regiment (294. Infanterie-Division). Advancing behind the thunderous barrage were the leading assault detachments of the Soviet rifle divisions and a large number of tanks from 2nd Guards Mechanized Corps. The preparatory fire caused heavy casualties to the defending troops in the forward line positions and destroyed whole sections of the trench system. The frontline battalions, although severely hammered by Russian artillery, initially held their positions. 6. Armee's intelligence had concluded before the attack that the Russians had concentrated the majority of their artillery and mortar detachments in this sector and the strength of the initial barrage was not unexpected. However, the heavy Russian fire caused particular difficulties due to the nature of the ground opposite Dmitrievka. The thin-soiled rocky ridges did not allow the infantry to dig in as deeply as would have been desired and the configuration of the terrain opposite Dmitrievka was not well suited for defense.

The Germans were handicapped by the need to use forward-slope positions due to the alignment of the ridgelines in the center, relative to the river. The three ridges across from Dmitrievka were not parallel to the Mius but instead stretched diagonally to the northwest. Because of this terrain configuration, the Germans were required to utilize many forward-slope positions in order to man a relatively straight line of defense and deny easy access to the Olkhovchik and Gerassimova Valleys. At many places, the Germans were not able to adequately shelter their infantry in the front lines and secondary positions because of a shortage of lumber for building bunkers and firing positions. Additionally, the Mius was shallow and could be crossed at many points without difficulty. Although the western bank of the river was in general higher than the eastern bank, which was characterized by flat ground, this advantage did not outweigh superior numbers of the Soviets.

The Germans not only had to endure the concentrated artillery fire of the Russians, but also were attacked by large numbers of Russian planes in this sector as well. The Soviet artillery was supplemented by swarms of Russian planes in groups of eighty to a hundred that roared in at low level to bomb key German positions. The Soviet planes dropped many phosphorus bombs which caused innumerable brush fires, resulting in large clouds of heavy smoke that obscured the defenders' vision and covered the advance of the Russian forces. Banks of smoke hung in the hot, humid air, mixing with the enormous amounts of dust stirred up by thousands of advancing feet and tank tracks. From out of the smoke issued the ominous sound of many tanks and the shouts of great masses of Russian infantry. In many areas, where smoke completely hid the Russian advance, the German machine gunners and infantry waited nervously as the Russians approached unseen. Infiltrating Russians appeared suddenly at many points behind the front lines, having made their way unseen through gaps blasted in the line created by artillery or lightly defended areas between strongpoints.

Waves of brown-uniformed Russian infantry overran many of the frontline German trenches in the first assaults. The tanks of 2nd Guards Mechanized Corps, following close behind their infantry, clanked over the main line of trenches and penetrated into the Olkhovchik and Gerassimova ravines. From there, the tanks approached the sides of the ravines under the cover of dust, smoke and terrain, followed by masses of Soviet infantry.

Stunned or broken by the weight of artillery and overrun by tank-supported assault groups at many points, the grenadiers of the two German infantry regiments were driven back to an average depth of four kilometers along the line of Hill 168.5–194.3–Gerassimova–173.4.[13] The Germans recovered and made a stand along this line, closely pursued by the Russians, and the issue remained in doubt for some time during the morning. The fighting on Hill 173.4 was especially severe, with the elevation changing hands several times before the Germans made a final counterattack and kicked the Russians off the hill. The fighting subsided at that point and allowed the Germans to organize their defenses and recover.

Although forced back to secondary positions, the German infantry surrendered ground grudgingly and inflicted heavy casualties on the Soviet rifle divisions. The ranks of Russian infantry were mowed down by machine-gun and mortar fire. 6. Armee's artillery batteries also destroyed stolidly advancing Soviets by the hundreds, but there were always more to take the place of those who fell. By later in the morning of the first day, the Russians pushed farther into the Gerassimova ravine and were threatening to force their way through the Olkhovchik as well. It was at this time that the Soviet command decided to deploy strong reserve armor. Leaving assembly positions in Dmitrievka, T-34s left the floor of the Gerassimova and climbed out of the valley toward the west, using large ravines to move up the slopes in concealment.

At this time (1030 hours), the Luftwaffe made a timely appearance over the battlefield and contributed to the stabilization of the situation in the center. Stukas descended in waves on the Russian tanks as they attempted to exit the Gerassimova Valley and knocked out fifteen Soviet tanks. Following the Stuka attacks on the Russian armor, the Russians faltered and the Germans were able to hold on to their line of hills and strongpoints. The Soviet rifle divisions continued to suffer heavy losses, again, due in large part to the excellent coordination of the available artillery, which on 17 July fired 1,430 tons of ammunition.[14] The Germans successfully defended the highest position on the middle ridge, Hill 213.9, in spite of strong Russian assaults on the hill with tanks and infantry. This elevation was to be the scene of bloody fighting and horrible casualties on both sides during the next few weeks of July and August.

All of the Soviet attacks on the hill were turned back with the Russian infantry being butchered by the hundreds. This key hill, rounded, and featureless, was defended stoutly by 306. Infanterie-Division's Ausbildungs-Bataillon (the divisional training battalion). The commitment of a division's training unit, although common on the Eastern Front after the first year of the war in Russia, was both an indication of the value of this position to 6. Armee and evidence of the shortage of infantry on the German side. Only in unusual situations should a division be required to commit its training formation into battle. In practice, however, training and replacement battalions were routinely used by the Germans as reserve forces and were thus utilized in battle at crisis points. Invariably, heavy combat decimated these battalions, and many disappeared entirely, with their surviving men then distributed to the regular infantry battalions. The acclimatization of replacement infantry was thus left to the efforts of the NCOs and veterans and battle experience. Unfortunately for the replacements, without adequate and realistic training, they often did not survive their first lessons.

Both sides obviously were aware of the importance of this point of high ground and the fighting there became increasingly bitter. As the day wore on, the combat around the hill remained intense. The hill afforded extremely good observation of all the surrounding terrain features and commanded the center ridge. Although relatively low, it was the highest elevation in that sector and dominated the center of the entire battlefield. Whoever held it could observe all of the other ridge crests and many of the tactically important hills for several kilometers around. The Germans fought stubbornly to hold Hill 213.9 and the Russians were equally determined to wrest it from their hands. The bodies of dead Russian infantry piled up like cordwood around the approaches to the hill, shot down by German machine guns or blown apart by artillery. Not until later in the evening did the fighting begin to die down around the hill strongpoints held by the two German infantry divisions that bore the brunt of the main attack in the center.

By the end of 17 July, both 294. and 306. Infanterie-Divisions had lost many men, with losses totalling 55 officers and 2,061 men killed, wounded, or missing.[15] Two things were quickly apparent to 6. Armee, and this awareness guided its planning over the next several days. First of all, it was clear that neither of these divisions could stand too many more days of such combat if losses continued to mount at that level. Second, Hollidt realized through analysis of battle reports that the Russians had lost a serious, though not crippling, amount of armor. He also knew that the Soviets had a significant amount of armor that was yet to reach the area. He was aware that 4th Guards Mechanized Corps was approaching and would be available soon, probably in a matter of days.

It was hoped that by the time this tank corps finally arrived in its entirety, the Russians would have lost so many tanks supporting the infantry in piecemeal commitments that they would continue to be forced to detach tanks from their mechanized corps in order to furnish close-support armor for their infantry. 6. Armee, accordingly, made every effort to destroy as many Russian tanks as possible, realizing that even though the Soviet infantry outnumbered the German grenadiers five or six to one, it was the mobile forces that posed the most dangerous operational threat. The potential for an armored breakthrough in 6. Armee's sector posed great dangers not only to the army itself, but to the German supply lines running farther to the east. A Soviet breakthrough toward Artemovka could turn south toward the Gulf of Taganrog and cut off rail supply to the German armies in the Kuban and Crimea. The rear areas were lightly defended and there were no mobile reserves that would be quickly available to counterattack such a breakthrough. At all costs, a successful Russian attack to the sea had to be prevented, because it would mean potential disaster to the Germans' entire southern flank of the Eastern Front. With only a weak panzergrenadier division in reserve, Hollidt would not be able to stop a strong Soviet mobile group that broke cleanly through his army to the west and turned south. The only hope of the army was to find a strategy to destroy or contain the Soviet tanks in the bridgehead.

6. ARMEE STRIKES BACK
In anticipation of a strong renewed effort by the Russians to break through the German defenses west of Dmitrievka and in order to take the pressure off the two weakened infantry divisions in the center, Hollidt decided to counterattack on 17 July with the only panzer formation then available, 16. Panzergrenadier-Division. Given the situation, Hollidt may have felt that he had little choice but to counterattack, without waiting for the arrival of additional armored strength, which was en route. Since the Russian build-up on the east bank had been detected, beginning 10 July, Hollidt made urgent requests to Heeresgruppe Süd for more panzer divisions. Now another panzer division, 23. Panzer, had been detached from XXIV. Panzerkorps and was on the way, although it would not reach the Mius until late on 18 July. Hollidt decided not to wait for its arrival.

At 1500 hours on 17 July, 16. Panzergrenadier-Division was ordered to assemble its combat units in the sector southwest of Kalinovka in preparation for an attack on the following day. From near Kalinovka, the division was to strike the southern flank of the Soviet

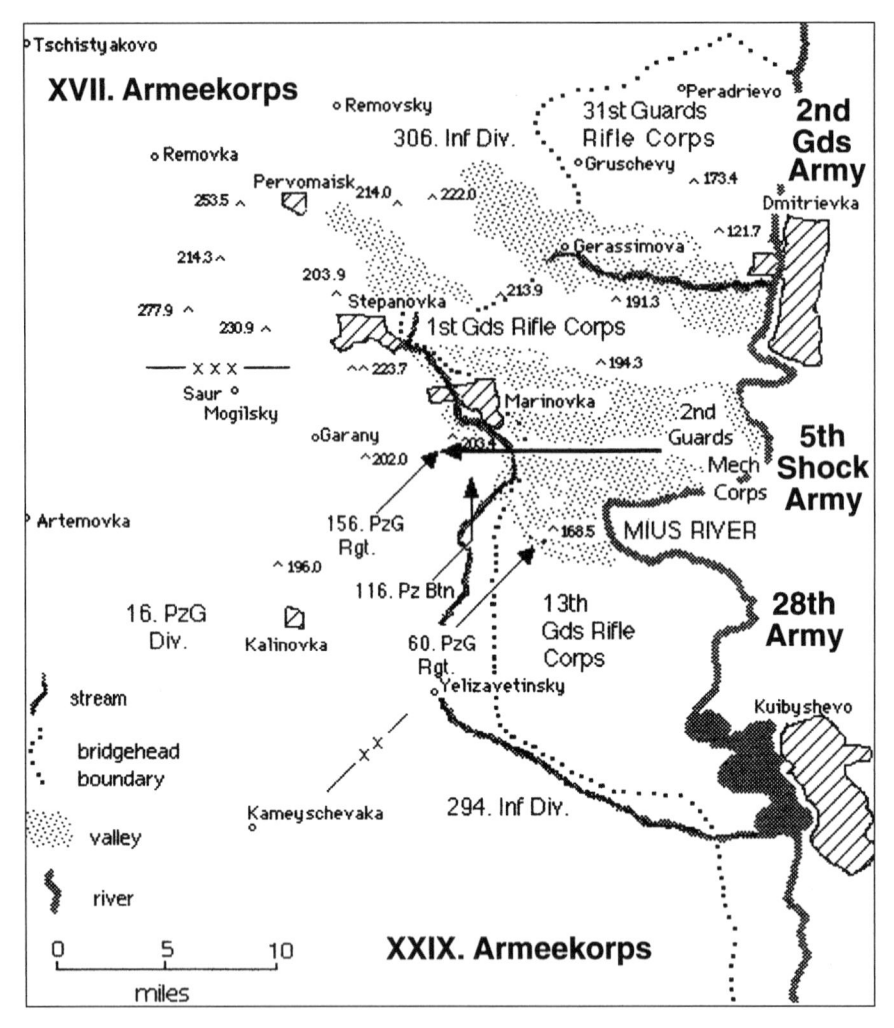

The counterattack of 16. Panzergrenadier-Division, morning of
18 July 1943.

penetration in the center by crossing the Olkhovchik Valley and attacking the Russian troops on Hills 168.5. and 194.3.

Hollidt probably made this decision based on three considerations. First, his infantry divisions could not be expected to stand up to many more days of losing men at the rate already suffered on the first day without collapsing under the weight of the Soviet attacks. Second, it was necessary to defeat the attack before Tolbukhin could bring up 4th Guards Mechanized Corps. Third, it was crucial to the success of German counterattacks that they be made without delay because of the skill and speed with which the Russians dug in and consolidated their gains. Any delay made the Germans' task more difficult and costly in terms of casualties and lost tanks. Accordingly, 6. Armee decided to aggressively counterattack with the only mobile force that it had on hand. 16. Panzergrenadier-Division began to move toward the battlefield from the Chistyakovo area, according to the orders issued on 17 July.[16] It was hoped that the division could strike the flank of the enemy forces south of Hill 213.9 and cut them off from the river. In light of the results of this attack, it may have been more prudent to wait for 23. Panzer-Division. As a continuation of the attack by the Soviets was obviously to be expected, 6. Armee may have benefited more from a stronger mobile defense directed against spearheads of the Soviet advance.

On the morning of 18 July, screened by its reconnaissance battalion, which was deployed southwest of Stepanovka, the division began its attack. On the right, 116. Panzer-Bataillon and 60. Grenadier-Regiment advanced from south of Kalinovka with the intention of driving through the Soviet positions defending the borders of the Olkhovchik Valley. Entering the southern edge of the valley near Yelizavetinsky, this Kampfgruppe drove toward its first objective, Hill 168.5. Its mission was to penetrate the Russian lines south of Hill 213.9 and roll up the flank from south to north.

The other assault group of the division, 156. Panzergrenadier-Regiment, began the day with a successful assault on Hill 203.4, which was located just to the south of Marinovka. From there, the regiment pushed past Marinovka and on into the Olkhovchik Valley, advancing on the left flank of the armored group. The initial objective of the regiment was just to the south of Hill 213.9. It was hoped that a penetration into the Soviet rear areas at this point would disrupt the subsequent Soviet attempts to take the important high ground on the center ridge. Hollidt hoped thereby to destroy the effectiveness of the anticipated renewal of the Russian effort there on 18 July.

Although the attack began successfully, with both attack groups able to penetrate the valley, it quickly ran into difficulties. The advance of 156. Grenadier-Regiment was struck violently on its right flank by a powerful tank and infantry force driving from the area southeast of Marinovka. The Russian attack stopped the German advance in its tracks and the grenadiers were abruptly compelled to go on the defensive. This development immediately escalated into a dangerous situation when the Soviet tanks penetrated the defenses and threatened to overrun the regiment and break through toward the west. After the strength of the Soviet attack became clear, the hard-pressed grenadiers radioed for help to 116. Panzer-Bataillon, then in operation on its right.

In order to prevent a Soviet breakthrough in the Marinovka area, which would endanger its own flank, the panzer battalion quickly reacted to the emergency situation. In order to go to the aid of the endangered grenadiers, it was necessary to withdraw its tanks from the attack on Hill 168.5. The panzers pulled back quickly, regrouped and swept north, taking the Russian tank and infantry force on its southern flank. In a sharp engagement, the Russians were halted by the German armor and the defensive fire of the grenadier regiment. After the arrival of the German armor, the situation was stabilized.

However, this success was countered by the subsequent failure of the attack on Hill 168.5. This attack did not continue to successfully advance without armored support. The regiment was soon forced to withdraw by Soviet counterattacks and heavy artillery fire. Although a crisis had been averted, the division's attack foundered in the face of subsequent attacks by strong Russian forces which were supported by large groups of attack planes. By late morning, 16. Panzergrenadier-Division found itself under ferocious pressure by overwhelming infantry strength with support from tanks of the 2nd Guards Mechanized Corps.

An attempt was made later in the day to get the division's attack moving again with little success. One below-strength panzergrenadier division was not enough to counter a Soviet force of more than a mechanized corps and twelve rifle divisions. Only by hard fighting did the division avoid being overwhelmed and destroyed.

While the attack on 18 July failed to accomplish its objectives, the command of 6. Armee took some satisfaction in the damage inflicted on Soviet armor. Russian armor losses were estimated to be a total of seventy-eight destroyed or damaged Soviet tanks for the day. Although the pressure on Hill 213.9 was not relieved, the main attack, made by elements of 2nd Guards Mechanzied Corps, was thrown back in the area south of Marinovka. The situation became less threatening there, in spite of the failure of the counterattack,

6. Armee Stands Fast

due to the hard fighting of units of 16. Panzergrenadier-Division. The Russians were forced to devote their attention to the defeat of the German counterattack, which prevented further westward expansion of the bridgehead on 18 July.

To the north, in the Gerassimova Valley and on the center ridge, the Soviets had more notable success. With their lines of communication not threatened by a decisive penetration of 16. Panzergrenadier-Division, the Russians continued to throw ever-mounting pressure against the depleted infantry battalions of 306. and 294. Infanterie-Divisions. As a result, several additional breakthroughs occurred when the German lines were penetrated by overwhelming numbers of Soviet infantry. Large formations of Russian planes were again over the battlefield all day at decisive points and made many attacks with bombs and cannon fire. Supported by attack groups that sometimes numbered 80 to 100 planes, the Russians captured Hill 213.9. The survivors of the training battalion were driven off the hill and pushed to the north by the tide of Soviet infantry and tanks. The men of 294. and 306. Divisions began to give way under the unrelenting pressure in the center. Gaps opened in the lines that could not be closed because the fighting of the preious day had eaten up the reserves of each unit. When these gaps were expanded, the Germans began to give way in the center. Later in the day, the towns of Marinovka and Stepanovka fell to the Russians. German troops were pushed out of the village of Grushevy and driven from the southern end of the Gerassimova Valley. The town of Gerassimova, located west of Dmitrievka, was captured also.

After the loss of Hill 213.9, the key position on the central high ground, Hollidt was faced with a serious crisis. The situation was made more critical by the heavy losses, particularly the casualties suffered by the grenadier regiments. Although the Soviet diversionary attacks on both flanks were quickly defeated, the center threatened to collapse under the weight of the main Soviet drive. Russian tanks and infantry had driven the 294. Infanterie-Division back in disorder on both sides of the central ridge and forced the 306. Infanterie-Division to give up several kilometers in the northern part of the penetration. This cleared the way for an advance up the length of the Gerassimova Valley and west toward the exit of the valley at Ssneshnoje. The danger of a major Soviet breakout to the west grew by the hour.

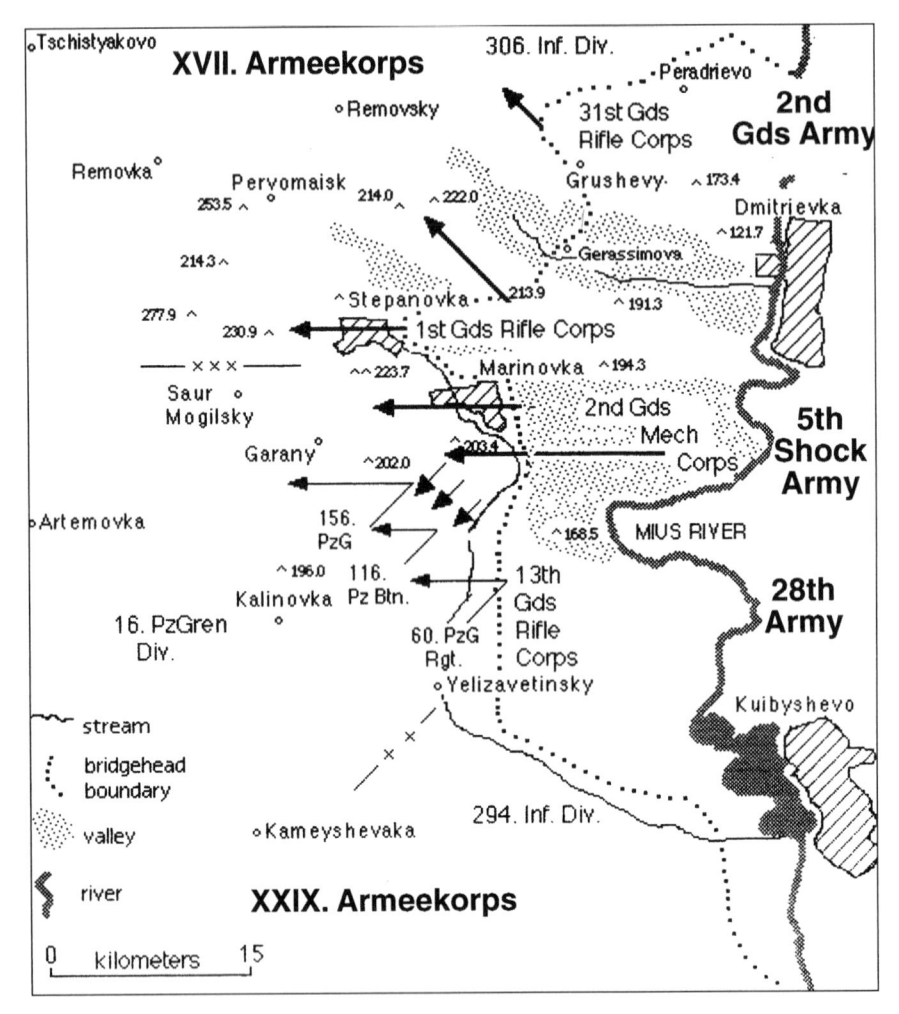

The failure of the counterattack of 16. Panzergrenadier-Division.

The 6. Armee did not have the panzer units necessary to stop a fast-moving Soviet mobile corps' penetration in the direction of Artemovka and Stalino. As no immediate help could be expected from other divisions of Heeresgruppe Süd, other than 23. Panzer-Division, such a breakout threatened Hollidt's army with collapse and destruction if not checked with the forces at hand. There was insufficient infantry on hand to build and man defenses in depth and so once the relatively shallow hard crust of defense was broken, there was little to slow the Russians down.

6. Armee Stands Fast

At this point in the battle, when the situation appeared to be very dark for the men of 6. Armee and disaster threatened, luck intervened on the German side. During the afternoon of 18 July, the Russian tanks and infantry flowed irresistibly over abandoned and blasted trenches, driving the Germans back in disorder until fortunate circumstance combined with the determination of the German infantry to halt the Soviet advance in the center. A training area, complete with an extensive system of trenches and bunkers, in addition to antitank obstacles and ditches, had been built on the road leading to the northwest along the crest of the middle ridge. This position had been constructed for combat exercises by army training battalions. Here the Germans rallied and brought the Soviet attack to a halt.

The T-34s rolled up the flanking valleys on either side of this position but on the center ridge, northwest of Hill 213.9, the Russians could not break the resistance of the troops entrenched in the training fortifications. There, the German infantry, supported by assault guns, narrowly staved off disaster. Columns of greasy black smoke from burning T-34 and T-70 tanks marked the limit of Soviet forward progress on the center ridge. At the end of the day, of the seventy-eight tanks that the army claimed had been knocked out, many were destroyed in front of the training area rallying point. By nightfall, when the attacks were finally halted for the day, Russian dead lay in piles among burnt out tanks A potentially fatal breakout was narrowly averted and the Soviet rifle divisions and armored strength were dealt severe losses.

23. PANZER-DIVISION ARRIVES ON THE MIUS

On the evening of July 18, 23. Panzer-Division arrived in 6. Armee's sector, concentrating in assembly areas around Removka and northwest of Pervomaisk. The division's armor was sorely needed by Hollidt's army. The reconnaissance battalion was immediately thrown out to the southeast in order to screen the division from an attack in that sector.[17] The division was not overly strong in armor, having only about fifty operational tanks on 18 July. However, it was significantly stronger than 16. Panzergrenadier-Division, as that division had only twenty operational tanks left after the fighting on 18 July.[18]

Manstein was evidently concerned with the deployment of the relatively weak panzer division. In communication with Hollidt, he suggested that a single additional panzer division of only moderate strength could not be expected to stem the tide of a full-scale breakout by Southern Front. He recommended that the division would be better utilized in a mobile defence as it could expect less than adequate support from the much weakened 16. Panzergrenadier-Division. To make matters worse, the division would have to attack essentially from the march, without proper reconnaissance or preparation. Manstein further suggested that it might be better to await the arrival of additional panzer forces before attempting a counterattack that was not reasonably sure of success.

Hollidt ignored this advice and ordered the attack to go ahead as scheduled. He was evidently very determined to regain his old defense lines before the Russians had time to consolidate their gains. His concern was understandable, but given the outcome of the counterattack, the army may have been better served if he had followed Manstein's advice. This was not to be the last time that Manstein questioned the use of armor by Hollidt during the fighting on the Mius. It may have been that he did not believe that 6. Armee's commander, with his background as an infantryman, was sufficiently skilled in the proper use of panzer divisions. The nature of the commitment of the II. SS-Panzerkorps armor later in the month would appear to confirm his concern.

During the night, both combatants regrouped for the next day. A renewal of the attack in the center was expected because fresh Soviet infantry reinforcements and tanks were observed streaming into the Dmitrievka area late on 18 July. After making a penetration approximately four kilometers deep, Tolbukhin had a bridgehead only marginally adequate to commit larger armored units in a more powerful attack to the west. The German command expected a strong push toward Artemovka and from there to the important rail center at Stalino. The primary concern of 6. Armee was that it avoid a deep penetration in the center of its front. A successful Russian thrust west of Dmitrievka resulting in the capture of Artemovka would sever the key railroad line running from there south to Taganrog and would split the army in half. Because his army was too weak in armor to recover from such a defeat, Hollidt may have been forced to make his decision based on weakness rather than strength.

German intelligence knew that 4th Guards Mechanized Corps was expected to arrive in the area at any time, adding its tanks to the Russian armor already in the bridgehead. Realizing that his army did not have the infantry strength to endure another day of attrition like the previous two days, Hollidt decided to counterattack on 19 July, in hopes that aggressive defense would stop the Russian drive before it could overrun the weakened infantry regiments. One of the few positive notes from the combat action on 18 July was the fact that the Russians had continued to endure substantial losses of tanks.

6. Armee ordered a three-pronged attack for the early morning of the 19 July, after being assured of sufficient air support by IV. Fliegerkorps. The support was to consist of fighter cover as well as ground-attack planes (primarily Stukas). The main effort was in the center, where 23. Panzer-Division was to attack down the length of the middle ridge, along both sides of the Ssneshnoje-Marinovka road. The divisional objective was the recapture of Hill 213.9. However, in order for this attack to have any chance of success, it was necessary to secure both flanks of the main route of advance by parallel thrusts on the right and left of the center ridge. The forces necessary to carry out these missions would prove to be inadequate.

An already weakened 306. Infanterie-Division, reinforced by 6. Armee's Sturmabteilung (an assault battalion attached to the army headquarters) was assigned the task of securing high ground to the north and east of the main attack by the capture of Hill 173.4. The 16. Panzergrenadier-Division was ordered to protect the south flank of the main attack by advancing past Hill 230.9 and recapturing Stepanovka in order to neutralize Russian infantry and artillery positions in and around the town. There was a particularly strong heavy antitank gun battery located near a road intersection to the east of Stepanovka. It was essential that it be eliminated because it was equipped with 76mm antitank guns and could direct fire on the right or southeast flank of the attack.

Without the capture of the flanking positions, 23. Panzer would have to attack while under intense antitank and artillery fire from the front and both sides. It was therefore crucially important that both flank attacks succeed. The two divisions entrusted with these tasks were weakened by the previous days of fighting, however, and it is a telling measure of the shortage of men and tanks that they were asked to accomplish tasks which would have been difficult for full-strength divisions. The 306. Infanterie-Division did not have sufficient offensive strength to carry out such an attack, even reinforced as it was, with 6. Armee's Sturmabteilung and a number of assault guns. However, given the army's deficiency of armor and lack of other options, Hollidt had little choice once he decided to attack in the center.

The 23. Panzer-Division's attack was doomed from the start, even given that it was an experienced and fresh division. The attack, moving as it did down the crest of an exposed ridge line, funneled the German tanks into what became a trap when the two supporting attacks failed. On the left of the attack, in its attempt to capture Hill

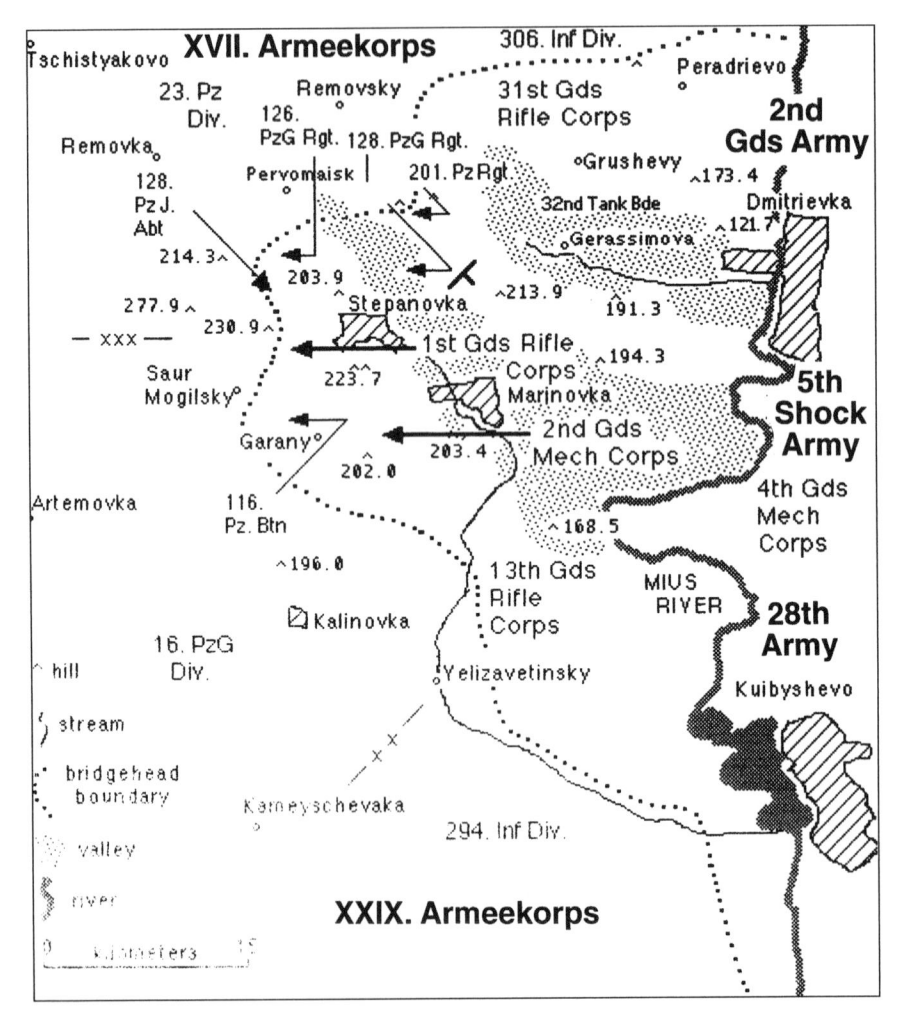

The counterattack of XXIV. Panzerkorps, 19 July 1943.

173.4 and the surrounding high ground, 306. Infanterie proved unable to overrun the Russian positions and withdrew with losses that it could ill afford.

On the right, 16. Panzergrenadier threw its twenty remaining tanks at Stepanovka with determination but was struck by a strong force of T-34s rolling west on a broad front of attack from out of the village itself. Hardly had the German tanks deployed for the advance when it was met head on by the Russian attack. T-34 cannon shells and a storm of antitank projectiles greeted the panzers from hidden positions in Stepanovka. In short order, the unexpected, violent counterattack immobilized or destroyed fifteen of the twenty German tanks. Then the Soviet tanks advanced from the environs of the village toward the stunned panzer battalion, maneuvering into position over the open ground and fanning out into a broad attack toward the west. Having very quickly suffered the loss of much of its armor, the division was forced to withdraw in order to avoid being overrun and completely destroyed by the Soviet assault. Shortly afterward, the attack began to break down at other points as well.

Following the withdrawal of the surviving German panzers, Russian tanks and infantry overran Hill 223.7, southwest of Stepanovka, which was defended by an engineer battalion. The engineers were forced to give up the hill after the Soviet armor and infantry overran their position. Outnumbered by determined Russian infantry and with T-34s inside their perimeter, the German troops abandoned their trenches. The Russians were quickly able to exploit the favorably developing situation, pushing farther to the west and capturing a small village named Garany. The efforts of 16. Panzergrendier-Division to support 23. Panzer failed completely, partially due to the delay of some of its formations north of Stepanovka, but primarily because of the inadequate force of the attack and the overwhelming strength of the Soviets.

On the left flank of 23. Panzer-Division's advance, 306. Infanterie-Division's attempt to take the range of hills to the northeast of Hill 213.9 was also a failure. The division made little progress against the Russians, halting after the lead battalions met strong resistance from small arms, artillery and armor.

Thus, early in the day, the supporting efforts on both sides of the attack in the center failed before the main attack was well under way. Lack of success in these parallel attacks resulted in 23.

Panzer-Division conducting its attack down an exposed ridgetop under fire from three sides. In addition, due to the collapse of the attack of 16. Panzergrenadier-Division, a Soviet counterattack punched a hole in the German lines east of the villages of Garany and Saur Mogilsky. Not only had the main attack by 6. Armee stalled, but a full-scale Russian counterattack with numerous tanks was on the move south of the center ridge.

The failure to neutralize either the strong Soviet antitank gun positions around Stepanovka or the artillery on the high ground around Hill 173.4 ended any chance of success for the attack on Hill 213.9. When the panzers had moved down the ridge crest toward Hill 213.9, they were hit by Soviet fire coming from the northeast high ground and from the southwest. Not only were 45mm and 76mm guns firing antitank shells, but a multitude of antitank rifles, which were supplied in great numbers to the Russian rifle divisions, directed a hail of smaller projectiles at the tanks. High-explosive shells from heavy artillery and salvoes of rocket fire blasted the approaches to the hill. The heavy shells exploded among the tanks; columns of black smoke and fountains of earth and sod erupted among the tanks. The tank commanders ordered their vehicles forward into the storm of shot and shell.

At the start of the attack, from the front, there was little reaction beyond fire from infantry antitank rifles. Heavier Soviet weapons, the camouflaged antitank guns and dug-in tanks, used excellent fire discipline and held their fire, while antitank rifle bullets showered the panzers, clattering off armor or richocheting into the sky. The multitude of light projectiles could not penetrate tank armor, but at close range, they could be dangerous if they hit a vision port, a track joint or an exposed tank commander's head. When the panzer regiment began its attack, rolling forward into heavy enemy fire, the other units of the division jumped off as well. However, the attack did not begin well at several points, as a result of which the division's advance as a whole got off to a poor start.

The attack was weakened at the onset when the advance of the division's Panzerjäger battalion was held up by Soviet fire from near Hill 214.3.[19] This delay removed the support of the mobile antitank guns from the attack at the very beginning of the day's action. The attack was further hampered when, after the initial advance, 126. Panzergrenadier-Regiment was also delayed by two factors. Soviet fire originating from the north of Stepanovka caused the first delay. Subsequently, the commanding officer of the regiment mishandled the attack by failing to advance in the proper direction to support the main attack. When the regiment then bogged down north of the town, Russian infantry moved against it in strength, attacking from Stepanovka. The regiment was forced to halt and dig in to repulse this assault.

Although these formations of the division were delayed, resulting in poor support of the division's main effort against Hill 213.9, the panzer regiment and 128. Panzergrenadier-Regiment began their attack on schedule. As the tanks neared the slopes of Hill 213.9, continually under fire from shells coming from the flanks, the Soviet positions to the front remained quiet, exhibiting extraordinary fire discipline. When the German tanks were very close, all of the Russian antitank guns and dug-in tanks opened fire from their well-concealed firing positions. The high corn and sunflower fields that spread over the ridgetop and the surrounding terrain at the approaches of the hill provided excellent camouflage, hiding the Russian guns and tanks from observation by the German tank commanders until it was too late.

The close-range wall of fire devastated the German tanks and the attack faltered quickly in the face of this heavy fire. The panzer regiment, weakened by the losses sustained while advancing down the ridge crest, was shocked by the close-range antitank gun fire and losses quickly mounted. The momentum of the attack was destroyed and the panzers maneuvered into cover. At this point, small groups of Russian tanks rolled out of hidden ravines that led to the top of the ridge, using clear lanes of advance to attack the flanks and rear of the Germans. A fierce tank battle took place in front of the forward approaches of the hill.

After losing twenty-eight tanks, the remnants of the panzer regiment were forced to withdraw at noon. Left behind on the forward approaches to the hill were a number of burning tanks, scattered along the ridge, each marked by a column of oily black smoke. Damaged panzers limped to the rear under cover of fire from their comrades. Even after regrouping, the regiment was unable to resume the attack due primarily to swarms of IL-2s that pounced on any vehicle that showed itself in the open. The Russians also directed artillery fire from heavy guns (17.2cm) against the assembly area.

Neither of the panzergrenadier regiments had been able to support the tank attack on Hill 213.9 satisfactorily—for different reasons. The 126. Panzergrenadier-Regiment remained stalled to the north of Stepanovka and fell behind the advance of the 128. Panzergrenadier-Regiment on the panzer regiment's left. The 128. Panzergrenadier-Regiment steadily continued to move forward and pushed across the Olkhovchik Valley to the foot of Hill 213.9, driving scattered groups of Russian infantry ahead of it. When the attack reached the base of the hill and the German infantry attempted to ascend the slope, they were suddenly hit by artillery, mortar and small-arms fire and were stopped cold, with heavy losses. Unable to continue to move forward and having lost contact with both the panzers and 126. Panzergrenadier-Regiment, the regiment finally pulled back later in the day. With the collapse of the attack of the panzer regiment upon Hill 213.9 and the failure of the two panzergrenadier regiments to accomplish anything decisive, the attack by 23. Panzer-Division petered out. In any event, the attack had little chance of success after the two supporting attacks failed to secure the flanks of the main effort on the center ridge. To make a difficult situation worse, the poor start made by some of its own units helped doom the division's efforts to failure.

The attempt to regain possession of the key center ridge had failed. In fact, Hollidt's situation worsened considerably after the Russians stopped the attack. Later into the afternoon, the Russians maintained pressure all along the front, trying hard to break out of the bridgehead toward the west. The Russians reacted quickly, exploiting loss of momentum by 16. Panzergrenadier-Division and pushed westward toward Saur Mogilsky and Kalinovka, expanding the depth of the bridgehead. The German counterstroke of 19 July, designed to destroy the Soviet forces before they could renew the attack, failed to accomplish its mission and actually resulted in lost ground at a high cost in tanks and men that the army could ill afford.

It was only by last-ditch resistance of emergency forces at Hills 202.0 and 230.9, west and southwest of Stepanovka, that the Germans destroyed a number of Russian tanks and were able to begin to plug the large dangerous gap that earlier in the day threatened to become unmanageable. The Russian advance to the north remained stalled in front of the training area, while, at strongpoints near Stepanovka and Marinovka, the Germans finally stopped the Russian armored advance in the center, with support from several assault gun batteries. After the Russian attack was halted in this sector, 23. Panzer-Division tried to salvage the day with an attempt to recapture Stepanovka at 1530 hours. Army artillery supported the attack well and Stukas bombed key Russian positions in the south. 16. Panzergrenadier-Division was not able to support the attack. It remained completely occupied with the effort to stop the Soviet attack in the Garany area.

The failure of the counterattack on 19 July and the resulting loss of armor resulted in a crisis for Hollidt. His army was now too short of tanks to have any hope of successfully counterattacking the Soviet bridgehead. Having incurred serious tank losses in both mobile divisions, Hollidt did not have sufficient armor resources to have any hope of a successful renewal of the operation. Manstein's worst fears about the weakness of the attack were realized and there was reason to doubt whether the army could survive a strong Russian attack if such an effort resulted in a major breakthrough or, worse, multiple breakthroughs. The mobile units of 6. Armee were too weakened to restore the situation if a strong Russian attack cracked the front open. The infantry strength of the army, of concern before the attack, had been reduced to a critical level. Such problems did not trouble the Soviets, however.

On the Russian side of the river, there was no lack of replacement troops and tanks, especially infantry. Tolbukhin had twelve rifle divisions in the center sector alone. In addition to the impending arrival of fresh armor from 4th Guards Mechanized Corps, German air reconnaisance reported the arrival of new rifle divisions at several railheads east of the river. These infantry reinforcements would quickly be available and could be across the Mius in a matter of hours. Soviet strength was growing while German manpower losses could not be replaced.

Hollidt decided on a change of tactics in view of the overwhelming superiority in numbers enjoyed by the Russians in the bridgehead area. Heeresgruppe Süd had previously informed 6. Armee that it could not move additional mobile forces (II. SS-Panzerkorps) to the Mius until the end of July. Manstein at first hoped that the II. SS-Panzerkorps could be used in 1. Panzerarmee's sector south of the Donets at Izyum, in combination with XXIV. Panzerkorps.[20] But Hitler specifically vetoed this plan and ordered the II. SS-Panzerkorps (minus *Leibstandarte*) to be sent to the aid of 6. Armee. After this decision was made, preparations began for the transportation and concentration of the SS divisions in 6. Armee's area. However, it was anticipated that it would take until 28–29 July to transport and assemble II. SS-Panzerkorps in the battle area.

This meant that 6. Armee would have to make do with what resources it had at hand until that time. Hollidt had to find a way for his army to survive until these reinforcements arrived. Given the situation, decisions were made out of bitter necessity, reflecting the problems resulting from shrinking manpower, a continuing shortage of armor and the period of time that would elapse before significant mobile reinforcements arrived.

The primary goal of Hollidt's new tactics was to inflict the maximum possible destruction on Soviet armor. It became necessary to make every effort to destroy Russian tanks at all given opportunities in order to reduce the chances of a massed armored attack at a critical point. Second, it was also necessary to find infantry to replace the losses of the most seriously weakened infantry divisions of the army, 294. and 306. Infanterie-Divisions. Infantry strength had to be maintained at all costs, even if it meant robbing the rest of the front in the quiet areas. All subsequent defensive measures were organized with these two objectives in mind. During the night of 19 July, emergency units were hastily organized from troops in the northern and southern sectors of the army and sent marching to the Stepanovka-Dmitrievka area. Additional antitank guns, heavy antiaircraft guns (88mm), and assault gun batteries were sent to the Dmitrievka sector.

Hollidt was able to take these measures because Tolbukhin did not renew with determination the diversionary attacks to the south or north of the main effort. As a result, after the Germans quickly defeated these attacks, they were able to devote their full effort in the center. The failure of 4th Guards Mechanized Corps to arrive in time to participate in the first days of fighting did not allow the Soviets to concentrate their armor. Tolbukhin was of course under the pressure of time and had to attack as soon as possible in order to influence operations of the panzer divisions in the Psel-Prochorovka area. It was necessary to assemble enough armor to sufficiently threaten the Germans and cause them to react, but given the role of Tolbukhin's mission, it was not required to assemble enough tank strength to give his army its best chance of success. Again, the element of time entered the equation, and thus, the Russians launched their assault across the Mius before the arrival of 4th Guards Mechanized Corps. Had the Russians advanced on a broad front with sufficient tank strength at two or more points, the problems presented to the Germans may well have been beyond their means to control. However, with the defeat of the attacks to the north and south of Kuibyshevo, which were began with insufficient armor support, 6. Armee was able to concentrate on the main assault at Dmitrievka.

Hollidt anticipated a resumption of the Soviet attack with the main effort, probably west of Stepanovka on the following day, 20 July. This assumption proved correct when the new day dawned. Again, from first light, the Soviet air force was present in strength, bombing and strafing in support of the tanks from 2nd Guards Mechanized Corps. Between Hill 196.0 and the Stepanovka area, Soviet armor supported a broad frontal attack by elements of nine rifle divisions. Two fresh divisions, 118th and 387th Rifle Divisions, crossed the Mius river during the night and reinforced the attack. The German infantry battalions, weakened from high casualties by three days of fighting, with their personnel physically tired and then under attack by thousands of massed infantry with armor, were forced back to the west, losing several key defensive positions. The Soviets captured Hill 214.3, just to the northwest of Stepanovka, on the road to Ssneshnoje. The village of Saur Mogilsky, situated southwest of Stepanovka, fell also, although not without stout resistance from its defenders.

More territory was lost when the reconnaissance battalion of 16. Panzergrenadier-Division was driven off Hill 230.9 by an assault led by many Soviet tanks with clusters of infantry riding on the tank decks. When this force continued to the west past the just captured hill, it was counterattacked by the 675. Pionier-Abteilung, moving to the attack from it's own positions atop of Hill 277.9. The attack of the German engineers on the Russian flank temporarily threw the Soviets into confusion and delayed the advance. When the Soviet tide was then temporarily halted, 23. Panzer-Division rallied quickly and launched an effective attack that recaptured Hill 214.3 and drove the Russians back. In other areas, the Russian spearheads gradually pushed the Germans out of their positions, with only the German artillery preventing outright collapse. The German infantry fought back with determination, surrendering their positions only when the vast numerical superiority in numbers became decisive. However, the

Soviet successes were won at a high price. The German strategy of destroying as many tanks as possible resulted in high tank losses by the Russians.

All through the day, the Germans blunted the advance of Soviet armored elements by the use of well-positioned antitank guns and Stuka attacks. Assault gun batteries were also particularly effective in the antitank role, but many of the Russian tanks were knocked out or immobilized by close-combat weapons of the infantry such as grenade clusters, mines placed under turrets or gasoline bombs. Experienced German infantry learned that tanks could not hurt them in well-constructed fortifications if they did not break and run, leaving the protection of their trenches and dug outs. In the open, they were vulnerable to machine-gun fire and grinding tank tracks, but hidden in their positions, it was possible to stealthily attack the enemy armor after it penetrated the trenches. First, however, it was necessary to separate the Soviet infantry from the tanks. This was accomplished by firing all automatic weapons and mortars at the infantry as they advanced on foot or riding on top of the T-34s and T-70s. This forced them to seek shelter and jump off of the tanks. Without infantry, the Russian tanks became vulnerable to close-combat attacks because the earlier T-34 tank models suffered from a lack of good observation ports to the sides. This inherent weakness resulted in blind spots which could be taken advantage of by infantry using close-combat antitank weapons.[21] Until later in 1943, the turrets of the T-34 did not have all-round vision cupolas for the tank commanders, which further handicapped them in detecting attacking close-quarter infantry and also location of targets and potential dangers of other types. Cooperation and command to the degree made possible in German panzers by the instant communication between individual tanks in the same unit was not possible in Russian tank formations.

The Russian army was still in the process of improving its force structure and perfecting its armor tactics and principles in the summer of 1943. The key element of armor, its mobility, was at times negated by the use of inflexible tactics and the poor communications capability of Soviet armored units at this point in the war. The inability of tank unit commanders to quickly communicate with their supporting forces hampered close cooperation and allowed the Germans to separate the tanks from the infantry and defeat each sep-

6. Armee Stands Fast 135

13th Guards Rifle Corps and 2nd Guards Mechanized Corps, 20 July 1943.

arately. Unlike the German (and American) armies, the Soviets never developed armored personnel carriers during the war, and as a result, the Russian infantry was vulnerable to small-arms, artillery and mortar fire during the early stages of an attack. This often resulted in the infantry being pinned down and unable to advance with the tanks. In the German panzer or panzergrenadier divisions, usually one battalion per panzergrenadier regiment was equipped with light armored personnel carriers that protected the infantry while advancing with armor. By contrast, Soviet infantry often accompanied attacks hanging on to tank decks or on foot and remained vulnerable to small-arms, mortar and artillery fire. If the Germans could survive preparatory artillery fires in sufficient numbers to man their machine-gun and mortar positions, grevious losses could be inflicted on the Russian infantry. The high rate of fire from the machine guns of the German infantry wreaked a terrible slaughter when manned by skilful crews. If the Russian infantry could be forced to halt and take cover, the tanks then became vulnerable to close assault by German infantry.

By the end of the day, 2nd Guards Mechanized Corps and 32nd Tank Brigade had lost so many tanks that Tolbukhin probably no longer had sufficient tanks to mount a dangerous breakout attempt. In order to create a bridgehead of sufficient depth and width, the Russian infantry needed supporting armor, the only source of which was the armored units then available. As a result, small groups of the Russian tanks were doled out to the rifle divisions, where they were knocked out or destroyed by the Germans. Thus, after the first days of the attack, the chances of producing a decisive breakthrough steadily diminished. Out of necessity, Tolbukhin's main body of armor was distributed along the entire front rather than concentrated at a critical point. When the rest of his armor arrived late on 20 July, the massive tank losses of the previous day's fighting had by then reduced the chances of successfully breaking the German line.

The Germans were aware of the arrival of 4th Guards Mechanized Corps as soon as its tanks began to assemble on the east bank due to information from aerial reconnaissance. Assuming that the logical objective of the principal Soviet attack was toward Artemovka and from there on to Stalino, 6. Armee prepared to meet the threat in the center. Anticipating that the Russians would try to break out of the bridgehead into the flat tank country west of Garany–Saur Mogilsky, Hollidt built up a blocking position to defend this area and prepared to meet the next Soviet threat.

THE ATTACK OF 4TH GUARDS MECHANIZED CORPS

By early in the day of 21 July, the three brigades of 4th Guards Mechanized Corps, the 12th, 13th, and 15th Guards Mechanized Brigades, had arrived in the Dmitrievka area. A mechanized corps had a normal establishment of approximitely 200 tanks, and thus, the arrival of this formation gave the Russians a sizeable advantage in tank strength. On this date, between its two mobile divisions, the Germans had a total of 36 operational tanks to oppose the Soviet tank force. There were 17 Panzer IVs and 19 Panzer Is still operational on that date. Almost immediately upon their arrival, some of the fresh Soviet armored units were thrown into action across the river. 4th Mechanized Corps' tanks made its first attack against the positions of 156. Panzergrenadier-Regiment at a point northeast of Kalinovka. However, the full strength of the corps was not committed. Nevertheless, this attack penetrated the thin German lines and pushed on to the south and east of the town. Reinforced by a Kampfgruppe from 294. Infanterie-Division, 16. Panzergrenadier-Division counterattacked the Soviet battlegroup south of Kalinovka and destroyed them. The Germans were able to regain their old positions in this sector. However, the Russians had more success at other points. The limited German mobile reserves, faced with too many crisis situations, could not be everywhere at once. Because of its losses, 16. Panzergrenadier-Division did not have the strength to conduct anything larger than such local counterattacks. The village of Grigorievka was captured by the Russians, and bitter seesaw fighting began in nearby Yelizavetinsky, with that hamlet changing hands repeatedly during the morning. German infantry battled fiercely to keep the village, counterattacking when they were driven out by the Russians. Each time, they pushed back into the ruined collection of huts. The fighting in Yelizavetinsky continued into the late afternoon.

Other Russian armor and infantry assault groups pushed to the north, against Peradrievo and Nikiforoff, where infantry of 306. Infanterie-Division, supported by an assault gun battalion, destroyed thirty to forty Russian tanks according to 6. Armee's estimates. The day ended without decisive success by either side although the Germans had been able to inflict more tank losses on the Soviet mobile formations, which again were dispersed in attacks along a broad front instead of concentrated at a decisive point. Hollidt had anticipated an attack by massed armor in the center on 21 July, due to the arrival of 4th Guards Mechanized Corps but it did not take place. In the meantime, however, three more Russian rifle divisions, 49th and 87th Guards Rifle Divisions and 320th Rifle Division, crossed the Mius.

However, even as fresh Russian troops were arriving, help also appeared for the Germans, in the form of 236. Sturmgeschütz-Abteilung (assault gun battalion), which was used to reinforce 16. Panzergrenadier-Division. An assault gun battalion normally had between twenty and thirty vehicles and possessed supply, communications and command detachments integral to the battalion. These battalions were attached to corps, army and larger HQ and were intended for use as a unit according to German tactical doctrine. Individual batteries were not organized to operate as separate units, although this frequently occurred.

Previously, 6. Armee had requested of Heeresgruppe Süd that it receive additional reinforcements in the form of the HQ and support units of XXIV. Panzerkorps. This request was granted and the command group of XXIV. Panzerkorps took over the defensive effort west of Garany on 22 July. Under the direction of this HQ, the Germans organized a strong blocking position on a line of Hills 253.5–214.3–277.9–196.0 and from there south to Kalinovka. At fortified strongpoints along this position, antitank guns, 88s, and assault guns were emplaced. A major attack by 4th Guards Mechanized Corps was expected to be committed in an attack toward these fortified hills on the following day.

Up to this point, 6. Armee had narrowly succeeded in surviving one crisis after another in spite of the overwhelming numbers arrayed against it, and it was likely that the next day would be decisive. Hollidt's tactics had been successful in destroying a large number of Soviet tanks during the first days of the attack and the Soviet infantry had been slaughtered in large numbers. However, with the arrival of 4th Guards Mechanized Corps and three additional rifle divisions, all indications pointed to a major attack in the center sector. Thus, on the evening of 21 July, 6. Armee was faced with a major decision. If the Germans correctly anticipated Russian intentions, Tolbukhin's attack would collide with a solid wall of 88s, antitank guns and the remaining German tanks and assault guns. Hollidt decided that the Russians would make their next major attack in the center. However, after five days of fighting, Hollidt's army was tiring and running critically short of infantry, even after receiving some reinforcements. With the Russians concentrating to attack with strong armored forces once again, the Germans had to correctly anticipate the location and direction of the expected attack on 22

July. If Tolbukhin's assault had struck in strength at another, unexpected point, the German defenses may well have collapsed.

Hollidt's army had weathered several difficult situations due to the courage of its soldiers and the emergency, measures initiated by 6. Armee during the previous four days. Essentially, all of the available German infantry were concentrated in the front lines. The reserves were already committed and largely used up. The surviving troops formed a formidable hard crust, but there was no depth to the defense. Had the Russians succeeded in breaking out to the west, the army would be hard pressed to avoid being cut up into fragments. It was of vital importance that the German command guessed correctly in regard to Russian intentions. Understandably, the night of 21–22 July was a time of nervous anticipation and great anxiety for the command of 6. Armee.

XXIV. PANZERKORPS DEFEATS THE SOVIET ATTACK

In the darkness of the early morning of 22 July, the Soviet attack began and escalated throughout the day with gradually increasing intensity. The main attack was preceded by platoon- and company-strength actions by Soviet infantry, accompanied by some tanks, which aggressively probed German defensive positions all along the line. At many points, the Russians attempted to break into the German lines behind heavy artillery fires. The direction of the main attack was not confirmed by the events of the first hours of fighting, as the Soviets did not commit large elements of 4th Mechanized Corps at first. Tolbukhin attempted to neutralize several formidable German strongpoints that were located in the center of the line. The strongest assaults were in the area of a line of hills northwest of Garany and Saur Mogilsky. This section of the line was defended by units of 23. Panzer-Division and XVII. Armeekorps elements.

Early in the morning, the Russians attacked 128. Panzergrenadier-Regiment's positions in the blocking line, making three attacks in battalion strength from 0400 to 0900 hours, with the *Schwerpunkt* (point of main effort) of the Soviet effort around Hill 277.9. Smaller forces struck elements of Panzer-Aufklärungs-Abteilung 23 in a wooded area southwest of the hill. The Germans repulsed the main attack, after which the Soviet troops were pinned down by artillery and counterattacked. The Soviet infantry were annihilated in close combat and artillery fire. At 1000 hours, the Soviets made another assault on this hill with two battalions and twenty-five to thirty tanks supported by very strong artillery support.[22] A battalion of 201. Panzer-Regiment was assembled west of the hill and, in close cooperation with elements of 16. Panzergrenadier-Division, smashed the Soviet force after the initial attack was stopped by the panzergrenadiers.

Soviet artillery hammered the German lines and severely damaged frontline positions but was less effective in destroying German guns in the main artillery positions which could not be fired upon with observed fire. At several points along the front, the Russian rifle divisions moved forward in seemingly endless numbers, advancing through thick smoke and dust. The German medium artillery (10.5cm) inflicted heavy losses on the Soviet infantry as they advanced toward the infantry positions. There were fewer Soviet tanks to support the infantry due to the high armor losses of the first day. Most of the tanks of 4th Guards Mechanized Corps were evidently concentrated for the attack in the center. Soviet planes dropped many phosphorus bombs, which ignited the tinder-dry vegetation of the sun-parched terrain. Smoke from these fires drifted in dense clouds over the battlefield at many points, mingling with dust and obscuring the Soviet advance at many points.

West of Garany, the battalions of 128. Panzergrenadier-Regiment, which defended the sector of the line dominated by Hill 277.9, bore the brunt of repeated infantry attacks. The Russians made a number of determined efforts to take the hill. The strongest attack was made at 1500 hours, when a Soviet rifle regiment, with about twenty tanks in support, appeared out of a wooded area northeast of Saur Mogilsky and advanced toward the hill. The Russian advance was aggressively counterattacked on its flanks by the 23. Panzer-Division's reconnaissance battalion, supported by artillery and a few tanks. Immediately, German artillery fell on the attack, tearing great gaps in the ranks of the Soviet infantry. Machine-gun fire reached out to clear the Soviet infantry off of the tank decks, but still the attack came on. Exhibiting tremendous courage and discipline, the Soviet infantry, although decimated in the open ground in front of the hill, continued to resolutely advance through high-explosive artillery and small-arms fire. However, when German antitank guns destroyed a number of the Russian tanks, the attack collapsed.[23]

6. Armee Stands Fast

Later in the day, it became evident that the Russians were making their main effort in the anticipated direction. The sound of large numbers of tank motors was heard, the vehicles concealed at first by the smoke and dust. It was a nerve-wracking situation for the German infantry and antitank gunners, who could hear the T-34 motors roaring in the distance and the tracks clanking as the attack pushed forward but could not see the Soviet armor. The Soviet tanks moved up under the cover of choking clouds of smoke and dust. The Russians again employed great numbers of their fighter-bomber aircraft in support of the attack, strafing and dropping phosphorus bombs. Fires caused by the phosphorus bombs added to the clouds of smoke laying over many points of the battlefield. Soviet artillery also laid down heavy smoke screens to further conceal the advance of the armor. Heavy barrages of high-explosive shells pounded the German front lines.

At 1530 hours on 22 July, approximately 140 Soviet tanks rolled forward on a broad front toward the southwest between Grigorievka and Saur Mogilsky. Swarms of Soviet infantry advanced in waves behind the T-34s or rode the tanks into battle, clinging to the turrets and decks. To the German commanders and the men in the trenches, the volume of Soviet artillery, large amount of air support and the number of tanks involved in the attack left little doubt that Tolbukhin's major effort was toward the Kalinovka-Yelizavetinsky sector, as expected. The main weight of the attack fell upon the positions of 16. Panzergrenadier-Division. By this time, the division barely had the combat strength of a regimental battlegroup. In the previous four days it had lost 10 small-unit commanding officers, 69 other officers, and 1,366 noncoms and men.[24] It had been strengthened to a degree by additional assault gun battalions and other units attached to XXIV. Panzerkorps headquarters, but had only a handful of operational tanks.

In the initial assault, most of the Russian tanks rolled right over the smoke-shrouded front lines. They were able to avoid early tank losses from long-range fire by German antitank guns and tanks because of the cover provided by the smoke and dust. However, the Russian infantry did not fare as well. When the Russian tanks advanced against the German lines southwest of Garany, the survivors of 294. Infanterie-Division proved that they had learned their lessons well, and they directed furious machine-gun fire and mortar attacks on the Soviet infantry riding on the tanks. Corps and divisional artillery dropped a curtain of high explosives in front of the German trenches and bunkers. Faced with this storm of shot and shell, the Soviet infantry quickly jumped off of the tank decks and took cover. The Soviet armor was now faced with a familiar dilemma: if they advanced alone, they became vulnerable to German tank killer teams and antitank-gun nests, but if they halted their advance, they became easier targets for German tanks and assault guns or the deadly 88s.

Characteristically, the Soviet tanks continued to drive westward, leaving the Russian infantry pinned down in front of the German lines, under fire from mortars and machine guns. Soon German forward observers zeroed in on the Russian positions and walked artillery fire back and forth over the trapped men. Mortar shells dropped among them and machine-gun fire made it suicidal to attempt to retreat or advance. In the meantime, the tank attack left the German strongpoint line, pushing farther to the west. As it did so, the tanks rolled out of the clouds of dust and smoke enveloping the frontline positions. The attack also advanced beyond most of the effective support of the Russian artillery.

When the Russian tanks emerged from the protective cloak that had enshrouded the front lines and secondary positions, they appeared in front of the German blocking positions. Now on open ground, in sight of the German gunners, they were struck by long-range fire from German tanks and assault guns waiting in the hills between Kalinovka and Saur Mogilsky. Antiaircraft batteries added the fire of 88mm guns with devastating effect. The 88 could hit a T-34 at a range of 3,500 meters or more, a distance at which they were relatively safe from the 76mm guns of the Russian tanks. The powerful 88mm armor-piercing round was capable of penetrating T-34 armor even at more than 3,000 meters, and a solid hit invariably left a burning wreck on the battlefield. The drawback to the use of these superb weapons in an antitank role was their height and relative lack of mobility, which made them vulnerable to armored attacks if they were not concealed and well supported by infantry and armor.

With high-quality optics and well-trained marksmanship, the German gunners poured a withering long-range storm of projectiles on the Russian tanks as they rolled over the grassy steppe. Soon burning Soviet tanks lurched to a halt all along the attack front, columns of smoke rising high into the air. Here and there ammunition detonated and thunderous explosions blew tanks apart. Those tank crews lucky enough to survive the white-hot stream of metal that penetrated armor and ricocheted around inside tank interiors leapt out of their burning tanks. They scurried for a hole or ditch and safety. Stuka pilots, now that they could find targets out in the open, turned their planes over in steep dives and dropped bombs or made strafing attacks with on board cannon.

As the German guns wreaked havoc on the Russian tanks, the attack continued to roll westward in spite of the destruction of one vehicle after another. The losses were ignored, until, in less than an hour, 130 burning or immobilized T-34s dotted the landscape in front of the high ground.[25] A few surviving tanks finally turned tail and made their way back over the burning grass, stopping now and then to pick up tank crew survivors who were sheltering around the shattered hulks. The Germans claimed the destruction of 93 Soviet tanks in the XXIX. Armeekorps' sector alone, with 23. Panzer adding 15 more tanks to that total.[26] In spite of the heavy losses of the previous days, the men of 16. Panzergrenadier-Division had held their ground in the face of an attack by two Soviet tank brigades and refused to break. Throughout the day, battle groups of the division were in combat at critical areas all along the front.

After the failure of the main armored attack, the Russians attempted to get their attack moving again with a renewed attempt to take Hill 277.9. In mid-afternoon, the situation remained undecided in the villages of Yelizavetinsky and Grigorievka, where German and Russian troops remained locked in furious fighting for possession of the two small villages. Large flights of Soviet planes supported the infantry at various points, and antiaircraft units of 294. Infanterie-Division shot down three of the planes. At 1700 hours, a battalion-strength attack hit I./128. Panzergrenadier-Regiment's position's again, and some twenty minutes later, a second attack struck the perimeter of the other battalion of the regiment. Both attacks were halted and then destroyed by counterattacks of reserve elements of the regiment. Other Russian infantry advanced from Stepanovka and assaulted the positions of 126. Panzergrenadier-Regiment west of Hill 230.9.

At 2000 hours, the Russian infantry that earlier had attacked Hill 277.9 regrouped and attacked again with ten to twelve tanks rolling out of the Olkhovchik in support. This assault was also turned back

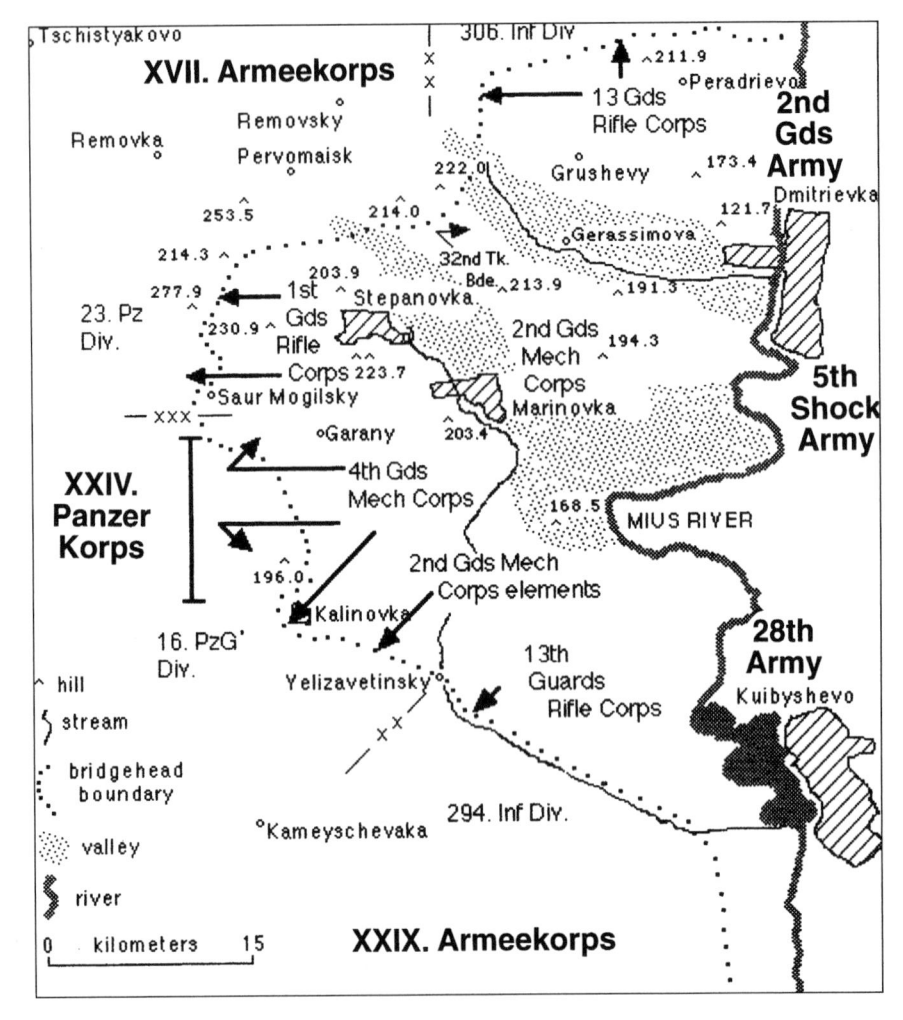

6. Armee scores a critical defensive success, 22 July 1943.

with heavy losses. Russian infantry captured the town of Kalinovka, but this small victory did not justify the high cost in destroyed armor that was inflicted on Tolbukhin's front during the day. His strongest armored formation, 4th Guards Mechanized Corps, had been smashed, and infantry losses were high, largely due to effective German artillery support. The Russian infantry, although obstinate in attack, suffered from poor coordination with the armor in the offensive operations on 22 July. Time and again, once Russian infantry went to ground, forced to take cover from well-sited machine-gun and mortar fire, the advance stalled in front of the German positions. At that point, the medium artillery and mortars went to work. Mortar units were particlarly active during defensive actions as evidenced by an expenditure of a total of 100 tons of heavy mortar shells by the Germans on 22 July alone. 6. Armee's machine-gun and mortar ammunition expenditures rose characteristically on days of heavy defensive operations such as on 22 July and were generally twice as high in comparison with days of offensive operations.[27] Light infantry gun ammunition expenditures were also heavier on days of defensive operations. In contrast, light and heavy field howitzers used less ammunition on days of heavy defensive fighting. In the period from 17 July to 29 July, 6. Armee's howitzers used an average of 74.8 tons per day. Later in the fighting, during counterattacks on the Soviet bridgehead, the army used an average of 88.6 tons of heavy and light howitzer shells. The availability of plentiful artillery ammunition was extremely important to the survival of Hollidt's army. Without adequate supplies of shells, it is doubtful that the weakened divisions could have turned back the numerous Soviet infantry.

Testifying to the grim efficiency of German artillery, dead Russian soldiers lay in great, grotesque piles in front of the German positions on 22 July. At points where Soviet armor was committed, burnt out T-34s were scattered over the blasted terrain, victims of accurate fire from the blocking positions west of Garany and Saur Mogilsky.

In spite of the victory of 22 July, Hollidt anticipated a renewal of the Soviet attack on the following day and viewed this prospect with concern. The units that had been at the point of main effort, 294. Infanterie-Division and 16. Panzergrenadier-Division, were in bad shape. The 16. Panzergrenadier had only 550 combat effectives among its two panzergrenadier regiments, and the 294. and 306. Infanterie-Divisions were reduced significantly as well. 23. Panzer-Division had also taken heavy losses in both men and tanks.

On 23 July, the crisis seemed to have temporarily passed when there were no large-scale Russians attacks at any point along the front. Instead, the Soviet contented themselves with probing reconnaissance sorties in a number of places, none of which were intended to gain any significant ground.

However, it was very clear to Hollidt that the army would be able to hold out against further strong Soviet attacks only if certain conditions were met. Hollidt was of the opinion that the men had done all that could be expected of them and were spent. He stripped all of the battalions from quiet sectors of the front that could be spared and had reported to Heeresgruppe Süd that if the Soviets were able to mass armor at an unexpected sector, it was likely their attack would be successful.

Emergency measures were utilized by 6. Armee in order to scrape together a few more replacements. Construction units and rear-area men who could be spared were hurriedly organized into scratch units and sent to the front in quiet areas in order to free up a few more

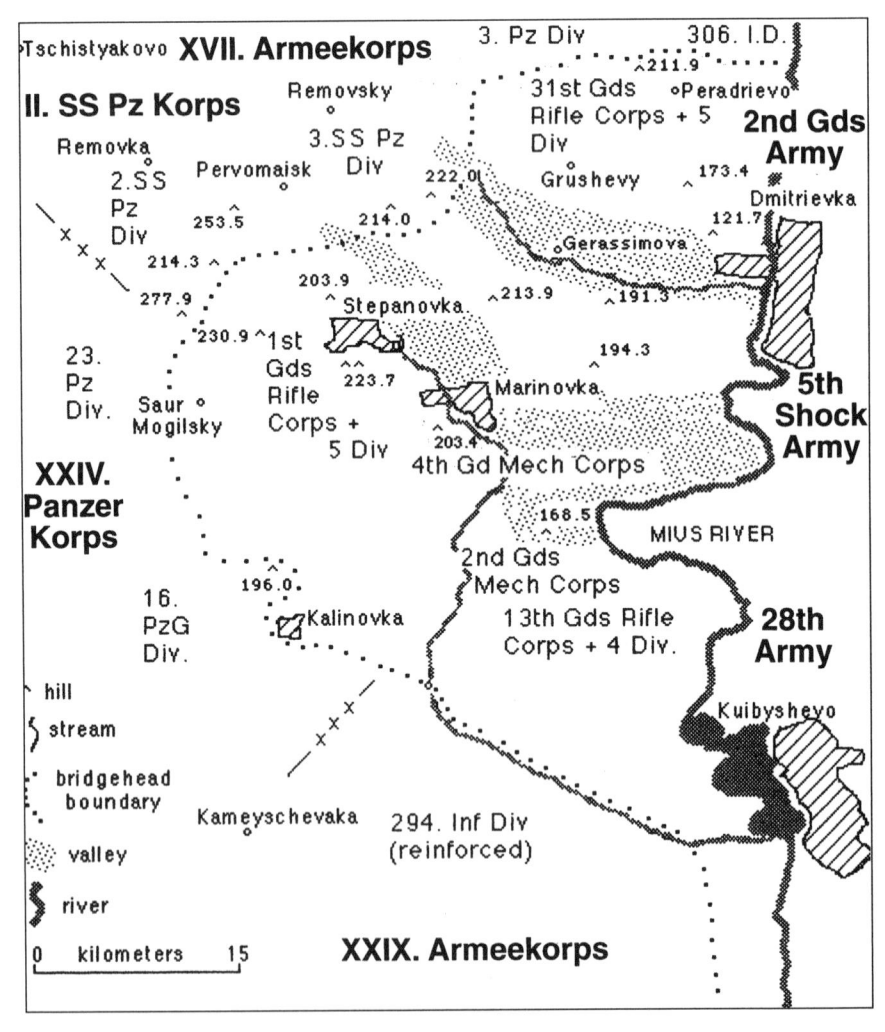

The situation on the Mius, 29 July 1943.

combat units to send to the critical bridgehead defense sector.[28] None of the makeshift formations were expected to be able to fight off anything stronger than routine patrol activity, but there was no other alternative available to replace the battalions sent to the endangered center sector. If the Russians attacked sections of trenches manned by cooks, bakers and military police with strong infantry forces supported by tanks, the result would have been disaster.

Using the lull in combat activity, the tank-recovery companies of 23. Panzer and 16. Panzergrenadier-Divisions performed miracles of repair by late 23 July, when the two divisions fielded thirty-three (eighteen Panzer IV and fifteen Panzer III) and twelve operational tanks, respectively. The army also had forty-seven Sturmgeschützen in four assault gun battalions in the Dmitrievka sector. The assault gun battalions had listed eighty-seven vehicles ready for action on 17 July; now, five days later, nearly 50 percent were out of action. The last reserves were already committed and all available armor was concentrated in the critical sector. This weakened other sections of the front, but it could not be helped. A renewal of the attack in strength lasting for even a few days, with the resulting casualties, would mean disaster for the army. The last barrel had been scraped; there were no more possibilities left. The already thin ranks of the infantry divisions left no strength for sufficient reserves, most of the men being on the front line. A Soviet breakthrough at any point was likely to cause a crisis that could not be mastered. Hollidt could only await the arrival of II. SS-Panzerkorps and hope that the Russians did not regroup before the SS tanks arrived on the Mius.

During the last days of July, there were a series of minor probing attacks made by the Russians with small groups of tanks and company- or battalion-strength infantry forces. It became evident to the Germans that the Soviet infantry was exhausted because they did not attack with their normal discipline and disregard for losses. However, Semenovsky was lost, and the Germans were pushed out of Yelizavetinsky and Grigorievka a final time. On 26 July, the Russians attacked 111. and 294. Infanterie-Divisions with moderate infantry forces, approximately ten tanks and aircraft, but accomplished nothing. Shortly afterwards, a stronger effort hit 16. Panzergrenadier-Division with thirty tanks, supported by as many as 100 planes. The Russians again made extensive use of rocket launchers in support of this attack. Under cover of the rockets and artillery, the Soviet tanks advanced in successive attacks by groups of eight to ten tanks, but seven were knocked out and the attack collapsed. A small penetration was made by infantry, but it was sealed off and destroyed. There were several weak attacks on 27 July, but these were halfhearted efforts and probably were only designed to harass the Germans.[29]

Hollidt's army had inflicted a sound defeat on the Russians, destroying hundreds of tanks, capturing 3,973 prisoners and capturing or destroying many guns, mortars and antitank guns. Russian dead and wounded numbered in the thousands, and several of the Soviet rifle divisions were essentially destroyed for the time being due to the extent of their infantry losses. However, plentiful manpower reserves resulted in rapid reconstruction of divisions. Many times German intelligence officers were shocked to discover a division facing them that had been reported destroyed in fighting at some other point on the Eastern Front only weeks before.

Major Francke, the Ia of Hollidt's 6. Armee, wrote in the report on the July 1943 fighting on the Mius River that the Russian defeat was due to "the high fighting qualities of the troops of all branches of the service and the heroism of officers, non-commissioned officers and enlisted men alike . . . and . . . the rapid transformation of the results of reconnaissance into orders, concentration of force . . . lightning concentrations of German artillery fire and fire from armor piercing weapons and model support by the Luftwaffe."

Hollidt's 6. Armee suffered casualties during the two weeks of combat which totalled 15,486 killed, wounded and missing.[30] There would be very few replacements for the army's losses. Without strong reinforcement, 6. Armee could not withstand another strong attack by Southern Front. The few German reserves were used up and now it remained to be seen which side could regroup first.

Feldmarschall Erich von Manstein, the commander of Heeresgruppe Süd during the battles in the summer of 1943. NATIONAL ARCHIVES

Totenkopf Panzer IIIs in action during the battle of Kursk. NATIONAL ARCHIVES

SS-Sturmbannführer Ernst Haussler (left) and the commander of III./Regiment *Theodor Eicke*, Karl Ullrich (right), observe the attack across the Psel River. Georg Bochmann, commander of SS-Panzer-Regiment 3, is in the center. NATIONAL ARCHIVES

The commander of 4. Panzerarmee, General der Panzertruppen Hermann Hoth, with officers of 2. SS-Panzer-Division. From left: Walter Krüger, division commander; Peter Sommer, division Ia; and Hoth (center).

MARK C. YERGER

SS Tiger tanks and Sturmgeschtütz IIIs advance through Russian artillery fire. German panzergrenadiers are riding into battle on the assault guns. NATIONAL ARCHIVES

An SS Tiger in action during the battle of Kursk. The II. SS-Panzerkorps had thirty-five Tiger tanks on 5 July 1943, the first day of Operation "Citadel." On 12 July, at Prochorovka, there were less than twenty still operational. Of those, ten belonged to 3. SS-Panzer-Division *Totenkopf.* These Tigers were committed to the fighting in the bridgehead across the Psel River and were not involved in the action against 5th Guards Tank Army. NATIONAL ARCHIVES

An SS Panzer IV tank crew watches a Russian tank burn in the distance after knocking it out. NATIONAL ARCHIVES

SS-Obersturmbannführer Hans-Albin von Reitzenstein, the commander of SS-Panzer-Regiment 2 of 2. SS-Panzer-Division *Das Reich* in July 1943. MARK C. YERGER

General der Panzertruppen Hermann Breith, the commander of
III. Panzerkorps (center, walking with his hands behind his back).
NATIONAL ARCHIVES

Oberstgruppenführer Paul Hausser, the commander of II. SS-Panzerkorps
during the battle of Kursk. Hausser is in the center with officers of
Das Reich. Walter Krüger and Hans-Albin von Reitzenstein are on the
left. On the right is Werner Ostendorff, the Ia of II. SS-Panzerkorps in
the summer of 1943. MARK C. YERGER

Georg Maier, here as an Obersturmführer, was the Ia of *Das Reich* during the fighting at Kursk. He later was the Ia of 6. SS-Panzerarmee under Sepp Dietrich. MARK C. YERGER

Otto Baum, here as an Obersturmbannführer, commanded Regiment *Totenkopf* during the summer of 1943. Baum was one of the most highly decorated soldiers of the Waffen SS. He won the 1st and 2nd classes of the Iron Cross and was awarded the German Cross in Gold in December 1941. For his leadership of III./SS-Panzergrenadier-Regiment 3 during the Demyansk fighting, he was awarded the Knight's Cross in 1942. On 12 August 1943, Baum was awarded the Oak Leaves to the Knight's Cross. He later won the Swords while commanding 2. SS-Panzer-Division *Das Reich*.

Kurt Ullrich, here as an SS-Sturmbannführer, commanded III./Regiment *Eicke* during the battle of Kursk. Ullrich was a highly decorated soldier of the Waffen SS. He was awarded both grades of the Iron Cross for his performance during the French campaign and later won the Knight's Cross as commander of SS-Pionier-Abteilung 3 during the fighting in the Demyansk encirclement. On 14 May 1944, he was awarded the Oak Leaves to the Knight's Cross.
MARK C. YERGER

SS assault guns (Sturmgeschütz IIIG) with SS infantry during the fighting in southern Russia during the summer of 1943. MARK C. YERGER

An SS Panzer VI Tiger tank advances toward the fighting in the distance. This photo was taken during the summer fighting, probably during the battle of Kursk. NATIONAL ARCHIVES

SS armor advances over typical Russian countryside of the type often seen in the Ukraine, particularly in the Prochorovka area. NATIONAL ARCHIVES

SS officers use a knocked-out British Churchill tank for shelter. The Russian army used British and American tanks furnished through Lend-Lease, but Russian tank crews preferred Soviet designs because of their superior armor and main gun. NATIONAL ARCHIVES

A captured Soviet T-34 in use by an SS tank crew. *Das Reich* fielded a number of these tanks while one of its battalions was in Germany being equipped with the new Panther tanks during most of the summer of 1943. NATIONAL ARCHIVES

SS armor—a Panzer VI Tiger and Panzer III—in the field during the battle of Kursk. On the right is what appears to be an Sd.Kfz. 263 command vehicle. MARK C. YERGER

German infantry attacking across open ground in Russia. The attack is supported by fire from a 37mm antitank gun in the foreground.
NATIONAL ARCHIVES

SS panzergrenadiers at rest in a captured Russian village. NATIONAL ARCHIVES

A good picture of a camouflage-painted Sturmgeschütz III. The StuG IIIs were originally equipped with a short-barreled howitzer for infantry support. As the war progressed, the Germans used these armored vehicles in a defensive role and equipped them with a long-barreled main gun that improved its antitank capability. NATIONAL ARCHIVES

German Panzer IVs moving toward the front during the battle of Kursk.
NATIONAL ARCHIVES

SS-Standartenführer Hellmuth Becker. Becker commanded SS-Panzergrenadier-Regiment *Theodor Eicke* during the fighting in the Psel bridgehead.
MARK C. YERGER

A German infantryman during fighting in Russia. The strain of battle is written in his face.
NATIONAL ARCHIVES

A Panther Ausf. A in the field. Contrary to popular belief, the SS divisions were not equipped with this tank during the battle of Kursk. *Das Reich* did not receive its Panther battalion until 22 August 1943. *Totenkopf* did not get its Panthers until even later in the year.
NATIONAL ARCHIVES

A column of Panzer IIIs moves past a Russian village on a typical road in southern Russia. In the summer of 1943, this tank still was used in large numbers by the German panzer divisions. The II. SS-Panzerkorps had 112 Panzer IIIs at the beginning of Operation "Citadel." NATIONAL ARCHIVES

General der Infanterie Karl Hollidt, the commander of Armee-Abteilung Hollidt. In the summer of 1943, Armee-Abteilung Hollidt was redesignated as the second 6. Armee. Hollidt was later promoted to Generaloberst. NATIONAL ARCHIVES

Marshal F. I. Tolbukhin, the commander of the Soviet Southern Front. He carried out the masterful diversionary operation at the Mius River in the first weeks of July 1943.

A German mobile 37mm antiaircraft gun with an ammunition trailer. The gun crew has just shot down a Soviet plane, which burns in the distance. This gun and the more numerous quad mounted 20mm were deadly versus low-flying ground-support aircraft. NATIONAL ARCHIVES

A Russian KV-1 heavy tank burns after its engine compartment was set afire. This tank was being phased out by late 1943. It was replaced in the heavy tank battalions of the Soviet army by the early versions of the Joseph Stalin tank. NATIONAL ARCHIVES

A Panzer IV of 23. Panzer-Division in the summer of 1943. This tank was the backbone of the German panzer divisions during this period of the war. It was never entirely replaced by the heavier Panther. JEAN RESTAYN

A rare sIG 33 of 23. Panzer-Division, a 150mm howitzer on a Panzer III chassis. Originally intended for street fighting, this vehicle was used for mobile, close artillery support of infantry and armor attacks. JEAN RESTAYN

A Russian T-34/76 knocked out during the Mius fighting. JEAN RESTAYN

Hermann Priess, the commander of 3. SS-Panzer-Division *Totenkopf* following the death of the division's first commander, Theodor Eicke. He was a Brigadeführer at the time of the Mius counterattack. MARK C. YERGER

A German artillery observer scans Hill 213.9 for targets. The low, featureless hill had few terrain landmarks that could be used for adjusting artillery fire. NATIONAL ARCHIVES

Paul Hausser, commander of II. SS-Panzerkorps, with Sylvester Stadler, the commander of SS-Panzergrenadier-Regiment *Der Führer*. Stadler played a key role in breaking the stalemate that existed at the Mius after indecisive fighting on 29–30 July. MARK C. YERGER

A Panzer III/L readied for rail transport. The armor of II. SS-Panzerkorps was transported by rail from the Kharkov area to a railhead near the Mius River. MARK C. YERGER

German armor losses were substantial during the battle of Kursk, although the losses of SS panzers at Prochorovka have been greatly exaggerated. Here the wreckage of a knocked-out Sturmgeschütz III smolders. NATIONAL ARCHIVES

CHAPTER 4

A Strategy of Deception

MASKIROVKA AND THE RELATIONSHIP BETWEEN THE MIUS RIVER BATTLE AND OPERATION "CITADEL"

After the conclusion of the Stalingrad campaign, the Soviet General Staff studied all operational data that had been gathered during the battle as well as afterwards, with the specific intention of using the information to correct deficiencies and codify successful tactics. This was an ongoing process in the Soviet army, probably to a greater extent than any other army of the war. It reflected the pragmatic approach to war that the Soviet military utilized throughout World War II, a process that dramatically changed the Soviet force structure during the war years. The Russian army, as a whole, was clearly *tactically* inferior in comparison to the German Army on a division-by-division basis from 1941 until late 1943 (at the earliest), although shrinking German manpower resources, frequent shortages of fuel or ammunition, and inferior industrial strength eventually resulted in a gradual decline of German combat efficiency. These factors, when combined with a continual, systematic improvement in Soviet mobile force structure and command experience, led to an evening of quality by the end of 1943 and certainly by 1944.

From analysis of the Stalingrad offensive and the factors that led to the subsequent reversals of Manstein's Kharkov counterattack, combat experience was used by the Russians to make conclusions that helped formulate the directives contained in the 1943 Field Regulation manual which governed the conduct of combat operations on the operational and tactical level. The Stavka chose surprise and the use of military deception, or *maskirovka*, as the *key* elements necessary for victory, even more so than the choice or direction of the main effort.

The Soviets defined *maskirokva* as the use of a broad spectrum of deceptive measures designed to conceal the preparations for attack, thus ensuring surprise in regard to time, forces and the point of attack. *Maskirovka* involved a "complexity of measures, directed to mislead the enemy regarding the presence and disposition of forces, various military objectives . . . and also the plans of the corrunand."[1] That the Russians had learned the methods of concealing the preparations of even front-level forces was evident in the surprise launching of the Stalingrad counteroffensive in late 1942, which led to the successful destruction of the first German 6. Armee in the ruins of Stalingrad. The Soviets were able to conceal the enormous gathering of reserves and supplies necessary for the launching of this counterattack. When it struck, the Russians achieved strategic surprise, a key factor in the shattering of the southern sector of the Eastern Front in the winter of 1942–43. Later in the war, during the decisive summer of 1943, the Russians massed an even larger strategic reserve under command of Steppe Front as well as two entire tank armies in the Orel area. The exact location, composition of the armies and even their existence were successfully concealed from the Germans until armies from Steppe Front began arriving in the south during the battle of Kursk and 3rd and 4th Tank Armies went into action against Heeresgruppe Mitte on 19 July.

The Soviet strategic reserve suffered great losses of men, tanks and equipment from 7 to 17 July. However, within just over two and a half weeks, Steppe and Voronezh Fronts were poised to begin the last battle of Kharkov. Both 1st Tank Army and 5th Guards Tank Army were moved, rebuilt and assembled north of Belgorod without the Germans being aware of these operations. The Germans did not believe that the Russians were capable of large offensive operations so quickly after the bloodletting of Operation "Citadel," a direct result of the ability of the Russians to conceal their intentions on the strategic level. The recovery and concentration of these forces were not detected, and this led to erroneous conclusions on the part of the German command. On 1 August, Manstein informed OKH that he believed the Russians to be exhausted and were not likely to begin offensive operations again for several weeks. Two days later, the Russians launched Operation "Rumyantsev," the main post-Kursk counteroffensive in the south of the Ukraine. Using the techniques of *maskirovka*, the Russians were able to assemble large forces without the Germans being able to detect their existence, location or strength.

A Strategy of Deception

In order to conceal their intentions and achieve this type of operational/strategic surprise, the Russians implemented very detailed, codified *maskirovka* principles. Among the most important requirements for achieving tactical and operational surprise were the below factors:

1. Concealing the actual movement and preparations for the movement of troops and supplies into the concentration area. This included concealing facilities for storage of fuel and supplies, troop shelters, road and bridge construction, etc.
2. Strictly limiting movement of these forces or supply units during the daytime.
3. Camouflage of the assembly positions and dispositions of the attack force.
4. Elimination of battle reconnaissance by units of the attacking force.
5. Strict radio silence of all arriving units, especially mobile forces.
6. No firing of artillery that was designated for the support of the attack for registration purposes. Registration was accomplished by having roving batteries or already sited guns provide this information.
7. Deceptive measures regarding operations of radio and other communication means.
8. Limiting knowledge of counteroffensive plans to as few people as possible.
9. Limiting effectiveness of German air reconnaissance.

There were other means of deception and concealment used as a matter of course in Soviet planning, deception not being a suggested measure but rather an *integral* part of planning. *Maskirovka* was utilized as a comprehensive measure to conceal Soviet operations on all levels, from fronts down to regulations concerning methods of camouflage for small-unit fighting positions. There were staff organizations within higher unit formations that were specifically charged with the planning, preparation, and incorporation of *maskirovka* tactics with all operations. *Maskirovka* was carefully planned and utilized as a fundamental and necessary element at all levels of Soviet operations during warfare, encompassing strategic, operational and tactical planning as a matter of normal operations. After Stalingrad, the revised principles of *maskirovka* were issued to the commanders as basic military principles necessary for victory. These directives were not lightly ignored in the Soviet army.

Why, then, given the above list of specific measures utilized to conceal Soviet intentions, were all of these principles violated by Tolbukhin's Southern Front during its preparations for the Mius River attack? Why was the build-up of forces across the river from 6. Armee so easily detected by the German intelligence detachments on the west bank? The Germans knew virtually every Russian formation's location and date of arrival. Much of the Soviet build-up was conducted in broad daylight and even troop movements conducted at night were compromised by seemingly poor security measures such as tank units arriving in the area at night with all their driving lights on. These were direct violations of Soviet principles of concealment. In addition, groups of Russian officers were observed conducting reconnaissance and studies of terrain in the attack areas. According to Soviet regulations, this was strictly prohibited, as only specially organized units of troops from formations identified by the Germans as already being in the attack area were to be utilized for this purpose.

Beginning on 10 July, 1943, only three days after Tolbukhin had been ordered to attack, the Soviet concentration of forces on the Mius began with a complete disregard for basic security measures, particularly in radio transmissions, from the first day of the build-up. The German command, at the height of the battle of Kursk, was aware of Soviet intentions in the 6. Armee area. Before 16 July, the Germans had essentially identified and pinpointed the location of all major Soviet formations. The concentration of forces, stockpiles of supplies and arrival of armor, all easily detected by the Germans, left no doubt that an attack was coming on 6. Armee's front. In addition, the point of main effort was clearly the Dmitrievka-Kuibyshevo area. From the very first, it was without doubt that the Soviet activity at Izyum and the Mius constituted preparations for attacks in sufficient strength to potentially threaten key lines of supply in the south. As expected, Hollidt hastily communicated his concerns to Manstein, apparently as early as 10 July. Thus, days before the battle of Prochorovka, through Heeresgruppe Süd dispatches, Hitler was aware of the diversionary attack preparations.

Apparently, neither Hitler nor the German High Command were suspicious of the sudden lack of Russian skill in concealing their intentions and preparations. This may have been due to the unwise, yet fairly common tendency of the Germans to underestimate the skill of the Soviets in conducting war or, perhaps simple arrogance. It did not occur to either 6. Armee or Heeresgruppe Süd to question why the Soviets were unable to conceal a concentration of forces much smaller than that gathered for the Stalingrad offensive just a few months earlier. Similarly, the impending attack of the Russians in 1. Panzerarmee's sector, at Izyum, was clearly anticipated by the Germans. In this sector, 15. Infanterie-Division observed masses of tanks and infantry, with heavy weapons, moving south toward Izyum along the west bank of the river. The Russian forces, in a strength that made it obvious that a concentration of some size was being built up, made no attempts to conceal their movements. An officer of the German division later wrote a report of the division's operations during this period of the war and remarked curiously about the Soviet failure to make any attempt to conceal their movements:

> Following the "Citadel" failure, it became evident that the Russians were concentrating troops in the vicinity of the town of Izyum across the river from the XL. Panzerkorps zone, south of the 15th Infantry Division. In broad daylight and in plain sight of the personnel of the 15th Division, Russian troops in dense columns marched southward along the highway. . . . Why the Russians did not try to hide this movement remained a mystery.[2]

The officer quoted above noted that the Russian troop movements were "continuously reported to higher headquarters," a result that the Russians obviously counted on. The answer to the "mystery" about why the Soviets ignored their own principles of war, principles that were integral to all levels of combat and were considered to be vitally important, is simple. The Mius and Izyum attacks were planned and deliberately obvious supporting diversionary operations. The primary objective was to draw German mobile reserves out of the Kursk sector and away from the planned counteroffensives on both flanks of the bulge. What was interpreted by the Germans as poor security measures by the Soviets was instead a deliberately planned lack of security measures. The Russian command wanted the German leadership to be aware, without a shadow of a doubt, that 6. Armee was about to be attacked. The offensive objectives of the attack by Tolbukhin's Southern Front were, of course, legitimate but the primary objective of the attack was to force Heeresgruppe Süd to withdraw armor from the decisive Belgorod-Kursk battles in order to send it to the Mius and Izyum. In Colonel David Glantz's study of *maskirovka* and the use of deception in warfare, *Soviet Military Deception in the Second World War*, he quotes Soviet sources on the importance of this diversion of German panzer divisions out of the 4. Panzerarmee sector:

> It is necessary, however, to understand that the Southern Front offensive was an important help to our forces in the Kursk Bulge: the enemy was not only unable to take one division from the Mius front in order to strengthen his forces at Kursk, but he was even forced to temporarily transfer to the Mius River his tank corps from Kharkov.[3]

This weakening of forces at the Psel-Prochorovka axis essentially brought "Citadel" to an end at a time when 4. Panzerarmee had superior numbers of tanks in that key sector. It was the death blow to any hopes the Germans had of affecting the course of the war in the East. Equally significant, it greatly aided the post-"Citadel" counterattacks of Steppe Front toward Belgorod and Southwestern Front toward Kharkov. When the Germans withdrew the II. SS-Panzerkorps in order to send *Das Reich* and *Totenkopf* (along with 3. Panzer-Division) to the Mius, the threat to the southern flank of the Soviet salient was ended at a critical time. This was critical to the Soviets because they had shot their bolt at Prochorovka while Heeresgruppe Süd still had a dangerous number of tanks and additional reserves. The Germans had a rare numerical superiority in tanks in the Prochorovka area and 4. Panzerarmee was in possession of the *Totenkopf* bridgehead over the Psel. It is important to remember that Heeresgruppe Süd also had the three uncommitted divisions of XXIV. Panzerkorps available at Belgorod on 13 July. However, not only was II. SS-Panzerkorps withdrawn from the Prochorovka area but the divisions of XXIV. Panzerkorps were moved south to the assistance of 6. Armee and 1. Panzerarmee. The result was that the Germans lost their last chance at a major victory in Russia and the Soviets were allowed to withdraw their battered armies for rebuilding and subsequent participation in Operation "Rumyantsev."

By deliberately revealing their attack preparations, the Soviets affected the commitment of a half dozen panzer divisions at an extremely critical stage in the war. The diversionary attack by Southern Front drew SS and army panzer divisions away from Heeresgruppe Süd's main effort to the north of Belgorod at the very moment that Manstein correctly believed Operation "Citadel" had reached its decisive point in the south.[4] The Russian leaders in the southern area of the bulge knew the stakes quite clearly and recognized the seriousness of the situation early in the course of the fighting. Nikita Khrushchev, Stalin's political officer in charge of overseeing the Soviet army and its performance in the southern combat area, was in Vatutin's Voronezh Front HQ on 5 July. As early as the evening of the first day, Khrushchev realized that the key sector was in the south, where the most important of the Soviet counterattacks planned for the summer of 1943 would take place. In a conversation with Vatutin, Khrushchev clearly stated what was surely the opinion of Stalin, giving an astute appreciation of the German gamble: "The next two or three days will be terrible. Either we hold or the Germans take Kursk. They are putting everything on one card. It's a matter of life or death for them. We must ensure that they break their necks."[5]

Khrushchev and the chief of staff of 1st Tank Army subsequently conferred on 8 July regarding the events of the day. It had been a bad day for the Russians as XXXXVIII. Panzerkorps and II. SS-Panzerkorps shattered the front of 6th Guards Army and drove back the lead elements of 1st Tank Army to begin the push toward Prochorovka and the Psel River. In *Scorched Earth*, Carell's epic history of the Eastern Front, he related the comments of Khrushchev and the operations officer of 1st Tank Army, Major General Shalin, regarding the events of the day. The two German panzer corps, supported by the "tank buster" Stukas of dive-bomber ace Hans-Ulrich Rudel, had smashed two regiments of armored infantry and tanks of 1st Tank Army's 6th Tank Corps, which had been committed with orders to halt the Germans at any cost. Khrushchev heard the unwelcome news that the attacking forces were destroyed in two hours. Lieutenant General Popel, the Military Council officer of 1st Tank Army, told him that "all that was left of them was their numbers."[6] Rudel alone destroyed twelve T-34s by attacking from behind, diving to within yards of the tank and firing 3.7cm cannon shells through the light armor covering the motor, which set the tank afire or put it out of action. 1st Tank Army's 31st Tank Corps had been put to flight and was falling back in some disorder to the west of Prochorovka. Khrushchev's terse comment in regard to the events of the first days was that if the Germans weren't stopped, they would take Kursk. Almost surely in response to orders of Stalin or Zhukov, major elements of the strategic reserves in the south, the armies of Steppe Front, were committed to the battle shortly thereafter.

In spite of strong objections by Steppe Front's commander (Koniev) that the piecemeal destruction of his armies would compromise the front's post-"Citadel" mission, the Soviet command at the highest levels clearly recognized the consequences if the panzer divisions of 4. Panzerarmee and Armee-Abteilung Kempf were not stopped south of the Psel. Saving 5th Guards Tank Army for future operations in the Kharkov-Belgorod sector would have been without purpose if the Germans encircled the Kursk salient with the resulting destruction of Soviet forces and the capture of Kursk. Rotmistrov's tank army was committed because it was the last chance the Soviets had to win the battle in the south. The fact that it was ordered toward the Psel by 8 July illustrates Stalin's concern from the first.

The Soviet dictator did not easily agree to commit reserves before the planned moment. Earlier in the war, he had built up reserves for the counteroffensive following the defeat of the Germans before Moscow, and in spite of the desperate fighting west of the city, he stubbornly refused to commit any large formations of that force regardless of the losses suffered by the defending forces until the time of his choosing. Yet in the summer of 1943, he allowed his reserves to be committed prematurely, beginning on the second day of the battle when infantry armies of Steppe Front were sent to the Psel-Prochorovka area. Nothing could emphasize the gravity of the situation more than the decision to utilize the armies that were to carry ou "Rumyantsev." The Russians realized that it was worth any risk to save the situation in that area, not only because of the danger of a German breakout over the Psel, but for the results of a German victory in the Ukraine. Stalin believed that the Germans planned to eliminate the Kursk salient in preparation for a renewed attack on Moscow; thus, any measure was acceptable in order to defeat the Germans in the south.

PLANNING FOR THE SOVIET COUNTEROFFENSIVE AT BELGOROD-KHARKOV, OPERATION "RUMYANTSEV"

Stalin had been persuaded by Zhukov and others to exhaust the German offensive through defensive fighting only by strongly reassuring the dictator that this would be a prelude to a large-scale general offensive leading to the destruction of German forces in the Ukraine. Stalin wanted to attack with the coming of warm weather, as he had done after the previous two winters. It was difficult for Zhukov to convince him to follow a defensive strategy because Stalin believed in attacking his enemies, not waiting for them to attack him. For Stalin to risk not having the forces available to conduct the main offensive operation of the summer speaks volumes in regard to how the Soviet supreme commander viewed the critical nature of events on the southern wing.[7]

As early as April 1943, Zhukov, in communication with Stalin, was supported by Lieutenant General A. I. Antonov, the chief of staff of operations for Stavka, when he wrote an assessment of the Soviet chances for success by first using a defensive strategy as prelude to attack in the Kursk sector: "I consider it inexpedient for our troops to launch a preemptive offensive in the near future. It would be better for us to wear down the enemy on our defenses, knock out his tanks, bring in fresh reserves, and finish off his main grouping with a general offensive."[8]

This was a realistic assessment, recognizing German superiority at the *tactical* level at this point in the war, if not in words, then implicit in the candid estimation of chances of success with a large-scale Soviet offensive before German strength was reduced by a defensive battle. Realizing that success was more likely if their offensive was launched after the Germans had exhausted themselves, enduring ruinous casualties, the Russians generals planned accordingly. This was a tacit acknowledgement of the fact that normally, if Soviet forces fought the Germans on anything near parity, the Germans could inflict a punishing defeat on the Russian offensive by utilizing very strong panzer reserves.

In the summer of 1943, the Germans remained superior to the Russian army in the conduct of fluid operational-level attacks, although the Soviets were constantly improving their command and force structure, as well as building a large core of experienced and skilled officers. The German superiority in armored battles on open ground, is illustrated by the slaughter of Rotmistrov's tanks at Prochorovka and a second annihilation of 5th Guards Tank Army (and Katukov's 1st Tank Army as well) that occurred during "Rumyantsev." This superiority was due to a number of factors, including superbly trained commanders at the battalion-regimental level and excellent, aggressive small-unit leadership by company commanders and NCOs. The German Army accomplished this by mission-oriented training which emphasized quick reaction to battlefield situations, flexible conduct of operations and personal initiative. German officers and NCOs were trained to utilize their own judgement of combat situations and lead accordingly. Soviet operations were sometimes characterized by execution of orders regardless of changing conditions in battle or the rigid formulation of attack by formula. The Germans were trained to find the best manner to carry out an assigned mission in accord with existing conditions and the forces at hand. The details were left to the commander on the scene, who was expected to know how best to accomplish his mission. Innovation and aggressive leadership were expected from German officers and NCOs. This situation changed later in the war, when Russian commanders demonstrated that they had learned their lessons well. In the first years, the Russians sometimes launched attacks at the same time and place, over the same ground in an identical manner until either the Germans were annihilated or the Russians ran out of men and tanks. By 1944, however, the Russian tank force was a formidable opponent and was recognized as such by German commanders with experience on the Eastern Front. Major General Mellenthin described this improvement in Soviet command in his study of armored warfare, *Panzer Battles*:

> It was not until 1944 that these large armored and mechanized formations developed into a highly mobile and keenly edged tool, handled by daring and capable commanders. Even the junior officers became remarkably efficient; they showed the determination and initiative, and proved willing to shoulder responsibility.

As we have seen, Russian tank officers were sometimes hampered by poor communications capability in the first years of the war. A Russian tank commander could thus find that he had little control over his unit once the battle began because he could not effectively communicate with the units under his command. There were other factors which hindered effective use of Soviet armor, including poor unit structure, which resulted in lack of sufficient support troops such as engineers, motorized infantry and adequately mobile artillery. These problems were recognized and the Soviet army continually and dynamically evolved during the war, becoming more effective with each passing year. However, in the summer of 1943, Soviet armored operations, although more skilful than in the first years of the war, were not up to the level exhibited by better-quality German panzer forces. The destruction of hundreds of Soviet tanks at Prochorovka was not an aberration. This occurred time and again during the early years of the war if German commanders were able to operate without interference from above that limited flexibility and conduct of defensive operations and had sufficient forces. In fact, in recognition that their forces were unable to engage the Germans on equal terms, Soviet tank corps commanders were at times actually forbidden to engage German armor in offensive operations on open ground and were ordered to fight from defensive positions. This happened after 12 July when Rotmistrov ordered his surviving tanks to dig in in support of the infantry.

In light of German tactical superiority, the Russian defensive strategy in the summer of 1943 was undoubtedly a correct one for the Soviet armor force structure of mid-1943. It was also, without question, clear evidence of Russian strategic superiority because it provided the Soviets with their best opportunity to win the war. The Russians' strategic and operational planning was the correct course of action in order to utilize their superiority in industrial capacity and the population base of the Soviet Union. The result was a strategy designed to provide the best chance of victory in the long run. The Soviet command at the higher levels recognized that the war would be a long-term affair and was not likely to be won quickly by either side, in contrast to Hitler, who planned to knock Russia out of the war in a matter of weeks and had no clear plan to win the war when this did not occur. Stalin realized that the Soviet Union, given time and taking into consideration the affects of attrition, using the vast Soviet numerical advantages in both men and machines, would defeat the Germans as long as the Soviet army avoided a fatal mistake.

Stalin bought the time he needed with the lives of literally millions of his soldiers and the destruction of tens of thousands of tanks and other war material. He and his commanders ruthlessly expended men and machines equally freely in order that the Soviet state would survive.

In contrast, Hitler refused to even discuss planning for events that he decreed would not occur. No clearer evidence need be cited in support of this statement than the failure to provide winter clothing for the German troops in the first winter of 1941–42, which resulted in the loss of thousands of men to frostbite and death due to exposure after the onset of an especially severe winter. It is interesting to note that SS divisions were better prepared for the winter and were furnished warm winter camouflage uniforms for the combat troops that were stockpiled on Himmler's orders.

In the summer of 1943, the failure of Operation "Citadel" resulted in the loss of initiative at the strategic level and condemned the German Army to a state of reaction to Soviet operational and strategic moves for the rest of the war. Instead of the formulation of a war plan based on strategic objectives and policies that were realistic, given German (and Russian) military capabilities, Hitler made decisions regarding the war in Russia that were based on political and racial objectives or on his own estimation of the situation and not on realities. As an example, one needs only to remember the political considerations that were given to Guderian as justification for launching Operation "Citadel," when, as events proved, the Germans would have been wiser to conduct a strategy of mobile defense in the East.

Soviet planning, in contrast, showed a much more accurate evaluation of the Soviet and German force capabilities. Accordingly, Soviet front missions for the spring of 1943 reflected planning that utilized the major Soviet advantages as well as correctly evaluating German intentions for the summer of 1943. The quality of Soviet intelligence information was markedly superior to that of the Germans as well. While Stalin knew German intentions for the summer and details about the planning and execution of the Kursk offensive, the Germans had insufficient knowledge of Soviet forces and the location or strength of Soviet strategic reserves.

All of these elements were blended by a unified Soviet command into formulation of the operational planning for the summer months. The defense of the southern sector of the Kursk bulge was but a prelude to the beginning of the counteroffensive in the Belgorod-Kharkov area, which was to be the main effort of the massive series of attacks launched after the defeat of "Citadel." Steppe Front was to concentrate east of Kursk with massive forces, in order to exploit the defeat of the German offensive by a decisive counterattack, whose ultimate goal was the defeat of German forces east of the Dnepr. It was the mission of both Southern Front and Southwestern Front to divert German panzer divisions from the most critical point, which was of course the Belgorod-Kharkov sector.

On 7 July, just two days after the beginning of "Citadel," Stavka issued General R. Y. Malinovsky, commander of Southwestern Front, a warning order for his attack across the northern Donets at Izyum. Tolbukhin, commander of Southern Front, was ordered to begin formal preparation for his attack on the same day. On 17 July, both fronts launched their attacks, after a concentration of forces, that was deliberately meant to be detected by the Germans. When the Russians, at both points, were confronted by a fully alerted defending force, the result was high losses and failure to hold the initial penetrations in either sector. Colonel General V. I. Chuikov, commander of 8th Guards Army at the Izyum bridgehead, reported that his attack was "smothered everywhere." German officers of 1. Panzerarmee, captured during the battle, revealed the information that they had been aware of the impending Soviet attack since before 12 July and that their intelligence had even been able to correctly pinpoint the approximate origins and even direction of the main attack. At the Mius, across the river from Dmitrievka, the Soviet build-up was also clearly detected from 10 July, and the danger of a penetration toward Stalin sounded alarm bells at the highest levels of the German command.

Neither of the operations were successful in terms of actual offensive gains. Both, however, were *extremely* successful in regard to their primary objective, which was to draw German forces out of Heeresgruppe Süd's attack sector. Had the forces of the two diversionary attacks been able to decisively penetrate the German front and subsequently join forces at Stalino, thus fragmenting Heeresgruppe Süd, the Soviets would have cheerfully accepted this outcome. However, both attacks suffered what were apparent defeats. The Soviet attacks at Izyum and the Mius were full-fledged dangerous situations, but neither would have been decisive in the larger sense had Manstein's panzer divisions broken free and taken Kursk. The destruction of the

Kursk salient and the resulting damage that this would have entailed would have made any gains of the Soviets at the two diversionary points superfluous.

In the context of the assessment of the situation by Khrushchev, the alignment of Soviet forces both in the south and north, and the relative tank strengths of the opposing forces on the Psel, the importance of the two diversionary attacks to the defeat of the Germans on the southern wing of Kursk is very clear. Had Hitler followed Manstein's advice—ignoring the Soviet build-ups at Izyum and the Mius and allowing Heeresgruppe Süd to commit XXIV. Panzerkorps at Prochorovka—the course of the battle could well have been changed in the south. Within days, II. SS-Panzerkorps and XXXXVIII. Panzerkorps would have been rested and ready to resume offensive operations. Hausser's II. SS-Panzerkorps had over 200 tanks back in action by 16 July. However, the SS panzer divisions were ordered to give up their hard-won gains. On 18 July, Hitler issued orders sending 23. Panzer-Division to the Mius and *Wiking* and 17. Panzer-Division to the Izyum bridgehead. On 19 July, the following day, the Soviet 3rd and 4th Tank Armies were sent into battle against Heeresgruppe Mitte. Within days, 1st Tank Army and 5th Guards Army withdrew from the Psel-Prochorovka area and relocated to the area north of Belgorod, where they prepared for the launching of "Rumyantsev." By 18 July, the two armies had been reduced to a total combined strength of approximately 200 tanks. However, on 3 August, having been allowed to withdraw and refit, the two armies were rebuilt to a strength of over 500 tanks each. As a result, the primary counteroffensive in the East for the summer of 1943, Operation "Rumyantsev," was able to go forward as planned. Although the operation did not result in a total success and the Germans were able to eventually recover and temporarily stabilize the situation once more, because of the losses suffered during the second half of the summer of 1943, Hitler's armies were weakened almost fatally. By the end of August 1943, the loss of southern Ukraine was only a matter of time. This was the legacy of Hitler's decisions following the first day of battle at Prochorovka.

CHAPTER 5

6. Armee Strikes Back

THE COUNTERATTACK OF THE SS PANZER DIVISIONS: A CHANGING ROLE

With the loss of strategic initiative on the Eastern Front, Germany was reduced to reacting to the operations of the Russian army for the rest of the war. Although there were many German tactical victories—because the panzer divisions were still dangerous opponents and the German infantryman fought with extraordinary stubbornness and skill—the Soviets essentially had the forces to remain on the attack until the fall of Berlin. When the advancing Soviet armies were thrown back temporarily or given a stunning local defeat, the units that were most often involved were the panzer divisions of the army or Waffen SS. Hitler turned to the SS divisions more frequently as the war dragged on to the end.

The first battle of the Waffen SS panzer divisions in this new role was the counterattack of Hollidt's 6. Armee against Tolbukhin's Southern Front. This bloody fight was typical of the battles that many of the SS panzer divisions engaged in during the last years of the war. It shared many characteristics of these desperate operations. First, the SS divisions were transferred, as was common, directly and with little recovery time, from a hard fight in another sector. Second, the objective of their operations was to restore an extremely serious situation with the whole front in danger of collapse. Third, the SS divisions faced a numerically superior enemy force which was either in established positions, as on the Mius, or engaged in an all-out attack against weak German forces. Last, the end result of these battles of 1943–45, regardless of whether the Germans were successful or not, were heavy Russian casualties and bloody losses as well for the SS men.

Because this battle contains all of these elements and was the first of the post-"Citadel" battles that typified the changing role of the

Waffen SS panzer divisions, I have chosen to study it in greater detail than that devoted to either the battle of Prochorovka or the later chapters dealing with the fighting of the SS divisions at Bogodukhov under command of III. Panzerkorps.

II. SS-PANZERKORPS ARRIVES ON THE MIUS RIVER

By 27 July, the three panzer divisions of II. SS-Panzerkorps concentrated near 6. Armee's sector (see appendix IV). The 3. Panzer-Division had reached its assembly points near Krasnaya Zwesda, SS *Das Reich* was assembled around Makeyevka, and SS *Totenkopf* was concentrated in the area of the town of Ordzhonikidze. Most of each division's main combat units reached their designated assembly areas during the period of 26–27 July, with the remaining formations arriving within a day or two. The staff of 6. Armee moved up to an advanced command post close to the front in preparation for the launching of the attack.[1] The Germans had won the race to act first on the Mius.

6. Armee, after an evaluation of the situation and a careful appraisal of its own forces, decided that even with the addition of II. SS-Panzerkorps, it did not have sufficient strength to attempt an envelopment on the eastern side of the Mius. The ideal plan would have been to penetrate the Soviet lines to the north of the bridgehead, cross the river and then close the envelopment on the eastern side of the river after reaching sufficient depth in the rear areas of Southwestern Front. In that manner, the Soviet forces on the west bank of the river, which were considerable, would have been caught from behind by an attack closing on them from the east. This would have prevented the escape of any Russian divsions that attempted to withdraw over the Mius to safety.

However, Hollidt estimated that he needed twice the amount of mobile divisions that were actually allotted, in order to have a good chance of penetrating the Russian lines deeply and quickly enough to trap the Soviet divisions in the bridgehead by encirclement east of the river. He judged that not only did his army have insufficient mobile divisions to carry out such an attack, but such an operation would have required logistical support that was not available. Hollidt therefore decided that the army would attempt to utilize a shallower attack by the II. SS-Panzerkorps, XXIV. Panzerkorps, and infantry battle groups organized from the various corps of the army. The main attack was to originate from the northwest quadrant of the battlefield with the attack direction to the southeast, in order to trap and destroy the enemy on the western side of the river.[2] Because of the narrow depth of the Soviet defensive lines, it would have been more desirable to make enveloping panzer attacks from both flanks of the penetration on the western side of the river, but even this course of action was judged not possible with the divisions available. The danger of an attack on a shallow bridgehead was that the enemy would escape if he were not cut off very quickly. Delays in reaching the river would be fatal, as it would allow the Russians the freedom to withdraw over the river and bring up additional forces.

It was decided to make a three-pronged attack from the northwest sector of the battlefield in a repetition of the attack of 19 July. An attack delivered in this manner over the terrain configuration of the bridgehead limited the degree of maneuver available to the SS panzer divisions, particularly *Totenkopf*. This division was given the unenviable task of attacking over the same terrain, and with the same direction of attack on Hill 213.9, as had 23. Panzer-Division on 19 July. It was not practical to drive across the ridges diagonally because this would concede the high ground to the Russians at successive points and would mean that the attack would have to capture consecutive ridges from west to east in a drive to the Mius. This was not tactically desirable. However, the decision to repeat the formula of parallel advances from the northwest meant that the attack would have to take the key high ground of Hill 213.9 for success to be possible. This in turn dictated that the flanking high ground on both sides of the central ridge had to be taken as a prerequisite to success in the middle.

Without the possession of the middle ridge and the observation advantages of the dominant height, it was difficult for the Germans to adequately direct artillery fire on targets in the depth of the penetration or into the two valleys. For this reason it was necessary to physically control the flanks of the main thrust because it was not possible to effectively suppress the Soviet gun positions on the flanks of the II. SS-Panzerkorps' advance with either artillery or air support. Stukas of IV. Fliegerkorps were given missions of support at points of attack, but evidently, there were not enough dive-bombers for the task of knocking out Soviet artillery and antitank gun positions on the flanks. Without good observation for artillery and inadequate air support, it was absolutely vital that the attacks protecting the main assault effectively eliminate or diminish the fire from the flanks. However, this did not prove to be an easy task.

Showing a lack of any tactical imagination, Hollidt could come up with nothing more likely to succeed than a repetition of an attack launched from the same area and over the same ground that had been tried earlier by a fresh 23. Panzer-Division (with notable lack of results). It is instructive, in view of what happened, to recall the admonition of Mellenthin about the severe penalties of failing to eliminate Russian bridgeheads. Given the time that the Russians had to fortify and prepare the key hill, it would appear to have been logical to realize that an attack force without sufficient strength on the flanks would not likely be able to successfully attack a Russian position that had been in their possession for nearly two weeks. "Hesitation will always be fatal . . . a delay of a day may mean a major catastrophe. Delay means disaster."[3]

In the course of the first days of the counterattack of II. SS-Panzerkorps, the two divisions of XXIV. Panzerkorps, although much weaker than either of the two SS panzer formations, were to have somewhat greater success than the two SS divisions, due to their commitment against objectives that were not as heavily fortified and manned. There was not a tougher point of attack than that against which Hollidt had decided to send *Totenkopf.* Had this division been committed against the objectives that were assigned to the XXIV. Panzerkorps on the first day, it is likely that the battle would not have become the bloodbath that it did, with the resulting delays and heavy casualties. In addition to *Totenkopf*'s attack against Hill 213.9, *Das Reich* was ordered to take the town of Stepanovka, all but guaranteeing that it would become bogged down in street fighting. Combat against Russian infantry who excelled in defensive fighting in built-up areas was always difficult and time-consuming.

After two days of carnage, from 30 July to 1 August, it would take a manuever around the main defensive hills and towns and a surprise attack directed against a less heavily fortified position to break the bloody stalemate that began with another doomed German tank attack on Hill 213.9.

The Russians had fortified the hill, as always, very quickly after its capture on 17 July. Using spade and pick, the Russians disappeared into the earth and dug their guns and firing pits into the rocky ground, skilfully using natural features of terrain to disguise their location. As a veteran commander with extensive experience in combat in Russia, Hollidt must have known that the Russian position on Hill 213.9 would be a tough nut to crack after the Soviets had been in possesion of the hill for that length of time. During this time, the Soviets had doubtless improved their defenses and brought up as many guns, tanks and troops as could be packed into the position. A veteran army panzer division attacked the hill nearly a fortnight earlier, when the hill had just been captured by the Russians and it had been thrown back easily, losing most of its armor in the first hours of the battle. The 23. Panzer-Division attack did not even penetrate through the minefields on the approaches to the hill and reach its base, due to its decimation by the flanking fire and the camouflaged guns and tanks of the defenses on the slopes of the hill itself.

Now, after the Soviets had been on the hill for nearly two weeks and had made the hill and its approaches into a killing zone of minefields, camouflaged gun positions, carefully registered artillery, and the antitank guns of one and a half antitank brigades, another German panzer division prepared to repeat a frontal attack over the exposed ground. The key to success was the elimination of the Soviet guns and batteries on the flanks. As difficult as an assault on the hill would have been even without Soviet guns in these positions, the task became tantamount to suicide when made along the featureless, bare ridge crest through fire coming from three directions.

6. Armee, using its limited resources, organized its battered and tired divisions to support the attack of the II. SS-Panzerkorps as best it could. South of Hill 213.9, on the extreme right flank of the counterattack, XXIX. Armeekorps created a battlegroup from units of 294. Infanterie-Division, a battalion from 111. Infanterie-Division and several other attached battalions in order to carry out the offensive mission assigned to it. This mission was to penetrate across the southern end of the Olkhovchik Valley and seize a key hill, Hill 168.5. This was the initial corps objective. After reaching the hill, the attack group was to turn north and establish a blocking position at the southern end of the valley, closing it as an avenue of retreat. The infantry of XXIX. Armeekorps were to be the anvil on which the hammer of the panzers of II. SS-Panzerkorps would drive the Russians and destroy them.[4]

In the center, *Totenkopf*'s panzer regiment and Panzergrenadier-Regiment *Totenkopf* were to deploy on both sides of the Ssneshnoje-Marinovka road, attack down the center ridge and drive the Russians off Hill 213.9. Regiment *Eicke* was given the objective of clearing the Russians from the Gerassimova Valley in a parallel attack on the left wing of the panzer group. This attack would serve to screen the inside flank of the XXIX. Armeekorps' attack from Soviet infantry or armored assaults originating from the eastern borders of the valley itself or from the high ground to the east and northeast of Dmitrievka.

On the left flank, the flank of the main attack was to be protected by advances of 3. Panzer-Division and 306. Infanterie-Division. The attack objective of 3. Panzer was Hill 211.5 and the surrounding high ground bordering the east edge of the Gerassimova. However, the division had just forty operational tanks, and only eleven of them were Panzer IVs.[5] The other twenty-nine were nearly obsolete Panzer III tanks, some of which were equipped with a long-barreled 5cm gun that fired a shell of higher velocity than the older weapons with which that model of tank had been fitted. Like the two SS divisions, this division, commanded by Lieutenant General Westhoven, was tired and weakened from the fighting at Kursk.

A XVII. Armeekorps battlegroup, consisting of elements from 306. Infanterie-Division, two battalions from 3. Gebirgs-Division, one battalion from 335. Infanterie-Division and 6. Armee's Sturm-Bataillon, was to attack on the left of 3. Panzer-Division and first capture Hill 173.4, where the Soviets had many gun positions. After this objective had been taken, the secondary mission of the attack group was to recapture the old trench line just to the north of Dmitrievka.[6] This was an overly optimistic goal given the condition of the infantry at this time, because both of the regiments of 306. Infanterie-Division and the attached battalions were decimated from the hard fighting of the preceding day. At the conclusion of the bitter fighting of the last two weeks in July, Hollidt had judged them not able to withstand another strong Russian attack even when assigned purely defensive tasks. In an evaluation of his forces delivered to Heeresgruppe Süd, Hollidt stated that even in this defensive role his battered divisions could hold the Mius positions only if the Russians did not receive reinforcements of men or armor. It is certain that they were not capable of offensive action, which meant that *Totenkopf* was likely to have little chance of effective support on its left flank.[7]

In the south, east of Marinovka and just west of Kalinovka, the two mobile divisions under the command of XXIV. Panzerkorps, 16. Panzergrenadier and 23. Panzer-Divisions, were given the objectives of penetrating the front to the west of Garany and the capture of Kalinovka. Their primary assignment was the protection of the right flank of II. SS-Panzerkorps' attack against Stepanovka and the upper Olkhovchik Valley. After assembling west of Garany and Saur Mogilsky, XXIV. Panzerkorps would attack immediately on the right flank of *Das Reich*'s attack on Stepanovka and the hill to the south of that town (223.7). Like the infantry divisions, these two panzer divisions of the army were not at full strength.

On 29 July, 23. Panzer-Division had just thirty-four operational tanks, only twenty of which were Panzer IVs. Even weaker was 16. Panzergrenadier-Division with just thirteen operational tanks. By 24 July, the two panzergrenadier regiments of this division were reduced to a total of 550 men. The two divisions had sustained a total of 464 dead, 2,582 wounded, and 255 missing in the fighting from 17 July to 29 July. Neither was in good condition after the losses of personnel and equipment that were suffered in the earlier battles.[8]

The right flank of *Totenkopf*'s attack on Hill 213.9 was to be covered by the attack of *Das Reich*. The division was instructed to capture Stepanovka and eliminate the 7.62 antitank guns in the eastern parts of the town itself and the dangerous antitank strongpoint east of the town. This position was located at a fork in the road that ran out of the town to the east before it split into two lanes that ran up the slope of the center ridge. One of these roads led almost to the base of Hill 213.9 and the other intersected the Ssneshnoje-Marinovka road just to the south of the hill. From the road fork gun position, the approaches to Hill 213.9 were in plain line of sight. The antitank guns dug in there were ideally situated to direct accurate flanking fire on any attacker that moved along the ridge top. In addition, other Russian antitank guns were hidden among the ravines and houses on the eastern perimeter of the town.

The existing conditions were almost certain to result in a slow, dogged battle of attrition, as was to be expected in a head-on assault on the fortifications of Hill 213.9 and the town of Stepanovka as well as the other fortified points and hilltops. The relatively shallow depth of the Soviet penetration dictated that the attack proceed quickly and according to the planned timetable or risk the danger that the Soviets would be able to simply withdraw across the river without being caught in the trap. Given this situation, the plan of attack ordered by Hollidt seemed to risk an outcome of less than ideal results.

THE ATTACK OF 3. SS-PANZER-DIVISION *TOTENKOPF* AT HILL 213.9

In the center, *Totenkopf* panzers prepared to make their attack past the hulks of 23. Panzer-Division's knocked-out tanks from the 19 July assault on the hill. The destroyed panzers lay blackened and burned out in the corn and sunflower fields in front of the Soviet fortifications. Surely, these must have been ominous harbingers to the SS tankers. In and beyond the huge fields of vegetation were extensive minefields laid in wide belts circling the hill. After an attacking force penetrated the mines and ran the gauntlet of fire from three directions, there lay before them the slopes of the hill itself. On the forward slopes, the Soviets had concealed batteries of heavy antitank guns (7.62cm), lighter guns of 4.5cm caliber, and literally hundreds of antitank rifles. There were also tanks, in earthen emplacements from which they could fire from a hull down position. The Soviet fortifications were formidable and very well camouflaged. Given the nature of the situation, the experienced commanders of the division were likely very apprehensive about the attack. A tank attack moving frontally on a narrow axis of advance, over exposed ground that funneled down to an extensively fortified defensive position, was not tactically advisable. However, the men of the Waffen SS divisions prided themselves on obeying orders, no matter how difficult the assignment. As a division, *Totenkopf* was aggressive almost to a fault in offensive operations, and over the next few days, its men and officers were severely tested.

By the third year of the war, it was an elite division, having been combat tested and equipped with outstanding personnel, both officers and men. The combat units of the division were commanded by a core of exceptional officers. A number of these men, who joined the division before it fought in Russia, became its most outstanding soldiers. These officers were best characterized by men such as

Karl Ullrich and Otto Baum, both of whom first served in the SS-Verfügungstruppe and were graduates of the SS-Junkerschulen. Other outstanding officers of the division included Kurt Launer, Max Seela, Erwin Meierdress, Josef Swientek, and Georg Boclunan, all of whom won the Knight's Cross.

Ullrich was a qualified mechanical engineer in 1933 and served briefly with the Reichswehr before joining the SS. In 1935, he attended the SS-Junkerschule Braunschweig, after graduation being commissioned as SS-Untersturmführer. He trained at an army engineering school before assignment to the SS-Verfügungsdivision, which was the first Waffen SS division organized for combat, in 1937. The division's first commander was Paul Hausser, who saw to it that his men were given first-class training and equipment. The Verfügungsdivision later became 2. SS-Division *Das Reich* in 1940.

In May 1941, Ullrich was transferred to 3. SS-Division *Totenkopf* and commanded SS-Pioniere-Bataillon 3. By this time, he had already won both classes of the Iron Cross. In 1942, Ullrich led a *Totenkopf* Kampfgruppe in the Demyansk fighting, where he won the Knight's Cross. When notified of the award, he somewhat sarcastically replied that he would rather have been given replacements for his dead and wounded. Ullrich's bravery, leadership and energetic command were particularly evident during "Citadel." His leadership and courage during the fighting in the Psel bridgehead figured prominently in winning him the Oak Leaves to the Knight's Cross in 1944. Later in 1944, he was given command of 5. SS-Panzer-Division *Wiking*, an assignment which he kept until the end of the war.

Otto Baum was another officer of the division who received his military training in the SS-Verfügungsdivision, under the tutelage of Hausser at Braunschweig, graduating in 1935. In 1938, he served in Regiment *Der Führer* before briefly tranferring to *Leibstandarte* in 1939. He saw combat in France with this division and began his duty with *Totenkopf* in 1941. Serving during the Demyansk encirclement, he distinguished himself as commander of SS-Infanterie-Regiment 3 and was awarded the Knight's Cross. In early 1943, Baum took over command of SS-Panzergrenadier-Regiment 5 (later renamed SS-Panzergrenadier-Regiment *Eicke*). Baum received the Oak Leaves to the Knight's Cross following the Kharkov campaign in February–March 1943. By June 1944, Baum commanded 17. SS-Panzergrenadier-Division *Götz von Berlichingen* until July of that year, when he was given command of *Das*

Reich. Baum remained with this division until November 1944, when he took over command of 16. SS-Panzergrenadier-Division *Reichsführer SS* and served in that capacity until the war's end. He was one of the most highly decorated soldiers of the Waffen SS, being awarded the Iron Cross, 1st and 2nd Class; German Cross in Gold; and Knight's Cross with Oak Leaves and Swords.

Many of the prewar officers of the division did not serve with it on the Eastern Front as they were replaced by better-qualified Waffen SS officers, most of whom were graduates of the Junkerschulen, were veterans of the Verfügungsdivision or even transferred army officers. Regardless of their background, most of the division's men, particularly the officers, shared similar qualities, one of which was a high degree of personal loyalty to Theodor Eicke, the first commander of the division, a characteristic that Eicke demanded from all who served under him. A second well-developed trait that was highly valued by the first commander of the division was obedience of orders, no matter how difficult the circumstances. This characteristic was tested by the events of the following days, as the division was to endure difficult and costly fighting once again.

The division, during 1941–42, demonstrated remarkable tenacity and aggressive dedication to orders, which resulted in high casualties. By 1943, the superb replacements given to the division had been forged in the fire of combat. Experience gained in France and the first years in Russia provided tempering factors that made *Totenkopf* a tough, skilled, and dangerous opponent. This elite status had been paid for with a great deal of blood as the division had suffered heavy casualties in all its operations. However, the division had endured more than just the loss of men and machines during the fighting of early 1943. Its spiritual leader, Eicke, who organized the division from regiments of Totenkopfverbände troops in 1939, was no longer with his division. As commander of *Totenkopf,* Eicke had led it through the fighting in France, the invasion of Russia and the bitter fighting in the Demyansk pocket in 1942. He was not a trained military commander and had little tactical expertise, but his influence on the toughness and tenacity of his men was pervasive. Eicke, like Dietrich of *Leibstandarte* and Hausser of *Das Reich*, put his personal stamp on the men of *Totenkopf.*

On the afternoon of 26 February 1943, Eicke was shot down while on a reconnaissance flight in a Fieseler Storch searching for

SS-Panzer-Regiment 3, which had been out of radio contact with the divisional HQ for some time. The plane strayed over a Soviet position and was shot down after being struck by a storm of small-arms fire. The SS troops who witnessed the destruction and blazing impact of the plane tried to reach the crash scene but could not get to it before dark, when the effort had to be called off. Early on the next day, a battle group of volunteers recovered the bodies of Eicke and the other occupants of the plane. Theodor Eicke thus died on the eve of one of the most stunning German victories on the Eastern Front, Manstein's Kharkov counterattack, in which *Totenkopf* played a major role.

The loss of Eicke removed an influential element of personal leadership that was much in evidence to the men of the division, who saw him as a leader who demanded no more of them than he demanded of himself. He was not a leader who sat safely in the rear and the combat troops respected him for this. However, Eicke's death did not adversely affect the performance of *Totenkopf*. The enduring legacy of its first commander was a division that could be absolutely depended upon to attack furiously or defend with remarkable tenacity, regardless of conditions or casualties. It retained this characteristic nearly until the end of the war. By that time, almost all of the old veterans were gone and even the elite SS divisions lost hope in the face of bitter reality.

In July 1943, *Totenkopf* was commanded by SS-Brigadeführer Hermann Priess. Priess was a Reichswehr veteran who had joined the SS-Verfügungstruppe in 1934. He later served with the artillery of SS-Standarte *Germania* and subsequently commanded II./SS-Artillerie-Regiment 2. Priess was transferred to *Totenkopf* in order to take over as commander of II./SS-Artillerie-Regiment 3 and in 1941 was appointed commander of the regiment.[9] On 26 February, he assumed command of the division. (See appendix V for the divisional order of battle.)

On 29 July, Priess concentrated the divisional units in preparation for the attack. Each of the regimental HQs moved forward and established their new locations close to their zones of attack. SS-Panzer-Regiment 3 HQ was located at the northern end of the center ridge in a group of houses near the Removsky mine.[10] The HQ location was very close to the Ssneshnoje–Marinovka road. On the following day, *Totenkopf* panzers would deploy to attack on both sides of the road, without reconnaissance or enough time for the SS engineer units to prepare a path through thick fields of mines laid down on the approaches to Hill 213.9. From the location of the regimental headquarters, the low, rounded hill, surrounded by fields of corn and sunflowers, could be seen in the distance.

The night before the battle was not a peaceful one for the men of the three divisions of II. SS-Panzerkorps as they tried to snatch what sleep they could before the bloody dawn. An SS gunner of 2./SS-Flak-Abteilung 3 remembered the restless night as the division settled in for the evening on 29 July: ". . . by the afternoon we had moved into our new position. Hard and rocky ground. During the night the IL-2's appeared once again and bombs fell very close to the battery gun positions. Muzzle flashes from our 2 cm Flak guns, apparently attracted the Russian pilots."[11]

All formations of the three divisions of the II. SS-Panzerkorps arrived at their assigned start positions by the night of 29 July and received the order confirming the attack from 6. Armee HQ on that night.[12] Just two weeks had elapsed since the fierce combat of the Kursk salient. The three divisions were about to plunge into bloody fighting that would equal and even rival the intensity and violence of combat during Operation "Citadel." Over the next four days, *Totenkopf* would suffer more casualties than the total number of killed and wounded lost during ten days of fighting in "Citadel."

Totenkopf would be particularly tested during its brief tour of duty at the Mius because of the nature of its assignment. Possession of Hill 213.9 would provide the Germans with an elevation from which they could observe both the Gerassimova and the Olkhovchik Valleys, as well as crossings of the Mius at Dmitrievka and north of Kuibyshevo. It was these crossing points by which supplies and men reached the Soviet bridgehead, although the river was so shallow it did not represent a difficult barrier at any point. Capture of the hill meant that German artillery could be employed with direct observation of many key sectors of the battlefield.

The task of capturing the hill was just one more difficult task for a division that had been given one bloody assignment after the other since 1942, a characteristic of the duties of the other Waffen SS divisions as well. A list of *Totenkopf*'s battles includes some of the most difficult engagements of a war that was characterized by hard and

6. Armee Strikes Back

vicious fighting in all sectors. The battles of Demyansk, Kharkov, and Kursk, as well as the subsequent bitter fighting of late summer and fall of 1943, had a common result with regard to *Totenkopf*'s involvement: hard fighting and long lists of killed and wounded.

Material and equipment losses from the Kursk fighting were high, although the division arrived on the Mius with adequate tank strength as listed below:

Panzer VI	10
Panzer IV	9
Panzer III	49
	68

The panzer regiment, besides suffering substantial losses in hard-to-replace tank crewmen, was reduced to about 60 percent of its pre-"Citadel" tank strength. The division listed 117 tanks as operational on 4 July 1943, the day before "Citadel" began, but now had less than 70 still running Although on 13 July *Totenkopf* tank strength had been down to 54 tanks, a number of tanks were left behind by *Leibstandarte* when it was transferred to Italy. The armor loss of early July constituted a less than crippling, but still substantial, loss of combat strength. However, a percentage of the damaged vehicles were undoubtedly in the divisional tank repair shops at the time and returned to action at a later date.[13]

Priess, in issuing an estimation of his division's combat status, reported that his unit was "in accordance with its strength, fit for all missions," but in truth, *Totenkopf*, after ten days of continuous combat during which it had taken heavy casualties (as well as substantial weapon and equipment destruction), was in a weakened state. A total of only 331 men and 43 officers had recovered enough from their wounds to leave the field hospitals and rejoin the division by 29 July.[14] There remained a deficiency of over 3,000 men and officers.

The weakened state of the division was of course normal for combat formations on the Eastern Front. In fact, the division had endured much more severe personnel losses earlier in the war, while in the Demyansk pocket, where it remained during the last months of 1941 and most of 1942. On 22 June 1941, the division had entered Russia with a strength of 17,265 men. Less than a year later, in May 1942, after enduring brutal conditions and five months of continuous combat in the Demyansk pocket, total manpower on hand was only 6,700, in spite of having received about 1,000 replacements early in the year and over 3,000 additional men in May of that same year. After fighting that lasted nearly a year in the Demyansk pocket, Eicke's division endured months of extremely harsh weather conditions and the mental stress of encirclement, while suffering approximately 14,000 dead, wounded or missing.[15] In spite of this, the division did not disintegrate. On the contrary, its combat units played a major role in the defense of the pocket and later units of the division maintained a supply corridor until the division was relieved in late 1942. During the fighting in the Demyansk sector, Eicke's men repeatedly held their positions, at times literally to the last man, under constant pressure from fresh divisions that the Russians threw against the pocket until the fall of 1942.

Not until October 1942, after more than ten months of brutal combat, were 6,400 survivors withdrawn, two thirds of whom were noncombatants: cooks, medical personnel, and specialized troops such as mechanics. Even these men were pressed into combat after losses in the grenadier, engineer, and mortar companies reached 80 percent on the average. The survivors were sick from trench foot, starvation, pneumonia, dysentery, and combat fatigue. By the time of their withdrawal, an SS doctor of Infanterie-Regiment 1, who examined 281 *Totenkopf* men, concluded that about 30 percent were not fit for further military service and resembled the concentration camp inmates that he had become familiar with during a tour of duty in the camps.[16]

Without a doubt, the fact that Eicke's men were able to continue to fight against overwhelming numbers in spite of absolutely brutal weather conditions, while starving and enduring the mental stress of encirclement, was one of the division's outstanding achievements during the war. Enduring the intense emotional strain of continuous heavy fighting, with the resulting catastrophic casualties, was, without question, proof of the toughness and exceptional unit pride that Eicke had created in the division. Study of the casualty reports of *Totenkopf* from this battle and others result in the conclusion that heavy casualties were a common result of the division's combat operations, partly due to the nature of the fighting to which it was committed and partly as a result of the high level of aggressiveness and fighting spirit exhibited by the division. Eicke saw to it that his men were infused with a potent mixture of intense commitment to the political goals of Germany, high unit morale and a healthy dose of pride in their toughness, which was carefully developed in the men of the original Waffen SS divisions. All of the division's service after the beginning of Operation "Barbarossa" took place on the Eastern Front with few respites from combat during the four years of the war in the East.

The division first fought as a complete unit in France, and although numerous shortcomings were exposed during the fighting in the West, the men greatly benefited from combat experience. It was evident from the very first that the division's officers and men were aggressive almost to a fault. In Russia, Eicke's division exhibited this same hard-driving aggressiveness, but it had been tempered by experience. Eicke became an adequate commander. He benefited greatly by the assignment of several outstanding men to the position of division Ia, although his simplistic, heavy-handed tactics were not admired by army officers.

Led by a hard core of aggressive officers and men and learning from the harsh experience of Eastern Front warfare, the division was a unique formation. With such leadership and with personnel imbued with indifference to hardship and suffering, trained to be scornful of danger and expected to unquestioningly obey orders with ruthless dispatch, it is not surprising that the division developed a military reputation for recklessness in attack and extreme tenacity in defense.

Eicke's—and, by extension, *Totenkopf*'s—military philosophy is aptly described by Sydnor as

> . . . concentrating all available mass and firepower in the forward units, and by reckless, zealous pursuit of the attack until the enemy surrendered or was annihilated. In the more complex and sophisticated theories of motorized operations, Eicke had neither the learning nor the slightest interest. In his blunt and impatient mind the rules were fixed plainly enough: concentrate every soldier, weapon and vehicle in the front line, then smash away at the enemy with relentless fury until he crumbled.[17]

The stage was set for a furious collision in the center of the attack sector, where *Totenkopf*'s men and tanks collided head on with the defenses on Hill 213.9. Opposing the panzer divisions in the center sector were the antitank guns of one and a half antitank brigades, five and a half rifle divisions, and elements of 4th Guards Mechanized Corps. The first objective for the attack of II. SS-Panzerkorps was a line extending from Hill 223.7 (near Stepanovka)–Hill 213.9–Hill 173.4. After reaching this line, the corps was to drive the Soviets into the blocking position established by the Kampfgruppe from XXIX. Armeekorps in the southern end of the Olkhovchik Valley. If *Totenkopf* smashed through the defenses on the hill without delay and the flanks were secured promptly, the attack had some chance for success. Whether the division had any better chance of taking Hill 213.9 than had 23. Panzer-Division ten days earlier, particularly when considering the time and effort the Russians had spent fortifiying the hills, was questionable. The advance of the divisions of XXIV. Panzerkorps, driving east toward the Olkhovchik Valley, would turn out to be as vital to success or failure as the parallel attacks of *Das Reich* and 3. Panzer-Division. Without a successful German advance into and across the Olkhovchik Valley, cutting the lines of supply and retreat of Hill 213.9 and the valleys on either side of it, *Totenkopf* would make a frontal attack against a near inpregnable fortress manned by Soviet troops and tanks secure from threats to their flanks or rear. In addition, it was unlikely that the attacks on the flank would be successful with the forces at hand.

In retrospect, the attack had the earmarks of an operation launched hurriedly and without the necessary strength or proper preparation. Hollidt knew that Manstein would take the three panzer divisions from him as soon as they were needed at Kharkov. It is probable that Manstein only allowed their commitment on the Mius because it was his opinion that the Russians had been weakened severely in the south by their losses during "Citadel." On 2 August, Manstein reported to OKH that he did not believe the Russians were recovered yet to the degree that they could launch offensive operations and he did not expect anything to happen for several weeks.

Manstein expected an attack in the near future at Belgorod-Kharkov, but he did not believe it was imminent on 2 August. Had he been aware of the build-up and concentration of 1st Tank Army and 5th Guards Tank Army, north of Belgorod, he may have left Hollidt's army to its own devices. By the time of his report to OKH, the two Soviet tank armies, which had been close to total destruction by

13 July, had a total of over a thousand tanks. The two armies, which Manstein had wanted to destroy before breaking off "Citadel," were ready for action again by the first days of August. This was one of the legacies of Hitler's decision to disperse the panzer divisions of Heeresgruppe Süd in the days after 12 July.

Hollidt probably ordered the immediate attack by the divisions of II. SS-Panzerkorps, literally from the march, because he was well aware that he would not have them long. In any event, there was not enough time allowed to the divisions to complete proper reconnaissance nor to locate and remove Russian mines which were laid by the tens of thousands in front of the main fortified positions. The three divisions were brought on line and issued their orders to attack as soon as they arrived.

On the night of 29 July, 3. SS-Panzergrenadier-Division *Totenkopf* received its instructions from II. SS-Panzerkorps. Hollidt had ordered the attack on Hill 213.9 for the next day.[18] On 30 July, in the early-morning hours, the counterattack of II. SS-Panzerkorps on the Mius River began.

CHAPTER 6

The First Day

THE ASSAULT ON HILL 213.9: THE DEATH RIDE OF SS-PANZER-REGIMENT 3

Early on the morning of 30 July 1943, the tanks and SS grenadiers of Regiment *Totenkopf* moved into their jump-off positions as artillery and mortar batteries shelled targets on the approaches to Hill 213.9. The men of Regiment *Totenkopf*, commanded by SS-Obersturmbannführer Baum, fell in behind the tanks of I./SS-Panzer-Regiment 3. The heavy tanks, the huge Tigers, ground slowly to the front, spearheading the attack with their 88mm guns and thick frontal armor. The Tigers were followed by the majority of the battalion's Panzer IVs. This force advanced west of and parallel to the Ssneshnoje-Marinovka road which ran generally north to south from Removsky. The road ran parallel to the Olkhovchik Valley and then led to the east edge of Marinovka.

Regiment *Eicke*, led by SS-Standartenführer Hellmuth Becker, advanced to the left of the armored group, easily penetrated the first line of Russian defenses to the southeast of Removsky and swept into the northern end of the Gerassimova Valley. Late in the morning, the upper end of the valley was cleared of Russian troops.[1] By 1305 hours, the northern segment of the valley was reported to be securely in German hands.

The assault battalions of Regiment *Eicke* pushed farther down the flat-bottomed valley until they reached the area north of the Nedadejewa Schlucht (ravine or deep stream bed), which was located just to the northwest of the village of Gerassimova. Like many villages and towns in Russia, Gerassimova was long and narrow and bisected by a dirt road that ran its entire length. The stretch of houses and small huts was closely bordered on the west edge by the Gerassimova stream. The small stream flowed the length of the valley before turning to the east and joining the Mius at Dmitrievka.

The Nedadejewa ravine ran from near the ridge crest road, down slope in a northeasterly direction before it opened into the Gerassimova Valley. From this point in the valley, only a few kilometers of ground remained between Regiment *Eicke* and the Mius River. To the east, the town of Dmitrievka could clearly be seen.[2] However, the passage through the remaining half of the valley was not to be quite as easy. Russian infantry were dug into the Nedadejewa, and when the German troops moved closer, they directed a large volume of small-arms fire at the SS grenadiers. Russian mortar fire, from medium and heavy tubes of 82 to 120mm, ranged in on the Germans. The impacting mortar rounds threw up sprays of dirt and stones, the crump of the explosions audible over the rattle of small-arms fire. When the bursts of mortar shells tore into the ground in the midst of their advance, the SS grenadiers were forced to halt and quickly take cover. As the men of Regiment *Eicke*, utilizing available cover, carefully worked forward, the armored assault against Hill 213.9 also came under heavy fire on the ridge crest.

Two armored groups, one headed by the Tigers and another, made up of lighter armor, on the right wing of the heavy group, rolled forward with grenadiers moving behind the tanks. The SS panzers, like Regiment *Eicke*'s attack in the Gerassimova, initially encountered light resistance. The principal Soviet reaction consisted of some desultory fire that originated from the northwest section of Stepanovka shortly after the attack began at 0810 hours. However, at the moment the attackers neared the approaches of Hill 213.9, just in front of the mine belts, a hail of projectiles of all calibers erupted from the front and flanking ridges. Dug-in Russian tanks, with only their turrets protruding above the ground, opened fire on the SS tanks. Artillery and heavy mortar shells exploded, raising clouds of fine dust and smoke. A storm of antitank rifle bullets clattered against the tank armor, richocheting off the armor plate into the air or whirring past the heads of the tank commanders, who quickly ducked for cover inside the cupola. The tanks continued to advance, undeterred by the antitank rifle shells that rattled against their armor or sailed past with nasty whines.

However, when the heavier 7.62cm Russian antitank guns began to fire from their gun positions, the German tanks manuevered into small depressions or behind hillocks to escape the Russian fire. Although the Soviets still equipped many of their divisions with rel-

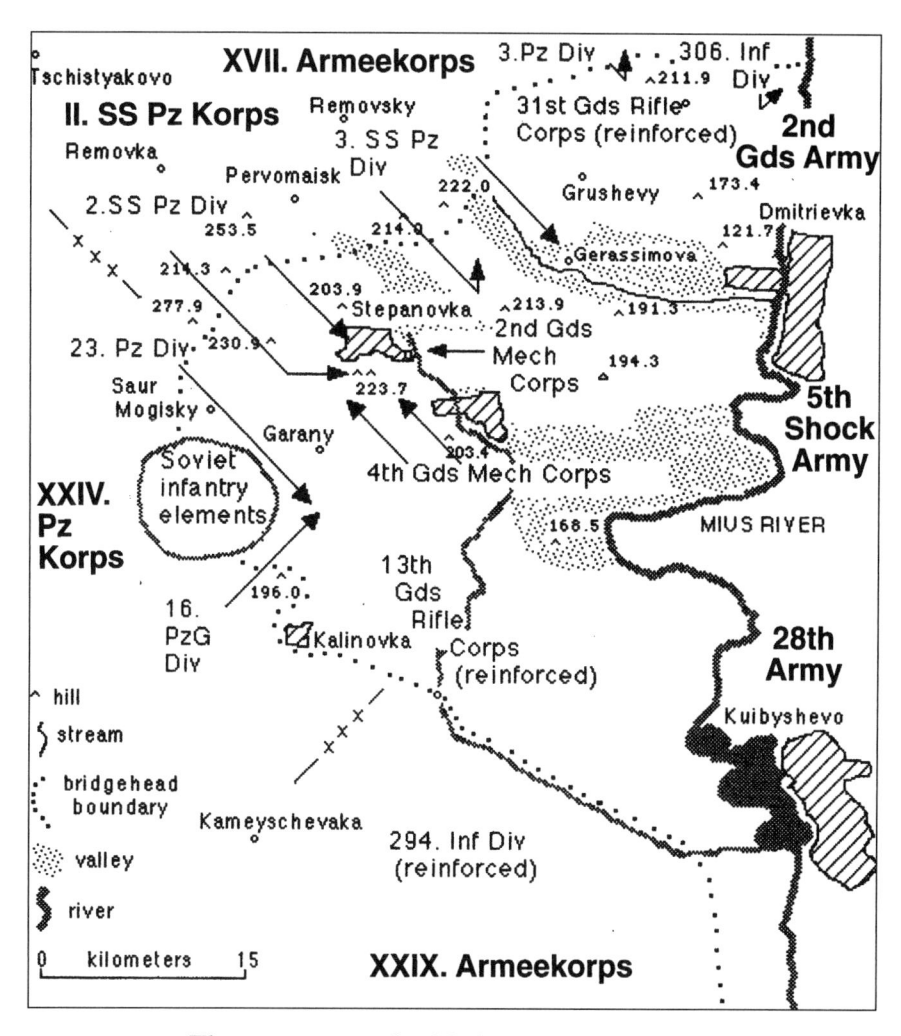

The caption: The counterattack of 6. Armee, 30 July 1943.

atively light antitank guns (4.5cm) in the summer of 1943, more of the heavy 7.62cm guns were making their presence felt. The 4.5cm guns of the Russians were not a great danger to penetrate the frontal armor of even the Panzer III, but they could be dangerous when striking the thin armor on the sides or rear of a tank. The hated *Ratsch-bumm* or 7.62cm antitank round was another story, however. Its high-velocity round could penetrate the frontal armor of the Panzer III and IV and, at close range, even the armor of the Tiger. When these guns began firing, with their distinctive report, the SS tank commanders took cover or fired off smoke and tried to find dead ground. In addition to the Russian antitank gun fire coming from the front, there was extremely heavy high-explosive shelling and long-range antitank gun fire from both flanks.

Larger Soviet artillery pieces began to find the range, firing from the northeast, where batteries of heavy artillery were emplaced in the area of high ground near Hills 173.4 and 121.7. These 17.2cm guns were capable of damaging a tank track or penetrating engine covers and setting the tank on fire if a chance hit struck one of these vulnerable points. Multiple hits could also sometimes stun the crew; however, the main damage was to the advancing German infantry, who were forced to find cover when the heavy shells thundered down on the ridge crest. When the mines and Soviet fire forced the German tanks to halt or slow down, small groups of Russian tanks left cover and moved down lanes cleared of mines and tried to work into position for a flank shot on the German tanks. A veteran of the *Totenkopf* Division, former SS-Oberscharführer Feichtner, described the action in front of the hill at this point of the assault:

> ... at this time, in the midst of heavy fire from the Russian PAK, a pair of Soviet tanks came down the hill. We halted quickly, protected by terrain, elevated our fire a little and left the pair of T-34s burning on the battlefield as we rolled on. At this time a message came over the radio to our tank commander. ... The tank of squad leader SS-Hauptsturmführer Richter has run over a mine and fallen out of the attack. He remained with his tank and furnished fire support to the advance. The Tiger of SS-Untersturmführer Schussler was also out of action and he had been blinded. Hours later, he died at the division field hospital.[3]

The spearhead of *Totenkopf*'s attack, seeking to find a way to penetrate the position, found itself in broad and dense minefields to the northwest of the hill. The assault force plowed straight into the mines before realizing that it had done so, losing tank after tank with damaged wheels or tracks. When the attack bogged down, any immobilized tanks made easy targets for the Soviet guns on the flanks if the damaged vehicle could not limp into the scanty cover. As a result of the losses to the mines and antitank gun fire, less than two hours after the start of the advance, all momentum was lost. The panzer regiment reported that it was under fire from 7.62cm guns and T-34s dug into the hill itself, heavy antitank fire from the northeast corner of Stepanovka, particularly from the fortified PAK position at the crossroads east of the town and devastating high-explosive barrages from the north and northeast. In addition, there was noticeably heavy artillery and mortar fire of all calibers from Hill 191.3.[4]

At 0940 hours, after the depth of the minefields became apparent, the order was passed to the rear to bring the SS engineer detachments forward to try to clear paths through the mines. All weapons that could be brought to bear were then utilized to provide covering fire for the engineers, who crept forward into the fields to begin the dangerous task of removing mines while under enemy fire. Following the German principle of leading from the front, the officers of the engineer company crawled into the fields to direct the mine removal personally. Untersturmführer Dahnert, the chief of the Panzer-Pionier-Kompanie, was soon wounded while leading his company and was subsequently taken to the rear. Continuing their dangerous work, even while under intense small arms and artillery fire, his men succeeded in digging out enough mines to enable the remaining mobile tanks to push forward again. Working forward in twos and threes, covering each other, the German tanks attempted to penetrate the outpost positions of the hill.

The Russian infantry in the forward positions fought stubbornly, often firing from one-man holes that were difficult to locate. Even when bypassed, the Russians fired on the German infantry from behind until the SS grenadiers cleared them from their holes with grenades and machine pistols or in close combat with spade or bayonet. The surviving Russians, those able to escape or withdraw, disappeared into the corn only to reappear behind the Germans or to man the next ambush.[5]

To the right of the heavy armored group, which was making its slow progress through the mines, the Panzer IIIs and Panzer IVs of II./SS-Panzer-Regiment 3 were also stopped. From their front, on the southwest slopes of Hill 213.9, heavy fire forced them to take cover. Several armored vehicles were already burning in front of the Russian positions. The two panzer attacks were in sight of each other but were not able to support each other by a successful breakthrough because both were mired in the minefields. Each group had lost the ability to manuever due to the undimimished volume of fire from the Russian guns. The minefields were situated so as to channel the German attack into the massed fire of the Soviet Pakfronts.

Because of the volume of fire from the right flank, from the direction of Stepanovka, it was evident that *Das Reich* had not been able to carry out its mission of neutralizing the eastern edges of the town. It was also clear from the amount of fire coming from the east and northeast that the attacks of 3. Panzer-Division and 306. Infanterie-Division were also stopped short of their objectives, Hill 173.4 and the adjacent high ground. The flank attacks, so important to the success of *Totenkopf*, were bogged down on both sides, with the result that the division advanced straight into a death trap for its tanks and men.

Later in the morning, the grenadiers of Regiment *Totenkopf* renewed their push forward in an attempt to reach the next line of fortifications, but this attack gained only a few yards of ground at a high cost. The SS grenadiers leapt forward, moving and firing, following the principle of no fire without movement and no movement without fire only to be greeted by a hail of mortar fire and small arms. In an attempt to place effective high-explosive fire on the hill, the SS Nebelwerfer (wheeled six-barrel rocket launchers) detachments moved closer to the forward units. The light-carriaged Nebelwerfers were hooked up to wheeled vehicles or halftracks and moved forward to new positions. The rockets were well suited for this kind of fire support due to the heavy volume of explosives that could be laid down on relatively large areas with indirect fire. Given the lack of high ground to correct observed fire and the difficulty of locating terrain features to adjust fire on the hill, this type of weapon proved valuable to the Germans. However, there were difficulties that hindered these efforts. The Nebelwerfer fired by electrical ignition, a system that normally worked well, having the advantage of allowing the crews to withdraw to shelter after loading the tubes and firing their rockets from cover. On this day, electrical system malfunctions caused the premature explosion of two launchers of the Werfer battalion's 3. Batterie, setting off thunderous explosions when all six tubes exploded. The casualties and confusion created by this accident distracted from the business at hand although the other batteries fired their salvos of screaming projectiles at the hill. The German artillery fired support as well, with the guns of II. SS-Panzerkorps added to those of 6. Armee.

Regardless of these determined German efforts, the Soviets maintained a continuous rain of shells of all types and calibers on the attackers. Adding to the difficulties faced by the SS men, the Russian air support was also strong. During the entire day, the IL-2s were overhead constantly, often roaring in over the field in flights of twenty to forty planes. In spite of the efforts of the German Flak units, not many of the Russian planes were reported shot down. Flak detachment gunners from *Totenkopf* claimed only one IL-2 shot down for the entire day. The large formations of Soviet fighter-bombers flew in at low levels over the battlefield and dropped fragmentation bombs on the SS grenadiers, inflicting additional casualties.[6] The Luftwaffe was not to be seen in the air other than for a flight of Stukas that gathered high over Removsky-Gruse before making dive-bomb attacks on the forward slopes of Hill 213.9. German fighter support was entirely lacking, leaving the Soviets free rein in the air on the first day of the counterattack.

In spite of the additional support of the Stukas and the Nebelwerfer unit, the SS tanks and grenadiers could not penetrate the main defensive line. The Soviet antitank gun fire was undiminished in either accuracy or volume, with the result that the SS panzers could not advance and punch through the Soviet line to create a decisive breakthrough. The tanks could not support the grenadiers with their main guns, which precluded an infantry breakthrough of the main defensive line. Any time that a German panzer left a covering depression or concealing fold in the ground, a storm of projectiles hit the tank. Even the massive Tiger tanks, almost invulnerable from the front due to their massive frontal armor plate, could be stopped by heavy antitank shells that struck the thinner armor on sides and the rear. High-explosive shells from the hills to the north rained down on the Germans. There was little sheltering terrain for armor on the ridge top except for small ravines and an occasional fold in the ground. In the process of manuevering to avoid shots from the front or while the tank crew worked to get in position to fire, the Russian Pakfronts on the adjacent ridges were able to fire at the flanks of the SS panzers from Stepanovka and the crossroads northeast of that town.

To the front, the antitank gun batteries held their fire until the Germans were very close, then opened up a barrage of fire directed by a single commander. Russian fire discipline and antitank tactics had improved since the earlier battles of 1941 and 1942 to the point that 6. Armee battle reports mentioned the improvement in Russian tactical antitank fire on Hill 213.9.[7] The Russian Pakfront commanders developed the tactic of directing all of the guns of their batteries to fire concentrations against one or two German tanks, firing shell after shell until the panzer ground to a halt or exploded into flame. If any of the German tank crews survived, they then had no choice but to bail out of their wrecked and blazing vehicles, leaping from the tank into the storm of shot and shell that flashed in at them from all sides. Panzers that were disabled in the open were sitting ducks for the Soviet gunners and were likely to be destroyed completely. When the Germans were hit by such a hail of shell fire, even from the lighter 4.5cm guns, they quickly steered for cover. In their haste, more of the SS panzers were disabled from striking mines. Soviet tanks continued to use narrow, cleared passages through their own minefields, manuevering down the hill to get a flanking shot at the SS tanks.

Soon columns of smoke from burning vehicles, both German and Russian, marked the forward limit of progress of each of the armored spearheads. Both quickly stalled, brought to a halt again by the mines, fire from the flanks and the heavy antitank gun fire from the hill itself. In an attempt to get the attack moving again the whole of *Totenkopf*'s artillery regiment, reinforced by an army mortar unit, fired on the hill shortly before 1100 hours. The machine-gun nests and mortar batteries had to be neutralized before the grenadiers could survive their assault in sufficient numbers to capture the Russian antitank gun positions or destroy the dug-in tanks. However, in spite of this additional artillery support, the grenadiers were not able to gain much ground. This failure prevented the surviving *Totenkopf* tanks from gaining any manuevering room. Until the Russian supporting artillery and volume of small-arms fire was at least suppressed to a survivable level, the SS grenadiers could not get into the main defensive positions and knock out the concealed 7.62cm antitank gun positions. They were nearly impossible for the tank commanders to see and their fire prevented the tanks from advancing into the defensive system.

The First Day

As the frustrated SS grenadiers tried to knock out camouflaged Russian machine-gun positions, they found them to be extremely difficult to spot, even from close range. The rounded, featureless nature of the hill and the skill with which the Russian troops had concealed their firing positions hampered effective artillery support. The commander of SS-Artillerie-Regiment 3, SS-Sturmbannführer Josef Swientek specifically noted the difficulties of providing adequate artillery support with regard to the terrain peculiarities of the hill:

> Our observers had few good opportunities to spot targets. They could see very little of the well concealed system of fortifications. The hills, especially 213.9, had rounded, soft terrain contours with no distinctive features. Thus it was hard to find good landmarks to adjust artillery fire missions. There were a large number of concealing ravines also.[8]

Under cover of the artillery, which fired concentrations just forward of the minefields, the SS-Panzer-Pionier-Kompanie was ordered to go forward again, to remove more mines from the line of advance. Ignoring their losses in dead and wounded, they again were able to locate and dig out many mines while under cover of artillery and small arms fire. However, the numbers of surviving engineers diminished quickly as shell fragments or bullets took their toll. The grenadiers provided some cover with small-arms fire, sweeping the ground ahead of the engineers with grazing fire from the MG-42s and machine pistols. On the slope of the hill above, the Russian antitank gun crews marked the sectors where the SS engineer units were at work. They were well aware that when the mine lanes were cleared the German tanks would soon appear. The Russian gun crews and commanders waited for the German tanks to leave cover and begin to move forward again.

Meanwhile, in the upper entrance of the Gerassimova Valley, Regiment *Eicke*'s battalions continued to make slow progress toward the south, fighting forward with difficulty. They continued to battle against great superiority in numbers and strong Russian positions. Small assault groups, under cover of fire from their comrades, leapt to the attack, clearing one position at a time. While the Soviet artillery and antitank guns still thundered and crashed at Hill 213.9, Regiment *Eicke* pushed the Russians off a fortified hill north of

Gerassimova. By 1305 hours, the regiment reported that it had penetrated into the sector just to the north of the village but was still involved in fierce fighting for possession of the hill itself. The Russians tried to regain possession of the hill by infiltrating the flanks of the German attackers, moving through the small ravines and water cuts that were common everywhere. These attacks were supported by heavy mortar fire. The SS grenadiers managed to turn back the Soviet attempts to retake the hill, stubbornly hanging on to their hard won ground in the face of unending counterattacks. Pressure from Russian infantry grew stronger later in the day, particularly coming from the east where the flank of the regiment was attacked repeatedly by assaults of company strength. Soviet strength became very apparent to the rapidly decreasing numbers of SS grenadiers, as a seemingly inexhaustible number of Russian infantry appeared as if springing from out of the ground itself.

On the approaches of Hill 213.9, two more paths had in the meantime been cleared through the mine belts. By early afternoon, the division regrouped and pushed forward again. Regiment *Totenkopf* grenadiers made another push up the hill at 1315 hours following a Stuka mission which had been called in to bomb the forward slope. The Stukas gathered in the air high above the hill, then one after the other turned over on a wing and screamed down, adding their bombs to the maelstrom that raged on the Soviet positions. Once more, the grenadiers dashed forward and tried to advance in the face of heavy machine gun fire and mortar barrages. SS tanks slowly and cautiously worked their way up the hill, firing as they moved from one position to the next. Coordinating their movements by use of their tank radios, the panzer crews worked forward with care, some firing to cover the advance while others found a way to move farther up the slope a few yards at a time.

Again antitank rifle bullets clattered noisily off the tank armor. This forced many of the tank commanders to pull their heads down again and use the cupola periscopes to locate targets. Without being able to see from their normal command spot, the commanders were not able to identify targets as well, nor detect potential dangers to the sides or rear of their vehicle. Dust and smoke, thrown up by burning vehicles and grinding tracks, made it even more difficult to see clearly.

The First Day

The attack on the hill slowly pushed forward in fits and starts, making only minor gains with no decisive success. The Russian artillery continued to fire barrages of high explosives and fragmentation shells from the batteries located on the hills and ridges around Hills 194.3 and 191.3. Black smoke and earth rose into the air in ugly fountains when the shells landed in the midst of the battered *Totenkopf* tanks or the rapidly alining ranks of the SS grenadiers. The Russian artillery observers had spotted the attackers up and moving above ground again and the shells tore gaps in the advancing grenadier companies.

After a hard-earned few hundred meters of progress, another minefield was encountered. Tanks struck mines, tracks were blown off and the suddenly crippled tanks tried to reverse out of the danger zone or limp into a depression or a small ravine.

Those who failed to take cover soon enough found themselves suddenly under fire by antitank rounds of all calibers flying through the air in storms of murderous shellfire, coming in from three directions. Tanks shuddered from the heavy blows of direct hits or the clang of glancing shots. Even hits that failed to penetrate tank armor sometimes caused splinters of steel or bolts to fly around inside the tank, wounding or killing the crew. The flanking fire was undiminished from any direction. When the German tanks were unable to advance, the Russians again made a number of counterthrusts with small groups of tanks.[9] A few T-34s again tried to slip down the hill to attack the panzers. Most were knocked out by the Germans before they caused great damage.

At 1745 hours, the division reported to II. SS-Panzerkorps headquarters that after three attacks, supported by Regiment *Totenkopf* and the divisional artillery, it had gained little ground in its attempt to capture the hill. The division requested and received another Stuka sortie at 1625 hours, although no appreciable effect was noticed and the Russan fire continued without slackening in amount. The strong 7.62cm antitank gun position located near the crossroad west of Stepanovka proved to be a deadly thorn in the side of *Totenkopf*'s advance down the center ridge. This position significantly troubled both *Totenkopf* and *Das Reich* tanks over the next days with its well-directed and accurate long-range antitank gun fire. Its location to the west of the forward approaches to Hill 213.9 made it ideally located to fire on German tanks moving toward the hill along the ridgetop. The men of SS Regiment *Deutschland* were fighting hard to get through Stepanovka to silence this group of guns and others on the east border of the town. The Russian resistance in the town showed no signs of weakening, and they were not only determinedly holding on to their fortified houses and strongpoints, but brought up fresh elements of several rifle divisions and launched counterattacks on the Germans in the town.

To the east of Hill 213.9, on the left flank of the division's attack, Regiment *Eicke* remained involved in difficult fighting to hold on to the gains that it had made during the initial advance down the Gerassimova Valley. In spite of attempts by the Russians to outflank the regiment with an attack of reinforced battalion strength, the German troops dug in and fought off all efforts to drive them out of the valley. The Russian attack, supported by heavy mortars and air support, hit the regimental left flank, defended by III./*Eicke*, at 1515 hours. It was only with difficulty that the Russians were driven back using small-unit counterattacks to disrupt the Soviet infantry.[10] Artillery and mortar shelling gradually became stronger after the main German attack on 213.9 stopped. Russian guns were then redirected to fire against Regiment *Eicke*. German losses continued to mount steadily from the constant shelling and relentless Soviet infantry attacks.

The already weakened SS grenadier companies suffered serious losses of officers and NCOs, in addition to severe losses to the grenadiers. Leading from the front and by example was the expected method of leadership and command in the classic SS divisions and was carried almost to a fault in *Totenkopf*. While this provided aggressive leadership and immediate and violent reaction to combat situations, it resulted in casualties to junior officers during heavy fighting. On the first morning of the battle, Regiment *Eicke* quickly began to suffer heavy losses of small-unit commanders. The regiment lost SS-Obersturmführer Hermann, commander of 7. Kompanie, and SS-Obersturmführer Müller, commander of 12. Kompanie, as well as Untersturmführer Krautmann and Untersturmführer Thiemann from other companies. Untersturmführer Wirth of II./*Eicke* and Untersturmführer Petersen and Untersturmführer Moth (both from 10. Kompanie.) were either killed or severely wounded in the early fighting on 30 July.[11]

The First Day

The attack of *Totenkopf,* like that of 23. Panzer-Division two weeks earlier over the same ground, depended on the elimination of the very active and numerous Russian gun positions that were located in Stepanovka, at the roadfork east of the town and northeast of the central ridge, near Hills 191.3, 121.7, and 173.4. However, in spite of all efforts by *Das Reich* and 3. Panzer-Division, the attacks by these two divisions were unable to accomplish much on either flank. The 3. Panzer-Division was stopped in its tracks after encountering extensive minefields around a fortified hill position northwest of the village of Peradrievo. The division was then aggressively attacked by small groups of Soviet tanks, well supported by heavy artillery. The Russians had dug-in tanks and antitank guns on the key hill, identified as Point 211.5, where the resistance on the hill halted the panzers before much progress could be made. During the whole day, the Soviet air force harrassed every move of the division, attacking vehicles as well as infantry positions.

The Soviet air force again made its presence felt continuously over the battlefield during 30 July, dropping fragmentation and high-explosive bombs on the spearhead units. Russian planes sowed further confusion by strafing and bombing the German artillery and mortar positions in the rear areas. Large groups of IL-2s and other types of Russian fighter-bombers roared in at low levels to attack tanks, vehicles and artillery positions with impunity because of the absence of Luftwaffe fighter support. These air attacks hindered but did not stop efforts to support the division's advance by the artillery and mortar battery crews with fire-support missions on the hill. In spite of the deployment of divisional Flak units, the SS gun crews were often forced to take cover from attacks by Soviet planes. The Flak batteries were apparently effective enough to prevent the Russian planes from completely disrupting the German attacks or knocking out any significant numbers of guns. The Russian ground-attack tactics were not as effective as those of the Allied planes in the West, most likely due to lack of adequate radio communication and poor coordination with ground units.

The most damaging hindrance to the momentum of the German attacks were the minefields. The Russians were well known to be capable of making extraordinary efforts in laying mines and could put down amazingly extensive fields overnight. During the many days that they had been able to devote to preparing the defenses of Hill 213.9, it was not surprising that the Germans encountered the number of deep mine belts ringing Hill 213.9 and other main Soviet defensive positions. This was particularly true of Hill 211.5, another strongly held and fortified elevation in the attack sector of 3. Panzer-Division. The great majority of the tank losses of the three panzer divisions of II. SS-Panzerkorps were due to running-gear damage from mines. The afternoon report by 6. Armee on the battle action for 30 July stated that *Totenkopf* lost forty-eight tanks during the course of the day, but that only one was a total loss, an indication that most of the German tanks were out of action due to repairable damage of the nature that could be expected from mine hits.[12]

This is interesting because accounts of the battle by *Totenkopf* veterans describe a number of burning tanks at the northwestern edge of Hill 213.9, where the Tigers and Panzer IV tanks of I./SS-Panzer-Regiment 3 made their assault on the defensive fortifications in front of the approaches to Hill 213.9. Other accounts by veterans of the division report the destruction of SS tanks as well as T-34s and the burning tanks may thus have been from both sides.[13] Tanks hit by multiple shots from 7.62cm guns were more likely to have penetrations of armor and as a result catch fire, which often resulted in a total loss due to exploding ammunition, damage which generally destroyed a tank completely.

Whatever the type of damage, the significant numbers of tanks, that were put out of action during the day severely reduced the heavy striking power of *Totenkopf*. Eight of the division's ten Tigers were put out of action due to various reasons, mostly running-gear damage. Other vehicle losses were high also, with twelve assault guns reported out of action and eight armored cars of various types destroyed or damaged. Some of these may have been the burning "tanks" that *Totenkopf* veterans remembered.

Human losses were high as well, particularly in the panzergrenadier companies, which were reduced to twenty to twenty-five men in some cases, down from an average of about ninety just before the battle. There continued to be many casualties among the company commanders of the panzergrenadiers. Regiment *Totenkopf* lost two company commanders to severe wounds. Losses of officers were particularly severe in the companies of II./*Totenkopf*. Two company commanders, Obersturmführer Blossl and 10. Kompanie's com-

The First Day

manding officer, Untersturmführer Jensen, were killed. The officer who assumed command of 10. Kompanie, Untersturmführer Bergner, was subsequently wounded.

Overall losses for the three divisions of II. SS-Panzerkorps after the fighting on the first day totalled 915 killed, wounded or missing. Altogether, 91 tanks out of a total of 211 were either destroyed or temporarily out of commission at the end of 30 July. *Totenkopf* was the most severely battered of the three divisions of the II. SS-Panzerkorps, losing 26 officers and 468 NCOs and men either killed, wounded or missing and forty-eight of the division's tanks (including eight Tigers). There were significant losses of assault guns and light armored vehicles also. *Das Reich* lost 18 officers and 300 other ranks while losing twenty-five tanks, most of which were repairable and presumably caused by mine damage. 3. Panzer-Division's personnel losses were 5 officers and 98 men and NCOs killed, wounded or missing.[14] Only nineteen of the division's original strength of thirty-seven tanks were still running after the fighting on the first day.

The only success for II. SS-Panzerkorps on the first day of the attack in the center, had been the penetration into the Gerassimova Valley by the grenadiers of Regiment *Eicke*. The flanking attacks of 3. Panzer-Division and *Das Reich* had not done as well as had been hoped for, and as a result, *Totenkopf*'s attack was not supported well. Given the lack of success on the flanks and the strength of the Russian defenses on Hill 213.9, the attack, as executed, probably had little chance for success in any event. In regard to the manner of the commitment of *Totenkopf* against Hill 213.9, essentially from the march, it is instructive to remember a corollary to Generalmajor F. W. von Mellenthin's admonition regarding the price of failure to eliminate a Russian position immediately after it had been established: "No artillery fire, however violent and well concentrated, will wipe out a Russian bridgehead which has grown overnight."[15]

The Russians, so adept at quickly creating effective fortifications, even overnight, had been given many days to prepare a death trap for any attacker who advanced over the open ground in front of Hill 213.9. *Totenkopf* had attacked over unfamiliar, extensively mined ground without any preliminary reconnaissance, while under fire from three sides. It was not realistic to expect the division to take a heavily fortified hill manned by over a brigade of antitank guns and elements of two rifle divisions in a frontal assault under those conditions. It was a recipe for failure for II. SS-Panzerkorps and death and disaster for the men of the three panzer divisions.

FAILURE ON THE FLANKS

On the morning of the attack, *Das Reich* had deployed into two battle groups for the assault on Stepanovka and Hill 223.7, to the south of the town. By 0400 hours, the troops arrived at the assembly positions and were prepared to advance. The panzer group, whose first objective was Hill 230.9, was supported by the panzergrenadiers of 111./*Der Führer* in the armored personnel carriers, mobile elements of the *Das Reich* reconnaissance battalion and 111./SS-Artillerie-Regiment 2 (self-propelled). On the division's left flank, assigned to capture Stepanovka and Hill 203.9, SS-Panzergrenadier-Regiment *Deutschland* was reinforced by one company of engineers, two batteries of the assault gun battalion and II./SS-Artillerie-Regiment 2. The artillery of the division was reinforced by the Nebelwerfers of Weiler-Regiment 52, temporarily assigned to the SS formation. Acting as the corps reserve were the remaining two battalions of SS-Panzergrenadier-Regiment *Der Führer*, which were still moving toward the sector.

On 30 July, the battalions, under command of Obersturmbannführer Sylvester Stadler, were south of Chistyakovo, some miles from the fighting.[16] Stadler was another of the exceptional soldiers of *Das Reich*, having already won both the 1st and 2nd Class of the Iron Cross and the Knight's Cross, awarded in April 1943 for numerous actions of resourcefulness and leadership. By the end of the war, he was also awarded the Oak Leaves and Swords to the Knight's Cross. Stadler and his regiment would play a key role in the final outcome of the battle on the Mius.

At 0800 hours, the attack groups of *Das Reich* jumped off from their starting positions and advanced toward their objectives. Behind the right flank of the division and screening to the south was the remainder of the reconnaissance battalion. On the division's left, Regiment *Deutschland* crossed the rounded hills to the north of Stepanovka, supported by artillery and rocket fire from the Nebelwerfer detachment. Initially, the *Deutschland* assault group pushed forward quickly, overrunning one of its first objectives, Hill 203.9, which lay just to the northwest of Stepanovka. Quickly overcoming initial resistance, the grenadiers successfully reached the outskirts of the town, although II./*Deutschland* received fire from Soviet tanks

The First Day

hidden among the buildings of the northwest section of Stepanovka. Here the regiment encountered the first tough fighting, as the volume of enemy small-arms fire began to grow stronger. Inside the town the Russian infantry opened fire from bunkers and concealed fighting positions. The SS grenadiers immediately were involved in difficult street fighting and close combat.

After the SS men pushed farther down the streets, they came under heavy fire from small arms, machine guns and mortars, from Soviet troops firing from difficult to detect positions. They fought their way forward, assaulting fortified postions concealed in houses and buildings, which could only be knocked out in close combat. By 1050 hours, *Deutschland* was completely involved in fighting throughout the town, near Hill 203.9 and to the north of the hill.[17] Once having entered Stepanovka, the SS grenadiers became bogged down in fire from automatic weapons, snipers and small arms of the Russians infantry. There were Soviet tanks in the town as well, adding to the problems of the Germans, although in the narrow streets the Russian armor was robbed of any advantage of mobility and was vulnerable to close attack. Heinz Macher, a Knight's Cross winner during the battle for Kharkov and a veteran of the engineer company of Regiment *Deutschland*, fought on the Mius River and was wounded by Russian heavy artillery at Hill 230.9:

> We were told to attack Stepanovka on the Mius. Two platoons of No. 16 Company were placed at the disposal of 2nd Battalion. . . . In open order we climbed a gentle slope on whose other side lay the objective; Stepanovka. Just below the crest of the reverse slope was 2nd Battalion's medical post. As I passed it I called out to Dr. Axmann that he should get his bandages ready because I would be back in a quarter of an hour. He shouted back, "You're mad." . . . A few minutes later a small piece of shrapnel from a 17.2cm shell hit me in the left forearm and our platoon stretcher bearer put on a field dressing. For a scratch like that one did not abandon one's mates. . . . Five minutes later, I fell to the ground. Another fragment from a 17.2 shell had hit me. . . . This one severed the nerve in my upper arm. . . . Dr. Axmann looked quite surprised when I was brought into the aid post on a motorcycle combination.[18]

Attacking to the west of Stepanovka, the *Das Reich* panzer battle group, supported by grenadiers of III./*Der Führer*, pushed the Russians off Hill 230.9 and out of several adjacent defensive positions. The III./*Der Führer* was armored, equipped with lightly armored personnel carriers (Sd.Kfz. 251), while the other battalions of the regiment were primarily transported by truck and heavy cars. The main fortified hill (230.9) was cleared and reported to be in German hands by 1000 hours. All units reported that the resistance of the Soviets at these points was aided by artillery fire from large-caliber guns. This artillery support was probably from gun positions around Dmitrievka and other sites on the east bank of the Mius.

In this sector, too, the Russians laid extensive minefields of great depth with the result being losses of twenty to twenty-five *Das Reich* tanks due to damage from mines.[19] As had happened with *Totenkopf* in the center, the attack was delayed until the SS engineers of *Das Reich* were able to clear paths for the tanks to move through. Once the tanks penetrated the mines, the attack resumed with success. From the secured high ground near Hill 230.9, the panzers pressed on to the southeast for a distance of 1.5 kilometers. Early in the afternoon, at 1345 hours, the panzer regiment reported that a second fortified hill, referred to as the "Doppelkopfhohe," had also been successfully overrun and that the Russians were routed from their fortifications and driven back to the east.[20] The double hill (223.7) was just south of Stepanovka and northwest about two kilometers from Marinovka. Stadler's two reserve battalions of *Der Führer* were ordered to move up from their position in the rear and were on the road at Hill 214.3, northwest of Stepanovka, at 1230 hours.

In Stepanovka itself, I./ and II./Regiment *Deutschland* continued to be embroiled in a vicious stalemate of street fighting.[21] The SS grenadiers engaged in fierce house to house struggles against Soviet infantry and armored elements. This type of fighting required elimination of individual strongpoints and machine-gun nests that mutually supported each other and was a characteristically hard and slow matter. The village had been turned into a large fortified position by the Soviet soldiers who fought from under the ruins of houses or in firing positions concealed under buildings. The Russian tanks emplaced in the ruins became instant armored strongpoints around which the infantry emplaced machine guns and concealed sniper nests.

Bunkers built under or into structures were extremely hard to spot even by infantry at close quarters and difficult to identify for artillery or air strikes. As a result, support from Stukas that were called in to make attacks on the Russian positions in the town did not deliver decisive help to the embattled SS infantry. It was clear that the Russians would have to be rooted out of their fortifications by close assault one position at a time. This was, as always, a costly business in both time and casualties for the attacker. Street fighting of this nature was familiar to *Das Reich* veterans of Kharkov, where the panzer-grenadiers of the division were involved in bitter house-to-house fighting in March 1943. Fighting in the ruins of that city cost the division many men killed and wounded, and the Germans had a healthy respect for the Russians when they defended a built-up area. The Russians were masters of this type of battle, stubbornly refusing to be rooted out of their holes and bunkers and often fighting until they were killed or wounded severely enough so that they could no longer resist or escape.

The Soviets stiffened their defensive postions in the town with automatic guns and heavier infantry weapons, such as heavy mortars, that could be used effectively even in the close quarters of an urban area. By late afternoon, the bitter Russian resistance began to take its toll on the SS grenadiers. The strain of fighting and the extreme heat of the Russian summer combined to stop the weary attackers. The German soldiers, who had been on the attack since early morning with little rest, halted to recover and regroup. They had not been able to capture more than the northwest section of Stepanovka before they halted temporarily. Casualties in the grenadier companies were serious and some of the *Deutschland* companies were reduced to the strength of a platoon. The attack of Regiment *Deutschland* ground to a halt in Stepanovka.

In order to get the attack moving again, the commander of the regiment, Obersturmbannführer Heinz Harmel, who was in the town overseeing the actions of his men, brought in light armored vehicles from the reconnaissance battalion. It was hoped that the firepower from their 2cm automatic guns and 75mm infantry guns mounted on Sd.Kfz. 251 half-tracks could be used effectively against the bunkers in the town and eliminate the stubborn Soviet defenders.[22] However, even with this heavier firepower, the SS infantry remained involved in slow, tortuous street fighting.

By late afternoon, the attacks of all three divisions of II. SS-Panzerkorps in the main attack sectors slowed. On the northern flank, 3. Panzer-Division encountered the same type of wide and deep minefields that caused so much damage and delay to *Das Reich* and *Totenkopf*. The key high ground in that sector, Hill 211.5, was ringed by three belts of mines comparable to the depth of the fields placed around 213.9. Under fire, the men of the division's 39. Pionier-Abteilung entered the minefields to clear lanes through the first belt for the tanks to advance. In spite of their efforts and the removal of 300 mines, many with wooden cases, 3. Panzer's tanks could not break through the antitank defenses around the hill. After the first minefield was penetrated, the tanks reached the second belt at about 1200 hours. When the German tanks slowed at this time, trying to extricate themselves from the mine belt, the Russians made a sortie from the hill with twelve tanks that emerged from the Russian lines to counterattack the panzers.[23] This armored thrust by the Soviets forced the German tanks and engineers to pull back before lanes could be cleared through the mines of the second belt. The result was a complete loss of attack momentum, for when the armor was forced back, the infantry could not advance and the attack fizzled out.

3. Panzer-Division's armor regrouped and made a second attempt to break through the Russian line, redirecting their advance over a nearby elevation, Hill 128.1, in order to attack 211.5 from another direction. Under intense Russian defensive fire and heavy artillery shelling, this attack broke down about 600 meters in front of the main position on Hill 211.5. At the same time, antitank gun fire hit the German tanks from the northeast, originating from a concealed position south of the village of Srubna. This village was located in the ridge line of hills on the northern border of the Gerassimova Valley. The division's advance halted on a line approximately between Srubna–Peresej–Hill 211.5.[24]

At 1715 hours, the division reported that seven of its panzers were out of action due to mine damage and four others from various projectile damage. By the end of the day, the division lost a total of eighteen tanks. Considering that it began the day with only thirty-seven operational tanks, this represented losses that severely reduced its offensive striking power. Adding to the personnel and equipment losses from the Soviet ground forces were casualties from strafing and bombing attacks by groups of fifteen to twenty IL-2s. The Russian planes were in the air constantly, attacking at low level, again without interference from the Luftwaffe. The Russians evidently were able to keep their planes over the field much of the day without significant loss from either the German antiaircraft guns or German fighters. The Luftwaffe did not provide fighter cover; its operations were limited to Stuka attacks and thus could not protect the German troops from the bombs and machine guns of Soviet aircraft in any sector of the attack by II. SS-Panzerkorps on 30 July.[25]

THE ATTACK OF XVII. ARMEEKORPS

The attack of 306. Infanterie-Division encountered effective Russian resistance, stalled in heavy defensive fire from artillery and came to a halt. The division's main objective was the capture of high ground around Hill 173.4. The Russians had positioned a large number of heavy mortars and artillery there. From Hill 173.4, the Russians had good observation points from which to shell the center ridge, as well as the Gerassimova Valley and Stepanovka. For this reason, it was necessary for the Germans to control this high ground, but the weakened division required reinforcement to have any hope of success. The assault group put together by XVII. Armeekorps was made up of the Sturmabteilung from 6. Armee HQ, two battalions from 306. Infanterie-Division, two battalions from 3. Gebirgs-Division and one battalion from 335. Infanterie-Division. German intelligence estimates placed the opposing Soviet forces as being at least one and a half rifle divisions, with some supporting armor.[26] Several of the German battalions were reduced to company strength by this date and many had lost most of their officers.

Before the attack had even begun, the Germans had to repel an aggressive Russian combat patrol that probed their forward outposts in the early-morning hours of darkness. The left-flank positions of 306. Infanterie-Division stopped the Russian assault troop, a platoon of thirty to forty men, after it attempted to penetrate the front lines at about 0310 hours. Failing in their attempt to get into a German forward position, the Russian patrol was pinned down in front of the main trenchline and destroyed by mortar and artillery fire.[27]

At 0810 hours, XVII. Armeekorps began its attack. At first, the main attack group, Kampfgruppe Holm, under command of Oberst Holm, made good progress. Holm reported that at 0845 hours, the leading assault detachment, commanded by Oberleutnant Ebe, was moving forward quickly, as was 579. Grenadier-Regiment (306. Infanterie-Division). Within the hour, the attack pushed farther toward the east, spearheaded by the progress made by Assault Detachment Ebe. The advance of the German infantry attracted the attention of Russian aircraft which bombed and strafed elements of the German attacks forces at mid-morning. However, the air attacks were evidently not able to seriously hold up the advance. By 1040 hours, Ebe's group reached a ravine about 2.5 kilometers southeast of Peradrievo. Here they were shelled heavily from guns located in the area to the southwest of the village. The artillery forced a halt in further offensive progress of the lead German units. Holm reported that due to the strength of the enemy artillery, further progress was not likely until the attack by 3. Panzer-Division could overrun the gun positions or force their withdrawal.[28]

In spite of the strength of Soviet artillery in its sector, the Feld-Ausbildungs-Battalion (Field Training Battalion) of 3. Gebirgs-Division took a ridge of high ground just to the south of Peradrievjo. Around these positions near Peradrievjo and the terrain to the south, Kampfgruppe Holm consolidated and prepared to renew its advance at the time when 3. Panzer-Division was able to push past Hill 211.5 and attack toward the village. Moving forward again, Assault Detachment Ebe regained a section of the old German main line of defence to the south of Peradrievjo, near a ravine just east of the river. At this time, unclear battle reports by neighboring German units led to a mistaken conclusion by the German corps command. It was incorrectly reported that the Field Training Battalion of 3. Gebirgs-Division, took a hill just three kilometers north of Dmitrievka on the flank of Assault Detachment Ebe. The attack seemed to be going better than could have been expected.

A battalion of 579. Grenadier-Regiment was able to move forward with a genuine success, reaching a hill just northeast of Peradrievo by noon. At this point, however, just as the Germans had made progress at several points, the attack began to break down. Oberleutnant Ebe's assault group was overrun and disorganized by a strong Russian counterattack. Communication was lost with Ebe and his unit, and Holm reported at 1245 hours that the situation was then unclear to his front. Shortly before 1300 hours, disturbing reports confirmed that things had gone badly for Ebe and his men. Divisional artillery

The First Day

observers reported that a strong enemy counterattack was advancing from the area where the battle group should have been. The Russian counterattack originated from the southwest of a ravine near Peradrievjo that had been taken by Assault Detachment Ebe earlier in the day.

The Russian counterattack had collided with Holm's spearhead and scattered the attackers. In the fighting, Oberleutnant Ebe, as well as another officer, were killed. The loss of these officers resulted in the collapse of the German advance in that area and the disintegration of the assault group. The situation broke down further when the Field Training Battalion of 3. Gebirgs-Division, which had established itself on the flank of Assault Detachment Ebe, lost contact with that unit entirely when it gave way due to the Russian counterattack.[29] The disintegration of Assault Detachment Ebe created a gap which Soviet infantry exploited quickly with a penetration to the west. The surviving remnants of Ebe's command were either driven to the west by the power of the Russian attack or captured. The Russians aggressively reacted and quickly pushed more troops into the sector in order to expand the gap. The confusion over exactly what was happening helped reduce the effectiveness and quickness of German reaction to this development.

Observing the progress of the Soviet advance, the artillery observers of the division reported that the Russian counterattack was at a point three kilometers southeast of Peradrievo and moving to the northwest. By specific order of 306. Infanterie-Division's commander, 6. Armee's Sturmabteilung was issued orders to halt the Russian counterattack at all costs. It promptly established a blocking position and dug in near Peradrievo to await the Russian force that had scattered Assault Detachment Ebe. After a sharp fight, the Russian counterattack was stopped by the German battalion, with the aid of good artillery support.[30]

After this situation became stabilized, the Ia of 3. Panzer-Division informed XVII. Armeekorps that it planned another attack for 1840 hours, with the objective being Hill 211.5 and the village of Grushevy. In addition to its own artillery, the panzer division requested the support of elements of the artillery of 306. Infanterie-Division. It was hoped that this effort, if successful, would enable Holm to get moving again, as all progress had slowed markedly by the middle of the afternoon.

Later in the day, another Russian attack hit the positions of the training battalion on the shoulder of the gap formed after the disintegration of Ebe's battle group, but the attack was weak. It seemed uncoordinated and was turned back by the Germans without difficulty. After the Soviet assault melted away, fighting in the sector tapered off, the Germans digging in to hold their meager gains and the Russians exhausted by the heavy casualties that were inflicted on the rifle divisions during their counterattacks against Ebe and Holm. Although a Russian breakthrough was avoided, the attack of XVII. Armeekorps had failed. This was due, at least in part, to the lack of success in 3. Panzer-Division's attack zone. The failure of 3. Panzer to make a decisive penetration at Hill 211.5 allowed the Russians to launch multiple counterattacks against the XVII. Armeekorps units. XVII. Armeekorps HQ ordered Holm to dig in, consolidate his positions and regroup overnight in order to prepare to support the renewal of 3. Panzer-Division's attack on the next day. II. SS-Panzerkorps scheduled the attack to begin again at 0530 hours on 31 July. XVII. Armeekorps command ordered the majority of the artillery of 306. Infanterie-Division to prepare to support the attack of 3. Panzer-Division on the next day.

XXIV. PANZERKORPS ON THE FIRST DAY

In the southern sector of the battlefield, the Germans were able to make small penetrations on the first day although neither XXIV. Panzerkorps nor XXIX. Armeekorps reached their assigned objectives during the first day of fighting. The XXIV. Panzerkorps objectives were the capture of Kalinovka and protection of the right flank of the attack by *Das Reich*'s armored group (SS-Panzer-Regiment 2 and III. [armored] Regiment *Der Führer*) south of Stepanovka.

Between them, the two army divisions had fifty-five tanks, twenty-eight assault guns, and seventeen self-propelled antitank guns. The antitank guns were 7.5cm PaK 40s mounted on either converted Czech tank or modified Panzer II chassis. In addition to the self-propelled guns, the two divisions had twenty-four towed (truck or half-track) 7.5cm or 7.62cm antitank guns (the 7.62cm guns were captured and modified Russian guns) available. All of the fifty-five tanks of the two divisions were Panzer III and IVs, of which twenty-six were Panzer IVs equipped with the long-barrelled, high-velocity 75mm gun.[31] Although the numbers of tanks available to XXIV. Panzerkorps were much less than the strength of II. SS-Panzerkorps, it was assigned attack areas that were not defended as strongly as in the center, where three quarters of the Soviet antitank guns were arrayed around Hill 213.9 and Stepanovka. The only Soviet armored formation in this attack sector was the remnants of 2nd Guards Mechanized Corps. Out of a total number of 160 artillery batteries located in the entire bridgehead area, the Russian command had grouped 31 of its batteries between Stepanovka and Hill 213.9 and 21 batteries in the Gerassimova-Dmitrievka sector.[32] The remaining guns were spread out in support of the rest of Tolbukhin's three armies. This reflected the importance that the Soviet command placed on the holding of Hill 213.9, Hill 211.5, and Stepanovka, which formed the center of their defensive position.

In the first hours of the attack, which began at 0810 hours after preparation by division and corps artillery, the tanks of 16. Panzergrenadier-Division, supported by the infantry of 156. Panzergrenadier-Regiment, made their way through a small wooded area to the north of Hill 196.0. The attack group succeeded in breaking through the Russian lines at this point. It then turned north, toward Hill 196.0, which was situated just north of Kalinovka and several kilometers southwest of Marinovka. The division cleared the area west of the hill with elements of the engineer battalion supported by a company of light armored vehicles of the division's reconnaissance battalion. Hill 196.0 was captured by the division after a brief fight, after which the attackers pushed on to join forces with the spearhead units of 23. Panzer-Division. That division also made good progress early in its attack.

The tanks of the panzer division's 201. Panzer-Regiment, with infantry in support, quickly moved through the area north of Saur Mogilsky, turned south and by 0930 hours arrived at a ravine 1.2 kilometers south of the village. From there, the attack quickly continued, with I./Panzer-Regiment 201, under command of Hauptmann Alber, pushing through Garany. Alber, without delay, drove on to Hill 196.0, where he linked, up with the elements of 16. Panzergrenadier-Division already on the hill. The panzergrenadiers, following the tanks at some distance, cleared out the remaining Russian troops still in Garany and secured a wooded area north of Saur Mogilsky. With the support of a number of assault guns, the panzergrenadiers were able to destroy Soviet units amounting to the strength of a regiment in the area north of the village and the attack seemed about to quickly reach its first objective for the day. However, at that time, the German armor had a disastrous encounter with Soviet tanks and antitank guns at Saur Mogilsky as a result of allowing itself to become separated from the infantry.[33] A number of Russian tanks were hidden in concealed firing positions among the huts and rough buildings of the village. The German armor approached Saur Mogilsky without waiting for the infantry to catch up with them and failed to detect the Soviet armor. The Russian tank commanders waited until the panzers were at close range before opening fire. As a result, the panzer regiment quickly suffered heavy losses of tanks and assault guns within the first moments after the Soviets opened fire. The surviving tanks of the regiment pulled back from the village, took shelter in a wooded area and waited for the infantry of the panzergrenadier regiments to arrive and clear the Russians out of the village.

At 0900 hours, infantry of 126. Panzergrenadier-Regiment moved up and assaulted the north edge of Saur Mogilsky. Shortly afterwards, other elements of the regiment fought their way into the houses on the west edge of the village. The Russians fought back with great determination and the fighting turned bitter as Soviet and German infantry fought for the possession of the small village. The houses and buildings were the scene of extremely hard close-quarters fighting as houses changed hands repeatedly, both sides fighting bitterly to secure the village. The panzer regiment pushed on toward the east and by 1130 hours reached the vicinity of Garany.

While the fight in Saur Mogilsky continued, spearheads of the two divisions consolidated their link-up in the area to the south and west of Garany at 1225 hours. The resulting encirclement trapped elements of five Soviet rifle divisions in a pocket west of Garany. The tiny hamlet of Semenovsky was cleared of Soviet troops by 1345. House-to-house fighting continued in Saur Mogilsky into the early-evening hours. At 1845 hours, 23. Panzer's armored group pushed towards the east with a few supporting grenadiers and attacked Hill 202.0. This hill was only a few kilometers southeast of Marinovka and just west of another of the fortified Russian hill strongpoints, Hill 203.4, which guarded the southern approaches to Marinovka. From Hill 203.4, the Russians had dominant high ground observation and could look down on anyone who attempted to penetrate the Olkhovchik Valley.

The First Day

Elements of 128. Panzergrenadier-Regiment assembled north of Saur Mogilsky in order to clean the Russians out of a ravine that lay south of the village. The division command evidently felt it was necessary to deal with these troops in order to secure lines of communication and supply to the spearhead units at Hill 196.0 and Garany which had halted in that area. With the involvement of the panzergrenadiers of both divisions in fighting for possession of villages and supply routes, and the armor halted, the momentum of the attack came to a stop. It is not clear to what extent these Russian infantry elements actually constituted a serious threat.

However, when XXIV. Panzerkorps halted its advance on the right flank of II. SS-Panzerkorps and failed to prevent Soviet elements from massing against the advance of *Das Reich*, it contributed to the failure of the attack in the center by II. SS-Panzerkorps.[34] XXIV. Panzerkorps allowed itself to become involved in reducing the pocket of trapped Soviet infantry west of Garany rather than penetrating the Soviet defenses on the right of *Das Reich* Although the town of Kalinovka was taken, due to the failure of XXIV. Panzerkorps to continue its advance, the II. SS-Panzerkorps' attack advanced with an open right flank. *Das Reich* was continually attacked on that flank during the first day by Soviet tanks and infantry. *Das Reich*'s armored group reached Hill 223.7, which was south of Stepanovka and thus was considerably east of the Garany pocket. The 23. Panzer-Division's failure to close up with the SS elements allowed the Russians to devote their full attention to stopping *Das Reich*'s mobile elements.

There may have been a simple reason for the lack of offensive progress on 30 July in XXIV. Panzerkorps' sector. The 23. Panzer-Division's panzer regiment had suffered severe tank and assault gun losses when it blundered into the Soviet ambush at Saur Mogilsky. Although 16. Panzergrenadier-Division reported that it still had eighteen operational tanks, a loss of only a few vehicles, 23. Panzer-Division had lost nearly half of its tank strength by the afternoon. Out of the thirty-seven tanks it had on the evening of 29 July, just twenty were left by late in the day. The division had only two assault guns left.[35] These losses, coming after the carnage of the attack on Hill 213.9 on 18 July and ten days of hard fighting, may have sapped the aggressiveness of the division. The failure to support the attack in the center was not balanced by any great tactical benefit derived from clearing out the pocket.

The encirclement of the Soviet rifle divisions west of Garany resulted in the destruction of eighteen antitank guns, many mortars, and forty-four antitank rifles, in addition to a number of trucks, large quantities of small arms and a few artillery pieces. Some enemy infantry and artillery units were observed to withdraw from the neighboring areas although, as a whole, the Russians were not forced to make any significant withdrawals east of the encirclement area. The destruction of Soviet infantry, regardless of their threat to XXIV. Panzerkorps supply routes, did not outweigh the consequences of the failure to close with the right flank of II. SS-Panzerkorps. This union was necessary in order to attack toward the Olkhovchik with the maximum possible concentration of armor. The resulting relatively narrow penetration by *Das Reich* did not produce a decisive breakthrough nor force any significant retreat of the Soviet defending forces. The few Soviet formations that did attempt to withdraw and regroup on the eastern bank of the Mius were spotted by a large number of Stukas as they attempted to cross the bridges in the area south of Dmitrievka. The Russian units, caught in the open, were hit very hard by the German planes.[36]

The last operations of the two divisions of XXIV. Panzerkorps for 30 July began in the late afternoon and continued throughout the night as substantial panzergrenadier and artillery elements of both divisions remained occupied with the destruction of the Soviet forces inside the Garany pocket. Saur Mogilsky was finally cleared of Russians by 1835 hours after infantry elements of 23. Panzer-Division eliminated the last village strongpoints and forced the survivors to surrender. Earlier, the village of Semenovsky was cleared of all Russian troops at 1345.[37] Supported by the corps artillery, the reduction of the encirclement itself lasted until early the next morning when the last Russians surrendered or escaped. The final count of Russian prisoners taken out of the pocket reached more than 3,000, although many had escaped during the night, filtering through German lines in the dark. Estimates of the dead were recorded as being substantially higher than the number of prisoners taken.

Large numbers of Soviet troops, individuals or in small groups, made their way into Stepanovka during the night in attempts to reach the Russian forces fighting there. Once into the town, they had to pass through *Das Reich*'s positions to reach their own lines. Some of these

The First Day

infiltrators inevitably bumped into the SS grenadiers in the town, and as a result, there was much confused fighting in the darkened streets between the Russians and elements of Regiment *Deutschland.*

While the clearing of the pocket was still in progress, the orders for the next day were received. The mission orders issued by XXIV. Panzerkorps for 31 July gave 16. Panzergrenadier-Division the task of advancing from Kalinovka, after which it was to drive to the river in support of the attack by XXIX. Armeekorp's 294. Infanterie-Division on Hill 168.5. The 23. Panzer-Division was to attack with its main force and take Hill 202.0, regroup there and advance on Hill 203.4, just to the south of Marinovka. This hill was another of the fortified hill positions that buttressed the Soviet defensive line. Other elements of the division were to mop up pockets of resistance remaining in the rear areas.[38]

XXIX. ARMEEKORPS

On the southern border of the Soviet penetration, attacking in a northeast direction, the main battle group of XXIX. Armeekorps had a relatively successful day of operations, in contrast to the other sectors of attack. This assault group consisted primarily of elements of 294. Infanterie-Division, reinforced by battalions from three other divisions and 15. Luftwaffe-Felddivision. In the valley across from this sector of the attack, 6. Armee intelligence estimated that the Soviet forces defended with a strength of two battalions at the point of attack. Soviet strength in the entire corps sector was estimated at four rifle divisions, in addition to some elements of 2nd Guards Mechanized Corps.

Mobile firepower for the assault was furnished by six assault guns, which provided close fire support for the infantry and supplemented the corps artillery and mortar detachments. The assault guns were assigned to III./514. Grenadier-Regiment (294. Infanterie-Division), which was to carry out the primary attack. A battalion of Luftwaffe troops, from Luftwaffe-Jäger-Regiment 30, was assigned to support the operations of the lead battalion.[39] The first objective of the main attack was to penetrate the defenses of the Olkhovchik on its western edge, at the southern end of the valley. After breaking into the Olkhovchik, the battle group was to advance to Hill 168.5 and, from that point, penetrate to the Mius west bank. The supporting battalions would mop up pockets of resistance after the initial breakthrough and establish defensive positions in the gap. In this manner, XXIX. Armeekorps was to seal off the southern exit of the Olkhovchik and prevent the escape of Russians driven south to the river by the attack of II. SS-Panzerkorps.

At 0810 hours, the attack began after artillery preparation by corps and divisional artillery. The reinforced battalion deployed behind the advancing assault guns and moved over the steppe. Almost immediately, the first mortar shells burst around them and machine-gun fire rattled in the distance. The battery of assault guns from Sturmgeschütz-Abteilung 243 furnished excellent fire support to the attack, which destroyed sixteen Russian antitank guns by the evening of 30 July. The main German assault group carried out a successful penetration of the first line of the Soviet defenses. At 1930 hours, the main assault group overran two Russian rifle battalions at the point of attack and captured 650 Russian prisoners, breaking into the Olkhovchik Valley. By the end of the day, a total of 750 captured Soviet soldiers were marching out of the battlefield from this sector alone. After this first penetration, the Germans pushed on across the valley floor toward Hill 168.5. Casualties began to mount as mortar shells and small-arms fire took their toll. After heavy artillery was brought to bear on the German advance, the Russian infantry began to fight with more resolve and many had to be rooted out of their holes one by one. Wounded Russian soldiers, left for dead or undetected, fired on the Germans from behind until they were silenced by a grenade or a burst of machine-gun fire.

The assault detachment losses were heavy. The casualties of 294. Infanterie-Division alone were 600 men, 150 being dead or missing, and the remaining 450 wounded. This number of wounded taxed the capabilities of the division's medical personnel and aid stations.[40] Many of these casualties were caused by heavy artillery fire from Kuibyshevo and the environs of the town. In spite of the efforts of German artillery and Stuka attacks, the Soviet gun positions in and around the town remained in action throughout the day without serious interruption. Although at many times the Soviet artillery seemed poorly directed and was not particularly effective in defensive operations requiring observed fire adjustments, it was dangerous when on target. Rocket attacks were also particularly feared because of the amount of high explosive that covered the impact area. While the attack in the center progressed steadily across the floor of the valley, the attacks were also going well in other sectors, although the losses were serious there as well.

A reinforced regiment of 336. Infanterie-Division fought its way forward through stout resistance. The regiment was supported by a battalion of infantry from 17. Infanterie-Division. The attack group in this sector was able to capture a small hill to the east of the village of Yelizavetinsky, a ruined collection of huts and shattered buildings four kilometers west of the north edge of Kuibyshevo. The village was reduced to little more than smoking ruins after the fierce fighting for its possession.

Fighting on the right of the main attack, II./95. Grenadier-Regiment (17. Infanterie-Division) also fought its way into the valley and battled slowly up the southern end, making steady progress against the Soviet infantry. The Russians were driven out of their positions and withdrew slowly back across the valley floor toward the east. Stubborn resistance of several rear-guard detachments delayed the German advance and hindered pursuit of the retreating Soviets.

At the end of the day, after hard fighting at all points, the infantry of XXIX. Armeekorps had made substantial gains in the southern end of the Olkhovchik Valley, although they had not yet been able to cross the valley and seal it off. The main objective, Hill 168.5, was not taken. This hill was strategically located in the center of the eastern edge of the valley mouth, which opened up on the banks of the Mius approximately two kilometers north of Kuibyshevo. It was around this hill that the blocking position was to be established. Without closing off the southern exit of the valley, the Russian troops pushed south or east of the attack of II. SS-Panzerkorps could reach the Mius and escape over the river to Dmitrievka. The wide valley also served as a main line of communication to Marinovka and Kalinovka and the Russian troops holding the center of the penetration. Given the lack of success attacking the fortified hills at other points, it would appear that XXIX. Armeekorps' sector would have been a more suitable area for the use of armor considering the flat terrain and lack of strongpoints studded with antitank gun nests. Given the success of an infantry attack supported by only a handful of assault guns, it would be logical to assume that had Hollidt committed strong panzer forces on the extreme southern flank on the first day, Hill 168.5 might have been taken early in the fighting. Although the German infantry made good progress on 30 July, it was at a heavy cost and did not close the valley to the Russians. What effect the securing of the valley might have had on the course of the subsequent fighting remains open to speculation.

AN INDECISIVE FIRST DAY
Taken as a whole, the first day of the attack was not a great success for 6. Armee although a total of 3,000 Russians were captured in XXIV. Panzerkorps' area of operations alone. The army reported that 16 Soviet tanks, 23 guns of various calibers, 112 antitank guns, and many small arms had been captured or destroyed.[41] However, inflicting casualties and material losses were not the primary objectives of the attack, which depended on speed in order to achieve maximum success. Without quick penetrations at all points, the Soviets were not cut off from the river. As a result, the Russian command could bring up reinforcements at will and withdraw over the river only if necessary. It was up to 6. Armee's command to recognize this and plan accordingly for the next day. However, Hollidt made few adjustments and repeated the assault on the Soviet center.

The main effort on the center ridge had not gone well, primarily due to the failure to successfully eliminate the flanking gun positions on either flank of the attack sector of *Totenkopf*. On the right of Hausser's attack, the inability to quickly take Stepanovka, in particular the eastern sections of the town, contributed significantly to the failure to take the key position on the center ridge, Hill 213.9. The strong Soviet antitank gun position east of Stepanovka commanded the center ridge and caused great difficulties for the SS panzers with its heavy 7.62cm guns. Regiment *Deutschland* fought on into the night, the SS grenadiers making temporary gains only to be driven back by Soviet counterattacks. House-to-house fighting continued into the night, as stragglers from the Garany pocket made their way stealthily through the town, contributing to confusion as the Germans often had to fight an enemy that appeared from the rear. A stream of fresh Soviet rifle battalions continued to enter the town on its east edge, moving up through the Olkhovchik Valley. The Russians remained able to bring up plentiful reinforcements, both men and tanks, in the relative safety of the valley floor, which could not be directly observed by the Germans due to Russian occupation of the surrounding high ground. The Soviets could move without serious interference from German artillery. The constant commitment of fresh troops allowed the Soviets to continually counterattack positions of Regiment *Deutschland*. When the SS grenadiers were able to fight their way forward, capturing a key house or strongpoint, Russians immediately attacked in attempts to regain their position. The regiment was hard pressed just to hold on to its small gains in the western half of the town and fight off the Russian attempts to throw it out of Stepanovka.

South of the town, the panzer group of *Das Reich*, with III./Regiment *Der Führer* (armored) still in support, also found itself at a halt and remained unable to break into the Olkhovchik. At 2015 hours, the division, according to orders received from II. SS-Panzerkorps, ordered SS-Obersturmbannführer Stadler's I./ and II./*Der Führer*, the corps reserve, along with elements of the division's reconnaissance battalion, to move toward the front and take up a position along a Hill 202.0–Hill 223.7 line. The attack at this point ended with the coming of darkness although the fighting in Stepanovka could plainly be heard toward the north. The night was to be spent in assembling the reserve for use at a favorable time and repairing damaged tanks.

In the Gerassimova Valley, Regiment *Eicke* continued to fight off the inevitable Soviet night infiltrations and reconnaissance in force. As expected, the German positions were allowed no rest but were probed during the night by battalion strength attacks supported by tanks. Small groups of T-34s rolled out of the dark followed by Soviet infantry firing automatic weapons and hurling grenades. In bitter fighting, the German troops fought off all attempts to drive them out of the valley. Russian planes attacked the Germans during the night, swooping in out of the night sky to drop bombs and attempt to strafe the German positions. Unable to bomb accurately in the dark, however, the Russian air attacks accomplished little more than to keep the SS grenadiers on edge.

On the center ridge, Regiment *Totenkopf* and the surviving tanks of SS-Panzer-Regiment 3 withdrew from the approaches of Hill 213.9 after the last attack failed, moving back to Removsky Gruse, northwest of the hill. In the panzergrenadier regiment, due to its heavy losses, particularly in company-grade officers and NCOs, it was necessary to reorganize and consolidate. Meanwhile, under cover of darkness, the tank recovery and repair company of the division worked without stop to remove crippled tanks from the battlefield and to repair those with minor damage in order to return them to action. Survivors from tank crews of the panzers that had been knocked out during the day crept out with the repair crews to search for their dead or to provide security.

Because of the failure to secure its flanks, the main attack force of *Totenkopf* at Hill 213.9 had been halted in front of the hill by Soviet mines, antitank guns and artillery. The tanks of *Totenkopf*'s panzer regiment had been forced by the plan of action ordered by 6. Armee, to attack down a constricted corridor, which by its nature severely limited the panzer regiment's ability to maneuver. This tactically unsound commitment of armor took away the primary tactical weapon of armor on the attack, its mobility. It exposed the German tanks to antitank gun fire from three sides while advancing over terrain with limited cover. The minefields channeled the attack, funneling the panzers into killing zones covered by the Russian Pakfronts.

As a result, the attack on the center ridge greatly reduced the tank strength of II. SS-Panzerkorps, although most of the tanks were able to eventually return to action. Most of the losses were caused by mine damage and only one panzer was a total loss. The attack had been sent forward without time to sufficiently reconnoiter the approaches of the divisional objectives or to make significant preliminary mine removal efforts. Once the tanks were halted in the minefields and forced to maneuver into cover by the Soviet antitank guns and artillery, any possible momentum was lost. In the face of the weight of artillery, mortar and small-arms fire that the Russians poured on the attackers, no success could be expected on the following day utilizing similar tactics. The supporting grenadiers were not able to fight their way into the defensive system and delays caused by the minefields exposed the German tanks to dangerous antitank gun fire. After pulling back in the afternoon, the men of the division realized how many of their comrades had been killed or wounded during the vicious fighting.

The SS panzergrenadier regiments had already been weakened considerably by the loss of unreplaceable company- or battalion-grade officers and experienced noncommissioned officers during "Citadel." Many of the men who took over these command positions were still new to their commands on 30 July due to the short time that had elapsed since their withdrawal out of the Kursk salient. Almost immediately after being withdrawn from the Psel area, the SS divisions had to prepare for the transport to the Mius, which did not allow time or opportunity for either extensive reorganization or training. In the short time between the withdrawal and arrival in 6. Armee's area, hardly any replacements had arrived and the few that trickled in were mainly those soldiers who returned after recovery from minor wounds. Many of these new officers were killed or wounded in the fighting on the Mius.

However, in spite of the first day's lack of success, heavy casualties and tank losses, 6. Armee did not change its tactics on the next day. On the evening of 30 July, it ordered II. SS-Panzerkorps to force the issue by making identical frontal assaults over the same ground on the morning of 31 July regardless of the strength of the Soviet positions in the center. *Totenkopf* was to attack over the same killing ground of the center ridge with its panzers and to once more try to penetrate the defenses of Hill 213.9. Regiment *Eicke*, in the Gerassimova, was to continue its efforts to clear the valley of Russian infantry forces and reach the Mius east of Dmitrievka.

Das Reich's objectives also remained the same. Regiment *Deutschland* was ordered to fight its way through the ruins, push the Russians out of Stepanovka and neutralize the gun positions east of the town. 3. Panzer-Division and 306. Infanterie-Division would resume their attacks on Hill 211.5 and the range of elevations east of that hill. In the south, XXIV. Panzerkorps was to drive east, into the Olkhovchik, with its primary mission the protection of the right or southern flank of *Das Reich*'s advance. In an odd parallel to the failure of III. Panzerkorps to secure the SS division's right flank south of Prochorovka on 12 July, once again a supporting attack by army panzer divisions would fail. This left *Das Reich* vulnerable to attacks by 2nd Guards Mechanized Corps from both the front and the right flank on 31 July.

CHAPTER 7

Deadlock

Totenkopf division commander, SS-Brigadeführer Herman Priess, decided to make another attempt to take Hill 213.9 in the early hours of 31 July while it was still dark, in hopes of catching the Soviets by surprise. Having failed to overrun the Russians in a daylight frontal attack, Priess hoped to avoid the smothering Russian artillery and mortar fire, attempting to utilize surprise to compensate for lack of numbers. An assault detachment was formed and assembled quietly. The German troops crept forward using narrow lanes through the minefields, past burnt-out tanks, the dead and wrecked equipment. They were able to approach the Russian forward positions without being detected. There was no artillery preparation as that would have warned the Russians that something was in the wind. At 0100 hours, the *Totenkopf* grenadiers launched a violent assault on the hill. SS troopers suddenly appeared out of the darkness, hurling grenades into bunkers and firing pits, leaping into the earthworks with machine pistols and spades. The forward strongpoints and bunkers erupted with automatic-weapons fire and the sounds of close combat and hand-to-hand fighting. At the instant it was certain that the assault troops were inside the Russian position, artillery and the SS Nebelwerfer batteries (rocket launchers) laid down blankets of fire on secondary positions of the Russian fortifications, attempting to interdict probable areas of assembly in order to disrupt Russian counterattacks.

Although surprise was successfully achieved in the initial assault, the Russians reacted quickly and were able to lay down artillery fire on their own positions. The sudden storm of high explosive thundering down on them forced the German assault teams to take cover before reaching the main line of defence. This quick response by the Soviet artillery doomed the attack to failure because the Germans could not move over the open ground between the forward trenches and fighting holes and penetrate to the next line of defense.

The Soviets lost no time bringing up strong infantry reserves, and the troops that had been routed out of the frontline positions by the surprise attack soon regained their composure. When the reserve units joined them, they began to aggressively move against the German flanks with attacks launched from communication trenches. Having lost the element of surprise and suddenly confronted with fully alerted defenders, the German attack broke down about 500 meters in front of the main defensive positions.[1] Heavy automatic-weapons fire swept over the trenches and mortar barrages began to range in on the German positions. Faced with this development, it was apparent that the attack had failed. In order to avoid being surrounded and destroyed, the SS assault teams withdrew back into the darkness from which they had come.

Although this attack was not successful, the attention of the Russians was diverted from other areas along the front. During the assault on the hill, *Totenkopf* engineer units were again hard at work under cover of darkness, removing more mines from the minefields located in the open ground leading to the hill. During the course of the night and early morning, 2,000 wooden-cased mines were removed from the northwest edge of the slope.

However, the now alerted Russians discovered this activity and small-arms fire and mortar shells began to hit some of the areas where the engineers were at work. More casualties were inflicted on the engineer companies. The commander of 1./SS-Pionier-Abteilung 3, SS-Obersturmführer Bachtler, was killed, and two section leaders, Oberscharführer Baunigartel and Oberscharführer Martini were wounded, Martini later dying of his wounds.[2] However, in spite of their losses, the SS engineers cleared lanes for the panzers to attack again with the dawn of the new day.

THE SECOND DAY OF THE COUNTERATTACK

After pulling back from the initial early-morning assault, Regiment *Totenkopf* regrouped in order to advance again following morning artillery and Stuka attacks on the hill. At 0915 hours, the entire strength of II. SS-Panzerkorps artillery began a forty-five-minute preparation fire against targets on the hill and identified or suspected strongpoints. To the east, over the high ground and hilltops that bordered the east edge of the Gerassimova Valley, a flight of

Stukas first gathered high in the air, then one after the other made their steep characteristic dives to bomb Soviet positions. Soon the Russian trenches were marked by the smoke and dust of the explosions of the bombs and shells. At the same time as the German artillery battered the forward slope, Nebelwerfer rockets screamed down on the crest of the hill. It was impossible to shell the rear areas or crest of the hill with precision or adjusted fires because the Germans did not possess observation positions with line of sight to the reverse slope of the hill.

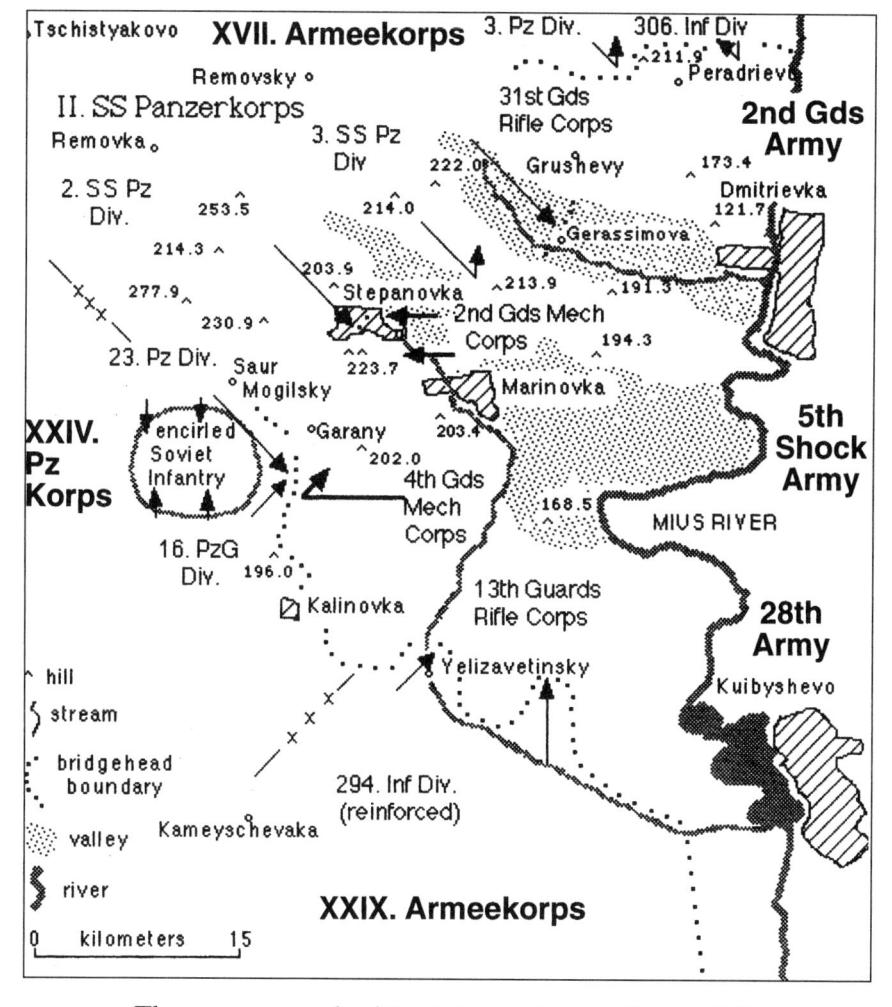

The counterattack of II. SS-Panzerkorps, 31 July 1943.

At 1000 hours, the tanks of the division, followed by widely spaced infantry, began the next attack, behind a rolling barrage. The attack advanced just in front of the falling shells, following the artillery as closely as possible. The veteran SS grenadiers knew that the closer they could move behind the moving wall of high explosives, the better. Ideally, the Germans wanted to be as close as possible to the Soviet trenches when the artillery lifted so that they could be in the position before the Russians had time to rush out of their bunkers and man their machine-gun and firing positions. While this occasionally resulted in casualties from their own artillery fire, veteran troops accepted this as a price less bitter than walking into withering defensive fire as a result of advancing too far behind the artillery. It was of utmost importance to have experienced artillerymen firing accurately, laying their concentrations of shells with precision and lifting the barrage in coordination with the infantry attack progress. Efficient radio communication was an absolute necessity due to the unforseen events of battle such as delays or unexpectedly quick advances. The attack had been shifted slightly to the northeast in hopes of finding mine belts that were not as wide or dense as those already experienced. Former SS-Unterscharführer Stettner, a veteran of the panzer regiment, recalled the attack:

> This time we attacked on the left of the hill and past the minefields of yesterday.... The grenadiers moved behind us. There was heavy enemy fire directed against the advance through the head high corn and sunflower fields. Enemy batteries threw their shells into the midst of the attack spearhead. Mortar fire tore gaps in the ranks of the advancing Grenadier companies. Everywhere fountains of earth rose into the air.[3]

Another *Totenkopf* panzer regiment veteran, Obersharführer Feichtner of 1./SS-Panzer-Regiment 3, remembered the second day of the attack on Hill 213.9: "We fought forward meter by meter. We got almost to hand grenade range of the Russian main position."[4]

The attack moved forward slowly, again with great difficulty in the face of heavy Russian defensive fire from small arms and artillery. The artillery and mortar fire finally forced the SS grenadiers to go to ground after they had gained only 200 meters. The attack was reported to be about 300 meters north of the hill itself when it slowed. At this point, the attackers on Hill 213.9 fought their way past the vast fields of corn and sunflowers that had presented so many problems for both grenadiers and tankers. The dense vegetation effectively concealed the Soviet fighting positions until the German soldiers advanced to point-blank range, at which time the Russian machine gunners opened fire with devastating effect. Mines were also easily concealed among the stalks of the plants, which complicated their detection and removal. Antitank gun positions were nearly invisible.

Such terrain greatly favored the defender, as each Soviet defensive position could mark out an assigned field of fire and cover it with a wall of mortar or automatic-weapons fire without it being necessary to see the advancing attackers. The Russian mortar detachments and artillery batteries had worked out coordinates for fire missions on likely avenues of approach and assembly. Antitank guns were sighted to provide flanking fire against advancing tanks. By contrast, the SS grenadiers had to push through the shell bursts and torrents of bullets seething at them from unseen origins, unable to locate the enemy until the survivors were right on top of them. The corn and sunflower fields covered many of the hill approaches like a featureless green sea. Until the German attack pushed through these fields in front of the hill, they were handicapped in coordination of fire support from the artillery or air.

The Soviet air force again appeared over the battlefield in large numbers, bombing and strafing the German advance as it fought its way toward the hill. It is interesting to contrast the effect that the Russian planes had on German operations with the well-documented effects of Allied air power in the West during and after Normandy. In France, during 1944–45, the Germans had great difficulty moving at all in the daylight. It often proved impossible for the Germans to conduct routine movement or supply operations during the day with the Allied fighter-bombers overhead. Attacks out in the open were often out of the question.

However, while 6. Armee and II. SS-Panzerkorps combat reports mention Soviet planes being active all over the battlefield from the first day on, it did not prevent the Germans from attacking during daylight hours at any time. The vast majority of the German tank losses were attributed by their own reports to be from mines, antitank guns or Soviet tanks and not from the Russian planes. Given the numbers of Soviet planes that were reported to be over the field virtually at all times of the day and night, this is hard to understand. It may have been due to difficulties in communication between ground troops and the Russian planes, which would drastically limit effectiveness of air support because it could not be directed to key points at the critical time. Given the lack of radio communication between Soviet tank commanders and individual tanks, which was not corrected until late in the war, this is conceivable. Whatever the lack of effectiveness can be attributed to, it was probably not due to efforts of German Flak units as very few Russian aircraft were reported shot down by the divisions. It is possible that while not actually shooting down Soviet planes, German antiaircraft fire may have been strong enough to force Soviet planes to avoid attacking key areas or prevented them from getting close enough to cause damage.

Tank commander Stettner described the panzer assault from the point where it left the corn and sunflower fields on the approaches to Hill 213.9:

> Before us was the Russian field position. We pushed the Russians out and took some of the enemy trenches. I moved forward. We're hit by an antitank gun round. Then we were hit again. Our tank caught fire. Nothing to do but get out! My gunner and loader were able to get out quickly. I received a couple of small burns. I heard my other two comrades, the driver and the radioman, who did not get out in time, as they burned to death in the blazing panzer. The Pak shot must have penetrated the frontal plate. We then worked our way to the rear.[5]

In the first minutes of the attack, the SS grenadiers pushed beyond the outpost positions and cleared the first line of positions on the hill. The tanks of the division, however, were again quickly struck by a hail of antitank gun fire. The Soviet Pakfronts used excellent fire discipline in directing their shells at individual tanks until they were knocked out, disabled or forced to seek cover. The tank losses from the numerous Russian antitank positions and the weakness of the grenadier companies combined to bring the advance to a halt after the first early successes. The grenadiers had won a few hundred meters more with their sacrifice, but the tanks still could not break through the storm of shot and shell directed at them when they emerged from the corn fields. Again, the Russian artillery fire and antitank shells from both flanks added to the devastation and made advance toward the main field positions very difficult The SS infantry soon was forced to go to ground in the face of undiminished Russian fire. Soon afterwards, they regrouped and rallied for another attack, only to fall back once more.

The SS troopers tried to storm the next line of trenches three times during the day, but each time, they were driven back, always with more casualties. By midday, Ullrich's III./*Totenkopf,* numbered less than a hundred men, reduced to the strength of a company.

The divisional engineers continued to work in the corn fields behind the infantry attacks on the hill, working to clear more of the forward slope of mines. Under cover of the grenadiers' advance, 1,200 more wood-cased mines were removed during the clearing operations on 31 July.[6] These type of mines could not be located with mine detectors and had to be found with probes before they could be dug up. This was a delicate and dangerous task, particularly while under fire. It was made doubly hazardous because Soviet mines were notoriously unstable, disliked by Russian mine-laying crews, who often removed German mines for their own use.

REGIMENT *EICKE* IN THE GERASSIMOVA

In the Gerrassimova Valley, Regiment *Eicke* tried to gain more ground to the south but was held up by Russian positions dug into the sides of two small ravines to the south of the Nedadajewa Schlucht and Point 128.1. By 1745 hours, the SS men were able to push a little farther down the valley but progress was difficult and the fighting consumed more men with no decisive gains. When the Nedadajewa ravine was cleared, the Germans pursued the retreating Russians farther to the south, only to find an unexpected nasty surprise. A second deep ravine, the Popova Schlucht, was located a few hundred meters south of the Nedadajewa and was defended by Russian infantry dug into the sides of the natural defensive position. When Regiment *Eicke* advanced against this position, it was brought to a halt by heavy small-arms and mortar fire.[7]

The combat in the valley turned into a hard-fought slugging match in which the SS grenadiers took one fortified ravine, only to find another in front of them. It was a fight that they could not ultimately win due to the great disparity in numbers. The nature of the terrain was a disadvantage to the Germans because it lent itself to defensive operations. As soon as the Russian infantry were driven out of their fighting holes, they could vanish down a small concealed ravine or stream bed, to regroup quickly and attack from a flank or the rear. The many ravines furnished ideal avenues for infiltration, tactics that perfectly suited the Russian soldiers. Because the Russians were numerically far superior, they were continually able to bring up fresh troops for counterattacks on the German lines, always supported by mortar, artillery fire and air attacks.

The Russians were able to direct accurate artillery fire on both flanks of Regiment *Eicke*'s advance because they controlled the high ground on either side of the German advance. This advantage enabled their heavy guns to support or cover any move that their infantry made and quickly counter any advance by the Germans. They were also able to cross the Mius at Dmitrievka and move fresh rifle battalions up the Gerassimova Valley with only minor interference from German artillery. In the face of stubborn resistance from the Soviet infantry and formidable heavy-weapons fire, Regiment *Eicke* was again halted and could not break through the Russian lines. While the German troops battled their way forward through machine-gun fire and mortar shells, clouds over the battlefield grew dark and the sky turned menacing.

At mid-afternoon, a violent storm signalled an end to the fighting temporarily when a tremendous cloudburst dumped so much water on the battlefield in this sector that all movement was paralyzed. In just minutes, the torrents of water were at knee level in trenches and ravines and completely flooded low areas. The ravines were swept by flash floods that inundated foxholes and headquarters positions, washing away radios, telephone lines and supplies. Observation for artillery was absolutely impossible because the artillery observers could not see anything through the inpenetrable curtain of rain. Communications were completely disrupted due to loss of radios or destruction of headquarters positions. Very quickly, the whole area was transformed into a sea of black, sticky mud.[8] In addition to communication disruptions, supply became impossible and even tracked vehicles could hardly move. Wheeled vehicles such as trucks or heavy cars were absolutely unable to plow through the mud. Combat ground to a halt on both sides by order of the forces of nature.

With the weather conditions preventing any operations, *Totenkopf* took stock of the situation. By the afternoon, at 1730 hours, the division reported to II. SS-Panzerkorps that it had only twenty operational tanks left, in addition to fourteen assault guns. These were the bitter fruits of the ill-advised attack on Hill 213.9 and the failure to support *Totenkopf* on either flank. The division had only one Tiger tank that was still capable of action, nine Panzer IVs still running, and just five Panzer IIIs, in addition to several Befehlpanzer (command tanks). Even during the hard fighting at Kursk, the division had never been reduced to this level of tank strength.

In late afternoon, because of the cloudburst and general exhaustion, operations remained at a halt as the division regrouped and tried to restore communication lines. The grenadier companies dried out their equipment and ammunition and reorganized from the day's losses. After nightfall, the tired soldiers of the division were harassed by the Russian air force. Soviet planes roared overhead in the night sky to bomb and strafe the firing positions of the artillery and flak guns and attacking known positions of the grenadiers. Although casualties from the air attacks were essentially very light, the raids were hard on the nerves of the Germans due to the large number of attack planes the Russians employed and the inability of the Luftwaffe to stop them.

STEPANOVKA: THE RUSSIANS COUNTERATTACK *DAS REICH*

Das Reich found itself absolutely unable to mount any offensive operations during the early-morning or daylight hours of 31 July. Its battalions were completely occupied reacting to one Soviet attack after the other in the rubble strewn streets of Stepanovka. In the town and to the south where the panzer group was located, the Russians threw constant counterattacks at the division continuing into the afternoon. The division was forced completely on the defensive and was hard pressed to fight off the strong Soviet infantry and tank forces, all of which were supported by swarms of Russian planes and artillery fire from heavy guns, mortars and rocket launchers. The panzer group was nearly overrun by a particularly aggressive tank assault from the area around Hill 202.0. It was only after a flanking counterattack by III./*Deutschland* over Hill 223.7, to the south of Stepanovka, that the situation was stabilized and substantial Russian forces in the area were scattered. At 1000 hours, another strong attack, made by

Soviet tanks and infantry, was turned back in cooperation with the tank destroyer battalion and 126. Panzergrenadier-Regiment of 23. Panzer-Division, which were in the area around Hill 196.0. In the air, Stukas gathered overhead and furnished well-coordinated air support, attacking the Russian infantry and tanks visible and moving in the open.[9]

On Hill 202.0 III./Regiment *Der Führer* fought off several Russian infantry attacks that were reinforced by over seventy tanks. The first counterattack in this sector came from the Krutaja ravine (which lay between the ruins of Garany and Marinovka), and it struck the German lines at 0330 hours. More than twenty Soviet tanks were destroyed in the darkness during this and subsequent attacks against *Der Führer* at 0715, 0950, 1030, and 1.00 hours.[10] All during the day, the Russians were able to move tanks and troops north up the Olkhovchik Valley and infiltrate to the west unseen and under cover by utilization of the deep ravines and broad valley. It was apparent from the strength and number of counterattacks originating from the Krutaja ravine that in this sector the Russians were determined to establish a stable defensive line to the east of Marinovka. Infiltrating units of Russian troops from assembly areas west of Marinovka also made energetic efforts to penetrate the German lines and retake Hill 202.0.

Regiment *Deutschland* continued to turn back all attempts by the Russians to drive it out of Stepanovka on 31 July. Reinforced by a few tanks that entered the town from the east edge of Stepanovka, elements of several Soviet rifle divisions attacked the SS grenadiers, infiltrating between the houses and engaging in what the division reported as "bitter house-to-house close combat."[11] The fighting raged back and forth in the village, with the grenadiers driven from their positions by overwhelming Russian strength, only to regain them with quickly mounted counterattacks. Although *Deutschland* was not able to make any consistent offensive headway due to this pressure, the SS soldiers refused to break and turned back all attempts to force them out of Stepanovka. The Germans inflicted great material and manpower losses on the Russians at all points. By the end of the day, *Das Reich* had destroyed a total of twenty-six Soviet tanks and captured 1,400 prisoners.[12]

In Stepanovka, the use of Soviet tanks caused particular problems because the Germans had no armor of their own in the town. However, tanks in built-up areas are very vulnerable to close attack. Their use requires well-coordinated infantry support and is not an ideal method of armor commitment. In the narrow streets and among the wrecked buildings of the town, the SS troopers attacked the Russian tanks with whatever antitank weapons were at hand. Later in the war, the German troops were issued large numbers of the extremely deadly Panzerfaust, which was the most effective handheld antitank weapon produced by any of the warring nations during World War II. At this point in the war, the Panzerfaust was not available in large numbers, although it became more plentiful by late 1943. Another weapon used by those with the courage to place it on a tank was a magnetic shaped-charge grenade which was very effective if placed properly. The soldiers used various makeshift weapons to destroy armor at close range.

Daring soldiers could leap onto Russian tanks with a bundle of grenades or satchel charge, emplace the explosives at a vulnerable place such as at the turret ring and explode them. If nothing else was available, gasoline in bottles or other containers with a burning wick attached could be thrown on top of engine decks. The flaming gasoline, if it flowed down into engine vents, could set the tank afire. These methods required great skill, courage and agility. Not only did the man who attempted to destroy a tank in this manner have to possess nerves of steel, he had to be agile enough to place the charge correctly and quick enough to get off the tank before it exploded. Sometimes mines were used to knock out tanks, placed by a daring soldier who positioned the mine under a turret edge and detonated it with a grenade.

Assaults on tanks required teamwork if these tactics were to succeed (and the attacker survive) because it was necessary to suppress the fire of accompanying Soviet infantry and of other tanks in order for an infantryman to survive an attempt to attack armor with such weapons. If the tank commanders could be forced to keep their heads down, the poor observation design of the T-34 made the task slightly easier because it was then possible to attack the tanks unobserved by their crew. Even the use of a Panzerfaust required nerves of steel. If the missile missed the tank, the trail of smoke and fire from the projectile pinpointed the location of the firer.

In these ways, some of the Soviet armor was knocked out when the Russian tanks attempted to support the counterattacking Russian infantry in Stepanovka. After the seemingly unending Russian attacks, the town streets were strewn with the wrecks of burnt-out tanks and Soviet dead. When darkness descended upon the town and the counterattacks subsided, *Deutschland* once again began to root the Russian rifle companies out of their bunkers and fortified houses. Lost ground was recaptured house by house, assaulting Russian strongpoints with grenades and machine pistols. There was vicious hand-to-hand fighting with bayonet, machine pistols and rifle butts. Both sides fought determinedly to destroy each other and gain sole possession of the blasted huts and debris-filled streets. Neither side took many prisoners. The Germans couldn't spare men to guard them and the Russians didn't bother to take many SS men alive.

Near the double hills to the south of Stepanovka, the grenadiers of III./Regiment *Der Führer* also had to fight off Russian counterattacks that were launched with strong artillery preparation and support. All of the Russian attempts to take the so-called *Doppelkopf* hills (223.7) and the neighboring German defensive positions near Hill 202.0 were accompanied by mortar fire from 82mm and 120mm mortar batteries organic to the rifle divisions. These infantry attacks originated primarily out of the Krutaja Schlucht. This ravine stretched between Stepanovka and Marinovka and served as a safe assembly area, allowing the Russians to bring up troops for attacks on Hills 223.7 and 202.0. The SS grenadiers, fighting from quickly constructed field defenses, fought off each attack. Russians troops attacked in waves over the grassy steppe and were mowed down by MG-42s and mortar fire. There were scores of Russian dead in front of *Der Führer*'s firing positions at the end of the day. However, the fighting took its toll on the defenders as well, with *Der Führer* reporting losses of 200 killed and wounded during the fighting on 31 July.[13]

Das Reich turned back a total of fourteen separate Soviet attacks on 31 July, six on the right flank and eight in the middle sector.[14] Its tank strength at the end of the day was reported as ten Panzer IIIs, twelve Panzer IVs, and one Tiger, in addition to twenty assault guns and five command tanks. While the divsion was not able to do anything offensively, the losses that it inflicted on the Soviets were enormous.

The same downpour that halted *Totenkopf*'s operations in the afternoon had a similar effect on combat in this sector as well. Torrential rains and the resulting floods caused nearly complete disruption of communications between the formations of the division for several hours. Small streams and ditches became rivers and the deep mud made even walking difficult. At 1445 hours, the ravine where the divisional HQ was located was washed out by a sudden, violent flash flood. The rushing waters destroyed communication connections and radio sets, washing away light vehicles and equipment. As a result, the divisional HQ remained out of contact with its subordinate units for some time. Due to this break in communications, in addition to the impossibility of directing artillery support and the difficulties presented by the rain and mud, offensive operations were not possible even had the situation allowed.[15] Not until later in the afternoon, when radios dried out and new cables were laid, were communications restored and the division prepared for further action.

3. PANZER-DIVISION

The resumption of the attack by 3. Panzer-Division on the second day resulted in very little ground gained and nothing to show for its efforts but more losses of tanks and men. After two attacks by Stukas and a fire mission by divisional and corps artillery, the attack began at 0615. The main effort was made against Hill 211.5, the supporting positions on the high ground near that hill and at Peresej. During the fighting, the division lost a total of ten tanks, primarily from tank and flanking antitank gun fire from a ravine near the village of Peresej. Russian artillery and mortar fire continued to operate without significant interference by the German preparatory artillery or air attacks. Lack of adequate ground observation sites for the German artillery forward observers restricted effective use of artillery in this sector as well. Possession of the high ground remained a key factor of the battle, as it was on the center ridge, around Hill 213.9. The main defensive point in the sector of 3. Panzer-Regiment attack was Hill 211.5, which was girdled by thick minefields and defended by Pakfronts and emplaced T-34s. From the beginning of the attack, strong Russian artillery fire fell on the division's advance when it reached the areas south and southwest of Nikiforoff.

At Peresej and near a fortified ravine adjacent to that village, the division advanced into a storm of heavy artillery and small arms fire. When the Russian fire broke up the first attack, the division regrouped and tried again. Both infantry and tank attacks failed, the panzers crippled by mines and well-directed antitank gun fire and the grenadiers turned back by inpenetrable artillery and mortar barrages.

The tank strength of the division melted away. After two days of combat the division had only nine tanks still operational by late afternoon of 31 July. Personnel losses were 196 killed, wounded, or missing for the day, which were moderate when compared with the casualties of XXIX. Armeekorps and the SS divisions.[16]

In the afternoon, following evaluations of the division's performance and condition, 6. Armee decided to withdraw 3. Panzer-Division from its attack sector and place it in reserve, temporarily at the disposal of XXIV. Panzerkorps. After its losses during the first two days of combat, without any decisive breakthrough, the division was judged as too weakened offensively to be expected to be successful on the following day. At 1600 hours, after speaking with the commander of 3. Panzer-Division, Generalleutnant Westhoven, Hollidt issued orders for the division to pull out of its positions during the night and organize its mobile units for a move to the Artemovka area.[17]

It was also decided to redirect the main effort of the II. SS-Panzerkorps from the center ridge to the right flank of *Das Reich*. The artillery of 3. Panzer-Division was to be detached temporarily and used to support the operations of XXIV. Panzerkorps and Hausser's SS divisions. Subsequently, the much-reduced 306. Infanterie-Division was assigned the duty of taking over the positions of the panzer division as it left the sector and moved into reserve. This operation was to be completed during the night and the early-morning hours of the next day.[18] After two days of hard fighting under the command of II. SS-Panzerkorps, Hollidt decided to place the army panzer division under command of army officers. The two Waffen SS divisions, after experiencing equally hard combat and more severe losses, remained in their assigned sectors, ordered to renew the fight on the next day.

During the whole night, the movements of 3. Panzer divisional formations were harassed by Soviet fighter-bombers.

THE NORTHERN FLANK REMAINS STALEMATED

In the XVII. Armeekorps' sector, 306. Infanterie-Division began its attack at 0530 hours, in hopes that 3. Panzer-Division's attempt to create a breakthrough in the Soviet lines south of Nikiforoff would be successful and reduce Soviet strength. In support of the armored group of the panzer division, the main effort by 306. Infanterie-Division was made north of Hill 211.5, where it was hoped the tanks could provide the necessary impetus to break through the Russian line. However, when the panzer division lost many of its few remaining tanks to Russian fire, it became clear to XVII. Armeekorps that the infantry attack would not be successful.[19] Without armor, there was no chance that the weakened infantry regiments could take the Russian positions in a frontal attack, much less force a breakthrough. When the panzers pulled back and withdrew from the fight, leaving several of their number burning in front of Hill 211.5, the attack by 306. Infanterie-Division collapsed as well. Neither the panzer division nor 306. Infanterie-Division could make any headway against the strong Russian defensive positions protecting the artillery and mortars situated on the high ground east of the center ridge. Heavy mortar and machine-gun fire inflicted casualties that the grenadier regiments could not afford.

The infantry of 306. Infanterie-Division and its supporting battalions were already weakened by the fighting that they had endured since July 17, to the extent that the attack group did not have the strength to take the Russian positions. After many days of intensive defensive combat, the men were exhausted physically and mentally, and as a result, the attack soon came to a halt. A breakthrough in the neighboring sector by 3. Panzer-Division could have diverted the Russian efforts and reserves and may have resulted in more success for the XVII. Armeekorps' attempts to capture Hill 173.4 and the surrounding terrain. An attack that captured a key point of high ground at some point could have led to a lessening of the Soviet artillery fire originating northeast of Hill 213.9 by furnishing an observation point for artillery observers. At this point also, the Germans were severely hampered by lack of high ground. As a result, Soviet artillery positions were able to operate without significant interference from German artillery.

These gun positions severely hammered the attacks by both army divisions and the main attack by *Totenkopf* on the center ridge. In the afternoon, 306. Infanterie-Division pulled its infantry back without having gained much ground. Shortly afterwards, the division learned of the redeployment of 3. Panzer-Division and the lengthening of its own front to close the resulting gap in the lines. It was impossible for the division to sufficiently man its own front at this time, much less the expanded length of the sector now assigned to it. 6. Armee sent its last infantry reserves to XVII. Armeekorps to ease the situation somewhat.

In order to help take the place of the withdrawing troops, XVII. Armeekorps ordered the Feld-Ausbildungs-Bataillon of 306. Infanterie-Division to move up from its reserve position and take over the line to the immediate left of the *Totenkopf* sector. Next to that unit, I./683. Grenadier-Regiment, 6. Armee's Sturm-Bataillon, and the Feld-Ausbildungs-Bataillon of 3. Gebirgs-Division manned the line from west to east, respectively. The left flank of the line anchored at a point near Hill 256.3.

Although 6. Armee's Sturm-Bataillon was already in position, the training battalion of 306. Infanterie-Division was just east of Pervomaisk at 1800 hours and was expected to arrive by march in order to replace I./394 Panzergrenadier-Regiment, the last of 3. Panzer-Division's units to leave the battlefield for the move to Artemovka. The battalion was supposed to extend its flanks to close the gap between it and 6. Armee's Sturm-Bataillon, which would hold the sector to its left. Given the aggressive patrolling habits of the Russians, it could be dangerous to be caught in a withdrawal from frontline positions, and so the battalion of the panzergrenadier regiment could not leave its positions until the replacement troops were at hand.

However, weather conditions affected the troop movements to a significant extent. The rain storm that struck the ridges in the late afternoon of 31 July, had turned the roads and march routes assigned to 3. Panzer-Division into quagmires and hindered the movements of all the German formations attempting to move into or out of the sector. Because of the mud, it was not until the following day that the last battalion of the panzer division was replaced in the line. The vehicles of the division were also slowed down by the mud but were able to arrive at Artemovka during the last hours of darkness on 1 August. Although the artillery regiment of the division remained in action, the other combat formations of 3. Panzer-Division would not play any further offensive role during the days leading to the conclusion of the battle for the Mius River positions.

XXIX. ARMEEKORPS PUSHES INTO THE OLKHOVCHIK VALLEY
In its attack sector, XXIX. Armeekorps followed up the good advances that it had made on the fast day by pushing farther across the Olkhovchik Valley floor in the direction of the west bank of the Mius, just above Kuibyshevo. The corps objective was Hill 168.5, which stood guard at the southern exit of the Olkhovchik. Its capture

would effectively seal off all the main lines of communication to Marinovka and threaten the line of supply of the Soviet rifle divisions fighting Regiment *Deutschland* in Stepanovka. With this objective in mind, the attack was launched on the morning of 31 July. During the early hours of morning, a number of strong Soviet patrols probed the German lines, which delayed the start of the attack.

The reconnaissance patrols were of about company strength and were supported by a few tanks. They originated out of the Olkhovchik Valley from south of Kalinovka, near Yelizavetinsky, where fighting still raged sporadically. The Russian probes were fought off, and shortly after they withdrew, reinforced elements of a 294. Infanterie-Division battle group managed to capture the southern half of Yelizavetinsky.

This battle group, designated as Kampfgruppe Haus, worked forward under artillery fire by utilizing the shelter of a stream bed until it got into position to assault the village. Storming out of the stream, the German infantry was able to take the Russians by surprise and quickly penetrated the defenses of the town. The fierce assault forced most of the Russians out of Yelizavetinsky. However, some elements of Soviet infantry remained dug in at various points in the northern half of the village, steadfastly refusing to be routed.[20] During the fighting for Yelizavetinsky, German artillery observers moved forward with the attack and spotted Russian artillery firing on their own forces as well as German troops to the northwest. Subsequently, a request was made to the Ia of the IV. Fleigerkorps for a Stuka attack on two Russian artillery positions south of Marinovka. This urgent request was made at 1025 hours, but after an hour, the German planes had not made the requested attack and the Russian guns continued to fire without interference.

In the meantime, the assault elements of XXIX. Armeekorps had been halted by Russian artillery due to the delay of both air and artillery support. The artillery batteries that were designated to support the attack were still in the process of moving to new firing positions. As a result, they were not able to provide the infantry with the support of their guns. An attack by Stukas, scheduled for the morning, did not materialize at the specified time. This was probably because of muddy airfields, which seemed to hamper the German planes more than they did the Russians, who seldom lacked for air support during the fighting on the Mius. As a result of this poor performance by the support elements, the infantry, which attacked on schedule, was slowed by Russian artillery.

However, just as it seemed the attack would flounder, the German planes made their appearance at 1150 hours. Dive-bomber attacks knocked out several Russian artillery positions, and shortly afterwards, the volume of Soviet artillery fire lessened appreciably. Subsequently, the attack was able to get moving again and pushed towards a Soviet defensive position about 500 meters in front of a group of four houses. Old German trenchworks were used by several assault detachments to infiltrate the Russian positions, which were shortly afterwards in German hands again. The capture of this position allowed the attack to make good progress toward two tactically important hills identified as the "Sternhohe" and "Kreuzhohe."[21]

When the German infantry advanced on these strongpoints, they drew a fierce Soviet reaction. The Russians counterattacked immediately but were driven back. They attacked several times during the day in reinforced battalion strength, later supported by several tanks.[22] These counterattacks were barely turned back. The Germans' defensive efforts were strengthened significantly by a number of assault guns from Sturmgeschütz-Bataillon 243, which destroyed seven Russian tanks in the fighting near the "Kreuzhohe."[23] Reports from the German infantry battalions to corps and division HQs made it evident that the Russians had suffered severe casualties during their attacks around the hills. In addition to the loss of hundreds of dead and wounded, 1,200 Soviet prisoners were captured by the Germans, and a total of twenty tanks was destroyed. German armored losses consisted of three assault guns, only one of which was listed as a complete loss.

Although most of the attack group made good progress early in the day, capturing part of Yelizavetinsky, its middle battalion lagged behind the flank battalions, remaining stalled in front of a fortified slope just southwest of Yelizavetinsky. The Russians put up a stout resistance in the center sector, fighting from trenches and firing pits dug into the ridge. On the left, the attack pushed to the northwest and reached the southern edge of Malo-Petrovsky, situated northwest of Yelizavetinsky. Over 250 prisoners were reported captured by the Germans at this point, and a further 350 were taken by the afternoon.

Even though Russian losses were heavy, the German attack halted short of Hill 168.5, under constant pressure by counterattacks of small groups of tanks and infantry. Without tanks, the Germans had great difficulty with Soviet armor, which made reckless attacks on the German infantry, and the momentum of the attack was repeatedly interrupted. The assault guns became involved in actions against Soviet armor and were not able to assist the infantry in reducing fortified positions.

The resistance of the fortified Russian infantry dug in on the hills and ridges was too difficult to overcome without the support of the assault guns. By late afternoon, XXIX. Armeekorps decided that its infantry had little chance of making continued progress without additional armor. This was due both to the fire of Soviet artillery and the heavy losses by the assault battalions of the infantry regiments during the morning fighting. By late afternoon, 294. Infanterie-Division reported that it had lost 18 officers, 123 non-commisioned officers, and 1,128 men killed, wounded or missing—severe losses for a division that was not at full strength to begin with. Accordingly, the division commander decided to consolidate his gains and wait for the link up with tanks of XXIV. Panzerkorps. The attack was to be renewed with the support of the panzers of XXIV. Panzerkorps. Unfortunately, the panzers of 23. Panzer-Division were involved in the final stages of mopping up the Garany pocket, a task that was not finished until 1100 hours. The attack groups of XXIX. Armeekorps dug in where they had been forced to stop, waiting until contact was established with 16. Panzergrenadier-Division, which had jumped off on time and was expected to push forward and link up with the infantry for a coordinated push to the river.

XXIV. PANZERKORPS

Before first light, assault groups of 16. Panzergrenadier-Division began their attack, encountering light Soviet resistance. They entered Kalinovka at 0345 hours, finding it abandoned by Russian troops. Two battalions of the division, along with the fifteen tanks of 116. Panzer-Bataillon, occupied the town by 0400 hours. In the continuation of its attack, the division pushed farther to the east and was able to capture two small villages, Malopetrovsky and Grigorievka, which lay only a short distance west of Yelizavetinsky. From there, the division pushed eastward toward the Olkhovchik with one battalion of infantry and a few assault guns. About one kilometer east of Hill 196.0, Soviet resistance stiffened and the ever-present artillery and mortar fire pinned down the advance. The Russian troops were solidly entrenched in two large ravines, the Krutaja and Kriwaja Schlucht. When the 16. Panzergrenadier units halted in front of these two ravines, Soviet tanks and infantry counterattacked from hills north of Malopetrovsky and Grigorievka. Throughout the rest of the day, the division remained stalled in front of the high ground and ravines west of the Olkhovchik and made no further advance into the valley.

During the night of 30–31 July, 23. Panzer-Division halted its offensive operations against the encircled Soviet troops in the pocket. In its morning communication with 6. Armee, the division reported that there had been little activity in the hours of darkness, beyond frequent air attacks by Soviet planes. At first light, the division renewed a series of concentric attacks against remnants of the Soviet divisions trapped in the Garany pocket. In spite of constant attempts to break out, none of the trapped Russians managed to escape as organized formations. At 1000 hours, from outside the pocket, the Russians unexpectedly attacked with a strong infantry/armor force that originated from southeast of Marinovka. The Soviets made every effort to crash through the German lines in an attempt to break into the encirclement and reach their comrades. All of their efforts failed, however, when, despite the strength of the rescue assault group, the Germans threw it back. Elements of *Das Reich*, which included the panzer group and III./*Der Führer*, on their own initiative, assaulted the retreating Russians from the flank, and in cooperation with 128. Panzerjager-Abteilung and 126. Panzergrenadier-Regiment of 23. Panzer-Division, drove the Soviet tank attack back toward Hill 202.0. In their wake, the Germans left a trail of burning T-34s and dead or surrendering Russians.

After the defeat of this attempt to free the encircled Russian troops, the units of 23. Panzer-Division renewed their reduction of the pocket in order to destroy the trapped Soviet troops. Artillery of the division and corps remained involved in firing on the enemy forces in the pocket. Stukas provided air support, bombing Soviet strongpoints and troop concentrations located in several deep ravines. Panzergrenadiers, tanks from 201. Panzer Regiment and the divisional reconnaissance battalion, along with supporting elements of the division, crushed the last Russian resistance at 1100 hours. All of the encircled Soviet divisions were destroyed as effective combat formations. By the end of the day, much material was either captured or destroyed, including a few tanks, fifty-two antitank guns, eleven automatic guns, and twenty-four field guns of various types. The Russian divisions destroyed in the pocket were identified as 3rd Guards Rifle, 33rd Guards Rifle, 315th Rifle, and major elements of 96th Guards Rifle Divisions. In addition, several mortar units and small detachments of motorized and armored troops were wiped out.[24] The division reported that Russian losses were apparently exceptionally high (*außergewöhnlich*) and its own casualties were considerable. Later, after assembling in the area west of Garany-Saur Mogilsky, 23. Panzer-Division prepared to renew its attack toward the west, much too late in the day to give much aid to the infantry of XXIX. Armeekorps, who had been fighting without armor support since early in the morning. By the afternoon, the division had relocated its artillery to the area west of Garany, where it organized firing positions and brought up ammunition.

On this date, the troops of 6. Armee first experienced a new Soviet weapon, one that was to become very familiar to them in the future. This was a heavy Russian assault gun built on the T-34 chassis and equipped with a powerful 15.2cm gun. Nicknamed the "animal killer" by the Russian tank crews, it had been quickly developed by the Russians to provide a counter to the heavy armor of the Tiger and Panther tanks. 6. Armee's account of the battle specifically mentions the first destruction and study of this type of Russian armored fighting vehicle on 31 July.[25]

The XXIV. Panzerkorps involvement in the fighting to destroy the encircled Russian divisions near Garany resulted in delay of the armored elements advance towards Marinovka. Of particular significance was that the artillery of the corps remained in position to furnish support to the effort to reduce the pocket and did not move to new firing positions, establish observation posts or organize the supply of ammunition to its subsequent firing positions until the afternoon. The division evidently did not intend to attack until all its units were assembled. The Russian relief operation that tried to punch its way through the German lines further held up 23. Panzer-Division. The major effect of these delays meant that the armor could not support XXIX. Armeekorps until later in the day and likely was a critical factor that limited the success of the operations in the southern Olkhovchik.

Because *Das Reich* did not advance from the positions occupied on 30 July, its flank was not further endangered due to the delay of XXIV. Panzerkorps' attack. However, the Russians were free to commit significant strength to counterattack the division in Stepanovka—forces that may not have been available if 23. Panzer-Division had made a strong push toward the river earlier in the morning. However, the lack of armor support for XXIX. Armeekorps was an important factor in the inability of the infantry assault battalions of 294. and 111. Infanterie-Divisions to penetrate the Soviet lines and reach their objectives. The failures of the panzer divisions were compounded by the performance of the artillery and the Luftwaffe units, which were not particularly skilful in their operations to suppress Russian artillery and mortar positions in the Marinovka area.

Although German artillery units were normally efficient and flexible in battle, the XXIX. Armeekorps artillery designated to support the attack of the infantry had difficulties in deploying as planned. It was delayed by muddy terrain, did not move forward to new firing positions quickly and was unable to give adequate fire support to the infantry early in the attack. This was a considerable handicap and resulted in less than the desired results. More importantly, the infantry suffered casualties that the army could ill afford.

The divisions of XXIV. Panzerkorps did not make much offensive progress during the latter part of 30–31 July, having difficulties disengaging their artillery from the perimeter of the Garany pocket and delaying the corps advance to deal with the encircled Russian forces. The divisions did not exhibit a great deal of aggressiveness in their attempts to carry out the primary mission of the corps, which was to support and screen the right flank of the attack by II. SS-Panzerkorps. At 2015 hours, XXIV. Panzerkorps reported that it was assembling and that it expected "strong enemy resistance on the following day." Study of the records of the XXIV. Panzerkorps provide a possible answer to the lack of offensive progress made by these troops on 31 July.

From 17 July through 29 July 1943, 16. Panzergrenadier-Division had lost 112 officers and 3,313 non-commissioned officers and men, with a further casualty total listed as 24 officers and 508 other ranks on 30–31 July. This was a total of just under 4,000 casualties suffered by a division that was not at full strength to begin with. By the end of the fighting on 31 July, the division had only twelve Panzer III/IV tanks still running, although it listed twenty-two assault guns available for action. The 23. Panzer-Division lost twenty-two of its thirty-seven tanks by 31 July, having only fifteen Panzer III/IVs still operational on that date and only one assault gun. In armor strength, it was a division in name only, having been reduced to the tank strength of a company.

Both formations had been involved in the fierce combat west of the Mius since the third week of July, with 16. Panzergrenadier-Division in action with 6. Armee since 18 July, when it first counterattacked the Soviet advance. It is without doubt that the constant fighting wore the men down mentally and physically and contributed to the failure to carry out their assigned missions with regard to the support of II. SS-Panzerkorps. It may well be that because 6. Armee was aware of its condition, the withdrawal of 3. Panzer-Division from its attack sector and placing it in reserve behind XXIV. Panzerkorps at Artemovka were precautionary measures directly attributable to the weakness of the two divisions. In an unfortunate repeat of similar failings at Prochorovka by an army panzer unit, *Das Reich* was again attacked on its southern flank when the flank remained unprotected by the failure of XXIV. Panzerkorps to advance farther to the east.

By the afternoon of 31 July, both divisions of XXIV. Panzerkorps were halted east of a line Hill 202.0–196.0–Malopetrovsky. On the evening of 31 July, air and ground reconnaissance spotted a group of fifteen to twenty Soviet tanks on the move south of Marinovka, heading toward the west. Heavy traffic of various other types of Soviet vehicles was also reported by air reconnaissance.

DEADLOCK ON THE SECOND DAY

At the end of the second day of its counterattack, 6. Armee evaluated the situation, with special concern for the lack of progress in II. SS-Panzerkorps' sector and could only react with discouragement. In two days, Hausser's three divisions lost 1,300 men and officers killed, wounded or missing. Twenty-four Panzers had been totally destroyed (ten Panzer IIIs and fourteen Panzer IVs). There were an additional twenty-seven Panzer IIIs, forty-five Panzer IVs, and nine Tigers temporarily out of action with repairable damage.[26] The heavy losses in men and material, if continued at that rate, would have quickly destroyed the divisions as effective formations. Manstein had feared this very situation, knowing that he would need the panzers of II.

SS-Panzerkorps later in the summer. If Hausser's corps was battered to pieces, it would be out of action at a time when it was desperately needed elsewhere. Evidently, this possibility was on Manstein's mind, and he kept a close watch on the progress of the attack. He appeared at Hausser's headquarters later in the day to question the use of the SS divisions.

On the other side of the ledger, the Russians had lost untold dead and wounded. In addition, they had lost more than 6,000 prisoners, sixty-eight tanks, and numerous guns and automatic weapons in their attacks against Stepanovka, the counterattacks on the high ground to the south of that village and the defense of the Soviet middle against the assaults by *Totenkopf*.[27] In spite of these losses, which Tolbukhin could afford, they were still firmly in possession of Hills 213.9, 203.4, and 211.5. At each point, the Russians had defeated 6. Armee's attacks and inflicted serious losses in armor and manpower on the Germans. Even after two days of combat, the Soviets were weakened very little at any of the main positions and they had prevented any significant breakthrough into the Olkhovchik. There were fresh rifle divisions on the east side of the river and Tolbukhin fed rested troops across the river in a steady stream. By contrast, the Germans were reduced to commitment of their divisional training battalions and 6. Armee HQ combat units in order to find enough troops to even adequately man defensive positions.

Manstein appeared at the headquarters of II. SS-Panzerkorps on 31 July to observe the progress of the attack. There he conferred with Hausser, *Das Reich* commander Kruger, and Obersturmbannführer Silvester Stadler, the commanding officer of II. SS-Panzerkorps' reserve, I./ and II./Regiment *Der Führer*. Stadler's two battalions, still in transit to the front, were significantly delayed by rain and mud on 31 July, a fact that concerned Manstein. The two battalions of *Der Führer* were motorized, which meant that they were primarily equipped with trucks and wheeled vehicles instead of half-tracks and had difficulty in navigating the muddy terrain after the torrential rain of the afternoon. All roads in the area, which were dirt, had become quagmires.

The transport of heavy weapons was also difficult, and as a result, Stadler's troops and equipment were not yet completely assembled, due to delays and vehicle breakdowns. These were direct results of the mud and the strains it imposed on vehicles and men. It is interesting to note that the Germans could not provide even their elite SS units with enough armored infantry carriers to fully equip each panzergrenadier regiment at this date and, in fact, were never able to do so. Later in the war, the situation became even worse, in spite of the fact that vehicle and tank production increased markedly in late 1943 and reached its highest levels in mid-1944.

After the disappointing results of the first two days, Manstein was not overly enthusiastic about continuing the attack. None of the reports received during the day had changed his opinion. Two days of fighting had produced nothing but extensive casualties and very little gain. There were other areas of crisis brewing along Heeresgruppe Süd's front, and Manstein did not want to destroy II. SS-Panzerkorps in further attacks without the chance of a quick success.

Manstein requested a report from Stadler in regard to the progress of the I./ and II./*Der Führer* toward the front, as he had already decided to withdraw the II. SS-Panzerkorps within a matter of days and there was some question as to whether Stadler's two battalions would be able to make their attack before the departure of the corps. When Stadler answered that the two battalions would arrive and be ready for commitment in about five hours, Manstein was of the opinion that this would be too late and too little, which brought a firm reaction from the young SS officer. Stadler forcefully expressed the opinion that his battalions would be in position and ready to take the key position that had been assigned to his men, which was Hill 203.4. The Feldmarschall, still not reassured, questioned the ability of two battalions to successfully turn the tide of battle when two days of combat by three full panzer divisions had not produced a success.[28]

Hausser spoke with Manstein and voiced his confidence in the fighting ability of both the men of *Der Führer* and its commander. In spite of his misgivings, Manstein left it up to Hausser and Hollidt to decide the course of action for the next day and returned to Heeresgruppe Süd HQ. It was decided to continue the attack on 1 August. Regiment *Der Führer* and Obersturmbannführer Stadler were given their chance. Stadler's men were to make the main effort, at Hill 203.4, the hilltop bastion guarding the west edge of the Olkhovchik south of Marinovka.

In view of the 31 July failure to eliminate the Soviet positions on either flank of the attack on Hill 213.9, 6. Armee belatedly realized (perhaps because of Manstein's obvious displeasure with events to that point) that to continue to hammer at the same points of attack was useless. Further frontal assaults would lead only to more casualties and lost equipment without chance of success. It was therefore decided to reinforce the right flank of II. SS-Panzerkorps and make the main attack in *Das Reich*'s sector. The division would attempt to break into the valley with Stadler's battalions and the divisional armor leading the assault. Artillery was regrouped, and during the night, Nebelwerfer units were moved from the center ridge to positions from where the rocket launchers could support the right flank of *Das Reich*.

The new direction of attack would be a drive to push across the southern sector of the Olkhovchik Valley east of Stepanovka and Marinovka. The main objective of the attack was Hill 203.4, the dominant high ground in that area. With the capture of the hill, the division hoped to penetrate the valley and strike Soviet troops on Hill 213.9. The success of this attack depended on the capture of Hill 203.4. With the Russians firmly in possession of that elevation, their observers were able to see the entire surrounding area with the result that they would be able to direct fire on any units attempting to enter the Olkhovchik. It was up to Stadler and his grenadiers to take the vitally important hill. Without its capture, the Olkhovchik could not be crossed at this point and Hill 213.9 could not be cut off from the river, with the result that the Russian forces dug into the hill would not be weakened to any degree.

After receiving his assignment, Stadler requested that he be allowed to conduct a personal reconnaissance of the hill and the terrain surrounding it. Hausser agreed and requested only that he retain the right to approve the plan of attack. After quickly making his way to the area south of Stepanovka, Stadler made an extensive and painstaking survey of the attack area, carefully noting the terrain features. Before speaking with Hausser again, he met with the battalion commanders of the units to be involved in the attack on the next day. The importance of the attack was evident to the commander of *Der Führer* and he decided that audacity and surprise were needed to capture the hill.[29] His plan called for a surprise attack in the early morning, screened on the flanks by thick smoke from the Nebelwerfer units, which at that time were not yet in place. Stadler's plan called for *Der Führer* to lead the assault with I./*Der Führer* echeloned on the right flank. Both battalions were to advance in silence to avoid alerting the Russians until the last possible moment. There would be no artillery preparation on the hill itself because Stadler decided that a preliminary bombardment would alert the Russians and the element of surprise outweighed the benefits of artillery preparation.

The importance of the attack by his regiment was quite clear to Stadler, who realized that success at Hill 203.4 might well be the decisive factor in whether the counterattack of II. SS-Panzerkorps would rectify the situation on the Mius.[30] It was also evident from Manstein's comments on the lack of a decisive success after the first two days of fighting that he would not allow the II. SS-Panzerkorps to continue to exhaust itself without a satisfactory result. It was only after Hollidt strongly urged the continuance of the attack, and Hausser so forcefully voiced his confidence, that Manstein allowed a resumption of the attack. The change in the point of main effort, the *Schwerpunkt*, of the attack may well have been the deciding factor that persuaded him to allow Hausser's divisions to remain under 6. Armee command for a few more days.[31]

It is likely that had the main attack been concentrated at this point on the first day, rather than at defensive sectors that the army knew to be extremely strong and heavily fortified (Hills 213.9, 211.5 and Stepanovka), the results of the fighting on 30 July might have been more favorable to the Germans. In committing *Totenkopf* to the main attack on Hill 213.9, 6. Armee's command was at least guilty of lack of imagination in the employment of the armor given to it.

In order to support the attack of *Das Reich*, XXIV. Panzerkorps was ordered to make a parallel drive on the right of *Das Reich*, the objective of which was to penetrate the Olkhovchik in the area south of Hill 203.4. This attack was intended to support the SS division and screen its southern flank by clearing the Krivaya and Krutaya ravines, breaking into the Olkhovchik Valley and advance between *Das Reich*'s attack and Hill 168.5. The spearheads of this attack were to link up with Stadler's battalions in the area of Hill 203.4 as well as support the attack by XXIX. Armeekorps on Hill 168.5.

A penetration across this section of the Olkhovchik would threaten the Russian troops in Stepanovka and on Hill 213.9 with encirclement and thereby force the Soviets to withdraw their forces to avoid encirclement. Marinovka was to be temporarily bypassed in order to avoid becoming entangled in house to house fighting, which would destroy the momentum of the attack. Hollidt evidently decided to avoid fighting such as that which *Deutschland* had been involved in since it entered the maze of strongpoints in Stepanovka.

Attacks on the northern flank of the army in 3. Panzer's former attack zone and in the sectors of *Totenkopf* and 306. Infanterie-Division were stopped. The roads and terrain were still extremely muddy and difficult to traverse. As a result of these conditions, 306. Infanterie-Division and the battalions under its command barely settled in after an exhausting night spent wading through knee-deep mud and wrestling vehicles and equipment through the muck when it began to grow light in the east.[32] The assault by 306. Infanterie-Division and the SS attacks against Hill 213.9 and Stepanovka were to wait until the new direction of attack resulted in a situation more favorable to renewal of the offensive by those units. Elements of SS-Aufklärungs-Abteilung 2 were brought up to support the ground attack on the right flank of the division with its 20mm automatic guns and self-propelled infantry howitzers. South of Stepanovka, the armored elements of *Das Reich* assembled to make a penetration of the Olkhovchik at that point. The panzer attack, supported by the remnants of III./*Der Führer*, was also accompanied by the divisional assault guns.

In the Gerassimova Valley, SS-Standartenführer Becker's Regiment *Eicke* screened the left flank of *Totenkopf* by an active defense of its sector, supported by a few tanks and several batteries of heavy artillery. In Artemovka, 3. Panzer-Division stood ready for possible commitment as XXIV. Panzerkorps' reserve for the action on 1 August.[33] The assault detachments of *Totenkopf* were ordered to be ready to attack 213.9 again at short notice if the attack in *Das Reich*'s sector was successful. Otto Baum, the commander of Regiment *Totenkopf*, reorganized his surviving troops into small assault groups. The only division reserve, the mobile guns and armored vehicles of SS-Aufklärungs-Abteilung 3 and the engineers of SS-Pionier-Abteilung 3, stood by for commitment to the fight at Hill 213.9.[34] In support of the attack, most of 6. Armee's artillery was to direct its fire on targets in the area south of Marinovka. IV. Flieger-Armeekorps was also assigned air support missions in the same area.

At 0600 hours on the morning of 1 August 1943, the attack was resumed, with the troops of *Der Führer* carrying much of the responsibility for providing the impetus toward the success or failure of the attack to destroy the bridgehead across the Mius. If a decisive breakthrough was not made and the battle concluded quickly, the attack would likely fail. The prospects for future success were unlikely, primarily because Hausser's divisions would not be available for much longer, with action in the Kharkov area imminent. Hollidt was of course aware of Manstein's intentions and realized that without the support of the three panzer divisions, his army had little chance of forcing the Russians back across the river. If a major counterattack took place in the Kharkov area, it was likely that all his panzer divisions might be taken from him. He also knew that the army could not hold its positions west of the Mius with the Russians in possession of the bridgehead on the western bank.

It was only a matter of time before Tolbukhin was able to bring up additional reserves, both infantry and armor. If the penetration could not be destroyed quickly, Hollidt's army would stand alone, battered and weakened from the weeks of fighting in the summer of 1943. Although the Mius itself proved a less than formidable physical barrier, the army needed the defensive positions that it had been preparing since the spring in order to have any chance of survival after the departure of the panzer divisions. The battle for the Mius was more than a fight to eliminate a Russian bridgehead—it was for the life of the army itself.

CHAPTER 8

The Decisive Day: 1 August

II. SS-PANZERKORPS

The early-morning hours did not pass peacefully for the men of II. SS-Panzerkorps and 6. Armee, knowing that the next day would again bring scorching heat and fierce fighting. Before moving to their new positions during the night, hampered by the mud and darkness, the last panzergrenadiers of 3. Panzer-Division were finally relieved and had to execute the difficult task of leaving their defensive positions without alerting the Soviets.[1] At the same time, the companies of 306. Infanterie-Division, moving as silently as possible, found their way to their assigned trenches in the darkness. Finding the correct sections of the line in the night, in unfamiliar terrain, without undue noise, was a slow process made unbelievably strenuous by the mud. Vehicles of the panzer division crawled through the muck with difficulty. Men cursed as they had to put their shoulders to trucks bogged in the slippery mire that had been a dry, dusty track only the day before. The units of the two divisions gradually passed each other; columns of exhausted, silent men wading through the muck while other exhausted, silent men struggled past in the blackness.

The Russians were aware of unusual activity in the sector and responded with reconnaissance probes of the division's front.[2]

The mobile elements of 3. Panzer-Division were unavoidably held up by the infantry columns of both divisions behind the divisional front. But with the exception of the one panzergrenadier battalion, all other units and staff of the division reached the assigned area southwest of Stepanovka by the early hours of the morning of 1 August.[3] The delays caused by the mud and other conditions resulted in the last movements of the withdrawals, attack preparations and assembly taking place just before daylight on 1 August. Feld-Ausbildungs-Bataillon 306, committed to frontline duty, occupied its assigned section of the line shortly before dawn and only established contact with its neighbor (Kampfgruppe Holm) at 0430 hours, having experienced numerous delays passing through the vehicle columns of 3. Panzer-Division. There was no offensive German combat activity in this sector during the morning while the divisions moved into their new defensive positions, preparing for the resumption of the advance if the main attack in *Das Reich*'s area was successful. During the withdrawal and relief movements, Russian aircraft had again been active over the front, harassing and attacking the moving formations of men and equipment. Fortunately for the Germans, there had been no significant activity by enemy ground forces.

Kampfgruppe Holm received much-needed reinforcements in the form of a battery of Sturmgeschütz IIIs detached from 302. Infanterie-Division in order to furnish additional close support. After moving into place near the frontline trenches, the right flank of the battery found that a gap of nearly 800 meters existed between it and the left flank of *Totenkopf*. However, a kilometer east of the northern part of the Gerassimova Valley, reconnaissance elements of 306. Infanterie-Division made contact with troops of Regiment *Eicke* in the valley itself.[4] A hastily mobilized battalion sized unit made up of various elements of 302. Infanterie-Division arrived to help man the expanded frontline positions of 306. Infanterie-Division.

REGIMENT *DEUTSCHLAND* FIGHTS ON IN STEPANOVKA

Meanwhile, in the ruins of Stepanovka, Regiment *Deutschland* continued to battle entrenched Russian infantry and roving Soviet tanks during the night and early-morning hours of 1 August. The SS grenadiers doggedly attacked, building by building, driving stubborn Soviet infantry out of one house after the other, gradually working eastward. Dug in amongst the ruined huts and smashed buildings, the Russians gave ground very slowly. At 0337 hours, as the darkness of morning was broken by flashes of machine-gun fire and shell explosions, the regiment reported that it had reached a line 150 meters east of the north-south road that ran through the middle of the town. Division reports to Hausser's HQ described the house-to-house fighting as "tough" and "hard" (*zahen und harten Hauserkampfen*).[5]

Due to the determined fighting of the SS grenadiers, after more than two days of continuous combat, the Germans controlled about two thirds of the town. In spite of the commitment of large numbers of fresh Russian infantry all during the previous day and night,

The Decisive Day: 1 August

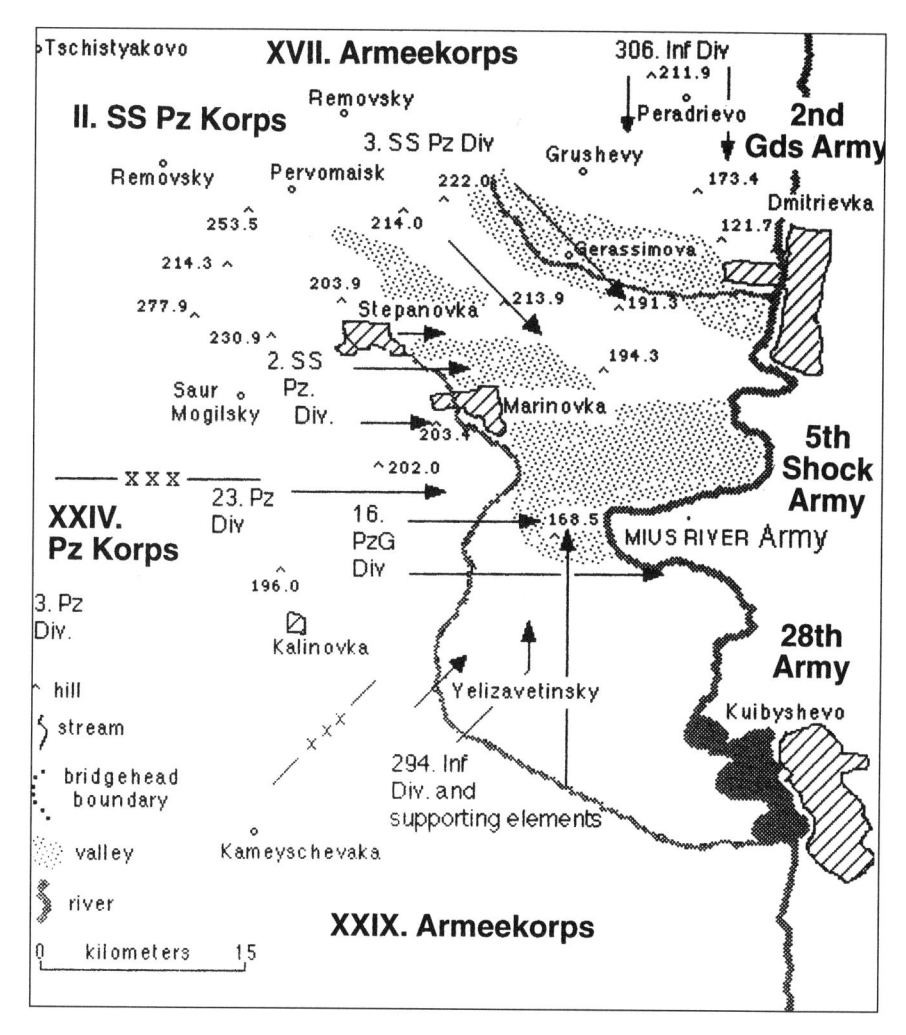

The decisive day, 1 August 1943.

Deutschland turned back eight counterattacks and then resumed its drive to the east edge of the town. Army intelligence indicated that the SS regiment had faced elements of three Soviet rifle divisions in Stepanovka and fought them to a standstill. The Russians had committed tanks and large amounts of artillery and mortar support without being able to drive the German troops out of the town.[6] In further attacks during the morning of 1 August, assaulting from the sector of the town east of the road, *Deutschland* forced its way into the southern and eastern sections of the village. The SS assault groups fought their way to the town's eastern perimeters by late morning, a sign that the resistance in the town was weakening. Whether this was due to the attrition of the Russian rifle division strength as a result of the losses on 30–31 July or a first sign of withdrawal from the town was not yet clear.

In *Totenkopf*'s sector, Soviet planes had been active in the night, making bombing raids on the positions of the division in the villages behind the front lines while the men tried to snatch some brief hours of rest. Positions of the artillery and Flak guns were apparently the main targets of these attacks. The Russian planes dropped bombs and made strafing runs with cannon fire. However, in the darkness, little damage was sustained.

Regiment *Der Führer* and the division's tanks were to advance and break into the Olkhovchik. Stadler's battalions were to assault Hill 203.4 and the armor was to attack south of Stepanovka. Artillery and air support was organized accordingly, although in the area of Hill 203.4, the artillery was to fire only after the attack began. Regiment *Der Führer* (I. and II. Battalions) prepared for the assault of Hill 203.4, after reaching their assembly areas in darkness.[7] The armored group of the division assembled just to the south of Stepanovka, with III./*Der Führer* in support. The *Das Reich* reconnaissance battalion was in position near Hill 202.0, ready to screen the advance of the SS tanks and reinforce the assault of 23. Panzer-Division if needed. The 23. Panzer-Division was to cross the Olkhovchik and furnish support to Stadler's assault into the valley after the capture of Hill 203.4

The assembly areas of the division were harassed by persistent Russian air attacks during the night and early morning, although again with very little effect. Harrassing fire from Soviet artillery in this sector during the night was minimal and mostly from lighter-caliber guns. It is possible that due to the constant German pressure of 30–31 July, the Soviets began to remove some of their artillery. The Stuka attacks and German artillery had silenced a few of the Soviet gun positions but no appreciable withdrawal of significant amounts of artillery or heavy equipment was observed. On the previous day, ground observation reported heavy Russian motor traffic at various times, particularly to the north of Kuibyshevo, but the nature of the Soviet activity was unclear. There was no evidence of significant withdrawals at any point. Given this, there was little to contradict the expectation of heavy fighting on 1 August.

When the new day dawned, the fierce battle for the Mius River still hung in the balance as the two armies faced each other, locked in a bitter stalemate. The attack of *Das Reich* would decide the success or failure of II. SS-Panzerkorps' counterattack against the Soviet bridgehead and determine the fate of the nearly exhausted 6. Armee.

ASSAULT ON HILL 203.4

After an artillery preparation that hammered the Soviet trenches and gun positions in the primary attack sector, the third day of the counterattack on the Russian penetration over the Mius River began. The assault reports of the fighting units from the previous two days of combat had been used to identify Soviet strongpoints in key areas and to plan artillery fire plans, information that had often been bought with blood. The German guns ranged in on the Russian batteries, although still handicapped at certain points by lack of good observation positions for their artillery forward observers. The artillery of 6. Armee, combined with the the detached artillery of 3. Panzer-Division and the guns of the SS divisions, was a formidable concentration of fire power, totaling nearly 600 guns. The fire plans worked out for 1 August were prepared to support the redirection of the attack with the majority of artillery strength assigned to support the assault of *Das Reich* and XXIV. Panzerkorps south of Stepanovka and in the Marinovka area.

The German artillery observers skilfully directed the fire from target to target, and quickly, the known Russian gun emplacements and fighting positions began to be silenced. In its evening report on 1 August, the HQ of 6. Armee's artillery estimated that eleven Russian artillery batteries were put out of action in this sector, in addition to several lighter gun positions destroyed through the combined efforts of artillery and Stuka attacks.[8]

Following the careful preparations of Stadler and his battalion commanders, the grenadiers of *Der Führer* received orders to make ready to go forward from their assembly areas just after 0400 hours. Soon they were moving toward the hill. The advance to the jump-off line was made in the sheltering darkness, with as little noise as possible. The ground was still wet and muddy in low places, and the dirt tracks that served for roads were still slippery. Although the soft terrain presented minor problems, the one benefit to the SS grenadiers was that they would not be tormented by choking dust during the heat of the day. Forty-five minutes later, the first screaming Nebelwerfer smoke shells passed unseen over their heads, striking in the distance, invisible to the men in the morning darkness. Aside from the Nebelwerfer shells that were employed to screen flanking fire from the main attack, there was no fire on Hill 203.4. Stadler did not want to alert the Russians with an artillery preparation on the hill.

The tanks, assault guns and vehicles of the armored group flared out into attack formation south of Stepanovka, moving forward from the assembly positions near Hill 202.0. On the right flank of the attack, elements of 23. Panzer-Division advanced from the area south of that hill. The concentrated artillery began its bombardment of the Russian positions, the shells whistling overhead to impact on targets along the western border of the Olkhovchik. The major portion of the assigned fire missions for the German artillery was concentrated in this sector. In particular, the medium guns were very active during offensive operations. During the attacks in 6. Armee's sector between July 30 and August 2, the 10cm guns alone averaged an expenditure of twenty-five to twenty-six tons of ammunition a day. By the end of the third day of the counterattack, the combined artillery under 6. Armee's command expended a total of 1,350 tons of artillery shells of all calibers in support of combat operations.[9]

As this massed firepower struck the Soviet lines up and down the front at the main points of attack, I./ and II./*Der Führer* began their attack on the Russian positions forward of Hill 203.4. Stadler's battalions moved to the attack toward the Soviet front line. In the distance, shrouded by dense clouds of smoke from Nebelwerfer rockets, lay the fortified hill.[10] In spite of all the difficulties presented by the mud and darkness, the Nebelwerfer units deployed to the requested sector during the early hours of 1 August and were in position to fire their rockets in time to support the assault.

Stadler's plan to take the Russian defenders by surprise through utilization of smoke and silent advance was successful. The SS grenadiers, deploying stealthily in the attack, burst out of the smoke and darkness, taking the Russians unaware in their forward positions. German stick grenades flew out of the night, exploding in bunkers, machine pistol fire rattled suddenly in the trenches and camouflage-uniformed shadows were suddenly in the midst of the Soviet positions. Russian and German soldiers fought each other in close combat. Assault detachments avoided strongpoints, quickly moving toward the hill before the Soviet soldiers were fully alerted. The violence of the attack shocked the Russian infantry, and after a brief, savage firefight, the startled Russian troops fell back, disorganized by the ferocity of the attack. The successful execution of Stadler's plan resulted in quick penetrations of the Russian positions in front of the hill. Before the Russians knew what was happening, the SS troopers were on the hill itself.

As happens so often in successful combat operations, the personal leadership and initiative of small-unit leaders decided the outcome of the battle. The commander of 4./*Der Führer*, SS-Obersturmführer Willi Grieme, exhibited just such skill and aggressiveness in the attack. He personally led his men in an attack against a key strongpoint on the hill, swiftly assaulting the Russian position and capturing it by storm. Instantly, he regrouped his men and led them against a second strongpoint and took it as well. The leadership exhibited by Grieme and the aggressive attack of his company, were important factors in breaching the defenses of the hill.[11] With the capture of these two key positions by the Germans, the forward-slope defenses on the hill were penetrated before the Russians could react. Other SS assault detachments, also moving swiftly, made penetrations at other points. As was so often experienced by German units in combat on the Eastern front, the Russian soldier, who was so resolute in defense when attacked in an expected manner, often was routed when taken unawares or attacked from an unexpected direction.

Shortly after the quick penetrations of the main defenses on the hill, the Russians abandoned the western slope of Hill 203.4. Quickly, the SS grenadiers pushed forward to pursue the retreating Russians from the crest of the hill down the length of the eastern slope, not allowing them to recover and organize a defensive position. In a short time, Stadler's attack had penetrated to a depth of nearly three kilometers, the hill itself being reported taken at 0845 hours.[12]

However, no sooner had the Russian infantry retreated than their artillery dropped a thunderous barrage of artillery on the forward slope and crest of the hill. The intensity of the shelling forced the Germans to take cover in Russian dug-outs and bunkers in order to survive. There was no question of further attack into the storm of fire that covered the top of the hill. In addition to forcing the SS grenadiers to take cover, the Russian shellfire created a very dangerous situation in regard to Stadler's communications, a development that threatened to undo his success in capturing the hill.[13]

Stadler had just established his regimental HQ under a destroyed T-34 tank and was preparing to direct the consolidation of the captured position when the heavy barrage of artillery crashed down. The command group was forced to take shelter under the knocked-out Soviet tank. Shortly afterward, a shell cut the telephone lines, and within seconds, another shell destroyed the HQ radio set. Stadler was suddenly without any form of communication with division or corps command. The Russian artillery fire was so murderous that even messengers were unable to get through the storm of exploding shells.

Out of communication with Stadler and not aware of the unexpectedly quick capture of the hill by his regiment, the German forward observers noted the intense Russian artillery fire and concluded that it was in support of a counterattack against *Der Führer*. Stadler's regiment, at that point, was believed to be still in front of the forward positions of 203.4. Operating on the mistaken assumption that Stadler was in need of artillery support to smash what was perceived to be a Russian counterattack, German artillery shelled the trenches and fortifications on the crest of the hill. Stadler and his men thus found themselves in the unenviable situation of being under fire from both Russian and German guns at the same time. In desperation, utilizing the only means of communication left to them, the Germans fired white flares into the air to signal their comrades that they were in possession of the hill. It was only after some time that the flares were recognized and the shelling by the German guns stopped. Weidinger records that Stadler's caustic comments regarding being shelled by his own artillery were "unrepeatable" (*einmaligen*).

In the meantime, while *Der Führer* remained immobilized under the barrage of artillery, a Russian counterattack was organized with the objective of throwing the Germans back down the western slope. The Soviets troops recovered from their initial confusion and quickly massed in order to prevent the Germans from penetrating farther into the Olkhovchik Valley east of Hill 203.4. A number of tanks also appeared at the base of the hill and crawled forward with the Russian troops, riding on the decks or walking in waves behind the tanks as they ground up the reverse slope. The Russian shells still smashed down on the hilltop as the counterattack moved up the hill under cover of the high explosives. Russian tanks and infantry overran the

German forward positions and threatened to break through and create a dangerous a gap in the line. Having just stopped his own artillery from crippling his regiment's attack, Stadler's communication breakdown now threatened to result in a lack of artillery support when it was needed at a critical moment.

At this point, things took a better turn for Stadler and his men when radio communication was reestablished. The facts of the situation were relayed to divisional HQs and German artillery soon made its presence felt as now the Germans could see into the valley.[14] The fire of the batteries was directed on the Russian attack on the reverse slope of the hill. Now in possession of high ground from which observation was excellent, Stadler directed the fire of his own guns with deadly effect. A short time later, German shells began to fall on the Soviet counterthrust and the high-explosive shells tore gaps in the ranks of the advancing Russian infantry. Long columns of brown-uniformed soldiers walked over the bodies of the fallen and the attack pushed inexorably up the hill, moving through the smoke and flying shell fragments.

It was only after the Russian infantry came under fire from the machine guns and mortars of *Der Führer* that the attack faltered. The high rate of fire from the German MG-42s washed over the T-34s, sweeping the Russian infantry off the tanks like a deadly broom. Rows of Russian soldiers, walking behind the tanks, fell under the hail of automatic weapons fire and mortar shrapnel. The Russian infantry finally went to ground after leaving piles of dead and wounded littering the eastern slope. The T-34s continued up the hill in spite of the loss of the escorting infantry.

When the Soviet tanks pushed onto the crest of the hill without the support of their infantry, German assault groups, equipped with machine guns and other automatic weapons, swiftly mounted counterattacks against the flanks and rear of the immobile Russian infantry. The aggressive tactics of the German troops, though outnumbered, routed the Soviet infantry. With the withdrawal of the infantry, the Soviet attempt to retake the hill began to fall apart. Veteran German troops knew that they had little to fear from tanks unaccompanied by infantry, especially when occupying adequate fortifications such as the well-designed Russian trench system. They simply hid from the T-34s, taking shelter as the tanks clanked over the trenches, then emerged stealthily to assault the Russian tanks, dropping grenades into open hatches or attaching magnetic antitank shaped charges to engine covers. A few assault guns had reached the hill and opened fire on the Soviet tanks.

After losing the close support of their infantry, the Russian tanks were severely handicapped and could not secure possession of the position by themselves. Under fire from the SS assault guns and under close assault by the aggressive SS grenadiers, the surviving Russian armor had little choice but to abandon the attack. The Russian attack faltered, then collapsed entirely, and the T-34s withdrew from the hill, leaving several of their number burning on the slope. *Das Reich*'s assault guns had by this time moved into position and fired on the Russian armor, their 75mm guns helping to repel the assault.[15] With the inherently poor observation characteristics of the T-34 and a common unwillingness of Soviet tank commanders to expose themselves by observing from the cupola of their tanks, the German assault guns found it easy to take up effective firing positions and direct their fire on the Russian tanks.

However, even as the their tanks withdrew, more Soviet infantry surged up the hill from the eastern slope in brown waves. These attacks were driven off as well, destroyed by artillery fire, and by noon, it was evident from the slackening of the fighting that the attempt to regain the hill had ended. At many points, the Russian dead lay in piles in front of the positions of the *Der Führer* grenadiers.

When the battlefield became quiet and he had time to look around, it was readily apparent to Stadler, from his HQ on the hill, why the German troops had had such a difficult time during the last few days in their attempts to take the fortified positions at Hills 213.9, 211.5, and 203.4. From his vantage point, he was able to clearly observe the entire surrounding terrain and had excellent lines of sight to many of the positions of *Das Reich* and II. SS-Panzerkorps.[16]

He could clearly see Russian troops withdrawing behind rearguard detachments and streaming over the Mius at several points east of Hill 203.4. Significant Soviet strength crossed the river unmolested except for Stuka attacks before the division could adjust the fire from its artillery and organize for a combined arms pursuit. *Der Führer* remained engaged in the mopping up of the last remnants of Soviet resistance and did not secure the whole hill until 1300 hours. The last elements of the Soviet infantry elements holding out on the eastern slopes were captured or destroyed. After the hill was secured, Stadler was forced to wait for 23. Panzer-Division to fight its way across the Olkhovchik to support his regiments attack to the east. For a time, the tardy advance of the army panzer division kept him waiting impatiently and the advance of *Der Führer* did not continue until 1430 hours, when the armored spearhead of 23. Panzer-Division reached the area south of the hill.[17]

THE BREAKTHROUGH INTO THE OLKHOVCHIK

South of Stepanovka, the panzer group of *Das Reich* made several attempts to penetrate into the valley, but each was broken up by intense concentrations of Soviet artillery. The Russian fire struck with such force that it held up the spearhead of the mobile assault force until after 1100 hours. At that time, divisional artillery and Stuka attacks silenced the Soviet guns. The western edge of the Olkhovchik, between Stepanovka and Marinovka, was again attacked by the armored group just after noon. The SS grenadiers dismounted and assaulted the fortified Soviet infantry positions along the western edge of the valley. With the support of their tanks and assault guns, the SS troopers broke into the Russian position and began to slowly root out the Soviet infantry. The Russian defenders fought bitterly to the end, the survivors only surrendering when the position was destroyed. The battalion-strength defending force was decimated, with about 300 prisoners taken captive.[18]

After the fighting, III./*Der Führer* was reduced to an average company strength of only thirty-five to forty men. The casualties in *Der Fuhrer*'s companies were replaced by men of the engineer battalion in order to maintain the battalion combat strength. With the capture of this fortified position, the armored group stopped to take on fuel and ammunition, delaying its advance. When the vehicles completed their resupply, the attack moved forward toward the valley, although not without difficulty.

When III./Regiment *Der Führer*, with the remaining *Das Reich* tanks, attacked between Hill 223.7 and the southern perimeter of Stepanovka, it came under defensive fire from weapons of all calibers. After German artillery and Stuka attacks again were called on to eliminate the Soviet artillery, the tanks and assault guns rolled forward, with the mounted grenadiers spread out in attack formation behind the heavier armored vehicles. Again the personal initiative of a small-unit commander provided valuable leadership, providing the impetus to break into the valley about two kilometers south of Marinovka. Three assault guns of 3. Batterie/SS-Sturmgeschütz-Bataillon 2, commanded by Hauptscharführer Alfons Stegmaier, destroyed two T-34s and several antitank guns on the western edge of the valley. After knocking out the Soviet gun position, Stegmaier led his battery into the Olkhovchik. His assault guns furnished support for the advance of the SS grenadiers as they drove the Russians across the valley. Stegmaier pushed on all the way to the western base of Hill 213.9 and was the first man of his division to make contact with men of *Totenkopf*. It was probably Stegmaier's battery that knocked out the antitank gun strongpoint at the crossroads east of Stepanovka. For his leadership and decisive command during the fighting south of Stepanovka and other, earlier successful actions, Stegmaier was awarded the German Cross in Gold.[19] On the right flank of the armored group, the successful capture of Hill 203.4 aided the advance, as it resulted in a weakening of Soviet artillery fire and neutralized a key Soviet observation point.

The lead units of *Das Reich* now threatened the western and rear slopes of Hill 213.9 and had cut off the Russian troops in Stepanovka. This penetration resulted in the first large-scale withdrawals of Soviet troops and heavy weapons. At 1655 hours, artillery observers and air reconnaissance of 6. Armee reported that it observed regiment-strength Russian units withdrawing toward the east, abandoning the reverse slopes of Hill 213.9.[20] At 1700 hours, the message came over the radios of *Das Reich* HQ groups that Hill 213.9 had been taken by *Totenkopf* assault detachments. The breakthroughs of Stadler's two battalions of Regiment *Der Führer* and the armored group had broken the back of the Russian resistance and directly resulted in the capture of Hill 213.9. With the loss of the high ground at Hills 213.9 and 203.4, the Soviets had suffered more damage than they could recover from.

REGIMENT *DEUTSCHLAND* CLEARS STEPANOVKA

In the darkness of the early-morning hours of 1 August, the men of Regiment *Deutschland* were still embroiled in house-to-house fighting amongst the ruins in the southern and eastern sections of Stepanovka. The *Deutschland* grenadiers, reacting to a slackening of Soviet pressure, renewed their drive to clear the Russians out of the southern part of Stepanovka. During the hard fighting to reach the eastern edge of the town, the SS grenadiers and attached units from the divisional engineer battalion destroyed five Soviet tanks in the rubble-strewn streets.[21] Subsequently, the SS grenadiers reached the road entrance on the north edge of a projection of the town that extended eastward into the Olkhovchik. By 1515 hours, *Deutschland* pushed beyond the perimeter of the town, reaching a ravine just east of the town. At that point, the Soviet troops on the western slopes of Hill 213.9 directed a storm of mortar and small-arms fire on the German assault units. The heavy fire held up the advance and forced *Deutschland* to call for Stuka attacks and fire support from artillery and the Nebelwerfer battalion. The advance of the grenadiers resumed after effective fire support from medium artillery and rocket barrages from Werfer-Regiment 52 knocked out many of the Russian positions. The same Nebelwerfer unit that had so effectively contributed to *Der Führer*'s success on Hill 203.4 contributed to the success of *Deutschland* in the Olkhovchik.

The last Russian nests of resistance were cleared out of the southern section of houses in Stepanovka in cooperation with a *Totenkopf* battery of assault guns from SS-Sturmgeschütz-Abteilung 3 and elements of *Totenkopf* engineer detachments. Many of the areas east of the town, from where the Russian antitank gun and artillery positions had caused such damage to both of the SS divisions, were taken and mopped up. Most importantly, the antitank gun position near the roadfork to the northeast of Stepanovka was captured and silenced. By 1730 hours, *Deutschland* pushed into the valley south of the town, driving out the last Russian infantry.[22]

XXIX. ARMEEKORPS ASSAULTS THE OLKHOVCHIK

At 0810 hours, as the assault groups of *Das Reich* jumped off to begin their attacks, 294. Infanterie-Division and its attached battalions began the third day of the counterattack with an initial triumph in the ruins of Yelizavetinsky.

A XXIX. Armeekorps battle group, led by a battalion of 21. Grenadier-Regiment (17. Infanterie-Division) began the day's action with an attack against the northern half of the village, where the Russians remained dug in. The battalion stormed the Russian foxholes and fortified houses, assaulting across the narrow village roads. Working from house to house, the attackers drove the Russian troops out of the northern half of Yelizavetinsky and pursued them into the area east of the village. In spite of flanking fire from the northern part of Kuibyshevo, which lay just across the Mius, the town was cleared of Russian troops by 0830 hours. Continuing its attack, the battalion advanced to the east, toward the Mius. The advance overran and destroyed a Soviet antitank position, located at a crossroads to the northwest of a small clutch of dwellings named Repechovataja.[23]

The Russians rallied quickly to counterattack the newly won German gains, but the Germans quickly dug in and established communication with their artillery observers. Several times, the Soviets massed strong infantry attacks supported by artillery, but were repulsed by infantry small arms and effective artillery support. The German guns and mortar units erected a wall of fire in front of their troops that could not be penetrated by the Soviet infantry. When the Russians withdrew and tried to regroup, their assembly area was shelled. The Soviet infantry made several weaker attempts to fight their way back into Yelizavetinsky, but each was broken up by artillery.[24] Near a group of four houses, close by a hill that was nicknamed the "Kreuzhohe," the Soviets made their only breakthrough. After artillery pinned the Russians down, the penetration was sealed off and eliminated by counterattack.

Later in the morning, battalions of 17. and 294. Infanterie-Divisions advanced across the southern mouth of the Olkhovchik Valley, driving Russian rear guard units before them. This battle group captured Hill 168.5, which was situated at a wide point in the valley northwest of Kuibyshevo. This victory marked the first time that German troops were able to successfully close off Russian lines of communication in the southern section of the valley. The hill lay just east of the Marinovka–Kuibyshevo road and its control by the Germans effectively cut that line of communication.

By early afternoon, reports began to arrive at the XXIX. Armeekorps HQ in regard to observation of columns of Russian artillery and other heavy equipment crossing the Mius at bridges and fords. The Russians had constructed bridges over the shallow river during the occupation of the west bank, heavier ones with the capacity to support tanks and artillery. There were many lighter bridges and fords provided for infantry. These retreating Russian units were probably units forced to abandon their defensive positions after the capture of Hill 168.5 and Regiment *Der Führer*'s penetrations into the Olkhovchik after the capture of Hill 203.4. Regiment *Deutschland*'s subsequent drive into the valley from the eastern edge of Stepanovka added to the already serious threats to the Soviet lines of communication. The capture of Hill 168.5, following the decisive breakthrough made by Stadler, created the opportunity for additional victories in the afternoon, although the German troops on the hill for a time found themselves under fire from their own artillery.

The advance across the valley proceded more rapidly than expected, and taking the hill quickly nearly meant disaster for the German infantry. In an incident similar to that which had been experienced by Stadler, German shells still fell on the hill after the Russians had abandoned it. The artillery batteries of II. SS-Panzerkorps were not aware of the fact that German soldiers were now on the hill. Just as had happened on Hill 203.4, prompt action had to be taken in order to avoid losses to friendly fire. By observation of the direction from which the shells were fired, forward observers realized that the artillery of II. SS-Panzerkorps was the likely source of the shelling. The Ia of 294. Infanterie-Division quickly informed 6. Armee that the hill was in German hands at that time and requested that the artillery of 6. Armee and II. SS-Panzerkorps be informed of that fact promptly.[25]

When XXIX. Armeekorps' battle groups tried to move farther across the Olkhovchik, they were halted after contact with Soviet troops firing from new defensive positions. The Soviet rear guard elements fought with great determination and, reinforced by a few tanks, refused to be routed. When the Germans halted to regroup and advance again on the Russian positions, they were assaulted ferociously by platoon-size counterattacks. Russian artillery began to drop shells on the assault group. Shortly afterwards, the intensity of the shellfire began to increase. In the face of this solid resistance by Soviet infantry and heavy artillery fire, the attack stalled.

The commander of 294. Infanterie, Generalleutnant Block, requested support from 16. Panzergrenadier-Division's armored elements and asked that it be committed at the confluence of the Krivaja with the Olkhovchik. It was, however, not possible to provide the requested armor, as at that time 16. Panzergrenadier-Division was involved in heavy fighting itself. As its commander, Generalleutnant Count Gerhard von Schwerin, reported in his answer to the request for armored support, the divisional attack groups were very weak and could not spare the vehicles. The concerns of Schwerin were entirely justified as there were only twelve tanks available to his division on 1 August. Due to the weakness of the combat units, the division had all it could do to maintain its own progress.

The only armor immediately available to send to the hard-pressed infantry division were twelve assault guns belonging to Sturmgeschütz-Abteilung 243, subordinate to XXIX. Armeekorps. But even this support was delayed after the appearance of sixty-seven Russian tanks near the "Kreuzhohe." The Soviet tanks were engaged by the assault guns west of Repechovataja, a small village that lay north of Kuibyshevo and the assault gun battalion remained involved in this fighting for some time. Without the support of the assault guns, the infantry attack lost its momentum after taking Hill 168.5.

XXIV. PANZERKORPS—1 AUGUST

In the first hours of the attack, XXIV. Panzerkorps encountered a number of difficulties on 1 August, due primarily to mud, however, and not the Russians. The movements of vehicles of the two divisions were hampered in the first hours of the attack due to the muddy roads and ravine crossings. This was particularly true in the case of 23. Panzer-Division, which lost a great deal of time due to the condition of the terrain. The last of its combat units were not able to reach their assigned assembly areas until 0800 hours. The division was already considerably late in beginning its attack by that time. The 16. Panzergrenadier-Divison, demonstrating more skill, or perhaps more resolve, had already jumped off and was advancing. Once more, delays by 23. Panzer Division were serious hindrances to the the success of the attack.

After the division finally managed to assemble, a battalion assault group of 128. Panzergrenadier-Regiment penetrated through the northern part of the Krutaya ravine and assaulted Russian positions inside the ravine from the flank, while the divisional armor attacked the ravine frontally. The Krutaya Schlucht (stream bed or water cut) was east of Garany and the Soviets had used it as an assembly point from which they had repeatedly launched attacks during the previous two days. When the panzers and panzergrenadiers stormed the Krutaja, Russian resistance was discovered to be relatively weak. The northern part of the ravine was cleared of Soviet troops and was completely in German hands at 1200 hours. After regrouping, the attack group pushed on toward the area of Hill 203.4, although the panzers were again delayed by a minefield encountered north of the Krutaja. The panzergrenadiers pushed on without the tanks, moving toward a long hedgerow, southeast of Hill 203.4. The grenadiers deployed and assaulted the hedgerow without the armor. The Russians stubbornly defended the hedgerow, and when the German infantry began to advance across the valley floor, machine-gun fire began to rattle and mortar shells immediately fell on the attackers. After sustaining a number of casualties, the German infanty withdrew and waited for the armor to rejoin them.

Moving against the Krutaja to the south of this attack group, 126. Panzergrenadier-Regiment and Kampfgruppe Henneberg also encountered obstinate resistance by detachments of Russian infantry, coming under fire from heavy Russian artillery, which caused numerous casualties. After reorganizing for the assault and receiving support from the divisional artillery, the German infantry made its attack into the face of the shellfire and strong small-arms fire, which poured on them from firing positions dug into the sides of the ravine. The grenadiers overran the defensive perimeter, broke into the ravine and penetrated into the midst of the Russian fighting positions. After brief fighting at close quarters, the western edge of the ravine was taken. This success was followed up by an attack on the eastern edge of the ravine slope. All organized resistance in the Krutaja soon collapsed. At 1845 hours, in a subsequent attack, the panzergrenadiers of the division captured an intact twenty-four-ton bridge over the Olkhovchik stream that flowed down the center of the valley floor.[26] Small groups of Russian infantry remained to be cleared out of the ravine and grenadiers did not finish mopping up the last pockets of resistance along the lower stretch of the Krutaja until nearly 1300 hours.[27]

At 1230 hours, the hedgerow south of Marinovka was taken by 128. Panzergrenadier-Regiment after the panzer group arrived and supported the attack. Once more on the move, the regiment continued its drive across the valley's western half, aiming for the heavy bridge still intact over the Olkhovchik stream. It became evident that Russian strength was weakening, although the rearguard elements continued to fight and delay the German advance. The Soviet artillery remained formidable, inflicting casualties on the division's assault units until later in the day when the division organized effective counterbattery fire on Soviet artillery positions east of the river.

Russian artillery batteries located in the Marinovka were also silenced or had withdrawn. The weight of fire directed against the regiment as it attempted to cross the valley visibly diminished.[28] The Soviets, at this point, were confronted with another gap in their defensive line.

The other division of XXIV. Panzerkorps, 16. Panzergrenadier-Division, began its attack with only mimimal delays in spite of the muddy conditions. The division's spearhead unit, a battalion of 60. Panzergrenadier-Regiment, deployed from Malopetrosky, a small group of huts east of Grigorievka, and advanced toward the Krivaya ravine. This small valley opened up on its eastern end into the Olkhovchik at a point between Yelizavetinsky and the south edge of Marinovka. Its western origin intersected the Krutaya just to the east of Hill 196.0. The Krivaya ravine, like the Krutaja, served as a sheltered route of supply and assembly for Soviet infantry and armor moving out of the Olkhovchik. The 16. Panzergrenadier-Division, after the elimination of the Soviet troops defending the ravine, was also in position to penetrate the Olkhovchik. A successful German entry into the valley at that point threatened the Soviet troops in the Marinovka area with encirclement and supported the attack by Stadler's regiment, which already had fought its way into the wide valley.

However, the advance of the panzergrenadier division was slowed by Soviet resistance and most of the morning passed before it reached the ravine edge. At 1200 hours, 60. Panzergrenadier-Regiment's lead battalion arrived at the western border of the Olkhovchik near a point northeast of the entrance of the Krivaya into the larger valley. A 156. Panzergrenadier-Regiment battle group cleared out Russian elements still occupying the Krivaya there and then pushed east from a point 500 meters north of the Krivaya's intersection with the Olkhovchik. The Russians then were faced with breakthroughs into the valley in several different sectors. By this time, it had become apparent that Russian resistance was weakening at many points.

Late in the morning, the chief of staff of 6. Armee, Generalmajor Bork, was close to the front, observing the progress of the spearhead units of Regiment *Der Führer* and XXIV. Panzerkorps. When it became clear to him that the Russian infantry fire and the volume of artillery had recognizably diminished in strength, he ordered *Das Reich* and 23. Panzer-Division to push across the southern section of the Olkhovchik with all possible speed without regard to any danger to their flanks. The acceleration of the attack was to prevent the Russian command from moving a stronger blocking force into the Olkhovchik and, more importantly, to prevent the Russians from withdrawing their forces safely over the river. The new objective of this attack by *Das Reich* and XXIV. Panzerkorps was the high ground east of Marinovka, around Hill 194.3. The capture of this hill, located just to the southeast of Hill 213.9, would result in the encirclement of the Soviet forces in Stepanovka and in the Marinovka area. The supply routes and communication lines to the key position in the center, Hill 213.9, would also be threatened by a penetration at that point because the Germans would be able to direct observed artillery fire into the valley east of Marinovka. Speed of action was essential in order to prevent the Russians from having time to dig in and build up a new line of defense or begin the withdrawal of additional forces out of the bridgehead.

Due to the capture of high ground by the Germans, they were able to command by fire all points of the collapsing Soviet bridgehead from the southern section of the Olkhovchik to the area between Stepanovka and Hill 213.9. Now that the Russians were forced out of their trenches and holes and moving above ground, they could be engaged by combined arms and destroyed. Those units moving across the valley in the open or crossing the river over its numerous fords were vulnerable to artillery and Stuka attacks. The Soviet infantry detachments left behind in the Olkhovchik did not have their previously overwhelming amount of artillery support, and they were mopped up by coordinated attacks of German infantry, armor and artillery, with Stuka support from IV. Fliegerkorps.

In the early afternoon of 1 August, XXIV. Panzerkorps consolidated its breakthroughs into the Olkhovchik. The diminishing strength of Soviet artillery was apparent. The lessening of Soviet artillery was due to a combination of the advances into the valley and counterbattery efforts of the German artillery and Stukas and greatly facilitated the attack of XXIV. Panzerkorps. When the reports of multiple German penetrations into the Olkhovchik became known to the Soviet command, it became necessary for Tolbukhin to begin to withdraw from the bridgehead in order to prevent the annihilation of his forces. He was faced with the choice of either counterattacking the gaps and attempting to restore a continuous front or withdrawing from his positions west of the Mius River.

THE LAST ASSAULT ON HILL 213.9

By late in the afternoon, it was clear that the Soviets had begun to react to multiple breakthroughs and the severing of their lines of retreat to the Mius by giving up the defense of the bridgehead. They were observed to begin substantial withdrawals at several points in late morning of 1 August, and for the first time, Soviet artillery units were observed crossing the river. The II. SS-Panzerkorps HQ alerted the assault groups of *Totenkopf*, which remained ready to resume their attack on Hill 213.9. At 1115 hours, the division received alert orders for the resumption of the attack and company commanders reported to the regimental command post. There they learned that Hill 213.9 was to be taken by assault later in the afternoon, after the attacks in *Das Reich*'s sector and in the southern sector of the Olkhovchik created a favorable situation for *Totenkopf* to resume attacks on the hill.[29]

The men of the division waited throughout the morning for the order to once more try to storm the hill that lay in front of them. Making use of the brief lull in combat that began with the end of fighting on 31 July, the tank repair company of *Totenkopf* worked nonstop to return tanks to action. On 1 August, the division reported that it had three Tiger tanks, eleven Panzer IVs, five Panzer IIIs, and six command tanks in working order, for a total of twenty-five tanks. There were also fourteen assault guns and sixteen self-propelled 7.5mm antitank guns on light armored chassis.[30]

The panzergrenadier regiments had suffered grievous casualties. Some companies numbered only eight to ten men, having been decimated by the fighting of the previous two days. The battalions were reduced to an average strength of 80 to 100 men by the losses sustained during ten days of fighting during "Citadel," but the Mius fighting was a bloodbath. Fragments of companies were combined in order to organize them into assault detachments. By 1 August, Regiment *Totenkopf* remained a regiment in name only, barely having the strength of a weak battalion.[31] Regiment *Totenkopf*'s attack was reinforced by II./Regiment *Eicke*, commanded by SS-Sturmbannführer Kurt Launer, as well as elements of the SS engineers and the reconnaissance battalion.

While *Totenkopf* prepared to attack once more, wings of Stukas assembled above the hill, and swooped down to bomb Soviet strongpoints in the front lines. The bombs raised great plumes of dark earth into the air. German artillery began to hammer the Russian forward

The Decisive Day: 1 August

positions to suppress Soviet defensive fire and Nebelwerfer rockets blanketed the hilltop with thunderous barrages of rockets. The company commanders returned to their men and gave them the word to prepare for the attack. A veteran of Regiment *Totenkopf*, former SS-Rottenführer Hax, remembered that moment: "Shortly before 1300 hours, the order was transmitted to the companies: . . . prepare to move, things are moving fast. Then came the call to get ready."

While the grenadiers had rested and waited in the hot morning sun, men of the SS panzer engineer companies were at work in the minefields long before daylight. They continued to remove mines all through the day, shielded from observation by the corn and sunflowers. In the afternoon, when the attack started again, concentrations of high-explosive shells burst on the Soviet forward positions, forcing the Russian infantry to keep their heads down. The mine-removal teams remained at work under cover of friendly fire. Hundreds of mines were removed from the northwest sector of the hill during the course of the day, as the SS engineers worked to create safe lanes of advance for their tanks.[32]

Because of the weakness of the SS grenadier regiments, there was no longer sufficient strength to have a divisional reserve infantry element for the attack. The only formation left to the division for use as a reserve was SS-Panzer-Aufklärungs-Abteilung 3 and several companies of the divisional engineers, SS-Pionier-Abteilung 3. Reserve armor was also nonexistent. In place of tanks, the tank destroyer battalion's motorized 7.5 antitank guns were to support the attack and move forward with the attack of the reconnaissance troops. Automatic 2cm guns on the armored cars and the 7.5cm guns mounted on armored cars and half-tracks of the reconnaissance troop could not replace tanks but were effective weapons against infantry and bunker positions.

At 1330 hours, the assault detachments began their attack and the remnants of Regiment *Totenkopf* again moved forward toward the first enemy positions 500 meters in front of the hill. Panzer motors roared as the SS tank commanders ordered their drivers to cautiously advance. The tanks moved forward, using any available cover that the terrain provided. Ahead of the tanks, a thin line of grenadiers walked behind assault guns, widely spaced and moving cautiously. When scattered Russian artillery shells fell on the attackers, they leapt forward in quick rushes, using assault troop tactics. Long-range machine-gun fire rattled and mortars began to drop on the SS troopers. The Germans hoped to advance under cover of their artillery and move nearer to the hill until they got close enough to assault the Russian fighting holes and antitank gun emplacements in the first defensive positions. The tanks were not to be committed until the grenadiers eliminated antitank gun positions on the forward slope. More losses of the surviving panzers were to be avoided at all costs.

Meanwhile, behind the attack, Flak units of the division fought off Soviet bombers and attack aircraft, putting their 2cm automatic guns to good use in the protection of artillery positions as well as the forward line. German fighter planes made a much-needed appearance over the battlefield, engaging the IL-2s before the Russian planes could disrupt the attack with strafing and bombing attacks.[33] Overhead, the Stukas were at work again as well. The gull-wing aircraft circled high in the air, locating their targets, before plunging down to drop their bombs on the hill crest. The artillery of II. SS-Panzerkorps concentrated its fire on selected targets on the hill and reverse slope assembly areas.

Advancing through the Russian machine-gun fire and light artillery, the SS assault detachments crept up the hill while armored cars of the reconnaissance battalion blasted machine-gun nests and fighting positions. When the assault squads were close to the Russian first line, they moved to attack, breaking into the positions at several points. Without stopping, bypassing strongpoints, they rapidly pushed toward the hill when suddenly a cloud of smoke, dust, and explosions struck in front of them as if a murderous curtain had been dropped on the hill. The Russians erected a wall of mortar and artillery fire between the attackers and the main line of defense. SS engineers and grenadiers threw themselves into holes and ditches, taking shelter from the shellfire. The Russian shells churned up the dusty ground, blasting clouds of dust high into the air. The German infantry found itself in shattered trenches and bunkers that had been destroyed by their artillery or Stuka attacks, bodies of Russians and Germans alike strewn around the bloody ground.

When the attack faltered, the Nebelwerfer batteries were ordered to fire on the hill again. While the German troops remained in their shelters, salvos of screaming rockets roared in over their heads and blasted Hill 213.9. Using the cover provided by the smothering blanket of high explosives and smoke, the SS troops moved forward again. Under the personal leadership of Obersturmbannführer Baum and Sturmbannführer Ullrich, the SS troopers renewed the assault of the Russian positions, infiltrating in small groups and penetrating the Soviet earthworks. Under cover of fire laid down by mortars and small arms, the combat groups moved forward, finding weak points or gaps that could be used to get into the main defensive positions. The assault groups eliminated bunkers and antitank gun positions with grenades or explosive charges that the engineers had provided. Gradually, the Germans gained control of the forward trenches near the top of the hill.

Relays of Stuka flights continued to bombard the hill, and the combined artillery of a number of 6. Armee batteries and II. SS-Panzerkorps artillery directed their fire onto Soviet artillery positions on Hills 191.3, 194.3, and 140.3 in order to silence Russian guns. The capture of high ground in the Olkhovchik gave German artillery observers line of sight ability to direct gun fire on the Soviet artillery positions to the east of Hill 213.9. By mid-afternoon, the results of the penetrations into the valley by *Der Führer* and XXIV. Panzerkorps were also evident by a slackening of the volume of Russian artillery fire on Hill 213.9. Some of the artillery that had been positioned in the high ground east of the valley and middle ridge had now been withdrawn and some had been silenced with counterbattery fire. Russian artillery fire was clearly weaker at all points. As the Russian artillery strength diminished, the German attack began to work over the crest of the hill, still having to overcome determined Russian defenders.

Now the enemy was not an unseen tormentor firing from camouflaged, nearly invisible holes and bunkers. The fighting was at close range and the Russian troops could be seen, firing from individual holes with their head and shoulders above ground or firing from dugouts and bunkers. The enemy was now visible and could be engaged and killed.

Although Russian artillery support was diminishing, the defenders of the hill still fought back with mortar fire and small arms. At about 300 meters from the main defensive positions on the right flank of the attack, SS engineer units and a battalion of *Totenkopf* grenadiers under command of SS-Sturmbannführer Ernst Haussler had to stop when a heavy Russian mortar concentration landed right on top of their advance. Once more, the Germans went to ground.

Again the Stukas swooped down, the bombs exploding thunderously close to the German assault troops. When the dive-bombers droned away, high in the summer sky, the attack groups pressed forward again until Nebelwerfer barrages impacted on the Russian positions just in front of them. The grenadiers hurriedly found any available shelter when the rockets hurtled over their heads with their distinctive screams. The shock waves from the explosions washed over the SS troops, crammed into any available cover. However, they quickly moved forward again, toward the main defensive position, while the Russians were momementarily stunned.

German artillery began to support the advance. Slowly, the attack again went forward as German light and medium artillery adjusted its fire from point to point as needed. At 1430 hours, *Totenkopf* reported that its assault had pierced the hill's main defensive fortifications. At 1530 hours, on the right flank, the SS engineer battalion reported progress west of the hill, while the reconnaissance battalion advanced on the left wing northwest of Hill 213.9.[34]

Artillery concentrations were adjusted and new fire plans were coordinated to smash Russian strongpoints. In this type of flexible support, the German artillery often remained superior to the Russian army nearly to the end of the war. The Soviets could lay down fearsome concentrations of artillery fire, augmented by rockets. However, their artillery was often slow to relocate and properly coordinate its fire to support the infantry when forced to move or the battle situation changes abruptly. The Soviet army frequently experienced shortages of trucks and prime movers, which hampered artillery relocation during the fast-moving events of war. The shortage of trucks, in spite of the thousands sent by the American and British Lend-Lease program, was to a large extent due to the Soviet decision to produce thousands upon thousands of tanks at the expense of other types of vehicles. Radio communication deficiencies were likely a factor as well.

By contrast, 6. Armee and II. SS-Panzerkorps were able to coordinate fire from five artillery battalions from several different divisions. The German artillery provided strong artillery fires for the main attack, suppressing Soviet positions on the flanks but was also flexible enough to redirect some of its batteries to support the assault troops on 213.9 and other points at the same time. The Nebelwerfer batteries also proved especially useful in the attack, utilizing both smoke

The Decisive Day: 1 August

and high-explosive shells. An example of the German ability to relocate and coordinate fire support is the use of the Nebelwerfer batteries to support Stadler's assault on Hill 203.4 in the morning and then regroup to support the assault on Hill 213.9 later in the day. The fire support group of 6. Armee in the center consisted of army batteries, the artillery regiment of 3. Panzer-Division and SS artillery, all of which were smoothly utilized with effectiveness and flexibility.

Because of the heavy tank losses in the previous days, the SS tanks had not been committed until the infantry assault cleared gaps which could be exploited with reduced threat of further tank loss. Only then were the panzers to move up, able to support the attack more effectively now that the crews could concentrate on fire coming primarily from the front. Because of heavy casualties to the SS tankers, many of the crews were put together from survivors of the last two days of fighting and had no experience working together. Former Unterscharführer Stettner, of 5./SS-Panzer-Regiment 3, commented on this aspect of the operations at the Mius:

> From the rear, our reserve Panzer Is moved to the front. I took over the old panzer of my chief, Hauptsturmführer Flohr, who died in combat yesterday. The panzer crew was a motley bunch. A Rottenführer from Vienna was the gunner. Forward was a driver from the division replacement battalion.[35]

Under the pounding of a total of about 600 German guns, the Russian artillery fire weakened even further by late in the afternoon and it became noticeably less coordinated, although the mortar fire was still dangerous. With much of the Russian flanking fire eliminated or becoming weaker, the attack on the center ridge gained forward momentum after the SS tanks were ordered to advance into the main defensive position. Working their way forward, tank guns eliminating bunkers and machine-gun nests, the engineer and grenadier companies of *Totenkopf* gained ground steadily.

The Stukas appeared over the front lines again, turned over on their wings and plunged down in screaming dives, released their bombs, and pulled out at the last second before roaring away into the afternoon sky. The SS tanks slowly moved up onto the hill, blasting stubborn nests of resistance with their cannon. All of the Soviet anti-tank guns and T-34s were not destroyed, however. The German tanks still drew fire and had to engage Russian tanks coming down the hill in counterattacks.

Former Unterscharführer Stettner again described the attack of the panzer regiment:

> To our right moved Oberscharführer Sepp Fischer, to the left was Uzelino. Behind us followed our engineer section. We formed the left flank. We aggressively moved toward the hill. Before us was a Russian antitank gun position. Uzelino's vehicle was hit and caught fire. Uzelino leapt from the turret and ran for cover behind our tank. The other members of his tank crew worked their way to the rear. A fire trail flashed over my turret and one hit Fischer's tank. Our panzer shuddered and then shuddered again. . . . Fireballs flew past our panzer. Like a scared rabbit we scuttled toward a small mound of earth to find cover. The gunner from Fischer's tank raced in behind us and called out, "Unterscharführer! Oberscharführer Fischer is behind the panzer with a leg wound. We need to carry him to the rear! We need some cover." I fired off a smoke shell.[36]

There was still dangerous antitank gun fire directed at the flank of the SS tanks, coming from the area southeast of Stepanovka. SS Nebelwerfers fired a barrage of smoke shells to screen the panzers from this threat. With clouds of thick smoke shielding their advance, the tanks and assault guns renewed their progress over the hill crest with the grenadiers and engineer sections working forward with them. The SS infantry fired tracer rounds or tossed smoke grenades to mark the location of Russian machine-gun nests and other nest of resistance for the armored vehicle crews. Tanks or assault guns moved up to the Russian fighting position and blasted it with high explosive shells at close range, then machine-gunning any Russian who tried to flee. In addition to the sporadic antitank gun fire, now largely ineffective due to the smoke shells laid in front of the crossroads east of Stepanovka, the SS tanks found that Soviet armor still posed a danger.

Stettner described the progress of his tank during the attack on Hill 213.9:

The Decisive Day: 1 August

> With all of our power we sped toward the Pakfront. . . . I ran over a PaK. Under our wheels and treads the metal crunched. We halted behind the enemy gun and raked every movement with the turret machine gun. To the right of us the last Tiger moves forward. I quickly call to my old friend Karl Sandler. We stalk along the hill's forward slope, making use of all cover. I then halted behind an old, wrecked Panzer
>
> I saw three T-34s moving to our left. "Turret! Eleven o'clock, range 400 meters. Panzer Granate 39, T-34." The gunner calls out, "Ready! Fire!" The shell hit the first T-34 under the turret. The turret hatch flew open but no one jumped out as white smoke rolled out of the hatch. The next round was loaded and ready. The second T-34 literally exploded into pieces. The next shell hit and penetrated the motor of the third T-34. It also caught fire and a black column of smoke rose high into the air.[37]

The panzers rolled toward the hill crest, passing through lanes in the mine belts, leaving burning and blasted bunkers and knocked out Russian tanks behind them. The panzer regiment reported to division headquarter that its tanks were on the main part of the hill at 1600 hours. At this point, when the German tanks were still involved in mopping up the defenses on the hilltop, the Russians rallied and counterattacked forward SS infantry elements on the eastern slope. Several battalions of Russian infantry surged up the hill toward the SS soldiers. The hundreds of Soviet soldiers threaten to overrun the Germans by sheer weight of numbers even though machine-gun fire swept many of them off their feet. Always more shouting, brown-uniformed figures moved forward in a line that seemed to stretch across the entire side of the hill. The SS companies, now reduced to mere handfuls of men, dropped into cover and began to fire at the attackers moving toward them. For the first time, a few tanks could also be seen, cautiously edging up the slope.

At that time, when the German assault seemed about to be stopped, it received timely help from the Luftwaffe. A flight of Stukas screamed down and dropped their bombs on the charging Russian masses. After the planes delivered their explosive cargo, they heeled over and screamed back down, attacking the Russian infantry with low-level machine-gun fire. The air attack broke up the counterattack before it could overrun the German troops on the east slope. Shocked by the surprise from the air, the stunned Soviet infantry scattered, fled back down the hill or surrendered by the hundreds.

By 1635 hours, the division reported that the west side of the hill was secure and the eastern slope was in the process of being cleared. While there were scattered pockets of Russian troops still on the hill, the position had essentially been taken. Some of the defenders fought to the last, while other Russians surrendered or scurried through gulleys and communications trenches to the rear. Due to the bitter nature of the fighting and the heavy casualties inflicted by both sides, the Russian troops were at times reluctant to show themselves after surrendering. The SS grenadiers were in no mood for nonsense, as too many of their comrades lay dead and shattered on the slopes behind them to be patient with reluctant enemy soldiers. In the heat of battle, they were quick to explode with reactions that only combat veterans truly know and understand:

> We had reached the Russian main defensive position. Now to clear the holes. "Come on out, bastards!" Then in Russian: "Ivan, *idi suda!*" Four hands came up out of the holes, then two heads appeared slowly. Then the rest of the body. From between the Russians two arms reached up, grabbed them by the collar and roughly pulled them down. "So it's like that!" Then a grenade flies toward us, but it goes overhead and strikes behind us. Naturally, we can do that also. Otto fires, and I toss an "egg" grenade into the hole. A blast! We go up and look in. Four men had been in the hole. Hugo Lechner had also thrown a grenade.[38]

The bitter fight for Hill 213.9 was over after three days of bloody combat. At 1700 hours, in a message to HQ of II. SS-Panzerkorps, *Totenkopf* reported: "Hill 213.9 taken . . . in spite of strong PaK and artillery fire."[39]

The Soviet command was threatened by a complete collapse of the bridgehead now that the main line was penetrated at so many points. Tolbukhin realized that he did not have enough reserve strength to successfully counterattack all of the German penetrations, but his main objective had long ago been accomplished and now he sought to disengage as much of his men and equipment as possible. By this time, the Russian withdrawal from the bridgehead was in full swing as artillery and other heavy equipment tried to get over the Mius before being cut off. As men were less valuable than cannons, mortars and tanks, rear-guard units were sacrificed in order to gain time for as much equipment to cross the river as possible. Tolbukhin bought that needed time with the blood of his rear-guard troops.

After the loss of Hill 213.9 and the failure of their counterattack, the Russians tried to build a blocking position on the reverse slope. A hastily manned line was thrown together around a number of quickly emplaced antitank guns. The Soviet command desperately threw men up the southeast slope, commiting an entire fresh rifle division to the effort to stop the German advance between Hill 213.9 and Hill 194.3, east of the Marinovka–Ssneshnoje road.[40] The division moved hurriedly into the area just to the southwest of Hill 191.3. There the men of the Soviet rifle battalions quickly dug fighting positions and prepared to meet the German attack. Other elements of Russian infantry advanced to the east of the new line, counterattacking the left flank of Regiment *Eicke*. This attack struck the middle of the regimental sector in the Gerassimova Valley and was accompanied by artillery support from Dmitrievka. Along with this artillery activity, the Soviets again committed large numbers of planes to harass and delay the German advance.[41]

According to SS-Rottenführer Hax of the reconnaissance battalion, "the Russians plastered us at that time with their 17.2cm howitzers, the 'Black Sow.' I had just left a hole and had to jump into a latrine ditch. . . . The Russians also fired phosphorus mortar shells at us."[42]

Das Reich and 23. Panzer-Division's assault groups pushed toward Hill 194.3 in the late afternoon, widening their breakthroughs. This threatened the left flank of the new Soviet blocking position southeast of Hill 213.9 and the Russians were faced with the choice of either regaining the hill by counterattack or abandonment of the bridgehead entirely. The blocking position was essentially untenable with the high ground advantage derived from the possession of the hill. The terrain, however, did not favor a successful counter thrust. Possession of the high ground on the center ridge allowed the Germans to use the heights to look down on any attack, with all of the advantages that this gave the SS and army artillery. The positions of the two opponents had been reversed!

After the loss of the center ridge and the multiple penetrations into the Olkhovchik, the Russians had essentially lost the battle for possession of the bridgehead. The penetrations across the Olkhovchik cut the lines of communications between the Soviet forces in Stepanovka-Marinovka and the river. Because the German forces in the Olkhovchik threatened the flank of the new blocking position that the Soviets attempted to maintain east of the Marinovka–Hill 213.9 road, the fresh rifle division that Tolbukhin rushed up to the makeshift line was confronted with an impossible situation. Without the commitment of strong armored forces, it was unable to hold the new line because of the penetrations on its flank by 23. Panzer-Division, *Das Reich* and XXIX. Armeekorps at Hill 168.5 in the southern end of the Olkhovchik.

Later in the day, the SS panzer divisions continued to push toward the river. A battalion of *Das Reich* tanks reached Hill 168.5 at 2215 hours after pushing across the Olkhovchik. Regiment *Deutschland* fought its way east of Stepanovka in the afternoon, with the left flank of the regiment in contact with *Totenkopf* to the east of the town. III./*Deutschland* advanced to just west of Marinovka at Fedorovka. Combat elements of *Das Reich* and *Totenkopf* maintained contact near Hill 194.3, building a secure position for the night, in order to furnish a jump-off line for the continuation of the attack on the following day.

It was the opinion of 6. Armee that the Soviet defenses had been pierced in too many places for the situation to be saved without the commitment of a strong armored force. At that time, the Russians did not have enough armor in the bridgehead or an immediately available reserve. The Soviet rifle divisions were so decimated that they had, for all practical purposes, no offensive value and Tolbukhin had little choice but to continue to withdraw over the Mius.

In German eyes, 6. Armee was on the verge of victory at the Mius, the Russian bridgehead defenses were pierced in many places, and Southern Front forces were beginning to withdraw back over the river in defeat. What was unknown to the Germans was that Tolbukhin had been extremely successful in accomplishing his primary objective, which was to threaten 6. Armee strongly enough to force Heeresgruppe Süd to draw German panzer divsions out of the Kursk offensive at a critical time. The battles of Kursk and the Mius River fighting are inseparably interrelated because of the influence that the latter had on German operations following the battle of Prochorovka.

In terms of strategy, the two battles were closely related because the attack of Southern Front across the Mius was a planned and integral part of the Soviet campaign to defeat Operation "Citadel" in the south. The diversionary battle and the program of deliberate lack of the normal *maskirovka* measures were of vital importance to the outcome not only of "Citadel" but the subsequent offensive at Kharkov-Belgorod. Without the diversionary attacks at Izyum and the Mius, the Soviet 1st Tank Army and Rotmistrov's 5th Guards Tank Army may have been destroyed by Hoth's panzer divisions in the days after 12 July.

The battle at the Mius River during this period of the war can be seen to be a microcosm of the war on the Eastern Front. German forces, often superior to the Russians on a division-to-division comparison, although vastly outnumbered, won a tactical victory at the Mius. However, the Soviets achieved their main objective, which was the removal of panzer divisions from a critical arena of the Kursk battle. In the larger scheme of the war as a whole, it was immaterial whether Tolbukhin defeated 6. Armee during July 1943 or in August or October of the same year. However, it was extremely important strategically that his attack influenced the operations and commitment of the panzer divisions of Heeresgruppe Süd from 17 to 29 July.

While Tolbukhin was forced to retreat across the river, the Soviets were able to make a reasonably orderly withdrawal across the Mius, saving much of their artillery and heavy weapons. The Germans succeeded in forcing the Russians out of the Mius bridgehead, causing Tolbukhin to abandon his earlier gains at Dmitrievka-Kuibyshevo. However, the counterattack of II. SS-Panzerkorps and 6. Armee was not a complete success. The quick strike that was to have encircled the entire bridgehead on the western bank and destroyed the bridgehead forces was not possible due to the failures of the supporting attacks on both flanks of the middle ridges and the terrific resistance put up by the defenders of Hills 213.9, 211.5, and 203.4 in the first days of the counterattack. XXIV. Panzerkorps, due to its losses of armor on the first day and the weakness of both divisions from the fighting earlier in July, did not properly support the right flank of *Das Reich*, getting involved in the reduction of the encirclement west of Garany, which delayed their advance at a critical time. As a result, the attack of the armored group of the SS division was not strong enough to break into the Olkhovchik on the first day. *Das Reich* was forced to fight off the attacks of several rifle divisions and the entire 2nd Guards Mechanized Corps on the second day of the attack. All momentum was lost on the first day and with it went the chances for a dramatic German success. It can be argued that Hollidt used his armor poorly and nearly destroyed the two SS divisions as a result. Manstein was well aware of the mishandling of the two panzer divisions, and this may explain why he took such on-the-scene interest in the fighting.

Even after the bridgehead began to collapse and Tolbukhin began the retreat, stubborn action by the Russian rear guards prevented Hollidt from destroying as many Russian troops as had been hoped for. On 1 August, although the Russians were beaten, they were not driven out of the bridgehead in disorder, and they aggressively maintained numerous delaying positions, shielding the withdrawal of the main Soviet forces. The Russians continued to hold their delaying positions actively, holding tired German troops at bay and counterattacking at many points along the front while at the same time the bridgehead perimeter contracted toward the river. After dark on 1 August, the Soviets continued to maintain their reverse-slope blocking positions south and east of 213.9, employing a reinforced rifle battalion and eight to ten tanks in a night attack against *Totenkopf*'s positions on Hill 213.9. At 2200 hours, *Totenkopf* reported that it had been attacked and was still engaged in close combat with Soviet troops. The surprise night attack materialized out of the darkness from the east and succeeded in penetrating the German lines but was not strong enough to push them off the hill. An unidentified veteran of 3./SS-Regiment *Totenkopf* remembered the events of the evening of 1 August:

> Our section, which numbered just eight men, had occupied a forward outpost. Suddenly, the Russians attacked with tanks and infantry and overran our position. About a hundred meters to my left, some of my comrades, Friedrich M., L., and Hans, a fellow north Silesian, tried to escape. With loud yells,

the Soviet soldiers advanced with fixed bayonets and overran the position. It was horrible to know what was happening and hear the shrill cries of my comrades and not be able to help them.[43]

After sharp fighting in the forward positions and the inevitable German counterattacks, the attack was turned back by 2250 hours. The defeat of the Russian attack ended the fighting on the third day and the rest of the night passed quietly on the hill. On 1 August, 3. SS-Panzergrenadier-Division had just twenty-five operational tanks left. There were five Panzer IIIs, eleven Panzer IVs, and three Tigers, in addition to six command tanks. Other armored vehicles included fourteen Sturmgeschütz IIIs and sixteen 7.5cm motorized antitank guns. *Das Reich* listed fifteen Sturmgeschütze and fifteen motorized 7.5cm antitank guns, along with eleven Panzer IIIs and thirteen Panzer IVs, with five command tanks.

II. SS-PANZERKORPS RECEIVES NEW ORDERS

On the morning of 1 August, at 1030 hours, while the fighting in 6. Armee's area still raged all over the battlefield, the Ia of II. SS-Panzerkorps received an order. The corps was ordered by Heeresgruppe Süd to prepare for the withdrawal of its three divisions for duty elsewhere on the Eastern Front. Transport officers of the Armeekorps HQ were directed to procede to Stalino in order to arrange for the rail transfer of *Das Reich*, 3. Panzer Division, and *Totenkopf* to the Kharkov area.[44] Manstein urgently needed the three panzer divisions to move north to the sector of the front west of Kharkov. Another situation was soon to become critical on the northern flank of Heeresgruppe Süd's front.

The Russians, until the last minute, had successfully concealed the concentration of forces for their attack against Kharkov, fooling even Manstein. Voronezh and Steppe Fronts prepared for the attack utilizing the whole range of *maskirovka* measures that were normally employed and concealed their build-up from the Germans even though it was on a huge scale. Vatutin's Voronezh Front had a total strength of over 450,000 men, 1,859 tanks, and General I. S. Koniev's Steppe Front had just under 200,000 men and 454 tanks. Each army was massively reinforced with antiaircraft divisions, artillery brigades and various units of engineers, antitank, mobile antitank and rocket launcher troops in detachments that varied from battalion to divisional size. In spite of the concentration of this enormous amount of troops, supplies, and equipment, Manstein mistakenly believed that the Russians had suffered such losses during "Citadel" as to make an offensive unlikely until later in the month, if not toward the end of the summer. This provides a valuable illustration of the ability of the Russians to create huge reserves in a surprisingly short time and their ability to conceal these concentrations of troops effectively.

Two Soviet fronts were massed for the attack on the Belgorod-Kharkov sector, Voronezh and Steppe Fronts. Voronezh Front's primary mobile elements consisted of 1st Tank Army and 5th Guards Tank Army. 5th Guards Tank Army, reduced to approximately 150 to 200 tanks after its destruction by Hausser's SS panzers at Prochorovka, had 503 tanks. 1st Tank Army, in possession of less than a hundred tanks after XXXXVIII. Panzerkorps and *Totenkopf* had decimated its three mobile corps, had 542 tanks, almost all of which were T-34s.[45]

These two armies were the armored reserves that Manstein had pleaded with Hitler to allow him to finish off after Prochorovka. In retrospect, Manstein's strong desire to destroy the Soviet tank formations around Prochorovka can be seen to have been the correct course of action in light of the events of August. The Soviet armies that had been in position to be destroyed on 13 July were again at full strength only weeks after their catastrophic losses at Kursk and ready to participate in the most important Soviet counterattack of the summer. Hitler's decisions regarding the employment of German armor after Prochorovka allowed the Soviet command to rebuild these two tank armies, the key offensive formations in the south Ukraine and commit them in the decisive sector of the Soviet summer counteroffensives for 1943.

It is interesting to note that while the Russians were able to very quickly reequip their tank armies with vehicles, even the vast manpower resources of the Russians could not make up for the enormous personnel losses of the Russian rifle divisions during "Citadel." On 1 August, the armies of Vatutin's Voronezh Front were 10 to 30 percent below established manpower strength, with the rifle divisions averaging only 7,800 men, which was approximately 75 percent normal strength. Koniev's Steppe Front was even weaker, with some of its armies at barely 65 percent of table of organization and equipment, with an average rifle division strength of just over 6,000 men (35 percent understrength).[46]

However, regardless of these deficiencies, the Russians, with a total of almost three quarters of a million men and and approximately 2,300 tanks faced German forces of about 200,000 men and less than 300 tanks in the Kharkov-Belgorod area on 3 August. While II. SS-Panzerkorps fought Tolbukhin's armies at the Mius River, 1st Tank Army and 5th Guards Tank Army lay north of Belgorod, ready to launch their phase of the Soviet counteroffensives of the summer of 1943. Thus, just after the battle on the Mius had been decided, the divisions of II. SS-Panzerkorps received orders that would bring them face to face with the two Soviet tank armies that three weeks earlier might have been destroyed if Hitler had not lost the will to commit his "last battalion" at Prochorovka.

During the battle of Kursk, SS armor and infantry advance across open terrain in an attack on the low ridge in the background. NATIONAL ARCHIVES

A German assault gun moves past a Nebelwerfer. The Nebelwerfer electrically fired rockets with warheads of high explosives or smoke charges. It was a light weapon and could be easily moved by half-tracks or light trucks. NATIONAL ARCHIVES

Vehicles of the Panzer-Nachrichten-Abteilung (signals battalion) of 23. Panzer-Division. The tubular structures on the vehicles are long-range radio transmission aerials. JEAN RESTAYN

A German machine gunner fires over the gun shield of a PaK 40 75mm antitank gun at infantry targets in the village in the background.
NATIONAL ARCHIVES

A 37mm antiaircraft gun in action against Russian ground-attack planes.
NATIONAL ARCHIVES

The Ju 87D Stuka dive-bomber was an effective weapon, furnishing tactical air support during attacks on Hill 213.9. NATIONAL ARCHIVES

Makeshift tank destroyer: a captured Russian 76.2mm antitank gun mounted on the chassis of a 38(t) tank and known as the Marder III. This vehicle belonged to the tank destroyer battalion of *Das Reich*.
MARK C. YERGER

SS-Sturmbannführer Josef Swientek, the commander of SS-Artillerie-Regiment 3.
MARK C. YERGER

Sylvester Stadler was the commander of SS-Panzergrenadier-Regiment *Der Führer* during the summer battles of 1943. Stadler won the Knight's Cross in 1943 as the commander of II./Regiment *Der Führer*. He later was awarded the Oak Leaves and Swords. MARK C. YERGER

SS infantry fire an MG-34 machine gun at attacking Russian aircraft.
NATIONAL ARCHIVES

SS grenadiers inspect a knocked-out T-34 tank.
NATIONAL ARCHIVES

A Panther Ausf. A of 23. Panzer-Division, probably in the fall of 1943. The division did not have any Panthers during the Mius fighting. Its panzer regiment was partly equipped with this model later in the year. JEAN RESTAYN

Three Knight's Cross winners of *Das Reich* during the Mius fighting. From left: SS-Hauptsturmführer Helmut Schreiber, SS-Obersturmbannführer Heinz Harmel, and SS-Sturmbannführer Gunther Wisliceny.
MARK C. YERGER

An example of a well-concealed Russian defensive fighting position. Holes such as these dotted the slopes of Hill 213.9.
NATIONAL ARCHIVES

A German 8cm mortar team in action. This standard mortar could fire a 7.5-pound shell up to 2,600 yards. Later in the war, after experience with the Russian 12cm mortars, the Germans produced heavier mortars as well. The German 12cm tube fired a shell that weighed nearly thirty-five pounds. NATIONAL ARCHIVES

A Tiger tank moves past resting SS infantry. NATIONAL ARCHIVES

SS panzergrenadiers, moving into action while mounted on a Sturmgeschütz III, are supported by two SS Tigers. NATIONAL ARCHIVES

Nebelwerfers launch a barrage of rockets toward Soviet positions. These rocket launchers were fired electrically so that the crews were not exposed to the blast of the rockets when fired. NATIONAL ARCHIVES

Erwin Meierdress, the commander of I./SS-Panzer-Regiment 3. Meierdress won the Knight's Cross in 1942 and the Oak Leaves the following year. MARK C. YERGER

Max Seela, here as an Obersturmführer, commanded SS-Panzer-Pionier-Abteilung 3 in mid-1943. He was a tank destruction specialist, having been awarded the Knight's Cross for the single-handed destruction of Russian tanks during combat in the Demyansk encirclement in 1942.
MARK C. YERGER

SS grenadiers of Regiment *Totenkopf* occupy Russian trenches after the capture of Hill 213.9. NATIONAL ARCHIVES

Das Reich Sturmgeschütz IIIs advancing toward the front during combat in the summer of 1943. NATIONAL ARCHIVES

Two SS troopers with magnetic antitank mines. When placed on a vulnerable spot on a tank—such as above the engine grill or on the thin upper hull plate—the shaped charge could penetrate armor and disable a tank or its crew.

A 150mm Hummel self-propelled howitzer, probably belonging to 5. SS-Panzer-Grenadier-Division *Wiking*. This self-propelled artillery vehicle mounted a 15cm howitzer, the sFH 18, which fired a ninety-five-pound projectile to a maximum range of more than eight miles.
NATIONAL ARCHIVES

Destroyed Russian T-34s knocked out during a Soviet attack against 2. SS-Panzer-Division *Das Reich* in 1943. MARK C. YERGER

Russian civilians move past a *Das Reich* Panther Ausf. A in a picture probably taken late in the summer or fall of 1943. MARK C. YERGER

A *Wiking* Panzer III. The Panzer III was gradually phased out during 1943, although the panzer divisions of both the Waffen SS and the army fielded some of these tanks until much later in the war.
NATIONAL ARCHIVES

A heavy artillery piece (150mm) in action supporting a German attack on the village in the background. NATIONAL ARCHIVES

A Wasp self-propelled howitzer, which mounted a 10.5cm gun. The Wasp and Hummel provided mobile artillery support for the German panzer divisions. NATIONAL ARCHIVES

In the distance, a Russian tank explodes and burns after being hit by a shell from the Panzer IV tank on the left of the photo. NATIONAL ARCHIVES

A Tiger in action on the flat steppes of the southern Ukraine. The picture was probably taken during the battle of Kursk. MARK C. YERGER

Motorcycle troops of *Das Reich* struggle to move along a muddy Russian path. Note the divisional and tactical markings. MARK C. YERGER

German officers shelter behind a Panzer IV. Note the aerials, which mark this tank as a command vehicle. NATIONAL ARCHIVES

A *Das Reich* Panzer III artillery observation tank transporting Russian prisoners. Note the Kursk-period divisional markings and the camouflage pattern, which was probably earth brown over base dark yellow.
NATIONAL ARCHIVES

An Sd.Kfz. 222 armored car armed with a coaxial 20mm gun and MG-34. These lightly armored vehicles were used by reconnaissance troops as scout cars. NATIONAL ARCHIVES

A smashed Russian artillery piece and a dead member of the gun crew.
NATIONAL ARCHIVES

A *Das Reich* Panther Ausf. D. Note the mud and worn coating of *Zimmerit* antimagnetic paste on the armor. One battalion of the division was equipped with the Panther by late August 1943. The other battalion fielded improved versions of the Panzer IV throughout the rest of the war. MARK C. YERGER

This Panther probably belonged to 5. SS-Panzergrenadier-Division *Wiking*. Note the light armor plate, known as *Schiftzen* (skirts), which shielded the tracks and running gear from hollow-charge antitank projectiles. NATIONAL ARCHIVES

Christian Tychsen (right), the commander of II./ SS-Panzer-Regiment 2 in summer of 1943. He was awarded the Knight's Cross in March 1943. Later in the war, he commanded the panzer regiment of 2. SS-Panzer-Division *Das Reich*.

MARK C. YERGER

CHAPTER 9

The Destruction of the Bridgehead

THE MIUS LINE RETAKEN

On 2 August, XXIV. Panzerkorps consolidated its positions, enlarging the gaps that had been punched in the Soviet defenses along the western edge of the Olkhovchik. South of Marinovka 16. Panzergrenadier-Division elements cleared the southern sector of the valley of Russian stragglers and remnants of rear-guard detachments. At the hedgerow south of Marinovka, a battalion of panzergrenadiers secured the breakthrough area. A portion of corps artillery was subordinated to II. SS-Panzerkorps' advance and supported elements of *Das Reich* near Hill 213.9 and east of Marinovka. The artillery was directed on a number of Russian batteries and silenced them or forced a change of position. Soviet artillery strength, along with infantry resistance, was obviously melting away at most points. By 2020 hours, 23. Panzer-Division pushed to within a kilometer of Hill 168.5 and built up a solid bridgehead of its own into the valley west of the captured bridge over the Olkhovchik stream. At dark, the forward line of 23. Panzer-Division ran from the mouth of the Krivaja Schlucht, where it opened into the Olkhovchik, to a point just west of Hill 168.5. The division reported capturing a total of 4,193 prisoners on 1 August.[1] The 16. Panzergrenadier-Division was not able to advance as far into the valley, probably a direct result of its offensive weakness. The divisional front extended from the hedgerow bridgehead south of Marinovka to north of Yelizavetinsky. Between the two divisions the entire corps had a total of only thirty-four tanks and about twenty assault guns.

After it became clear that the Russian bridgehead was decisively penetrated at multiple points on 1 August, II. SS-Panzerkorps issued mission directives accordingly for the following day. With 3. Panzer-Division effectively under command of 6. Armee, the orders concerned only *Das Reich* and *Totenkopf*. Both divisions were to concentrate their attack toward the river, with the first objective being Hill 194.3 and the hills and high ground near that point. Several flanking elevations sprawled randomly from there north to the area just west of Dmitrievka. After *Das Reich* elements cleared out the last Russian pockets of resistance encircled in and around Marinovka and the high ground east of the town, the two divisions were to push to the east of a 194.3–213.9 line. The final objective of the attack for 2 August was the capture of Hill 191.3 and occupation of the old main German defensive line along the west bank of the river (see appendix II).

The panzer group of *Das Reich* and III./*Der Führer* were to advance from their positions around the Marinovka area and drive to the northeast with their left flank boundary the south slope of 213.9 and its right flank on Hill 194.3. *Totenkopf* would move from the south slope of 213.9, make contact on the right flank with *Das Reich* and join with the other division in an attack to the river in an advance parallel to its neighbor to the south, XXIV. Panzerkorps. The main point of effort was to be on *Totenkopf*'s right and along the whole of *Das Reich*'s front. The left-flank units of Regiment *Eicke* remained in their defensive positions in the Gerassimova. Their mission was to secure the northern flank of II. SS-Panzerkorps and deny the use of the Gerassimova to any Russian formations. The artillery support was directed to prepare for fire missions with the initial point of main effort being east and northeast of Marinovka.[2]

Shortly before dawn on 2 August, on a day that would again be hot and humid under clear skies, the attack was resumed. At 0520 hours, Regiment *Totenkopf* grenadiers moved out of the captured fortifications on Hill 213.9 and advanced behind the artillery fire of 6. Armee and II. SS-Panzerkorps batteries. SS tanks and assault guns rolled forward with the sparse ranks of grenadiers spread out in thin lines behind them. Everywhere Russian resistance was feeble or dissipating quickly. A weak attempt to delay the German advance was made by the Russians with a few tanks near Hill 194.3, just before 1000 hours. With the full weight of the artillery of both the SS divisions (including the guns of 3. Panzer-Division) and 6. Armee, in addition to the support of the Luftwaffe, this small force was brushed aside quickly. Stuka squadrons worked in close cooperation with the SS spearheads, bombing pockets of resistance and attacking small groups of retreating Soviet troops.

The Destruction of the Bridgehead

At most points, the advancing Germans were opposed by little more than remnants of delaying detachments covering the withdrawal of the last remaining Russian troops of the main body. The Russians that were still hurriedly crossing the Mius now had to contend with the fact that the Germans were in possession of high ground which afforded observation advantages previously denied them. Soviet units abandoning the bridgehead were now completely visible to German artillery observers as they crossed the river and were mercilessly shelled, causing a large number of casualties.

Like vultures descending upon carrion, flights of Stukas gathered to attack the fleeing Soviets. The planes first concentrated, circling high over the crossings and then swooped down to bomb and strafe the retreating Russians. The German planes, with the Russian air force suddenly not in evidence near the river, caused much destruction and disruption to the retreating columns of men and equipment. In its daily report, *Totenkopf* recorded that Russian air activity was very light in the areas where bridges and fords crossed the Mius; thus, German planes attacked the Russians with little or no interference from Soviet fighters. Watching the slaughter of the Russians, one *Totenkopf* soldier was reminded of another scene of air attacks on men in the water. *Totenkopf* Unterscharführer Blechinger, a witness earlier in the war of the Dunkirk evacuation, commented on the masses of Soviet soldiers who tried to escape by bridges or fords across the Mius: "It was like at Dunkirk, bombs and shells struck among the enemy troop columns."[3]

At 0740 hours, *Totenkopf* advance detachments moved toward Hill 191.3, opposed only by desultory small-arms fire and shortly afterward occupied the hill in cooperation with assault guns from *Das Reich*. Later in the morning, also with little Russian resistance in evidence, Hill 194.3 was captured.[4] After its armor helped turn back the abortive Soviet tank counterthrust near 194.3, *Totenkopf* panzers renewed the offensive by 1000 hours, pushing toward the high ground around Hill 173.4 and 121.7. These elevations had been the sites of Soviet heavy artillery and mortar positions and had caused much grief to both SS divisions during the previous few days. This was particularly true of the attacks by *Totenkopf* against Hill 213.9. Now the guns were gone, blasted by Stuka attacks or pulled back over the river before they could be cut off from the crossings over the Mius.

Shortly after 1115 hours, minor pockets of Russian resistance on both hills were being mopped up and Soviet prisoners were being herded to the rear in long lines. Everywhere the Soviet resistance melted away totally, as most of the rear-guard units had either been destroyed or had delayed the Germans long enough to satisfy the letter of their orders. The few remaining survivors escaped over the river if they were able. Standing on the newly captured hills and looking to the west, the men of the SS divisions could clearly see, as had Stadler on Hill 203.4, why the Soviets had been able to direct such accurate artillery fire on them in the days just past. From the fortified high points, all the surrounding terrain could easily be registered for artillery, with any movements clearly visible to an artillery observer.

Totenkopf reported that its forward elements arrived at the old Mius trenchline by 1720 hours, when the remnants of Regiment *Totenkopf* on the right and Regiment *Eicke* elements on the left, occupied the old trenches and fortifications built by 6. Armee on the west bank of the Mius. The HQ units of the division set up quickly behind their regiments, both panzergrenadier regimental HQ groups taking up positions east of Stepanovka. The panzer regiment command detachment moved into the Olkhovchik Valley along with the command groups of both SS-Artillerie-Regiment 3 and the engineer battalion.[5]

By early morning, Marinovka had been cleared, after II./*Deutschland* arrived on the northern border of the town at 0715 hours. Shortly afterward, I./*Deutschland* reached the west edge. At once, the regiment threw out screening detachments to the east, into the Olkhovchik, but there were no Soviet attempts to counterattack. *Der Führer* grenadiers encountered stronger Russian resistance in its attack toward the old Mius position in its initial attack, which got under way at 0830. The Soviets put up a determined fight for a short time, delaying the drive to the northeast until SS tanks joined the grenadiers. With the arrival of the divisional panzer group, under command of SS-Sturmbannführer Christian Tychsen, the Russian will to fight quickly vanished and resistance collapsed. Surviving Russian troops melted away toward the river. The German attack then turned to the east and drove without serious opposition to the west bank of the Mius. There was no attempt by Soviet ground troops to further delay the advance of *Das Reich*. By mid-morning, Tychsen's panzer group reached the old Mius fortifications opposed only by artillery fire from the east bank of the river.

In the air, however, the Russian air force finally managed to send a few of their ground-attack planes against the German troops. Soviet planes harassed the advancing German columns with a minor bombing and strafings from IL-2s. The primary Russian air effort was directed against the pursuing German columns and apparently little effort was made to protect the Soviet men and equipment moving over the river. The Russian troops still crossing the Mius were left to fend for themselves, against the attack of German planes.

The *Das Reich* divisional battle report for the day listed seven separate air attacks by a total of approximately sixty planes. The antiaircraft units of both SS divisions utilized their 20mm and 37mm gun fire to defend their spearhead units and no significant German losses to Russian air attacks were noted in the records of II. SS-Panzerkorps. On this date, the battle report of the *Totenkopf* Division recognized that 4./SS-Flak-Abteilung 3 shot down its hundredth enemy plane since the unit's first deployment to the Eastern Front.[6]

The Russian artillery on the bridgehead side was virtually nonexistent by then as all of the batteries that could move had been transported over the river to escape the pursuing German tanks and infantry. However, significant Soviet artillery fire came from the east bank of the river, from firing emplacements in Kuibyshevo and Dmitrievka. This fire bore little resemblance to the murderous artillery that the Soviets had been able to direct against the German attacks earlier in the fighting, in either volume or accuracy. With the loss of the high ground, the fire from the Russian guns was considerably hampered by lack of good observation points. Observation from the east was affected substantially due to the fact that the Soviet side of the river was lower in elevation than the west bank.

By late in the afternoon, both divisions of II. SS-Panzerkorps had reoccupied the old defensive positions of 6. Armee on the western side of the river. The two divisions had only a remnant of operational tanks left. *Totenkopf* reported at the end of the day that it had twenty-three tanks still running, a total that included fourteen Panzer IIIs and IVs and three Tigers. *Das Reich* listed twenty-two tanks, with ten Panzer IIIs, eight Panzer IVs, and four command tanks.[7]

After the destruction of the Russian bridgehead on the Mius River, 6. Armee listed 17,895 Russian soldiers captured and estimated that the dead were several times that number, citing as evidence the piles of rotting Soviet corpses that lay at all points where the fighting had been intense. 6. Armee itself lost 154 officers missing or dead, 480 officers wounded in action, 3,168 noncommisioned officers and men dead, and 15,817 wounded in action. There were, in addition, over 2,000 missing noncoms and men. Total casualties for 6. Armee units from 17 July to 3 August, including those of support troops, added up to 21,369 killed, wounded, or missing.[8]

Casualties sustained by II. SS-Panzerkorps were also severe, but in *Totenkopf*'s case, they had been catastrophic, particularly in the main combat units. The soldiers themselves were painfully aware of the destruction and death that their division had sustained in the terrible fighting on the Mius. A *Totenkopf* veteran, former Oberscharführer Steiger of 1./SS-Panzer-Regiment 3, remembered the losses: "The cost of the fighting on the Mius was terrible. The grenadier companies had all shrunk to just a few men. Non-commissioned officers were company commanders. A battalion didn't even have the strength of a company."[9]

The division's losses from 30 July to 2 August 1943 totaled 1,458 killed, wounded, and missing. Fourteen officers were killed, and fifty had suffered wounds. The panzergrenadier and panzer regiments, of course, suffered the heaviest losses in the fighting. The casualties among the junior officers of the division were especially critical, coming at a time when the division had just sustained extensive losses of these ranks during "Citadel."

Of the total of 64 officer casualties, 38 were from either the panzergrenadier regiments or the panzer regiment. In the panzergrenadier regiments, the losses of noncoms and men were also particularly high, testifying to the fierce combat that had taken place in just a few days time. In the two SS panzergrenadier regiments of *Totenkopf*, the dead and missing totalled 99, and there were 605 wounded—for a total of 704 infantry casualties. The panzer regiment lost 49 dead or missing and 127 wounded. The engineer units suffered casualties that were extremely severe in relation to their unit size, losing 32 dead and 135 wounded, including both officers and men. These losses reflect the difficult nature of the operations the engineer units were called upon to execute during the battle for the Mius. The dangerous task of clearing extensive minefields

The Destruction of the Bridgehead 327

while under enemy fire resulted in significant casualties. To the credit of these men, they performed prodigious feats of mine removal in front of Hill 213.9. The Russian small-arms, artillery and mortar fire had decimated the SS engineers as they worked in the minefields in front of the hill. The large amount of mines that were removed, in spite of casualties suffered by all ranks, clearly illustrates the determination to carry out mission orders that characterized combat operations of the elite divisions of the Waffen SS during the war in Russia.

It is interesting to compare the manpower losses that *Totenkopf* suffered from 30 July to 2 August 1943 on the Mius with the total casualties suffered by the division from 1 July to 2 August 1943, which included those losses sustained during the battle of Kursk. In four days of combat in the Mius bridgehead, the division lost 1,458 men (219 dead, 1,193 wounded, and 46 missing).[10] For that entire month, the division listed a total of 2,120 men killed, wounded, and missing. Subtraction of the Mius casualties from the 2,120 lost during the whole month results in a total of 662 casualties lost during "Citadel."[11] The division, ordered by 6. Armee to frontally attack the strongest point of the Soviet defense while under fire from three sides, thus suffered over twice as many killed and wounded in the four days of the Mius battle as it lost in nearly ten days during "Citadel." This is a stark testament to the intensity of the terrible combat in front of Hill 213.9 and in the Gerassimova Valley.

Das Reich endured grievous losses of its own, losing 2,811 men between 1 July and 1 August (551 dead and 2,236 wounded), although the exact losses of the division on the Mius river could not be determined from the records of II. SS-Panzerkorps. The total figure for II. SS-Panzerkorps casualties for the month was 7,958 killed, wounded, and missing, including 40 additional casualties from various support troops integral to the corps or HQ personnel. However, this total includes *Leibstandarte* losses as well. That division was spared the slaughter on the Mius, but it lost nearly as many men during "Citadel" as had *Das Reich*. *Leibstandarte*'s casualties during "Citadel" totalled 2,750 men and officers.

Just after the conclusion of the battle for the Mius line, General der Infanterie Hollidt issued the following order of the day to 6. Armee and II. SS-Panzerkorps:

The July defensive battle on the Mius front has ended with our victory.

In a fortnight of heavy defensive engagements, the front-line divisions, the reserves which were brought up, and the emergency alert units succeeded in sealing off the penetration near Dmitrievka against the resistance of enemy troops eight times their own strength. The enemy units attacked in great number and suffered heavy losses in personnel and material. Of tanks alone, 585 were knocked out of action, some of them in close fighting. It was thanks to the heroic fighting of the above troops that, after bringing up new forces, the army was able to begin a counterattack on the front arc of the penetration on 30 July. The old main line of resistance was regained after four days of heavy fighting. Enemy forces that had penetrated in other places of the front had been beaten back in courageous counterattacks.

The commander in chief of Army Group South, Generalfeldmarschall von Manstein, has expressed his thanks to me today for the performance of the troops of the Sixth Army and their officers.

I feel the desire to express my thanks to the officers and men of all the units concerned for their tenacity in defense and for the model elan with which they carried out their attack and overcame the difficulties of their missions. Faithful to the last, every foot of terrain, every village, and every hill was defended. The deeply echeloned enemy defensive system was destroyed in a daring attack and a step by step advance. In spite of the burning sun, our soldiers held out as long as the order required it of them and they attacked undauntedly as soon as they were given the opportunity. Here many a new stanza was added to the epic of German heroism.

The enemy penetration has failed; strong enemy forces have been annihilated.

As usual, the cooperation of our comrades in the Luftwaffe was ideal. Continuously flying against the foe, attacking him just in front of our infantry or in the depth of the battlefield, vigilantly following all his movements, the Luftwaffe brought the army constant relief in its heavy struggle. In grateful and appreciative words I have again confirmed the comradely assistance of our sister service to the commander in chief of the Luftflotte, the commanding general of the Flieger Armeekorps, and the commander of the Anti-Aircraft Division.

The army bows in reverence before those of its comrades who gave their blood and their lives in the heavy fighting. They guaranteed us our final victory.

The main point now, soldiers of the Sixth Army, is to keep what has been won and to defend it stubbornly when the enemy attacks again, I know that you will hold the Mius-Donets front and protect the industrial region of the Donets, which is so important to the war effort.

Sieg heil der Führer!

The bitter combat and suffering of the men who died or were wounded in the fighting west of Dmitrievka were not reflected in the language of the official reports about the battle. Hollidt spoke of "epic German heroism" during the "courageous counterattack" and paid tribute to the "model elan" of the army and II. SS-Panzerkorps. Doubtless, the dead and wounded of *Totenkopf* and *Das Reich* would have preferred a more imaginative and realistic plan of attack with which to display their elan and courage. Surely the words describing "epic German heroism" must have brought to mind bitter images from the surviving *Totenkopf* panzergrenadiers and tank crews who were ordered to suicidally attack Hill 213.9 while under fire from three sides. Hollidt was undoubtedly familiar with the problems involved in an attack on such a fortified position if for no other reason than 23. Panzer-Division's previous attack on the hill on 19 July with notable lack of success and heavy tank and personnel losses. As a veteran of the war in the East, he was surely aware of the skill that the Russians had in regard to digging in and defending a position once they had been taken it.

The command of 6. Armee ignored the lessons of experience that Mellenthin and other veteran officers declared was an essential principle of warfare on the Eastern Front. Once the Russians were allowed to consolidate a position, only the best planned and executed attack could succeed in throwing them out and only then with significant losses. Frontal attacks would always result in high casualties because the Soviets would be organized to defend frontally in short order after their capture of a position. Hollidt chose to throw the three divisions of II. SS-Panzerkorps into tactically ill-advised frontal attacks against an enemy superbly entrenched behind mines, wire and machine guns. This was reminiscent of the murderous trench-warfare tactics that resulted in the slaughter of whole infantry divisions in World War I.

As a result, 3. Panzer-Division was stopped in its tracks, mired helplessly in minefields, having lost many of its armored vehicles to concentrated antitank gun fire. *Das Reich* was committed to street fighting in Stepanovka, which was guaranteed to bog it down, and its armor attacked fortified hills south of the town. *Totenkopf*, living up to the SS motto of "My honor is my loyalty," attacked resolutely into the death trap that was Hill 213.9 almost to the point of destruction. It was only after two days of slaughter, which gained nothing, that it became apparent to Hollidt, perhaps due to suggestions from Manstein, who could be acidic in his criticisms, that he was accomplishing little by battering II. SS-Panzerkorps into fragments. Manstein's concerns are described by Weidinger in his history of *Das Reich*. In any event, Hollidt redirected the attack to a less heavily defended area, which resulted in a decisive day of attack.

The stalemate was only broken when Regiment *Der Führer*, under command of an imaginative leader utilizing sound reconnaissance and daring tactics, successfully carried out a surprise attack and penetrated the Russian line. It appears that Stadler's assault on Hill 203.4 was only narrowly allowed to go on after the assurances of Obersturmbannführer Stadler convinced Manstein that the deadlock might yet be broken. With the Soviet attack at Belgorod imminent, it is interesting to note Manstein's presence at the Mius. Manstein may have had little confidence that the commander of 6. Armee would use his armor correctly. It is also interesting to note that while Hollidt was content to let the two SS divisions fight to destruction after the second day, he quickly removed 3. Panzer-Division from SS command. After the second day of fighting, he placed it under the command of XXIV. Panzerkorps, where it remained in reserve.

Manstein, on the scene at 6. Armee HQ after two days of fighting had produced little except for dead men and crippled tanks, was doubtless worried that the three divisions of II. SS-Panzerkorps would be too weakened to be of immediate use after the Mius battle was concluded. He could not afford to let II. SS-Panzerkorps be destroyed. On 1 August, Manstein reported to OKH that he expected a Soviet attack on that city in the near future, possibly having received additional intelligence that contradicted his earlier belief that the Russians would not be able to launch large-scale attacks so soon after Kursk. In any event, he had already recognized that when the Russians did begin their attacks on the Belgorod-Kharkov axis, he would need the three panzer divisions in that area. The orders to begin transporting the divsions of II. SS-Panzerkorps to the Kharkov area were issued on 1 August. Manstein may have been intent on making sure that he would have something left to transfer.

However, the Russians did not give him the time that he had originally expected, and on 3 August, the attack began, two to three weeks sooner than Manstein had predicted.[12] At Kharkov and in the sector west of the city, 4. Panzerarmee and Armee-Abteilung Kempf were aligned on the north flank of Heeresgruppe Süd with fifteen understrength divisions, having only three relatively weak panzer divisions available at the time.

Fortunately, the "elan" and "heroism" of Regiment *Der Führer* helped break the stalemate and gave Hollidt the decisive victory at Hill 203.4, which, along with the other penetrations into the Olkhovchik, broke the back of the Russian defense. The OKW dispatch in regard to the battle of the Mius, released on 4 August 1943, was not as full of the same rhetoric as Hollidt's report and made these comments on the battle:

> In the battle on the Mius, infantry and tank units of the army and the Waffen SS under the leadership of Generalfeldmarschall von Manstein and General der Infanterie Hollidt, excellently supported by units of the Luftwaffe led by General der Flieger Dessloch, foiled the repeated attempts of strong enemy forces to break through and in a spirited counterattack defeated the enemy forces which had penetrated into the area north of Kuibyshevo.
>
> By 2 August, 17,895 men had been captured in these engagements; 730 tanks, 703 guns, and 398 mortars, as well as numerous other weapons and great amounts of material, were captured or destroyed. The number of enemy soldiers killed in action is many times that of the prisoners.[13]

In a matter of days after the conclusion of the main fighting, the SS divisions, along with 3. Panzer-Division, were on their way to Kharkov. The HQ units of II. SS-Panzerkorps were ordered to Italy and were soon on their way west. The three divisions formerly under its command were to be placed under the command of III. Panzerkorps, then operating in the Bogodukhov sector. Even after the demands placed on the divisions at Kursk and the great slaughter on the Mius battlefield, the men of the three divisions had little time to recover before being ordered to the next crisis. As they left the blood-soaked valleys and ridges, back along the same route of march on which they had arrived only days before, elements of 16. Panzergrenadier-Division and 23. Panzer-Division moved into the positions of II. SS-Panzerkorps on 3–4 August in the old defensive line along the river.

After the withdrawal of the three panzer divisions of II. SS-Panzerkorps, there was some continued small-scale fighting. Over the next few days, the Russian brought up a few fresh tanks and men in moderate numbers. 2nd Guards Mechanized Corps received sixty new tanks to replace the horrendous vehicle losses that it had suffered. On 4 and 5 August, supported by artillery fire and large numbers of planes, a number of these Russian tanks made a small breakthrough in the forward lines of 294. Infanterie-Division. Some mobile elements of this attack force penetrated all the way to the edge of Stepanovka, but after they were separated from their supporting rifle units, they were destroyed by antitank guns or assault guns. The rifle battalions that supported the Russian tanks were isolated and destroyed by counterattacks, and 130 prisoners were captured. Forty-nine of the sixty new tanks of 2nd Guards Mechanized Corps were destroyed in this attack in an abortive effort to keep II. SS-Panzerkorps in the bridgehead. This was a wasted effort, as the divisions were already in the process of leaving. All along the line, during the next several days, the Soviets continued to make small spoiling attacks of about battalion or company size.[14] However, the issue had already been decided.

Essentially, the battle was tactically lost for the Russians when the breakthroughs spearheaded by Regiment *Der Führer* caused the collapse of the Russian center. On 1 August, Tolbukhin was confronted by more German penetrations than his front could counter, due to crippling tank losses and massive casualties inflicted on the rifle divisions. In view of the main objective of Southern Front's attack, there was no more reason to press the defense of the bridgehead. The fighting that took place from 3 to 5 August was no more than ineffective attempts to delay the withdrawal of units of II. SS-Panzerkorps. Tolbukhin, on 1 August, ordered the withdrawal of his front and he soon found out that the battle on the Mius was regarded as a success by the Soviet High Command.

Stalin, however, was far from displeased. Marshall Vasilevski arrived at Tolbukhin's HQ to inform the front commander that Southern Front's attacks had fulfilled their role perfectly—the German command could not move divisions up to Kursk and had even brought armor down from the north to bolster the Donbas, first-class divisions which would have made their presence felt on the "Belgorod-Kharkov axis."[15]

On 4 August 1943, 6. Armee received the following message:

The attack by 6. Armee against the area of penetration around Dmitrievka, prepared and ordered by the commander in chief Heeresgruppe Süd and executed by the 111. Infanterie-Division, 294. Infanterie-Division, 306. Infanterie-Division, 3. Panzer-Division, 23. Panzer-Division, 16. Panzergrenadier-Division, SS *Reich*, SS *Totenkopf* and attached units under the command of the XVII. Armeekorps, XXIX. Armeekorps, XXIV. Panzerkorps, and II. SS-Panzerkorps, has resulted in a great success and great amounts of captured material.

I assure the command and the troops of my full appreciation.
(signed) Adolf Hitler
The Commander in Chief, General der Infanterie—Hollidt[16]

AFTERMATH OF THE VICTORY ON THE MIUS

The function of Tolbukhin's Mius attack was to ensure the victory of Russian forces in the southern and most important sector of the Kursk salient. Through his successful conduct of this operation and the attack at Izyum, the Russians, utilizing deception and superior numbers, succeeded in preserving a win at Kursk, as much by influencing Hitler to abandon the fight in the Prochorovka-Psel area as by force of arms. In fact, the plan to draw German strength out of the southern area of the Kursk salient may have been the most important

Soviet success, at least in the south. The attack in the north was essentially stalemated after the first few days and 9. Armee had no uncommitted panzer divisions available by 12 July. Thus, there was no reasonable expectation that Model would be able to get its attack going again. Only in the south did the Germans have any chance of victory and only in the south did the Soviets go to such great lengths to ensure their victory.

This period of the war has been misunderstood due to mistaken beliefs regarding SS tank losses and ignorance of the interrelation between the battles of Prochorovka, the Mius and, later, the fighting at Bogodukhov. It is without question that "Citadel" resulted in a decisive German defeat and was characterized as such by Guderian, who, perhaps influenced by the calamitous tank losses of the army panzer divisions, stated that the panzer divisions were unemployable for a long time to come. While it is certainly true that all of the German panzer divisions had suffered, Guderian's statement can only be called true if he was refering to the army panzer divisions.

The fact is that 6. Panzer, 19. Panzer, and 11. Panzer lost almost all of their tanks during the battle of Kursk. The 7. Panzer-Division and 3. Panzer-Division were not in much better shape. In contrast, the Waffen SS divisions suffered fewer losses, although in continuous heavy action from 5 to 17 July, and made the deepest penetration of any panzer corps during the battle.

Das Reich and *Totenkopf* were to be committed to constant counterattacks for the remainder of the month of August while under command of III. Panzerkorps. During this time, 3. Panzer-Division, and, later, 5. SS-Panzer-Division *Wiking* were used in primarily defensive operations. *Das Reich* and *Totenkopf* were utilized in mobile operations against their old enemies, 1st Tank and 5th Guards Tank Armies, in the fighting around Bogodukov. They played a key role in the restoration of the crisis situation that existed west of Kharkov by 5–7 August.

These units were supposedly destroyed as effective fighting formations at Prochorovka by their enormous losses of tanks, a belief that has been used to justify criticism of the Waffen SS divisions and their commanders. However, the losses at Prochorovka are a myth, and in fact, the Waffen SS divisions retained sufficient fighting power to destroy Tolbukhin's Mius bridgehead in July and later help III. Panzerkorps fight the Soviet 1st and 5th Guards Tank Armies to a standstill at Bogodukhov. The next chapter deals with the fighting of the divisions during the remainder of August, side by side with 3. Panzer-Division and *Wiking*, led by Felix Steiner, the first commander of Regiment *Deutschland*. In the days immediately after the conclusion of the counterattack on the Mius, these divisions of the Waffen SS, in cooperation with army panzer divisions, particularly 3. Panzer and *Grossdeutschland*, began weeks of intense combat in the area west of Kharkov. They met their old opponents, 1st and 5th Guards Tank Armies, in desperate fighting west of Kharkov. At stake was the very existence of the entire southern wing of the Eastern Front east of the Dnepr River.

CHAPTER 10

The Battles for Bogodukhov

THE SS PANZER DIVISIONS

The battle of Kursk was the last time that the three oldest and most experienced Waffen SS divisions served together under the same corps command or a Waffen SS corps commander. For the rest of the war, the divisions were sent into action at many points of combat in the East as well as on the Western Front. At times, they were under command of the army and, at times, under SS corps command or SS army-level headquarters. When *Das Reich* and *Totenkopf* left the Mius River area, *Leibstandarte* was already en route to Italy. It was assigned to Heeresgruppe B and was soon under the command of II. SS-Panzerkorps again. Immediately after the end of the fighting on the Mius River, II. SS-Panzerkorps HQ units left Russia for the West, under orders to assume command of *Leibstandarte*, 65. Infanterie-Division and 25. Panzer-Division, effective 14 August 1943. By that date, the HQ units had completed their transfer to the West and were situated in the Reggio area.[1] Although both *Leibstandarte* and *Das Reich* were in France by the time of the D-Day landings in 1944 and fought as part of Sepp Dietrich's 6. Panzerarmee in the Ardennes counteroffensive, *Totenkopf* never left the Eastern Front for the remainder of the war.

During the rest of the summer, *Das Reich*, *Totenkopf*, and 3. Panzer-Division remained in action on the Eastern Front and were entangled in a sprawling battle against major elements of 1st Tank Army and 5th Guards Tank Army. The last three weeks of August 1943 saw these divisions, and *Wiking*, involved in near continuous fighting against overwhelming odds as they battled the armored spearheads of Katukov's and Rotmistrov's reconstituted tank armies. The III. Panzerkorps was ordered to close the huge gap between Hoth's 4. Panzerarmee and 8. Armee (formerly Armee-Abteilung Kempf).

On 3 August, the German front lines, from a point fifteen kilometers north of Belgorod to the sector northwest of Tomarovka, had been crushed by massive infantry attacks of 6th Guards Army, 5th Guards Army and 53rd Army, supported by over 500 tanks integral to the armies. Overwhelming infantry strength, massive armor support and a crushing amount of artillery destroyed entire German infantry divisions in a matter of hours. The nearly 1,100 additional tanks of the two Soviet tank armies, committed into the breakthrough between Belgorod and the Tomarovka area, ripped open a huge gap in the lines during the first days of Operation "Rumyantsev." (See appendix V for the order of battle of the Soviet forces that carried out "Rumyantsev.") West of Tomarovka, on a 100-kilometer-long front, three additional rifle armies, with over 550 tanks in support, attacked the thinly held front of 4. Panzerarmee on 5 August. To the west of Belgorod, the Germans defended a line along the eastern bank of the northern Donets River. This line ran through the city of Belgorod itself and followed the course of the river, due south for sixty kilometers, to the region east of Kharkov. The German defenses behind the river line were attacked by major elements of 69th Army, 7th Guards Army and 57th Army, supported by about 250 tanks. In reserve were two additional armies, each of which had a tank corps.

THE LAUNCHING OF OPERATION "RUMYANTSEV"

The Soviets packed enormous forces into the main attack sector of Operation "Rumyantsev." The attack zone extended from north of Belgorod to a point about thirty-five kilometers to the west, just slightly northwest of the town of Tomarovka. Between Belgorod and the Tomarovka area, arrayed from west to east, were 6th Guards Army, 5th Guards Army, 1st Tank Army, 5th Guards Tank Army, and 53rd Army. The front lines lay about fifteen kilometers north of Belgorod and only ten kilometers north of Tomarovka.

The area west of Belgorod was defended by 4. Panzerarmee's LII. Armeekorps in the Tomarovka area and XXXXVIII. Panzerkorps on a sixty-kilometer-long front stretching to the west. In the main zone of the Soviet attack were five German infantry divisions of average strength—for that time period of the war in Russia—and two relatively weak panzer divisions. On the far left flank of 4. Panzerarmee was 255. Infanterie-Divison, holding the sector of the line west of

The Battles for Bogodukhov

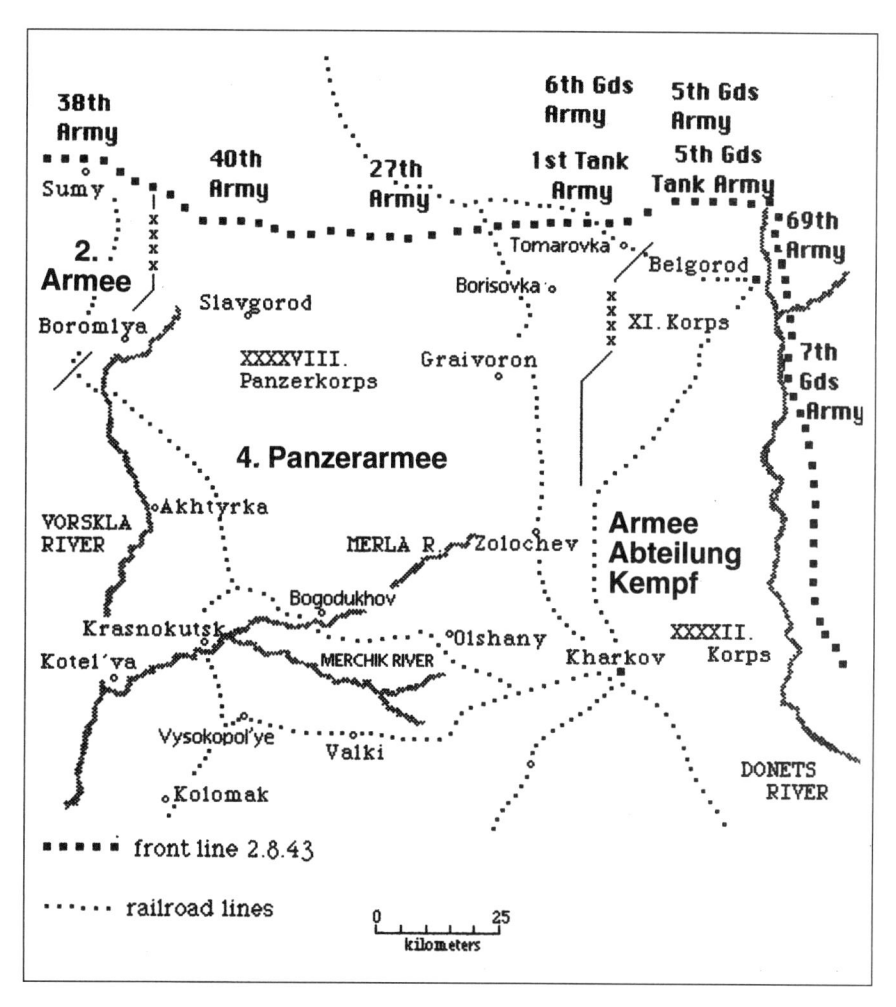

The situation in the Kharkov-Belgorod area, 2 August 1943.

Tomarovka. North of the town, the defenses were manned by 332. Infanterie-Division. On the extreme right flank of the front held by 4. Panzerarmee, a single division, 167. Infanterie-Division, defended approximately fourteen kilometers of front, with two infantry regiments in line. Behind them was a single panzer division, 19. Panzer-Division. West of Belgorod, another weak panzer division, 6. Panzer-Division, was in reserve.

The XI. Armeekorps of Armee-Abteilung Kempf defended the sector directly north of Belgorod and a part of the line that stretched south of the town behind the northern Donets. To the right of 4.

Panzerarmee's 167. Infanterie-Division, XI. Armeekorps' 168. Infanterie-Division occupied positions directly north of Belgorod. The front lines bent sharply to the south from that point, following the line of the northern Donets River through Belgorod and on to the south. The 198. Infanterie-Division held the river line on the northen outskirts of the city and 106. Infanterie-Division defended the river immediately south of Belgorod. Below the city, on the right flank of 106. Infanterie-Division, the line was held by 320. Infanterie-Division.

The unfortunate 332. and 167. Infanterie-Divisions defended the section of the line which had been chosen by the Soviet command to be the point of main effort. The divisions were attacked by the infantry of seven rifle divisions of 5th Guards Army, led by the armor of two integral tank regiments. An artillery division, mortar division and various detachments of antitank, self-propelled artillery, assault guns, and rocket units of brigade and regiment size, supported the attack.

A waiting avalanche of armor belonging to 1st Tank Army and 5th Guards Tank Army, a force of over 1,000 tanks, was echeloned behind 5th Guards Army. Russian tank strength in this sector was about 1,200 tanks, which was opposed by two panzer divisions of LII. Armeekorps. 6. Panzer-Division, in reserve seven to eight kilometers behind the front, had 50 tanks. 19. Panzer-Division had only about 28 tanks. The two panzer divisions were reinforced with an attached panzer battalion, Panzer-Abteilung 52, with about 10 Tigers. Thus, the entire German tank strength was about 90 operational tanks in this sector. The Soviets outnumbered the German armor by a factor of twelve to one.

Early on 3 August, 5th Guards Army, 5th Guards Tank Army and 1st Tank Army, after a long artillery preparation, launched an overwhelming attack of infantry and tanks that overran the infantry battalions of 332. and 167. Infanterie-Divisions in the front line. The assault began just to the west of the boundary between 4. Panzerarmee's right flank and Armee-Abteilung Kempf's left flank. It smashed into the front lines, broke through at many points and crushed the regiments of the two German infantry divisions. These divisions were good-quality units and not badly understrength for this period of the war in the East, but the enormous weight of Soviet firepower, hordes of infantry and hundreds of tanks simply overran them both.

The huge amount of guns, rockets and mortars had an operational density of over 100 guns/tubes per kilometer on the day of the attack. Voronezh Front's command carefully organized its artillery support preparations for the point of main effort in the center and Stavka provided their artillery batteries with the required trucks and shells for support of an operational breakthrough, support of the advance and fire missions to facilitate a deep breakthrough by the mobile groups. The fire plan called for a 170-minute artillery preparation before the assault and subsequent fire on targets in the depth of the German defenses.[2] Under the crushing weight of this firepower, the German forward defensive lines literally disappeared. When the first barrage lifted, Russians sapper units began to clear mines in front of the German lines. After a brief pause, the rain of high explosives began again and this time was joined by waves of ground-attack planes that swept over the field into the depths of secondary positions. Hundreds of Soviet tanks rolled over the wreckage of the German trenches, breaking through quickly, barely delayed by the weak efforts of the stunned defenders. At all key points, overwhelming Soviet air support was evident, with fighter-bombers and attack planes bombing and strafing strongpoints, crossroads and other tactically important targets.

Within the first hours of the attack, the two divisions were effectively destroyed, reduced to disorganized fragments incapable of cohesive resistance. The front of 167. Infanterie-Division was shattered, and the Russian attack penetrated the entire front. The 332. Infanterie-Division was also overrun, large masses of Soviet infantry and tanks passing through the German lines at that point as well. West of Belgorod, 6. Panzer-Division deployed hurriedly and counterattacked the penetration in the 167. Infanterie-Division's area but was unable to halt the Russian flood. Panzer-Abteilung 52, with its Tiger tanks, and 19. Panzer-Division were also shouldered aside by the strength of the Russian armored attack although both reported the destruction of significant amounts of Soviet armor. German air support made its presence felt after the initial penetrations of the front lines reached a depth of about three kilometers, attacking Russian tanks and infantry assault groups.

Shortly before noon, 1st Tank Army and 5th Guards Tank Army were committed and passed through the lead elements of the infantry attack. By the end of the first day, the two tank armies penetrated to an average depth of fifteen kilometers, although 1st Tank Army experienced difficulties crossing the Vorskla River. Near Tomarovka, determined resistance slowed the advance of the tanks. Later in the day, German counterattacks hit the lead armored elements of the attack, covering the withdrawal of the infantry elements toward Tomarovka. Forward elements of 5th Guards Tank Army rolled past the German strongpoints and by nightfall cut the Belgorod–Tomarovka road, penetrating to an average depth of more than twenty kilometers.

Against the assembled might of the Russian offensive, the German front was quickly broken west of Belgorod. Voronezh Front's 5th Guards Army and the tanks of 5th Guards Tank Army smashed open a deep hole in the front, located at the boundary between Armee-Abteilung Kempf and 4. Panzerarmee. German forces were pushed back toward Tomarovka on the Soviet right and thrown back to the east on the left.

On 4 August, the situation rapidly got worse for the Germans. Soviet armored elements drove deep into the rear areas, the German command struggling unsuccessfully to restore a shattered front. 200th and 49th Tank Brigades of 1st Tank Army's 6th Tank Corps moved rapidly past Tomarovka and crossed the Tomarovka–Belgorod road early in the day. Elements of 19. Panzer-Division counterattacked Soviet divisions along with remnants of 332. Infanterie-Division. They were able to delay the Russian advance on Tomarovka sufficiently to force the diversion of additional armor from 1st Tank Army in order to reinforce the Soviet rifle divisions fighting to take the town. The most dangerous initial penetration of the day was made by 5th Guards Tank Army, which pushed nearly fifteen kilometers southeast of Tomarovka, along the boundary between 4. Panzerarmee and Armee-Abteilung Kempf.

By nightfall of 4 August, 1st Tank Army's leading elements, 6th Tank Corps and 3rd Mechanized Corps, in a renewal of their assault, pushed fifteen kilometers farther south of Tomarovka. The two corps roughly paralleled the advance of Rotmistrov's 18th and 29th Tank Corps. However, 5th Guards Tank Army's spearheads were not as successful on the second day and were held to an advance of only four hard-earned and bloody kilometers. This was mainly because of the defensive efforts of 6. Panzer-Division. With only a fraction of the armor of the Soviet forces facing it, this division counterattacked the

The Battles for Bogodukhov

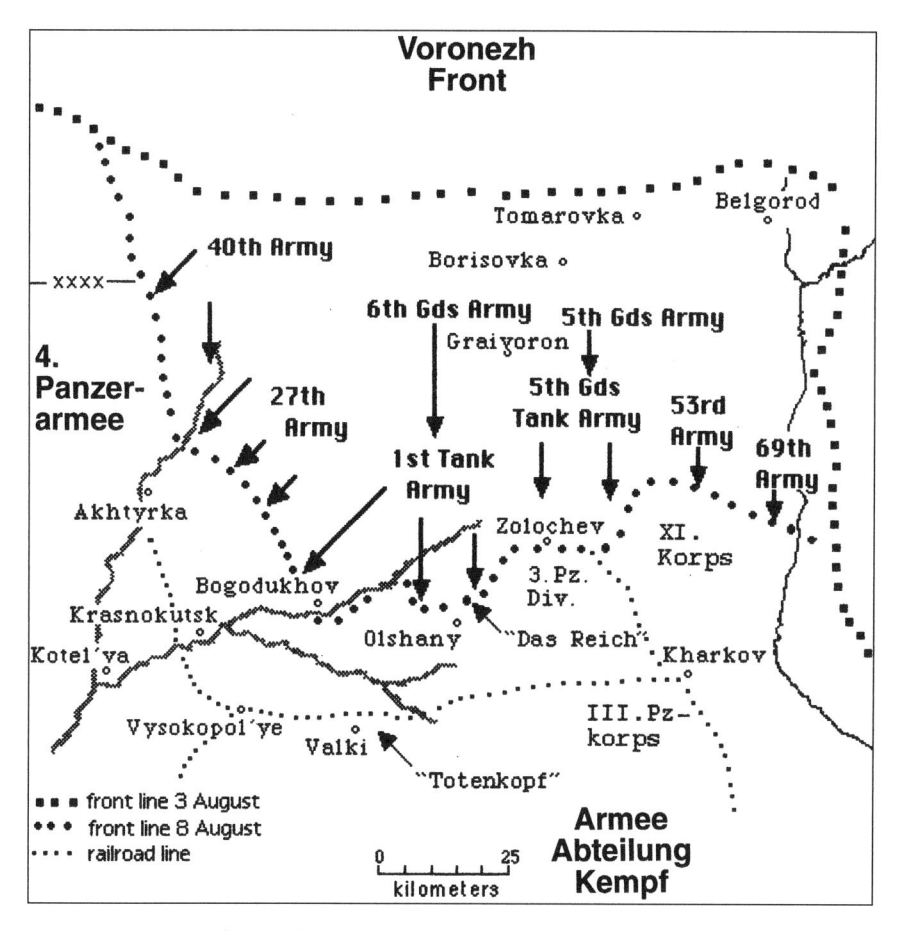

Operation "Rumyantsev," 8 August 1943.

Soviet armor ferociously during the whole day, striking back without pause and blunting one Soviet advance after the other. However, sheer weight of numbers still forced the division to give ground steadily, falling back to the south. The German forces defending Tomarovka now had major Soviet elements in their rear areas and were close to being encircled.

THE DEFENSE OF BELGOROD

At Belgorod, the Soviet 53rd Army and elements of 69th Army, with five rifle divisions, broke the defenses of 168. Infanterie-Division and attacked 198. Infanterie-Division, which defended the northern approaches to the city. Each of the five Soviet divisions attacking the city was assigned a tank regiment for infantry support. A mechanized corps was held in reserve by the army for exploitation of any offensive success or support where necessary.[3] When the attack began, the Soviet infantry, in spite of great numerical superiority, had difficulties advancing quickly enough to suit the Soviet command. 53rd Army's mobile reserve, 1st Mechanized Corps, with three brigades of armor, was committed early on the first day after the infantry bogged down in the artillery and machine-gun fire of the German defenders.

All during 3 August, Soviet attempts to throw bridges across the Donets River south of Belgorod failed because of accurate German artillery fire which broke up every effort by Russian engineers to bridge the river. Soviet pressure was unrelenting, however, and by 4 August, the Germans were forced slowly back to a prepared defensive line manned by elements of 168. and 198. Infanterie-Divisions and 6. Panzer-Division. The Russians pushed the Germans back to the perimeter of the city after a day of slow, difficult fighting, their infantry stung by repeated local counterattacks by small battle groups of German tanks and infantry. Again dissatisfied with the progress of the attack, the Soviet command detached armor from 5th Guards Tank Army to supplement 53rd Army's tanks in an attack south of the city. This attack was designed to sever German communication lines entering Kharkov from the south and southwest. 5th Guards Mechanized Corps was removed from Rotmistrov's command, over his strenuous objections, and transferred to Belgorod, with orders to drive southeast from its position on the Belgorod–Tomarovka road, penetrate the front of 6. Panzer-Division and cut the road entering Belgorod from the southwest. By nightfall of 5 August, 5th Guards Mechanized Corps, attacking with strong infantry support, reached the Belgorod–Kharkov road and cut it at a point ten kilometers due south of the town. The city was nearly encircled.

Under attack from three sides, and with Soviet mobile units on the move in their rear, the Germans prepared to evacuate the city. On 5 August, the Soviet infantry attacks penetrated into the city for the first time. Bridging was finally thrown over the Donets by Soviet engineers and 5th Guards Mechanized Corps pushed hard to cut German communication lines south of the city. Threatened with complete encirclement, the Germans evacuated the city and Belgorod was in Russian hands by late in the afternoon.

To the west of Belgorod, the German defenders in Tomarovka were threatened with encirclement by 6th Guards Army to the immediate southwest and the deeper penetration by 1st Tank Army, whose spearhead tank corps were approaching Bogodukhov. West of Tomarovka, the Soviet 27th Army pushed south, squeezing the lines of communication of the town in that direction. The Soviet attacks on both sides of the town created a narrow corridor stretching to the southwest. The narrow strip of land remained open on a Tomarovka-Borisovka-Graivoron line, due largely to 19. Panzer-Division counterattacks and firm defensive resistance.

On 6 August, the Germans withdrew from Tomarovka, moving southwest to Borisovka, which was already under attack. Elements of 97th Guards Rifle Division seized a key road position south of Borisovka and established a road-block defense there, holding on in spite of furious attempts by the Germans to eliminate this threat. True to form, the Russians made an all-out effort to strengthen this bridgehead and brought up substantial reinforcements during the day. A strong force consisting of a reinforced rifle battalion and about a dozen tanks also was able to take Khotmyzhsk, an important rail station which was south of Borisovka. Recognizing the seriousness of the situation, the Germans made every effort to eliminate the Russian battalion dug in around the rail station. By late in the afternoon, all of the Russian tanks were destroyed or driven off, but the rifle battalion, bolstered by artillery, mortar, and antitank units, held its position. In the evening of 6 August, 13th Guards Rifle Division threw additional infantry elements into the area around Golovchino.

By nightfall, the Germans decided to fight their way out of Borisovka, after realizing that the Russians had nearly completed its encirclement. On 7 August, elements of 19. Panzer-, 255. Infanterie-, and 332. Infanterie-Divisions began a harrowing two-day fight through the Russians toward the southwest and their own lines. Blundering into one strongly defended Soviet position after another, the Germans desperately searched for a gap in the quickly closing noose. By now, Soviet aircraft were on the scent of the Germans and descended upon retreating columns, shooting up trucks and other vehicles and adding to the confusion and destruction Small units of Germans became separated from the main body in the confusion while searching for a way out of the trap. They became victims of

Russian planes or were attacked by Soviet assault columns pushing in from all directions. Marauding columns of T-34s, laden with machine pistol–equipped infantry, and accompanied by assault guns, pursued retreating groups of Germans. There was no front and no clear idea where the Russians might be and groups of Soviet tanks and motorized infantry were liable to appear at any time and place. Russians and Germans came upon each other unexpectedly in the fluid situation. Through one such chance meeting, 19. Panzer-Division lost its commander.

On the afternoon of 7 August, the commander of the division, Generalleutnant Gustav Schmidt, left the HQ of XXXXVIII. Panzerkorps with his divisional staff units, planning to return to Akhtyrka over a road that division elements had traveled safely during the entire day. The HQ column passed unknowingly through the positions of 13th Guards Rifle Division, which deployed its 39th Guards Rifle Regiment in an ambush designed to destroy the German column. On a wooded road, General Schmidt and his men ran into the Soviet ambush without warning.

> General Schmidt was driving at the head of the column in his command tank. His radio operator was twiddling the knobs and remarking to Lieutenant Kohne, the ADC, "An unusual amount of Russian radio traffic. They're jabbering as excitedly as if they were in the middle of a battle."
>
> Kohne had no time to reply. Like lightning from a clear sky, hell was suddenly let loose. The crash and flames of antitank shells. They were coming from the woods along both sides of the highway. They burst open. Sheets of flame. The smell of burning. Smoke. . . . T-34s now appeared on the road and within a few minutes had shot up the column.[4]

Overrun by the Russian attackers, and without hope of escape, General Schmidt and his aide shot themselves rather than allow themselves to be captured alive. After the capture of survivors of the HQ group, the Russians allowed the general's driver and radio operator to bury their dead officer before being marched off into captivity.

The gap west of Belgorod had been expanded by the Russians to a width of over thirty kilometers wide. The objective of 1st Tank Army was Bogodukhov, which lay to the west of Kharkov. A successful attack at that point was intended to split the front apart between 4. Panzerarmee and Armee-Abteilung Kempf, without hope of repair. At the same time as the Russians were fighting to reduce the German defenses at Tomarovka and Borisovka, other elements of the Russian attack were making contact with elements of 3. Panzer and 2. SS-Panzer near Zolochev.

THE III. PANZERKORPS ASSEMBLES

To counter a critical breakthrough at the boundary, Manstein gathered his armor in from all other areas, realizing early in the first days of the Russian offensive that the most dangerous point of the Russian attack was the penetration southwest of Belgorod, where the Soviets threatened to create a gap too large to close and thereby shatter the German front. Undoubtedly, it was anticipation of this possible course of events that had been on Manstein's mind when he conferred with Hollidt, Hausser, and Stadler at 6. Armee HQ several days earlier. He had come close to ordering the two SS divisions out of the Mius bridgehead at that time, in order to send them north to counter the expected attack in 4. Panzerarmee's sector. Had Manstein suspected that the attack would come as early as 3 August, it is likely that he would never have allowed II. SS-Panzerkorps to be sent to Hollidt in the first place. When the Russians began their offensive, these divisions were many kilometers to the south, getting chewed up in a fierce battle against Tolbukhin's Southern Front. As a result, they arrived only after the offensive had begun and considerably weakened at that.

By 5 August, 3. Panzer-Division was north of Kharkov, *Das Reich* units were arriving west of the city and *Totenkopf* was underway and had some elements in the area already. The three divisions were concentrated in order to counterattack the eastern flank of the Russian armored spearheads driving toward Bogodukhov. At the same time, 4. Panzerarmee prepared to attack the western flank, with Panzergrenadier-Division *Grossdeutschland* leading this effort. That division had been ordered back to Manstein's Heeresgruppe Süd. The attack was to be made under command of XXIV. Panzerkorps. Another elite division of the Waffen SS, 5. SS-Panzergrenadier-Division *Wiking*, commanded by Felix Steiner, was on its way to the battlefield also. Manstein planned to use his panzer divisions to slice through the communication lines of the lead Soviet mobile units and destroy their momentum. In the past, the Germans had been able to accomplish this many times on the Eastern Front, aided by Soviet transportation and supply deficiencies. Although the Soviet army was vastly different in mid-1943 from the army of 1941, it had still not mastered all of the organizational skills necessary for sustaining deep operations. South of Belgorod, the Russian offensive would begin to run out of steam again, suffering from familiar problems such as lack of sufficient infantry transport to move rifle divisions with the tank units and slow relocation of artillery.

Manstein gathered the battered panzer divisions for one more supreme effort, calling on his "fire brigade" units to rescue the situation once again at a crisis point on the Eastern Front. More and more frequently, Hitler sent the SS divisions, on his personal orders, to battle the Russian armies driving to the west and Germany. He believed in the supreme importance of "will" and was always concerned with obedience and "political reliability" of men and divisions—characteristics that, in his mind, were best found in the Waffen SS divisions.

The average Waffen SS grenadier or tank crewman, struggling through the mud, exhausted and dirty, fought on with determination on the Eastern Front during the fall of 1943 for other reasons, believing in his cause and country. It is not likely that the young Waffen SS soldiers were motivated to storm fortified Russian hills in the face of machine-gun fire and mortar shells by the social and racial notions of such people as Heinrich Himmler. Many in the rank and file of the combat divisions repeatedly ridiculed the unmilitary and unimpressive Reichsführer-SS. The SS panzer commander going into action against Soviet tanks, outnumbered five to one or even eight to one, was not not likely to be greatly motivated by political considerations or notions of reliability of political will when masses of T-34s charged toward him, rolling out of clouds of smoke, fire and dust. They fought like most ordinary soldiers, for their commander and their comrades, political ideas having scarce practical value in the daily life of the soldier at the point of the bayonet, where survival and the honors of war leave little room for other concerns. However, it is without doubt that the men of the elite, early divisions of the Waffen SS and some of the later formations as well, demonstrated a remarkable degree of unit "toughness." These divisions fought well and were dangerous opponents well after the war was irrevocably lost. They were

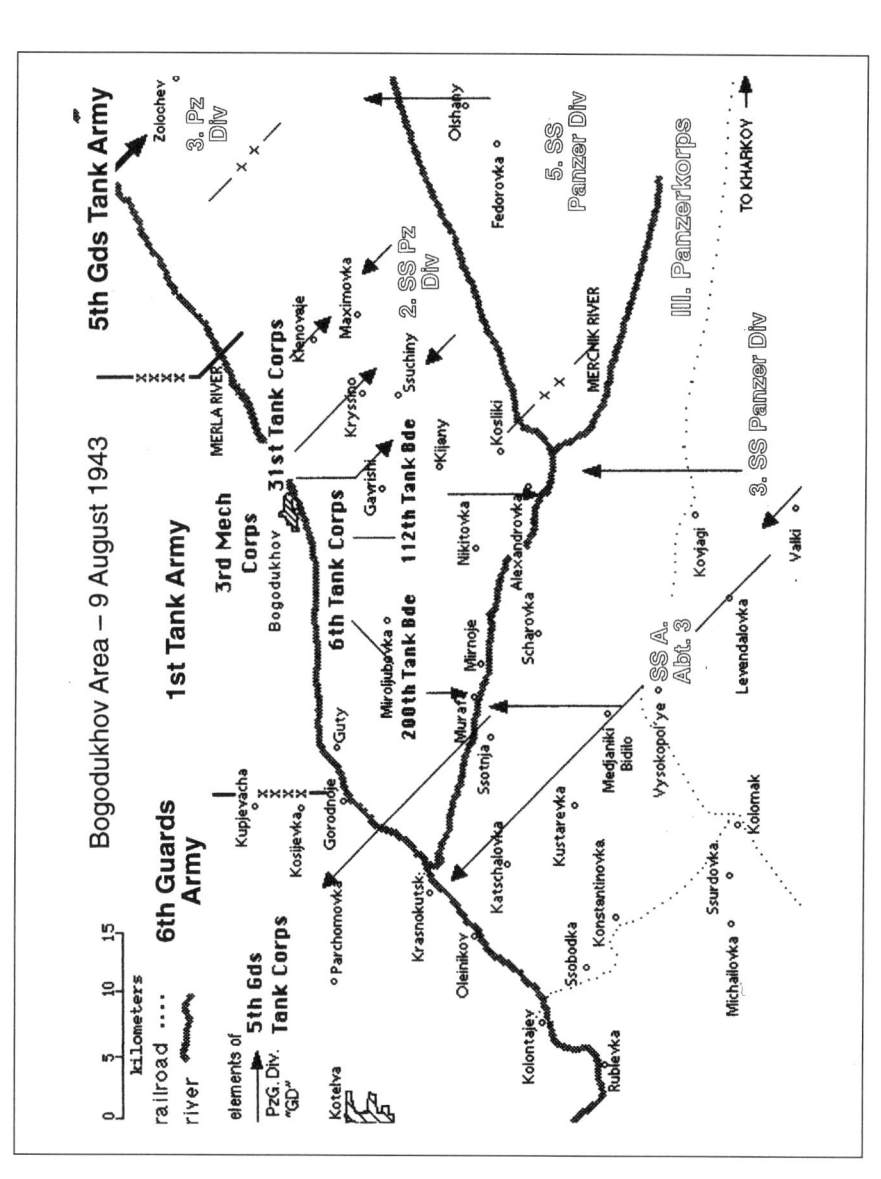

Bogodukhov area, 9 August 1943.

hardened further by grueling training of a modern nature. By the summer of 1943, the surviving personnel of these divisions had been forged in the fire of combat experience. They were at the peak of their effectiveness before the battle of Kursk, with better than average replacement personnel commanded by officers and NCOs who lived through the first years of the war in Russia. Although the number of these experienced warriors constantly declined due to death and wounds, there were still enough to lead the divisions during the harsh combat of the late summer and fall of 1943.

The men of *Das Reich*, 3. Panzer-Division, and *Totenkopf*, in the first days of August, had been in nearly continuous combat since 5 July and were without a doubt mentally and physically tired by the time they were ordered to move to the Kharkov area. The panzer regiments of the divisions had only a fraction of the tanks that each had been equipped with before "Citadel" and there had been many casualties. Now, in the first week of August 1943, the three divisions that had fought together on the Mius, stood ready to fight their old enemies from the Psel-Prochorovka battles, 1st Tank Army and 5th Guards Tank Army. Their mission was to stop the armored Soviet juggernaut, fresh from victories at Belgorod and Tomarovka.

III. PANZERKORPS PREPARES TO COUNTERATTACK

By 6 August, the Russian command believed that the Germans in the city and to the west of Kharkov were on the verge of collapse and did not think that Manstein could change the situation with the troops at hand. This conclusion was based on estimation of German tank losses and the destruction inflicted on the German infantry divisions as well as the great advantage in men and materiel that the Russians possessed. After the capture of Belgorod, Steppe Front consolidated, then moved south and began to position itself for the attempt to capture Kharkov. The German infantry divisions were in most cases too weak and stretched over too great a defensive frontage to hold back the Soviet steamroller. This forced the German command to commit the panzer divisions to defense of frontline positions instead of being used in mobile operations. As a result, the 19., 11., and 7. (Rommel's old unit) Panzer-Divisions held sectors that should have been the responsibility of infantry divisions. Although this was a necessity that could not be avoided, it did not allow for proper use of mobile divisions against attacking forces.

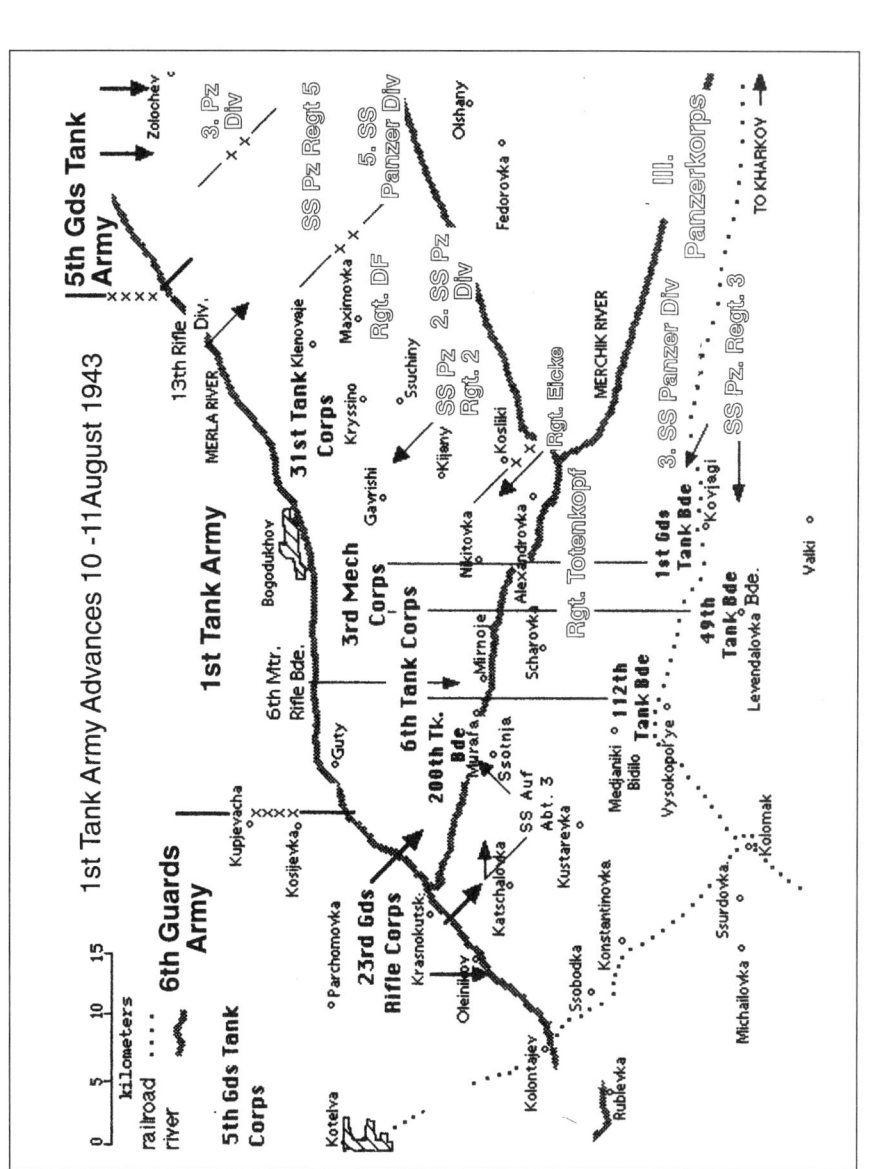

1st Tank Army advances, 10–11 August 1943.

The Soviet 5th Guards Tank Army and 1st Tank Army continued to push strongly to the south, slicing deeper into the German rear areas. The Russian armored groups drove toward Zolochev and Bogodukhov, deflected to the west somewhat by the stubborn defense of Kharkov. However, when the two tank armies advanced so quickly to the south, the rifle divisions were left behind, first due to a lack of enough transport and, second, to deal with the task of reducing the pockets at Tomarovka and Belgorod. After cleaning up these areas, the Soviet rifle divisions were worn down further by casualties and unable to catch up with the armor. As a result, prodded on by the front commanders, the Soviet tank and mechanized corps became separated from most of their infantry and outran the bulk of their artillery as well.

Just northeast of Zolochev, during the night of 5 August, 5th Guards Tank Army's 18th Tank Corps moved west of the defensive positions of the Germans in an attempt to flank the town. At first light, the entire Russian tank corps attacked positions defended by 3. Panzer Division, which was assembled along a Zolochev–Kasatscha Lopanj line. The fighting continued into the evening, with the Germans destroying eight Soviet tanks and throwing the Soviet infantry back with heavy losses. Russian troops supported by tanks fought their way into Zolochev late in the day. They pushed the defenders back to the southern edge of the town, but could not clear the town of all of the stubborn German infantry and fighting continued into darkness. Soon, other 5th Guards Tank Army formations, the brigades of 29th Tank Corps, advanced west of 18th Tank Corps and made contact with elements of 3. Panzer-Division also.

West of Zolochev, at Kasatscha Lopanj, the advance of 29th Tank Corps was halted by solid defenses anchored by the veteran troops of the panzer division. In response to the new situations, Rotmistrov began to deploy 5th Guards Mechanized Corps to the south in order to assist 29th Tank Corps and infantry elements of 5th Guards Army in their attack on 3. Panzer-Division.

In spite of these minor delays, 1st Tank Army had already penetrated more than fifty kilometers south of their start line, wreaking havoc with German rail line traffic and other communication lines. Katukov concentrated his armor on 6 August in preparation for an attack on the key railway center located at Bogodukhov, which was defended by a few German supply troops and other odds and ends. In the afternoon, 6th Tank Corps elements reached the outskirts of Bogodukhov, taking the Germans troops in the town and railway station completely by surprise. The Germans in the town fled south. By 1800 hours, the town was successfully occupied by 6th Tank Corps troops, the Russians capturing large stores of fuel and supplies.[5] Shortly afterward, Russians secured the town and pushed several mobile columns farther south. At this point, the Soviets first began to see evidence that new German panzer divisions had arrived in the area. The easy victory of 6th Tank Corps at Bogodukhov contrasted with the situation of 3rd Mechanized Corps north of Olshany. There, the Russian spearhead elements struck solid resistance in the form of SS battle groups on the move. One Russian attack ran head on into two march columns of *Das Reich*. The division was ordered to throw back the massive Soviet juggernaut bearing down on Bogodukhov.

The two *Das Reich* columns that 3rd Mechanized Corps made contact with were an eastern column, made up of a tank company and supporting grenadiers, and a western column, made up of I. and II./*Der Führer*. The two battalions of Regiment *Der Führer* were reinforced with some motorcycle detachments and elements of SS-Aufklärungs-Abteilung 2. Most of the rest of the heavy weapons and armor of the division were still in transport by rail from Stalino and had not arrived. The eastern column of *Das Reich* panzers deployed against the armor of 3rd Mechanized Corps' 1st Guards Tank Brigade in a meeting engagement just to the north of Olshany while elements of 10th and 3rd Mechanized Brigades attacked the western column of *Das Reich*. Troops of *Das Reich*'s reconnaissance battalion destroyed three Russian tanks and other vehicles in fierce combat around the village of Klenovje. The SS panzers inflicted significant losses on the Russians, but the small German detachments, under the assault of forward elements of a full mechanized corps, were forced to fall back toward Olshany in order to consolidate a stronger defensive position and await the heavy weapons of the division.[6]

Rotmistrov decided to renew his attack with an attempt to break through the German lines and envelop 3. Panzer-Division's positions at Zolochev, attacking the east flank of the division with armor. At the same time, he planned to fix the Germans in place by a frontal attack. The abundance of Soviet tanks was becoming apparent to the

Germans at this point. Air reconnaisssance observed two Soviet columns of tanks moving toward the division with a total of fifty to sixty tanks. Although units of 3. Panzer-Division continued to arrive, most of the artillery and the Flak battalion had not been able to assemble. Elements of the reconnaissance battalion holding the line Schuravlovka–Kasatscha Lopanj–Zolochev were reinforced by the staff of I./Panzer-Regiment 3 and one company of tanks. Formations of Soviet infantry and tanks were observed to gradually assemble in front of the division's lines throughout the afternoon and night, as it became evident that the Russians intended to attack at this point on the following day. In the area between Hills 227.2, 290.8, and 213.6, a total of about seventy Russian tanks were observed by reconnaissance elements of the division.[7]

By morning of 7 August, the Soviets assembled several tank or mechanized brigades, including elements of 5th Guards Mechanized Corps, and threw them at 3. Panzer-Division. 29th Tank Corps attacked Kasatscha Lopanj throughout the day with little success. Meanwhile, 5th Guards Mechanized Corps and 18th Tank Corps assaulted 3. Panzer-Division positions around Zolochev. Soviet tank losses at Zolochev were high, the German division claiming the destruction of thirteen Soviet tanks for the day. Despite its losses, 5th Guards Mechanized continued to attack from the east while 18th Tank Corps maintained pressure on the division from the west.

Recognizing that more armor was needed at the front, III. Panzerkorps was given five Tiger tanks from the Armee-Abteilung Kempf panzer training school, a welcome addition considering the avalanche of Soviet armor gathered against the still assembling German panzer divisions. (See appendix III.)

All during the day of 7 August, in *Das Reich*'s sector, the Russians launched continuous attacks on the defensive line established by *Der Führer*. In particular, Soviet attacks concentrated on the boundary area between II./*Der Führer* and another position of the regiment. At this point, they were able to break into the SS defensive lines and reached a group of houses near a point designated as 158.2. Realizing the danger of this breakthrough, Obersturmbannführer Stadler personally directed the counterattack against the Soviet breakthrough and was able to drive the Russian troops back and restore the original line.[8] By the time darkness fell over the battlefield, the SS troopers had repulsed numerous additional Soviet attacks and the defensive line, although severely battered, held firm. The Soviet 3rd Mechanized Corps made further assaults against the German positions on Hill 213.6 during the night with infantry elements reinforced by tanks, but was unable to drive the SS panzergrenadiers from their fortified hills and positions.

The fighting grew hard and vicious, the intensity of the Russian attacks providing stark evidence that they were determined to eliminate the SS troopers or drive them back. The men of *Der Führer* were just as determined not to give up their positions, even if it meant their death. An eight-man combat group of 7./*Der Führer*, entrenched around a machine-gun position near a wooded area west of a small village fought off repeated company-strength Soviet attacks supported by tanks during 8 August. After inflicting heavy losses on the Russians, the small group was overrun before it could be reinforced. Fighting to the last man, all of the SS grenadiers were killed. The fighting on 8 August continued to be very heavy, with the tanks and infantry of both 3rd Mechanized Corps and subsequently 31st Tank Corps trying to bludgeon their way through *Das Reich*. However, in spite of every effort, the Russians were driven back with substantial losses and forced to go over to the defensive by the aggressive, counterattacking defense of the German division. The Soviet columns pushing south met the SS battle groups in meeting engagements characterized by violent fighting. The Russian columns initially pulled back in surprise at encountering sudden resistance. However, as a picture began to form of the location of German units, Russian armor continued to move south and assemble to move against this new threat. Late on 7 August, the Russian command concentrated its armored strength in preparation for an attack.

5th Guards Mechanized Corps again attacked 3. Panzer-Division early in the day and was able to push to the southeast of Zolochev. To the southwest of the German positions, 18th Tank Corps also managed to make a penetration to the village of Rogozyanka.[9] Assaulted by two Soviet corps, the division could not hold at all points. Although, at Kasatscha Lopanj, the Russian attack was repulsed, overwhelming pressure finally pushed the German line away from the southern outskirts of Zolochev on the embattled eastern flank. The defenders were forced to withdraw to the south along the rail line leading out of the town, closely followed by elements of both Soviet corps.

At Kasatscha Lopanj, 29th Tank Corps was not as successful in its efforts to take the town on 7 August. A breakthrough into the western sector of Kasatscsha Lopanj was counterattacked by 3. Panzer tanks and panzergrenadiers and destroyed. In spite of several strong assaults by the Russians, 3. Panzer-Division held so firm that 29th Tank Corps, after suffering heavy losses, was ordered to stop its futile attempts to take the town and regroup to the southwest on the following day. It was withdrawn and sent to reinforce the Soviet efforts to destroy the 3. Panzer formations that were conducting phased withdrawals to the south of Zolochev. A division of 33rd Guards Rifle Corps, 6th Guards Airborne, replaced 29th Tank Corps in order to secure the tank corps flank. In spite of the attacks by elements of tank and rifle corps, 3. Panzer-Division was able to maintain unit cohesion and withdrew its left flank to defensive positions to the southeast of Zolochev.

The division was pursued by the Russians, who pushed forward with tanks and infantry in attempts to catch and overrun the Germans before they could organize their defense. On 8 August, 1st Tank Army advanced in three columns with the intention of outflanking 3. Panzer-Division and pushing south of Bogodukhov in order to cut the Poltava-Kharkov railroad at the towns of Kovjagi and Vysokopol'ye. 31st Tank Corps advanced on the left flank of the army southwest of Zolochev. In the center, 3rd Mechanized Corps attacked toward Kovjagi rail station and 6th Tank Corps, on the right, pushed south toward Vysokopol'ye. Katukov had hoped to push into the gap west of Zolochev and find that 3. Panzer-Division's left flank was open. However, when 3rd Mechanized and 31st Tank Corps advanced west of Zolochev, they had run into elements of *Das Reich*. That division was moving up on the left of 3. Panzer-Division, screening the division's west (or left) flank. All along the front, Soviet units recoiled, their advance halted and then driven back by counterattacks from *Das Reich*.

By 8 August, *Das Reich* had assembled more of its force with the exception of some divisional armor, just in time to face attacks along iti front by armor of 31st Tank Corps. At 0300 hours, attacks on Zapovka and a fortified hill, Hill 213.7, were turned back by SS grenadiers and assault guns. Nearby, at Hill 207.5, five Russian tanks and infantry broke through the SS positions, only to be stopped by antitank guns of the division, which destroyed three of the tanks.

Shortly afterward, near the village of Maximovka, 600 to 700 Soviet infantry, with several tanks, attacked *Das Reich* positions without success. Hill 213.5 was assaulted again at 1030 hours, this time by considerable armor along with Russian infantry. The attack was turned back after the loss of seven T-34s, one T-60 and three assault guns. The Soviets tried to take the hill again at 1200 hours and occupied the hill for a short time before a counterattack threw them off and destroyed eight more Russian tanks and several assault guns.

Soviet armor gained strength throughout the day and the attacks on *Das Reich* became noticeably stronger. At 1625 hours, Zapovka was attacked again by Russian infantry, this time with approximately twenty-five tanks in support. After destroying two T-34s and heavily damaging another, the SS troops forced the Soviets to withdraw. Following a regrouping of their force and the arrival of more armor, the Soviets pushed to the south of the village with about forty tanks and infantry. This attack force was pounced upon by Stukas and its advance was significantly disrupted by the dive-bombers. On this date, the only available *Das Reich* armored vehicles were four Tigers and about twenty assault guns. The main body of the panzer regiment was still in transit to the battle area at that date.[10]

Katukov's 6th Tank Corps, on the right, did not encounter much resistance and its lead reconnaissance forces, spearheading the advance of two tank brigades, reached the Merchik River, south of Bogodukhov. There the Russians forced weak German security detachments to withdraw back over the river to the south. *Das Reich* had not extended its front to this point west because it was in the sector that *Totenkopf* had been assigned. The division was at that moment assembling in order to attack toward the river and, by this operation, protect the sector west of *Das Reich*'s left (west) flank. A gap temporarily existed in the front south of Bogodukhov that was not covered by any German forces besides bridge security detachments and small groups of reconnaissance troops. However, 1st Tank Army was not able to exploit this situation to its advantage due to several factors. 6th Tank Corps was short two tank brigades on 8 August because one, 112th Tank Brigade, was still involved in fighting around Graivoron, while a second tank brigade was holding positions at Bogodukhov. Second, the bridges over the Merchik had been destroyed by the Germans. The lack of a bridge was not a drawback to Soviet infantry, as they habitually crossed by boat or raft, clinging to anything that floated, or even by swimming. However, tanks were another matter entirely. Evidently, the Russians did not feel they had enough strength to cross the river and hold a bridgehead on the south bank with only their infantry. Unable or unwilling to cross at this time, the Russians regrouped to take the crossings at the town of Alexsandrovka, on the north bank. 6th Tank Corps, frustrated in its attempts to cross the Merchik and cut the rail line at Vysokopol'ye, which was several kilometers south of the river, waited for the assembly of its other two tank brigades and prepared to attack the river again on 9 August.

In the meantime, after 29th Tank Corps was repulsed at Kazach'ya Lopan by 3. Panzer-Division's stubborn resistance, 5th Guards Tank Army spent most of the evening and night of 8 August reorganizing for a resumption of the attack on the following day. 6th Guards Airborne Division replaced 29th Tank Corps during the morning, while that unit withdrew its tank brigades and moved them under cover of darkness toward Zolochev. By nightfall, 29th Tank Corps was in combat south of Zolochev, fighting 3. Panzer-Division and *Das Reich*. In spite of the amount of Soviet armor arrayed against these two German divisions, the Russians could not make any significant progress. This led to a great deal of impatience at the upper level of the Russian command. It was now apparent to the commanders of the Soviet 1st Tank Army and 5th Guards Tank Army that German armor was quickly concentrating to the west of Kharkov, primarily via the Poltava-Kharkov rail line. 1st Tank Army reassembled the tank units of 6th Tank Corps during the night of 8 August with the intention of severing that key railroad line at a point south of Bogodukhov.

Katukov had anticipated a higher degree of success than had been subsequently possible. While 6th Tank Corps was stalled by destroyed bridges at Alexsandrovka, 3rd Mechanized Corps and 31st Tank Corps had actually lost ground to attacks by advance elements of *Das Reich*. The SS division had not completely assembled yet, but was able to blunt the attack by two Soviet corps. The army commander was thus justifiably concerned with the slowed rate of advance south of Bogodukhov and stubborn German resistance west of Kharkov. At higher levels, the Soviet command was also concerned.

The Stavka realized that the Germans in Kharkov were aided to a great extent by the railroad lines running into the city from the west and south. The arrival of the panzer divisions from the Mius was also a concern. Accordingly, a new directive was issued to 1st Tank Army and 5th Guards Tank Army with these developments in mind:

> The Stavka of the High Command considers it necessary to isolate Kharkov by means of a rapid cutting of the main rail and road lines of communication in the direction of Poltava, Krasnograd, and Lozovaya to speed the liberation of Kharkov. For that aim, Katukov's 1st Tank Army will cut the main routes in the Kovyagi and Valid area and Rotmistrov's 5th Guards Tank Army, while enveloping Kharkov from the southwest, will cut routes in the Merefa area.[11]

Strongly urged to action by this directive, on the morning of 9 August, both 5th Guards Tank Army and 1st Tank Army renewed their attacks. 1st Tank Army renewed the attack against the Merchik River and the rail lines south of Bogodukhov, with the objective of severing this key route of supply. Katukov ordered 6th Tank Corps to force a crossing of the Merchik River, supported by a weakened 31st Tank Corps, which was to advance on the left of 6th Tank Corps from it's positions southeast of Bogodukhov. By 8 August, 31st Tank Corps had only fifty tanks left after the fighting near Tomarovka, less than half of what the other Soviet tank and mechanized corps listed as operational. 6th Tank Corps attack moved toward the Merchik in two columns, one led by 200th Tank Brigade and the other spearheaded by 112th Tank Brigade. Katukov held 3rd Mechanized Brigade in reserve on the left flank. The right flank of the attack was screened by 163rd Rifle Division of 23rd Guards Rifle Corps, the lead infantry elements of 6th Guards Army. Early on 9 August, 6th Tank Corps armor, supported by motorized infantry, attacked Alexsandrovka.

Totenkopf had brought additional combat formations of the division up to the line during the night of 8 August, deploying them in an arc west of Alexsandrovka. Regiment *Totenkopf* held defensive positions at Shuravli and in the town of Alexsandrovka itself. Regiment *Eicke* occupied a wooded area near Olschany and SS-Panzer-Regiment 3 deployed around the Kovjagi rail station area. The reconnaissance battalion threw out a light defensive screen of mobile detachments west of Alexsandrovka. Elements of the reconnaissance battalion held positions around the village of Katschlovka, which was about fifteen kilometers west of Alexsandrovka and near the junction of the Merchik with the Merla River. The reconnaissance detachments were isolated and out of contact with any other *Totenkopf* troops, waiting for the Russian advance to make contact.

A second detachment of Aufklärungs-Abteilung 3 crossed the Merchik near Murafa and searched for crossings on the Merla River above the town of Krasnokutsk. Other elements of the division continued to arrive during 8–9 August.

One battalion of the artillery regiment had assembled early on 9 August, along with a panzer company of twelve tanks. As a division, *Totenkopf* had a total of fourteen Panzer IIIs in operation on that date and twenty-seven Panzer IVs, although all of the panzer regiment was not on hand until after 9 August. Still to be brought up were the heavy weapons of both the panzergrenadier regiments, I. Regiment *Totenkopf*, the last elements of the panzer regiment and I./SS-Artillerie-Regiment 3.

Regiment *Totenkopf* prepared to defend Aleksandrovka. Reconnaissance had reported unmistakable evidence of gathering Soviet armor. The SS grenadiers did not have long to wait. On the afternoon of 9 August, 6th Tank Corps' spearhead, 112th Tank Brigade, attacked the town. Immediately, fierce combat broke out in the northern section of the village. Soviet tanks with infantry advancing behind them assaulted the SS positions. Heavy defensive fire drove the first attack back.

When the Russians recoiled from the initial contact, *Totenkopf* assault teams immediately counterattacked 112th Tank Brigade, which, forced to withdraw, reorganized and made a second attack. Tanks and infantry struck the lines of Regiment *Totenkopf* at Alexsandrovka under cover of a sudden cloudburst of torrential rains. Several T-34s and infantry broke through the defenses and were able to occupy part of the northern section of the town.[12] The Soviet force inside the town was destroyed after the SS grenadiers knocked out three tanks and scattered the infantry. Later in the day, it became evident that the Soviets had large forces in the area and probably intended to make a strong effort to take the town and attack south of the Merchik.

In radio communications with reconnaissance detachments, it was reported that Soviet tanks were spotted occupying several villages west of Alexsandrovka and between the main body of the division and the reconnaissance detachments west of Alexsandrovka. Cut off by these advances of 6th Tank Corps, the reconnaissance battalion detachments filtered back toward the east, making their way between or around Soviet columns.

All day long on 9 August, 112th and 200th Tank Brigades of 6th Tank Corps tried to fight their way across the river. 112th Tank Brigade attacked Alexsandrovka for a third time and 200th Tank Brigade moved on Merefa, which was farther to the west. However, Regiment *Totenkopf* fought off the Soviet attacks and prevented the establishment of a bridgehead on the south bank. Confronted by these active defensive efforts and local counterattacks by *Totenkopf* at the Merchik, the Soviets were not able to force a crossing of the river at Merefa or Alexsandrovka on 9 August, although Merefa, which lay on the northern bank of the river, was captured by the Soviets. The fords and crossings to the west, along the course of the Merchik toward Krasnokutsk, remained undefended by German troops, however.

While III. Panzerkorps battled to hold the river line south of Bogodukhov, a large gap still existed to the west toward the junction of the Merchik with the Merla. Hoth's 4. Panzerarmee had begun a drive from the west to join hands with III. Panzerkorps elements south of Akhtryka, in the Kotel'va–Parchomovka area, but strong Soviet forces were pouring south into the huge gap west of the Olshany area. At Olshany, 3. Panzer-Division and *Wiking* were engaged in bitter fighting against 5th Guards Tank Army. The two divisions anchored a shoulder forming the eastern boundary of the huge gap west of Kharkov. Into this gaping hole torn in the German lines, the Soviet armies, led by mobile groups of the tank armies, drove southward.

From Olshany, the gap stretched to Bogodukhov where the three corps of 1st Tank Army drove toward the railroad line from Poltava to Kharkov. West of 1st Tank Army's spearheads, 6th Guards Army pushed south, on a line parallel to the course of the Merla River. North of Krasnokutsk, the river course ran north before bending to the west, toward Bogodukhov. On the right flank of 6th

Guards Army's attack groups, 27th Army attempted to advance from the Akhtryka area toward Kotel'va. At Akhtryka, XXXXVIII. Panzerkorps' defenses formed the western shoulder of the breakthrough. Between Akhtryka and Olshany, a huge seventy-five-to-eighty-kilometer hole existed between Armee-Abteilung Kempf and 4. Panzerarmee.

In search of information regarding Soviet units in the gap, and to protect the divisional left flank, fast-moving reconnaissance forces of *Totenkopf*'s reconnaissance battalion had already reached the Merchik River east of Krasnokutsk, at a point about fifteen kilometers southwest of Akhtryka. The SS recon detachments motored far from the security of their own frontline positions, seeking to make contact with Russian forces in the area north of the Merla River, towards the Kotel'va-Parchomovka area. Above Krasnokutsk, these units crossed the Merla River. Once over the river, the SS detachments were only about ten kilometers from Akhtryka, where XXIV. Panzerkorps was assembling. 4. Panzerarmee planned to attack toward the southeast in an attempt to join hands with III. Panzerkorps and chop off the forward units of 6th Guards Army. 6th Guards Army's spearhead formation was 5th Tank Corps, which was in the Kotel'va area by 8–9 August.

On 9 August, *Totenkopf* reconnaissance detachments established contact with lead elements of XXIV. Panzerkorps' Panzergrenadier-Division *Grossdeutschland* at Kupjevacha, southwest of Akhtryka.[13]

While *Totenkopf* battled with the southern elements of 6th Tank Corps along the Merchik, intense fighting broke out in the area to the division's right, in the defensive sector of *Das Reich* and 3. Panzer-Division. Early on 9 August, Rotmistov's 5th Guards Tank Army renewed its attack from the area north of Olshany. The attack immediately ran up against stubborn resistance from *Das Reich*, 3. Panzer-Division, and elements of 5. SS-Panzergrenadier-Division *Wiking*. In spite of throwing his army's full strength against the German divisions, Rotmistrov had no decisive success and could not make significant breakthrough at any point on 9 August. However, the Soviet numerical strength slowly pushed the Germans back and threatened to create crisis situations at a number of points. While there were no large breakthroughs, several local penetrations forced the SS troops to make tactical withdrawals.

Later in the day, *Das Reich*, under strong pressure from the Soviets, withdrew to a new defensive position, inflicting heavy losses on the Russians as it moved back. Katukov kept the pressure on, urging his commanders forward, and by the early afternoon, the Soviets assembled armor for an attack against the towns of Dolshik and Zapovka. The assault on Dolshik was driven off, the Russians losing several tanks in the process.

Behind a smothering amount of artillery fire, the Russians captured a key elevation, Hill 209.2, driving the SS defenders off the hill after bitter fighting. Attacks by Stukas and fighter planes and shelling of suspected assembly areas failed to weaken the Soviet advance. *Das Reich* turned back a Soviet attempt to take Zapovka at 1410 hours. However, a Soviet tank and infantry attack punched through the defenses between 3. Panzer and *Das Reich*, creating a gap at the divisional boundary. Counterattacks by SS armor and III./*Der Führer* sealed off the penetration.

Combined with a few tanks or a handful of assault guns, III./*Der Führer* served as the divisional reserve. The battalion counterattacked Soviet penetrations at several points during the day. However, the battalion was already worn down and suffered additional casualties. The situation was extremely dangerous for the division because it did not have all of its tanks yet. This lack of armor hampered the SS division in dealing with Russian armor that supported the infantry attacks.

However, the last elements of the division's panzers were arriving. In the afternoon of 9 August, the division reported that additional elements of its panzer regiment were unloading and could be expected to join the fight during the evening. There were sixteen assault guns available to the division, in addition to the tanks that had already arrrived. The tank destroyer and engineer battalions were not at full strength either, with elements of both still to arrive. While the division assembled, piece by piece, the Russians were on the move during the night of 9–10 August.

Vatutin, concerned that his offensive was beginning to stall, issued orders for 1st Tank Army to continue the attack south of the river, toward the critically important Poltava-Kharkov rail line. Katukov was ordered to take Vysokopol'ye and Valid and sever the railroad supply line by 11 August.[14] Katukov pulled 31st Tank Corps out of its positions on the left flank of his army and assembled it to support a renewed attack across the Merchik on the morning of 10 August. The armor was replaced in the line by a rifle division.

Before first light, the Soviets renewed their drive to the south, attacking all three panzer divisions of III. Panzerkorps along the whole front. However, the Russians continued to lose more tanks to the German tanks and antitank guns, with 3. Panzer-Division reporting the destruction of seven Russian tanks south of Zolochev during morning attacks. There were gaps in the divisional front, however, that could not be defended due to the relative weakness of the division. The lack of infantry strength was particularly serious because all of the infantry of the panzergrenadier regiments were in the front lines. There were no reserves of any kind. The division's reconnaissance, assault gun and mobile antitank gun battalions were already in action as well. Soviet reconnaissance units alertly found the undefended areas between the divisional strongpoints. Flexibly directing its forward detachments into these gaps, 31st Tank Corps penetrated the German defenses. The division could do little to stop the Soviet mobile groups.

A Russian tank force was observed moving along the Dergatschi–Zolochev road. However, it could not be stopped because the division had nothing left with which to launch a counterattack. The division reported to Armee-Abteilung Kempf that judging from the concentration of Russian armor moving through their front, further attacks toward Kharkov could be expected.

A Russian assault group of tanks and motorized infantry which penetrated the boundary position between 3. Panzer and *Das Reich* could not be thrown back. The division was forced to call on support from its neighbor, *Das Reich*. By this date, most of the heavy weapons of the SS division had arrived, including the last tanks of the panzer regiment. The SS armor immediately went into action, counterattacking the Soviet armor with the support of panzergrenadiers of III./*Der Führer*. The counterattack stopped the Russian attack cold, throwing it back and destroying a large number of T-34s. The division claimed the destruction of sixty-six Soviet tanks by 10 August.

Earlier in the day, *Das Reich* had repelled an attack near Hill 210.6, knocking out or damaging four T-34s. This attack was followed by stronger Russian efforts near Dolshik, with large numbers of infantry and twenty-five to thirty tanks that emerged from concealment out of a wooded area near that village. The attacks were broken

The Battles for Bogodukhov

up and fifteen Soviet tanks remained on the battefield, burning or disabled. All along the divisional front, Soviet infantry and tanks probed one area after the other, particularly against the section of the line held by I./ and II./*Der Führer*. None of the Russian efforts created any significant breakthroughs.

The positions of I./ and II./*Der Führer* were shelled heavily throughout the day and were probed by strong reconnaissance patrols constantly. The division was again forced to send III./*Der Führer* to the assistance of 3. Panzer-Division when the boundary between the two divisions was attacked at the same spot as on the previous day. Although the Soviet penetration was sealed off and the attackers dispersed, the division reported that a section of the rail line between Maximovka and Bogodukhov was destroyed.[15] A makeshift airfield, with several light planes which indicated the presence of a HQ group, was reported near one of the small villages occupied by the Soviets. Russian air activity remained light although a position of the division was bombed once in the morning. The division had thirty-three operational tanks and twenty-two assault guns on 10 August.

Of the four divisions of III. Panzerkorps, 3. Panzer-Division was hardest hit during 10 August. Infantry detachments from 168. Infanterie-Division, which was reduced to a regiment-size battle group, reinforced the panzer division's infantry. The remnants of 394. Panzergrenadier-Regiment were particularly hard pressed at Dolbino. Russian infantry, after heavy artillery bombardments, broke into the town along with a number of tanks. The German panzergrenadiers fought back desperately for several hours, until finally the last elements of Russian infantry withdrew from Dolbino. However, the infantry of the division's panzergrenadier regiments was exhausted and Soviet pressure began to force it fall back. Several defensive positions were flanked by Russian battle groups, and in order to prevent their encirclement, the division withdrew part of its defensive line. Divisional assault gun batteries and a few tanks screened the retreat.

The division withdrew its left flank to Hill 194.8. The Russians closely pursued the German troops in spite of the efforts of the reconnaissance battalion, which sustained severe casualties in counterattacks against the advancing Soviet tanks and infantry. Early in the evening, at 1800 hours, the Russians assaulted the right flank of the division with a force estimated at a strength of five battalions.

This attack, however, was turned back after bitter fighting. The 3. Panzer-Division estimated that it had destroyed forty-six Russian tanks during the day. It inflicted bloody losses on the resolute Soviet infantry at all points, but there was a high cost to the Germans as well. The vehicle strength of the reconnaissance battalion and the manpower of 394. Panzergrenadier-Regiment were dangerously low.

Russian attacks were beaten back at one point, only to be renewed at other sections of the line, always supported by numerous tanks. The division was hard pressed by relentless Soviet attacks that continued during the night. The heavy pressure forced the entire division to withdraw to a new defense line, where it organized for the assaults that were sure to come on the following day. The division took some degree of comfort in the amount of Soviet armor it knocked out during the fighting. It was estimated that the Russians lost 110 tanks in the attacks on the division in the period from 7 to 11 August. Elsewhere on the front of III. Panzerkorps, the fighting was just as hard.

In the sector defended by *Totenkopf*, 6th Tank Corps' 112th Tank Brigade renewed its attempts to get across the Merchik in the morning hours of 11 August. With elements of 3rd Mechanized Corps in support, the tank brigade forced a crossing. In spite of counterattacks by Regiment *Totenkopf*, the Russians succeeded in establishing a foothold across the river near Alexsandrovka. 1st Tank Army had its first bridgehead on the south bank of the Merchik. *Totenkopf* was spread too thin along its front to be able to stop the Soviet onslaught. The armor of the division was in operation south of the river, near the railroad station at Kovjagi and could give no support to Regiment *Totenkopf*.

Regiment *Eicke* was attacked by tanks and infantry south of Pavlovo in the afternoon. At 1515 hours, the Soviets forced a breakthrough in the defenses of the regiment, and three tanks with about 100 infantry penetrated on the left flank. Learning of this dangerous development, SS-Sturmbannführer Kurt Launer, commander of II./*Eicke*, led a counterattack against the breakthrough. In vicious fighting, sometimes hand to hand, the Russian penetration was cut off and destroyed.

At Murafa, a crossing site on the Merchik to the west of Alexsandrovka, a Russian attack nearly succeeded in capturing a bridge over the river before German troops could blow it up. The Soviets advanced from a nearby village named Kosijevka, rolling fast toward the bridge with infantry clustered on the tanks. Dismounting and firing their submachine guns at anything that moved and with the support of machine-gun fire from several tanks, Russian infantry were on the bridge almost before the engineer detachment defending the crossing was aware of the attack. The first attempt to destroy the bridge with placed charges failed when damp electrical connections did not function properly. Men of the reconnaissance battalion, also defending the bridge, swept the span clean of Soviet soldiers and allowed SS engineers to leap from cover and place a fuse on the charges. By this daring action, the demolition charge was set off and the bridge destroyed. However, under cover of cannon and machine-gun fire from the tanks, Soviet infantry worked their way across the small river using the cover of the bridge wreckage.

A steady stream of Russian soldiers stumbled and clawed their way to the south bank while T-34s shelled German positions from the north bank. Dead and wounded Soviet soldiers crumbled into the water, knocked down by German small-arms fire, but others took their place and continued to cross. Spreading out to either side of the ruined bridge on the south bank, Soviet infantry dug in and built up a bridgehead. After more Russian troops crossed the river, assault teams crept down the river banks on either side of the bridge and attacked SS positions across open cornfields that covered much of the southern bank. Soon piles of dead and dying Russians lay in front of the German firing positions, but a seemingly inexhaustible number of Soviet soldiers continued to expand the small bridgehead. While the Russians built up their crossing site at Murafa, 112th Tank Brigade, at Alexsandrovka, brought up its main elements and prepared to attack south of the river.

After consolidating the Alexsandrovka bridgehead defenses, the Soviets began preparations for the drive toward Vysokopol-ye, Kovjagi, and the railroad. The commander of the 112th Tank Brigade, Colonel M.T. Leonov, organized a battle group of twenty-six tanks, a battery of self-propelled guns, and several antitank guns to lead the advance toward the rail line. Spearheads of 3rd Mechanized Corps also crossed the Merchik at the Aleksandrovka bridgehead and quickly drove toward Kovjagi, east of Vysokopol'ye. The lead elements of 3rd Mechanized Corp's 49th Tank Brigade, with about ten tanks and infantry riding on the T-34s, reached the rail station at

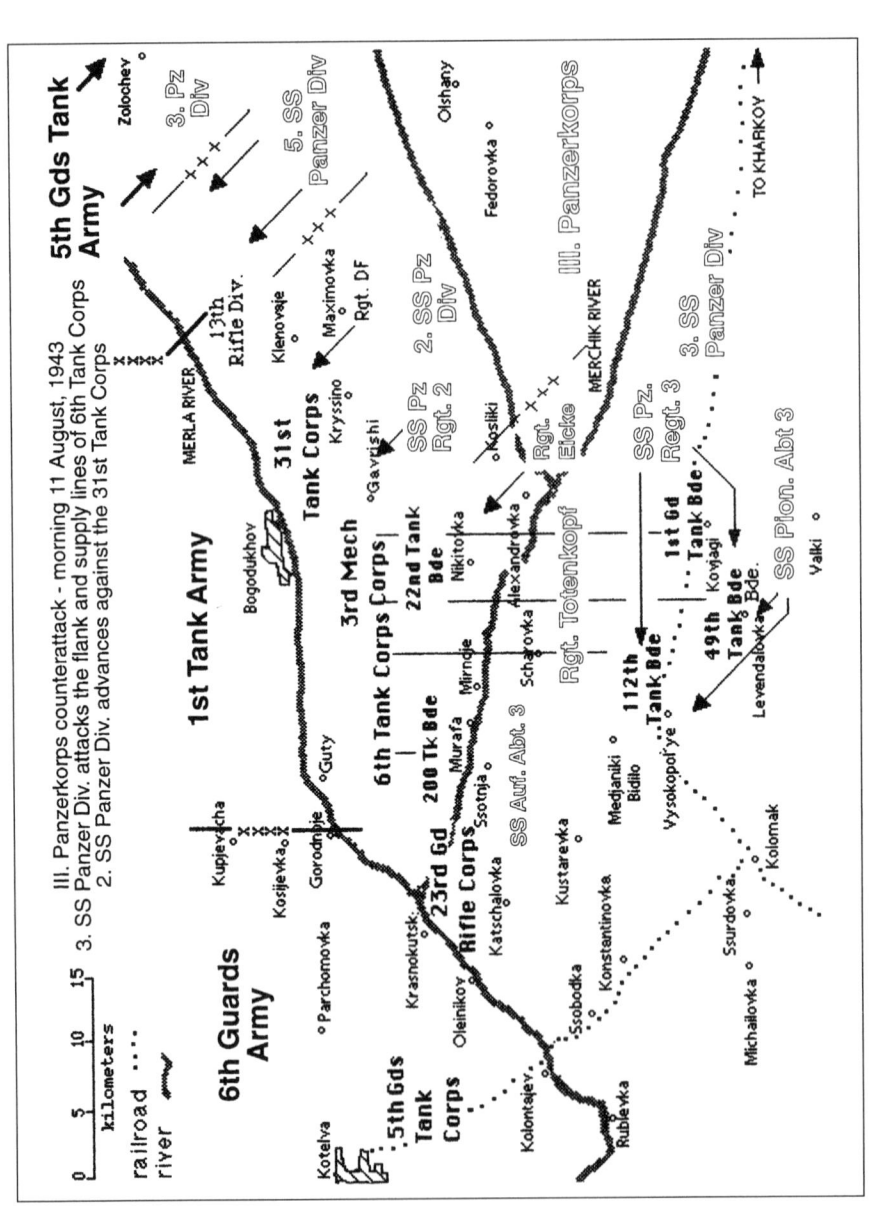

The counterattack of III. Panzerkorps, morning of 11 August 1943.

The Battles for Bogodukhov

Kovjagi early in the morning. After the reinforced 1st Tank Brigade also reached the station, 49th Tank Corps' battle group pushed on and at 0900 hours took a small village, Levandalovka, south of Kovjagi. Reserve units of Regiment *Totenkopf*, elements of the divisional reconnaissance battalion, and the assault gun battalion reacted quickly to the penetrations across the river. They assembled and launched counterattacks on the communication lines of the Russian battle groups below the river. Panzers of SS-Panzer-Regiment 3 prepared to attack the Russian mobile elements north of the village of Valid.

One of counterattacks was against 1st Guards Tank Brigade, at Kovyagi. Tanks of I./SS-Panzer-Regiment 3 counterattacked the Soviets forces at the Kovjagi rail station. The *Totenkopf* panzers advanced in two battle groups and plunged into vast cornfields that surrounded the station area, laying down heavy machine-gun fire to sweep the Soviet infantry out of the fields. The panzers cautiously moved through the corn toward the village. The commander of one of the *Totenkopf* battle groups, SS-Obersturmführer Burgschulte, was decapitated by a direct hit to the cupola of his command tank, leaving the unit without an experienced commander. Learning of this situation, SS-Obersturmführer Riefkogel left a field hospital bed where he was recovering from previous wounds and came forward to take over command of the Kampfgruppe. He led a detachment of four tanks in an attempt to push the remaining Soviet troops out of Kovjagi, losing one of the tanks while overrunning a group of five Russian antitank guns. The fighting around Kovjagi continued on into the afternoon as SS tanks and infantry battled elements of 1st Tank Corps and 17th Tank Regiment.

Later in the afternoon, after being strafed by a German aircraft, which mistook the *Totenkopf* tanks for Russian vehicles, Riefkogel was wounded in the head by a splinter of shrapnel. It was his seventh wound in action while serving with *Totenkopf*. After receiving this wound and since he was not yet fully recovered from a wound suffered during the Mius fighting, Riefkogel was evacuated. While he was being taken to the rear in a light car, his vehicle was met by the panzer regiment commander, Georg Bochmann, and the commanding officer of I./SS-Panzer-Regiment 3, Edwin Meiderdress, who presented him with the Knight's Cross for bravery in action on 11 July, during "Citadel."

With the loss of Riefkogel, neither of the two panzer groups at Kovjagi had an experienced commander at hand. The commander of the second group, Obersturmführer Altemiller, was also killed earlier in the attack, and it was necessary for a *Totenkopf* Ordonnanzoffizier to take command of both battle groups. This situation starkly illustrates the severe losses of small-unit officers that the division had suffered beginning with the fighting at Kursk in July and the even worse casualties at the Mius.[16]

III. PANZERKORPS OPPOSES TWO OLD ENEMIES

During the hard fighting from 6 to 11 August, the Russians had not gained as much ground in the sector west of Kharkov as Vatutin had hoped for. The four panzer divisions of III. Panzerkorps repelled all attempts by 1st Tank Army to cut the critical Poltava–Kharkov railroad line south of Bogodukhov. Rotmistrov's 5th Guards Tank Army was slowly driving the Germans back in the Olshany sector but had lost large numbers of tanks in the process.

The defensive efforts of 3. Panzer-Division and *Wiking* around Zolochev and Olshany had slowed the southward rate of advance of Rotmistrov's 5th Guards Tank Army. Meanwhile, *Totenkopf* and *Das Reich* parried or cut off 1st Tank Army's thrusts to reach the rail line south of the Merchik. With the Soviets temporarily off balance, Armee-Abteilung Kempf prepared to launch a counterattack with *Das Reich, Wiking,* and *Totenkopf.* 3. Panzer-Division was to play a primarily defensive role over the next few days while the SS panzers struck back at the overextended Soviet armored columns south of the Merchik. In addition to the Soviet armored units building up at the bridgeheads over the Merla and south of Bogodukhov, 5th Tank Corps of 6th Guards Army was moving toward the confluence of the Merchik with the Merla. Pushing south from the Krasnokutsk area, the tanks of 5th Tank Corps moved toward the town of Kotel'va. South of Kotel'va, there were no German troops other than railroad or village security detachments. A yawning and undefended gap remained between 4. Panzerarmee and Armee-Abteilung Kempf. The armor of three Soviet armies was entering the gap north of the Merchik River. Their plan was to split the two German armies apart.

The objective of III. Panzerkorps was to chop through the lines of 1st Tank Army toward the west and link up with 4. Panzerarmee's

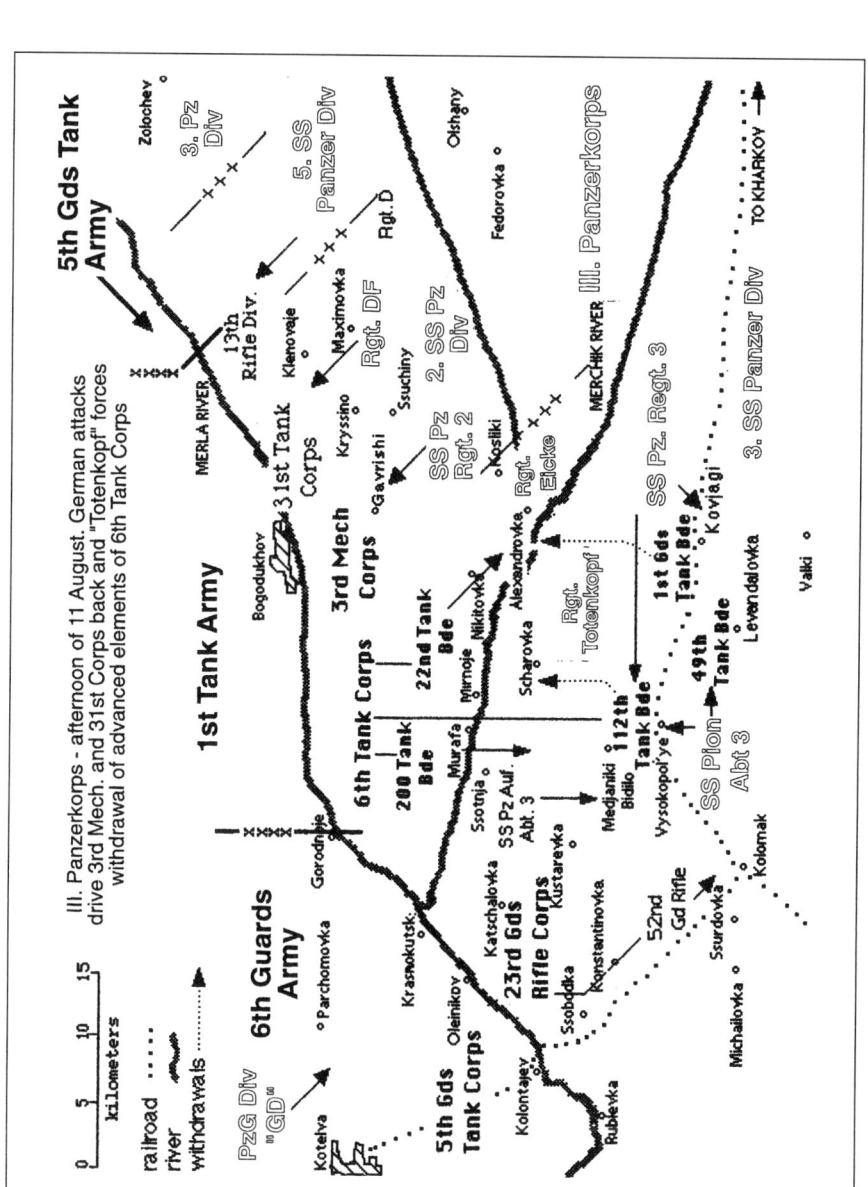

III. Panzerkorps, afternoon of 11 August 1943.

XXIV. Panzerkorps, which had already launched an attack from the Akhtryka area toward the towns of Kotel'va and Parchomovka. This attack, led by Panzergrenadier-Division *Grossdeutschland* and 10. Panzergrenadier-Division, had already established contact with reconnaissance elements of *Totenkopf* north of the Merla River. But this was a tenuous connection at best and did not cut the lines of supply of 5th Guards Tank Corps or other elements of 6th Guards Army. Moreover, it was threatened by the continuation of 1st Tank Army's offensive south of the Merchik.

By 11 August, the SS and army panzer divisions of III. Panzerkorps had assembled their component units. While *Totenkopf* battled columns of Soviet armor and mechanized infantry south of the Merchik and *Das Reich* fought off Soviet attacks in the Olshany area, *Wiking* deployed north of Olshany and took over sections of the front manned by *Das Reich*, freeing that division's combat units for offensive operations. *Wiking* found itself in the thick of the fighting as soon as it arrived on the front, confronting elements of 5th Guards Tank Army literally from the march.

On 11–12 August, the attack by III. Panzerkorps met the renewed efforts of the Russians to cut the railroad line of supply west of Kharkov in attacks along the entire length of the Merchik from south of Bogodukhov to west of Krasnokutsk.

CHAPTER 11

The Counterattack of III. Panzerkorps

THE FIGHTING ON THE WESTERN SHOULDER
While Armee-Abteilung Kempf's III. Panzerkorps struggled to contain the Soviet armor thrusting south out of the Bogodukhov area, the Soviet 5th Guards Tank Corps, which had been detached from 6th Guards Army and given to 1st Tank Army, continued its penetration between 4. Panzerarmee and Armee-Abteilung Kempf. By 11 August, 5th Guards Tank Corps was pushing toward the confluence of the Merla and the Vorksla Rivers. The section of the Vorksla south of Akhtyrka roughly formed the western shoulder of the gap between the two German armies. Behind the Vorskla, 4. Panzerarmee manned firm river-line defenses that stopped the Russian advance to the west below Akhtyrka. 4. Panzerarmee's defense of the river had channeled the Russian advance into a penetration sector to the south of Akhtyrka, toward the towns of Kotel'va and Parkomovka. On the right flank of the attack by 5th Guards Tank Corps, the Soviet 27th Army's attack had encountered problems north of Akhtyrka.

The Soviet 27th Army's mobile element, 4th Guards Tank Corps, attempted to advance in a parallel attack on the right flank of 5th Guards Tank Corps. However, it remained delayed in sustained fighting twenty to thirty kilometers north of Akhtyrka, opposed by Panzergrenadier-Division *Grossdeutschland*. On 7 August, 4th Tank Corps, attempted to attack southwards along both banks of the Vorskla River and found its advance contested stoutly by elements of *Grossdeutschland*. The German division gave ground slowly, forced back by the attack of three Soviet tank brigades, until east of Akhtyrka, near a railroad line, *Grossdeutschland* built up a solid defensive position studded with antitank gun positions, 88s and assault guns.

27th Army was ordered to take Akhtyrka in order to secure the western flank of the attack through the gap between Akhtyrka and Krasnokutsk. However, *Grossdeutschland* successfully turned back the heavy Soviet frontal assaults. Having failed to crack the division's defenses in this manner, 27th Army decided to outflank the German position. While continuing to conduct limited frontal attacks in order to pin *Grossdeutschland* in place, 13th Guards Tank Brigade moved south of the town, turned west and attacked on the German right. This assault forced the Germans to withdraw to the west toward Akhtyrka. Under heavy pressure by the Soviets, *Grossdeutschland* executed a difficult but orderly withdrawal of its right flank and occupied defensive positions east of the outskirts of the town. On 10 August, the division was forced to withdraw its entire front to a defensive perimeter around the Akhtyrka. The following day, 4th Guards Tank Corps again assaulted the defenses of Akhtyrka.

On 11 August, tanks and infantry of 12th Guards Tank Brigade penetrated the defenses of the town but were driven out during the evening hours when the Germans cut off the attack group, forcing them to fight their way back out of the town. *Grossdeutschland* was also able to fight off Soviet attacks originating from the southeast, preventing any penetrations into the town from that direction. The Russians made a subsequent attempt, later on 11 August, to capture Akhtyrka with 13th Guards Tank Brigade. The brigade attacked the town from the southwest but was similarly unable to crack the German defenses. The timetable of the advance of 27th Army's armored group was thrown off by the stubborn defense of the town. In order to catch up with and support the attack of 5th Guards Tank Corps, 27th Army ordered 4th Tank Corps to break off their attack.

Frustrated by its inability to break into the town with the forces at hand, 27th Army assembled additional infantry formations in Trostyanets, north of Akhtyrka. These new forces were ordered to maintain the pressure on the Germans, while 4th Guards Tank Corps was ordered to bypass the German perimeter to the south, turn west and cut lines of communication into the town.[1] On 12 August, it moved south against light resistance and took the town of Kotel'va on the following day. Elements of *Grossdeutschland* engaged the Soviet force and halted its attack.

The situation stabilized at this point after attempts to encircle the town were defeated. A last effort to break through the German lines in the Trostyanets sector, north of Akhtyrka, was mounted by two Soviet rifle divisions against the defensive positions of 57. Infanterie-Division. Quickly, 7. Panzer-Division moved into the threatened sector and reinforced counterattacks by the German infantry division, and after two days of bitter fighting, the two divisions were able to stabilize the front. It became clear to the Russian command that the forces they had at hand were not sufficient to crack the German front on the western shoulder in the Tostyanets-Akhtyrka sector. The commander of 27th Army had not concentrated his forces in an orderly manner and had allowed 4th Tank Corps to become bogged down in the fighting for Akhtyrka. He had used his artillery poorly in support of the attacks by 4th Tank Corps on the town. As a result of this ineptitude and German defensive stubborness, the Soviet attack in the area of Akhtyrka and Kotel'va ran out of steam by 12 August.

THE SITUATION ON 12 AUGUST

By 12 August, although armored elements of the Soviet attack had made serious penetrations in great depth between Kharkov and Akhtyrka, dogged German resistance on both flanks of the Soviet attack tied down many Russian rifle divisions and their supporting artillery. The Soviet infantry divisions were involved in grinding, costly fighting at Belgorod and Tomarovka. This was followed by heavy combat at Kharkov in the east and Graivoron and Borisovka in the west. In the days that followed the initial breakthroughs, Soviet infantry became largely separated from the fast-moving elements of 1st Tank Army, 5th Guards Tank Army and the mobile elements of 27th and 6th Guards Armies, which pushed below the Merchik and Merla Rivers. In spite of the fact that Vatutin's mobile spearheads had penetrated as much as 100 kilometers to the south and Kharkov was under concentric attack by powerful forces, the battle had reached a familiar decisive moment. By prodigious efforts, the Germans had been able to channel the Soviet breakthrough and gather a force of panzer divisions on both flanks. The Soviet rifle divisions, although held up significantly, were in a position on 12 August to be able to begin concentrating in support of the armored advance within twenty-four to thirty-six hours.[2] However, until they were able to do so, the Soviet spearheads were overextended and did not have the necessary infantry and artillery strength to sustain the operation.

The situation presented an opportunity to the Germans if they could gather sufficient mobile divisions to cut off and destroy the extended Soviet tank forces before the rifle divisions could reinforce the advance mobile groups and erect firm defenses on the flanks of the penetration. The Soviets still had difficulty moving their heavy artillery and the infantry of their rifle corps in sufficient numbers to quickly support a deep penetration by armor. This was primarily because of an inadequate number of trucks and artillery prime movers. As had happened before on the Eastern Front, this shortcoming gave the Germans a window of opportunity to strike, if it could be done before Soviet infantry caught up with the mobile forward detachments.

The German command realized that the situation was at a critical juncture and that time was of the essence. Accordingly, on 12 August, it prepared to counterattack with panzer divisions from both flanks of the penetration, cut off and destroy the Soviet armored units and thus achieve a decisive victory, such as at Kharkov, earlier in the year. 4. Panzerarmee, by 13 August, had halted the Russian attacks in the Akhtyrka-Koterva sector and prepared to launch its counterstrike, under command of XXIV. Panzerkorps. The attack element was made up of Panzergrenadier-Division *Grossdeutschland*, 7. Panzer-Division, and 10. Panzergrenadier-Division. *Grossdeutschland*'s forward elements maintained their contact with *Totenkopf* reconnaissance units southeast of Akhtyrka, at Parchomovka.

The "fire brigade" formations of the German Army, the army and Waffen SS panzer divisions, prepared once again to destroy a major Soviet attack and restore the situation on the Eastern Front. Confidence was high, as the panzer divisions had been in this situation on many occasions during three years of combat in Russia and always had succeeded in cutting off and destroying overextended Soviet armored spearheads.

THE BATTLES SOUTH OF BOGODUKHOV—12–17 AUGUST

By 11 August, the Soviet armored groups had lost many tanks and much equipment and were growing short of motorized infantry. As a result of determined defensive operations by the panzer divisions of

III. Panzerkorps, the Soviet attacks lost their momentum in the Merla-Merchik Rivers area. The Soviet spearheads of 6th Tank Corps south of the Merchik were in danger of being cut off by attacks of *Das Reich* and *Totenkopf*. Rotmistrov's 5th Guards Tank Army had also been frustrated in its attempts to decisively cut off German lines of communication to the southwest of Kharkov, on the right flank of III. Panzerkorps. The efforts of the panzer divisions of III. Panzerkorps and scattered elements of several German infantry divisions, now joined by *Wiking*, resulted in little progress by Rotmistrov's army by the end of 11 August.

On 12 August, dissatisfied with the progress of 5th Guards Tank Army, Zhukov ordered Rotmistrov to pull back over the Merla River and assemble north of Bogokukhov. From there, his army was to support 1st Tank Army in a decisive push south of the Merchik. Rotmistrov promptly refused to obey the order, replying succinctly that if he withdrew from the area east and south of Bogodukhov, the Germans would capture it. It may be that Zhukov was not aware of the reasons for the slowed pace of the Russian attack. Voronezh Front's commander, Vatutin, was a notoriously optimistic man who had gotten in trouble in the past because of the misinterpretation of information that did not fit his perceptions of reality. This had happened in the Kharkov area in February–March when he ignored the reports of his own tank commanders regarding the weakness of their formations and interpreted the evidence of gathering German armor as preparation to cover a withdrawal. The result was the catastrophic defeat at Kharkov at the hands of II. SS-Panzerkorps and XXXXVIII. Panzerkorps under direction of Manstein.

The situation was fast becoming disturbingly familiar to the Russian tank commanders at the points of the advance. Their tank brigades were infantry poor, in need of maintenance and had suffered severe losses. Their lines of communication could not be adequately secured until the infantry corps caught up with the lead mobile elements and established defensive positions on the shoulders of the penetrations. The concerns of the Soviet tank commanders were born out on 11–12 August when the Germans began a counterattack against 1st Tank Army. III. Panzerkorps attacked from the Olshany-Dolshik-Merchik sector. (See appendix VI for III. Panzerkorps order of battle.) XXIV. Panzerkorps attacked from south of the Akhtyrka area and drove toward the Merchik.

By 10 August, the panzer divisions had already received their mission orders for the attack. *Wiking* was to secure the north flank of III. Panzerkorps, in the area from Klenovoje to the Merla sector, and replace *Das Reich* elements west of Dolshik. *Das Reich* was to concentrate all its strength on its left or southern flank and advance to the west, with the objective of destroying the Russian forces advancing from Bogodukhov. The division was instructed that if circumstances were favorable, it was to take the town itself, but only if it could be done quickly. On arrival at the south bank of the Merla River, it was to reconnoiter across the river toward Bogodukhov and evaluate Soviet strength. *Totenkopf* was ordered to attack toward Murafa after reaching Nikitovka and to clear the south bank of the Merchik. 3. Panzer-Division, after its severe losses during the previous days, was to hold its positions south of Zolochev around Olshany.

III. Panzerkorps' plan was to attack in two parallel advances, with *Das Reich* pushing west, after clearing the sector south of Bogodukhov by driving 31st Tank Corps back to Bogodukhov. This attack would cut the lines of communication of the Soviet 6th Tank Corps. *Totenkopf* was arrayed to the south of the Merchik, facing north against the advance of 6th Tank Corps at Alexsandrovka and Murafa. Its mission was to hold the positions of Regiment *Totenkopf* south of the river at Alexsandrovka while attacking westward toward the Krasnokutsk-Konstantinovka area. This would cut off the forward elements of 6th Tank Corps south of the Merchik. On the night of 11–12 August, *Wiking* occupied the line at Olshany. *Das Reich* concentrated for the attack during the night. However, some elements of Regiment *Deutschland* remained in the line until *Wiking* took over the entire sector. On 11 August, *Wiking* had thirty-three tanks, *Totenkopf* thirty-nine (including seven Tigers), and *Das Reich* fifty-one (with eight Tigers). Schwere-Panzer-Abteilung 503, assigned to support *Totenkopf*, had thirteen Tigers.

The timing of the German counterattack was disturbed somewhat by developments on 11 August, below Bogodukhov, particularly south of the Merchik. When the Soviet 1st Tank Army went over to the offensive again on that day, after being prodded into action by Zhukov, it forced some elements of *Totenkopf* on the eastern flank of the division to defend themselves against Soviet battle groups advancing in the area south of the river. Advance elements of Soviet mobile groups drove south toward the railroad and stations along the line.

The Counterattack of III. Panzerkorps

Russian tanks carrying infantry, made contact with German troops unexpectedly, meetings which resulted in chaotic fighting at several points along the rail line below the Merchik.

An example of the type of fighting that occurred during 11 August was a meeting engagement between supply troops of *Totenkopf* and a small detachment of Soviet tanks. The Russian troops, which were probably advance elements of 49th Tank Brigade, intercepted the supply and ordnance train of SS-Panzer-Aufklärungs-Abteilung 3, west of Kovjagi. The security detachments of the supply troop reported hearing the sounds of tank motors and withdrew to a small village nearby, deploying in a hedgehog defensive alignment. The *Totenkopf* troopers fought off infiltrations by Russian infantry who tried to make their way into the village after the raiding group of tanks continued on. The Soviet armor was more intent on penetrating farther to the south than losing time fighting in the village. The tanks did not get involved in the fighting and instead continued to the west. By evening, 49th Tank Brigade detachments had reached the village of Levendalovka, near units of I./SS-Pionier-Abteilung 3.

All along the sector south of Alexsandrovka and west to the Merla, *Totenkopf* fought off groups of Soviet tanks driving south from the Merchik toward the rail line. At several places, Russian troops tore up rails in order to hamper train traffic. The Tigers of the division counterattacked a breakthrough in Regiment *Totenkopf*'s sector that resulted from an attack at 0400 hours near the village of Kosliki. The reconnaissance battalion occupied a bridge position at Krasnokutsk before 0800 hours.

In *Das Reich*'s sector of the front, Russian tanks and infantry were observed to be concentrating at the southern edge of Dolshik, under cover of a forest south of the village and around Hill 209.2. Shortly afterward, *Das Reich* had to repel a strong Soviet attack by infantry supported by several tanks that originated from the forest assembly area at 0530 hours. The attack was broken up, and four T-34s were destroyed. However, it was soon apparent that the Russians were regrouping for a second attack. At 0845 hours, *Das Reich* turned back a stronger attack from the woods, knocking out eleven of the force of twenty-five to thirty supporting T-34s. A third attack was also stopped, leaving four burning tanks on the field. Throughout the day, the whole front of the division was assaulted by Russian tanks and infantry—in particular, the sections held by Regiment *Der Führer* and the reconnaissance battalion. Some of the Russian battle groups found gaps in the German lines and penetrated to a rail line south of Dolshik. In the afternoon, reconnaissance elements of the division reported that rails and ties were blown up at a point near the village of Gavrieky.[3]

Similarly, *Wiking* was engaged in fighting against 5th Guards Tank Army elements before it was fully organized for the defense of its new defensive line. *Wiking* was not able to move all of its strength into line in place of *Das Reich* before the panzer regiment was heavily engaged near Olshany. At that point, it was required to go to the assistance of *Das Reich* elements fighting off attempts by Russian mobile units to wrest a range of hills north of Sinkovsky from German possession. At 0945 hours, *Wiking* panzers, with a company of its reconnaissance battalion and infantry of Regiment *Germania*, attacked Hill 209.5, encountering strong Soviet resistance. Shortly afterwards, the right flank of the division was attacked by a battalion-strength assault near Dolshik. Elements of Regiment *Westland* defeated the Russian attack on the right, and by 1315 hours, the panzer group pushed past Hill 209.5 toward another range of high ground occupied by the Russians. While *Wiking* and *Das Reich* engaged 5th Guards Tank Army forces north and west of Olshany, *Totenkopf* continued to battle mobile elements of Soviet spearheads south of the Merchik.

Pavlovo was captured by 1455 hours, by Regiment *Eicke*, followed shortly afterward by the capture of two more small villages after Soviet troops withdrew abruptly. Vysokopol'ye remained occupied by the Russians and fighting there continued into the night, with neither side gaining a decisive advantage.[4]

In the evening, a *Totenkopf* battle group under command of Knight's Cross winner SS-Sturmbannführer Max Seela engaged the troops of 49th Tank Brigade and 17th Tank Regiment that held Levandolovka. The SS combat engineers of 1./Pionier-Abteilung 3 assaulted the village, broke into the perimeter and destroyed a number of the Soviet tanks with antitank weapons in close combat. Only a few survivors of the Russian force were able to escape to a wooded area northwest of the village. The sixty to seventy men of Kampfgruppe Seela continued north from the village, reached the railroad line near a rail station at Vodjanaja and worked slowly down the length of the railroad toward the west.[5] The battle group of 112th

Tank Brigade that had occupied Vysokopol'ye continued to fight off attacks by other elements of the SS engineer battalion that attempted to drive them from the town.

South of the Merchik, the attacks by *Totenkopf* forced some of the Soviet forward detachments to retreat to the river. Some were unable to escape and were encircled and destroyed by SS assault groups. Farther west of the area south of Murafa, the reconnaissance battalion was attacked by Soviet tanks operating east of Krasnokutsk at river crossing sites on the western section of the Merchik. At Krasnokutsk, Russian tanks and infantry crossed the Merla despite the efforts of the SS reconnaissance troops and the left flank of the battalion was forced back to the village of Katschlovka. Other Russian units moved into the town of Oleinikov, north of Krasnokutsk.

To the southeast of Bogodukhov, *Das Reich* was on the move also, beginning its advance at 0800 hours, along both sides of the rail line south of Maximovka, where it immediately encountered heavy resistance from 1st Tank Army.[6] Russian tanks and SS panzers clashed on the open ground, and after heavy fighting, the Soviets withdrew back towards the Merla. West of Maximovka, *Das Reich* broke through the Soviet positions on a broad front and pushed the Russians back on the Bogodukhov-Kharkov railroad in attacks during which the division claimed the destruction of seventy tanks and a great deal of equipment.

At the end of the day on 11 August, the situation in the area of 1st Tank Army was extremely serious. Contrary to expectations, Katukov's tank army had not gained control of the sector south of the Merchik. In fact, it had been pushed away from the rail lines which were so vital to the Germans. His army had lost 134 of the 268 tanks it had begun the day with and was driven back over the Merchik at many points. Its extended spearheads to the south of the river had either been cut off, dispersed or were forced to withdraw to avoid encirclement and destruction. The remains of the 112th Tank Brigade battalion commanded by Colonel Leonov was forced to attempt a fighting withdrawal out of Vysokolpol'ye. It fought its way out of the town and escaped north to Sharovka, which lay on the Merchik. Most of Leonov's battle group was destroyed during the fighting. It lost all of its antitank guns and left most of the original force of twenty-five tanks behind, out of fuel or knocked out.

The defensive operations of *Totenkopf* and *Das Reich* on 11 August blunted the advance of lead elements of 1st Tank Army. The two SS divisions drove the Russians back and created an extremely dangerous situation for the Soviets on the night of 11–12 August. The Soviet rifle divisions were still en route to join the main armored elements. The Soviet tank corps, which were deficient in artillery and infantry strength and had been weakened considerably, found it hard to adequately defend their gains. Compounding the problem was the fact that Russian air support was not effective at this time, which contributed significantly to the setbacks suffered by 1st Tank Army south of Bogodukhov.

Katukov committed his last reserve forces to attacks against the German panzers in an effort to stave off utter disaster. He reinforced the right flank of 6th Tank Corps and ordered reserve units to the relief of 112th Tank Brigade at Sharovka, where Colonel Leonov's battered troops were under continuing heavy pressure by *Totenkopf.* Katukov ordered 31st Tank Corps to regroup and attack again late in the day, sending it against the breakthrough made by *Das Reich* along the rail line east of Olshany. The commitment of the remnants of 31st Tank Corps and elements of 3rd Guards Mechanized Corps motorized infantry finally brought the advance of *Das Reich* to a halt late on 11 August.

As early as 10 August, it had been clear that 5th Guards Tank Army was at a standstill and Vatutin realized that the army was not likely to succeed in the fight against 3. Panzer-Division at Zolochev, in spite of the losses that had been inflicted on the German division. Believing that his chances of success were better in the Merla–Merchik River area, he decided to discontinue Rotmistrov's unsuccessful attacks on Zolochev in order to assemble all possible strength near Bogodukhov. Vatutin intended to use 5th Guards Tank Army to contain the German counterattack on the right flank of 1st Tank Army and provide additional forces to support the renewal of Katukov's attack. Vatutin ordered 1st Tank Army to continue to push to the south over the Merchik with the objective of cutting German lines of communication into Kharkov from the southwest. Katukov prepared to resume his attack on the following day.

12 AUGUST—5TH GUARDS TANK ARMY CONTINUES THE ATTACK

The Soviet 1st Tank Army was severely damaged by the fighting of 11 August. The attack by *Totenkopf* tanks on the left of 6th Tank Corps drove the flank in and it was necessary for Katukov to hurriedly throw much of his remaining infantry strength against the SS division in order to stop the Germans. During the night, the fighting died down and the Russians regrouped in order to continue their operations on the next day.

In order to regain the momentum of 1st Tank Army's attack, Vatutin ordered 5th Guards Tank Army to withdraw and during the night of 11 August move by forced march to assembly areas north of Bogodukhov in order to position it to support the renewed operations of 1st Tank Army south of the Merchik and Merla Rivers. Rotmistrov planned to conduct attacks on the junction of *Das Reich* and *Wiking* and the western flank of 3. Panzer-Division.

THE GERMANS STRIKE BACK ON 12 AUGUST

By early on the morning of 12 August, 5th Guards Tank Army reached its jump-off positions near Bogodukhov, preparatory to beginning its attack toward the Kovjagi-Valki sector with the mission of severing the German lines of communication west of Kharkov and supporting the attacks by 1st Tank Army. Rotmistrov deployed 18th and 29th Tank Corps (II. SS-Panzerkorps' old opponents at Prochorovka) forward, keeping 5th Guards Mechanized Corps as reserve.

The two Soviet tank corps, expecting to begin their attack through secure positions south of the Merchik River, were surprised when their leading detachments came under attack by *Totenkopf* battle groups near the Alexsandrovka bridgehead and other points south of the river. Instead of beginning the attack below the Merchik through the secure positions of 1st Tank Army, the Soviet spearhead units were counterattacked by German battle groups of SS tanks and panzergrenadiers. German and Russian divisions began a chaotic day of fighting during which the two opponents penetrated frontline positions, counterattacked each other's penetrations at many points and engaged in fighting all along the river. The confusion forced the Soviets to regroup. Unable to get his attack properly underway, Rotmistrov pulled his two leading tank corps back late in the morning, under pressure by *Totenkopf*'s assaults and renewed attacks by *Das Reich* south of Gavrishi.

In spite of the failure of 5th Guards Tank Army's initial advance, Katukov ordered his armor to again cross the Merchik at several

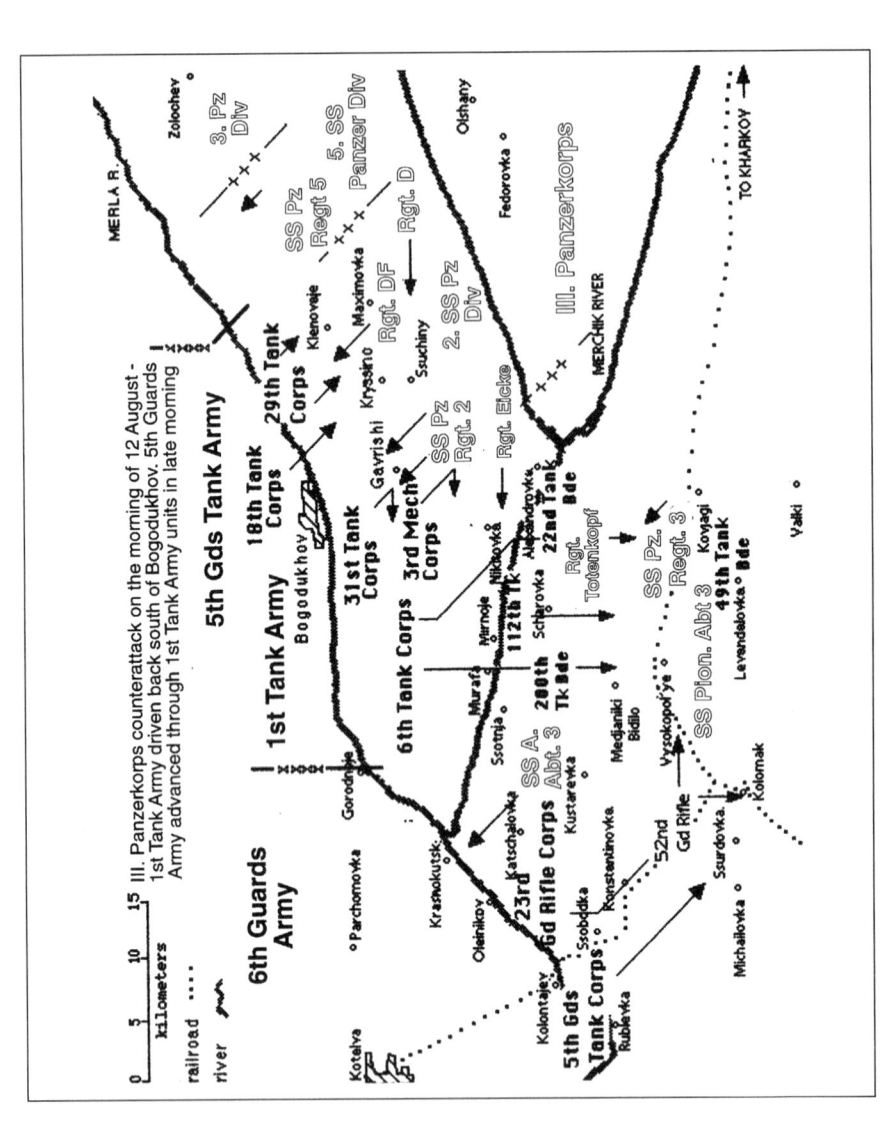

The counterattack of the III. Panzerkorps, morning of 12 August 1943.

points and strike south, toward the railroad. Tanks of 6th Tank Corps, accompanied by motorized infantry, crossed the river and advanced toward Vysokopol'ye once more. At 0345 hours, two battalions of 3rd Mechanized Corps infantry, with supporting armor, moved out of the Alexsandrovka area, penetrated the German front and reached the area north of the town. In Vysokopol'ye itself, Soviet tanks and infantry continued to fight 1./SS-Pionier-Bataillon 3. Elements of 6th Tank Corps' assault force reached the rail line at about 1300 hours.

North of the river, in the sector of Regiment *Eicke,* near the village of Kosliki, leading tanks of 3rd Mechanized Corps came under fire by Tiger tanks, probably belonging to schwere-Panzer-Abteilung 503, and a number were knocked out. Several T-34s also broke through the German lines near Mimoje, where Regiment *Totenkopf* grenadiers were dug in, but these Russian tanks were quickly attacked by tank destroyer squads with close combat antitank weapons and were destroyed at that point. SS armor first engaged Soviet tanks at 0420 hours in the Vysokopol'ye area when *Totenkopf* tanks drove back a probe by Russian tanks near Kovyagi Station. 6th Tank Corps' attempt to reinforce the troops encircled at Vysokopol'ye failed when *Totenkopf* cut off the relief elements and destroyed them. The survivors retreated to the north.[7]

At Krasnokutsk, a Soviet assault group threatened the left flank of the division but was brought to a halt by elements of SS-Panzer-Aufklarungs-Abteilung 3. Dug in around the buildings of a village, with machine-gun positions strongly supported by 88s and mobile antitank guns, the *Totenkopf* troopers turned back several assaults during the day, inflicting heavy casualties on the Soviet infantry attacking through open fields in front of the firing positions of the defenders.

A Regiment *Eicke* battle group, made up of a motorcycle detachment, a company of panzergrenadiers, three assault guns and two tanks, counterattacked elements of 3rd Mechanized Corps and the surviving tanks of 112th Tank Brigade at the village of Novy-Merchik, on the north bank of the Merchik, forcing it to withdraw.[8] The panzergrenadiers and assault guns, following the repulse of the Soviets, caught up with them at the village of Pavlovo and drove them further toward Alexsandrovka. The Germans pursued the retreating Soviet force and by the early afternoon advanced to the eastern edge of the town. The Soviets, at this point, brought up a number of tanks and readied them for an attack. However, additional assault guns of the *Totenkopf* assault gun battalion arrived in time to inflict serious losses on the Soviet counterattack. The Germans estimated Soviet tank losses as twenty-five vehicles. At 1455 hours, Pavlovo was taken and the defending Soviet troops were routed, followed by the capture of two other villages, Kosliki and Bendjuky.[9]

The Soviet infantry and tanks in Vysokopol'ye continued to hold their positions and await rescue by reinforcements that never arrived. An attempt made by 6th Motorized Rifle Brigade to break through to the encircled battalions with additional armor of 6th Tank Corps was unsuccessful. The Soviet force lost two thirds of its armor in the attempt. By evening, the SS engineers fought their way into the village, supported by a few panzers and began rooting out the Russian infantry. Five Soviet tanks were destroyed in the house-to-house fighting, although the Russians infantry stubbornly fought to hold on to the village.[10]

1st Tank Army's lead elements south of the Merchik were struck on their eastern flanks by the *Das Reich* attack beginning from the southeast of Bogodukhov. Stukas and fighters of the Luftwaffe supported the attacks of the division at key points. Parts of 49th Tank Corps and 3rd Mechanized Corps elements were driven several kilometers to the west or north. The *Das Reich* attack, led by Regiment *Deutschland*, advanced on both sides of the railroad line running from near Olshany to Bogodukhov, arriving at 0940 hours in the Gavrishi area, there joined at 1030 hours by Regiment *Der Führer*. The SS panzergrenadiers and tanks attacked a fortified state farm near Gavrishi, which was defended by the armor of 29th Tank Corps and Russian infantry. The German advance was held up by heavy Soviet artillery fire and rolling barrages of rocket fire. Soviet resistance remained strong and flanking fire from the north gave *Der Führer* grenadiers problems in their advance toward the west. Later in the day, III./*Der Führer*, attacking through heavy frontal fire, breached Soviet lines and stormed Hill 195.5 as well as two small villages near the farm.[11] The SS tanks, with I./*Der Führer* then moving to the attack, drove the Russians back to the village of Suchliny, where Soviet tanks mounted an attack on the German advance. A group of about forty T-34s engaged the SS panzers, advancing from the north. These tanks were probably from 5th Guards Tank Army, that army having been expressly ordered by Vatutin to resume its attack regardless of the conditions after their initial setback in the morning. By late afternoon, *Das Reich* had only twenty-two operational tanks in addition to a few Tigers of schwere-Panzer-Abteilung 503 and twenty-three assault guns.

All along the axis of advance of *Das Reich*, Soviet tanks and supporting infantry were either destroyed or forced to withdraw. Both 18th and 29th Tank Corps of 5th Guards Tank Army hurriedly organized to counterattack in the afternoon. This attack was reinforced by the addition of two rifle divisions from 32nd Guards Rifle Corps. At this date, the first significant arrivals of Soviet rifle divisions had thus begun to occur and were to have an important influence on the fighting.

5th Guards Tank Army struck back in the afternoon. Immediately, losses began to mount. The counterattack was characterized by German reports of heavy Russian losses of men and material. The commander of 31st Tank Corps, General Chernienko, was killed leading his tanks against the SS panzers. The German attack threatened to reach Bogodukhov if unchecked. *Das Reich*'s advance was only brought to a halt when it reached the defensive positions of 32nd Guards Rifle Corps, which had dug in south of the city. The positions of the infantry were studded with antitank guns and hastily emplaced tanks.

Only by commitment of strong reserve elements of rifle and mobile units had the German drive toward Bogodukhov been halted. The SS division counted seventy Soviet tanks destroyed in the fighting during the day's operations. The Soviets were still hampered by lack of strong air support. In contrast, German aircraft were still able to operate over the battlefield with little opposition from Soviet fighters. However, Soviet planes began to appear in some numbers for the first time and the SS Flak detachments shot down several of them.[12]

Wiking began its attack also on the morning of 12 August, but without similar success. The division's panzer battalion, with a company of the reconnaissance battalion, attacked over Hill 209.5 against Soviet defensive positions along a line of several fortified hills. Regiment *Germania*, attacking on the flank of this force, closed up with the attack of the SS tanks from Hill 209.5, moving forward until stout Soviet resistance brought the attack to a temporary halt. At 1315 hours, the *Wiking* tanks advanced again against the range of hills held by the Russians that lay beyond Hill 209.5, but gained little ground.[13]

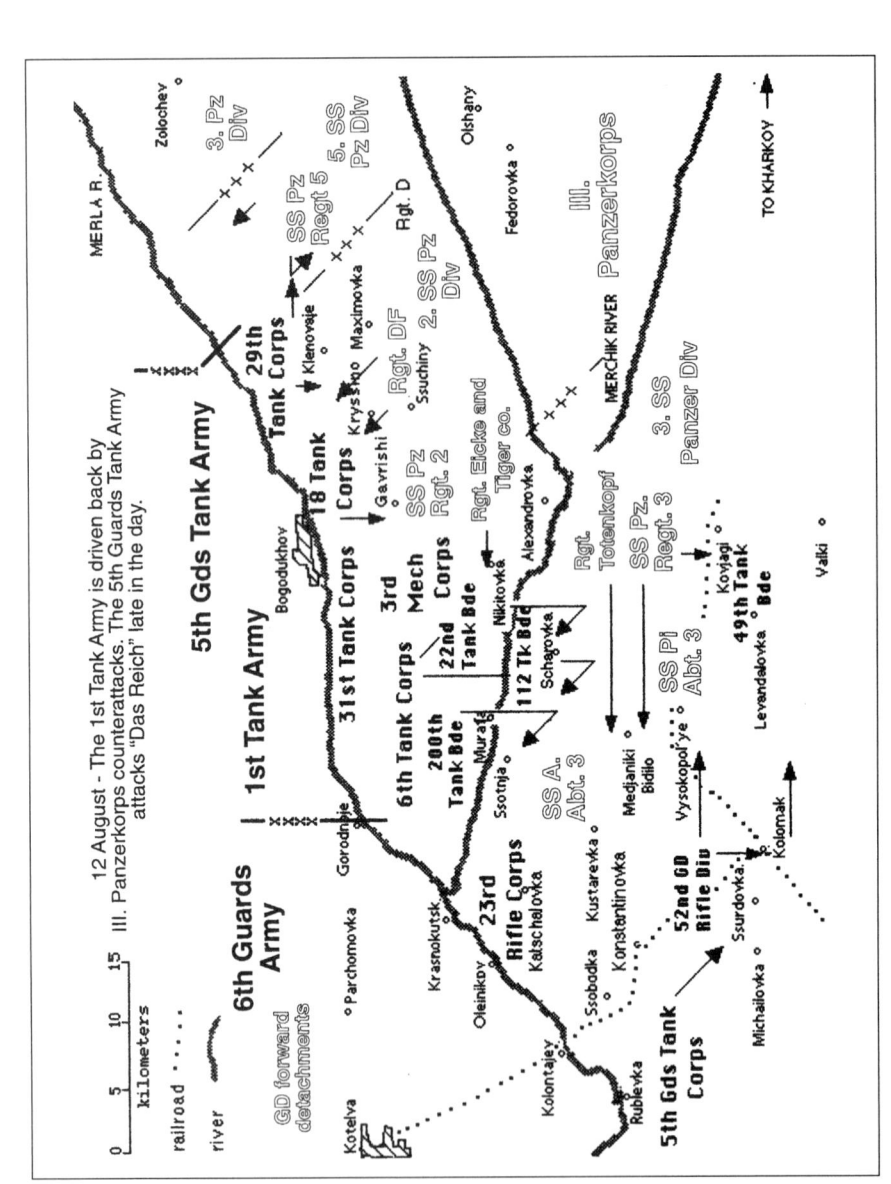

1st Tank Army is driven back, 12 August 1943.

When the German attack halted again, the Russians counterattacked the right flank of Panzergrenadier-Regiment *Westland*, the attack originating from the Dolshik area. The SS division and Russians defenders of the fortified hills sparred on into the night with the situation in this sector remaining essentially unchanged on 12 August.

VATUTIN ORDERS A COUNTERATTACK

By nightfall on 12 August, the two opposing armies were nearly exhausted after a long day of hard fighting. *Totenkopf* and the armored elements of 1st Tank Army, entangled with each other below the Merchik, halted operations temporarily except at Vysokopol'ye, where the fighting continued on into the night. In *Das Reich*'s sector, the Germans were brought to a halt only a few miles to the south of Bogodukhov. The earlier concern by Rotmistrov that the Germans would capture the town of Bogodukhov if he moved his armor as instructed by Vatutin was probably legitimate. Rotmistrov's refusal to withdraw the tank divisions that were defending the town's southern and southeastern approaches likely saved Vatutin the embarassment of having to retake Bogodukhov after he had again underestimated the dangers posed by panzer divisions on his flanks. *Wiking* and 3. Panzer-Division held their positions in the Dolshik-Zolochev area, fighting off the attempts of 5th Guards Tank Army to drive them out of their defensive positions.

1st Tank Army was reduced to a remnant of its former tank strength, which had been more than 500 tanks just eight days previously. The army had substantially less than 150 remaining tanks. 6th Tank Corps, 31st Tank Corps and 3rd Mechanized Corps were badly battered and weakened in both numbers of operational tanks and men. The army was short of infantry also, but that situation was changing because Soviet infantry columns and convoys were steadily arriving in the area. Rotmistov's tank army had also experienced hard and costly fighting. His 29th Tank Corps fought *Das Reich* in the Kijany-Kryssino area and it can be assumed that many of the tanks reported destroyed by the SS division were lost by 29th Tank Corps. 18th Tank Corps counterattack at Gavrishi, conducted through the battered units of 31st Tank Corps, was driven back by *Das Reich* with heavy losses. The withdrawal was not halted until two brigades of 5th Guards Mechanized Corps, 10th and 12th Mechanized Brigades, were brought up and thrown into the battle. It can be assumed that

18th Tank Corps' losses for the day were substantial because Rotmistrov's army as a whole only had 100 operational tanks by the end of 12 August. When the fighting stopped for the day, elements of the Russian armies and III. Panzerkorps remained intertwined throughout the sector.

During the night of 12–13 August, while Rotmistrov issued orders to his battered divisions that they should plan to hold their positions on the following day, Vatutin formulated other plans. The front commander was determined to renew offensive operations on 13 August, reinforced with fresh rifle divisions that were now arriving in the area, in cooperation with armored elements of 5th Guards Tank Army. Interpreting German attacks by the SS panzer divisions as cover for a withdrawal toward the Psel, Vatutin ordered fresh attacks by 1st Tank Army, in spite of its losses. Several of the rifle divisions were used to reinforce the defences south of Bogodukhov late on 11 August. Vatutin planned to strike *Totenkopf* hard by advancing in strength south of the Merchik, attacking through the secure positions of Soviet rifle divisions now firmly entrenched on the north bank of the river. On the next day, he planned to send his rifle divisions and armor in attacks against *Totenkopf* units at Vysokopol'ye and around Kovyagi. He took this course of action in spite of misgivings by Zhukov, who counseled Vatutin to be aware of the danger of overextending his forward elements with German armor poised on the flank of 1st Tank Army. Vatutin also considered a thrust west utilizing mobile units from Rotmistrov's army to reinforce 27th Army and 6th Guards Army forces attacking south of Krasnokutsk.

After receiving reports of a German force moving along the rail line toward Vysokopol'ye (most likely formations of 223. Infanterie-Division), Vatutin decided to attack with elements of 5th Guards Mechanized Corps and infantry of 6th Guards Army. He planned to advance against the flank of the German force in the railroad area by attacking south of Krasnokutsk toward the rail line leading to the town of Konstantinovka. From there, he planned to advance to the Kolomak area, attack the Germans forces from the rear and position his armor on the flank of III. Panzerkorps. From Kolomak, Vatutin planned to attack east and hit *Totenkopf* on its west flank. At the same time, 6th Tank Corps was to cross the Merchik and again attack toward Vysokopol'ye and Kovyagi station.

The Counterattack of III. Panzerkorps

Early on 13 August, the Soviet attack began. South of Bogodukhov, *Totenkopf* elements defending the railroad line south of the Merchik were driven back near Alexseyevka by 52nd Guards Rifle Division. Advance detachments of the Soviet division occupied positions along the line, once more cutting that route of communication into Kharkov. 6th Tank Corps' 6th Motorized Rifle Brigade, supported by elements of 200th Tank Brigade, pushed to Vysokopol'ye and took possession of the village again. In the first hours of the renewed Soviet attack, 5th Guards Mechanized Corps successfully crossed the Merchik and prepared to move south. On the western flank of *Totenkopf*'s sector, the Russians attacked from bridgeheads on the Merla and Merchik Rivers.

Scattered units of *Totenkopf*'s reconnaissance battalion, struck by the Russian attack from out of the Krasnokutsk area, gave ground and withdrew eastward or to the south. The left flank of the division was hard pressed early on 13 August and the reconnaissance battalion was forced to withdraw several kilometers south of the river. The mobile units could not hold their positions but succeeded in delaying the Soviet advance.[14] 6th Guards Army attack, led by 22nd Guards Rifle Corps and 5th Guards Tank Corps, pushed south toward Kolomak. At least two Soviet rifle divisions and major elements of another occupied positions in the Konstantinovka–Kolomak area. Armor from 5th Guards Tank Corps reinforced the Soviet infantry. However, the Russians did not adequately secure their communication lines in the area between the Merchik and the railroad line, and this was to cost them dearly. Zhukov's warnings about the dangers of German panzer divisions poised on the flank of Vatutin's new attack were realized in the coming days.

As the Soviets pushed across the Merchik, threatening the left flank of *Totenkopf*, the right wing of the SS division attacked the Russian positions northeast of Nikitovka at 0430 hours on 13 August. After a strong preparatory barrage from two battalions of artillery, a battery of 88s, and two batteries of Nebelwerfers, the SS panzers rolled forward with elements of Regiment *Eicke*. In reserve, near Maximova, *Totenkopf* held its panzer engineer battalion and mobile elements of the Flak units of the division. The grenadiers of Regiment *Der Führer*, accompanied by *Das Reich* assault guns, attacked northeast of Nikitovka, on the right flank of Regiment *Eicke*.[15] The Tiger tanks of Panzer-Abteilung 503 supported the attack of both divisions with their 88s.

The advance of Regiment *Eicke* against two tactically important hills near Nikitovka, Hill 195.1 and 188.2, began at 0730 hours. The grenadiers of III./Regiment *Eicke* stormed the Soviet defensive positions on 195.1 and II./Regiment *Eicke* assaulted Hill 188.2. Artillery support was furnished by IV./SS-Artillerie-Regiment 3, which had reached new firing positions earlier on the same morning, moving from near Valid to the area of the attack by 0600 hours. The artillery battalion, in position only 400 meters behind the front lines, set up their guns in a field that stank with the bodies of Russians killed by Stuka attacks in earlier action. Destroyed Soviet vehicles and tanks were scattered over the area, the bodies of the crews laying in or beside the shattered machines.[16]

In the meantime, *Totenkopf* grenadiers, with Sturmgeschütz III assault guns in support, began an assault toward Alexsandrovka, fighting through a wooded section of the front against firm Soviet resistance. The German efforts during the preceding days had been supported by numerous attacks of Stukas on the Russian troop and vehicle concentrations. Soviet fighter cover had been scarce during the preceding days and the German planes had been able to strafe and bomb the Soviet infantry columns and destroy significant numbers of tanks and other vehicles without much interference.

The attack by the two German divisions quickly gained ground in the morning. By 0840 hours, Regiment *Totenkopf* reached a stream bed south of Nikitovka and by 0905 was fighting in the southern outskirts of the town. Behind them, destroyed Russian tanks and equipment littered the battleground. The wreckage of Soviet war material, left in the wake of the advancing grenadiers, Stuka attacks and the supporting artillery fires, was strewn along roads and fields. SS soldiers participating in the fighting south of Bogodukhov remembered "vast quantities" of destroyed vehicles and equipment (*unmengen von Kriegsmaterial und zahlreiche Panzer sind vernichtet*) in the drive toward Nikitovka.[17] North of the Bogodukhov-Kharkov rail line, *Der Führer* captured Hill 202.1 in the afternoon. A Soviet counterattack to retake the hill was broken up with the help of rocket barrages from the SS-Werfer-Abteilung and mobile 88mm guns moving up from Maximovka.

The Counterattack of III. Panzerkorps

By 1030 hours, II./*Eicke* broke into Nikitovka, and shortly afterward, III./*Eicke* reached the north end of the town. Under assault from two sides, and threatened to the northeast by German armor, the Russian defensive efforts in the town collapsed. The fighting was over by 1050 hours, when the last Soviet resistance from strongpoints in the center of the village ended, and Regiment *Eicke* took control of the town.

After the capture of Nikitovka, II./ and III./*Eicke* continued their advance toward a number of wooded hills northwest of the town. There the SS battalions came in contact with strong Russian defensive positions on two hills, 197.4 and 199.8. At 1800 hours, the two Russian positions were reported to be in German hands, in spite of intense flanking fire from the vicinity of Hill 197.1, which lay just to the northwest of these two elevations. Regiment *Totenkopf*, assaulting from its position to the south of Nikitovka, attacked Hill 160.0 near the village of Scharovsky-Sanat. The Russians defended the hill with infantry and tanks, but in spite of bitter fighting by the Soviet forces, by evening *Totenkopf* was in possession of the hill. With the coming of darkness, the fighting ended in the woods west and north of Nikitovka.

In contrast to the successful course of the fighting near Nikitovka and on the right flank of *Totenkopf*, the day had not gone as well for *Totenkopf*'s reconnaissance battalion, strung out in screening positions on the division's left flank. The battalion was defending a lengthy front between Katschlovka and Murafa, without the necessary strength to hold that amount of ground. When 6th Guards Army advanced to the south in the narrow penetration zone west of Vysokopol'ye on 13 August, they threw out strong forces along the flank of the attack facing west toward the SS divisions. *Totenkopf*'s reconnaissance detachments thus came under pressure from the Krasnokutsk area, while their left flank was pushed to the east by Russian forces attacking from Konstantinovka, from along a railroad used as a supply line to the forces penetrating south of Konstantinovka. This rail line was able to supply the attacking Soviet elements driving to the south toward Kolomak on III. Panzerkorps left flank.

The reconnaissance battalion, under attack by overwhelming numbers of Russian tanks and infantry, gave ground to the south and southeast. By late afternoon, it was pushed back to the area a few kilometers northwest of Vysokopol'ye, where elements of the division's engineer battalion were still in combat with 6th Tank Corps elements in the village, fighting which continued to rage.[18] However, the serious turn of events on *Totenkopf*'s left flank was the only flaw of the day for the two SS divisions.

The attack of *Das Reich*, advancing on *Totenkopf*'s right, also began well on 13 August, quickly penetrating the Russian line and moving to the northwest from the attack area north of Nikitovka. Early in the morning, the division took Hill 202.1, which lay several hundred meters north of Nikitovka, along a road running toward Bogodukhov. Soviet air strength evidently was more apparent on that date, at least in the attack sector of *Das Reich*, because the division reported that its Flak detachments shot down three Soviets planes during the day. Two of the planes were the ever-present IL-2s and the other was a fighter, a Yak-1. The division also reported destroying large numbers of Soviet tanks and other vehicles, estimating that, between itself and *Totenkopf*, the two SS divisions destroyed a total of 190 to 200 Russian tanks between 11 and 13 August. In its summary of the situation to Armee-Abteilung Kempf, III. Panzerkorps believed that the Soviet 3rd Mechanized Corps and 32nd Guards Rifle Corps were nearly destroyed, while 6th Tank Corps and 29th Tank Corps were greatly reduced.[19]

Das Reich's advance significantly threatened Bogodukhov after attacks by that division and *Wiking* drove 97th Rifle Division back toward the perimeter of the town. The Soviet infantry division withdrew to a line that it could hold about ten kilometers south of the town. Just eight kilometers south of Bogodukhov, 29th Tank Corps was driven back from defensive positions that it held near Gavrishi State Farm. The withdrawal of these forces exposed the western flank of 5th Guards Tank Army and forced Vatutin to react quickly. It appeared that the Germans were about to capture Bogodukhov or turn east and attack the lines of communication of 5th Guards Tank Army. The army probably had less than 100 operational tank remaining by this time, down from nearly three hundred just several days before.[20] The threat of German panzer divisions attacking his supply routes and the weakened state of his army must have caused consternation in the HQ of 5th Guards Tank Army, exacerbated by the constant demands from above ordering Rotmistrov to attack.

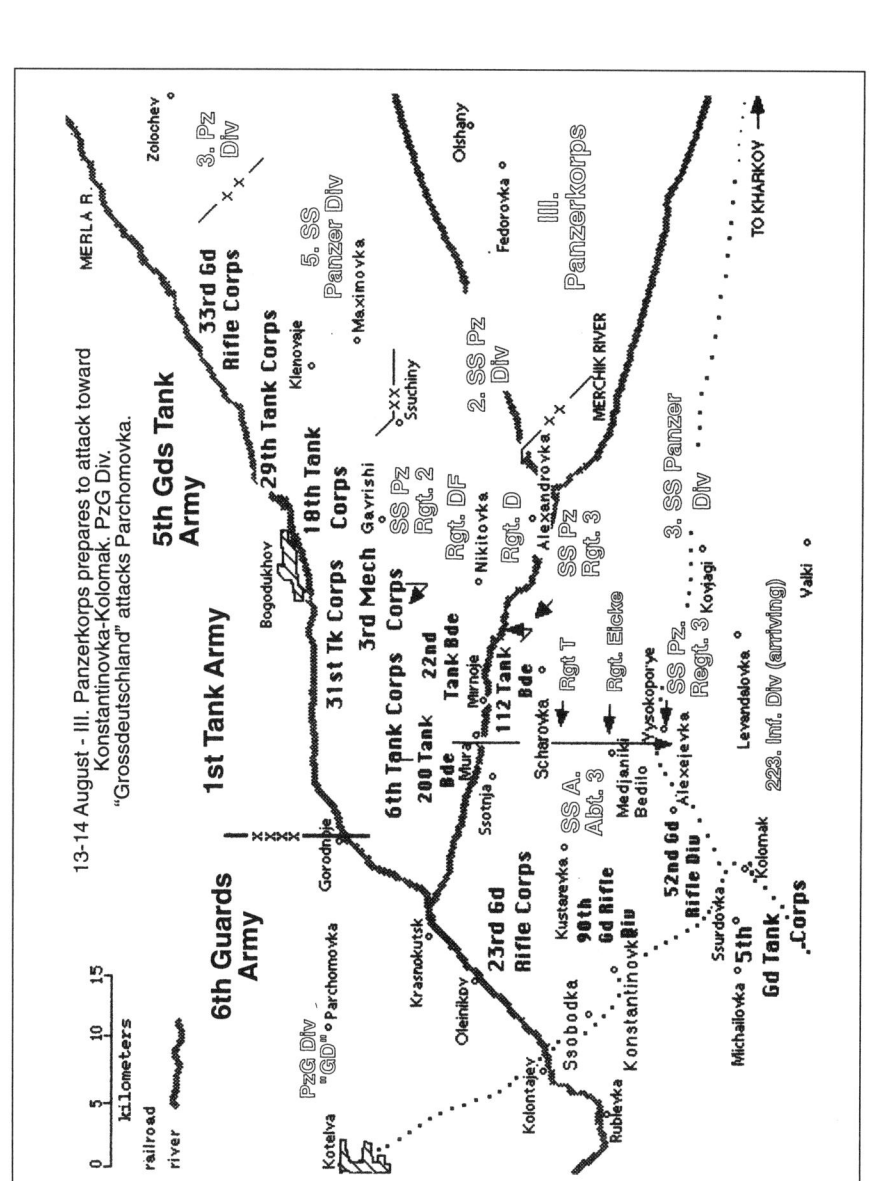

III. Panzerkorps prepares to attack, 13–14 August 1943.

Totenkopf's advance south of the Merchik toward Konstantinovka made good progress and supported the attack of Regiments *Eicke* and *Deutschland* at Nikitovka. SS armor made contact with Soviet tanks at several points. A Soviet tank force collided with the panzers of SS-Panzer-Regiment 3, commanded by Georg Bochmann, south of the attack by Regiment *Deutschland*. Near Scharovka, southwest of Nikitovka and just across the river, the German panzer group entered a small village just after it had been abandoned by ten or twelve Russian tanks. The village was still occupied by Soviet infantry. The SS panzers motored to the outskirts of the village and began to maneuver into firing positions, much to the distress of the Russians, who promptly scattered in all directions. After firing at the withdrawing Russian tanks as they scuttled away in the distance, Bochmann's battle group moved out to the northwest of the village in an inverted wedge formation. At that time, from a distance of about 2,000 meters, a group of approximately forty Soviet tanks was observed to deploy for attack. The T-34s attacked on line and moved directly at the German tanks.

In their path was an enormous field of sunflowers, the stalks of which were sometimes six to eight feet high. As they charged to the attack, the Russian tanks disappeared into the sunflower field. The Soviet tanks were almost completely hidden, their tracks mowing down the plants like huge, invisible reapers. Bochmann deployed his Tigers and Panzer IVs on line facing to the front, ordering them to fire at will when the Russian tanks emerged from the sunflower field. The Panzer IIIs of the group were deployed to the German right flank in order to take the Soviets from their left side. The lighter gun of the Panzer III was more effective against the thinner side armor of the T-34.

Unable to observe the German maneuvers due to the concealing high vegetation, the Soviet tank force was not aware of the flanking movements of the Panzer IIIs. The Tiger and Panzer IVs opened fire on the Russian tanks when they emerged into the ambush. The German tanks on the flank began to fire also. In short order, the terrain was full of burning T-34s destroyed by the 88s of the Tiger or struck by the 50mm cannon of the German tanks firing from the left flank. Russian tanks that were not hit in the first moments tried to escape the trap by maneuvering to safety. SS tanks knocked out many of the Russian vehicles as they tried to withdraw.[21]

The Counterattack of III. Panzerkorps

This engagement is an example of small-unit encounters that occurred between the numerically superior Russian armor and the much smaller German forces in the fighting around Bogodukhov in August. The Soviet tank commander made several tactical errors that resulted in the destruction of his unit. The first mistake occurred when the Soviets lost visual contact with the German tanks by advancing through the sunflower field. Second, the Soviet commander did not deploy any of his force in an overwatch position that could have protected his flank. These mistakes allowed the Germans to maneuver elements of their force to the flank of the Soviet attack. The experienced Bochmann, a veteran of years of tank combat, made his decisions very quickly and quickly deployed his tanks in order to take advantage of their armament to a maximum degree. The ability of German commanders to communicate with their tanks via radio enabled the SS panzers to quickly deploy to advantageous positions to oppose the Soviet attack. The result was the destruction of the larger force.

This incident, one of many such small-unit actions that took place around Bogodukhov, illustrates some of the reasons why 1st Tank Army and 5th Guards Tank Army were reduced to about two hundred tanks by 14 August. This occurred in spite of having over 1,000 tanks in the two tank armies alone at the beginning of Operation "Rumyantsev." There were other tank corps operating in the gap between Armee-Abteilung Kempf and 4. Panzerarmee as well, notably 4th Tank Corps and 5th Guards Tank Corps. The Soviet armored formations were opposed by four German panzer divisions which seldom had more than twenty-five to fifty tanks per division. However, in spite of the losses inflicted on the Soviet tank corps by the Germans, the arrival of additional Soviet infantry strength allowed 6th Guards Army to push farther south for a time. While the Soviets advanced successfully south of Kotel'va and west of Krasnokutsk, around Bogodukhov, the events of battle favored the Germans.

The attacks by III. Panzerkorps in the Nikitovka sector and the area south of Bogodukhov drove Russian troops back at all points on 13 August. In spite of the threat that this posed to the lines of communication of 6th Guards Army's forces south of Krasnokutsk, the Soviet command urged the attack to continue in the Kolomak area. Along the rail line between Kolomak and Vysokopol'ye, 52nd Guards Rifle division pushed east in an effort to link up with 6th Tank Corps elements attacking south from the Merchik. 90th Guards Rifle Division occupied positions between Katschlovka and Konstantinovka. To the southwest of Krasnokutsk, 5th Guards Tank Corps continued its drive to the south, although the tempo of the advance was slowed after elements of the corps were used to support the Soviet infantry in the Kolomak area and along the rail line.

On 14 August, these attacks continued to push in the left flank of *Totenkopf*. Additional Soviet infantry crossed the Merla and marched down the rail line leading out of Konstantinovka and turned south and west. Some of these troops moved to Kolomak while other infantry elements advanced due east toward a line of Vysokopol'ye–Murafa. Lead elements of 23rd Guards Rifle Corps penetrated thirty kilometers south of Krasnokutsk. *Totenkopf* was barely able to slow down the Russian advance with a number of stubbornly fought rear guard actions by the only forces it had in the area, the reconnaissance detachments. The reconnaissance battalion withdrew slowly before the Soviet advance. During the night of 13–14 August, reinforced by assault guns and antitank guns, it formed a solid defensive position west of Alexseyevka. Fighting from these defenses, it turned back Soviet attacks by infantry and tanks that originated from wooded areas north of the village.[22] Alexseyevka was only a few kilometers west of Vysokopol'ye. The Soviet attack along *Totenkopf*'s left flank threatened at that point to link up with the encircled elements in that town.

Late in the day, the fighting around Nikitovka temporarily subsided as the III. Panzerkorps realigned for its attack toward the Kolomak-Konstantinovka area, toward the threat on *Totenkopf*'s left flank. Although the situation remained favorable for the Germans on III. Panzerkorps' right and center, the Soviets continued to push farther south and east on the left flank. Essentially, there were no German troops in the gap that could oppose the Soviet advance. The deep Soviet penetration remained narrow however, and that offered III. Panzerkorps an opportunity to cut off the Soviets troops located south of Konstantinovka and between the rail line and Vysokopol'ye. This situation was created by the dilution of the attack strength of 5th Guards Tank Corps and the failure to move adequate infantry and artillery strength into the flanks of the penetrations. These failures created a situation which was favorable to the Germans and perilous to the Russians. Adding to the Soviet command's concerns was the

The Counterattack of III. Panzerkorps

steadily decreasing numbers of operational tanks and increasing infantry casualties.

The armor of both 5th Guards Tank Army and 1st Tank Army was decimated by this point. By 14 August, the two Russian tank armies were short of armor. The remaining Russian tanks were spread out from Bogodukhov, where they were fighting *Das Reich* on the German right, to the elongated penetration south of the Merchik. After just a few more days of combat, 5th Guards Tank Army would be reduced to less than 100 tanks following ten days of fighting. The infantry strength of the Russians, although several corps of infantry were now in the area, was declining as well. Several of the rifle divisions that had been in continuous combat in the Bogodukhov area for several days were reduced to well below 50 percent of their establishment strength by 14 August.

The long days of fighting, characterized by costly Soviet attacks and constant counterattacks by the Germans, had tired out the Russian troops. This may have been a factor in the events of the next day, when Soviet infantry was overrun at many points by SS panzers and routed by numerically inferior German infantry assaults.[23] At nightfall on 14 August, the deep Russian penetration south of Krasnokutsk presented an inviting target because of the slender supply corridor extending from Kotel'va to Konstantinovka and from there to Kolomak.

The III. Panzerkorps regrouped during the night of 14–15 August in order to cut off these extended Soviet advance elements with an attack on Konstantinovka. After reaching the rail line at that town, the attack would then turn south and advance along the line toward Kolomak. If successful, the attack would sever the supply lines of 6th Tank Corps south of the Merchik and penetrate into the rear areas of the Soviet forces in the Konstantinovka–Kolomak–Vysokopol'ye sector. While 3. Panzer-Division and *Wiking* were to hold their positions on the right flank of the corps, *Das Reich* and *Totenkopf* prepared to advance on 15 August.

By late on 14 August, *Totenkopf* battle groups were on the march, moving to assembly positions on a line south of Nikitovka. The division had twenty-nine operational tanks, only one of which was a Tiger, and seven command panzers. On *Wiking*'s front, the Russians remained on the defense, although the front was active with small to moderate Russian reconnaissance attacks all along the line of the

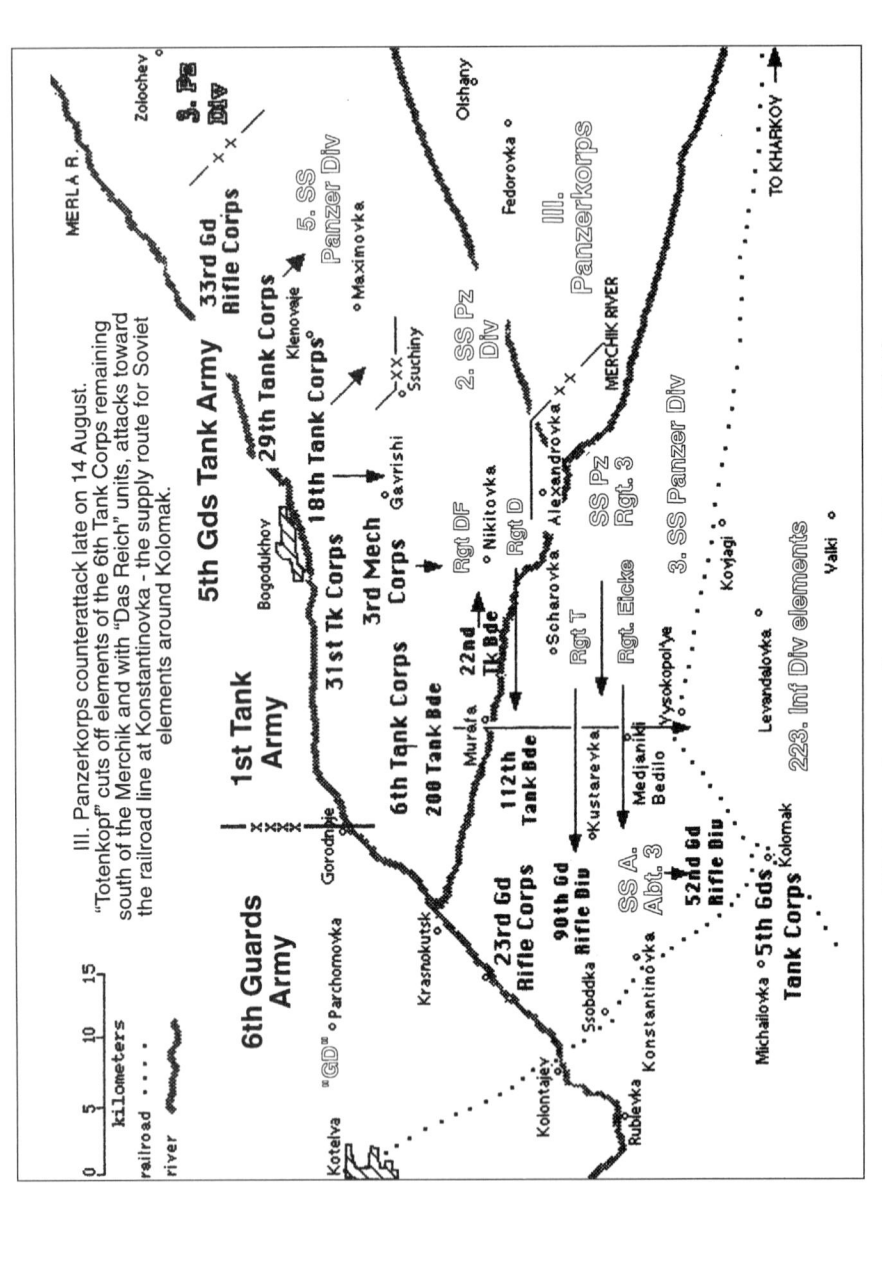

III. Panzerkorps, afternoon of 14 August 1943.

division, probing constantly at the panzergrenadier positions. Regiment *Westland* was attacked by two companies of infantry on its right flank at 0600 hours. Later in the morning, the regiment was hit with battalion-size attacks in the Kolchos–Hill 195.5 sector. Regiment *Germania* and Bataillon *Narwa* were struck by company-size attacks repeatedly throughout the day, sometimes supported by a few tanks. There was no concentrated offensive effort by the Russians in the *Wiking* sector and the small-scale activity was probably to cover Soviet regrouping and collect information for a coming attack. Russian troop concentrations were observed in several places and in front of Regiment *Germania*; the Russians were dug in with organized artillery positions.[24] The division had to extend its positions to the west and replace *Das Reich* units in order to allow that division to support the attack by *Totenkopf* on 15 August in the area south of Krasnokutsk.

During the night, *Das Reich* realigned its attack elements and armor in order to replace Regiments *Eicke* and *Totenkopf* in the Nikitovka area on the following morning. After moving into the town, the division moved to secure the north flank of *Totenkopf* while that division assembled south of Nikitovka under cover of darkness and aligned facing west for its attack toward Konstantinovka. Regiment *Deutschland* remained involved in fighting to secure wooded high ground to the west and northwest of Nikitovka. *Deutschland* positions northwest of the town, on Hills 197.4 and 199.8, were reinforced with antitank guns. In the afternoon, the regimental positions were attacked by Soviet tanks that had earlier been observed regrouping at Miroljukovka. At 1530 hours, about thirty Russian tanks advanced on a broad front from Miroljukovka, west of the rail line that ran south from Bogodukhov, attacking toward Hills 197.4 and 199.8. The fighting at that point continued to rage throughout the day. *Der Führer*, assembled southeast of Gavrishi, to the west of Maximovka, turned back a weaker attack originating from south of Bogodukhov in the afternoon of 14 August. On that date, *Das Reich* tank strength was twenty-six tanks (including six Tigers), four command tanks, and nineteen assault guns.[25]

While *Das Reich* fought off Soviet attacks south of Bogodukhov, *Totenkopf* brought its two panzergrenadier regiments on line northeast of Vysokopol'ye, just south of Murafa. By 1830 hours, the jump-off positions for the next day were secured and the SS grenadiers were reinforced with a tank battalion and several assault guns. Also supporting the attack were the Tigers of schwere-Panzer-Abteilung 503.

Meanwhile, the reconnaissance battalion remained under constant pressure west of Vysokopol'ye as the Soviet 22nd and 23rd Rifle Corps continued to attack in that sector, unaware that German forces were massing for an attack on the following day that would cut them off from their line of supply. Under continual attack by groups of Soviet infantry and a few tanks, the battalion slowly gave ground. A Russian column pushed by its left flank at Alexseyevka and reached the small village of Gwosdew, just southwest of Vysokopol'ye. It was the intention of the Soyiets to break through to Vysokopol'ye and rescue their comrades of 6th Tank Corps still fighting in the town.

The German objective for 15 August was to first take the town of Konstantinovka, then turn to the southeast and attack toward Kolomak along the railroad line. The capture of Konstantinovka would cut the rail line that was exposed to attack by the Soviet advance of 13 August. From there, the turn to the southeast would attack the rear of the Soviet forces advancing to Vysokopol'ye. The Stukas and fighters of VIII. Fliegerkorps would support the attack of the SS panzer on 15 August. The Luftwaffe had been in combat with Soviet planes during 14 August. There had been aerial fighting against Russian planes that had appear in strength during the day. There were a number of Soviet air attacks on the SS troops on 14 August.

THE GERMAN COUNTERATTACK OF 15 AUGUST

The jump-off of Regiment *Eicke* was nearly upset on the morning of 15 August, when a strong Russian infantry attack hit the regiment at 0300 hours in the Medjaniky-Bidilo area. The Soviet attack was driven off and the advance continued. The SS panzergrenadiers pushed forward several kilometers and, accompanied by SS panzers, were able to capture their initial objectives quickly. Mobile artillery, which consisted of Wasp 10.5cm guns and Hummel 15cm guns, advanced and provided fire support. Attacking from Hill 162.3, Regiment *Totenkopf* assaulted and seized the village of Kustarevka at 0830 hours. At the same time, on the left, Regiment *Eicke*, advancing parallel to this attack, reached the outskirts of Ssachalin. The town was defended by a large number of Soviet infantry, estimated to be as many as two regiments. The *Eicke* grenadiers assaulted the village, encountering fierce resistance from the Russians, which took until 1000 hours to

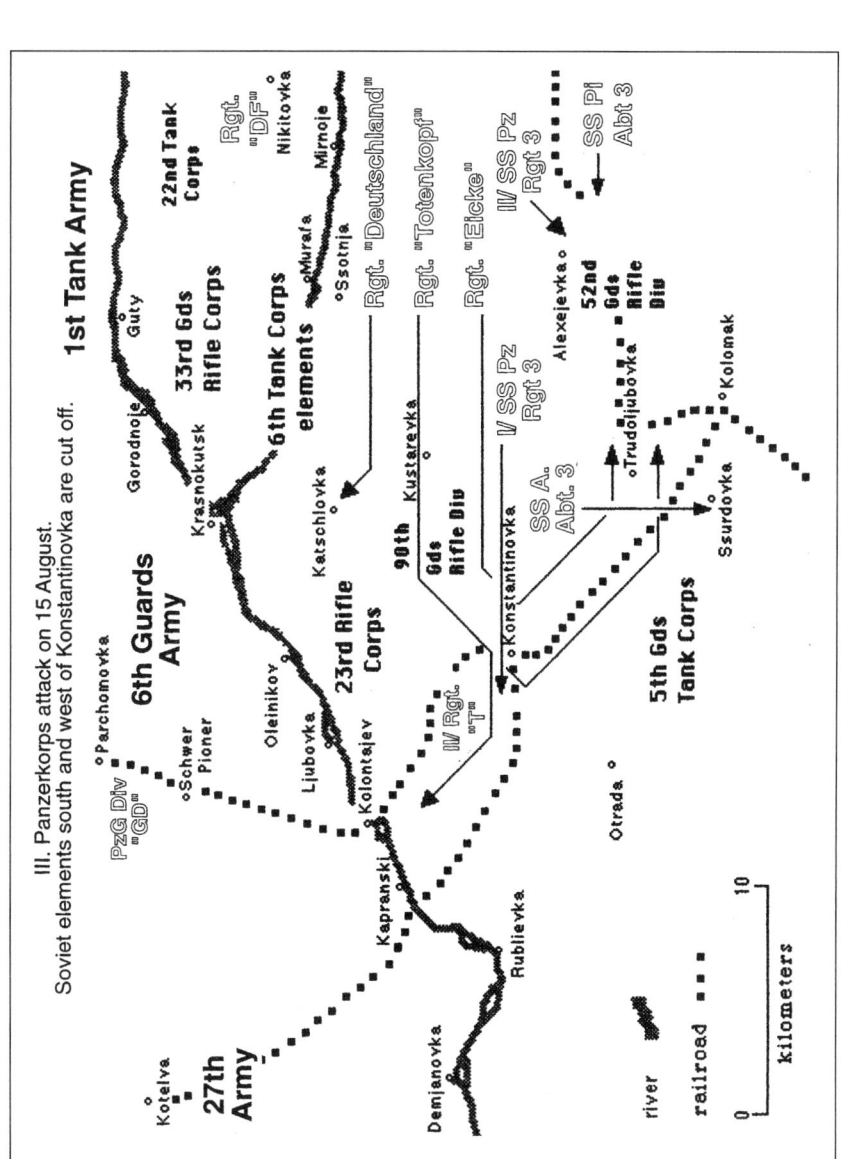

III. Panzerkorps, 15 August 1943.

break. The surviving Soviet troops fled north, leaving their heavy weapons behind. They were pursued by the shells of the mobile artillery of the division. The SS batteries moved forward in phased jumps, one battery always in position and ready to fire support, while the other batteries relocated behind the advance of the SS panzers and grenadiers.[26]

Moving west from Kustarevka, Regiment *Totenkopf* stormed the next village, at 1030 hours, after panzergrenadiers of Regiment *Eicke* crushed the Soviet resistance in Ssachalin. These advances positioned both regiments only a short distance from Konstantinovka and the vital rail line. At 1115 hours, elements of I./SS-Panzer-Regiment 3 assaulted Konstantinovka from the west, while, in support of the panzers, *Totenkopf* attacked the northern edge of the town. The fighting was brief and Soviet resistance was crushed quickly. After the town was secured, II./*Totenkopf* advanced out of the town, moving farther toward the northwest from Konstaninovka. By noon, the battalion cleared the village of Sslobodka of Russian troops.[27]

On the *Totenkopf* right flank, III./*Deutschland* screened the attack, advancing south of Murafa with elements of the panzer regiment. The battalion turned back a Soviet attack moving toward the flank of Regiment *Totenkopf* at Ssotnaja.

After driving the Soviet forces out of Konstaninovka and cutting the rail line, *Totenkopf* continued its attack into the rear areas of the Russian forces in the Vysokopol'ye–Alexseyevka–Kolomalc area. Less than an hour after the capture of Konstantinovka, the main elements of Regiments *Totenkopf* and *Eicke* moved down the railroad line toward the railroad station at Kolomak. All along the line of advance, Russian defenses collapsed. Moving parallel to each other, *Totenkopf* on the left and *Eicke* on the right, the attack pushed south, scattering Soviet troops before their advance. By early afternoon, the lead elements of the regiments arrived in the area west of Vysokopol'ye, where the Russians defended a number of villages. A Regiment *Eicke* assault group took a hill to the northwest of Trudoljubovka at 1340 hours, regrouped and moved against the village itself shortly afterward.

At about the same time, Regiment *Totenkopf* linked up with elements of the reconnaissance battalion northwest of Ssurdovka and deployed to attack from the march. Supported by covering fire of the reconnaissance troops, the grenadiers assaulted a rail line embankment which lay parallel to the road. The Sd.Kfz. 251s and light

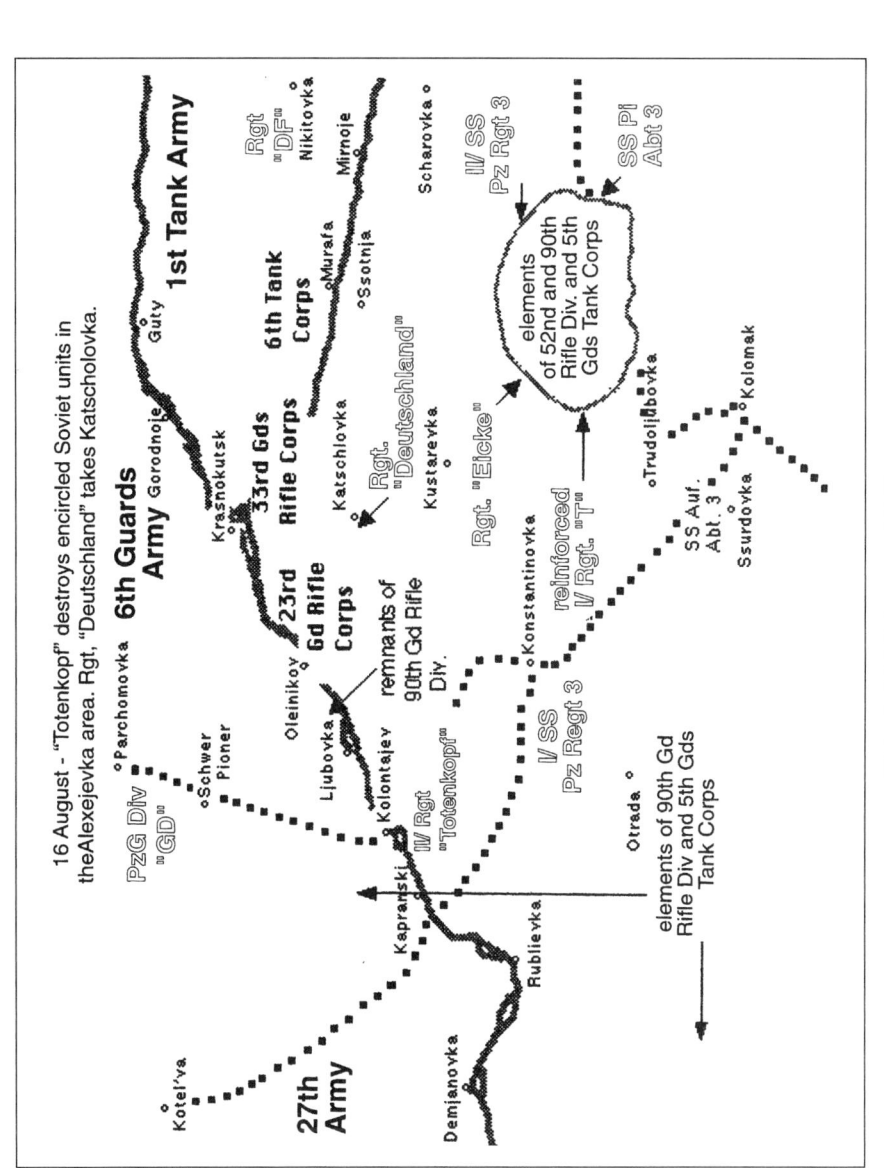

Totenkopf, 16 August 1943.

armored vehicles swung to the left and cautiously moved toward the embankment. A storm of fire erupted from concealed Soviet firing positions dug into the embankment and the surrounding fields. Advancing under covering fire from 20mm automatic guns, machine guns and light howitzers of SS-Aufklärungs-Abteilung 3, the attackers overran the Russian position. As the SS troopers mopped up pockets of resistance, groups of Russians abandoned their positions and fled in panic. They ran into the open fields that surrounded the village, many shot down as they tried to escape through corn stalk–stubbled expanses of ground. Others surrendered in large numbers as the assault continued to the edge of Ssurdovka. The SS men waved the prisoners to the rear, unable to take the time to deal with them.

Pressing farther toward the strongly held village, the column encountered opposition from several Soviet positions, located, as usual, on a number of small hills. Deploying to attack the village, the lighter vehicles advanced in a frontal attack while the main body of the panzers swung out on the flank and, under cover of the reverse slope of another nearby hill, attacked the Soviet infantry positions from the rear. The shock of an assault from behind by German armor was too much for the Russians and their defenses began to collapse at several points. A group of Russians dug in near a windmill, however, were more resolute and put up a stout fight. Utilizing the mobility of the reconnaissance vehicles, the Germans attacked a flank of the Russian position with heavy machine-gun and automatic-weapons fire from 20mm cannons. The defenders were routed and the windmill captured. With the fall of their strongpoint, the Russian defenses collapsed. Soviet troops abandoned the village and it was under German control by 1510 hours.

Just after midday, tanks of I./SS-Panzer-Regiment 3 arrived east of Kolomak, after having brushed aside weak efforts to stop them along their path of attack, the advance covering forty kilometers by that time. The tanks were moving without infantry support and had a few anxious moments when Soviet infantry fired on them with light anti-tank weapons from positions concealed in large sunflower fields. The panzers left the road and crushed through the field toward the gun positions, the Soviet infantry fleeing as soon as the panzers opened fire with machine guns and cannon. Near Kolomak, the battalion was attacked by a number of Russian tanks supported by infantry in a desperate attempt to stop it. As the two forces closed, in preparation to attack, the Germans were able to call in a flight of Stukas against the Russian tanks. Three T-34s were destroyed by direct hits from the dive-bombers and the remaining four were destroyed or driven off by the SS panzers. The German armor scattered the accompanying Soviet infantry and pushed on to Kolomak, where they encountered more determined defensive resistance, some of which came from Russian women's battalions.[28]

By the afternoon, the Russian lines of communication from the Merla to 6th Guards Tank Corps had been severed and SS battlegroups had encircled Soviet troops at Kolomak and other areas west of Vysokopol'ye. Shattered, and searching only for a route of escape, remnants of Soviet units filtered out of the path of *Totenkopf* and *Das Reich*, some making their way to safety over the Merchik to the north. Others withdrew to the west and joined divisions of 27th Army that established a reorganized line of defense east of the Merla. Some of the advance units of 6th Guards Army were not able to escape, their line of retreat closed off by the German spearheads attacking from their rear. During this fighting, the gunners of *Totenkopf*'s assault gun battalion, commanded by SS-Hauptsturmführer Ernst Dehmel, recorded its hundredth enemy tank destroyed in combat since 5 July 1943. This tank probably belonged to 5th Guards Tank Corps.

In Vysokopol'ye, unable to withdraw from the town, 6th Tank Corps units in that village were finally wiped out, destroyed by the combat engineers of Kampfgruppe Seela with the help of several Tiger tanks of schwere-Panzer-Abteilung 503. 52nd Guards Rifle Division was encircled and battered to destruction, and only a few of its survivors fought their way out or infiltrated through the German lines in small groups. A regiment of 90th Guards Rifle Division, fighting in the Alexseyevka area, was also surrounded and crushed by *Totenkopf* tanks and supporting units, after panzers and Stukas destroyed supporting Russian armor on the perimeter of the town.[29] 6th Tank Corps units south of the Merchik were virtually all destroyed.

With the pressure on the left flank of III. Panzerkorps relieved by *Totenkopf*'s destruction of the Russian forces in the Vysokopol'ye–Konstantinovka sector, the plans for the counteroffensive against 1st Tank Army's penetration proceeded with a secure flank to the east. For the following day, 16 August, *Das Reich* was given the mission of holding the Mirnoje-Katschlovka area and the crossings of the Merchik at that point and securing the Merla crossing at Krashokutsk. Meanwhile, elements of *Totenkopf* were given the task of destroying the isolated Soviet security and rear-guard detachments to the northwest of Konstaninovka. Elements of the division were to block the crossings of the Merla at Ljubovka and Kolontajev. This was in preparation for a III. Panzerkorps attack across the Merla toward Kotel'va and Parchomovka. III. Panzerkorps intended to link up with major elements of XXIV. Panzerkorps in the Kotel'va–Parchomovka sector and cutoff 27th Army and 6th Guards Army units south of the Merla. Meanwhile, the fighting wound down in the Kolomak area during 16 August.

Remnants of Soviet units and small groups of Russian soldiers continued to attempt to break out of the trap that the Germans had built in the battle area of Kolomak–Vysokopol'ye–Ssurdovka by the encircling attack made by *Totenkopf* on 15 August. Many of these units tried to use the cover of darkness to make their way north to the Merchik during the night. In wooded areas to the north of Alexseyevka, Regiment *Deutschland* fought off many attempts by groups of Russians to infiltrate through their lines, inflicting heavy losses on the retreating Soviet forces.

III. PANZERKORPS—17 AUGUST
With the critical situation on *Totenkopf*'s flank rectified, III. Panzer realigned for an attack over the Merchik during the night of 16–17 August and mopped up remaining pockets of resistance south of the Merla. By morning, elements of Regiment *Totenkopf*, with twenty-one tanks of the panzer regiment and reinforced with SS engineers and sixteen assault guns, were on the march toward Alexejevka in order to support the attack of Kampfgruppe Tyschsen toward Katschlovka. The armor was required because Soviet armor was starting to appear in the area around Krasnokutsk and the SS divisions were starting to run out of sufficient infantry to accomplish their tasks.

Having attacked first west of Nikitovka and Kovjagi on 12–14 August, southeast toward Vysokopol'ye on the 15–16 and forty kilometers to the Konstantinovka-Kolomak area, *Totenkopf* now prepared to attack back to the north, cross the Merchik, and assault the Merla River. The preparations of the divison were complicated by mopping-up operations against groups of Russians trying to reach their own

The Counterattack of III. Panzerkorps

lines. Beginning late in the night of 16 August and continuing on into the daylight hours, isolated groups of Russian tanks and infantry made attempts to break through to the north in order to reach the Merchik crossings at Mimoje. Just before midday, the *Totenkopf* battle groups began to encounter some of these isolated Soviet units in a wooded area to the northwest of Alexseyevka. Caught between the two German forces in the forest, the Russians were cleared out, leaving 250 dead amongst the trees and over 300 prisoners.[30] In the offensive operations of III. Panzerkorps for 15-16 August, led by *Totenkopf* and *Das Reich*, the corps HQ estimated that through the actions of the two divisions, the Soviets had lost 4,500 dead, twenty-one T-34s knocked out, and various numbers of antitank guns, artillery pieces, and mortars captured or destroyed. The two SS divisions had chopped up major elements of four Soviet rifle divisions and two tank corps during two days of fighting.

Das Reich attacked toward the river crossing at Krasnokutsk from south of the Merchik with a battle group of tanks and infantry led by SS-Sturmbannführer Christian Tychsen, commander of II./SS-Panzer-Regiment 2. From south of the Mirnoje area, the battle group was at first opposed only by light artillery and mortar fire. However, when Kampfgruppe Tychsen approached the village of Katschlovka, Russian infantry and antitank gun fire became heavy. A panzer company and one company of grenadiers from *Deutschland* attacked Katschlovka at 1315 hours and stirred up an even stronger Soviet reaction. Antitank gun fire from the west, near the village of Karaikosovka, held up the attack for a time. Artillery from the southwest of Krasnokutsk was also heavy. At 1610 hours, led by the panzers, SS infantry broke into the village and reached the northern outskirts after destroying ten antitank guns and scattering a battalion of Soviet infantry.

By early afternoon, other elements of Regiment *Deutschland*, attacking north of the Merchik, advanced on Mirnoje, which was situated on the north bank of the river several kilometers west of Nikitovka. At 1620 hours, Regiment *Deutschland* pushed to the edge of Mirnoje, fighting through heavy Soviet small-arms and antitank gun fire, which was eventually silenced by SS artillery. After moving north of Mirnoje, in an attempt to bypass the village, the attack received heavy fire from Hill 181.1, which was directly north of the village. Elements of the engineer battalion advanced with several Tigers, pushing forward towards the hill when Russian armor suddenly appeared and close-quarters tank-to-tank fighting broke out. Soviet T-34s and KV-1 heavy tanks battled the German tanks. Two Tigers were knocked out, one of which was totally destroyed. However, Russian losses were heavier. After the Russians lost four T-34s and one KV-1, their counterattack collapsed. Shortly afterward, their defenses on the hill were broken as well, when the Tigers and SS infantry overran the hill. At Mirnoje, the fighting remained heavy, and Russian resistance was supported by strong artillery fires and small groups of tanks emplaced around the town. The fighting continued into the afternoon at both Mirnoje and Katschlovka.

After midday, *Totenkopf* formations not involved in combat began to organize for further action, as the divisional units were somewhat dispersed due to the previous day's operations. In the west, *Totenkopf* units were spread out from several kilometers west of Ssurdovka to the area around Kolomak. In the south, the engineer battalion (with schwere-Panzer-Abteilung 503) was at Vysokolpol'ye.

A battle group built around the reconnaissance battalion and its support troops pushed to the Merla through the villages of Otrada and Beresovka, which were reported to be free of Russian troops by the advance units of the battle group. The II./*Totenkopf* was ordered to push to the Merla and build a bridgehead over the river to the right of the reconnaissance troops, near the town of Kolontajev.[31] The 10./ and 11./SS-Artillerie-Regiment 3 were allocated to support the bridgehead troops. About 1700 hours, II./*Totenkopf* sent out a reconnaissance force to probe marshy, wooded terrain west of Sslobodka. At that point, there were three elevated earthen causeways which had been built across the soft ground. Just beyond the causeways was the village of Kolontajev. Like many Russian villages and towns, it stretched along both sides of the road that ran from the earthen bridges down through the center of the village. Behind the village, there was a small hill which commanded the entire area as the rest of the swampy ground was flat and without cover or concealing terrain features. From positions built into the hillock and the village, the Russians commanded the bridges and surrouding terrain. At the approach of the forward elements of II./*Totenkopf*, the defenders unleashed a storm of machine-gun fire and 7.62cm cannon fire (the Russian antitank gun that German troops nicknamed the *Ratschbumm* for peculiar sound of its high-velocity shell) that halted the small recon force.[32]

The Counterattack of III. Panzerkorps

The main body of the battalion arrived somewhat later, and it was decided to storm the three bridges and overcome the Soviet defenses around them with a night assault supported by Stuka attacks. Once across the bridges, the attack group was to push into the village and secure it. The Stuka attack was to be directed by an officer serving as a ground observer and using a radio from an armored personnel carrier to communicate with the Luftwaffe planes. In the last several days, when fighting flared along the forested roads, in the multitudes of villages and along rail lines all over the front, the Luftwaffe support had generally been excellent. However, there were problems of unit identification commonly associated with close air support in such conditions, particularly when the confusing series of battles found German and Russian columns attacking and counterattacking over the same ground again and again. Several times, *Totenkopf* troops narrowly escaped being attacked by Stukas only by frantically firing off orange rocket flares that signalled the presence of German troops to the pilots of the dive bombers. The attack that earlier wounded Reifkogel during an attack was an example of mistaken identification and Stuka attacks on German troops. In the darkness of the sector around the Kolontajev bridges, the German planes again attacked their own men by mistake.

At 0200 hours, the Stukas reached the target, circling the area in the dark skies. Hearing the planes overhead, the waiting ground troops fired off parachute flares to guide their attacks. In the darkness, due to the difficulties involved in the correct identification of the target areas, the planes bombed and strafed their own troops, destroying the vehicle of the ground observer and thus ending any possibility of communication with the Stukas in order to properly furnish information to the planes. Because of the losses from the Stuka bombs and the resulting confusion, the assault group did not begin its attack as planned and it was not until 0245 hours that the assault finally began. The first bridge was quickly taken, but at the second one, the SS grenadiers encountered machine-gun and mortar fire that killed or wounded many of the men of the assault detachments. The grenadiers were forced to take shelter in pools of water or in cover around the base of the bridge embankment. Under heavy Russian fire, the attack immediately bogged down.[33]

Artillery was brought to bear at that time since all elements of surprise had been lost by that stage of the attack. However, the artillery fire was ineffective due to the skill of the Russians in building well-concealed positions. The forward observers had great difficulty in adjusting the fire because of the rain of machine-gun and mortar fire that made observation difficult and dangerous. When the attack stalled at the second bridge, the Luftwaffe was again requested to attack the Russian positions with a flight of Stukas. However, the bombing did not significantly reduce Soviet resistance and the remaining members of the assault group, nearly all of whom were wounded, remained pinned down in the swampy ground around the second earth bridge, unable to advance or withdraw. The wounded were finally removed by SS engineers in rubber rafts under cover from the fire of all weapons that could be brought to bear on the Russian positions. The first attempt to get over the river and establish bridgeheads for further advances toward the north and Bogodukhov had come to a standstill.

A second attempt by *Totenkopf* to cross the Merla on 17 August began at 1345 hours, with attacks by both III./ and II./*Eicke*. The first attempt, by II./*Eicke*, advanced north toward the river before it was halted by a Russian counterattack on its right flank at 1430 hours.[34] After maneuvering to outflank the Russian thrust and destroy it by counterattack, the forward elements of *Eicke* pushed to the northwest of Turovo. There it was attacked by a battalion-strength assault of Soviet infantry from the southwest. II./*Eicke* was forced take defensive positions. The Soviet pressure grew to the extent that the battalion was forced to call on I./*Totenkopf* for help in repulsing the Soviet attack. Regiment *Totenkopf* elements from Sslobodka hurriedly advanced and helped to surround and stop the Russian assault force. Having been under attack from several points during its advance, II./*Eicke* was not able to make much progress during the day advancing about two kilometers north west of Turovo.

Meanwhile, III./*Totenkopf* came to the relief of II./*Totenkopf* at Kolontajev, hoping to push through the marshes around the three bridges. However, a renewed attempt to force the crossing at 1500 hours was not successful either, as the Russians were now firmly established in strong defenses and the Germans were beginning to become worn down after the continual combat. Not only were the men starting to show the effects of fatigue, but the machines were breaking down as well. The panzer regiment was in transit toward the fighting on the Merla in order to support the attempts to get across the river, but its tanks were in need of repair and in bad shape mechanically. One *Totenkopf* panzer regiment veteran described the tanks as being "in miserable condition" (*sind einem miserablen Zustand*). The men of the regiment were not much better off, having been without water during the whole day, roasting under the Ukrainian summer sun beating down on them from clear, cloudless skies.[35] Fatigue was beginning to show, with the corresponding lessening of vigor in attack. The earthen bridges at Kolontajev remained in Soviet hands.

17 August ended with III. Panzerkorps still locked in combat with the armor and rifle divisions of 1st Tank Army and 5th Guards Tank Army, as well as divisions of 6th Guards Army and 27th Army. With their efforts, the army and SS panzer divisions had prevented the encirclement of Kharkov by a penetration of 1st Tank and 5th Guards Tank Armies, swinging wide to the west from the bridgehead south of Bogodukhov. From the first week in August, the panzer divisions had been involved in fighting against elements of three Soviet armies and had fought them to a standstill, destroying hundreds of Russian tanks and thousands of infantry during the series of battles. Although greatly outnumbered in both men and machines, the Germans launched a swirling series of attacks and counterattacks, primarily led by *Totenkopf* and *Das Reich*, that kept the Russians off balance, as they continually were forced to react to German battle groups slicing into rear areas or suddenly appearing on the flank of a Russian attack. Because of the lack of progress in this sector, largely due to the efforts of the offensive efforts of the two SS divisions and 3. Panzer-Division's stubborn defensive fighting, Koniev implored Zhukov to take 5th Guards Tank Army away from Voronezh Front and give it to his Steppe Front.

Koniev's divisions were worn down also, after fierce fighting on the Zolochev-Olshany-Kharkov axis, with many of his rifle divisions having only 3,000 to 4,000 men left. 7th Guards Army was left with only twenty operational tanks by 18 August and 1st Mechanized Corps had only forty-four, while 53rd Army divisions were down to 50 percent of their established strength.[36] With the additional armor obtained from Rotmistrov's 5th Guards Tank Army, Koniev planned to launch another drive to encircle the city. This time, the attack was to be launched closer to the city and in coordination with an assault on the German perimeter as well. However, for the time being,

Zhukov decided to leave Rotmistrov's tank army under command of Voronezh Front and to make one last effort to crack the German line in the Bogodukhov area.

Zhukov pressed Vatutin to break III. Panzerkorps' defenses, ordering him to go over to the offensive on 18 August. During the night of 17–18 August, as a result of orders from Vatutin, Rotmistrov realigned his tank army toward the boundary line between *Das Reich* and *Wiking* near Olshany and prepared to attack on the next day. The attack was led by 29th Tank Corps, with two supporting rifle divisions in the first echelon and the other two tank corps of 5th Guards Tank Army in reserve. The attack did not begin well, starting off with an ineffective artillery preparation and rapidly bogging down in heavy German artillery fire in front of strong defensive positions. In the early hours of the Soviet offensive, Rotmistrov committed his second echelon of reserves, 5th Guards Mechanized Corps, but this did not result in a penetration of the German positions at Olshany, and Rotmistrov issued orders to his last mobile reserves to prepare to join the fight. However, events on the western flank of the Soviet penetration caused Rotmistrov to cancel the attack.

On the morning of 18 August, while III. Panzerkorps continued to attempt to force crossings at the Merla, Hoth's 4. Panzerarmee launched its counterattack from Akhtyrka against the western flank of 6th Guards Army. This assault was under command of XXIV. Panzerkorps HQ, moved up from the Mius on 15 August, and spearheaded by Panzergrenadier-Division *Grossdeutschland*. On 18 August, the division had about seventy tanks and assault guns. In regard to equipment, the division was basically combat ready for a panzer division at this point in the war, but it suffered from insufficient infantry strength. The panzergrenadiers of the division were decimated by the hard fighting of the Kursk salient. Although *Grossdeutschland* was an excellent unit, its losses during the summer fighting, like those of the SS panzer divisions, were to limit its ability to hold ground and sustain its attacks.

The attack by *Grossdeutschland* was supported by 7. Panzer-Division and 10. Panzergrenadier-Division. In addition, there were several attached assault gun units and a heavy tank battalion with a few Tiger tanks. Screened by 7. Panzer-Division on the left and 10. Panzergrenadier on the right, *Grossdeutschland* was to attack from the south of Akhtyrka toward the area north of Krasnokutsk. These two divisions had about forty tanks between them.

The corps objective was to sever the communication and supply lines of the Soviet 27th and 6th Guards Armies. The advance by XXIV. Panzerkorps was to be coordinated with the III. Panzerkorps attack over the Merla with the objective of linking up near Parchomovka in order to complete the encirclement of the two Russian armies. It was in preparation for this attack that *Totenkopf* and *Das Reich* worked to secure crossings of the Merla. Before the operation could be launched, however, attacks by the Soviet 40th Army on 4. Panzerarmee defenses threatened to endanger the success of the German counterattack from Akhtyrka. On 17 August, some sixty kilometers to the west of III. Panzerkorps' sector, on 4. Panzerarmee's left wing, the Russians began a new offensive west of Akhtyrka. This was a renewal of an assault that had earlier failed to make any serious dent in the German defenses.

On 13 August, 40th Army, commanded by Lieutenant General K. S. Moskalenko, had attacked VII. Armeekorps in the Boromlya area with little success. The attack made slow and costly progress, opposed by heavy German artillery fire and stout resistance by German infantry. In three days of fighting, 40th Army's assault penetrated only about four kilometers. It became apparent, after the attack broke down completely, that the forces involved were insufficient to crack the German lines.

The Soviet command planned to resume the attack on 17 August. This time, 40th Army was reinforced by the fresh 47th Army. 47th Army had about 200 tanks of 3rd Guards Mechanized Corps available to exploit a breakthrough and support the infantry. The attack was be made to the southwest with the intention of penetrating the German front that was aligned along the western flank of the Soviet penetration west of Kharkov. The bulwark of this shoulder was the Akhtyrka salient, which the Soviets had been unable to destroy, in spite of hard fighting there since the early days of "Rumyantsev." At the same time, the Soviet 27th Army was to drive west of Kotel'va, breaking out of the penetration. The objective of these attacks was to encircle the German divisions in the Akhtyrka area, on the western flank of 27th Army. Enveloping and destroying this German strongpoint would tear a huge hole in 4. Panzerarmee's lines and eliminate the possibility of XXIV. Panzerkorps joining hands with

III. Panzerkorps as the German panzer divisions would be diverted to the gap created by the Akhtyrka group's destruction. The lines of communication of both 27th Army and 6th Guards Army units would then be secured and the western shoulder defenses shattered.

On the morning of 17 August, Voronezh Front began its attack with an enormous artillery and rocket bombardment. The weight of fire tore gaping holes in the thinly held lines of two German infantry divisions. Soviet assault groups of 40th and 47th Armies fought their way into the German positions and overwhelmed the defenders. The assault quickly opened a large gap in the front. Three hours later, exploiting the initial breakthrough, Soviet armor advanced to the west, creating a penetration of up to twelve kilometers in depth.

By the afternoon of 18 August, the German infantry divisions at the point of main effort had lost most of their lieutenants and many key NCOs as they tried vainly to stem the Soviet tide. In two days, both 57. Infanterie-Division and 68. Infanterie-Division were reduced to little more than regimental strength. They were not even designated as divisions on the German situation maps.[37] A counterattack by infantry elements of 112. Infanterie-Division and the few remaining tanks of 11. Panzer-Division could not stop the overwhelming strength of the Soviet offensive, but the Russians were slowed down. By 18 August, 47th Army's advance was halted by defensive efforts of 112. Infanterie-Division and the counterattacks of the remnants of German armor.

Thus, 4. Panzerarmee found itself in a critical situation on 17–18 August due to the Soviet attack on its western (left) flank. Hoth had to decide whether to launch the scheduled attack by XXIV. Panzerkorps south of Akhtyrka or to use his armor to restore the situation on 4. Panzerarmee's left. On the flank, the Soviet 40th and 47th Armies, with ten rifle divisions and approximately 300 tanks, were certain to eventually break the weakened German infantry divisions if allowed to hammer them to pieces. The infantry divisions of the army were too weak to prevent breakthroughs and there were few reserves. The only other armor available to Hoth was the handful of tanks possessed by 11. Panzer-Division. This division was limited in its ability to help because its main infantry and artillery units were already committed to limiting the width of the breakthrough. The essential problem was that the army did not have enough panzer divisions to effectively counterattack south of Akhtyrka and in the breakthrough area at the same time.

Hoth decided to react aggressively and to attack 27th and 6th Guards Armies southeast of Akhtyrka, leaving his embattled infantry divisions to face the new Soviet attack without much help from German armor. Hoth gambled that if the counterattack succeeded, it would compel Voronezh Front to react to the German counterattack by moving formations out of their 40th and 47th Army attack area and move them to the Kotel'va–Parchomovka–Krasnokutsk sector.

On the morning of 18 August, XXIV. Panzerkorps began its attack and achieved quick success. German success was aided by command deficiencies of 27th Army, which had also been weakened by the previous days of hard combat. The Soviet army had also been caught in an offensive organization and alignment as it prepared to attack in support of 40th and 47th Armies. By early afternoon of the first day, the spearhead elements of *Grossdeutschland* penetrated twelve kilometers to the southeast, cutting the communication lines of 27th Army and threatening to encircle the divisions southwest of Akhtyrka. Vatutin ordered 4th and remnants of 5th Guards Tanks Corps to counterattack the shoulder of the German attack from north of Akhtyrka. However, elements of these formations were involved with the renewed attack by *Totenkopf* from its bridgeheads on the Merla.

By nightfall of 18 August, XXIV. Panzerkorps pushed over twenty kilometers to the southeast of Akhtyrka, approaching the Kotel'va–Parchomovka area. While *Grossdeutschland* and 10. Panzergrenadier-Division of the 4. Panzerarmee attack group drove through 27th Army's front, III. Panzerkorps renewed its attack to cross the Merla, led by *Totenkopf* tanks and grenadiers attempting to advance to the northwest and meet *Grossdeutschland*. Elements of that division, by late on 18 August, were approaching Parchomovka, only ten to fifteen kilometers directly north of Kolontajev, where *Totenkopf* fought to cross the Merla. *Das Reich*'s attack to the west, spearheaded by Kampfgruppe Tychsen and Regiment *Deutschland*, remained stalled in front of Katschlovka and at Mirnoje.

Throughout the day of 18 August, *Totenkopf* was unable to enlarge its toeholds on the north bank of the river, in spite of several efforts and considerable losses. On the right flank of III. Panzerkorps, the front was generally quiet, with *Das Reich* pushing elements forward at several points around Nikitovka, while the Soviets shelled *Das Reich* positions with harrassing fire. The division's engineer battalion battled to clear the Russians out of a forested sector to the south of Hill 209.5. The SS engineers worked slowly through the wooded area, driving the Russians out of their positions, after tough fighting. Survivors retreated to the north and east, fleeing the German advance. Throughout the day, pockets of stragglers continued to fight and were eliminated in bitter close combat. Russian artillery was very strong in the area and hindered the movements of the Germans. A few Soviet tanks appeared and were engaged with 88s brought up to provide increased antitank defense. Several Russian tanks were destroyed by their deadly accurate fire. On 19 August, after the fierce fighting against 1st Tank Army tank brigades south of Bogodukhov, *Das Reich* had only twenty-eight operational tanks, including four Tigers, in addition to nineteen assault guns.[38]

Wiking repulsed an attack launched in the darkness of early morning on 19 August that broke through the front lines in a wooded sector of its front. The attack was cut off and destroyed, after elements of Bataillon *Narwa* counterattacked and cleared out the Russians still occupying the forested area from which they had come. The Russians reconnoitered the division's front at several points during the day with attacks ranging in strength from platoon-level probes of thirty to forty men to company-size attacks. Soviet tanks were observed assembling in villages at many points and Russian fighter-bombers were overhead constantly. *Wiking* reported to AOK 8 (HQ of Armeeoberkommando 8, which was formerly Armee-Abteilung Kempf) that its battle strength was critically reduced. As a result, gaps of up to two kilometers existed between the division's strongpoints on the front lines and could not be adequately defended.[39] Bataillon *Narwa* continued to fight to restore the situation in the forested section of the front where the early-morning attack had been launched.

TOTENKOPF ASSAULTS THE MERLA

After trying unsuccessfully to expand its two small bridgeheads during 19–20 August, at 1050 hours on 20 August, Regiment *Eicke* assault groups succeeded in enlarging the two river crossings sites over the river north of Kolontajev. South of the town of Oleinikov, two companies of III./*Eicke*, commanded energetically by Obersturmführer Kurt Franke, built up a defensive perimeter on the north bank. Soviet artillery and mortar fire began to fall on the German positions almost immediately. For his leadership at Oleinikov and other accomplishments, Franke was awarded the Knight's Cross on 3 October 1943.[40] Slightly north of Franke's position, other elements of the regiment, under command of SS-Sturmbannführer Max Kühn, enlarged a bridgehead near the north edge of the village.

Almost immediately, the Russians attacked Kühn's battalion with troops that came from Krasnokutsk. The SS grenadiers dug in near Oleinikov and engaged the Soviets force. Kühn reported at 2049 hours that his battalion was under constant attack. Russian counterattacks, artillery fire and air attacks prevented the Germans from getting more men and equipment across the river but the Soviets could not eliminate the German positions. The division reported that due to the strong defensive efforts of the Russians at both Kolontajev and Oleinikov, it could not get enough forces across the river to further expand the two small bridgeheads.[41] In order to break the stalemate, having been unable to get heavy weapons across the river near Kolontajev, division commander Priess decided to use maneuver and surprise to get across the Merla and flank the Russian positions along the river from crossings west of Kolontajev.

The reconnaissance battalion assembled at Beresovka and rolled to the southwest, following the southern bank of the Merla toward the Rublievka-Truchanovka area with the intention of finding an undefended ford or bridge. To reinforce a crossing of the Merla by the reconnaissance battalion, a battle group made up of I./*Totenkopf*, I./SS-Panzer-Regiment 3, and a few self-propelled antitank guns was assembled near Konstantinovka. On the night of 19 August, it began a march toward Rublievka, which lay due north of Konstantinovka, where it arrived on the morning of 20 August.

Earlier, during the afternoon of 19 August, the reconnaissance battalion arrived at Rublievka without significant contact with Russian troops, although discovering that the bridge was destroyed. One company raced farther to the southwest and seized an undefended but damaged bridge near Ssolonizevka at 1100 hours. SS engineer detachments with the column immediately began work to repair the bridge. Meanwhile, at Rublievka, 3. Kompanie (equipped with Schwimwagen amphibious cars) of the reconnaissance battalion crossed the Merla against light resistance. From there, this company advanced to the west toward the village of Demjanovka and captured a second bridge, securing it for the crossing of the battle group. By

1615 hours, 3. Kompanie had turned to the east from Demjanovka and arrived at Hill 136.4, northwest of Marinskoje. In the meantime, at Rublievka, 2. Kompanie crossed the river and advanced to the northeast along the river, reaching the village of Marinskoje. Moving rapidly along the northern bank toward the northeast, it reached Kapranski, just a short distance from Kolontajev, where their comrades fought to hold their small bridgeheads.[42]

A small detachment of the reconnaissance troops motored north and attempted to establish contact with forward elements of *Grossdeutschland* at Parchomovka during the night. The rest of the company dug in around the Marinskoje-Kapranski area at Hill 146.2. During the night, Russian motor traffic could be plainly heard, moving in strength, and Soviet tanks and motor vehicles passed unseen through the darkness. The detachments lay quietly as the Russian troops moved on, unaware of the presence of Germans. Shortly after first light, German air reconnaissance spotted the same Russian column of twenty tanks, armored cars and other vehicles traveling in the early morning toward Kotel'va, away from the German troops. Later in the day, the Soviet column would run into an armored attack from units of *Grossdeutschland*.

In the morning of 20 August, the *Totenkopf* grenadiers at Oleinikov, hung on to their hard-won gains in spite of Russian attempts to blast the SS troopers out of their position with artillery, mortars and antitank gun fire. Russian infantry attacked their positions repeatedly during the night in small groups but all of the Soviet assaults were repulsed.

Southwest of Kolontajev, the panzer battle group crossed the Merla at Ssolonizevka, earlier secured by 1. Kompanie of the reconnaissance battalion, and moved east along the river toward, the fighting at Kolontajev.[43] Shortly afterward, it reached Kapranski and began to assemble for the attack. At that time, a Soviet artillery barrage abruptly struck the tanks and SS grenadiers. The commander of the panzer battalion, Hauptsturmführer Erwin Meierdress, received his fifth wound in action, struck by a shell splinter in the leg. Despite this loss, the attack moved forward through the Russian artillery and reached Hill 163.8 northwest of Kolontajev after fighting through stout Soviet resistance. Two companies of I./*Totenkopf* attacked Kolontajev, breaking through the southern perimeter of the town at 1336 hours. The advance slowed, as the SS troopers had to fight their way

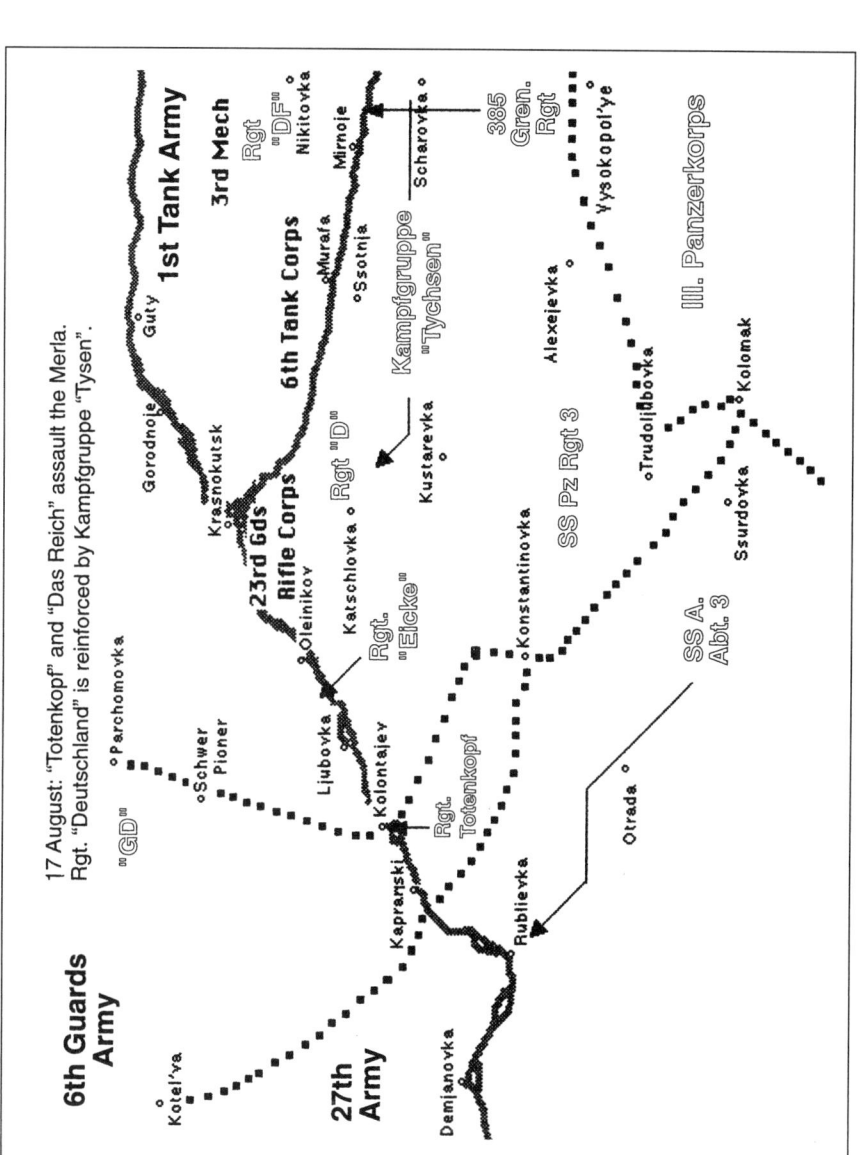

Totenkopf and *Das Reich* assault the Merla, 17 August 1943.

forward, battling down the narrow, wreckage-strewn streets in house-to-house fighting. Elements of the reconnaissance battalion turned north, toward Parchomovka, and cut the Kotel'va-Kolontajev road later in the morning.

Meanwhile, the remainder of I./*Totenkopf* continued to fight Soviet troops occupying Hill 163.8. They were unable to push the defenders off their hill and became pinned down by heavy defensive fire originating west of Kolontajev. The attack on the town stalled until help arrived in the form of the ubiquitous companies of the reconnaissance battalion. 3. and 4. Kompanie of the reconnaissance battalion, having assembled west of the town, assaulted Kolontajev from the northwest at 1336 hours. The noise of fighting from that unexpected direction was a clear indication to the defenders that they were under attack from three sides. Soviet resistance began to collapse quickly. From the bridgehead, German troops launched an attack to break into the town from the river. By 1400 hours, the town was taken.[44] After the fall of Kolontajev, a battle group was hastily organized to assault Hill 163.8 from the rear. In this attack, several of the SS panzers were destroyed and the battle group commander, Obersturmführer Herbatschek, was blinded by shrapnel. But the attack was successful and the hill was overrun by the German tanks, supported by SS grenadiers and the reconnaissance troops. While the last pockets of resistance were mopped up, the panzer battle group assembled a force to move to the assistance of the SS infantry holding the tiny bridgeheads at Oleinikov.

At 1750 hours, elements of the reconnaissance battalion, II./*Totenkopf*, and SS tanks advanced east toward the sound of the fighting in Oleinikov and captured another small town, Ljubovka. At this time, there was no report from the elements of the reconnaissance battalion that had attempted to establish contact with *Grossdeutschland* to the north, at Parchomovka. However, within an hour, a patrol of 3. Kompanie reported that it observed tanks and other vehicles moving from Parchomoka towards them but were not able to identify the column as German or Russian. When the first vehicles came closer, it became apparent that the unit was German as Panzer IIIs and IVs were identified in the forefront of the column. The XXIV. Panzerkorps had closed with III. Panzerkorps at Parchomovka. The contact with *Grossdeutschland* was reported to III. Panzerkorps at 1830 hours.[45] After meeting the *Totenkopf* reconnaissance troops, the commander of the *Grossdeutschland* battlegroup, Oberst Graf von Strachwitz, reported that the armored formation of Russians that was observed moving in the Kotel'va area earlier in the morning had been destroyed by his battle group.

To the east of Kolontajev, at Oleinikov, the struggle for the bridgeheads was still underway, but at 2030 hours, the *Totenkopf* panzer group, after it advanced along the northern bank of the river, assaulted the Russian defenses. SS grenadiers riding on tanks and vehicles of the reconnaissance battalion dismounted, assaulted behind the tanks and broke through the Russian lines. The division bridgeheads along the Merla River were linked together. The day was filled with success for *Totenkopf*. It had gained the north bank of the Merla and made contact with *Grossdeutschland*. The tank strength of the division for 20 August was reported as forty-one Panzer III and IVs and five Tigers, with about twenty mobile antitank guns of various calibers. Although this number of tanks was adequate, the infantry strength of the combat units, in particular the panzergrenadier regiments, remained low. After nearly six weeks of continuous combat, the division was dangerously worn down.

Das Reich continued to hold its ground south of Bogodukhov at Nikitovka, fighting off small probing attacks of one or two companies near Hill 209.5 and at other strongpoints occupied by its troops. In the west, in front of Regiment *Deutschland*, Soviet troops were observed moving into the area around the villages of Katschlovka and Pavljukovka, strengthening their defenses with antitank guns and mortars. Although there was little combat along the front, the Russians fired harassing barrages from light artillery and mortars at several sectors of the line. On 20 August, the division ceased any offensive actions by order of III. Panzerkorps, in order to prepare to move east toward Kharkov, where the Russians were massing armor west of the city for an attack on 3. Panzer-Division and *Wiking*. In order to reinforce *Wiking*'s depleted panzergrenadier ranks, I./*Deutschland* sent a company of its grenadiers to the SS division. *Das Reich*'s tank strength had improved slightly and the division reported that it had thirty-four tanks, five command panzers, and twenty assault guns, as well as fifteen motorized 7.5cm antitank guns and twenty-one towed 5cm antitank guns.[46]

Wiking prepared itself for the expected onslaught of Russian armor on 20 August, while under heavy pressure along its whole front from one Soviet attack after another. Some of the attacks were reinforced with a few tanks while others were not, although all were accompanied by air support. Most of the Soviet attacks were in the strength of two to three companies up to a battalion, with the most serious effort supported by about twenty tanks. It was only by the action of the divisional artillery, in cooperation with a Nebelwerfer battalion, firing accurate and timely barrages, that *Wiking* was able to turn back all of the Soviet attempts to penetrate its front on 20 August. The armored strength of the division was severely reduced as *Wiking* reported having only twenty tanks, three Sturmgeschütz, and one command tank, in addition to twenty-six 5cm antitank guns, eight towed 7.5cm PaK 40s, and three 7.5cm PaK 40s on self-propelled mounts. While the combat in the sector defended by *Wiking* continued, the fighting began to grow in intensity in the Kotel'va-Aktitryka area.

The link-up by *Grossdeutschland* and *Totenkopf* resulted in a tenuous encirclement of 166th and 71st Rifle Divisions and 4th Guards Tank Corps in the area around Akhtyrka. German air attacks immediately began against the trapped Soviet divisions, destroying most of the vehicles of 4th Guards Tank Corps and causing significant casualties to the rifle divisions. 166th Rifle Division took such heavy losses that it stopped all attempts to break out to the north and remained on the defensive.[47] 5th Guards Tank Corps was able to escape to the north, however, with lighter losses in men and machines. None of the three surrounded Soviet formations was totally destroyed.

4th Guards Army and 27th Army elements northeast of the *Grossdeutschland*–*Totenkopf* corridor continued to press in from the north with increasing pressure on *Grossdeutschland*'s left flank. North of Parchomovka, on the morning of 20 August, Voronezh Front ordered 4th Guards Army and 1st Tank Army to attack toward the Akhtyrka area, supported with an advance by 3rd Guards Tank Corps. The attack was clumsily executed and began without adequate artillery fire to suppress German defensive efforts. 3rd Guards Tank Corps' 13th Tank Brigade began its attack without proper reconnaissance and made little progress. Air support was also lacking in many key areas. Plagued by these deficiencies, the attack moved slowly. Heavy losses in men and equipment were sustained by some of 27th Army's formations.

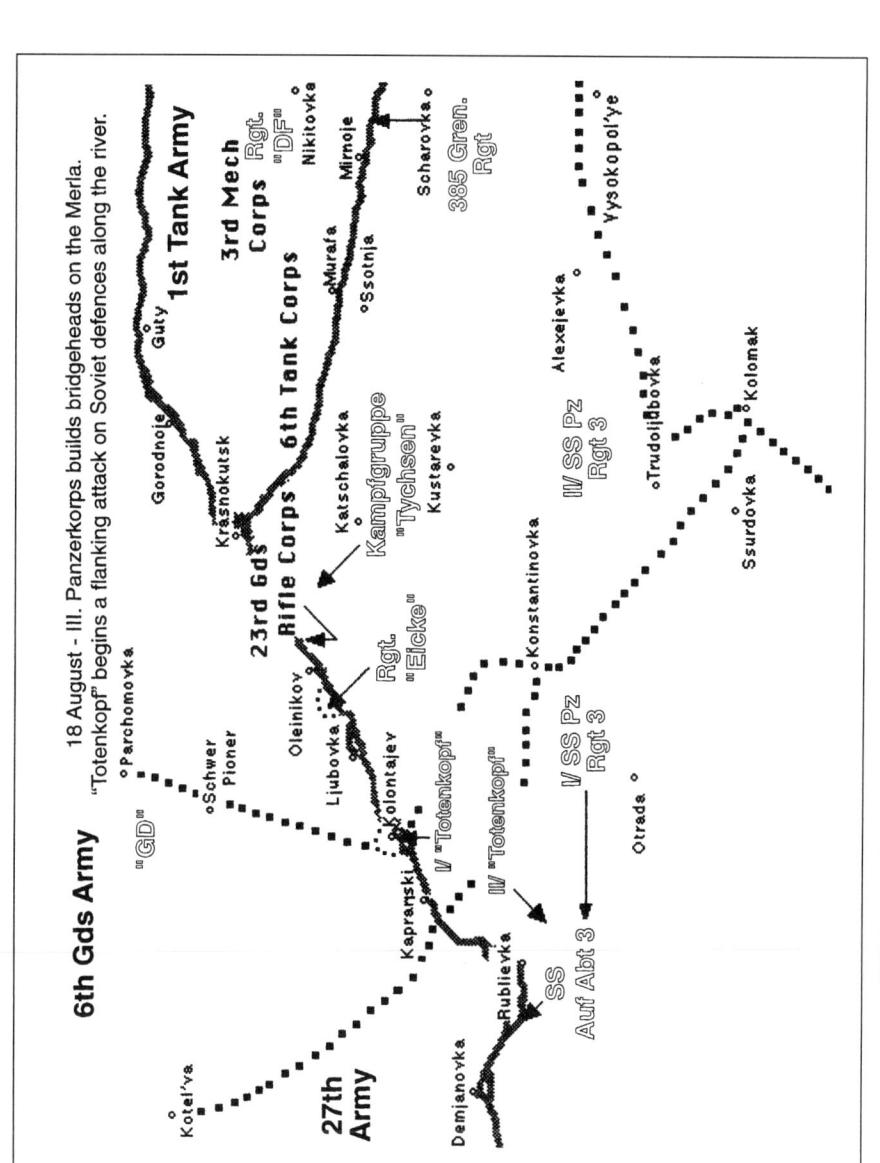

III. Panzerkorps bridgeheads on the Merla, 18 August 1943.

At Kaplunovka, however, a determined and more skilfully mounted assault by 5th Guards Airborne Division forced *Grossdeutschland* to withdraw. Under the threat of encirclement, the division pulled back to new positions south of a large state farm. In addition, the Soviet 47th Army was pressing 4. Panzerarmee hard on its northern flank. This pressure ultimately forced the Germans to move reserves out of the Akhtyrka sector.

On 19 August, the German forces north of the Psel River withdrew under Soviet pressure to the south bank. On the same day, 19. Panzer-Division was forced to make a fighting retreat from its positions, closely pursued by the forward elements of 126th Rifle Division and armor of 10th Tank Corps. These setbacks forced 4. Panzerarmee to remove 10. Panzergrenadier-Division from the command of XXIV. Panzerkorps and send it by forced march to the aid of 11. and 19. Panzer-Divisions. These two formations were by that time reduced to only a handful of tanks between them.

The timely arrival of 10. Panzergrenadier-Division, in addition to infantry reinforcements and an assault gun battalion, brought the Russian attack to a halt. 4th Guards Army and 27th Army, due to poor leadership and ineffective coordination of its attacks, suffered heavy casualties in the fighting. The commander of 4th Guards Army was sacked for his poor performance. The army sustained additional losses from German air attacks, but the fighting went on during the night of 20–21 August, with Soviet battle groups attacking north of Parchomovka and pressuring *Grossdeutschland* heavily. Fresh Soviet reserves continued to arrive on the front, including 20th Rifle Corps, with several crack Soviet airborne divisions and additional elements of 3rd Guards Tank Corps. The Soviet tank corps assembled east of Akhtyrka and attacked the SS bridgeheads on the Merla.

Near the bridgehead at Kolontajev, Soviet armor of 5th Guards Tank Corps, with supporting infantry, struck *Totenkopf* perimeter defenses and broke through, several tanks penetrating into the village accompanied by infantry. In the darkness, fighting broke out suddenly and violently and the situation was unclear at first. Sounds of Soviet tanks had been heard in the area south of the village. This evidence of a Soviet preparation for an attack was followed by an assault by Russian infantry. Startled SS troops soon found themselves involved in close-quarters street fighting against Russian assault groups led by tanks. German tanks fired at point-blank range at

The Counterattack of III. Panzerkorps

T-34s rattling cautiously down the dark, narrow village streets. The *Totenkopf* units in the village were under command of SS-Sturmbannführer Otto Baum, who personally led the counterattack against the Russians in the village. When he was wounded, SS-Sturmbannführer Ullrich took over command and directed the efforts to eliminate the Soviet penetration. After hard house-to-house fighting with grenades and machine pistols, the Russian troops were forced out of the village, leaving over 100 of their comrades behind as prisoners, most of whom were wounded.[48] Several T-34s that were immobilized in marshy ground were taken under point-blank fire by a light field howitzer and destroyed after they continued to try to cover attempts by Russian infanty to escape. At 0630 hours, after energetic leadership by SS-Sturmbannführer Ullrich, the Soviet assault was driven back and the last Russian troops in the bridgehead were eliminated.

At this time, elements of 1st Tank Army joined the battle against *Totenkopf* when Katukov's 3rd Mechanized Corps attacked Parchomovka from the north. Under great pressure from Soviet armor and infantry, the *Totenkopf* reconnaissance battalion was forced back and lost contact with the fusilier regiment of *Grossdeutschland*, which was still defending the small town. The command of *Grossdeutschland* became increasingly uncomfortable, primarily due to threats to its lines of communication by the attacks to the west of Parchomovka from 5th Guards Airborne Division. 4. Panzerarmee, hard pressed by the attacks of 40th and 47th Army attacks north of the Kotel'va–Parchomovka area, decided to pull the fusilier regiment back. The Soviet attacks against *Grossdeutschland* increased in tempo.

Retreating under heavy pressure, screened by its rear-guard units, the division was hard pressed to conduct an organized withdrawal. A Soviet mechanized column penetrated the divisional front and reached the Merla River just west of Kolontajev. This Soviet force hurriedly attempted to entrench in a small wooded area but was attacked by a few *Totenkopf* tanks supported by an engineer company and destroyed before it could organize the position. Some of the survivors tried to escape by swimming across the Merla River to the south bank. However, it was a case of out of the frying pan and into the fire for these unfortunate Russians because they were attacked and scattered by other elements of *Totenkopf* engineers, with many prisoners being taken.

Other attacks struck the German positions along the river. At Ljubovka, I./*Eicke* was attacked by 4th Guards Tank Corps' 14th Guards Tank Brigade early on 21 August. With the support of six tanks, an assault force of 14th Tank Brigade made an attempt to drive the SS grenadiers off a defensive position on Hill 177.6, situated to the north of the town. This attack failed, but the Russians tried again later in the day after trying to soften up the SS defenders with intermittent artillery fire. The next Soviet assault struck the left flank of the battalion at 1355 hours and succeeded in breaking through the defensive perimeter. Immediately, the Russians were thrown back by a counterattack. Later in the afternoon, Soviet infantry and tanks were observed regrouping in a wooded area northeast of Hill 177.6. This assembly area was taken under fire by artillery and mortars. However, this measure failed to discourage the Russians, and another attack was mounted by the Soviets from northwest of the town. Other action took place at Oleinikov, where Russian troops assaulted the east perimeter of the *Totenkopf* bridgehead near the town. Divisional artillery pinned down this force and then hammered it to pieces. Artillery units at Kolontajev and Ljubovka took the Soviet troops under direct fire and dispersed them.

After turning back these Soviet attacks, *Totenkopf* quickly organized a counterattack to hit the Russian forces remaining in the Kolontajev and Oleinikov areas. With support from SS tanks, II./*Eicke* advanced to the north against the Soviet elements at Parchomovka, in order to maintain contact with *Grossdeutschland* elements now slowly withdrawing to the west. Russian aircraft hit the German spearheads hard, bombing and strafing the German tanks and infantry. After advancing to the west, toward Parchomovka, the Germans unexpectedly ran into a defensive line of Soviet strongpoints.

The Russians had built up defensive positions in a hilly, wooded area with about 1,000 meters of open ground in front of it. Once again, *Totenkopf* found itself involved in attacks against Soviet troops on a chain of small fortified hills with infantry and Pak positions concealed in fields of high sunflower plants. However, by 1840 hours, the lead elements of the *Totenkopf* battle group pushed as far as the little village of Schwer Pioner, just one kilometer south of Parchomovka. After fighting their way north for another hour, *Totenkopf* tanks reached the town and made contact with *Grossdeutschland*'s rear guard. The reconnaissance battalion deployed south of the town in

The Counterattack of III. Panzerkorps

order to defend the narrow corridor of supply to Parchomovka. After the fighting of the last few days, the battalion was exhausted and had sustained heavy casualties in men and officers. As a result, sergeants commanded companies while corporals led platoons.

At the end of the day on 21 August, the losses of all the combat elements of *Totenkopf* had reached extremely serious proportions. A high percentage of the experienced, superbly trained officers and men that began Operation "Citadel" were by that date dead or wounded. The fighting strength of the panzergrenadier regiments had declined markedly due to losses to small-unit leaders and the rank and file. The situation had become so critical that III. Panzerkorps informed 8. Armee of the situation and requested reinforcements. Priess, the divisional commander, had informed the corps HQ that additional infantry strength was required if the division was to hold its positions. An hour later, III. Panzerkorps received the answer from 8. Armee. There would be no replacements and *Totenkopf* was to actually lengthen its front and take over the defense of Parchomovka from *Grossdeutschland*. II./*Totenkopf* was ordered to move to Parchomovka during the night and relieve the last elements of *Grossdeutschland* still in the town, a battalion of light infantry.

The losses of the other panzer divisions of III. Panzerkorps were also serious. *Das Reich* was dangerously reduced in strength, particularly in the panzergrenadier regiments. By this time I./*Deutschland* had just sixty surviving men. The panzer regiment had only thirty operational tanks. *Wiking* and 3. Panzer-Division were also in a weakened condition due to losses in manpower in the combat units of the divisions. The infantry manpower situation in the sector was only slightly relieved by the arrival of elements of 223. Infanterie-Division, beginning on 18 August in the sector around Nikitovka. The arrival of this division was delayed by the Russian attacks on the rail line between Kolomak and Vysokopol'ye.

On 20 August, it became evident from reconnaissance information that the Russians were massing on the right wing of III. Panzerkorps for a major attack in the sector immediately west of Kharkov. The Soviet forces that were detected were the lead formations of 5th Guards Tank Army. During the night of 20–21 August, Rotmistrov moved major elements of his army to the east, out of the Bogoduldiciv area. The army concentrated in the Korotich sector in preparation for an attack toward the Poltava-Kharkov railroad in order to finally cut this line of supply into Kharkov. At 0900 hours on 21 August, 5th Guards Tank Army began its first attacks, led by 18th Tank Corps and 5th Guards Mechanized Corps.[49] However, the attempts by armored units of 18th Tank Corps to cross the Udy River were stopped by a combination of factors, including mud, failure to clear adequate paths through minefields in the attack sector and effective German artillery fire. These setbacks in 5th Guards Tank Army's attack preparations resulted in the postponement of the operation until 22 August, although Soviet infantry got across the river and established bridgeheads at several points. The delay allowed *Das Reich* to withdraw its armor from the Krasnokutsk area and move to the right flank of III. Panzerkorps. The division was replaced by elements of 223. Infanterie-Division. *Das Reich* assembled its armor and antitank units to meet Rotmistrov's attack, which was expected on 22 August.[50] As a result, when bridges were finally thrown over the Udy and the Russian tanks rolled forward, they advanced toward a German panzer division, dug in and waiting.

5th Guards Tank Army attacked with nearly 120 tanks in the sector held by *Das Reich*. The assault began at 0500 hours, after a heavy artillery preparation and was supported by additional armor belonging to 1st Mechanized Corps. All day long, Rotmistrov's tanks threw themselves at *Das Reich* without success. Attack after attack was turned back, always with more Russian tank losses. The Luftwafffe was also operating in some strength, attacking the Russian tanks with determination. Whenever the Soviet attacks paused, *Das Reich* launched aggressive counterattacks with small battlegroups of tanks and SS grenadiers. The fighting was furious on both sides as Rotmistrov's army repeatedly attempted to break through the SS division's front without success. The town of Korotich was captured by 5th Guards Mechanized Corps tanks in the afternoon, but the Germans counterattacked quickly and threw the Russians out. The Poltava-Kharkov rail line was finally cut, this time for good, although the Russians could not take Korotich on 22 August. In spite of every effort of 5th Guards Tank Army, they could not break into the town again, and by the evening, both sides were content to quit fighting, exhausted by the furious combat. The capture of the town itself was of secondary importance when compared to the severing of the rail line, for that was an important lifeline to the Germans in Kharkov. The loss of this line of communication, while not fatal in

The Counterattack of III. Panzerkorps

itself, was a serious blow to the ability of 8. Armee to defend the city from the Russian attacks. Their infantry weakness forced the Germans to rely on their artillery to make up for manpower deficiencies. The delays in supplying artillery shells thus had serious consequences for the defense of the city. What few replacements arrived had to travel a more roundabout route to the city, entering from the south. However, this line of supply was also seriously threatened by the advance of the Soviet 57th Army from the southeast of the city on 22 August.

The constant earlier Soviet threats to the two rail lines and the knowledge that their loss would cut supply into the city had caused nerves to fray at the highest level of command in Kharkov. As early as mid-August, General der Panzertruppen Werner Kempf, aware of the strength of the Russian armies arrayed against his troops, had asked that he be given the freedom to abandon the city before his army was encircled. Kempf had no desire to preside over a second Stalingrad. He had radioed Manstein on 12 August, proposing to evacuate Kharkov. At that time, Manstein did not express any objections to the proposal. However, Hitler subsequently vetoed any suggestion of a withdrawal from Kharkov and promised reprisals against any person or unit who showed less resolve than he considered adequate. Kempf, expectedly, was not mollified and continued to protest. Two days later on 14 August, after Kempf again requested that he be allowed to evacuate Kharkov, Manstein removed him from command on Hitler's order. He was replaced by Manstein's own chief of staff, General der Infanterie Otto Wohler.[51] Armee-Abteilung Kempf had been renamed 8. Armee on that date. Manstein, describing this incident in *Lost Victories*, commented on the change of command very briefly, saying only that he did not oppose the change.

Wohler, recognizing the hopelessness of the situation, did not prove any more resolute, in view of the harsh realities facing the defenders of Kharkov. The artillery was running out of shells and the depleted infantry regiments could not hold their positions without copious artillery support. Two days after taking command of 8. Armee, Wohler also asked Manstein's permission to abandon the city.[52] Regardless of Hitler's demand that the city be held, Wohler found that he agreed with his predecessor on what he saw as the only remaining course of action. The city could not be defended for long, given the diminishing German strength and the overwhelming number

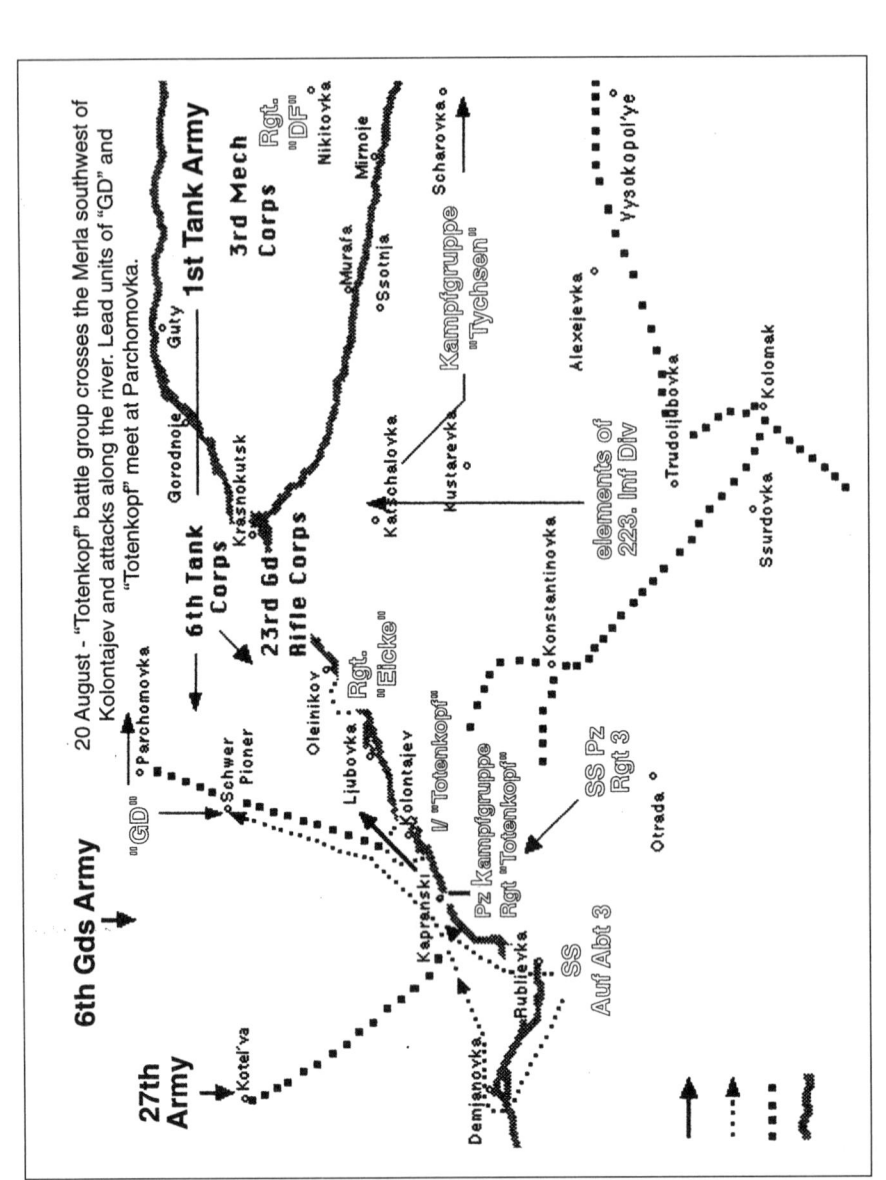

Totenkopf crosses the Merla.

and size of Soviet reserves. On 21 August, Manstein gave Wohler his consent to withdraw from Kharkov. The largely destroyed Soviet city, which changed hands several times during the war, was about to be recaptured by the Russians for the last time. During the night of 22 August, the Germans began their exodus from the city under great pressure from the Russians.

57th and 69th Soviet Armies pushed in from three sides with the coming of daylight. The Soviets sensed that the Germans were evacuating Kharkov, due to the lessening of artillery fire and diminishing resistance in the front lines. Later in the day, thunderous explosions were heard as ammo dumps were blown. Large German columns were then observed leaving the city and the Russian troops pushed into the town itself. Moving out of Kharkov to the south, the Germans desperately fought to hold open a corridor through which a withdrawal could be made. All along the corridor through which the German divisions evacuated Kharkov, Soviet artillery and mortars pounded the withdrawal. Russian planes gathered for the kill and attacked the German columns leaving the city, strafing and bombing the men and vehicles. After dark, 89th Guards and 107th Rifle Divisions broke into the interior of the city, driving the last German rear-guard detachments before them. Enormous fires were set by the Germans in hopes of delaying the Russian advance. The city became a hellish place of fire and smoke, artillery fire and desperate combat, punctuated by the explosions of supply dumps. By 0200 hours on 23 August, elements of 183rd Rifle Division pushed into the city center, reached the huge Dzerzhinsky Square and met men from 89th Rifle Division. The victorious Soviet troops hoisted a red banner over the city once again. By 1100 hours on 23 August, Kharkov was in the hands of the Russians. The fourth and final battle for the city was over.[53]

AFTER KHARKOV—RETREAT TO THE DNEPR

After the fall of Kharkov, the fighting continued on III. Panzerkorps' front for several days as Rotmistrov was determined to break through the German defenses west of the city. After furious attacks and counterattacks, Rotmistrov, having committed his last reserves, called a halt to further attacks. He had little choice because the army was exhausted. The troops were physically drained and the army had suffered the loss of more than 80 percent of its tanks. *Das Reich, Wiking,* and 3. Panzer-Division held firm at all points against weakening Soviet determination. German troops recognized that attacks were not pressed home with the characteristic Soviet disregard for losses. The Russian infantry became tentative in their attacks and any breakthroughs that did occur were counterattacked immediately, sealed off and destroyed. On 25 August, 5th Guards Tank Army reported that it had only fifty tanks still operational, down from a total of over 500 on 3 August. The army lost about sixty to seventy tanks in the fighting against *Das Reich* from 21 to 25 August.[54] Once again, Rotmistrov's army had been decimated in combat against the panzer divisions of the army and Waffen SS. While gifted in defensive operations, Rotmistrov seems to have had less talent for offensive actions conducted at the army level. Within the space of little more than a month, his army was nearly destroyed in fighting at Prochorovka and again during "Rumyantsev." In the fighting during Operation "Bagration," in June 1944, 5th Guards Tank Army would again suffer heavy losses fighting German panzer divisions. The destruction of the army's tanks during this fighting probably cost Rotmistrov his command. Later in the summer of 1944, he was removed from command of 5th Guards Tank Army.

The loss of Kharkov and the subsequent retreat to the Dnepr could not be prevented, however, by the efforts of the SS and army panzer divisions and the sacrifice of the German infantry divisions. Heeresgruppe Süd could no longer hold the key sector of south Ukraine on the Kharkov-Belgorod axis. This was in spite of the fact that 4. Panzerarmee and 8. Armee were able to reestablish a continuous front from the Udy River south of Kharkov extending to south of Akhtyrka. The Soviets, after suffering the loss of so much of their armor, became very hesistant to penetrate southwest of Bogodukhov with German panzer forces remaining on both flanks.

This hesitancy probably cost them an even more significant victory because the front between *Totenkopf* and *Grossdeutschland* was occupied by little more than two weakened regiments of SS infantry belonging to *Totenkopf,* a handful of tanks and elements of 223. Infanterie-Division. However, there was to be little rest for the Germans, because the Russian hydra, thwarted at one place, sprouted armored heads in other sectors.

The Soviet attack on 4. Panzerarmee's front slowly forced Hoth to withdraw behind the Vorskla River after Russian attacks breached the river-line defenses in a number of sectors. Hoth lashed back at the Soviets and counterattacks restored some order by 27 August. Although the situation was temporarily stabilized on the northern flank of Manstein's army group at that point, the front to the south of 8. Armee's sector flared up once more.

Tolbukhin's Southern Front crossed the Mius River again on 18 August. This time, using normal *maskirovka* principles, Tolbukhin's army was able to bring reinforcements into the Dmitrievka area without the Germans detecting their presence. 6. Armee's intelligence officers, perhaps waiting for the clear signs of a build-up as seen in early July, were apparently fooled this time by a complete lack of evidence with which to predict a Soviet attack.

All along Heeresgruppe Süd's sector, the front was under pressure by the Soviet or, as in the case of 6. Armee, in the beginnings of a crisis. In spite of the destruction of Soviet forces by the panzer divisions of the SS and army during the defensive operations and counterattacks from 6 to 25 August, the Soviets could always replace their losses in tanks quickly. However, even with their enormous population reserves, the Russians had difficulty finding enough replacements to rebuild their infantry divisions, ground down by continuous costly fighting from the first week of July to the end of August. Steppe Front's rifle divisions were reduced to an average strength of 3,000 to 4,000 men, many of whom were not combat troops. The Soviet infantry had perished in the tens of thousands in battles from the fighting at Kursk to the battles south and west of Bogodukhov. They had been thrown at German armored attacks, chopped up by repeated counterattacks by panzer divisions and fought to the death defending their positions in the Kursk salient. The enormous losses suffered by the Russian rifle divisions resulted in emergency measures.

The Russians conscripted untrained males of any age. Sometimes whole Ukrainian villages were forcibly stripped of men. These unfortunates were given a few brief instructions on how to use their weapons, fitted with a piece of a uniform or helmet and sent into combat. By these ruthless methods, the Soviet command was able to maintain their rifle divisions numbers, although the casualties among the raw recruits must have been catastrophic.

The German infantry divisions were also in bad condition. Many were reduced to the size of a weak regimental battle group. The panzer divisions also lost heavily in tanks and men, their panzergrenadier regiments shrunk in size to less than that of a full-strength battalion. All of the panzer and panzergrenadier divisions operated with only a fraction of the number of tanks of a full-strength division, in many instances having only twenty to thirty panzers in operation. In some cases, the divisions were reinforced with a battalion of Tiger tanks or a few batteries of assault guns. Most of the time, however, Soviet armor greatly outnumbered the German tanks. The German Army in Russia, from the beginning, was routinely faced by an enemy that outnumbered it by a ratio of five to one or greater in manpower and tank numbers. By the end of the summer of 1943, this disparity in numbers became even greater. To make matters worse, it was becoming evident that the Russian armored formations were constantly improving in terms of the quality of leadership and the use of armor in battle. German combat quality began to decline after mid-1943 due to irreplaceable losses in trained and experienced men and officers and the inability of Germany to produce sufficient numbers of tanks and assault guns. Soviet armored personnel and officers, from that point on, survived in sufficient numbers to pass on their experience and knowledge.

However, the German divisions in Russia continued to fight on, dealing out death and destruction out of proportion to their numbers. Long after victory was a forgotten dream, the German Army in the East continued to resist when by all rights it should have disintegrated. Fragments of infantry divisions effectively continued to fight, even when they were reduced to 20 percent of their established strength. Battered panzer divisions knocked out many Russian tanks for each one of their own lost in combat. The ability of the German Army to fight as long as it did, after the war was essentially lost in Russia, is one of the fascinations of the history of the Eastern Front for the student of warfare during the Second World War.

The reasons that the Germans retained such unit cohesion and were able to continue to fight effectively after suffering extremely high unit casualties are beyond the scope of this work. However, this ability has been noted by many students of the war. A study of the German Army's fighting effectiveness in the war, made by Martin van Creveld, concluded from the evaluation of seventy-eight battles of various natures that the Germans routinely inflicted casualties on their opponents at a 50 percent higher rate than those they received. This was true whether they won or lost the battle, whether fighting on offense or defense, and was true no matter how outnumbered the German divisions were in any of the engagements studied.[55] Creveld's book was based on calculations of battle casualties fighting against British and American troops in the West, no comparison being made of battles on the Eastern Front as unavailable numbers regarding Soviet casualties and lack of other information may have prevented accurate conclusions. The tactical superiority of better-quality German divisions was still clearly evident in the battles in the Ukraine during July and August 1943, when the mobile divisions and corps of the German Army repeatedly fought against Soviet armies, often elements of several armies, and inflicted enormous losses on their opponents.

It is instructive to note that tactical superiority, better training and various other qualities of its military organization did not result in victory for Germany in the East. The German Army, given all its military expertise and tactical skill, could not win a war waged against a nation that simply had more men, guns, and machines to sacrifice until time became a factor in achieving victory. The Soviet leadership understood the strengths and limitations of their military instrument and, accordingly, designed a long-term strategy that gave Russia the opportunity to win the war. The sacrifices of millions of Soviet soldiers and civilians during the first years of the war enabled Russia to survive until the constant efforts of the Soviet army to improve its force structure and command quality bore fruit.

Under Stalin's leadership and through the conduct of a centralized national effort, the Soviet Union remained focused on one goal, that of defeating Germany at whatever cost necessary. Stalin directed Russian conduct of the war in a cold-blooded, pragmatic manner. No sacrifice was too great or too bloody. When it proved necessary to commit even untrained conscripts to battle, the Soviet army threw such troops into the meat grinder with the inevitable resulting carnage. As late as mid-1943, the Soviets were promoting farming tractor drivers to tank commander status based solely on their experience in driving tracked vehicles. These are measures that Western nations find nearly inconcievable, and yet they resulted in victory. In contrast, Germany, under Hitler's leadership, launched an ill-advised attack on Russia that failed in large part because of decisions that Hitler made at a number of critical stages in the war. Hitler was often guided by political considerations that were in opposition to sound military principles and advice provided by his finest military leaders.

When the Soviets defeated the German attack on Moscow during the winter of 1941, time began to run out on Hitler's legions in the East. From that point in the war, Soviet strategy became a matter of surviving a series of dangerous situations until attrition of German strength became one of the factors that eventually provided victory. In the following year, the debacle at Stalingrad resulted in losses that the Germans could not afford. By the summer of 1943, the Germans had only the barest of chances to still inflict a major defeat on the Russian army that could have produced a lengthy operational stalemate. The last opportunity to achieve this goal, Operation "Citadel," failed and the war was lost.

In August 1943, after the cream of the elite divisions of the army and the first-line SS divisions was lost in a series of desperate, bloody battles in the Ukraine, the Soviet tide was never turned back. From that point on, it rolled inexorably westward in spite of the fact that the better German units, particulary the elite panzer/panzergrenadier divisions of the army and SS and first-rate infantry divisions, remained dangerous opponents. The German Army was still capable of inflicting startling numbers of casualties on the Soviets even though severely depleted in men and machines. The battles at Kharkov and in the Bogodukhov area illustrate this fact.

The operations of III. Panzerkorps, led by *Totenkopf* and *Das Reich*, and the actions of XXIV. Panzerkorps, led by *Grossdeutschland*, largely destroyed two complete Russian tank armies and decimated the infantry divisions of other Soviet armies in these battles. Katukov's 1st Tank Army had only 120 tanks left on 23 August, down from a strength of 542 on 3 August. Rotmistrov's 5th Guards Tank Army tank strength was only 50 operational tanks by 25 August and his mobile corps suffered severe losses in officers and men as well. His army, by the end of the fighting west of Kharkov, had lost approximately 60 percent of its staff officers and 85 percent of its company and battalion commanders. Many Soviet rifle divisions numbered significantly less than 4,000 men.[56]

Although the Soviet counteroffensives following Kursk were temporarily blunted west of Kharkov, the constant fighting never allowed Hitler to build a reserve large enough to regain the upper hand in the East. The Soviets, on the other hand, proved able to rebuild whole armies in a matter of weeks. Examples of this remarkable characteristic of the Soviet army include the reconstitution of both 1st Tank Army and 5th Guards Tank Army after Prochorovka and the conscription of tens of thousands of Ukrainians by the rifle divisions during the march across Ukraine in the summer of 1943. The failure of "Citadel" doomed the Germans to the loss of operational initiative on the Eastern Front without any hope of regaining it, although Hitler seems to have been unaware or unwilling to recognize this reality. The terrible losses in manpower that the Germans suffered in July and August were ultimately fatal and left the armies of Heeresgruppe Süd and Mitte too weak to do anything but delay the inevitable. Operation "Rumyantsev" marked the first time in the war that the Germans were not able to defeat a major Soviet offensive during the summer months and regain their lost ground and the strategic initiative.

After "Citadel," there was no real alternative for the Germans except to withdraw to the Dnepr River and defend the river line. Ideally, this could have been done from prepared positions with the panzer divisions arrayed behind the river to counterattack Soviet penetrations. An orderly withdrawal across the river that provided time to fortify defensive positions on the western bank was the correct and obvious decision. It was the course of action advocated by Manstein and Kluge, but Hitler did not agree. His continual orders to hold ground regardless of the conditions of the divisions and the dubious military value of much of the territory forced Heeresgruppe Süd to order its armies to stand and fight. These orders doomed Manstein's army group to a series of battles that it could not win, a disaster that it could not avoid, and condemned it to a race for the safety of the Dnepr that it could not afford to lose.

CHAPTER 12

Aftermath: 6. Armee Retreats from the Mius

After the divisions of II. SS-Panzerkorps left 6. Armee, the Russians continued to probe the German lines around Dmitrievka, perhaps trying to keep the SS panzer divisions in the area as long as possible. None of these attacks were in any way a threat to Hollidt's army, most being merely company- or battalion-level reconnaissance operations.[1] The obviously weak attacks by the Russians in 6. Armee's area were recognized as little threat to the Mius position and were judged, probably correctly, as belated attempts to force the German command to use the panzer divisions in 6. Armee's sector to rectify a dangerous situation. Because of the weakness of the attack, even 6. Armee in its weakened state was able to master the situation. In any event, in Manstein's opinion, obviously the more dangerous situation was then on the northern wing of Heeresgruppe Süd during the first week in August 1943.

Only once did the Soviets put together any armor for an attack at the Mius in the days immediately after the conclusion of the battle, but it was evident that this was not a full-scale crossing of the river. On 4–5 August, after receiving about sixty replacement tanks, 2nd Guards Mechanized Corps attacked again at Dmitrievka. Russian artillery strongly supported the attack and many Soviet ground-attack planes were in action also, IL-2s operating in large groups over the attack zone. The attack hit positions of 23. Panzer-Division and 294. Infanterie-Division and penetrated their lines opposite and south of Dmitrievka. The German artillery and small-arms fire succeeded in separating the Soviet infantry from the tanks, and as usual, when this occurred, the attack failed. Leaving their infantry behind, the Soviet armor blindlly rolled on toward the west, losing numbers of tanks to antitank gun fire and assault guns. By the time the surviving Russian tanks reached the east edge of Stepanovka, the Germans had destroyed forty-nine of the sixty Soviet tanks and the attack collapsed. Surviving T-34s withdrew and made their way back over the river as best they could.

With the Russian armor eliminated, the Germans turned their attention to the pinned down Soviet infantry, which were destroyed with artillery and counterattacks. About 130 prisoners were taken, but many of the Russian infantry can be assumed to have infiltrated back over the river. In the following days, there was some suspicious activity along the front at several points, but 6. Armee could make no conclusions from the information available to it. Aerial reconnaissance detected the presence of additional tanks assembled in Dmitrievka, but the Russians made nothing stronger than a series of battalion-size reconnaissance attacks along the German perimeter west of the town.

In the area south of the town, a shallow but wide Soviet bridgehead across the Mius remained occupied by Russian infantry forces. Now that the main penetration was taken care of, 6. Armee turned its attention to eliminating this position also. The Russian troops still on the west bank of the river, south of Kuibyshevo, were attacked by XXIX. Armeekorps on 9 August. After some sharp but brief fighting, the Russians were driven back across the river by the next day. Thus, by 10 August, the entire former defensive system on the Mius was back in the hands of 6. Armee.[2]

Although driven out of the penetration at Dmitrievka-Kuibyshevo with heavy losses, Tolbukhin's attack had served its primary purpose. The main objective of the attack was to pull significant German forces (primarily the panzer divisions) out of the Heeresgruppe Süd attack in the Prokhorovka-Psel sector. Had Tolbukhin been able to break 6. Armee and penetrate to Artemovka or even better, Stalino, the Russian command would have been delighted. As it was, the diversionary attack on the Mius, and to a lesser extent the Izyum attack, succeded even better than the Soviet command could have hoped. In this context, the result of the Soviet attacks south of the Psel was enormous, significantly affecting the course of the war on the Eastern Front in the critical summer of 1943.

After Hollidt's army wearily settled into its old bunkers and trenches along the Mius, 6. Armee counted up the casualties of the fighting from 17 July to 3 August. The army suffered 3,298 dead, 15,817 wounded and 2,254 missing, for a total of 21,369 casualties in seventeen days of fighting. The army on the Mius was much weaker than it had been only weeks before, reflecting the losses taken in the July–August fighting, even considering the normal understrength conditions typical of the German Army at this point in the war on the Eastern Front. Manstein had already complained to Hitler that Heeresgruppe Süd had over 100,000 unreplaced casualties, a complaint that did not result in any improvement of the situation as there were simply no men available. The Russian offensives in the south, intended to divert German reserves to Izyum and the Mius, had slowed or halted by the end of August. During the short span of time between the defeat of Tolbukhin's 17 July attack at Dmitrievka-Kuibyshevo and the end of August, the southern flank of Heeresgruppe Süd, anchored by Hollidt's 6. Armee, was quiet while the battles around Bogodukhov raged. As a result, what resources were available to Manstein went to 4. Panzerarmee or Armee-Abteilung Kempf.

After the situation on the northern flank in the Akhtyrka-Bogodukhov area slowly stabilized during the third week of August, the Russians prepared to again turn their attention to the Mius. 6. Armee remained short of armor and few of its infantry casualties were replaced. The Soviet command was of course obviously aware of the departure of II. SS-Panzerkorps and XXIV. Panzerkorps from 6. Armee's area. In the meantime, the Russians had brought up replacements for Tolbukhin's decimated rifle divsions, rebuilding the formations without bringing up new divisions. This tactic enabled the Russians to bring large quantities of infantry into the assembly areas without the Germans being aware of their arrival. 6. Armee was not able to identify the radio traffic of new units or observe troop movements with air reconnaissance. Ground observation did not produce any significant intelligence. This was in stark contrast to early July when observation posts spotted Russian officers with maps studying the terrain in broad daylight and when 2nd Mechanized Corps arrived at night with its driving lights on.

The Soviets replaced their losses, pouring fresh infantry and new tanks into the sector. However, Hollidt's army was in much worse condition than it had been in early July. The army had 200 kilometers of front to defend and even fewer infantrymen than it had before the last attempt of the Russians to cross the river and break out to the west toward Stalino. The army was short of both men and equipment and could not count on receiving help from any other quarter as a result of the need for all possible reserves in the Kharkov area.[3] Hollidt's army received only 3,312 men to replace the 23,830 that it had lost from 17 July to 10 August, a shortfall of 20,000.[4] With the whole Eastern Front in action at various levels of intensity, from Kaluga in the north to the Black Sea in the south, 6. Armee faced the coming storm with the strength at hand. To make matters worse, by 16 August, the army did not have a single tank. All of the mobile divisions that participated in the counterattacks in July and August were gone, dispatched to other hot spots. 23. Panzer-Division was transferred to 1. Panzerarmee's XXXX. Panzerkorps and was fighting against a second Russian attack at Izyum. The decimated 16. Panzergrenadier-Division was in reserve for 1. Panzerarmee and was exhausted by the Mius fighting. Of course, 3. Panzer, *Totenkopf* and *Das Reich* were in the area west of Kharkov under command of 8. Armee.

In mid-August, 6. Armee began to detect a few indications that the Soviets were building up for another assault over the river when some activity could be recognized. Both XXIX. and XVII. Armeekorps detected heavier than normal communications traffic on their fronts on 13 August. The army considered a resumption of Southern Front's attempt to force the Mius as a possibility in the near future, although the strength of the Soviet forces at hand was not clear and it did not appear that anything was imminent. Additional intelligence was not conclusive and the substantial numbers of troops arriving in the sector were not detected. Tank reinforcements remained in concealed assembly areas undetected, as this time Soviet *maskirovka* precautions were in effect and concealed the arrival of armor to the Dmitrievka sector. German air reconnaissance was not able to provide much additional information during the period because bad weather limited the effectiveness of the aerial cameras and visual sightings of troop movements. The Soviets would not have moved any forces into the area during the daylight in any event, and air reconnaissance would thus have been inconclusive.

6. Armee reported to the Ia of Heeresgruppe Süd on 16 August, relating their scanty information in support of the suspicion of

a Soviet build-up for a new attack in the area of Dmitrievka-Kuibyshevo. There was nothing like the amount of information that it had been able to amass in July, when the Russians wanted the Germans to unmistakably know that an attack was in the making. Due to the limited forces available to Hollidt, the preparations by 6. Armee for a possible Soviet attack consisted solely of regrouping the artillery of XVII. Armeekorps to meet an attack in the Dmitrievka area.

On 17 August, even light Soviet communications traffic subsided completely on 6. Armee's front. Other evidence of possible attack preparations, such as build-up of troops in the trench system and the detection of motor noise was lacking. Hollidt concluded, incorrectly, that the Russians had merely been engaged in a diversionary operation to attract German reserves from the Izyum area.[5]

Early on the morning of 18 August, at 0500 hours, Soviet artillery began a massive bombardment of the German frontline positions, accompanied, in addition, by attacks from large groups of ground-attack planes. Air attacks were conducted against unit HQs and important strongpoints. Hundreds of Soviet guns and mortars pounded the frontline defensive positions of the infantry divisions into ruins. Concentrations of rockets howled over the river, impacting with thunderous destruction on second-line strongpoints and assembly areas. It was immediately evident that Tolbukhin had assembled an extremely large number of guns, due to the amount of shells falling on the front lines.

The Russian artillery strength was grouped most strongly opposite the positions of 336. and 294. Infanterie-Divisions and the right flank of 306. Infanterie-Division. Under the weight of this bombardment on the trench line and shallow bunkers, many sections were entirely destroyed and casualties were heavy in the units occupying the forward positions. The shelling collapsed any fortification not dug deeply into the ground or buttressed strongly with scarce heavy timbers on concrete. The shells blasted gaps in the wire and completely wrecked many forward-slope positions.

The 294. Infanterie-Division's regiments crumbled under the intensity of the rocket fire, air bombardment and high-explosive shelling. Decimated by the weeks of intense fighting in the first defense of the Mius, the companies of the grenadier battalions were only a fraction of their established strength. The loss of junior officers and NCOs reduced unit cohesion and morale to a marked degree. All of these factors contributed to a sudden collapse of the regiments at the point of main effort. When 2nd Guards Army's rifle divisions surged across the Mius following the end of the artillery preparations, the German defenders gave way quickly. The strongest attack was led by seventy tanks in close support of the Soviet rifle battalions and hit the frontline positions of 514. Grenadier-Regiment. Broken by the force of the shelling and the shock of the attack of tanks and hordes of Russian infantry, the regiment disintegrated. Although the units on either side of the breakthrough temporarily held firm, at least during the first hours, the collapse of this regiment created an initial breakthrough which was exploited skilfully by the Russians. Reserve armor and infantry was quickly thrown into the gap. This situation swiftly resulted in a crisis early on the first day, one that 6. Armee had few reserve forces to meet.

Tolbukhin's attack tore a three-kilometer-wide hole in the front and subsequent attacks attempted to widen the breakthrough. The Soviet attack penetrated the German front lines in the center to an average depth of seven kilometers by the afternoon of 18 August, advancing to the west edge of Kalinovka. From there, the Soviets swung to the south toward Krynka, threatening the rear areas of 336. Infanterie-Division. This forced XXIX. Armeekorps to detach troops from frontline positions of that division in order to secure its northern flank with an attempt to build a firm shoulder along the flank of the penetration. The 336. Infanterie-Division was able to turn back all Russian attempts to break its frontline, but the division's left flank remained seriously threatened by the penetration in the adjacent sector.

During the night, the Soviets continued to attack and shovel reinforcements into the gap, using the cover of night to their advantage. In addition, late on the first day, a second gap was punched in the German lines near Kalinovka, where 111. Infanterie-Division's front was penetrated. This Russian attack struck toward Semenovsky, supported by armor that was brought up undetected under cover of darkness and thrown into the gap. In short order, the villages of Alexseyevka, Kamyschevaka and Jamschtschizky were overrun and occupied by the Russian infantry and tanks.[6] The fighting continued into the night as the Soviets brought up more troops and armor.

The German troops in Kolpakovka were pressured by strong Soviet armored and mobile infantry elements in the early hours of 19 August and squeezed into a small perimeter around the village. At this village, the Germans managed to build a makeshift defensive strongpoint buttressed by a few antitank guns, but the defenders were isolated by the Soviet tide that swirled around it on both sides.

Attacking through the initial assault by 2nd Guards Army, 5th Shock Army extended the penetration to ten kilometers in depth by the end of the first day. There was nothing tactically complex in the Soviet tactics. They simply bludgeoned straight ahead until they broke the defender's will to fight, without regard to losses of men or machines. However, once a gap was created, the Soviets reacted quickly and were able to exploit the situation before the Germans could react.

Instead of advancing on a broad front as was normal Soviet practice, Tolbukhin began to push one division after the other into the larger of the existing gaps. The Soviets were well aware of the fact that there was no German armor at hand to pinch off the neck of the penetration by counterattacks from the shoulders. Unconcerned by any threat of counterattack from the German infantry divisions, the Russians flowed into the narrow gap like a flood and spread out behind the German front.[7] Once the crust of the defense was broken, there was little to stop the Soviet advance. To the west, the way was open toward Artemovka and beyond to the major rail center of Stalino. The Germans reacted with weak counterattacks by small infantry units that were ineffectual.

The Soviets repulsed the feeble attempts to close the gap by elements of 294. Infanterie-Division and 3. Gebirgs-Division. As 5th Shock Army pushed west in the breakthrough area, the defending German units on the penetration shoulders were gradually rubbed out and the gap expanded to a width of twelve kilometers by 20 August, more as a result of German losses than efforts of the Soviet to widen the rift. By that date, a bridgehead was pushed over the Krynka River, which lay approximately fifteen kilometers west of Dmitrievka. Soviet forces occupied Krinitschka and Artemovka. This was the first major breakthrough into the rear areas of 6. Armee and caused serious disruptions, aggravated by the lack of sufficient motor transport to relocate German troops and the meager reserves of the army. The speed with which the Soviet advance was accomplished was an ill omen of worse to come for Hollidt's troops. The rampaging battle groups of Soviet tanks and infantry overran German units so quickly that they were not able to withdraw and they were often cut off and forced to surrender or were destroyed.

In one such incident, the majority of the artillery strength of 294. Infanterie-Division was destroyed when overrun in its positions due to the speed of the Russian advance. By late 19 August, the Soviets were for the first time threatening to completely sever the communication lines of XXIX. Armeekorps from its supply bases at Stalino-Uspenskaya.[8] The XXIX. Armeekorps scoured its rear areas for all the men it could find, giving bakers, guard detachments, village security units and butchers weapons and sending them to the front in a last-ditch effort to delay the Russians. There were no reserves left. No more telling example is necessary to illustrate the critical lack of manpower on the Eastern Front and the effect this shortage had on the combat effectiveness of the German infantry divisions. These makeshift reserves tried to hold the shoulders of the penetration in combat against battle-hardened infantry and tanks of 4th Guards Mechanized Corps. They were swept aside quickly.

6. Armee moved combat units of 3. Gebirgs-Division, then commanded by Generalmajor Picker, to the Saur Mogilsky area to serve as the basic unit of a Kampfgruppe for a counterattack on the northern edge of the Russian penetration. The elements of the division that left the divisional sector and moved to the penetration area could not be replaced. The remaining units of the division merely stretched their fronts to cover the gap created when the troops were withdrawn to the Dmitrievka sector. Attached to the battle group were six batteries of artillery, one assault gun battery and two tank destroyer companies. Late on 20 August, the Germans, aware of the narrowness of the penetration, which lay between the flank of 111. Infanterie-Division on the north and Kalinovka to the south, made an attempt to cut through the base of the Soviet penetration and close the gap. As unsatisfactory as this expedient measure was, having no significant motorized elements or armor, it remained the only course open to the army. The fate of 6. Armee clearly depended on the success of its emergency improvisational tactics which had become necessary due to the powerful Soviet force operating in the depth of the

sector. With even a small amount of armor, the German command would have felt more confident that they could have dealt some damage to the Russian lines of communication and supply. Intelligence information obtained from a captured Russian officer with documents concerning the tank strength of 5th Shock Army indicated that the Russians did not have as much armor as first suspected. Significant tank losses had already been inflicted on the Soviets, further reducing the number of operational tanks available to Tolbukhin.

Weak as it was, the counterattack by XXIX. Armeekorps was able to gain some ground in the initial stages of the operation on 20 August. As usual, the German assault troops were well supported by their artillery, which was to a significant degree responsible for the initial gains of the attack. Semenovsky was recaptured early in the day, but the attack slowed down at Hill 188.4, just south of that village, when it was delayed by hard fighting before fmally driving the Russians off the hill. The Germans destroyed a number of Russian tanks even without strong armored support, claiming a total of forty-three tanks knocked out in the early hours of the advance, most probably due to the operations of assault guns or tank destroyer companies.

Once the Soviets were aware that their lines of communication were threatened by the German counterattack, 4th Mechanized Corps, which had passed through the hole punched in 6. Armee's front, turned around and attacked the German forces from the west on 21 August. Kampfgruppe Picker, the 3. Gebirgs-Division's battle group, was unexpectedly attacked on its flank by Soviet armor but fought back bitterly, destroying more Russian armor in close combat and with heavy weapons. However, the overwhelming strength of the Soviets was too great. By evening, 4th Guards Mechanized Corps tanks and infantry rolled over the German infantry, pushed through to the east and reopened the gap, enlarging it to nearly nine kilometers in width.[9] Semenovsky and Hill 188.4, the scene of such heavy fighting and sacrifice on the day before, were both lost again to the Russian attack.

Not until 20 August was Manstein able to find a panzer division that could be spared for duties with 6. Armee. 13. Panzer-Division, from Heeresgruppe A, was ordered to move from the Crimea to Heeresgruppe Süd's command. Elements of the division were on the way almost immediately. However, it was to be several days before the units of the division arrived in Heeresgruppe Süd's area. By that time, it was too late to provide the armored punch that would have been so valuable earlier in the fighting. Had it been available to 6. Armee in time for the first counterattack, it would have been almost sure to have been able to seal off the Russian penetration, given the progress made by even weak German infantry elements in the failed counterattack. Whether the Germans could then have prevented 4th Guards Mechanized Corps from reopening the penetration again is problematic. It can be assumed that the Russian attacking force, confronted by even a small amount of German armor, would have suffered heavier tank losses. 6. Armee's counterattack, with only a makeshift battlegroup available on 20 August, supported with just a single assault gun battery and some antitank guns, destroyed nearly fifty Russian tanks. A few tanks and additional assault guns would have almost certainly have inflicted heavier losses on the Soviet armor.

After the failure of the counterattack of 20 August, XXIX. Armeekorps was forced to extend the flank of 15. Luftwaffe-Felddivision and 336. Infanterie-Division to the west, paralleling the breakthrough in an attempt to provide a defensive front strong enough to keep the gap from widening in the rear of the army. The two already weak divisions spread themselves even thinner, extending to the west at a 90-degree angle to the river in order to channel the Soviet penetration. Hollidt was undoubtedly aware that at some point, the divisions would not be able to continually extend their defensive lines to the rear and hold ground to the front as well. The army desperately fought to survive until German armor could arrive.

THE COUNTERATTACK OF 13. PANZER-DIVISION

Elements of 13. Panzer-Division, a battle group of regimental strength, made up of one panzergrenadier regiment and three companies of tanks, were the first mobile reinforcements to arrive in 6. Armee's area to counter Tolbukhin's new offensive on the Mius River. The division vanguard arrived in XXIX. Armeekorp's area on 22 August, assembling southwest of Saur Mogilsky. It received attack orders as soon as its vehicles and men unloaded from the train. The division immediately prepared to counterattack the northern flank of the penetration. The attack direction was to be toward Krinitschka with the objective of destroying 4th Guards Mechanized Corps elements at that point, some of which were taking on supplies and were stationary. The main objective was to close the gap between XXIX. and XVII. Armeekorps north of Semenovsky.[10] Kampfgruppe Picker of 111. Infanterie-Division was again to support the attack of 13. Panzer-Divison by advancing west of Semenovsky and attacking Hill 188.4. This force was given the mission of serving as flank security for the Panzer division's advance.

In the two days after the earlier counterattack by 6. Armee, the Russians continued to push west and frustrate the feeble attempts of the Germans to limit the width of the breakthrough. By the time 13. Panzer-Division began its counterattack, the gap in 6. Armee's front was again over twelve kilometers in width. The seriousness of the situation that 6. Armee found itself in on 22 August was underscored by communication from Heeresgruppe Süd, which made it clear to Hollidt that he could expect no more help after the arrival of 13. Panzer-Division. His army had to survive by its own efforts in the meantime. It was a familiar message.

The attack began well enough, supported by accurate artillery fires and the panzers gained six to seven kilometers before encountering stiff reaction from the Soviets. Once the Russians were aware that German armor was moving in the area, armored elements from the spearhead groups turned around again and attacked back to the east. Under heavy assaults by Soviet armor and infantry, and having encountered a strong defensive position west of Alexseyevka at Hill 157.3, the division's attack ground to a halt. One regiment-size battle group was not enough to close the gap and the remaining six kilometers proved too much for the German forces to cover.

It was a case of too little, too late—just two days late, in the opinion of the command of 6. Armee. What small resources the army had been able to throw at the Russians were used up and the continuing Russian expansion of the bridgehead left Hollidt without enough men to physically man a constantly lengthening defensive line. In fact, under the unrelenting Soviet pressure, there was fast becoming no position left to defend as the rear areas of the army were carved up. Communication and supply were increasingly disrupted, resulting in lack of ammunition and food. On 22 August, the Soviets built a bridgehead over the Krynka River, west of Saur Mogilsky, and were obviously planning to encircle German elements attempting to stop the attack west of the river. Hollidt's army was in danger of being overrun and cut up into isolated fragments before it could withdraw from its positions. From 22 to 25 August, 13. Panzer-Division continually made thrusts that occupied the Russians in the area of the base of the gap in determined attempts to keep the Soviets off balance. The division continued to tie down Soviet armor and thus delay the westward progress of the Soviet flood.

By 25 August, much of the strength of the division had been used up. However, the unit was well led, evidently had good morale and was still dangerous in the right circumstances. One such incident took place near the village of Lissitschj when elements of the division took a group of Russian tanks and infantry by surprise. Due to poorly organized perimeter security, the Soviets were surprised when the panzers struck without warning, promptly scattering men and machines and knocking out many tanks. The Russians lost 300 men as prisoners and much of the equipment of the Soviet unit was captured or destroyed.[11] The panzer division, over the next three days, skilfully operated as best it could considering its declining strength, making raids and parrying Soviet advances on the flank of XXIX. Armeekorps. Hollidt knew that these were stopgap measures and that his army could not seal off or contain the Soviet attack. Disaster was the only possible outcome if the army was ordered to hold the present position to "the last man."

The decline in the numbers of German infantry, serious in July, was by then disastrous. The infantry of XXIX. Armeekorps were spread out with a density of only 86 men per kilometer of front, while IV. Armeekorps was a little better off, with about 100 men per kilometer of front. 6. Armee estimated that the Russians still had approximately 100 tanks in XXIX. Armeekorps' sector, while 13. Panzer had only a handful of tanks left by 24 August. The Russian rifle divisions outnumbered the German infantry by a margin of eight to one.[12] The Russians were forced to pause for a short time after the counterattacks by 13. Panzer-Division, and 2nd Guards and 4th Guards Mechanized Corps regrouped on 24 August. To add to Hollidt's concerns, air reconnaissance spotted a new Soviet mobile unit assembling in the southern sector of the breakthrough. These were identified as elements of 4th Guards Cavalry Corps and were obviously preparing for commitment in the near future.

On 25 August, the Ia of both 6. Armee and 1. Panzerarmee, which was also beset by extreme Soviet pressure to the north of the Mius front, flew to meet with Manstein at Heeresgruppe Süd headquarters. Both officers realized that the only chance to save their armies was a withdrawal to a defensible line without delay. If Tolbukhin broke free to the west, the road to the Dnepr was open to the Russians and the entire Donets basin could be lost. More significantly, if the Russians were able to reach the river, spread out on the eastern bank and capture the crossing sites on the Dnepr, a major disaster would ensue for the divisions of both 6. Armee and 1. Panzerarmee. In this event, not only would these forces be cut off and likely destroyed, but the German 17. Armee, at that time in the Kuban bridgehead, as well as the troops in the Crimea of Heeresgruppe A, would be cut off from retreat or supply by land. Manstein realized that once again, the fate of hundreds of thousands of German soldiers (as well as the Eastern Front itself) was in the hands of Adolf Hitler.[13] An order from Hitler to stand and fight could potentially result in the virtual annihilation of Heeresgruppe Süd and the destruction of the southern wing of the Eastern Front.

Manstein, in radio communication with Hitler, bluntly informed him that without fresh divisions, including panzer divisions, the Donets basin could not be held with the tired and weak forces at hand. He explained that if OKH could not provide these units, then he must request that he be given freedom of movement to pull back to a shorter, more easily defensible line. While he did not believe that Hitler would agree to this proposal, before leaving his headquarters, he gave instructions that both armies should begin plans and preparations for a withdrawal to the "Tortoise Line" east of Stalino.[14] Hitler, of course alarmed by the phrase, "freedom of movement," which in his mind meant lack of will to stand and die if need be, promptly gave his answer to Manstein. His message? "Do nothing. I am coming myself." Doubtless, this reply did little to reassure Manstein.

Hitler left his East Prussian HQ and flew to the Ukraine, where he met with Manstein at the "Werewolf" HQ complex, where in better days the offensive campaign of the summer of 1942 had been directed. The bunkers and communications buildings were located in Vinnitsa and there Manstein brought with him officers who he hoped could explain to the Führer the realities of the frontline conditions on the Eastern Front. The commander of 23. Panzer-Division,

General von Vormann, whose men had been so instrumental in the defense of the Mius, came with Manstein. So did the commander of XL. Armeekorps, General Erhard Raus, and Hollidt of 6. Armee. The testimony of these soldiers of unquestioned bravery and experience, in Manstein's hopes, would be believed.

Manstein opened the conference by giving Hitler a summary of the situation and then proceeded to present him with two choices for the conduct of the defense of south Ukraine: "I presented Hitler with the clear alternatives: either quickly providing the army group with new forces—in any case not less than twelve divisions—and exchanging our tired divisions with others from quiet stretches of front, or abandoning the Donets area to release forces within the army group."[15]

Manstein made every attempt to get Hitler to realize just how weak his forces were and how it was absolutely necessary to shorten the lines or receive fresh divisions in order to provide for the creation of reserve forces able to react to the situations as necessary. In addition to explaining 6. Armee's manpower deficits, Manstein also gave the casualty-replacement figures for 1. Panzerarmee. That army's recent losses totalled 27,291 men while only 6,174 replacements had been received, which left a total of over 20,000 unreplaced losses.[16] At that point in the conference, he asked Hollidt to provide Hitler with the intelligence estimates of the Russian strength that faced each of his decimated corps:

> "General Hollidt, will you please give the Führer a comparative picture of the enemy's and our own strength?"
>
> "My XXIX Corps has 8,706 left. Facing it are 69,000 Russians. My XVII Corps has 9,284 men; facing it are 49,500 Russians. My IV Corps is relatively well off. It has 13,143 men, faced by 18,000 Russians. Altogether 31,133 Germans against 136,500 Russians. The relative strength in tanks is similar: Tolbukhin yesterday had 165 tanks in operation; we had 7 tanks and 38 assault guns."
>
> [Manstein continued:] ". . . The enemy is stepping up his pressure. With our available forces the Donets region cannot be defended, my Führer. Things are no better at First Panzer Army. Nor will Eighth Army and Fourth Panzer Army be in a

position to prevent a Russian breakthrough to the Dnieper in the long run. . . . Either you let us have fresh forces, and that means twelve divisions, or the Donets region must be abandoned. . . . I see no other solution."[17]

Hitler did not give in immediately, as Manstein almost certainly could have predicted, nor did he acknowledge the seriousness of the facts that had just been related to him. Instead, the dictator remained evasive as always, taking refuge in rhetoric and questions about minor matters of no real concern to the critical matters at hand. This was a common tactic of Hitler, invariably utilized when he was faced by decisions that he did not like to make. While he acknowledged that the situation was indeed grim and thanked the gathered commanders for their efforts over the past weeks, Hitler did not want to make a hard decision and instead retreated to another old strategem, delay. He again made it plain that there could be no retreat: all ground must be held until the enemy exhausted himself with attacks upon defenders who by will alone, if need be, resisted the attack.

Hitler remained distracted at the time by the course of events in the Mediteranean. Italy had collapsed, as he had forseen, and he was extremely concerned with the possibility of the Western Allies invading the Mediterranean coast at some point east of the Italian penisula. This would have threatened southeastern Europe, an event that he considered might bring Turkey into the war against Germany. Of course, the concerns of what might happen next month or next spring were of no concern to Manstein and his generals. They were determined to get the Führer to address the events that were absolutely sure to happen in their sectors within a matter of days.[18]

When Manstein adamantly stuck to his guns and refused to be turned from his arguments, Hitler changed his tactics. Where was he to find reinforcements, he asked Manstein? The Feldmarschall had a ready answer and replied that Heeresgruppen Mitte and Nord should give up any units that they could spare, making them available for redeployment to the southern front. Finally, pressed to make a decision, and without question not wanting to give up the Donets basin, Hitler agreed to make immediate transfers of divisions from Heeresgruppe Mitte. With that concession, Manstein and his generals returned to their HQs, much relieved and ready to plan for the coming reinforcements. They found, upon their arrival, that disturbing new events had taken place while they had been pleading with Hitler for a decision on the situation in the south. Bad news awaited them on their return from the conference.

XXIX. ARMEEKORPS: ENCIRCLEMENT AND BREAKOUT

While they had been at the Führer's headquarters in Vinnitsa, events had taken a turn for the worse in 6. Armee's sector. After pausing for two days to rest and regroup, the Soviets moved 2nd Guards Mechanized Corps and major elements of 4th Guards Mechanized Corps toward the western edge of the penetration. It was obvious that the Russians were prepared to attack through the positions of 3rd and 13th Rifle Corps. The attack was intended to encircle the entire XXIX. Armeekorps by penetrating the corps front, turning to the south and driving to the coast of the Black Sea.

On 27 August, after receiving replacements and new tanks, the two mechanized corps burst out of the breakthrough area toward the south and Mariupol, sweeping through the rear areas of XXIX. Armeekorps. The Germans could do little to stop the Russians. Here and there a detachment of security troops or a makeshift battle group, managed to slow the Russian onslaught for a few hours. However, unopposed by serious resistance, the attack slashed twenty miles to the south on the first day. It was immediately obvious to the Germans that the Russian objective was the Gulf of Taganrog and the encirclement of XXIX. Armeekorps. The Soviet advance to the coast created an immediate crisis with only one course of logical action left open to 6. Armee. No help from Heeresgruppe Mitte would arrive in time to change the situation because the Soviets had moved first, before the Germans were able to react. This was due in large part to the difficulty of getting Hitler to make decisions that were not to his liking or understanding. Hollidt directed the corps to break out of the encirclement to the west on the evening of 27–28 August.

Once again, 13. Panzer-Division was called upon, this time to stop the attack of two entire Soviet mechanized corps. The division, with infantry from 111. Infanterie-Division in support, attacked Russian lead elements near Novo Ivanovka, but was unable to accomplish much other than to force a momentary pause in the Russian advance. Once again, 6. Armee scraped together a few fragmentary reinforcements, sending them to 13. Panzer-Division. Security detachments of Kavallerie-Regiment Süd, mobile elements of Flak-Abteilung 91 and a few hurriedly repaired tanks were thrown together in a makeshift combat group to strengthen the breakout attempt. Additional help would eventually arrive, but the Germans troops caught in the encirclement could not wait and began to fight their way toward the north and German lines.

By 29 August, Manstein obtained two divisions from Heeresgruppe Mitte, the remnant of 9. Panzer-Division and a worn-out infantry unit, 258. Infanterie-Division. Units of the two divisions were dispatched toward the area of 6. Armee, hastily thrown together and rushed from Orel in order to supply badly needed reinforcements to Hollidt. The new divisions were both very weak, having been engaged in continuous fighting for some weeks during the hard fighting that took place during and after Kursk. Neither of the divisions were anywhere close to divisional size.

The infantry strength of the battle group was augmented by elements of 3. Gebirgs-Division. The mission given by 6. Armee to this force, which didn't have the strength of a normal division, was to break through the Russian front, drive to the south and link up with the attack of XXIX. Armeekorps. The XXIX. Armeekorps was to break out of the Soviet encirclement and push to the north. 302. and 306. Infanterie-Divisions of XVII. Armeekorps organized small assault groups in order to attempt to occupy enemy attention by conducting attacks on the northern flank of the Soviet penetration.[19]

The Soviet drive toward the sea continued without interruption, the feeble efforts of the Germans not able to signficantly delay the advance of two Soviet mechanized corps. On 29 August, the Russians reached the coast and cut 6. Armee in half. XXIX. Armeekorps was encircled in a pocket to the west of Taganrog, divided from the rest of the army. In the encirclement, the only thought now was to break through the Russian lines before the Soviets could begin an organized reduction of the pocket. The Soviet encirclement was not air tight at that point. Gaps still existed and it was possible to fight through and reach their comrades of XVII. Armeekorps. In the pocket were 111. Infanterie and 17. Infanterie-Divisions, later joined by the remaining elements of 336. Infanterie and the men of 15. Luftwaffe-Felddivision The ragged and tired survivors of these shattered units fought their way through Soviet forces to join the survivors of the other two divisions, who were in somewhat better condition.

The breakout by XXIX. Armeekorps to the north depended primarily on the attack of 13. Panzer-Division and the supporting diversionary attacks of IV. Armeekorps, for it was not strong enough to accomplish this task unaided. The fifteen-kilometer-wide pocket was under attack from three sides at this point. The Russians were making every effort to collapse the defensive perimeter and destroy the German divisions before they could escape.[20]

The attack of 13. Panzer-Division was reinforced by the firepower of Sturmgeschütz-Bataillon 259 and supported by the Stukas of Hans Rudel's air wing.[21] On 30 August, the tanks of 13. Panzer-Division began the first phase of the breakout operation. The division attacked at dawn and XVII. Armeekorps alerted the main combat elements of 306. Infanterie-Division on the western flank of the corps boundary in order to act as a reserve where needed. The 13. Panzer-Division battle group, weak though it was, punched through the Soviet lines, opening a narrow passage to freedom on the afternoon of 30 August. The XXIX. Armeekorps had in the meantime destroyed all of its heavy equipment that could not be taken out, lined up in three columns, each headed by assault guns or mobile Flak units, and marched north. Desperate to escape the ring of Soviet armor and rifle divisions that were closing in on them, the Germans stormed forward with grim determination. The Russians were somewhat deceived by the large clouds of dust that the three columns raised and interpreted the clouds to be German armor on the move. When the columns met Soviet defenses, the fighting was violent and brief. In some instances, Russian infantry broke quickly, perhaps anticipating the attack of German panzers. Each column, fighting with the intensity of desperate men, broke through the Russian lines.

Reacting quickly to the breakout attempt, the Soviets attacked 13. Panzer-Division with cavalry formations and some tank forces. However, the division continued to battle forward, in spite of all attempts to stop it. The tank repair detachment of the division sent even partially repaired tanks forward to join the panzer regiment, making every effort to get as many tanks as possible in running condition. Extraordinary efforts had been called for outside of the pocket as well as inside. Fighting to help their comrades escape the encirclement, 13. Panzer-Division continued its gallant attack from the west. The division maintained its forward momentum and resisted attacks from the flanks to close the gap through the Soviet lines. The efforts of this division critically shortened the distance that the columns of XXIX. Armeekorps had to cover before reaching German lines.

The last remnants of XXIX. Armeekorps divisions escaped from the steadily shrinking pocket perimeter during the night of 30–31 August. A small battlegroup had remained behind in Taganrog to destroy war material and vital installations of military value to the Soviets and only narrowly made its escape. The small detachment, under command of an Oberstleutnant Kalberlah, crossed over the Mius on the Mackensen Bridge, which was north of the city, and fought its way toward the moving XXIX. Armeekorps pocket. Kalberlah and his men made their way over a small river, the Mokrij Jelantschik, and reached safety after two harrowing days of flight and combat.

The desperate situation confronting the men of XXIX. Armeekorps caused men like Kalberlah and many others who are unknown to react with great determination. In some cases which are recorded, instances of individual bravery were almost incredible. A lone anti-tank gunner of 14./Grenadier-Regiment 55 (17. Infanterie-Division), an Obergefreiter Riess, reacted with calm resolve when his unit was attacked by a large number of Soviet tanks. He and his gun crew destroyed ten of the twenty-seven attacking tanks that broke into the sector manned by this unit. For his bravery under fire, Riess was awarded the Knight's Cross.[22]

The divisions that emerged from the encirclement were shadows of even their former reduced strength. The 336. Infanterie-Division and 15. Luftwaffe-Felddivision were essentially destroyed, having a total of only 500 combat effectives left after the breakout. Because of the loss of all types of heavy and transport equipment and the disorganization caused by the severe number of casualties, neither of these units had any appreciable combat value. Even a defensive mission was beyond the two divisions if attacked in force due to the lack of heavy weapons, sufficient numbers of fighting troops and the absence of even tactically sufficient armor. The fighting strength of those divisions that still maintained some unit cohesion was so reduced that 6. Armee did not consider them strong enough to meet the next serious crisis that had to be met.

However, XXIX. Armeekorps was faced with just such a crisis immediately upon completing its breakout. It was necessary that the corps quickly integrate itself with IV. and XVII. Armeekorps defenses in order to restore a unified front to the army and to resist Russian attempts to encircle the corps again. Cognizant of the weaknesses of XXIX. Armeekorps, 6. Armee ordered surviving elements of the recently arrived 17. Panzer-Division, the battle group of 9. Panzer-Division and an infantry regiment of 258. Infanterie-Division to reinforce XXIX. Armeekorps' attempts to establish a continuous front.[23] These units provided much-needed heavy weapons and, probably more importantly, mental and emotional resolve to the troops who had just undergone the strain of the breakout operation after many weeks of heavy combat on the Mius.

Having failed to completely destroy XXIX. Armeekorps, the Russians turned their attention to the rest of 6. Armee, XVII. Armeekorps in the center and IV. Armeekorps on the northern flank. After pausing to regroup, Tolbukhin's Southern Front ordered its mobile elements to smash through the boundary gap between the two corps on 30 August. In short order, Stepanovka, Chistyakovo, and the smaller towns of Sugress and Charzyssk were taken by the Russians. Battle groups of Russian tanks and infantry penetrated the front and broke free into the rear areas against little organized resistance. The German divisions maintained only a thin crust of widely dispersed infantry on the front line of defense and the only troops to be found behind the front lines were small security detachments and administrative and supply units located in villages and towns, rear-area units not organized for combat. The Russians cut the Chistyakovo–Charzyssk road, which was a main supply route of XVII. Armeekorps, on the first day of this attack. Roaming Soviet battle groups, made up of tanks and supporting infantry, appeared unexpectedly behind the front lines, routing security troops and overrunning unit HQs. The corps reserves were meager, and once the defense was penetrated, there was little that could be done to combat the rampaging Soviet tanks and motorized infantry.

One such group, made up of ten tanks and supported by about 600 men of a rifle battalion, surprised the divisional staff of 258.

Infanterie-Division during the night of 30 August. The HQ group was stationed in a village and did not expect an attack so far from the front. Security was evidently very lax. Approaching under the cover of darkness, the Russians overran the HQ and inflicted heavy casualties on the staff of the division. The division IIa (divisional adjutant) and O1 (chief ordnance officer) were killed and the Ia was severely wounded. While confusion reigned in the town and staff officers of the division tried futilely to restore some degree of order, another German unit saved the situation.

Stationed a short distance from the HQ, personnel of Flak-Regiment 24 quickly reacted to the situation. The counterattack, speedily organized and personally led by the commander of II./Flak-Regiment 24, recaptured the town, drove the Russians out and captured 100 prisoners. On his own initiative, the Flak regiment commanding officer had gathered together the troops at hand, utilizing them as supporting infantry for his guns and attacked the Russians. The counterattack hit the Soviet troops while the situation was still chaotic and the Russians, still flushed with their successful storming of the HQ position, were caught by surprise. Not yet organized for defense, the Russians lost two of their tanks and another armored vehicle before they realized what was happening. The attack, supported by the potent fire of the Flak battalion's 20mm automatic guns and deadly 88s, routed a superior Soviet force and restored the town to German hands. This is another example of a small German force conducting an immediate counterattack on Soviet troops and succeeding in routing a superior force.

In spite of a few German tactical successes such as the above incident, the attack by the Soviets in the center of 6. Armee threatened to split the army in half and drive on to Stalin or even penetrate to the Dnepr. Already, there was the dangerous situation in the south in which Russian infantry built three bridgeheads over the Krynka River and were advancing once again on XXIX. Armeekorps. The Krynka, generally narrow and shallow, intersected the Mius River below Kuibyshevo, then meandered to the north. It flowed through Chistyakovo, which was roughly northeast of Kuibyshevo. Faced by the Soviet bridgeheads over the Krynka, 6. Armee first attempted to erase the still small Russian bridgeheads that were established on the west bank. With these enemy troops driven back over the stream, 6. Armee planned to rally at the Krynka and organize for defense. This small river, although not much of a physical obstacle, was to be used as a barrier to quickly build up a defensive line.

With this goal in mind, the army ordered 306. Infanterie-Division to free up enough troops to attack toward the river from the northern flank of the Soviet bridgeheads over the river. The attack was to provide time and opportunity for XVII. Armeekorps to extend its flanks westward along the northern shoulder of the penetration to banks of the Krynka. A German infantry division thus had to provide the limiting shoulder on the flank of a Soviet offensive when it could barely defend itself to the front. Time and time again, the army asked its divisions to accomplish tasks that were beyond their capabilities and yet, more often then not, the divisions accomplished them. By this date, all of the infantry divisions were little more than regiment-size battle groups except for those on the extreme northern flank.

Hollidt, perhaps too optimistically, planned to drive the Soviets back across the river and use the extension of the right flank of the XVII. Armeekorps by 306. Infanterie-Division as an assembly area for an attack to close the gap between the two corps. It was the objective of XXIX. Armeekorps to hold the Krynka and then extend its front along the Krynka to the north and establish a union with its neighboring corps. Whether either could withstand another strong attack by Southern Front forces that were pushing toward the Dnepr was another question.[24]

In order to drive back the bridgeheads at the Krynka, 17. Panzer-Division was directed to swing behind Charzysak and attack the crossing sites on 1 September. This was in conjunction with the attempt of 306. Infanterie-Division to extend XVII. Armeekorps' flank west to the town of Sugress. These desperate maneuvers were the last gasps of a severely wounded army, trying to maintain a continuous front without the manpower to accomplish the task. Every operation by 6. Armee was conducted with forces too small and too weak to be normally expected to succeed in their assigned mission. Miraculously, however, the makeshift battle groups and shattered divisions accomplished their tasks and enabled Hollidt's army to piece together a front once again. It was a race against time for the army. If it was not allowed to withdraw in time and could not reach the Dnepr and relative safety, it would eventually be too weak to do anything but stand and die or disintegrate under Soviet assaults. This was the consequence of Hitler's order to stand and fight regardless of the realities of the situation, ignoring the disparity in strength between the Russians with their almost limitless resources and the ever-shrinking German manpower base.

In Manstein's mind, the situation was crystal clear and there was no question in regard to 6. Armee's inability to resist the next Soviet attack from its present positions given the manpower situation. On 31 August, he gave the order to retreat to the Kalmius River to a hastily prepared line called the Tortoise Line (*Schildkroten-Stellung*), after which he communicated with Hitler that night on his decision to withdraw 6. Armee, hoping that it was not too late to save some remnant of Hollidt's divisions. With little real choice, Hitler reluctantly approved the move, but only after insisting that it be done "provided, that the situation absolutely demands it and there is no other possible alternative."[25] There was, of course, no other real option remaining open to Manstein. In fact, there was serious doubt about whether the one remaining logical course of action, withdrawal, could be done successfully at that point. Manstein commented in regard to the lost opportunities to have salvaged the situation by prudent and timely decisions:

> If only it had been given this freedom of movement a few weeks earlier, the army group would have been in a position to fight the battle on its southern wing more economically. It could have freed formations for the vital northern wing and still halted the enemy advance on a shortened front, possibly even forward of the Dneiper. Now, however, freedom of movement served only to preserve the southern wing from defeat. Even so, it remained doubtful whether a proper front could still be established forward of the river.[26]

A collection of Organization Todt workers and whatever army engineers, conscripted civilians and rear-area men that could be put together, hastily worked to prepare the Tortoise defensive position. The new line was to protect the key city of Stalin and bar the rest of the Donets region from the Russian onslaught.

As if to underscore Manstein's doubts about the ability of 6. Armee to successfully withdraw to the new line, the Russians launched an attempt to break XXIX. Armeekorps' front on 3 September. An armored attack hit the corps with the objective of breaking through and driving toward the Dnepr. Once again, the emergency reaction battle groups and the battle-weakened, though still combat-worthy, 13. Panzer-Division saved the day, coming up with a stunning defensive effort that blunted the main Soviet tank attack against XXIX. Armeekorps. This gave the corps the desperately needed time to continue to organize a cohesive front. The Russian armored spearhead was smashed and sixty-three Soviet tanks were listed as destroyed in what 6. Armee rightly considered a "great defensive success."[27] A smaller attack against 258. Infanterie-Division, which had by 3 September already reached the Tortoise Line, was also turned back. A counterattack by infantry of that division, supported by a Panther tank battalion, restored the situation on 4 September. This allowed the main part of XXIX. Armeekorps and most of XVII. Armeekorps to reach the Tortoise Line by the following day. The pursuit of the Russians was halted by the unexpected presence of German armor. The Panthers knocked out many Soviet tanks, which blunted the spearhead of the armored attack and forced the Soviets to pause. This second delay gave the last elements of XVII. Armeekorps the chance to conduct a fighting withdrawal. The remnants of the corps reached the line on 5 September, along with the survivors of 13., 17., and 9. Panzer-Divisions. Each of the three panzer divisions was reduced to the strength of a regimental battle group or smaller.

With the occupation of the Tortoise Line, the Germans withdrew from the Mius River area for the last time in the war in the East. The sacrifices of the troops of 6. Armee (over 23,000 total casualties), II. SS-Panzerkorps (over 2,500 casualties, including 1,458 in *Totenkopf* alone) and the additional losses of corps support troops during the combat from 17 July until 10 August served to delay the Soviet capture of the river and its defenses for little more than a month. In the end, the Germans had to give up the Mius line anyway and begin the retreat to the Dnepr when Tolbukhin made his second attack and overwhelmed Hollidt's army. This time, there were insufficient available panzer reserves to send to the aid of 6. Armee. After the fighting of July and August, there was little fight left in the battered infantry divisions and their meager reserves were used up. Had Hollidt's army been allowed to withdraw earlier in the summer before the hard

Aftermath: 6. Armee Retreats from the Mius

fighting of 17–30 July, it could have made a coordinated retreat to the Dnepr and, with the aid of the panzer divisions, likely would have reached the river intact and with the ability to conduct an effective defense. Its losses would have been significantly reduced from the 23,000 that it lost in the defensive battles on the river and the subsequent counterattacks.

What could probably have been done with discipline and a reasonable chance of success in July was nearly impossible by mid-August. There was not enough infantry strength to even hold a defensive position then, much less to conduct a disciplined withdrawal in close contact with an aggressive enemy. However, perhaps unaware of the extent of German weakness, the last-gasp counterattacks by small German armored elements apparently stunned the Soviets on 4 September and there was no strong follow up of the attack on the next day. The Germans were allowed time to organize in their new position, although the temporary stabilization of the front did not last long. There were a few more days of calm, during which reports from deserters informed the Germans that the Soviet army had conscripted between 50,000 and 80,000 Ukrainian civilians in its march across the Ukraine. The forcibly drafted Ukrainians, civilian men of all ages, were given rudimentary training, then issued a rifle.

With the Russians sure to resume their offensive within days, Hollidt was not sure how long his army could hold out when finally attacked. His neighbor to the north, 1. Panzerarmee, was by then also in a crisis situation and could not furnish any help to 6. Armee. When 1. Panzerarmee was forced to withdraw from its positions along the western bank of the Donets River, the divisions were too weak to hold a line in open country. Southwest Front advanced quickly over the river and allowed 1. Panzerarmee no rest. While Southern Front temporarily gathered itself, Southwest Front continued to exert pressure against 1. Panzerarmee and did not let the army establish itself in the Tortoise Line position north of the section of the line held by 6. Armee.

Southwest Front, on 6 September, maintained its attacks on the Germans, striking just north of the southern boundary of 1. Panzerarmee, that adjoined the left flank of 6. Armee. In a matter of hours, a full Soviet mechanized corps, with overwhelming infantry support, broke through the German lines and created a bridgehead. Neither 6. Armee nor 1. Panzerarmee had the strength to do much about it. On the following day, 23rd Tank Corps rammed its way out of the gap along with 1st Guards Mechanized Corps and drove hard to the west. The Soviets were led by a strong tank group and soon penetrated nearly fifty kilometers behind the German front lines, reaching the village of Postyschevo in a largely unopposed advance. Faced with the prospect of being encircled again by this deep penetration, 6. Armee began to abandon the Tortoise Line, with assault gun detachments anchoring one flank of the withdrawal and 33. Panzer-Regiment of 9. Panzer-Division the other flank. XVII. Armeekorps and troops of Kampfgruppe Sieler also began to pull out of the line, withdrawing behind weak rear guards. The German defensive line melted away, and when rear-guard units on the flanks of the penetration disintegrated, a gap opened up to over twenty kilometers wide. Only the remnants of a few German units still fighting on hopelessly or disorganized groups of survivors scrambling to reach German lines remained in the gap. Soviet troops drove west, sometimes encountering no German resistance at all for many miles. There was no organized effort by an adequate rear guard and the Soviet tanks and motorized infantry flowed through the gaps between each division.

By 8 September, the lead elements of the two Russian mobile corps were only thirty miles east of the the Dnepr, approaching the Pavlograd area. Once again, due to insufficient numbers of trucks and infantry personnel carriers, the main body of infantry attached to the Soviet tank and mechanized corps was left far behind. While the Soviet tanks pushed forward, the infantry of the rifle divisions and slower heavy artillery formations were still consolidating the situation in the breakthrough area.[28] The lack of progress of these units was surely not helped by the great numbers of inexperienced infantry just integrated into the Soviet rifle divisions. The familiar Soviet problem of sustaining deep penetrations by mobile groups was still evident. The mechanized spearheads lost their tank strength due to attrition of armor and normal wear and tear. The problem of the lack of sufficient motorized infantry and heavy weapons was still not solved. Had a few normally equipped panzer divisions been available, it is likely that the Soviet spearheads would have been chopped off

Aftermath: 6. Armee Retreats from the Mius

and destroyed piecemeal. But there were no panzer divisions available except those that were mere remnants of their former strength. The Soviet penetrations were not as effective as they might have been because they continued to lose tank strength due to either mechanical and supply problems or German pockets of resistance. However, regardless of this situation, the prospect of mobile Soviet formations reaching the Dnepr before the German divisions were able to withdraw behind the river constituted a genuine crisis. All along the front of the two armies, Soviet attacks shattered German defensive positions. When a tank corps faltered, a mechanized corps or cavalry corps took its place, advancing through the stalled unit and continuing the attack.

In response to Manstein's urgent request of 7 September, in which he evidently successfully conveyed the seriousness of the situation to Hitler, the German leader met with Manstein at Zaporoshye. Also attending this meeting with Hitler were Kleist, commander of Heeresgruppe A, and the commander of 17. Armee in the Kuban, General Ruoff. Manstein explained again the desperate straits of Heeresgruppe Süd and the enormous numerical advantage of the Soviets. Hitler, evidently sufficiently impressed by the reports of Manstein and the other generals, agreed to allow Heeresgruppe Süd to withdraw toward the Dnepr if "absolutely necessary." The fact that Hitler did not recognize that the withdrawal was absolutely necessary at a point much earlier in the summer illustrated the degree to which he was out of touch with the situation as it existed. It is another example why the German commanders were forced into reacting too late with too little on the Eastern Front. By this date, of course, the question was not whether the German forces should withdraw, but whether they still could successfully withdraw at all. In order to help conduct the retreat to the Dnepr, Manstein again hoped to receive reinforcements from Heeresgruppe Mitte, which was in his mind the only way that he would be able to stop the Russians east of the river. Failure to reach the Dnepr before the Soviets took the main crossings and their invaluable bridges would constitute a disaster of the highest order. Manstein told Hitler that he needed additional forces to secure the main crossings as well as reinforcements to delay the Soviet pursuit of 6. Armee and 1. and 4. Panzerarmee.

Before leaving the meeting, Hitler promised Manstein that he would see to several measures that would alleviate the problems of Heeresgruppe Süd substantially. First, he agreed to order Heeresgruppe Mitte to assemble two more panzer divisions and two infantry divisions on Manstein's north flank and relieve pressure at that point by executing a counterattack on the north flank of the Soviet attack. Second, Hitler agreed to provide more divisions for Heeresgruppe Süd—if necessary, taking them from Kluge—in order to secure the Dnepr crossings. Manstein knew that if the Soviets took the bridges over the river, cutting off both supply and retreat, the destruction of the southern wing of the German Army in Russia was likely. In that event, the entire Eastern Front would collapse. Hitler also promised that he would evacuate the Kuban, thereby allowing the escape of 17. Armee and the use of these divisions in Heeresgruppe Süd's area of operations.[29]

After Hitler left the meeting, Manstein and his staff, much relieved that decisions had apparently been made to help the army group, ordered 6. Armee and 1. Panzerarmee to begin to withdraw to the west. It appeared that Heeresgruppe Süd would be able to conduct the withdrawal as it saw fit and the crossings of the Dnepr would be defended and held until the arrival of Manstein's tired and weakened divisions. This was not to be the case, however.

On the following day, it became apparent that the appropriate orders had not been issued, Hitler having either changed his mind or again delayed decisions that he did not want to make. Again the dictator abandoned thousands of his soldiers to their fate. There was no counterattack by Kluge on the northern flank. Kluge insisted that he could spare no more than three divisions although at the time he was under less pressure than Manstein. The only person who could have ordered Kluge to provide a few divisions, Hitler, remained unable or unwilling to unequivocally make that decision and issued contradictory orders to Kluge.

The race to the river was on, with some doubt as to who would get there first, the Germans or the Russians. The key bridges across the Dnepr were held only by security detachments and whatever scraps of units could be made available. If Soviet tanks reached them before 6. Armee and 1. Panzerarmee, the entire southern wing of the Eastern Front would be encircled. Disaster loomed for Heeresgruppe Süd.

The southern Ukraine east of the Dnepr was already lost irrrevocably before this point, after "Citadel" failed and 4. Panzerarmee and 8. Armee subsequently could not regain the territory lost to "Rumyanstev." But now, in addition to these ultimately decisive setbacks of the summer of 1943, the German armies east of the river faced the prospect of their utter destruction.

By the middle of the month, Heeresgruppe Mitte was being pushed back after a renewal of Soviet offensives in its sector. 9. Armee's front was penetrated by a Russian cavalry corps and 4. Armee expected an attack toward Smolensk at any time. Kluge's 2. Armee front was on the verge of collapse as well.

On 14 September, West Front's attack on Smolensk began and Kluge received the news that Manstein had ordered 4. Panzerarmee to begin its withdrawal toward the Dnepr. By that evening, convinced that he had no other choice, Kluge ordered both Model's 9. Armee and 2. Armee to retreat. The following day, after setbacks all along the front of both army groups, Hitler ordered Kluge and Manstein to meet with him again. At this meeting, he told Kluge to begin to conduct a slow pullback to the Dnepr in carefully executed phases of withdrawals. Manstein, although relieved that his army group was to be allowed to withdraw, faced a great challenge in pulling his armies out of their positions without precipitating a complete collapse. The 4. Panzerarmee, more mobile than the other armies, was able to fall back quickly. Beginning on 16 September, Hoth disengaged his divisions in two days and succeeded in restoring some order on his front. On the other hand, 1. Panzerarmee, 6. Armee and 8. Armee were all in various degrees of disarray and would have difficulty making the retreat to the river intact. There were only five crossings available to Heeresgruppe Süd across the wide Dnepr, which had bridges of sufficient strength to support tanks and other heavy weapons. These bridges were located at Cherkassy, Dnepropetrovsk, Kremenchung, Kiev, and Kanev. The military problems of the armies withdrawing to the Dnepr were increased by Hitler's insistence that they evacuate thousands of cattle and tons of supplies taken from the countryside in attempts to deny the Soviets food and other goods.

On 19 September, at the section of the Dnepr where the Pripet River joined the larger river, Soviet troops began to cross the river. At first, only small units or groups of individuals crossed over, floating on barrels, using boats or makeshift rafts and clamoring ashore against little German resistance. When the company-size or smaller units linked up with each other, narrow bridgeheads took shape on the western bank. On 20 September, mobile groups of Kalinin Front and Central Front penetrated Heeresgruppe Mitte on each flank and Kluge's gradual withdrawal turned into a precipitate retreat. Everywhere the Soviets pressed west as fast as they could, anxious to prevent the Germans from reaching the river and establishing a defensive position on the western bank.

Leading units of 3rd Guards Tank Army crossed the Dnepr on 22 September in small groups. From the east, Soviet engineers arrived and began to construct bridges, along with columns of infantry, tanks and artillery that gradually crawled toward the river as the army gathered itself. On 26 September, Voronezh Front built a bridgehead across the Dnepr and there were several small bridgeheads established by Steppe Front. To the east of the river, German troops fought and retreated to the west, while Soviet spearhead elements were already at the Dnepr. However, in spite of winning the race to the Dnepr at several points, the Russians were not able to bring enough infantry and artillery up to the river to keep the Germans from reaching the west bank.

In the last days of the month, Heeresgruppe Süd finally got the last of its battered divisions across the river. Once on the west bank, the weary troops spread out to either side, often too weak to eliminate even small Soviet bridgeheads. Shortly afterwards, Kluge's Heeresgruppe Mitte completed its withdrawal to a new defensive position named the Panther Line, which was generally behind the Sozh River east of the Dnepr. The most valuable portion of the Ukraine, the grain-rich southern area, with its enormous harvests of corn and wheat, was lost to the Germans and there was no possible prospect of regaining it. The staffs of Kluge's and Manstein's armies, having watched the ragged, exhausted German soldiers that trudged across the Dnepr bridges, were under no illusions regarding their ability to retake the Ukraine, although they hoped to be able to defend the Dnepr.

However, the German withdrawal began too late, because of Hitler's insistence on allowing no retreat until there was no other alternative. Even then, the divisions were often too weak or deficient in motor transport to conduct a organized withdrawal while in contact with the enemy. As a result, the Soviet tank spearheads were not to be delayed by the pitiful rear guard elements that opposed them. The T-34s, infantry clustered on their engine decks, broke through the German lines almost at will and motored to the west. Often they found undefended gaps between the retreating German divisions and encountered little resistance at all.

When the Russians reached the river ahead of the retreating German armies, Manstein did not have the strength to eliminate the bridgeheads, and thus, the Dnepr defensive position was penetrated before it was even occupied. Attempting to hold the territory east of the river, while lacking the strength to do so, cost the Germans men and equipment they could not afford and these losses doomed the defense of the river to failure. While the divisions of Manstein's and Kluge's armies were reduced to mere remnants, ruined by Hitler's insistence on holding militarily valueless ground or standing fast when it was operationally suicide to do so, the Russians brought up fresh or rebuilt reserves constantly. The Führer's orders to hold the southern Ukraine at all costs, the ruinous casualties of the summer of 1943 in the south and his interference with military operations during the period from July to August ultimately cost him the entire Ukraine and thereby the war.

CHAPTER 13

Conclusions and Review

GERMAN DEFEAT IN THE SOUTHERN UKRAINE

The summer of 1943 was a critical period in the Russo-German War and thus of the war as a whole. Despite their stunning successes in the early days of the war in the East, the Germans had failed to take Moscow or knock the Russians out of the war in 1941–42. After the losses sustained during the Stalingrad debacle, the Germans were able to stabilize the situation by the late winter. The brilliant counterattack at Kharkov, in March 1943, which was engineered by Manstein, gave the Germans one last opportunity to score a major strategic victory in the East.

By the summer of 1943, the last slim hope that the Germans had of winning the war was to force a stalemate in Russia. A strategic defeat of the Russians, resulting in a pause of sufficient duration to allow the transfer of major elements of the army to France, was Hitler's last hope. The German command anticipated that the invasion would come in 1944 and realized that there were simply not enough divisions, vehicles and fuel available to successfully conduct a two-front war. Three years of fighting against the Soviets bled the German nation of its manpower reserves. The casualties sustained in 1941–43 had an important effect on the war in the West, because the number of divisions that Hitler was able to keep in France were greatly reduced by the needs of the Eastern Front.

The losses of the German Army in Russia and the costly nature of combat on the Eastern Front prevented the Germans from stationing more than fifty combat divisions in France. This manpower situation was the direct result of the casualties inflicted on the Germans during 1941–43 by the Russian army. There were fifty-three German divisions spread out across France, Holland, and Belgium, including seven training divisions of little combat value. Of the remaining divisions, fifteen were static units without vehicles, some of which were fleshed out with Russian, Polish or Ukrainian conscripts of dubious value and fully twenty were newly formed divisions made up of overage reservists, Luftwaffe personnel, or fragments of units destroyed in Russia. Only four infantry divisions on the entire Western Front were combat experienced as entire units. All four had been devastated in Russia and were recovering from their losses. There were three parachute divisions of good fighting ability and eleven panzer or panzergrenadier divisions. Three of these were newly established and had never seen combat as a division. The other eight mobile divisions were rebuilding from ruinous losses suffered in Russia during the last half of 1943 and the winter of 1944. This included *Das Reich, Leibstandarte,* and 16. Panzergrendier-Division, which had been reorganized as a panzer division. It was now designated as 116. Panzer-Division.

Thus, the British and American armies that invaded France almost a year after the Kursk, Mius, and Bogodukhov battles directly benefited from the sacrifices of the Russian army in the previous three years.

OPERATION "CITADEL"

By mid-1943, a German victory in World War II was only possible if a stalemate was reached on the Eastern Front that allowed Hitler to transfer sufficient divisions to the West to defeat the invasion of the Western Allies. An Allied landing in France with Russia still in the war and active meant an inevitable loss of the war. Hitler hoped to engineer a stunning Soviet defeat in the southern Ukraine during midsummer of 1943 in order to force the Russians to halt offensive operations for a significant period of time.

The plan he chose to accomplish this objective was Operation "Citadel." The offensive was a great gamble given the condition of the German Army after two and a half years of war in Russia. It is doubtful whether even a decisive victory at Kursk would have accomplished the desired results. Certainly, the offensive would have had to have been completely successful in order to have inflicted losses of sufficient magnitude on the Red Army to force a static situation of any duration. Hitler agonized for months over the timing, preparations and whether to launch the attack at all. He postponed the offensive on several occasions. In spite of the doubts of Guderian, Model and others, Hitler chose to go ahead with "Citadel." Soviet plans for the summer of 1943 also centered around the Ukraine, with their main defensive effort as well as the most important planned counteroffensive operations being planned for the Orel-Kharkov area.

The concentration of Soviet forces in the sectors of Voronezh-Central Front—in particular, the strength of the strategic reserve, Steppe Front—leaves no doubt as to where the Soviet command felt the most critical operations of the summer would take place. Nearly one third of the total manpower available to the Russian army was concentrated either in or on the flanks of the Kursk salient Almost one half of all tanks and other armored vehicles of the Red Army were concentrated in the Kharkov-Orel area.[1] Rotmistrov's 5th Guards Tank Army alone had 600 to 650 tanks even before 2nd Tank Corps and 2nd Guards Tank Corps were attached to it for the battle at Prochorovka.

The ability to establish and conceal enormous strategic reserves was a characteristic of Soviet operational battles during the war in the East. The Germans were seldom able to detect their presence from the first winter of the war around Moscow. If such concentrations were detected, the information regarding them was incomplete. The result of the ability of the Russians to conceal enormous concentrations of troops and supplies was a series of nasty surprises for the Germans. During "Citadel," one new formation after the other arrived on the battlefield, appearing out of nowhere. The commander of 19. Panzer-Division made the following observation regarding this situation: "We knew too little about the strengthening of the Russians in this region (Oboyan and Korocha) prior to the beginning of the offensive.... We did not assume that there was even one fourth of what we had to encounter..."[2]

In contrast to the lack of German intelligence, due to Russian skill in concealing their intentions and capabilities, Stalin and his generals had very good intelligence regarding Hitler's plans for the summer of 1943 and the forces available to carry out the operations. The Soviets were not surprised by the German attack. In an analysis of the defeat of the summer offensive, Guderian reported to Hitler that "Surprise as a vital prerequisite for a successful panzer offensive was not achieved because the enemy was expecting the attack and was fully prepared to defend himself."[3] The common thread of Soviet intelligence and strategic planning runs through the events of the decisive summer of the war.

The three Eastern Front battles examined in this study—Prochorovka, the Mius and Bogodukhov—were key, interrelated events in the decisive fighting for possession of southern Ukraine in 1943 that began with the launching of the German offensive. There is a fascinating web of Soviet plans, deceptions and German response in the summer of 1943 that link each of the three battles to the other. These battles shaped the course of the war in the south Ukraine during the summer of 1943 and thus are important in the broader context of the war in Russia as a whole. At the end of August 1943, it became clear to all, perhaps even Hitler, that the Ukraine could not be held with shattered divisions and broken armies. The retreat to the Dnepr began, and with the abandonment of southern Ukraine, the war in the East—and thus the war as a whole—was irrevocably lost.

The study of these events illustrates the ultimately decisive strategic planning of the Soviets contrasted with the tactical superiority of the German Army. The Russians utilized their advantages, which were primarily a vastly superior industrial production capability and a large population base, in a manner that enabled them to win a war of attrition. The centralized Soviet state was mobilized for total war industrially, militarily and economically under the direction of Stalin. He ruthlessly sacrificed Soviet manpower and war material in whatever amount was necessary, in single-minded pursuit of one goal, the defeat of Nazi Germany. In contrast, under the direction of Hitler, a decentralized, compartmentalized German nation and military structure could not overcome the Soviet Union without a strategic plan that utilized the primary German advantage, which was a superbly trained military machine that was a tactically superior military force.

German tactical superiority during the first years of the war is clearly shown by the ability of the first-class panzer divisions of the SS and army to inflict catastrophic losses on Russian armored formations even when greatly outnumbered. This superiority continued essentially until the latter part of 1943. From that point on, German mobile division quality declined in general, while Soviet armored units steadily improved as a result of a number of factors. The dynamic Soviet programs of the study of war, intended to recognize its own shortcomings, transformed the Russian armored formations into high-quality units capable of defeating the German panzer divisions in 1944–45. The summer of 1943 was the last time that the majority of the German panzer and panzergrenadier divisions operated with a clear superiority on the Eastern Front. This advantage in quality is illustrated by the events of the summer at different points.

In two of the battles studied in this work, Prochorovka and Bogodukhov, a handful of German panzer divisions fought entire Soviet tank armies to a standstill and destroyed hundreds of Soviet tanks. The army and SS panzer divisions nearly destroyed 1st Tank Army and 5th Guards Tank Army during "Citadel." On 12 July, a single German panzer corps, Hausser's II. SS-Panzerkorps, met the main proportion of the 850 tanks belonging to Rotmistrov's 5th Guards Tank Army. The SS panzer divisions destroyed hundreds of Soviet tanks in one day of fighting. Rotmistrov's own account of the battle, published in a 1984 history of 5th Guards Tank Army, confirms this conclusion. In this book, he states that his army lost over 400 tanks to repairable damage by 13 July. He does not state how many were completely destroyed or not recoverable at the time.

On the Mius, five battered panzer divisions defeated an offensive by three Soviet armies and more than two entire mechanized corps. This was in spite of the fact that the three divisions of II. SS-Panzerkorps were involved in nearly two weeks of fighting during "Citadel" and were transferred to the Mius with little rest and few replacements.

In August, just after the fighting ended in the sector of 6. Armee, under command of III. Panzerkorps, several of the same German divisions literally destroyed 1st Tank Army and 5th Guards Tank Army a second time.

Tactical superiority, however, did not constitute a plan to achieve strategic or operational success over an opponent that could trade men and territory in order to gain time until attrition and improvements in force structure and command quality made their effect felt. The war in Russia and Germany's defeat clearly illustrated this fact. It is without doubt that the Russian military became a vastly improved engine of war during the war in the East. The improvements made by

Stalin's armies and officers were not the decisive factor in the war, however. Essentially, the numerical superiority in men and machines and the ability of the Russian nation to continue to fight after suffering enormous losses were decisive. The war was lost by Germany before the military improvements made by the Russians reached the point where its primary offensive weapons, the tank and mechanized corps, became equal to or better than the German panzer units. The summer of 1943 marked the last summer of German armored superiority in Russia. The events and long term affects of the battles in the south Ukraine in the summer of 1943 are reviewed below.

THE ROAD TO PROCHOROVKA

When 9. Armee failed to break through the Soviet tactical defenses, "Citadel" threatened to become a disaster. By 12 July, the date on which the battle in the south reached its climax, Model's attack had no hope of success on the northern shoulder. The defeat of 9. Armee, regardless of what happened in the south, meant that Germany had lost the war. However, while "Citadel" as a whole was a failure by 12 July, some degree of success was still possible in the south on that date. This was due for the most part to the fighting capabilities of the divisions of the army and SS, particularly the panzer divisions when wielded by commanders such as Manstein, Hoth, and Hausser. This was a factor that could not be controlled by Russian plans or deceptions. At Prochorovka, the tactical skill of German combat units, in this case the SS panzer divisions, threatened to create a breakthrough into the strategic depths of the salient. As a result, in spite of their many advantages, the battle of Kursk nearly ended in disaster for the Russians in the south.

By the third day of the battle of Kursk, in the south the worst fears of the Russians appeared possible. 7th Guards Army was shoved back across the Koren River by Armee-Abteilung Kempf's advance. 5th Guards Army was brought up and thrown against 4. Panzerarmee, and 69th Army moved southeast of Prochorovka and attempted to hold the line along the Donets River. After bitter fighting, it was clear that neither army could stop Hoth's advance although they significantly delayed Kempf's panzers. Katukov's 1st Tank Army, the operational mobile reserve in the south, was mangled by the panzer divisions of 4. Panzerarmee and by 11 July was a shadow of its former strength.

Conclusions and Review

It was apparent to the Soviet command that more armor was needed, the armor of Steppe Front's 5th Guards Tank Army, the strategic armored reserve in the Ukraine. The specter of German panzer corps penetrating Voronezh Front and moving against the flank and rear of Central Front while it was engaged fighting Model's army resulted in decisive reaction. On 9 July, Rotmistrov's army was ordered to assemble south of the Psel River in the Prochorovka area and prevent II. SS-Panzerkorps from capturing that town and crossing the Psel in force. The seriousness with which the Russians viewed the situation can be judged by the comments of Khrushchev when he stated that the Germans would reach Kursk if they weren't stopped south of the Psel–Oboyan–Prochorovka axis. The Soviets had little choice but to use their last reserves in a last-ditch attempt to stop the Germans from crossing the Psel in force.

On the night of 11 July, Rotmistrov's 5th Guards Tank Army, with 850 tanks, concentrated for an attack on a fifteen-kilometer front west and south of Prochorovka. Concerned by fears of the range and power of the 88mm guns mounted on the Tigers and not realizing how few of the heavy tanks were actually available to the Germans, Rotmistrov made the crucial tactical error of ordering his tanks to attack at high speed and drive straight at the SS divisions. His intention was to negate the advantage of the 88s by advancing toward the German tanks as quickly as possible and closing to point-blank range where the guns of the T-34s could penetrate even the armor of a Tiger.

In doing so, he condemned large numbers of his tank crews to death because the Russian tanks could not fire accurately while moving at high speed. German tanks, few of which were hit by the wild fire of the onrushing Soviet tanks, began retaliating as soon as the Russians began their charge across the open ground west of Prochorovka. Their accurate fire destroyed many tanks at long to medium range. The result was massive initial losses of Soviet armor in the sector between the Psel and the rail line west of Prochorovka. It appears from the reports of II. SS-Panzerkorps that the fighting in the sector defended by *Das Reich* was not characterized by reckless massed charges of Soviet armor. These reports indicate that the Soviets advanced in battle groups of tanks and infantry at many points along the line held by the division. However, Soviet tank losses were also high in this sector.

The fighting along the entire front resulted in the near destruction of 5th Guards Tank Army on 12 July 1943. The wrecks of hundreds of Soviet tanks littered the battlefield and Rotmistrov's army was reduced to a total of about 150 operational tanks by the following day. Soviet losses were so great that an initially skeptical Hausser arrived to inspect a sector of the battlefield to verify the reports of destroyed Soviet tanks that were claimed by his divisions.

On 13 July, Rotmistrov ordered his tanks to dig in and 5th Guards Tank Army never attempted any large scale armored operations for the remainder of the battle of Kursk. He may have been ordered not to engage in any offensive actions by Stalin, who was reportedly shocked when informed of the tank losses suffered by Rotmistrov's army after the first days of fighting. According to a letter to the author from Colonel David Glantz, it was rumored that Stalin made his displeasure known after the battle. He was said to have asked Rotmistrov, "What have you done to your magnificent tank army?" Not willing to risk further angering Stalin, it is possible that Rotmistrov realized that additional losses of armor would cost him the command of the army and so ordered his army to assume a defensive posture.

Following the battles of 12 July, Manstein held a temporary numerical superiority in armor in the Psel-Prochorovka area. As he possessed a still uncommitted panzer reserve, there were several offensive options still open to him. However, III. Panzerkorps' inability to advance and attack 5th Guards Tank Army's southern flank on 12 July was a great disappointment and a critical failure. The Russians delayed the link-up of III. Panzerkorps with II. SS-Panzerkorps elements until 14 July. This delay allowed Rotmistrov to attack Hausser's panzer divisions with his southern flank secure.

The failure of Breith's III. Panzerkorps resulted in a decisive weakening of the attack by II. SS-Panzerkorps on Prochorovka on 12 July. Instead of advancing toward the town on the right flank of *Leibstandarte*, *Das Reich* was forced to defend itself from attacks by 2nd Tank Corps and 2nd Guards Tank Corps. These attacks forced the division to defend its right flank and front instead of concentrating its efforts on capturing the town. Hausser's panzer corps was not able to conduct a concentrated attack on Prochorovka due to the efforts of these two Soviet tank corps. Had III. Panzerkorps been able to attack the southern flank of 5th Guards Tank Army as planned, the Russians may have been forced to commit 2nd and 2nd Guards Tank Corps against Breith's attack. In this event, it is possible that the Germans could have taken Prochorovka and completely destroyed Rotmistrov's army as well. However, the ferocious Russian counterattacks along the whole front of II. SS-Panzerkorps, despite enormous Russian losses, critically slowed the German advance toward Prochorovka. This lack of progress surely contributed to the decision that Adolf Hitler made on the following day.

He could see that II. SS-Panzerkorps had not taken the town and he received nothing but reports of tank losses from the panzer divisions of Kempf's army, Russian counterattacks and Model's defeat. It was evident that the German attack in the south slowed down everywhere on 12 July. Had Hitler received a report from Manstein that Hausser and Breith had successfully destroyed 5th Guards Tank Army and taken Prochorovka, the decisions that he subsequently made may have been different.

A VICTORY THROWN AWAY?

On 13 July, Hitler ordered Manstein and Kluge to meet with him. At this meeting, he explained that he intended to cancel "Citadel." Manstein reacted with dismay. It has been assumed that Manstein's account of the meeting with Hitler and his belief that Heeresgruppe Süd was on the verge of victory in the south on 13 July were postwar attempts to paint himself in a better light and place the entire blame for the failure of "Citadel" in the south on Hitler. Given the mistaken belief that the Germans had little suriving armor with which to renew the offensive, this seemed to be the only explanation for Manstein's statements. However, in fact, Manstein had local armor superiority, in both numbers and quality. In addition, he had an ace in the hole, XXIV. Panzerkorps. The situation was thus favorable for a renewed attack on 1st Tank Army and 5th Guards Tank Army, even given the failure of Breith's attack.

1st Tank Army, the Soviet operational armored reserve in Voronezh-Steppe Front's sector, was a shadow of its former strength.[4] On 11 July, Katukov's 31st Tank Corps suffered such heavy tank and officer losses that it panicked and retreated in disorder after a mauling by German armor. Much of his remaining armor was decimated during the fighting in the Psel bridgehead. Katukov's 6th Tank Corps had only fifty tanks still in action before the battle of Prochorovka, from a total of more than 200 on 4 July. The Soviets thus had no uncommitted armored reserves in the area, were in a defensive posture and had lost the option of manuever. In contrast, Manstein had several available options at this point. The entire XXIV. Panzerkorps could have been committed through the bridgehead over the Psel in an attack toward Kursk. A second possibility was the use of XXIV. Panzerkorps as reinforcement for *Das Reich*'s attack south of Prochorovka, with the objective of bypassing the town to the southeast before driving north again. In a third alternative course of action, the attack by III. Panzerkorps could have been reinforced with the reserve armor in an attempt to reach and cross the Psel east of Prochorovka.

It is clear that Manstein realized he had the opportunity to trap and destroy the remaining armor of two Soviet tank armies and he understood the importance of this development. In light of the subsequent use of these two tank armies in the main Russian counteroffensive of the summer, "Rumyantsev," Manstein's opinion was obviously correct. This statement can be made in the context of what is now known about Soviet plans for the summer in the south Ukraine, the facts regarding the battle of Prochorovka and the true purpose of the Soviet diversionary attacks at Izyum and the Mius.

In order to grasp the significance of the situation in the attack sector of 4. Panzerarmee following 12 July, and the impact that Hitler's cancelation of "Citadel" had on subsequent events in the south, one has to understand that accepted accounts of the number of tanks lost by the Germans, in particular the SS divisions, are a myth. In spite of this, in the final analysis, tank losses by either side were not the key factor that determined the cancellation of the offensive toward Kursk in the south.

It is instructive to remember that Manstein was not alone in his estimation of the seriousness of the threat posed by a successful offensive by 4. Panzerarmee and Armee-Abteilung Kempf. The statements made by Nikita Khrushchev in regard to the likelihood of the Germans taking Kursk if they were not stopped south of the Psel adds support to the opinion of Manstein. It is all the more significant because it came from the Soviet side of the table. In effect, this statement tacitly admits that the Russians had played their last card in the south when Rotmistrov's army was brought up from reserve. When taken in the context of the facts of the situation at the Psel on 13 July, Manstein's belief that some degree of success was in his grasp rings a great deal more likely than has been previously believed. He places the blame for the loss of a possible victory in the south squarely on Hitler's shoulders, and that is where it belongs.

In spite of the complete lack of surprise, the collapse of the northern attack, the appearance of unexpectedly large Soviet strategic reserves and German intelligence failings, Manstein's divisions were in position to deliver at least a partial victory on 13 July. There is, at the very least, a good chance that had he been given the freedom to act as he saw fit, the battle would have had a different ending. In the final analysis, it was the decisions made by Hitler on the day following Prochorovka that doomed the German Army to defeat in the south.

Renewed attacks by II. SS-Panzerkorps, supported by XXIV. Panzerkorps, may have disrupted the Soviet plans for use of Central Front's armored reserve against Heeresgruppe Mitte. The timing of the commitment of 3rd Guards Tank Army and 4th Tank Army against Heeresgruppe Mitte seems to be at least partially related to the situation in the south. Although both tank armies mentioned were available for use, neither was actually committed until the night of 18–19 July, after some wrangling among the Soviet command about where they were to be used. This was the day after II. SS-Panzerkorps evacuated the Psel bridgehead. What effect a critical change in Soviet fortunes in the south would have had on the use of these two tank armies will never be known. At the very least, the Soviet conduct of the counteroffensive in the north could have been modified to some extent. It can be seen that had the Germans broke through the Russian defenses at the Psel and reached Kursk, this event would have had serious consequences that may have affected Soviet plans for the summer. Stalin may have been forced to transfer one or both of the Soviet tank armies from the northern sector and use them to stop the German attack in the south. There would have also been other ramifications as well.

A successful German drive across the Psel and on to Kursk would have cut many of the lines of communication and supply to five infantry armies in the western section of the bulge. The critical manpower situation in the German infantry divisions may well have kept them from establishing a solid enough line to prevent the majority of Russian personnel from filtering back east or north. However, without fuel, it can be assumed that many tanks, vehicles and artillery pieces would have been left behind. This would have represented a major setback for the Russians as enormous numbers of divisions would have been in no shape to conduct combat operations for some time. Most serious would have been the loss of the two tank armies around Prochorovka.

The Russian powers of recuperation were vast but they were not limitless. The destruction of Katukov's and Rotmistrov's armies would have been a serious blow to Stalin's offensive plans in southwest Ukraine in the summer of 1943. Replacing large numbers of tanks in a short time was routinely done by the Soviets and crews were always found somehow, but replacing the entire command and support structure of an army is another thing. Without these two formations, Operation "Rumyantsev" would either have been postponed or carried out with different forces which would necessarily have been taken from another operational area.

A limited German success in the south thus could have had far-reaching effects on the conduct of the war in the east for the remainder of the summer and possibly longer, if not the final result of the war. The precise length of time it would have taken the Soviets to recover from a setback of this magnitude remains an unknown factor. The worst-case scenario for the Allies, a stalemate on the Russian Front lasting through the summer of 1944, was probably beyond the capabilities of the Germans once the attack on the northern flank failed. However, even a lull of several months could have allowed the Germans the opportunity to partially rebuild their strength after the bloodletting suffered by their divisions during "Citadel." They may even have been able to transfer a few more divisions to the West and tank reserves could have been built up because Albert Speer's reorganization of German war industry began to bear fruit in late 1943 and early 1944.

But the German manpower base would have remained inadequate to replace losses on the scale suffered in Russia. It is logical to assume that the Germans would have been in much better shape to resist the Russian counteroffensives along the length of the front than they were in the summer of 1943 immediately after the bloodbath of Kursk. However, it is likely that this fact would only have postponed the inevitable Götterdämmerung in Germany. The road to Berlin would have been paved with many thousands of dead Soviet soldiers who otherwise survived the war, but the final result would have been the same.

The lesson of the summer of 1943 is that tactical superiority, weapon quality and a high level of training does not constitute strategy. These factors are not necessarily enough to win a conflict against a determined enemy when the elements of time, numerically superior forces and the effects of attrition come into play. In modem warfare, assuming a large-scale non-nuclear conflict, tactical superiority is not sufficient to deliver a victory if employed without a long-term strategic plan developed with absolutely realistic, attainable goals and a centralized, unified military and national effort. This is particularly so when the opponent has a clear strategic plan designed to maximize his chances of winning by utilizing whatever advantages he possesses. In the case of the Eastern Front during World War II, the Soviet army, commanded by a constantly improving centralized command structure, overcame the tactically superior German Army through utilization of the advantages of the Soviet Union. These necessary qualities were enormous industrial strength, large human reserves, and the iron will necessary to sacrifice the lives and material of the nation in whatever quantities were necessary to attain victory.

PROCHOROVKA AND POSTWAR MYTH

A great deal of attention has been focused on the SS panzer divisions and their performance at Prochorovka by most accounts dealing with the history of the Eastern Front. It has long been an accepted belief that Hausser's II. SS-Panzerkorps lost hundreds of its tanks to the valiantly charging T-34s of Rotmistrov's 5th Guards Tank Army who raced in among the Tigers and Panthers and destroyed the SS heavy tanks in close combat, ramming them if necessary in brave, fatal gestures of sacrifice. With the loss of 300 or 400 panzers, including 70 or 100 Tigers (depending on the account), the SS divisions were driven from the field of battle, leaving their destroyed tanks scattered all over the battlefield. On the following day, the battle of Kursk was over, a resounding Russian victory, due to the resurgent Soviet tank force which had thus proved its superiority in combat. While very dramatic, essentially none of the above paragraph is true.

Almost without exception, accounts of the battle of Prochorovka quote similar figures pertaining to SS panzer losses, mentioning large numbers of destroyed Tiger and Panther tanks. The records of II. SS-Panzerkorps and 4. Panzerarmee, which document the daily tank strength of each division by type of tank, clearly show that the largest percentage of armor lost by Hausser's divisions took place in the days before Prochorovka. From a 4 July maximum strength of 327 (plus 25 to 30 command tanks), the number of operational SS tanks declined to 211 and 21 command tanks by 11 July. This is a loss of 139 tanks, approximately 35 percent of the 5 July corps strength.

The records of 4. Panzerarmee and II. SS-Panzerkorps show that the three SS divisions possessed a total of 163 panzers on 13 July, the day after the battle. This is a total net loss of only 48 tanks, but German losses were higher than that figure. *Totenkopf* and *Leibstandarte* lost a total of 62 tanks during the battle. The losses of *Das Reich* are more difficult to determine because the division had more tanks on the day after the battle than it did the day before. Whether this was due to receiving a few new tanks or repaired vehicles returning to action is unknown. If we make the assumption that it lost approximately 20 to 25 tanks while fighting southwest of Prochorovka, which is probably high, we can see that II. SS-Panzerkorps lost about 70 to 80 tanks on 12 July. Most, if not all, of these tanks that were repairable were likely recovered because II. SS-Panzerkorps remained in possession of the battlefield until the night of 17–18 July. While the above estimation of German tank losses can be debated, it is obviously more accurate than the often quoted figure of 400 tanks. This number has long been accepted as fact because it appeared to explain the failure of the Germans to defeat the Russians at Prochorovka.

If there were actually 400 tanks removed from the Prochorovka area after the battle, it is almost certain that the great majority of them were Russian. Besides the records of II. SS-Panzerkorps, there is information from Russian sources that tend to support this conclusion. According to Colonel David Glantz, in *From the Don to the Dnepr*, 5th Guards Tank Army was reduced to less than 200 tanks (he gives

Conclusions and Review 487

the figure as 150 to 200) on 13 July, from a strength of 850. This represents losses of approximately 650 tanks. This figure is supported by Rotmistrov's own account of the battle, published in 1984, in which he states that by 13 July his army had 400 tanks out of action with repairable damage. This total does not include tanks that were damaged but not recovered or the number of vehicles that were total losses.[5] Given that SS tank losses amounted to about 70 to 80 vehicles, it is thus plain to see whose tanks made up the majority of the hulks removed from the blasted earth of the battlefield. It is also logical, given the political situation in the Soviet Union in the postwar period and Khrushchev's role as the chief political officer in south Ukraine during the battle of Kursk, why these destroyed tanks were identified as German vehicles in postwar accounts.

A second mistaken belief regarding the SS panzer divisions at Kursk is that the three divisions employed great numbers of Tiger and Panther tanks at Prochorovka. The best German tank of the war, the Panzer V or Panther, was in service in time for Kursk, but none were issued to the SS panzer divisions. All of the new tanks were under command of the elite army division *Grossdeutschland*. *Das Reich* was able to add a Panther battalion in late August 1943, but *Totenkopf* did not receive its Panthers until later than that date, and so there were no SS Panthers lost at Prochorovka. There were, of course, SS Tigers in action during the battle. However, postwar accounts of the battle accepted Soviet reports that the II. SS-Panzerkorps lost 70 to 100 Tiger tanks at Prochorovka, whereas in reality on 11 July the two divisions that fought west of the town, *Das Reich* and *Leibstandarte*, had only 5 Tigers in action. *Totenkopf* reported having 10 Tigers on 11 July, but that division's armor was primarily involved in the fighting for possession of the Psel bridgehead and was north of the river. Since there were only 15 of the heavy tanks still in operation on 12 July, it is not possible that 70, much less 100, SS Tigers were lost during the battle.

Another myth essentially resulted from the acceptance of the above figures, among other factors, and thus seemed to be a logical conclusion. The SS panzer divisions have been judged to be inferior to the panzer divisions of the German Army and, as such, a waste of superb personnel and equipment. The losses of SS tanks at Prochorovka have been cited in support of this argument. In reality, II. SS-Panzerkorps on 12 July destroyed approximately eight Soviet tanks for every SS tank lost. If the measure of excellence is a function of the ratio of friendly tanks lost compared to enemy tank destruction, the SS panzer divisions performed extremely well. In fact, tank loss figures seem to contradict the belief in the superiority of the army panzer divisions.

Most of the army divisions lost a much higher percentage of their tanks than the Waffen SS divisions during the battles of Kursk. This is particularly true of Kempf's III. Panzerkorps and, to a lesser extent, XXXXVIII. Panzerkorps. *Grossdeutschland*, which possessed 300 tanks on 4 July, had only 91 left by 13 July. Many of these losses were among the 200 Panther tanks of 10. Panzer Brigade, which was attached to the division to strengthen it for "Citadel." However, heavy casualties, tank losses, and equipment destruction on the Eastern Front are a poor yardstick to judge skill, combat effectiveness, and training. High losses of men and machines were the norm for all German divisions that saw extensive combat in Russia during the bitter fighting of World War II. If competency of divisions and officers of the German armed forces that served in the East was evaluated only by the number of men or tanks lost in combat, then scarcely any unit or commander would have been considered adequate.

Study of the three battles covered by this work supports the argument that the SS panzer divisions were remarkably resilient, tactically excellent and dangerous opponents even after weeks of heavy fighting. During the summer of 1943, these divisions fought nearly continuously in difficult terrain conditions for months at a time and often, if not always, fought an enemy that had the advantage of enormous numerical superiority. When utilized correctly, such as at Prochorovka or Bogodukhov, these units consistently knocked out large numbers of Soviet tanks, often seemingly accomplished the impossible and were responsible for the destruction of many Soviet units and untold tens of thousands of Russian war dead. At the Mius, *Das Reich* and *Totenkopf*, although utilized clumsily, fought with determination and great sacrifice, providing the decisive breakthroughs that rectified the situation in the sector of 6. Armee.

6. ARMEE AND THE MIUS BATTLES

The battles of Hollidt's 6. Armee were a microcosm of the German situation on the Eastern Front and the problems faced by the Ger-

Conclusions and Review

man Army in Russia by mid-1943. Massive Soviet numerical superiority was pitted against a German Army that was characterized by understrength infantry divisions and lack of sufficient armored divisions. Nevertheless, Hollidt's army survived the attack by Tolbukhin's Southern Front through dogged determination, skilful conduct of defensive operations and the use of every last resource available to it. The German defensive effort was helped immeasurably by the intelligence available to 6. Armee due to the intentional lack of normal *maskirovka* procedures by Tolbukhin's Southern Front during the build-up of forces preceding the attack. It was possible for the Germans to detect the probable location of the main Soviet effort at Dmitrievka and prepare for it. Even after the battle began, 6. Armee showed a marked talent for anticipating Russians attacks and positioning its reserves at the correct time and place.

The overwhelming strength available to Tolbukhin and his subsequent failure to defeat Hollidt's weak army underscore the tactical superiority of the German Army that still existed in 1943. The failure of the Soviet attack during July and early August also is evidence of poor planning or overconfidence by the Soviet front commander. It seems apparent that if Tolbukhin had pressed his attack strongly at two or more separate points, Hollidt would have been faced with insurmountable problems. If the Russians had mounted determined diversionary attacks during the first days of the battle at multiple sectors of the front, it is unlikely that 6. Armee could have mastered the situation. However, Tolbukhin made only halfhearted attacks north and south of the main effort at Dmitrievka-Kuibyshevo and abandoned each when they met stubborn resistance. The obvious relocation of the main Soviet forces in the center allowed Hollidt to pull reserves from the flanks to reinforce the Dmitrievka area and hold the Russian attack at bay until reserves reached the area. This was in spite of the fact that the Russians had an enormous advantage in infantry and armor strength.

Tolbukhin initially had an entire mechanized corps at his disposal, with approximately 200 tanks, of which 120 were T-34s. 32nd Independent Tank Brigade was also on hand with about 50 tanks, although probably most of these vehicles were T-60s and not the heavier T-34s. The only German armor on hand initially was several assault gun battalions. The army reserve, 16. Panzergrenadier-Division, was in action by the second day of the battle. However, it possessed only 36 Panzer IIIs and IVs. Later, 23. Panzer-Division, a division of XXIV. Panzerkorps, Manstein's Heeresgruppe Süd panzer reserve, was sent to the 6. Armee area, having about 60 tanks on 17 July. Within days, 4th Guards Mechanized Corps arrived at the front, with an additional 200 or more Soviet tanks. All told, the Russians employed more than 450 tanks during the battle for the Mius line. This great superiority in numbers was partially negated when Tolbukhin dispersed his armor in small groups to support the infantry attacks. The one large-scale armored attack, that of 22 July, failed due to the insufficient depth of the bridgehead and astute placement of a blocking position of German armor and antitank guns, supported by strong artillery. The correct anticipation of the time and place of the Soviet attack by 6. Armee was a key factor.

Hollidt conducted the defensive operations of his army well but showed less skill in the proper use of armor. 6. Armee's conduct of the counterattacks on 18–19 July by 16. Panzergrenadier and 23. Panzer-Divisions and, later, the use of II. SS-Panzerkorps' divisions were questionable. On 18 July, Manstein suggested that Hollidt wait for the arrival of 23. Panzer-Division and use it and 16. Panzergrenadier-Division in mobile defensive operations. Hollidt ignored this advice and attacked with 16. Panzergrenadier-Division on 18 July, supported only by weak infantry attacks. The operation was too poorly supported to accomplish much except for the destruction of most of the division's tanks. Hollidt's determination to regain the old main line of defense by counterattacks in whatever strength available was sound tactically in the short run because he may have believed that only by regaining prepared positions was it possible for his army to hold its ground. However, the attacks resulted in a waste of armor, as Manstein had foreseen. The use of the SS panzer divisions in the counterattacks on 30–31 July was also less than skilful.

These attacks have all the earmarks of a hurried and poorly prepared operation. The three divisions were ordered to attack over poor terrain for the use of armor and without consideration of the Soviet defensive strength. The result was a catastrophic loss of tanks, primarily due to track and running gear damage in the minefields. Hollidt evidently did not feel that he would be allowed to have II. SS-Panzerkorps for a long period of time because he knew Manstein would soon require Hausser's divisions for the defense of Kharkov-Belgorod. His decision to attack from the northwest quadrant of the battlefield was thus not based on proper principles of the use of armor but was launched as it was because it was the quickest route of approach for an attack. Otto Weidinger's account of the meeting between Hollidt, Hausser and Manstein reflects the concern of Manstein that the panzer divisions would be mauled too severely to be effective in the coming battles around Kharkov.

It also appears that Hollidt was willing to accept severe casualties when they were suffered by SS divisions but felt differently about an army panzer division. On the second day, he transferred 3. Panzer-Division to the control of 6. Armee, pulled it out of the line and designated it as the army reserve under command of XXIV. Panzerkorps.

It is interesting to note that Stadler's properly planned attack on Hill 203.4 was successful when the earlier, hurriedly launched attacks failed at all points. Stadler requested that he be allowed to conduct a proper reconnaissance and carefully organized his attack. On the following day, the attack penetrated the main Soviet defensive position successfully. Organized defensive resistance quickly fell apart on the hill although XXIV. Panzerkorps failed to advance in time to properly support the attack. Regiment *Der Führer* held the hill until the panzers of *Das Reich* penetrated the Olkhovchik and 16. Panzergrenadier-Division also fought its way into the valley. At that time, the Soviet line was pierced in too many places and Tolbukhin no longer had enough armor to restore the situation. The subsequent withdrawal of the Soviets was a tactical victory for 6. Armee, although, unknown to the German command, Tolbukhin had won a strategic victory of much greater importance.

THE BATTLES FOR THE MIUS: A DECISIVE USE OF SOVIET DECEPTION?

The most important Soviet objective of the Mius operation was essentially reached before the fighting even began, when shortly after 10 July, the build-up around Dmitrievka became known to Hitler and the seed of impending crisis was planted. Undoubtedly, the clear evidence of the Soviet preparations to attack on the Mius and at Izyum, combined with Hitler's concern over the situation in Sicily and with the crisis north of Orel, was a primary reason for his orders on 13

July. Within days of Hitler's conference with Manstein and Kluge on that date, the withdrawal of II. SS-Panzerkorps from the Prochorovka area, *Grossdeutschland*'s transfer to Kluge and the use of XXIV. Panzerkorps divisions at Izyum and the Mius ended any chance the Germans had of achieving even a partial victory in the south. The most significant result of the operations along the Mius River beginning from 10 July was that five Heeresgruppe Süd panzer divisions ultimately ended up on the Mius River instead of remaining available for action in the Prochorovka-Psel sector.

The battles of 6. Armee on the Mius River and the counterattack of II. SS-Panzerkorps can be considered to be an integral part of the battle of Kursk, although it has not been recognized as such before now. Only after the strategic importance of this diversionary operation becomes clear from study of material concerning Soviet military deception operations during the latter stages of "Citadel" is this fact apparent. Just as 4. Panzerarmee and Armee-Abteilung Kempf began to battle their way through the Soviet armies south of the Psel on 7 July, the preparations made by the Soviets for the two planned diversionary attacks became immediately apparent to the Germans. This happened because the build-up at the Mius and Izyum were conducted with the intentional absence of any *maskirovka* measures. In his fascinating book on Soviet *maskirovka* operations, *Soviet Military Deception in the Second World War*, Glantz addressed this seemingly peculiar fact and the important relationship these operations had on the German conduct of the "Citadel" offensive in the south after Prochorovka:

> The Southern and Southwestern Fronts and their component armies were experienced combat formations, commanded by effective commanders. They were subject to the same regulations that governed the use of other Soviet forces. Within the context of improving Soviet *maskirovka* techniques the Mius and Izyum operations were aberrations. Here, at a time when Soviet fronts elsewhere over a considerable period successfully masked major portions of their force, the Germans had a crystal clear picture of what was going to occur.
>
> The explanation for these aberrations rests in the strategic context in which the operations occurred. Viewed out of con-

text, the two operations were mere clumsy and unsuccessful sideshows. In context, however, the operations were essential cogs in a strategic plan without which the plan might have failed.[6]

Thus, at the time when the "Citadel" offensive in the south was fast approaching its climax, the command of Heeresgruppe Süd received a deluge of reports about the concentrations of Soviet armored forces at Izyum and the Mius. Neither of the diversionary attacks produced a tactical victory, although each freely spent resources Stalin had in abundance, the lives of his infantrymen and hundreds of tanks. This constitutes stark and compelling confirmation of the cold-blooded, pragmatic conduct of war as practiced by the Soviets under Stalin. It was recognized that a serious effort had to be made at each spot in order for the deception to work. If the concentration of forces appeared too weak, the Russians risked the chance that the Germans may have concluded outside reinforcement was not necessary. Similarly, an attack that was quickly defeated in the opening stages would not have posed a sufficient threat to pull panzer reserves out of the critical Psel-Prochorovka area. This meant that blood had to be spilled in sufficient quantity to seriously threaten the Germans at both Izyum and the Mius. It was not necessary for either attack to succeed tactically, although success would have been cheerfully accepted. It was for this reason that Tolbukhin could not wait to have 4th Guards Mechanized Corps on hand when he first attacked. Although the failure to concentrate his forces was perceived to be an error by the Germans on the part of Tolbukhin, in the context of the purpose of his attack, it was not. On the contrary, he had little choice given the critical turn of events at Prochorovka from 12 to 16 July. The reason for his seemingly hasty use of insufficient armor is obvious when considering both the staggering losses of tanks suffered by 1st Tank Army and 5th Guards Tank Army and, most importantly, Southern Front's primary objective, the diversion of armor from the southern flank of the salient.

In that sense, the attack by Southern Front over the Mius may have been the most successful of the *maskirovka* measures that the Soviet utilized in the summer of 1943. At the worst possible time for the Germans, Hitler responded to these real, but potentially less than critical Soviet threats by making the absolutely worst decisions he could have made, ignoring the sound advice of Manstein. Within days, the Führer ensured the defeat of his southern wing by removing eight panzer divisions from the command of Heeresgruppe Süd by 17 July. Thus, the diversionary attacks of Southern and Southwestern Fronts succeeded to a degree that must have been beyond any hopes of the Soviet command.

It is not surprising then that on 1 August, Marshall A. M. Vasilevsky appeared at Tolbukhin's HQ to congratulate him on the successful conduct of the operation on a day when Tolbukhin's army was withdrawing back across the Mius in apparent defeat.[7] As a key overseer of all that went on in the planning for the operations during and subsequent to Operation "Citadel," Vasilevsky was in a unique position to understand the vital importance of the Mius and Izyum operations. He had also been given the assignment of overseeing the defense of Prochorovka on 11 July. Given this fact, it is obvious why he turned up at Southern Front HQ on 1 August to convey his appreciation to Tolbukhin for a job well done. Only in the context of *maskirovka* operations and the importance of the diversion of German panzer forces could the battles at the Mius River be considered a successful operation. Tolbukhin was congratulated because he had carried out his assignment perfectly.

THE BATTLES SOUTH OF BOGODUKHOV

The series of complex battles south and southwest of Bogodukhov pitted the forces of III. Panzerkorps against overwhelming numbers of Soviet forces. The four German panzer divisions of the corps, along with some infantry support, fought two entire Soviet tank armies as well as major elements of several rifle armies. These battles began in the first days of August 1943 and continued thoughout the month. While the fighting for the possession of Kharkov raged to the east, III. Panzerkorps fended off the attempts of 1st Tank Army, 27th Army, 5th Guards Tank Army and 6th Guards Army to penetrate to and cut the Poltava-Kharkov railroad line south of Bogodukhov.

The main Soviet armored forces that spearheaded "Rumyantsev" were 1st Tank Army and Rotmistrov's 5th Guards Tank Army, the armored reserves that Manstein had pleaded with Hitler to be allowed to finish off after Prochorovka. These two Russian tank armies were old enemies of the Waffen SS panzer divisions as they had fought against each other at Prochorovka and in the Psel bridgehead.

In the fighting that took place on both sides of the Merla and Merchik Rivers, the superiority of the German panzer divisions was clearly evident, in spite of being involved in combat operations almost continuously since 5 July. While *Wiking* and 3. Panzer-Division conducted primarily defensive operations, *Das Reich* and *Totenkopf* repeatedly blunted the attacks of Soviet elements south of the rivers and Bogodukhov. As at Prochorovka, the Russians enjoyed tremendous numerical superiority in tanks. Both 1st Tank Army and 5th Guards Tank Army began the operation with over 500 tanks each, while the SS divisions never had more than about 30 to 50 tanks each at any time during August. In spite of this, all Soviet attempts to penetrate to the railroad line were repulsed with bloody losses in men and tremendous loss of tanks. Katukov's 1st Tank Army thrusts south of the Merchik were repeatedly cut off and destroyed by III. Panzerkorps. The attempts by Rotmistrov's army to penetrate to the rail line from east of Bogodukhov were frustrated by 3. Panzer-Division and *Wiking*, with key defensive fighting by elements of *Das Reich*.

Totenkopf executed a masterful attack that cut off elements of infantry and armor from 27th and 6th Guards Army south of Krasnokutsk and then rolled down the line of supply toward Kolomak, south of Konstantinovka. Subsequent attacks encircled disorganized elements of several Russian divisions and destroyed major portions of them after brief fighting. Subsequently, *Totenkopf* drove to the Merla and forced a crossing of that river and linked up with 4. Panzerarmee spearheads at Parchomovka. However, when *Grossdeutschland* was forced to withdraw from that town by Soviet pressure on its northern flank, this success could not be followed up.

Das Reich also conducted successful counterattacks south of the Merchik. It defeated the full strength of an entire Soviet tank corps supported by additional armor and a rifle corps south of Bogodukhov, driving the Soviets back on both sides of Gavrishi. Not only did the division drive back the Soviet attack, it continued to gain ground north of Gavrishi and also to the southwest of Bogodukhov. In support of Regiment *Eicke* and *Totenkopf* Tigers, elements of *Das Reich* took the town of Nikitovka and turned back continuous armored thrusts by the Soviets west of that town. From 14 to 16 August, a panzer battle group supported *Totenkopf*'s attack toward Konstantinovka and Kolomak and reached Krasnokutsk, securing the right flank of *Totenkopf*. Before the panzer group could cross the river, it was recalled and sent to counter a renewed attack by Rotmistrov's 5th Guards Tank Army west of Kharkov. There the division met Rotmistrov's remaining tanks and after two days of fighting turned back this attack as well, inflicting heavy armor losses on 5th Guards Tank Army. During this fighting south of Bogodukhov, battlegroups of the division were repeatedly detached in order to restore crisis situations in the defensive sectors of 3. Panzer-Division and *Wiking*.

Both *Wiking* and 3. Panzer-Division held the line around Zolochev against the assaults of 5th Guards Tank Army and did not give up their positions until the army was forced to withdraw after the loss of Kharkov. The entire strength of Rotmistrov's army was employed in the Zolochev area in attacks against the salient held by these two divisions. The losses inflicted upon the Soviets eventually forced Rotmistrov to pull back from Zolochev and attack at another point because of the failure to crack the defensive line manned by these two divisions.

It was primarily due to the efforts of the divisions of III. Panzerkorps that the gap torn into the German line between 4. Panzerarmee and Armee-Abteilung Kempf was first limited and then closed. In spite of the greatly superior forces available to the Russians, they were not able to execute a decisive breakthrough south and southwest of Bogodukhov. This evidence conclusively illustrates the fact that the SS divisions were not destroyed at Prochorovka. Even though *Das Reich* and *Totenkopf* were in near continuous combat throughout July and August, they retained the will and ability to fight and defeat Russian armor even when outnumbered by factors of five to one or greater. Although not all of the Soviet tanks that were lost during "Rumyantsev" were knocked out in the fighting against III. Panzerkorps, hundreds were lost in the fighting around Bogodukhov.

THE WAFFEN SS PANZER DIVISIONS AFTER THE SUMMER OF 1943

For the remainder of the war after Kursk and the battles that immediately followed, Hitler often used the veteran SS panzer divisions, as well as the newer SS armored divisions, as his "fire brigades." When a crisis arose, particularly on the Eastern Front, more often than not the SS panzers were sent in, combined with army formations or with other SS units. He viewed the SS divisions as more reliable in terms of obedience to orders and in having that key ingredient that he believed in more than any other, the will to fight and endure and, if need be, die according to his orders. In addition to the first four SS panzer divisions, there were three other full-strength panzer divisions by late 1943. These SS compiled a respectable combat record on both the Eastern and Western Fronts after Kursk. The 9. SS-Panzer-Division *Hohenstaufen* and its sister division, 10. SS-Panzer-Division *Frundsberg*, were first used in Russia early in 1944, where both were under command of Hausser during battles around Tarnopol. Later in the year, the divisions were transported west to France. During the battles in France and the subsequent retreat, both divisions were battered severely and were withdrawn for refitting at Arnhem. The remnants of the divisions saw heavy fighting in battles with Allied paratroops during Operation "Market-Garden."

A unique SS division, built around veteran SS cadre withdrawn from *Leibstandarte*, was activated in early 1943 and began training in Belgium in February of that year. This was 12. SS-Panzer-Division *Hitlerjugend*. The personnel of the division were mainly sixteen-to-eighteen-year-old former Hitler Youth members. It was commanded by thirty-five-year-old Brigadeführer Fritz Witt, a former regimental commander from 1. SS-Panzer-Division *Leibstandarte*. Although this division sustained upwards of 60 percent casualties in fighting against Allied divisions in Normandy, it retained its cohesion and fighting spirit. The young soldiers of *Hitlerjugend*, led by hardened SS veterans, established a formidable fighting reputation in the bitter battles of Normandy fighting against Canadian divisions.

The panzer divisions of the Waffen SS won 71 percent of the Knight's Crosses awarded to Waffen SS personnel during the war. The number of Knight's Crosses awarded to *Leibstandarte* personnel was fifty-two while *Das Reich* had seventy-two, *Totenkopf* forty-six, and *Wiking* fifty-four. The second wave of SS panzer formations won their share of awards as well, with *Nordland* having twenty-seven Knight's Cross winners, *Hitlerjugend* fifteen, *Frundsberg* thirteen, and *Hohenstaufen* twelve.

Prior to the Kharkov and Kursk battles, the panzer divisions of the SS had been counted upon as good-quality mobile units that provided additional offensive mechanized striking power in combination with army panzer divisions during the 1941 and 1942 summer offensives in Russia. After Kursk, that role changed as a result of the loss of strategic initiative by the German Army on the Eastern Front. From that point of the war until the end, the role of the mobile divisions of the SS was to fight endless delaying actions or launch desperate counterattacks against the vastly superior numbers of Allied men and tanks on both fronts. The dazzling sweep of the summer campaigns of 1941 and 1942 was never regained, although every now and again, like the counterattack of *Totenkopf* in the Konstantinovka-Kolomak drive, it was like the "old days" once more, and SS panzers swept all before them. This was the exception, however. In place of the former great offensives came long months of constant retreat. The divisions regrouped to counterattack again and again, suffering from the inevitable heavy casualties of this type of combat.

The tough, battle-hardened divisions retreated, fought, and retreated once more, tenaciously maintaining their will to fight. The quality divisions remained dangerous opponents until the end of the war, led by young, aggressive officers who had been forged by years of fighting experience on the Eastern Front into hard, ruthless men, practiced in carrying out warfare as they learned it in Russia. By 1944, however, the splendid manpower that had characterized the rank and file of the Waffen SS elite divisions in the early years was gone. In the end, during the fighting in Hungary around Lake Balaton and the final days of the war, even the old dash was finally gone from the survivors, crushed by the bitter realization that the war was lost and the deaths of their comrades had been in vain. Guderian commented on this last great counteroffensive in the East, spearheaded by several SS divisions, the attempt of 6. SS-Panzerarmee to break the siege of Budapest in January 1945: "Hitler expected great results from this attack. . . . I was skeptical since very little time had been allowed for its preparation and neither the troops nor the commanders possessed the same drive as in the old days."

The accomplishments of the Waffen SS divisions during the last months contributed to a prolongation of the war and inflicted suffering and death on the Allied armies of both fronts. This fact was not lost on the Russians. At the end, the Waffen SS divisions made every attempt to surrender to the British or Americans. They were under no illusion as to their likely fate if they were captured by the Russians. In the case of the men and officers of 3. SS-Panzer-Division *Totenkopf*, even surrender to the Western armies did not keep them out of the hands of the Soviets. On 9 May 1945, after a fighting withdrawal to the north of Vienna, that division surrendered to U.S. Army troops, but shortly afterward, all these men were handed over to the Russians. The last commander of the division, Hellmuth Becker, led his troops into captivity and died while held prisoner in a work camp of the Soviet Union. Not until 1955 did the last few survivors of the division return to Germany.

In the summer of 1943, however, long months of war still lay ahead and many situations would arise when Hitler would call on the Waffen SS divisions. As a result, these divisions took part in many of the most important battles of the war in the East (as well as in the West). Although the SS divisions constituted less than 5 percent of the German ground forces, the mobile divisions of the SS made up approximately 25 percent of the total number of German panzer divisions and about one third of the panzergrenadier divisions. This fact guaranteed that they would see action at critical junctures in a frequency out of proportion to their numbers when compared to the army as a whole.

The history of the Eastern Front cannot be told accurately without recognition of the efforts of the SS panzer divisions on all fronts, particulary from 1943 until 1945. Objective study of these units, which were remarkable fighting formations, has been made difficult by incorrect association of all SS units with the concentration camps and atrocities committed against the inmates of these camps. The fact of the matter is that most of the Waffen SS veterans were simply soldiers during the Second World War. There were men who served in the Waffen SS who had also been associated with the camps, either before or during the war, but the numbers of such men were relatively small in relation to the size of the Waffen SS.

A total of approximately 25,000 SS men and women served in the various concentration, labor and death camps before the end of the war, while about 900,000 men served in the Waffen SS.[8] Those who were experienced in the methods of the camps system tended to stay there although an unknown number of transfers, sometimes Waffen SS personnel wounded in action, did occur from combat units to the camps and back again. However, simple arithmetic serves to show that the majority of the men of the Waffen SS never saw the inside of a camp and the characterization of all Waffen SS men as members of a criminal political organization is simplistic.

In any event, I have attempted to present a factual account about the military campaigns of several of the classic Waffen SS divisions on the Eastern Front during the critical summer of 1943 and to illustrate the crucial role that they played during the battles for the possession of the southern Ukraine. Their sacrifices and combat performance in extremely difficult fighting are somewhat unknown, except for several of the better-known battles on the Russian Front. However, even the histories of these battles have been colored with inaccuracies. I have presented evidence in hope of correcting several false beliefs in regard to the losses of the SS divisions at Prochorovka and the outcome of that critical battle. The popular conception that the SS panzer divisions were poorly trained, led incompetently, or were mediocre fighting formations does not hold water when the facts are known. *Das Reich* exhibited first-rate training from the first, fighting well in the division's first actions. This was primarily due to Paul Hausser's skill, experience, and organizational talents. *Leibstandarte* and *Totenkopf*, whose seminal units were created for purposes other than military operations in the field, benefited greatly from combat experience in 1939–41 and the infusion of trained officers and noncoms from Hausser's SS schools and the army. The physically exceptional personnel of these divisions and *Wiking* were superbly motivated, confident to the point of arrogance and always aggressive. Only first-rate, well-trained, and resolute formations could have fought as they did on the Eastern Front during the critical summer of 1943, in combat for months at a time, while enduring tremendous casualties. The combat history of these units warrants study and judgment of their military prowess according to the facts, rather than biased opinions based on poor research, prejudice and judgments based on inaccurate information.

THE CONSEQUENCES OF THE LOSS OF THE SOUTHERN UKRAINE

The Ukraine was of great, even decisive value to both sides throughout the war in Russia. This was particularly true in 1943. From the Soviet point of view, the operations in this part of the Eastern Front during the summer and early fall were obviously of vital imporance. The southern Ukraine was the most critical arena in the east during this period, for it was there that the Soviets decided to make their main effort of 1943. The strategic and military advantages of possession of the Ukraine were of enormous benefit to the Russians. A successful Soviet counteroffensive from the Kharkov-Orel-Kursk would have divided the German front, splitting apart the two strongest army groups in the East, Heeresgruppe Mitte and Süd. Movements of reserves between the army groups would thus have been extremely difficult and the southern wing of the Eastern Front, including 6. Armee, 1. Panzerarmee, and Heeresgruppe A would have been threatened with the loss of its lines of communication and supply. From the Ukraine to the heart of Germany, the path to victory lay in a straight line, through countries of Eastern Europe that Stalin already cast his eyes upon. It is almost certain that he felt the Soviet Union had paid in blood for the rights to any territory that it could wrest from the possession of the Nazis.

Beyond its military importance, the recapture of the Soviet "breadbasket" was significant for political and economic reasons as well. The vast grain and agricultural resources of the Ukraine were urgently needed to alleviate shortages of food and supplies in the Soviet Union. There was also the benefit of the large Ukrainian population, which was needed to provide replacements for the enormous casualties suffered by the Russian army. By August 1943, the advancing Soviet army reaped this human harvest, when it conscripted tens of thousands of Ukrainians, literally from the march, as it moved westward.

The loss of the southern Ukraine was an ultimately fatal setback for the Germans. Politically, it was a final blow to the confidence of Hungary, Rumania and Italy and signaled that the German tide was definitely receding. Germany's allies saw the writing on the wall and were reluctant to sacrifice more of their countrymen's lives for a lost cause. It became evident to the Axis allies that the initiative had passed to the Russians and Germany was reduced to reacting to the moves of the Soviets, which did not constitute a plan for achieving victory.

After the cancellation of "Citadel," the German Army could no longer win the war in Russia, and thus, the war as a whole was lost. Although the main Soviet counteroffensive, "Rumyantsev," was brought to a halt west of Kharkov, the Germans could not regain the territory lost during the summer. In that sense, although "Rumyantsev" failed to accomplish its most ambitious goals, it signified more than just the beginning of the reconquest of the Ukraine with the attendant rewards. It would mean that the German Army had been defeated in the summer months, an accomplishment that was beyond the abilities of the Russian army in the first two years of the war. The psychological advantage to the Russian command and soldiers was equalled by the negative impact on German confidence.

The defeats in southern Russia during the summer of 1943 sealed the fate of Germany, beyond any hope of turning the tide once again. While Germany still had to be actually beaten in the West, as well as physically driven from European Russia, its armies permanently lost the strategic initiative in the East after Prochorovka. Hitler's subsequent decisions concerning events on the southern flank of the Eastern Front during the summer of 1943 guaranteed the collapse of the defense of the southern Ukraine, which was accompanied by further unnecessary loss of men and equipment due to his orders to hold ground at all costs. The Germans were driven from the southern Ukraine, retreating to the Dnepr, closely pursued by the Russians, losing rear guards and encircled units all the while. The losses incurred during the battles of the summer of 1943 and the retreats of autumn, when combined with Hitler's failure to allow either Manstein or Kluge the necessary operational freedom dictated by the military situation, ultimately resulted in the loss of the Dnepr line as well. The weakened German divisions reached the Dnepr River without time to recover or dig in to defend the river. Thus, Heeresgruppe Süd began a doomed fight to hold the western Ukraine with ruined infantry divisions and exhausted panzer divisions. Hollidt's 6. Armee and its withdrawal after the loss of the Mius line was typical of the predicament that the German armies were in by this date.

Shortages of manpower, fuel, and tanks could not be alleviated, no matter how successful Manstein might have been in the days after

Conclusions and Review 503

Prochorovka. The forces necessary to defeat the Soviet colossus were certainly not available to the Germans after July 1943. However, Hitler's armies undoubtedly would have been able to utilize a pause in the fighting of several months to their benefit. The exact course that the war would have taken in this event cannot be known. It is clear, however, that the history of the war on the Eastern Front, if not the outcome, would have been different.

APPENDIX I

A Soviet Tank Army as Established during Early 1943

The exact structure varied according to the needs of the armies and their assigned objectives. Strengths of tank and mechanized corps varied slightly. By the summer of 1943, the Soviets tried to equip all of their tank corps with T-34s, but shortages of this robust tank design forced them to utilize T-60s and T-70s to some extent. Lend-Lease Shermans and M3 Grants were also used to equip some of the Soviet tank brigades. A tank army had about 45,000 to 50,000 men and 500 to 800 tanks. The tank armies created in 1943 included 1st Tank Army, 2nd Tank Army, 3rd Guards Tank Army, 4th Tank Army, and 5th Guards Tank Army.

1943 SOVIET TANK ARMY

Tank Corps	Tank Corps	Mechanized Corps
Tank Brigade (65 tanks)	Tank Brigade (65 tanks)	Tank Brigade (65 tanks)
Tank Brigade (65 tanks)	Tank Brigade (65 tanks)	Tank Brigade (65 tanks)
Tank Brigade (65 tanks)	Tank Brigade (65 tanks)	Tank Brigade (65 tanks)

ATTACHED SUPPORT TROOPS
Reconnaissance regiment (motorcycle/light car troops)
Two antitank regiments or brigade

Attached heavy tank regiment (In 1943, this detachment was made up of the heavy KV-1 tanks or possibly the improved model of the T-34, the T-34/85. Later in the war, the new Is-1 and Is-2 [Joseph Stalin] tanks replaced the KVs.)

Guards mortar regiment (equipped with rocket launchers)

Heavy artillery regiment

Antiaircraft regiment

Engineer battalion

One to two mortar regiments with 120mm or heavier mortars

Self-propelled antitank battalion or regiment (In 1943, many of these units were equipped with SU-76s.)

OTHER SUPPORT TROOPS

Supply, construction, tank maintenance, signals, and communications battalions as required to accomplish the mission of the army.

APPENDIX II

Typical Organization of Soviet Tank Corps in the Summer of 1943

2ND TANK CORPS
26th Tank Brigade (65 T-34s plus motorized rifle battalion)
99th Tank Brigade (65 T-34s plus motorized rifle battalion)
169th Tank Brigade (65 T-34s plus motorized rifle battalion)
58th Motorized Rifle Brigade
1502nd Anti-Tank Regiment (20 45mm guns)
269th Mortar Regiment (36 120mm mortars)
307th Guards Mortar Battalion (8 motorized rocket launchers)
83rd Motorcycle Battalion
74th Sapper Battalion
804th Signals Battalion
1698th Anti-Aircraft Regiment (16 37mm guns)

18TH TANK CORPS OF THE 5TH GUARDS TANK ARMY
110th Tank Brigade (65 T-34s and T-70s)
170th Tank Brigade (65 T-34s and T-70s)
181st Tank Brigade (65 T-34s and T-70s)
32nd Motorized Rifle Brigade
36th Guards Heavy Tank Regiment (KV-1 heavy tanks)
1000th Anti-Tank Regiment (24 76mm guns)
1694th Anti-Aircraft Regiment (16 37mm guns)
292nd Mortar Regiment (36 120mm guns)
736th Anti-Tank Battalion (12 motorized 85mm guns)
115th Sapper Battalion
419th Signals Battalion

APPENDIX III

Tank Strength of II. SS-Panzerkorps during the Battle of Kursk

5 JULY 1943

	Pz II	Pz III	Pz IV	Pz VI	Befehlspz.	T-34
1. SS-Pz.-Div.	4	11	79	12	9	
2. SS-Pz.-Div.		48	30	12	8	18
3. SS-Pz.-Div.		59	47	11	8	

Total medium and heavy tanks—327. Total Panzer IIs and Befehlspanzers—28.

11 JULY 1943

	Pz II	Pz III	Pz IV	Pz VI	Befehlspz.	T-34
1. SS-Pz.-Div.	4	5	47	4	7	
2. SS-Pz.-Div.		34	18	1	7	8
3. SS-Pz.-Div.		54	30	10	7	

Total medium and heavy tanks—211. Total Panzer IIs and Befehlspanzers—25.

13 JULY 1943

	Pz II	Pz III	Pz IV	Pz VI	Befehlspz.	T-34
1. SS-Pz.-Div.	4	5	31	3	7	
2. SS-Pz.-Div.		43	20	1	8	11
3. SS-Pz.-Div.		32	17	0	5	

Total medium and heavy tanks—163. Total Panzer IIs and Befehlspanzers—24.

16 JULY 1943

	Pz II	Pz III	Pz IV	Pz VI	Befehlspz.	T-34
1. SS-Pz.-Div.	4	5	42	9	6	
2. SS-Pz.-Div.		37	18	5	7	11
3. SS-Pz.-Div.		30	27	9	7	

Total medium and heavy tanks—193. Total Panzer IIs and Befehlspanzers—24.

Source: microfilmed records of II. SS-Panzerkorps at National Archives—Record Group T-354, roll 605, Reports of corps 1a to 4. Panzerarmee.

APPENDIX IV

Order of Battle of III. Panzerkorps, August 1943

Attached units are included.

3. PANZER-DIVISION
1 company Schwere-Panzerjäger-Abteilung 560
Eisenbahn-Panzer-Zug 62
8. Armee Sturmabteilung

SS-PANZERGRENADIER-DIVISION *DAS REICH*
Werfer-Regiment 52

SS-PANZERGRENADIER-DIVISION *TOTENKOPF*
Eisenbahn-Panzer-Zug 28

SS-PANZERGRENADIER-DIVISION *WIKING*

PIONIER-REGIMENT STAB 674

ARKO III. PANZERKORPS
Corps artillery

UNITS ATTACHED TO III. PANZERKORPS
schwere-Panzer-Abteilung 503 (Tigers)
Nachrichten-Abteilung 43 (signals battalion)
Feldgendarmerie-Abteilung 682 (military police)
Feldgendarmerie-Abteilung 403
Korpskommandostab (HQ company)

Source: Gliederung des III. Panzerkorps am 11.8.43; Report of Abteilung Ia on 10 August 1943; National Archives Record Group T-314, reel 201, frame 580.

APPENDIX V

Organization of 3. SS-Panzer-Division *Totenkopf* in the Summer of 1943

SS-PANZER-REGIMENT 3
HQ detachment
Tiger company
Signals company
Panzer maintenance company
I. Abteilung
II. Abteilung

SS-PANZERGRENADIER-REGIMENT *THEODOR EICKE*
I. Bataillon
II. Bataillon
III. Bataillon

SS-PANZERGRENADIER-REGIMENT *TOTENKOPF*
I. Bataillon
II. Bataillon
III. Bataillon

SS-STURMGESCHÜTZ-ABTEILUNG 3
HQ battery
3 batteries

SS-PANZERAUFKLÄRUNGS-ABTEILUNG 3
3 companies
motorized support units

SS-FLAK-ABTEILUNG (SELF-PROPELLED)
88mm battery
37mm battery
20mm battery

SS-ARTILLERIE-REGIMENT *TOTENKOPF*
150mm and 105mm battalion (self-propelled)
2 105mm battalion
150mm and 105mm battalion

SS-PANZERJÄGER-ABTEILUNG

SS-PIONIER-ABTEILUNG

Also included were military police, supply, medical, maintenance/repair, and communications detachments, as well as a divisional HQ group.

APPENDIX VI

Soviet Order of Battle for Operation "Rumyantsev"

VORONEZH FRONT
38th Army (5 rifle divisions)
40th Army (6 rifle divisions, 2nd Tank Corps, 10th Tank Corps)
27th Army (6 rifle divisions, 4th Guards Tank Corps, 93rd Tank Brigade)
6th Guards Army (6 rifle divisions, 5th Guards Tank Corps)
5th Guards Army (7 rifle divisions, 28th Tank Regiment, 57th Tank Regiment, 13th Artillery Penetration Division)
1st Tank Army (2 tank corps, 1 mechanized corps, 28th Anti-Tank Brigade, 8th Anti-Aircraft Division, assorted mortar, engineer, antitank, and motorcycle battalions)
5th Guards Tank Army (2 tank corps, 1 mechanized corps)

Total strength: 30 rifle divisions—458,000 men; 8 tank corps plus assorted armored units of smaller size—1,859 tanks

STEPPE FRONT
53rd Army (7 rifle divisions, 1st Mechanized Corps, 4 additional tank regiments)
69th Army (7 rifle divisions)
7th Guards Army (8 rifle divisions)

Total strength: 22 rifle divisions—198,000 men; 1 mechanized corps and assorted armored formations—454 tanks

SOUTHWEST FRONT
57th Army (7 rifle divisions, two tank brigades)

Total strength: 7 rifle divisions—60,000 men; 2.5 tank brigades—109 tanks

STAVKA RESERVE

47th Army (6 rifle divisions, 3rd Guards Mechanized Corps—213 tanks)

4th Guards Army (6 rifle divisions, 3rd Guards Tank Corps—200 tanks)

TOTAL FORCES COMMITTED DURING OPERATION "RUMYANTSEV"

71 rifle or airborne divisions—approximately 1.2 million men
13 tank or mechanized corps—more than 2,800 tanks
Other armored vehicles—more than 100

Source: Glantz, *From the Don to the Dnepr.*

APPENDIX VII

Waffen SS Ranks and U.S. Army Equivalent Ranks

Waffen SS Rank	U.S. Army Rank
Enlisted Men	
SS-Grenadier	Private
SS-Oberschütze	Private First Class
SS-Sturmmann	No precise equivalent
SS-Rottenführer	Corporal
NCOs	
SS-Unterscharführer	Sergeant
SS-Scharführer	Staff Sergeant
SS-Oberscharführer	Technical Sergeant
SS-Hauptscharführer	Master Sergeant
SS-Stabsscharführer	First Sergeant
SS-Sturmscharführer	Sergeant Major
Officers	
SS-Untersturmführer	Second Lieutenant
SS-Obersturmführer	First Lieutenant
SS-Hauptsturmführer	Captain
Field-Grade Officers	
SS-Sturmbannführer	Major
SS-Obersturmbannführer	Lieutenant Colonel
SS-Standartenführer	Colonel
SS-Oberführer	No equivalent

Waffen SS Rank	U.S. Army Rank
Generals	
SS-Brigadeführer und Generalmajor der Waffen SS	Brigadier General
SS-Gruppenführer und Generalleutnant der Waffen SS	Major General
SS-Obergruppenführer und General der Waffen SS	Lieutenant General
SS-Oberstgruppenführer und Generaloberst der Waffen SS	General

Notes

INTRODUCTION
1. Earl F. Ziemke and Magda Bauer, *Moscow to Stalingrad: Decision in the East*, 39.
2. Klaus Reinhardt, *Moscow: The Turning Point: The Failure of Hitler's Strategy in the Winter of 1941–42* (Oxford: Berg Publishers), 128.
3. Ibid., 176.
4. Ziemke and Bauer, *Moscow to Stalingrad*, 42.
5. Reinhardt, *Moscow*, 221.
6. Ziemke, *Moscow to Stalingrad*, 397.

CHAPTER 1: HEERESGRUPPE SÜD AND ARMEE-ABTEILUNG HOLLIDT: RETREAT AND RECOVERY IN THE UKRAINE
1. Dana V. Sadarananda, *Beyond Stalingrad: Manstein and the Operations of Army Group Don* (New York: Praeger, 1990), 149.
2. Col. David Glantz, *From the Don to the Dnepr: Soviet Offensive Operations, December 1942–August 1943* (London: Frank Cass and Co., 1991), 93.
3. Glantz, *From the Don to the Dnepr*, 111–12.
4. Feldmarschall Erich von Manstein, *Lost Victories*, (Novato, CA: Presidio, 1982), 368.
5. Ibid., 368.
6. Glantz, *From the Don to the Dnepr*, 85.
7. Manstein, *Lost Victories*, 409.
8. John Erickson, *The Road to Berlin* (Boulder, CO: Westview Press, 1983), 52.
9. Earl F. Ziemke and Magda Bauer, *Stalingrad to Berlin: The German Defeat in the East* (Washington, DC: Center of Military History, U.S. Army, 1968), 88.
10. Glantz, *From the Don to the Dnepr*, 188–89.
11. Paul Carell, *Scorched Earth: The Russian German War, 1943–44* (Atglen, PA: Schiffer Military History, 1994), 44.
12. Glantz, *From the Don to the Dnepr*, 121.
13. Carell, *Scorched Earth*, 188.
14. Ziemke and Bauer, *Stalingrad to Berlin*, 137.
15. Victor Madeja, *The Russo-German War*, vol. 31 (Allentown: Valor Publishing Company, 1987), 50.
16. Samuel W. Mitcham Jr., *Hitler's Legions: The German Army Order of Battle, World War II* (Briar Cliff Manor: Stein and Day, 1985), 433.
17. Ibid., 215.
18. Madeja, *Russo-German War*, vol. 31, 51.
19. Omer Bartov, *Hitler's Army: Soldiers, Nazis, and War in the Third Reich* (London: Oxford University Press, 1991), 39.

20. Madeja, *Russo-German War*, vol. 31, 76.
21. Mitcham, *Hitler's Legions*, 384.
22. Madeja, *Russo-German War*, vol. 31, 50.
23. Foreign Military Studies, United States Army Europe, FMS #D-154, *Experience with Russian Methods of Warfare and Their Utilization in Training at the Waffen SS Panzergrenadier School.*
24. Ibid., 14–15.
25. Geoffrey Jukes, *Kursk: Clash of Armour* (New York: Ballantine, 1968), 119–20.
26. Foreign Military Studies, United States Army Europe, FMS #C-078, *Sixth Army, Russia*, 1–3.
27. Ibid, 8.

CHAPTER 2: FROM PROCHOROVKA TO THE MIUS: III. PANZERKORPS AND II. SS-PANZERKORPS

1. Ziemke and Bauer, *Stalingrad to Berlin*, 128.
2. Alan Clark, *Barbarossa: The Russian-German Conflict, 1941–1945* (New York: William Morrow and Company), 234.
3. Col. Albert Seaton, *The Russo-German War, 1941–45* (New York: Praeger Publishers, 1971), 356.
4. Robin Cross, *"Citadel": The Battle of Kursk* (New York: Sarpedon, 1993), 98.
5. Carell, *Scorched Earth*, 21.
6. T-313, reel 368, frame 654268, Tagesmeldung XXXXVIII. Panzerkorps an 4. Panzerarmee—4.7.1943.
7. Madeja, *Russo-German War*, vol. 31, 93.
8. T-354, reel 605, frame 470, Tagesmeldung an 4. Panzerarmee vom II. SS Panzerkorps am 4.7.1943.
9. T-314, reel 720, frame 186, Tagesmeldung of GenKdo XXIV. Panzerkorps, 5.7.1943.
10. T-314, reel 720, frame 271, XXIV. Panzerkorps tagesmeldung an 4. Panzerarmee, 13.7.1943.
11. Janusz Piekalkiewicz, *Operation "Citadel": Kursk and Orel: The Greatest Tank Battle of the Second World War* (Novato, CA: Presidio Press, 1987), 159.
12. Jukes, *Kursk*, 112.
13. Cross, *Citadel*, 223.
14. Wolfgang Vopersal, *Soldaten-Kämpfer-Kameraden*, vol. 3 (Osnabrück: Truppenkameradschaft der 3. SS-Panzer-Division, 1990), 373–75.
15. NA/T-313, reel 368, frame 654360, Tagesmeldung II. SS-Panzerkorps an 4. Panzerarmee am 11.7.1943; and T-354, reel 605, which give identical lists of operational tanks for that date.
16. Seaton, *Russo-German War*, 363.
17. From II. SS-Panzerkorps situation map showing the various Soviet attacks on 12 July 1943 from the hours of 1140 to 1700. Reproduced in Silvester Stadler, *Die Offensive gegen Kursk: II. SS Panzerkorps also Stoßkeil im Großkampf* (Osnabrück: Munin Verlag, 1980).
18. Erickson, *Road to Berlin*, 110.
19. NA/T-354, reel 605, frame 636, Tagesmeldung der II. SS-Panzerkorps an Panzer AOK 4, 10.7.1943.
20. Jukes, *Kursk*, 102.
21. Franz Kurowski, *Panzer Aces*, 204–5.

22. A. L. Getman (commander of the 6th Tank Corps), *Tanki idut na Berlin*, quoted in Erickson, *Road to Berlin*, 664
23. NA/T-354, reel 605, frame 636, Tagesmeldungen der Divisionen an Panzer AOK 4, 10.7.1943.
24. Kurowski, *Panzer Aces*, 124–25.
25. Rudolf Lehmann, *1. SS Panzer Division "Leibstandarte Adolf Hitler,"* vol. III (Winnipeg, Canada: J. J. Fedorowicz Publishing, 1993), 237.
26. T-354, reel 605, frame 678, Tagemeldung GenKdo II. SS Panzerkorps vom 12.7.1943.
27. Charles Sharp, *Soviet Order of Battle—"School of Battle"—Soviet Tank Corps and Tank Brigades, January 1942 to 1945*, vol. 2 (West Chester: George F. Nafziger, 1995), 1.
28. NA/T-354, reel 605, frame 673-4, Tagesmeldung 2. SS-Panzergrenadier-Division "Das Reich" an GenKdo II. SS-Panzerkorps, 12.7.1943.
29. Madeja, *Russo-German War*, 44.
30. Glantz, *From the Don to the Dnepr*, 361.
31. NA/T-313, reel 368, frame 654385, Tagesmeldung 4. Panzerarmee, 13.7.1943.
32. *Die Geheimen Tagesberichte der Deutschen Wehrmachtführung im Zweiten Weltkrieg, 1939–1945*, vol. 7, 118.
33. NA/T-354, reel 605, frame 699, Tagesmeldungen 2. SS-Panzergrenadier-Division an GenKdo II. SS-Panzer-Korps, 13.7.1943.
34. NA/T-354, reel 605, frame 698, Tagesmeldung SS-Panzergrenadier-Division "LAH" an 4. Panzer Armee vom 13.7.1943.
35. From the recommendation of Ullrich for the Oak Leaves to the Knight's Cross, awarded on 14 May, 1944. Courtesy of Mark C. Yerger.
36. NA/T-354, reel 605, frame 702, Tagesmeldung 3. SS-Panzergrenadier-Division "Totenkopf" an II. SS-Panzerkorps, 13.7.1943.
37. NA/T-354, reel 605, frame 701, Tagesmeldung 3. SS-Panzergrenadier-Division "Totenkopf" an IL SS Panzerkorps, 13.7.1943.
38. NA/T-354, reel 605, frame 704, Tagesmeldung 2. SS-Panzergrenadier-Division GenKdo. SS Panzer Korps, 13.7.1943.
39. NA/T-354, reel 605, frame 705, Oberbefehlshaber 4. Panzerarmee an II. SS-Panzerkorps am 13.7.1943, 21.00 Uhr.
40. NA/T-354, reel 605, frame 761–762, Tagesmeldung der Divisionen an GenKdo II. SS-Panzerkorps, 16.7.1943.
41. Seaton, *Russo-German War*, 365.
42. Ziemke and Bauer, *Stalingrad to Berlin*, 128.
43. Manstein, *Lost Victories*, 449.
44. Glantz, *From the Don to the Dnepr*, 361.
45. Madeja, *Russo-German War*, vol. 31, 93.
46. Ziemke and Bauer, *Stalingrad to Berlin*, 138.
47. NA/T-354, reel 605, frame 761 and 768.
48. Erickson, *Road to Berlin*, 112.
49. Seaton, *Russo-German War*, 367.
50. Jukes, *Kursk*, 101.
51. Erickson, *Road to Berlin*, 110–11.
52. NA/T-354, reel 605, frame 470, Tagesmeldung II. SS-Panzerkorps an 4. Panzerarmee, 4.7.1943.

53. NA/T-313, reel 368, frame 654360 and 654361, Tagesmeldung 4. Panzerarmee am 11.7.1943.
54. NA/T-313, reel 368, frame 6543.85, Tagesmeldung 4. Panzerarmee am 13.7.1943.
55. Clark, *Barbarossa*, 337–38.

CHAPTER 3: 6. ARMEE STANDS FAST
1. Foreign Military Study, United States Army Europe, FMS #C-078, *Sixth Army, Russia*, 4 (hereafter cited as FMS #C-078).
2. Ibid., 5.
3. 50th Guard; 87th, 302nd, 346th Rifle Divisions; and a mortar regiment.
4. FMS #C-078, 9.
5. NA/T-314, reel 815, frame 981, Morgenmeldung der Division an 6. Armee, 17.7.1943
6. FMS #C-078. 11.
7. Ibid., 9.
8. F. W. Mellenthin, *Panzer Battles: A Study of the Employment of Armor in the Second World War* (New York: Ballantine, 1960), 223.
9. FMS #C-078, 13.
10. Mellenthin, *Panzer Battles*, 223.
11. Generalleutnant der Waffen SS Max Simon, *Experience Gained in Combat with Russian Infantry*, FMS #C-058, 17.
12. FMS #C-078, 16.
13. Ibid. 20.
14. Ibid., appendix.
15. Ibid., 20.
16. Madeja, *Russo-German War*, vol. 31, 54.
17. FMS #C-078, 25.
18. Madeja, *Russo-German War*, vol. 31, 54.
19. FMS #C-078, 26.
20. Manstein, *Lost Victories*, 452.
21. Erich Schneider, *Anti-Tank Defense in the East*, FMS #D-253, 25.
22. NA/T-314, reel 720, frame 488, Zwischenmeldung 23. Panzer-Division an XXIV. Panzerkorps, 21.7.43.
23. NA/T-314, reel 720, frame 516, Tagesmeldung 23. Panzer-Division an XXIV. Panzerkorps, 17.30 Uhr, 22.7.1943.
24. NA/T-314, frame 518, see Tagesmeldung 294. Infanterie Division and 16. Panzergrenadier Division an XXIV. Panzerkorps on 22.7.1943.
25. FMS #C-078, 37.
26. NA/T-314, reel 720, frame 520, Nachtrag zur Tagesmeldung an A.O.K. 6, 22.7.1943.
27. FMS #C-078, appendix 1, 69.
28. Ibid, 41.
29. FMS #C-078, 44.
30. In order to put this casualty total into some perspective, it is interesting to compare the U.S. Army casualties that were suffered during the D-Day landings. The U.S. First Army, including the 82nd and 101st Airborne Divisions, lost 6,603 men in the landings. British and Canadian losses increase the number to about 10,000. It is a measure of the enormous scope of the fighting on the Eastern Front that during a relatively small and largely unknown battle, the Ger-

mans lost more casualties than were suffered by the Allies during the invasion of Europe in 1944. Russian losses are unknown but surely exceeded German casualties, which meant that significantly more than 30,000 men were killed or wounded during the fighting. By the end of the first week of August, in continued fighting on the Mius, a further 8,500 German soldiers became casualties, and untold more Russians were lost in battle.

CHAPTER 4: A STRATEGY OF DECEPTION
1. Col. David Glantz, *Soviet Military Deception in the Second World War*, 2.
2. Madeja, *Russo-German War*, vol. 31, 48.
3. Glantz, *Soviet Military Deception*, 171.
4. Ibid., 174.
5. Cross, *"Citadel"*, 181.
6. Cross, *"Citadel"*, 181.
7. Boris Solovyov, *The Turning Point of World War II (The Campaigns of Summer and Autumn 1943 on the Soviet-German Front)* (Moscow: Progress Publishers, 1973), 73–74. Solovyov reports on conversations between Zhukov and Marshal A. M. Vasilevsky in April 1943 regarding operational strategy for the critical summer of 1943.
8. S. M. Shtemenko, *The Soviet General Staff at War, 1941–1945* (Moscow: Progress Publishers, 1970), 152.

CHAPTER 5: 6. ARMEE STRIKES BACK
1. FMS #C-078, 53.
2. Ibid., 48.
3. Mellenthin, *Panzer Battles*, 223.
4. FMS #C-078, 49.
5. NA/T-354, reel 605, frame 922, Miscellaneous SS Records: Einwanderzentrastelle, Waffen SS and SS Oberabschitte. Tagesmeldung vom 29.7.1943, GenKdo II. SS-Panzerkorps.
6. FMS #C-078, 51.
7. Ibid., 40–41.
8. Ibid., 46.
9. Mark C. Yerger, *Knights of Steel: The Structure, Development and Personalities of the 2. SS-Panzer-Division "Das Reich,"*, vol. 1 (Hershey, PA: Horetsky Publishing, 1989), 197.
10. Vopersal, *Soldaten-Kämpfer-Kameraden*, vol. III, 422.
11. Ibid., 421.
12. NA/T-354, reel 605, frame 922, Tagesmeldung GenKdo. der II. SS-Panzerkorps 29.7.1943.
13. For the pm-Citadel figures see 4. Panzerarmee records NA/T-313, reel 368, frame 654235 or T354, reel 605, frame 470, Tagesmeldung GenKdo II. SS-Panzerkorps vom 4.7.1943.
14. Vopersal, *Soldaten, Kämpfer, Kameraden*, vol. III, 422.
15. Charles Sydnor, *Soldiers of Destruction: The SS Death's Head Division, 1933–1945* (Princeton, NJ: Princeton University Press, 1977), 221–35.
16. Ibid., 242 and footnote same page.
17. Ibid., 65.
18. NA/T-354, reel 605, frame 927, Tagesmeldung vom 29.7.1943, GenKdo II. SS-Panzerkorps.

CHAPTER 6: THE FIRST DAY

1. Vopersal, *Soldaten-Kämpfer-Kameraden*, vol. III, 424.
2. NA/T-354, reel 605, frame 928, Zwischenmeldung vom 30.7.1943. GenKdo II. SS-Panzerkorps.
3. Vopersal, *Soldaten-Kämpfer-Kameraden*, vol. III, 426.
4. NA/T-354, reel 605, frame 928, Zwischenmeldung an GenKdo II. SS-Panzerkorps vom Ia, SS-Panzergrenadier-Division "Das Reich."
5. Vopersal, *Soldaten-Kämpfer-Kameraden*, vol. III, 427.
6. Ibid., 428.
7. FMS #C-078, 55.
8. Vopersal, *Soldaten-Kämpfer-Kameraden*, vol. III, 429.
9. FMS #C-078, 55.
10. NA/T-354, reel 605, frame 930, Tagesmeldung vom 30.7.1943–1730 hours.
11. Vopersal, *Soldaten-Kämpfer-Kameraden*, vol. III, 431.
12. FMS #C-078, 55.
13. Vopersal, *Soldaten-Kämpfer-Kameraden*, vol. III, 428–30.
14. Otto Weidinger, *Division Das Reich: Der Weg der 2. SS-Panzer-Division "Das Reich,"* vol. IV (Osnabrück: Munin Verlag), 437; Meldung fiber Verluste am 30.7.1943, 2330 hours.
15. Mellenthin, *Panzer Battles*, 223.
16. Weidinger, *Division Das Reich*, vol. IV, 238.
17. Ibid., 240.
18. James Lucas, *Das Reich: The Military Role of the 2nd SS Panzer Division*, 113.
19. Weidinger, *Division Das Reich*, vol. IV, 240.
20. NA/T-354, reel 605, frame 929, report of Division Ia of "Das Reich"- Generalstaboffizier Sturnibannfilluer Maier to GenKdo II. SS Panzerkorps -1755 hours, 30.7.1943.
21. Weidinger, *Division Das Reich*, vol. IV, 243.
22. Ibid., 243.
23. NA/T-354, reel 605, frame 928, Zwischenmeldung auf II. SS-Panzerkorps vom 30.7.1943.
24. Ibid. frame 931, Tagesmeldung II. SS Panzerkorps - 1730 hours, 30.7.1943.
25. NA/T-354, reel 605, frame 929, Tagesmeldung der II. SS Panzerkorps on 30.7.1943.
26. FMS #C-078, 51.
27. NA/T-315, reel 2029, frame 941, Tagesmeldung XVII. Armeekorps - 30.7.1943.
28. NA/T-315, reel 2029, frame 942, Tagesmeldung XVII. Armeekorps - 30.7.1943.
29. Ibid. frame 941, Tagesmeldung—30.7.1943.
30. NA/T-315, reel 2029, frame 942, Tagesmeldung XVII. Armeekorps - 30.7.1943.
31. NA/T-314, reel 720, frame 820, Zwischenmeldung XXIV. Panzerkorps, 1500 hours, 30.7.1943.
32. FMS #C-078, 52.
33. NA/T-314, reel 720, frame 821, Zwischenmeldung der XXIV. Panzerkorps, 1500 hours, 30.7.1943.
34. FMS #C-078, 51.
35. Op cit.
36. FMS #C-078, 56.
37. NA/1-314, reel 720, frame 822, Zwischenmeldung XXIV. Panzerkorps an A.O.K. 6, 30.7.1943.
38. NA/T-314, reel 720, frame 826, Tagesmeldung an A.O.K. 6, 30.7.1943.

39. NA/T-314, reel 815, frame 1074, Morgenmeldung der XXIX. Armeekorps an A.O.K. 6—30.7.1943.
40. NA/T-314, reel 815, frame 1076, Abendsmeldung der XXIX. Armeekorps auf la 6. Armee, 2245 hours, 30.7.1943.
41. FMS #C-078, 56.

CHAPTER 7: DEADLOCK

1. Vopersal, *Soldaten-Kämpfer-Kameraden*, vol. III, 432; and Morgenmeldung—Artillerie Kdr. 122 an II. SS-Panzerkorps, 31.7.1943.
2. Vopersal, *Soldaten-Kämpfer-Kameraden*, vol. III, 433.
3. Ibid.
4. Ibid.
5. Ibid.
6. NA/T-354, reel 605, frame 946, Tagesmeldung an GenKdo. II. SS-Panzerkorps—31.7.1943.
7. Ibid., frame 942, Zwischenmeldung II. SS-Panzerkorps vom 31.7.1943.
8. NA/T-354, Tagesmeldung 2. SS-Panzer-Division an GenKdo. II. SS-Panzerkorps—31.7.1943.
9. NA/T-314, reel 720, frame 888, Tagesmeldung XXIV. Panzerkorps—31.7.1943.
10. NA/T-354, reel 605, frame 942, Zwischenmeldung der II. SS-Panzerkorps—afternoon 31.7.1943.
11. NA/1-354, reel 605, frame 936, 2. SS-Panzer-Division an GenKdo. II. SS-Panzerkorps—31.7.1943.
12. Weidinger, *Division Das Reich*, vol. IV, 247.
13. NA/T-354, reel 605, frame 945, Tagesmeldung la SS-Panzergrenadier-Division "Das Reich" an GenKdo II. SS Panzerkorps, 31.71943.
14. FMS # C-078, 58; and Weidinger, *Division Das Reich*, vol. IV, 247.
15. Weidinger, *Division Das Reich*, vol. IV, 249.
16. NA/T-354, reel 605, frame 952, GenKdo. II. SS-Panzerkorps, la KTB, Nr. 686/43 g. Kdos.
17. NA/T-315, reel 2029, frame 945, Tagesmeldung der XVII. Armeekorps—31.7.1943.
18. Ibid., frame 956, Morgenmeldung II. SS-Panzerkorps vom 1.8.1943.
19. NA/T-315, reel 2029, frame 944, Morgenmeldung der XVII. Armeekorps auf 306. Infanterie-Division, 31.7.1943.
20. NA/T-314, reel 815, frame 1081, Morgenmeldung, la, 294. Infanterie-Division an XXIX. Armeekorps on 31.7.1943.
21. Ibid., Morgenmeldung auf la , 111. Infanterie-Division to XXIX. Armeekorps, 31.7.1943.
22. NA/T-314, reel 815, frame 1082, Chef 111. Infanterie-Division to A.O.K. 6, 1235 hours, 31.7.1943.
23. Ibid., frame 1085, XXIX. Armeekorps an 6. Armee, 2200 hours, 31.7.1943.
24. NA/T-314, reel 720, frame 887, Tagesmeldung 23. Panzer-Division an XXIV. Panzerkorp, 31.7.1943.
25. FMS #C-078, 57.
26. FMS #C-078, 58.
27. FMS #C-078, 58.
28. Weidinger, *Division Das Reich*, vol. IV, 251.
29. Ibid., 252.
30. Op cit.

31. Madeja, *Russo-German War*, vol. 31, 59.
32. NA/T-315, reel 2029, frame 946, Morgenmeldung 306. Infanterie-Division an XVII. Armeekorps for 1.8.1943.
33. FMS #C-078, 59.
34. Vopersal, *Soldaten-Kämpfer-Kameraden*, vol. III, 437.

CHAPTER 8: THE DECISIVE DAY: 1 AUGUST
1. NA/T-315, reel 2029, frame 946, Morgenmeldung 306. Infanterie Division an XVII. Armeekorps 1.8.1943.
2. NA/T-354, reel 605, frame 956, Morgenmeldung II. SS-Panzerkorps an A.O.K. 6, 1.8.1943.
3. NA/T- 315, reel 2029, frame 946, Morgenmeldung 306. Infanterie-Division and XVII. Armeekorps, 1.8.1943.
4. Op cit.
5. NA/T-354, reel 605, frame 956, Morgenmeldung SS-Panzer-Division "Das Reich" an II. SS Panzerkorps, 1.8.1943.
6. NA/T-354, reel 605, frame 953, GenKdo II. SS-Panzerkorps- Feindlage am 31.7.1943.
7. NA/T-354, reel 605, Morgenmeldung SS-Panzer-Division "Das Reich" an II. SS-Panzer Division, 1.8.1943.
8. NA/T-354, reel 605, frame 964, Artillerie Kommandeur 122—Abendmeldung vom 1.8.1943.
9. FMS #C-078, 69. Appendix with detailed figures on shell expenditure for various days in the period from 17.7.1943 and 2.8.1943. See also the comparison of artillery use versus mortar expenditures during offensive and defensive operations.
10. Weidinger, *Division Das Reich*, vol. III, 251.
11. Ibid., 252.
12. NA/T-354, reel 605, frame 962, SS-Panzer-Division "Das Reich"—Tagesmeldung an II. SS-Panzer Armeekorps, 1.8.1943.
13. Weidinger, *Division Das Reich*, vol. III, 252.
14. Ibid., 254.
15. Ibid., 253.
16. Op cit.
17. NA/T-354, reel 605, frame 692, Tagesmeldung SS-Panzer-Division "Das Reich" an II. SS-Panzerkorps, 1715 hours, 1.8.1943.
18. NA/T-354, reel 605, frame 970, Tagesmeldung GenKdo II. SS-Panzerkorps, 1.8.1943.
19. Mark C. Yerger, *Knights of Steel: The Structure, Development, and Personalities of the 2. SS-Panzer-Division "Das Reich,"* vol. 2 (Lancaster, PA: self-published, 1994), 137.
20. Weidinger, *Division Das Reich*, vol. IV, 260.
21. NA/T-354, reel 605, frame 962, SS-Panzer-Division "Das Reich"—Tagesmeldung, 1.8.1943.
22. Vopersal, *Soldaten-Kämpfer-Kameraden*, vol. III, 445.
23. FMS #C-078, 60.
24. Ibid.
25. NA/T-314, reel 815, frame 1089, Morgenmeldung auf XXIX. Armeekorps an 6. Armee, 1.8.1943.

Notes

26. NA/T-314, reel 720, frame 1004, Morgenmeldung 23. Panzer-Division, 2.8.1943.
27. Ibid., frame 938, Tagesmeldung XXIV. Panzerkorps, 1.8.1943.
28. FMS #C-078, 62.
29. NA/T-354, reel 605, frame 961, Femmeldung—Befehl an SS-Panzer-Division "Totenkopf," 1.8.1943.
30. NA/T-354, reel 605, frame 971, Tagesmeldung GenKdo. II. SS-Panzer-Division KTB, 1.8.1943.
31. Vopersal, *Soldaten-Kämpfer-Kameraden*, vol. III, 446.
32. Ibid., 440.
33. Ibid., 439.
34. NA/T-354, reel 605, frame 963, Tagesmeldung an II. SS-Panzerkorps from 3. SS-Panzer-Division, 1.8.1943.
35. Vopersal, *Soldaten-Kämpfer-Kameraden*, vol. III, 440.
36. Ibid., 441.
37. Ibid., 441.
38. Ibid., 443.
39. NA/T-354, reel 605, frame 966, Feindlage meldung an GenKdo. II. SS-Panzerkorps, 1.8.1943.
40. FMS #C-078, 63.
41. NA/T-354, reel 605, frame 963, Tagesmeldung 3. SS-Panzer-Division "Totenkopf" an II. SS-Panzer-Armeekorps, 1.8.1943.
42. Vopersal, *Soldaten-Kämpfer-Kameraden*, vol. III, 445.
43. Ibid., 446.
44. NA/T-354, reel 605, frame 959, Femspruch Ia, A.O.K. 6 an GenKdo. II. SS-Panzerkorps. 1.8.1943.
45. Glantz, *From the Don to the Dnepr*, 225.
46. Ibid., 224.

CHAPTER 9: THE DESTRUCTION OF THE BRIDGEHEAD

1. NA/T-314, reel 720, frame 941, Tagesmeldung XXIV. Panzerkorps an A.O.K. 6, 1.8.1943.
2. NA/T-314, reel 720, frame 965, 2.8.1943. GenKdo. II. SS Panzerkorps to the two divisions, 1.8.1943.
3. Vopersal, *Soldaten-Kämpfer-Kameraden*, vol. III, 448.
4. NA/T-354, reel 605, frame 976, Zwischenmeldung zum 2.8.1943, SS-Panzer-Division "Totenkopf," afternoon 2.8.1943.
5. NA/T-354, reel 605, frame 979, Tagesmeldung SS-Panzer-Division "Totenkopf," 1720 hours 2.8.1943.
6. NA/T-354, reel 605, frame 963, Tagesmeldung SS-Panzer-Division "Totenkopf," 2.8.1943.
7. Ibid., frame 982, Tagesmeldung GenKdo. II. SS-Panzerkorps Ia KTB, 2.8.1943.
8. FMS #C-078, 65.
9. Vopersal, *Soldaten-Kämpfer-Kameraden*, vol. III, 449.
10. NA/T-354, reel 605, frame 1002, Verlustübersicht nach Waffengatungem vom 30.7 bis 2.8.1943
11. Weidinger, *Division Das Reich*, vol. IV, 267. Personelle Verluste des SS-Panzerkorps in der Zeit vom 1.7.1943 bis 1.8.1943—(Kursker Schlacht und Schlacht am Mius)—GenKdo. II. SS-Panzer-Armeekorps, Ia, Tätigkeitsbericht Abt. IIa für die Zeit vom 1.7. bis 31.7. 1943.

12. Ziemke and Bauer, *Stalingrad to Berlin*, 151.
13. FMS #C-078, 65.
14. Ibid.
15. Erickson, *Road to Berlin*, 116.
16. FMS #C-078, 70.

CHAPTER 10: THE BATTLES FOR BOGODUKHOV
1. Lehmann, *1. SS Panzer Division*, vol. III, 267.
2. Glantz, *From the Don to the Dnepr*, 237.
3. Ibid., 258.
4. Caren, 301.
5. Glantz, *From the Don to the Dnepr*, 291.
6. Weidinger, *Division Das Reich*, vol. IV, 288.
7. NA/T-314, reel 201, frame 456, Morgenmeldung II. Panzerkorps an Armee-Abteilung Kempf, 7.8.43.
8. Weidinger, *Division Das Reich*, vol. IV, 289.
9. Glantz, *From the Don to the Dnepr*, 295.
10. NA/T-314, reel 201, frame 502, Tagesmeldung III. Panzerkorps an Armee-Abteilung Kempf, 8.8.1943.
11. Glantz, *From the Don to the Dnepr*, 298.
12. Vopersal, *Soldaten-Kämpfer-Kameraden*, vol. III, 461.
13. NA/T-314, reel 201, frame 529, Tagesmeldung SS-Panzergrenadier-Division "Totenkopf" an II. Panzer-Armeekorps, 9.8.1943.
14. Glantz, *From the Don to the Dnepr*, 298.
15. NA/T-314, reel 201, frame 571, Tagesmeldungen der Divisionen an II. Panzerkorps, 10.8.1943.
16. Vopersal, *Soldaten-Kämpfer-Kameraden*, vol. III, 463.

CHAPTER 11: THE COUNTERATTACK OF III. PANZERKORPS
1. Glantz, *From the Don to the Dnepr*, 304.
2. Ibid., 312.
3. NA/T-314, reel 201, frame 570, Tagesmeldung der Division an III. Panzerkorps, 10.8.1943.
4. Vopersal, *Soldaten-Kämpfer-Kameraden*, vol. III, 465.
5. Ibid., 466.
6. Weidinger, *Division Das Reich*, vol. IV, 291.
7. Vopersal, *Soldaten-Kämpfer-Kameraden*, vol. III, 467.
8. Ibid., 468.
9. NA/T-314, reel 201, frame 657, Tagesmeldungen SS-Panzergrenadier-Division "Totenkopf" an III. Panzerkorps, 12.8.1943.
10. Vopersal, *Soldaten-Kämpfer-Kameraden*, vol. III, 467–68.
11. NA/T-314, reel 201, frame 658, Tagesmeldungen SS-Panzergrenadier-Division "Das Reich" an Panzerkorps am 12.8.1943.
12. Weidinger, *Division Das Reich*, vol. IV, 291.
13. NA/T-314, reel 201, frame 648, Zwischenmeldung SS-Panzergrenadier-Division "Wiking" an III. Panzer-Armeekorps, 12.8.1943.
14. Vopersal, *Soldaten-Kämpfer-Kameraden*, vol. III, 471.
15. Weidinger, *Division Das Reich*, vol. IV, 292.
16. Vopersal, *Soldaten-Kämpfer-Kameraden*, vol. III, 471.

17. Ibid., 472.
18. Ibid.
19. Weidinger, *Division Das Reich*, vol. IV, 293; and NA/T-314, reel 201, frame 722, Anfrage Chef des Generalstabes Armee-Abteilung Kempf am 13.8.1943.
20. Glantz, *From the Don to the Dnepr*, 318, from P.Ya Yegorov et al., *Dorogami pobed: boevoe put' 5—gvardeiskoi tankovoi armii* (Moskva, Voinizadat), 58.
21. Vopersal, *Soldaten-Kämpfer-Kameraden*, vol. III, 475.
22. Ibid., 472.
23. Glantz, *From the Don to the Dnepr*, 323.
24. NA/T-314, reel 201, frame 754, Tagesmeldunen der Divisionen an III. Panzerkorps am 14.8.1943.
25. Ibid., frame 755,Tagesmeldungen der Divisionen an III. Panzerkorps am 14.8.1943.
26. Vopersal, *Soldaten-Kämpfer-Kameraden*, vol. III, 478.
27. Ibid.
28. Ibid., 482.
29. Glantz, *From the Don to the Dnepr*, 320.
30. Vopersal, *Soldaten-Kämpfer-Kameraden*, vol. III, 486.
31. NA/T-314, reel 201, frame 879, Tagesmeldungen der Divisionen an III. Panzerkorps, 17.8.1943.
32. Vopersal, *Soldaten-Kämpfer-Kameraden*, vol. III, 490.
33. Ibid., 491.
34. NA/T-314, reel 201, frame 879, Tagesmeldungen der Divisionen an III. Panzerkorps, 17.8.1943.
35. Vopersal, *Soldaten-Kämpfer-Kameraden*, vol. III, 494.
36. Glantz, *From the Don to the Dnepr*, 330.
37. Ziemke and Bauer, *Stalingrad to Berlin*, 156.
38. NA/T-314, reel 201, frame 983, Tagesmeldung der Division an III.Panzerkorps, 19.8.1943.
39. Ibid. frame 984, Tagesmeldung der Division an III. Panzerkorps, 19.8.1943.
40. Jost W. Schneider, *Their Honor Was Loyalty! An Illustrated and Documentary History of the Knight's Cross Holders of the Waffen SS and Police, 1940–1945* (San Jose, CA: R. James Bender Publishing), 110.
41. NA/T-314, reel 201, frame 1056, Tagesmeldungen der Divisionen an III. Panzerkorps am 20.8.1943.
42. Vopersal, *Soldaten-Kämpfer-Kameraden*, vol. III, 498.
43. Ibid., 497.
44. NA/T-314, reel 201, frame 1056, Tagesmeldungen der Divisionen an III. Panzerkorps, 20.8.1943.
45. NA/T-314, reel 201, frame 1102, Tagesmeldungen der Divisionen an III. Panzerkorps, 20.8.1943.
46. NA/T-314, reel 201, frame 1056, Tagesmeldungen der Divisionen an III. Panzerkorps am 20.8.1943.
47. Glantz, *From the Don to the Dnepr*, 342.
48. Vopersal, *Soldaten-Kämpfer-Kameraden*, vol. III, 506.
49. Glantz, *From the Don to the Dnepr*, 354.
50. By 21 August, 223. Infanterie-Division had assembled both its infantry regiments, the division staff, and 1. and 2. Kompanie of the Panzerjäger-Abteilung in the Merchik sector.

51. Ziemke and Bauer, *Stalingrad to Berlin*, 153.
52. Manstein, *Lost Victories*, 456.
53. Erickson, *Road to Berlin*, 121.
54. Glantz, *From the Don to the Dnepr*, 359, from P.Ya Yegorov et al., *Dorogami pobed: boevoe put' 5—gvardeiskoi tankovoi armii* (Moskva, Voinizadat), 58.
55. Martin van Creveld, *Fighting Power: German and U.S Army Performance, 1939–1945*, 6.
56. Glantz, *From the Don to the Dnepr*, 364.

CHAPTER 12: AFTERMATH: 6. ARMEE RETREATS FROM THE MIUS
1. FMS #C-078, 65.
2. Ibid., 66.
3. NA/T-312, reel 1468, frame, Die Abwehrschlacht der 6. Armee zwischen Mius and Dnjepr vom 18.8.–20.9.1943.
4. Carell, *Scorched Earth*, 312.
5. NA/T-312, reel 1468, frame 39, Die Abwehrschlacht der 6. Armee.
6. NA/T-312, reel 1468, frame 42, Die Abwehrschlacht der 6. Armee.
7. Ziemke and Bauer, *Stalingrad to Berlin*, 160.
8. NA/T-312, reel 1468, frame 43, Die Abwehrschlacht der 6. Armee.
9. Ziemke and Bauer, *Stalingrad to Berlin*, 161.
10. NA/T-312, reel 1468, frame 47, Die Abwehrschlacht der 6. Armee.
11. NA/T-312, reel 1468, frame 49, Einkesselung und Ausbruch des XXIX. Armeekorps bei Taganrog—27.8.1943–4.9.1943.
12. Ibid., frame 52.
13. Carell, *Scorched Earth*, 311.
14. Ziemke and Bauer, *Stalingrad to Berlin*, 162.
15. Manstein, *Lost Victories*, 459.
16. Carell, *Scorched Earth*, 312.
17. Ibid., 314.
18. Seaton, *Russo-German War*, 372–73; and Carell, *Scorched Earth*, 316.
19. NA/T-312, reel 1468, frame 53, Einkesselung und Ausbruch des XXIX. Armeekorps bei Taganrog.
20. Ibid., frame 54.
21. Ziemke and Bauer, *Stalingrad to Berlin*, 162.
22. NA/T-312, reel 1468, frame 55–56, Einkesselung und Ausbruch.
23. Ibid.
24. NA/T-312, reel 1468, frame 57, Einkesselung und Ausbruch, Absetzen auf die "Schildroten" Stellung.
25. Manstein, *Lost Victories*, 460.
26. Ibid.
27. NA/T-312, reel 1468, frame 58, Absetzen auf die "Schildroten" Stellung, 27.8.1943.
28. Ziemke and Bauer, *Stalingrad to Berlin*, 164.
29. Manstein, *Lost Victories*, 463–64.

CHAPTER 13: CONCLUSIONS AND REVIEW
1. Solovyov, *Turning-Point of World War II*, 79.
2. Glantz, *Soviet Military Deception in the Second World War*, 154.
3. Militararchiv der Deutschen Demokratischen Republik, No. 02, 14/2, 340, quoted in Solovyov, *Turning-Point of World War II*.

Notes

4. Erickson, *Road to Berlin*, 104.
5. P. A. Rotmistrov, *Stal'naya gvardiya* (Moscow: Voenizdat, 1984), quoted in Richard M. Armstrong, *Red Army Tank Commanders: The Armored Guards* (Atglen, PA: Schiffer Military History, 1994).
6. Glantz, *Soviet Military Deception*, 171.
7. Erickson, *Road to Berlin*, 116.
8. Robert L. Koehl, *The Black Corps: The Structure and Power Struggles of the Nazi SS* (Madison, WI: University of Wisconsin Press, 1983), 167.

Bibliography

Much of the basis for this book was primary material, although a large number of other sources were utilized as well. The major primary material source was the microfilmed German records available at the National Archives in Washington, DC. These reels of film can be located by utilizing the finding guides that are available in the microfilm room. If one studies the sources and bibliographies of most books on the campaigns and history of the SS divisions that were not written by former soldiers of the Waffen SS, it will be apparent that few of these authors have utilized primary records. Most cite earlier books almost exclusively as their sources, choosing not to do any original research or, in some cases, being guilty of sloppy work. It is this lack of proper research that contributed to the acceptance of incorrect information regarding the battle of Prochorovka. When these "facts" appeared in print in the first histories of the Eastern Front, they were simply accepted as fact by subsequent authors. However, the information found in the records of II. SS-Panzerkorps force one to reevaluate the accounts of what actually happened during this important battle.

A factor that contributed to this situation was the unavailability of the operational records of the Waffen SS divisions that fought on the Eastern Front until 1978. The last National Archive finding guide listing these microfilm records was not published until 1981. The earliest guide to the captured records of the Waffen SS divisions that were on microfilm at the National Archives, listed only the micro-film reels involving Western Front operations. It is volume 27 of the captured German records guides and provides information regarding record group T-354, Miscellaneous SS Records; Einwandererzentralstell, Waffen SS and SS Oberabschnitte. It was published in 1961.

Later finding guides list the operational records of Waffen SS units that fought on the Eastern Front. The records are incomplete for most of the divisions and the daily combat reports compiled by the Ia (operations officer) are often missing for most of the war, particularly those records of units that fought in Russia. Small-unit battle reports (*Kriegstagesbücher* for regiments or battalions) are almost non-existent for any of the divisions. Much material was either lost, destroyed by the divisions before their surrender or fell into the hands of the Russians and is currently unavailable. However, an enormous amount of information was micro-filmed and is in the National Archives, available to anyone who takes the time to search for it.

Secondary sources of information that were of the greatest value to me consisted of books by former soldiers of the Waffen SS and German Army. Two of these were extremely important in fleshing out the accounts of battles with a wealth of detail and 1st person accounts. Wolfgang Vopersal's enormous eight-volume history of 3. SS-Panzer-Division *Totenkopf* is full of reports, pictures, maps, and information taken from division-, corps, and army-level records. It contains verbal accounts by former members of the division describing the actions and battles of the division from their experience. This remarkable work is the most extensive unit history that I am aware of and any student of the Waffen SS would be well advised to collect all eight volumes. This work is currently out of print and somewhat difficult to obtain but well worth the effort and expense. Otto Weidinger, a veteran of 2. SS-Panzer-Division *Das Reich*, wrote an excellent history of his old division and its operations during the war and these volumes were also a source of much information.

A large number of other secondary sources are listed in the bibliography but particular mention needs to be made in regard to two books written by Colonel David Glantz. The first, entitled *Soviet Military Deception in the Second World War*, provided me with the information that linked the battle of Kursk with the battles of 17 July to 3 August on the Mius River. It describes the Soviet concept of military deception, which is known as maskirovka and gives many examples of its use during the war. A second Glantz volume, *From the Don to the Dnepr*, deals with Soviet offensive operations from late 1942 until summer of 1943. It furnished invaluable information about Soviet planning, the remarkable improvements in force structure, operational accounts and conduct of battle during the 1943. The description of the events of Operation "Rumyantsev" were particularly valuable. These are fascinating books and are absolutely basic reading for anyone who wants to begin to understand the war in Russia from the Soviet point of view.

I utilized the available primary sources whenever possible. However, the vast majority of this information is of German origin, either from the captured German records or books and studies written by German officers and men who fought during the war. A vast empty gulf exists in regard to what happened on the Russian side of the hill. There are various memoirs written by Soviet commanders such as Zhukov, Vatutin, and others, but none of these furnish the day to day detail necessary for in depth studies of the battles of the Eastern Front. There is a great deal of information available, however, but it is almost all in Russian and translation has been slow. Thanks to the efforts of Colonel Glantz and others, Soviet studies and accounts are being translated. As this information becomes more available, it will contribute to a greater understanding of the events of the Second World War in Russia.

MICROFILMED CAPTURED GERMAN RECORDS FROM THE NATIONAL ARCHIVES OF THE UNITED STATES (ARCHIVES II AT COLLEGE PARK, MARYLAND)
Record Group T-312, Records of German Field Commands, Armies
    Armeeoberkommando 6 (formerly Armee-Abteilung Hollidt): reel 1468
    Armee-Abteilung Kempf: reel 54
    Armeeoberkommando 9: reel 321
Record Group T-313, Records of German Field Commands, Panzer Armies
    Panzer Armeeoberkommando 4: reel 368
Record Group T-314, Records of German Field Commands Army Corps
    Generalkommando DI. Panzerkorps: reel 201
    Generalkommando XXIV. Panzerkorps: reel 720, 721, 722
    Generalkommando XXIX. Armeekorps: reel 815
    Generalkommando XXXXVIII. Panzerkorps: reel 1170
Record Group T-315, Records of German Field Commands, divisions
    KTB of 306. Infanterie Division: reel 2029
Record Group T-354, Miscellaneous SS Records
    Einwandererzentralstelle, Waffen SS and SS Oberabschnitte
    Generalkommando II. SS Panzerkorps: reel 605

MEMOIRS, DIVISION HISTORIES, AND BOOKS BY WEHRMACHT OR WAFFEN SS VETERANS
Befehl des Gewissens: Charkow, Winter 1943 Osnabrück: Munin Verlag, 1976.
Das Regiment "Deutschland," 1934–1945. "Deutschland" Regiment kameradschaft, 1987.
Die Geheimen Tagesberichte der Deutschen Wehrmachtführung im Zweiten Weltkrieg, 1939–1945, vol. 7. 1993.
Guderian, Heinz. *Panzer Leader.* London: Michael Joseph, 1952.

Lehmann, Rudolf. *1. SS Panzer Division "Leibstandarte Adolf Hitler,"* vol. III. Winnipeg: J. J. Fedorowicz Publishing, 1993.
Manstein, Erich von. *Lost Victories.* Novato, CA: Presidio, 1982.
Mellenthin, Generalmajor F. W. *The 48th Panzercorps: November 1942 to July 1944.* Germantown: Ostfront Publishing, 1994.
——. *Panzer Battles: A Study of the Employment of Armor in the Second World War.* New York: Ballantine, 1960.
Stadler, Silvester. *Die Offensive gegen Kursk: II. SS Panzerkorps als Stoßkeil im Großkampf.* Osnabrück: Munin Verlag, 1980.
Steiner, Felix. *Die Freiwilligen: Idee und Opfergang.* Göttingen: Plesse Verlag, 1958.
Ullrich, Karl. *Wie ein Fels im Meer—Kriegsgeschichte der 3. SS Panzerdivision "Totenkopf,"* vols. 1 and 2. Osnabrück: Munin Verlag, 1987.
Vopersal, Wolfgang. *Soldaten-Kämpfer-Kameraden: Marsch und Kämpfe der SS-Totenkopfdivision,* vol. III. Osnabrück: Truppenkameradschaft der 3. SS-Panzer-Division, 1990.
Weidinger, Otto. *Division Das Reich: Der Weg der 2. SS Panzer Division "Das Reich."* Osnabrück: Munin Verlag.
——. *Kameraden bis zum Ende: Das SS Panzergrenadier Regiment 4 "Der Führer" 1938 bis 1945,* vol. IV. Göttingen: Verlag K. W. Schutz, 1987.

BOOKS

Armstrong, Col. Richard N. *Red Army Legacies: Essays on Forces, Capabilities, and Personalities.* Atglen, PA: Schiffer Military History, 1995.
——. *Red Army Tank Commanders: The Armored Guards.* Atglen, PA: Schiffer Military History, 1994.
Bartov, Omer. *Hitler's Army: Soldiers, Nazis, and War in the Third Reich.* London: Oxford University Press, 1991.
Bender, Roger James, and Hugh Page Taylor. *Uniforms, Organization, and History of the Waffen SS.* 5 vols. San Jose, CA: R. James Bender Publishing, 1986.
Carell, Paul. *Scorched Earth: The Russian-German War, 1943–1944.* Atglen, PA: Schiffer Military History, 1994.
Clark, Alan. *Barbarossa: The Russian-German Conflict, 1941–45.* New York: William Morrow and Company.
Cross, Robin. *"Citadel": The Battle of Kursk.* New York: Sarpedon, 1993.
Erickson, John. *The Road to Berlin.* Boulder, CO: Westview Press, 1983.
Gilbert, Felix. *Hitler Directs His War.* London: Tandem Books, 1950.
Glantz, Col. David M. *From the Don to the Dnepr: Soviet Offensive Operations, December 1942–August 1943.* London: Frank Cass and Co., 1991.
——. *Soviet Defensive Tactics at Kursk, July 1943.* Combat Studies Institute: U.S. Army Command and General Staff College, 1986.
——. *Soviet Military Deception in the Second World War.* London: Frank Cass and Co., 1989.
Jukes, Geoffrey. *Kursk: The Clash of Armour.* New York: Ballantine, 1968.
Keegan, John. *Waffen SS: The Asphalt Soldiers.* New York: Ballantine, 1970.
Koehl, Robert L. *The Black Corps: The Structure and Power Struggles of the Nazi SS.* Madison, WI: University of Wisconsin Press, 1983.
Krausnick, Helmut, et al. *Anatomy of the SS State.* New York: Walker and Co.
Kurowski, Franz. *Panzer Aces.* Winnipeg: J. J. Fedorowicz Publishing, 1993.
Lucas, James. *"Das Reich": The Military Role of the 2nd SS Division.* London: Arms and Armour Press, 1991.

Luther, Craig W. H. *Blood and Honor: The History of the 12th SS Panzer Division.* San Jose, CA: R. James Bender Publishing, 1987.

Madeja, W. Victor. *The Russo-German War.* Vol. 31. Allentown: Valor Publishing Company, 1987.

Mitcham, Samuel W. *Hitler's Legions: The German Army Order of Battle, World War II.* Briar Cliff Manor: Stein and Day, 1985.

Newton, Steven H. *German Battle Tactics on the Russian Front, 1941–1945.* Atglen, PA: Schiffer Military Publishing, 1994.

Niehorster, Dr. Leo W. G. *German World War II Organizational Series.* Vol. 3/II. Hannover: Germany,1992.

Piekalkiewicz, Janusz. *Operation "Citadel": Kursk and Orel: The Greatest Tank Battle of the Second World War.* Novato, CA: Presidio Press, 1987.

Reinhardt, Klaus. *Moscow: The Turning Point: The Failure of Hitler's Strategy in the Winter of 1941–42.* Oxford: Berg Publishers.

Reitlinger, Gerald. *The SS: Alibi of a Nation.* London: Arms and Armour Press, 1981.

Sadarananda, Dana V. *Beyond Stalingrad: Manstein and the Operations of Army Group Don.* New York: Praeger, 1990.

Sajer, Guy. *The Forgotten Soldier.* Baltimore, MD: The Nautical and Aviation Publishing Company, 1967.

Seaton, Albert. *The Russo-German War, 1941–45.* New York: Praeger Publishers, 1971.

Sharp, Charles C. *Soviet Order of Battle: "School of Battle"—Soviet Tank Corps and Tank Brigades, January 1942 to 1945.* Vol. 2. West Chester: George F. Nafziger, 1995.

Schneider, Jost W. *Their Honor Was Loyalty! An Illustrated and Documentary History of the Knight's Cross Holders of the Waffen SS and Police, 1940–1945.* San Jose, CA: R. James Bender Publishing.

Shtemenko, General of the Army S. M. *The Soviet General Staff at War, 1941–1945.* Moscow: Progress Publishers. 1970.

Solovyov, Boris. *The Turning-Point of World War II (The Campaigns of Summer and Autumn 1943 on the Soviet-German Front).* Moscow: Progress Publishers, 1973.

Spaeter, Hellmuth. *The History of the Panzerkorp "Grossdeutschland."* Vol. I and II. Winnipeg, Canada: J. J. Fedorowicz Publishing, 1992.

Stein, George H. *The Waffen SS: Hitler's Elite Guard at War, 1939–1945.* London: Cornell University Press, 1966.

Sydnor, Charles W. *Soldiers of Destruction: The SS Death's Head Division, 1933–1945.* Princeton, NJ: Princeton University Press, 1977.

Tsouras, Peter G., ed. *The Anvil of War: German Generalship in Defense on the Eastern Front.* London: Greenhill Books, 1994.

Van Creveld, Martin. *Fighting Power: German and U.S. Army Performance, 1939–1945.*

Wegner, Bernd. *The Waffen SS: Organization, Ideology, and Function.* Oxford: Basil Blackwell, 1990.

Williamson, Gordon. *Infantry Aces of the Reich.* London: Arms and Armour Press, 1991.

Wray, Major Timothy A. *Standing Fast: German Defensive Doctrine on the Russian Front during World War II.* Combat Studies Institute, U.S. Army Command and General Staff College, 1986.

Yerger, Mark C. *Knights of Steel: The Structure, Development, and Personalities of the 2. SS-Panzer-Division "Das Reich."* Vol. I. Hershey: Horetsky Publishing, 1989.

———. *Knights of Steel.* Vol. II. Lancaster, PA: Self-published, 1994.

Zhukov, Marshal Georgi K. *Marshal Zhukov's Greatest Battles.* New York: Harper and Row.

Ziemke, Earl F. and Magda Bauer. *Stalingrad to Berlin: The German Defeat in the East.* Army Historical Series. Washington, DC: Center of Military History, U.S.Army, 1968.

INTERVIEWS OF GERMAN OFFICERS CONDUCTED BY THE U.S. ARMY AFTER THE SECOND WORLD WAR (FOREIGN MILITARY STUDIES)

C-058, *Experience Gained in Combat with Russian Infantry.*

C-078, *Sixth Army, Russia.*

D-154, *Experience with Russian Methods of Warfare and Their Utilization at the Waffen SS Panzergrenadier School.*

D-228, *Russian Artillery in the Battle for Modlin and German Countermeasures.*

D-253, *Anti-Tank Defense in the East.*

Acknowledgments

This book could not have been written in its present form without the help and encouragement of many individuals who contributed to the research, writing and production of the manuscript.

I want to thank Mark C. Yerger, author of a number of books on the Waffen SS, including two comprehensive volumes on the personnel and history of 2. SS-Panzer-Division *Das Reich*, who graciously responded to my letters and made available to me his extensive collection of records, documents and photographs. He helped in many ways, patiently answered many questions and in general, provided a great deal of encouragement. Mark loaned me copies of the personnel records of Waffen SS veterans as well as various reports or decorations forms describing wartime actions of these men. This material helped flesh out the accounts of fighting with personal touches from the individual point of view. Many of the photographs of Waffen SS men, vehicles and officers in this book are from his files. His knowledge of what information regarding the Waffen SS combat records is available on microfilm at the National Archives was a great help and saved me large amounts of research time and effort. All of his efforts have been greatly appreciated.

The staff of the library at Arkansas Tech University in Russellville, Arkansas, patiently tolerated my unending requests for books and material through interlibrary loan. They helped me obtain some of the early basic research and their efforts are also appreciated. I would also like to thank the courteous staff of the National Archives in Washington, DC, who helped me complete research of the microfilmed captured German war records during my visits to that facility.

Several individuals read and critiqued the manuscript in its early stages and made sound suggestions that improved its quality in each instance. Special thanks goes to Colonel Darryl W. Nash, U.S. Army, who edited and proofread the manuscript on a number of occasions and provided valuable advice in a number of areas. He generously made himself available to discuss my research at every stage. His knowledge of the German army and military history of the Second World War proved invaluable. Suggestions made by Colonel Nash, early in the writing process, contributed greatly to a needed tightening and restructuring of the book.

A number of other individuals supplied advice and help during the three years of writing and research. Dr. Hugh Moomaw read early drafts and provided editorial advice that aided in the organization of the material at the earliest stage of the work. My brother, James Nipe, also read the first typewritten drafts and made many significant contributions to the quality of the writing. Most valuably, he encouraged his computer-illiterate brother to become part of the computer age. Without my trusty MacIntosh, this work would have never been completed. My friend and roommate from college, John F. Loving, graciously allowed me to bore him on numerous occasions with my discussions about my research and in general provided encouragement that aided in the completion of this book.

I want to especially thank both of my parents, who provided a home in which reading was an important part of everyday life. From my earliest years, they fostered my love of books and reading. My desire to study history was inevitably influenced by the presence in their home of shelves full of books on many periods of history. My father's love of history has always been evident and his influence was an important factor in my desire to write this book.

Finally, I want to thank my wife, Linda, and my son, George III, who put up with my trips to the National Archives, the many hours spent on the computer and the piles of paper, copies of German war records, and stacks of books which clutter our house. I deeply appreciate their love and patience. Without their encouragement and belief, this work may never have been finished.

Index

air activity, Soviet, 103, 106–7, 109, 114, 121, 213, 241–42, 245, 250, 268, 270, 288, 325, 345–46, 387, 402.
See also individual aircraft types
Akhtyrka, 373, 374, 375, 414, 415, 416, 417, 424, 426, 434, 443
Alexsandrovka, 358, 359, 360, 361, 366, 367, 378, 385
Alexseyevka, 391, 398, 402, 404, 407, 408, 409, 446, 451
Antonov, A. I., 177
armies, German
  1. Panzerarmee, 1, 2, 88, 99, 131, 173, 174, 181, 453, 454, 465, 466, 467, 501
  2. Panzerarmee, 22, 31
  4. Panzerarmee, xi, xvii, xx, xxii, 26, 27, 31, 32–37, 41, 62, 63, 70, 75, 80, 81, 91, 174, 176, 331, 337, 338, 339, 347, 370, 373, 397, 415, 417, 427, 434, 478, 482, 486, 492
  6. Armee, x, xiii, xxi, xxii, xxiii, 1, 7–12, 14, 15, 16, 17, 19, 20, 93, 95–148, 170, 172, 173, 174, 183–99, 207, 214, 223, 229, 232, 234, 241, 252, 256, 259, 260, 261, 263, 267, 271, 272, 281, 284, 290, 296, 297, 299, 321, 322, 325, 327, 329, 333, 347, 435, 441–71, 477, 488–94, 501, 502
  8. Armee, xi, 331, 434, 435, 444, 469. *See also* Armee-Abteilung Kempf
  9. Armee, xx, 22, 25, 29–32, 71, 334, 469, 478
  18. Armee, xiii
armies, Soviet
  1st Guards, 2
  1st Tank, xi, 28, 31, 32, 34, 35, 36, 37, 45, 64, 66, 76, 87, 91, 170, 175, 176, 178, 198, 300, 301, 334, 337, 340, 341, 342, 346, 350, 352, 356, 357, 358, 359, 363, 370, 377, 378, 380, 382, 389, 390, 397, 399, 407, 413, 418, 427, 438, 439, 477, 478, 481, 493
  2nd Guards, 111, 446, 447
  3rd, xvii
  3rd Guards Tank, 75, 76, 483
  3rd Tank, 2, 22, 30, 31, 36, 170, 182
  4th Tank, 22, 30, 31, 36, 75, 76, 176, 182
  5th Guards, xi, 36, 50, 182, 338, 340
  5th Guards Tank, xi, 22, 28, 34, 35, 36, 37, 38, 39, 40, 54, 58, 59, 62, 63, 72, 74, 78, 85, 92, 170, 176, 198, 297, 301, 334, 337, 340, 341, 342, 344, 350, 352, 358, 359, 370, 380, 382–83, 389, 394, 397, 413, 414, 430, 434, 438, 439, 475, 477, 479, 480, 481, 485, 486, 493, 494
  5th Shock, 111
  6th Guards, xi, 2, 7, 28, 31, 32, 34, 75, 175, 338, 361–62, 375, 413, 494
  7th Guards, 31, 54, 56, 57, 58
  8th Guards, 181
  10th, xix
  16th, xvii
  27th, xi, 72, 373, 374, 375, 413, 415, 417, 424, 426
  38th Guards, 28, 75
  39th, xx
  40th Guards, 28, 32, 75
  53rd, 338, 343, 344
  60th Guards, 28
  64th, 2
  65th Guards, 28, 75
  68th Guards, 75
  69th Guards, 54, 57, 64
  70th Guards, 28

army detachments, German
  Armee-Abteilung Hollidt, x, 2, 4, 7–12. *See also* armies, German, 6. Armee
  Armee-Abteilung Kempf, 26, 31, 32–37, 39, 55, 56, 61, 70, 75, 176, 331, 337, 339, 340, 347, 354, 362, 364, 370, 394, 397, 418, 431, 478, 492, 496. *See also* armies, German, 8. Armee
army groups, German
  Heeresgruppe A, 3, 449, 453, 467, 501
  Heeresgruppe B, 1, 2, 337
  Heeresgruppe Don, xxii, xxiii, 1, 2, 3. *See also* army groups, German, Heeresgruppe Süd
  Heeresgruppe Mitte, xiii, xiv, xv, xvi, xvii, xviii, xix, xxi, 20, 21, 31, 32, 75, 170, 182, 455, 456, 467, 469, 470, 483, 501
  Heeresgruppe Nord, xiii, xxi, 455
  Heeresgruppe Süd, ix, x, xi, xiii, xxiii, 1, 3, 5, 6, 8, 9, 20, 21, 26, 28, 32, 35, 40, 64, 70, 71, 74, 88, 96, 117, 122, 131, 138, 172, 173, 174, 175, 181, 182, 199, 261, 296, 297, 299, 333, 347, 434, 435, 439, 441, 443, 444, 449, 450, 451, 453, 467, 468, 469, 470, 481, 490, 492, 493, 494, 501, 502
Artemovka, 122, 124, 252, 259, 447
artillery, German, 35, 103, 104, 115, 140, 145, 194, 209, 216, 223, 232, 238, 240, 262, 272, 274, 280, 289, 290, 291, 296, 344, 392, 402, 430
artillery, Soviet, 13–14, 15, 16, 40, 56, 91, 140, 141, 204, 211, 218, 230, 237, 240, 243, 270, 273, 277, 283, 284, 291, 321, 323, 325, 327, 340, 341, 376, 433
assault guns, German, 26, 27, 96, 98, 100, 110, 112, 131, 138, 147, 224, 230, 276, 278, 279, 282, 286, 287, 386, 401, 407, 424
  Brummbär, 25, 84
  Elephant, 26, 84
  Sturmgeschütz III, 26, 28, 299

balka, 97
Baum, Otto, 191–92, 201, 264, 289, 427
Becker, Helmut, 499
Belaya Gora, 99, 110, 111
Belenichino, 67
Belgorod, ix, 21, 28, 29, 36, 174, 175, 176, 181, 182, 198, 297, 300, 301, 330, 333, 338, 340, 342, 348, 350, 352, 375, 434, 491
  defense of, 343–47
Beresovka, 419
Berlin, 183
Black Sea, 444, 456
Bochmann, Georg, 396
Bock, Fedor von, xiii, xiv, xviii, xix, xx
Bogodukhov, 87, 91, 184, 332, 334, 335, 345, 347, 443
  assault of *Totenkopf* on Merla River, 418–20, 422–24, 426–31, 433
  counterattack of III. Panzerkorps at, 350, 353–67, 369–70
  counterattack of 5th Guards Tank Army at, 382–83
  battles around, x, 337–72, 474, 476, 477, 488, 494–96
  fighting on western shoulder, 373–75
  fighting south of, 376–82
  Germans counterattack (15 August), 402, 404, 406–8
  Germans strike back (12 August), 383, 385–87, 389
Borisovka, 345, 347, 375
Bork, Max, 284
Brauchitsch, Walter von, xx
Breith, Hermann, 27, 39, 40, 54, 55, 60, 63, 85, 480, 481
Busch, Ernst, xiii

casualties, 19, 326, 370, 436, 443, 445, 464, 473, 488
  effect on Wehrmacht, 11–12
Cherkassy, 469
Chistyakov, I. M., 32
Chuikov, V. I., 181
corps, German
  II. SS-Panzerkorps, x, xxiii, 7, 26, 32, 33, 35, 38, 39, 40, 41, 42, 47, 50, 52, 55, 58, 62, 64, 65–70, 78, 80–82, 83, 85, 86, 87, 89, 91–93,

Index

124, 131, 132, 147, 174, 175, 182, 184–90, 194, 198, 199, 207, 214, 215, 216, 220, 221, 224, 225, 227, 231, 234, 238, 241, 245, 250, 258, 259, 260, 261, 262, 263, 267–68, 271, 276, 281, 286, 288, 290, 294, 297, 299–301, 321, 322, 325, 326, 327, 330, 331, 332, 333, 337, 347, 377, 441, 443, 464, 477, 479, 480, 481, 483, 485, 487, 490, 492
  III. Panzerkorps, x, xi, 27, 32, 33, 37, 39, 40, 42, 54, 55, 56, 58, 59, 60, 63–64, 72, 86, 87, 91, 184, 235, 332, 334, 337, 347–48, 350, 352, 352–67, 369–70, 370, 372, 373–79, 477, 480, 488, 494, 496
  IV. Armeekorps, 8, 96, 460
  IV. Fliegerkorps, 125, 185, 253, 264
  XI. Armeekorps, 339, 340
  XII. Armeekorps, xvii
  XIII. Armeekorps, xvii
  XVII. Armeekorps, 9, 10, 15, 95, 96, 99, 110, 139, 188, 221–24, 250, 251, 252, 444, 445, 451, 457, 458, 460
  XX. Armeekorps, xx
  XXIV. Panzerkorps, xviii, 28, 64, 69, 70, 72, 74, 78, 79, 87, 96, 131, 138, 139–48, 174, 184, 186, 189, 198, 224–29, 232, 250, 255–59, 264, 271, 282–85, 289, 297, 321, 322, 330, 333, 347, 362, 372, 376, 377, 415, 417, 422, 426, 443, 481, 482, 483, 491
  XXIX. Armeekorps, 9, 15, 96, 99, 100, 101, 102, 103, 104, 108, 110, 143, 187, 188, 198, 224, 229–32, 250, 252–55, 257, 258, 263, 279–82, 333, 442, 444, 448, 449, 450, 452, 456–71
  XL. Panzerkorps, 173
  XXXXI. Panzerkorps, 25
  XXXXVI. Panzerkorps, 25
  XXXXVII. Panzerkorps, 25
  XXXXVIII. Panzerkorps, xxiii, 7, 26, 32, 33, 34, 39, 45, 62, 84, 175, 182, 300, 338, 346, 377, 488
  LVI. Panzerkorps, xvii
corps, Soviet
  2nd Cavalry, xviii

  2nd Guards Mechanized, 15, 95, 105, 109, 111, 113, 120, 133, 136, 225, 229, 235, 298, 332, 441
  2nd Guards Tank, 37, 40, 42, 55, 59, 63, 475, 480
  2nd Tank, 33, 37, 38, 40, 42, 54, 57, 59, 63, 475
  3rd Guards Mechanized, 5, 28, 32, 34, 382, 415
  3rd Mechanized, 342, 353, 355, 356, 358, 367
  4th Guards Mechanized, 104, 105, 116, 118, 124, 131, 132, 133, 136–39, 198, 449, 450, 451, 490, 493
  4th Mechanized, xxiii
  4th Tank, xxiii, 2, 373, 375
  5th Guards Mechanized, 38, 40, 42, 45, 46–47, 54, 57, 60, 61, 352, 354, 355
  6th Tank, 28, 342, 353, 356, 357, 358, 359, 363, 364, 378, 382, 385, 386, 393, 394, 397, 407
  9th Tank, 29
  10th Tank, 29, 33, 426
  18th Tank, 38, 40, 41, 42, 43, 44, 46, 55, 60, 61, 62, 63, 82, 352, 389, 390, 430
  29th Tank, 38, 40, 41, 42, 46, 55, 60, 61, 63, 82, 352, 356, 358, 394, 414
  31st Tank, 28, 34, 35, 43, 50, 65, 66, 74, 378, 382, 389
  33rd Guards Rifle, 65, 74
  33rd Rifle, 34, 35, 51
  49th Tank, 369
Crimea, 117, 453

deception, Soviet. *See maskirovka*
Dietrich, Sepp, 192, 337
Dmitrievka, 95, 96, 100, 104, 109, 121, 124, 132, 133, 136, 147, 172, 181, 188, 194, 201, 202, 225, 228, 231, 235, 244, 295, 297, 322, 325, 329, 435, 441, 442, 443, 444, 445, 448, 489, 491
  attack at, 111–17
Dnepr River, xiii, 181, 335, 434, 439, 461, 462, 464, 465, 466, 467, 468, 469, 470, 471, 502
Dnepropetrovsk, 2, 469

Dnepropetrovsk-Mariupol railway, 3
Dolbino, 365
Don River, xix, 2, 36
Donbas River, 333
Donets River, 2, 35, 39, 56, 57, 58, 59, 61, 99, 131, 181, 329, 338, 339, 340, 344, 453, 455, 463, 465, 478
Dunkirk, 323

Eastern Front, ix, x, xiv, xxiii, 1, 3, 7, 8, 16, 17, 19, 22, 25, 37, 48, 70, 71, 79, 87, 89, 90, 107, 108, 110, 111, 117, 148, 170, 175, 183, 192, 193, 195, 197, 325, 329, 335, 337, 348, 376, 437, 442, 473, 476, 485, 488, 497, 498, 499, 500, 501, 503
Eicke, Theodor, 192–93, 196, 197
engineers, 34, 35, 51, 194, 205, 238, 264, 286, 287, 290, 327, 367, 418, 419

Fedorovka, 296
"fire brigades," 91, 348, 376, 497
Franke, Kurt, 418–19
fronts, Soviet
 Bryansk Front, xiv, 30
 Central, 29, 470, 479, 483
 Kalinin, 470
 Reserve, xiv
 Southern, 4, 5, 92, 124, 148, 172, 174, 181, 183, 296, 297, 333, 347, 435, 444, 465, 489, 493, 494
 Southwest, xiv, 2, 7, 181, 184, 465, 494
 Steppe, 28, 32, 34, 58, 72, 170, 174, 176, 299, 300, 350, 435, 470, 475, 479
 Voronezh, 2, 170, 175, 299, 300, 341, 377, 413, 414, 417, 475, 479
 West, xiv, xvii, 30, 469

Garany, 138, 140, 189, 225, 226, 227, 228, 232, 246, 257, 282
Gerassimova Valley, 113, 114, 115, 121, 201, 209, 212, 215, 220, 233, 238, 243–45, 268, 295, 322, 327
Golikov, F. I., 2
Golovchino, 345
Grigorievka, 137, 143, 147

Guderian, Heinz, 180, 334, 475
 opposes "Citadel," 22–24, 25
Gulf of Taganrog, 117, 456

Harmel, Heinz, 59, 219
Hausser, Paul, 26, 38, 40, 50, 61, 62, 65, 68, 69, 70, 77, 78, 80, 83, 85, 89, 182, 191, 192, 232, 260, 262, 262, 265, 268, 300, 347, 477, 478, 480, 481, 485, 486, 491, 497, 500
Heeresgruppen. *See* army groups, German
Himmler, Heinrich, xvi, 348
Hitler, Adolf, x, xi, xiii, xiv, xv, xvi, xvii, xix, xx, xxi, xxii, 2, 3, 4, 26, 63, 64, 91, 93, 172, 173, 179, 182, 300, 301, 333, 348, 437, 438, 439, 443, 453, 471, 473, 474–75, 476, 481, 482, 483, 491, 492, 493, 496, 502, 503
 attention turns elsewhere at critical stage, 70
 consequences of decisions, 76–77, 88
 creates new 6. Armee, 7
 decides to launch "Citadel," 22–25
 loses will to continues "Citadel," 88
 makes decisions disregarding reality, 180
 makes poor decisions after Stalingrad, 1
 meets with Manstein, 453–56, 467–68, 469
 meets with Manstein and Kluge, 70–72
 orders II. SS-Panzerkorps to aid 6. Armee, 131
 pulls back II. SS-Panzerkorps, 32
 relies on SS divisions, 183
 vetoes withdrawal from Kharkov, 431
Hoepner, Erich, xx
Hollidt, Karl, x, 2, 3, 4, 7, 8, 10, 20, 95, 96, 101, 102, 112, 116, 117, 118, 119, 122, 123, 124, 125, 130, 131, 132, 136, 137, 138, 139, 145–46, 147, 148, 172, 183, 186, 187, 188, 190, 198, 199, 232, 250, 261, 263, 327–29, 330, 331, 333, 347, 441, 442, 443, 444, 445, 448, 450, 451, 452, 454, 456, 457, 462, 464, 488, 489, 490, 491, 502

Index

Hoth, Hermann, xxii, 3, 26, 32, 34, 35, 36, 39, 40, 54, 58, 62, 63, 337, 361, 414, 416, 435, 478

Ilyushin-2 (IL-2), 50, 106–7, 129, 194, 207, 213, 221, 288, 325, 394, 441
infantry divisions, German
  15., 173
  17., 100, 231, 279, 280, 457, 459, 464
  57., 375, 416
  65., 337
  68., 416
  106., 56, 340
  111., 9, 108, 147, 187, 258, 333, 446, 451, 456, 457
  112., 416
  117., 9
  167., 26, 57, 67, 69, 339, 340, 341
  168., 56, 57, 340, 343
  198., 340, 343, 344
  223., 429, 434
  255., 338, 345
  258., 457
  294., 10, 96, 104, 109, 112, 113, 116, 121, 132, 137, 141, 145, 147, 187, 219, 230, 253, 255, 280, 281, 332, 333, 441, 445, 447, 448
  302., 9, 98, 268, 457
  304., 8, 9, 10, 98
  306., 9, 113, 115, 116, 121, 125, 127, 132, 137, 145, 206, 221, 223, 224, 235, 250, 251, 264, 267, 268, 333, 457, 458, 462
  320., 56, 340
  332., 339, 341, 345
  335., 8–9, 10, 99, 221
  336., 100, 103, 231, 446, 450, 457
  375., 188
  state of, 10–12
intelligence, German, 113, 148, 172, 229, 331, 435
  detects Soviet build-up, 15–16
  signal intereception, 15
intelligence, Soviet, 180. *See also* maskirovka
Ivanovka, 99
Izyum, 131, 173, 181, 297, 333, 443, 445, 482, 491, 492, 493

Kalinovka, 117, 119, 130, 137, 141, 142, 144, 189, 224, 227, 253, 255, 446, 448
Kalmius River, 463
Kaluga, 444
Kampfgruppe Haus, 253
Kampfgruppe Henneberg, 283
Kampfgruppe Holm, 221–22, 223, 224, 268
Kampfgruppe Picker, 449, 451
Kampfgruppe Recknagel, 108, 109
Kampfgruppe Seela, 380, 407
Kampfgruppe Tychsen, 409, 417
Kaplunovka, 426
Katschlovka, 409, 410, 417
Katukov, M. E., 32, 36, 46, 87, 178, 337, 352, 356, 357, 358, 359, 363, 381, 382, 383, 427, 438, 478, 481, 484, 495
Keitel, Wilhelm, 24
Kempf, Werner, 26, 27, 36, 37, 54, 56, 58, 62, 431, 478, 481, 488
Kharkov, x, xi, xxiii, 21, 36, 87, 91, 174, 181, 198, 265, 297, 334, 335, 338, 344, 346, 347, 350, 358, 359, 364, 370, 372, 375, 377, 413, 423, 429, 430, 431, 433, 434, 444, 473, 494, 496, 498, 501
  battles for, 170, 193, 195, 219
  German abandonment of, ix
  Manstein's counterattack at, 5–7
  Soviet attempts to encircle, 2
Khotmyzhsk, 345
Khrushchev, Nikita, 34, 73, 85, 175, 176, 182, 479, 482, 487, 495
Kiev, xiii, xiv, 469
Kluge, Günther von, xx, xxi, 22, 24, 31, 70–72, 75, 439, 468, 469, 470, 471, 481, 492, 502
Knight's Cross, 191, 192, 216, 217, 369, 380, 459, 497
Knobelsdorff, Otto von, 26, 33
Kolomak, 390, 391, 397, 399, 406, 407, 408, 429, 495
Koniev, I. S., 72, 176, 299, 300, 413
Koren River, 56
Kotel'va, 373, 374, 397, 415, 417, 420, 422, 423, 424, 427
Krassny Luch, 96
Kremenchung, 469

Kruger, Walter, 41, 260
Krynka River, 461, 462
Kuban, 117, 453, 467, 468
Kuibyshevo, 99, 100, 104, 108, 109, 110, 111, 133, 172, 194, 231, 252, 270, 280, 282, 297, 325, 331, 442, 445, 461, 489
Kursk, 175, 176, 181
   battle of, 25, 39, 46, 73, 75, 76, 107, 170, 172, 174, 195, 245, 297, 300, 332, 333, 350, 474, 485, 497, 498, 501. *See also* Operation "Citadel"
   counterattacks after, x
   reaches climax, 16–17
   salient, 37

Lend-Lease aid to Soviets, xv, 39, 290
Leningrad, xiii, xiv
Luftwaffe, xii, xiii, 10, 16, 36, 65, 102, 106–7, 115, 148, 207, 213, 221, 293, 322, 328, 402, 411, 412, 430, 474
Luftwaffe field divisions
   15. Luftwaffe-Felddivision, 9, 229, 450, 457, 459

Makeyevka, 184
Malaya Nikolayevka, 96
Malinovsky, R. Y., 181
Manstein, Erich von, xxiii, 3, 26, 28, 31, 34, 63, 74, 75, 76, 79, 89, 90, 91, 131, 169, 172, 181, 182, 193, 198, 199, 259–60, 263, 265, 328, 330, 347, 348, 350, 377, 431, 433, 435, 439, 441, 443, 453, 471, 473, 478, 480, 481, 482, 483, 490, 491, 492, 494, 502
   believes "Citadel" reaches critical point in south, 175
   believes Soviets exhausted on 1 August, 170
   believes Soviets suffered crippling losses, 300
   believes success is possible on southern wing, 73
   comments on the crisis on the Eastern Front, 3–4
   concerns about Mius operations, 123–24
   conference with Hoth and Kempf, 39–40
   continues attack, 58
   counterattacks at Kharkov, 5–7
   expects attack on Belgorod, 330–31
   loses chance to break into tank country, 64
   meets with Hitler, 70–72, 453–56, 467–68, 469
   not enthusiastic about continuing attack, 261
   obtains two divisions from Heeresgruppe Mitte, 457
   orders retreat to Kalmius River, 463
   postwar statements, 78
   proposes to move Armee-Abteilung Hollidt to Mius, 2
   stabilizes southern flank of front, 1
   takes command of Heeresgruppe Don, xxii
   voices caution ahead of "Citadel," 22, 24
Marinovka, 119, 120, 121, 130, 193, 201, 225, 246, 248, 253, 256, 258, 259, 263, 264, 271, 277, 280, 283, 285, 295, 296, 321, 322, 324
maskirovka, 36, 88, 169–76, 299, 435, 492–93, 494
Maximovka, 357, 365, 381, 392, 401
Mellenthin, Friedrich von, 53, 108, 110–11, 178, 186, 215
Merchik River, xi, 357, 358, 359, 360, 364, 366, 367, 370, 372, 377, 378, 380, 381, 382, 383, 385, 386, 389, 390, 391, 396, 398, 399, 407, 408, 409, 495
Merla River, xi, 361, 362, 370, 372, 373, 377, 378, 381, 382, 383, 398, 407, 408, 412, 414, 415, 419, 420, 423, 427, 495
mines, 97, 103, 194, 199, 205, 206, 209, 211, 213, 218, 220, 238, 243, 293, 326, 330
Mirnoje, 409, 410, 417
Mius River, 3, 4, 5, 12, 70, 89, 91–93, 172, 173, 174, 181, 182, 184, 185, 194, 195, 199, 201, 202, 216, 217, 229, 231, 235, 244, 252, 253, 264,

Index

271, 280, 285, 295, 296, 301, 441, 442, 443, 444, 445, 446, 454, 459, 460
- aftermath of victory along, 333–35
- battles along, x, xi, 95–148, 474, 476, 477, 482, 488–94
- battle as microcosm of Eastern Front, 297
- connection of battle to Kursk campaign, 297
- description of area, 12–14
- Hollidt prepares to defend, 7–12
- line retaken at, 321–33
- needs panzer divisions to move west of Kharkov, 299
- quiet descends upon, 17
- retreat to, 9

Model, Walter, 22, 24, 25, 26, 29, 30, 36, 71, 334, 469, 475, 488

Moscow, xv, xvi, xvii, 438, 473, 475
- drive to capture, ix, xiv, xviii

Moskalenko, K. S., 415

mountain divisions, German
- 3. Gebirgs-Division, 8, 188, 221, 222, 223, 252, 447, 448, 449, 457

Nebelwerfer, 206, 207, 216, 237, 239, 262, 272, 279, 286, 288, 290, 291, 292, 391, 424

Nikitovka, 378, 391, 392, 393, 394, 396, 397, 398, 401, 408, 417, 423, 429

Normandy, effects of Allied airpower in, 241

Oberkommando der Wehrmacht. *See* OKW

Oberkommando des Heeres. *See* OKH

OKH, xiv, xviii, xix, 24, 25, 170, 198, 371, 453

OKW, 331

Oleinikov, 418, 419, 423, 428

Olkhovatka, 29

Olkhovchik Valley, 113, 114, 118, 119, 143, 187, 189, 194, 198, 201, 226, 229, 230, 231, 232, 246, 252–55, 257, 261, 262, 263, 264, 270, 274, 277–78, 279, 280, 281, 283, 284, 285, 286, 289, 296, 298, 321, 324, 331, 491

Operation "Bagration," 434

Operation "Barbarossa," xiii–xx, 11

Operation "Citadel," ix, x, xi, 8, 12, 17, 70, 71, 72, 76, 82, 85, 91, 170, 173, 174, 175, 176, 180, 181, 191, 194, 195, 199, 234, 286, 297, 300, 326, 327, 350, 369, 429, 438, 439, 469, 481, 488, 492, 494, 502
- advance of 9. Armee slows, 29–32
- formations involved in, 25–29
- Germans closer to victory than believed, 90
- Hitler cancels, 70–72
- Hitler's role in launching, 22–25
- preparations for, 19–22
- reaches critical stage, 95
- review of, 474–78
- southern wing of, 32–37

Operation "Rumyantsev," 22, 76, 170, 175, 176, 177–82, 415, 434, 439, 469, 482, 494, 496, 502
- launching of, 338–43

Operation "Typhoon," xiv

Orel, 21, 30, 31, 36, 71, 75, 170, 457, 475, 491, 501

Organization Todt, 463

"Panther Line," 470

panzer divisions, German, xxi, 20, 23
- 3., 26, 87, 91, 174, 188, 206, 213, 215, 220, 222, 224, 306, 249–50, 251, 259, 267, 271, 291, 299, 321, 322, 330, 332, 334, 335, 347, 350, 352, 353, 354, 355, 356, 363, 364, 365, 366, 370, 378, 382, 423, 429, 434, 495, 496
- 6., xix, 27, 56, 57, 58, 61, 334, 342, 344
- 7., xix, 27, 56, 57, 61, 334, 350, 375, 376, 414
- 9., xvi, 457, 464, 466
- 11., 26, 334, 350, 416, 426
- 12., 25
- 13., 449, 456, 457, 458, 459, 464, 450–56
- 17., xviii, 28, 96
- 18., 25
- 19., 27, 56, 57, 334, 339, 340, 341, 342, 345, 346, 350, 426, 475

23., 28, 29, 96, 117, 119, 122, 123–36, 139, 140, 145, 147, 182, 185, 186, 187, 189, 190, 198, 213, 227, 229, 246, 255, 256, 258, 259, 270, 272, 277, 282, 284, 295, 296, 321, 329, 332, 441, 444, 453
25., 337
116., 12, 479
Hermann Goering, 9
panzergrenadier divisions, German, 20, 23
1. SS *Leibstandarte Adolf Hitler*, 26, 35, 37, 40, 41, 42, 43, 45, 46, 47, 49, 51, 52, 55, 60–63, 65, 67, 68, 69, 70, 72, 73, 74, 80, 81, 82, 83, 86, 87, 92, 191, 192, 327, 337, 474, 480, 486, 487, 497, 500
2. SS *Das Reich*, 26, 35, 37, 41, 43, 45, 46, 47, 55, 59, 60, 63, 64, 65, 67, 68, 69, 70, 73, 74, 80, 81, 82, 83, 86, 87, 91, 92, 174, 184, 186, 189, 191, 192, 211, 213, 215, 218, 219, 220, 224, 227, 228, 235, 245–49, 256, 258, 259, 260, 262, 263, 264, 268, 270, 271, 276, 278, 279, 284, 285, 286, 295, 296, 298, 299, 321, 322, 323, 324, 325, 327, 329, 330, 334, 337, 350, 353, 355, 356, 357, 358, 362, 363, 364, 370, 372, 377, 378, 379, 380, 381, 382, 383, 386, 387, 389, 391, 394, 399, 401, 407, 409, 413, 414, 415, 417, 418, 423, 429, 430, 433, 434, 438, 474, 479, 480, 482, 486, 487, 491, 495, 497, 500
3. SS *Totenkopf*, 26–27, 34, 37, 40, 41, 46, 47, 50, 51, 55, 62, 64, 65, 66, 68, 69, 70, 72, 74, 77, 80, 81, 82, 83, 86, 87, 91, 92, 174, 184, 185, 186, 188, 189, 190–99, 204, 206, 207, 208, 214, 218, 220, 232, 234, 237, 238, 240, 243, 248, 251, 252, 260, 264, 268, 270, 278, 279, 286, 289, 290, 291, 294, 296, 298, 300, 322, 323, 324, 325, 326, 327, 329, 333, 334, 337, 347, 350, 357, 359, 360, 361, 362, 369, 370, 372, 376, 377, 378, 379, 381, 382, 383, 385, 386, 389, 390, 391, 392, 393, 394, 396, 398, 399, 401, 407, 408, 409, 410, 412, 413, 415, 417, 419, 422, 423, 424, 427, 428, 429, 434, 438, 486, 487, 488, 495, 496, 497, 498, 499
5. SS *Wiking*, 28, 91, 96, 182, 191, 335, 337, 347, 362, 370, 372, 377, 378, 380, 383, 387, 389, 389, 414, 418, 423, 424, 429, 433, 495, 496, 497, 500
10., 25, 414, 426
16., xxi, 8, 12, 20, 95, 101, 112, 117, 119, 120, 121, 123, 124, 125, 127, 128, 130, 137, 140, 141, 143, 145, 147, 225, 227, 255, 256, 259, 281, 284, 321, 332, 333, 474, 489, 490
17. SS *Götz von Berlichingen*, 191
Grossdeutschland, 26, 71, 84, 335, 362, 372, 373, 374, 376, 414, 417, 420, 422, 423, 424, 426, 427, 428, 429, 434, 438, 487, 488, 492, 495
partisans, xvi
Paulus, Friedrich von, xxi, xxii, xxiii, 1, 7
Peradrievo, 213, 222, 223
Pervomaisk, 123
Petropolye, 100, 101, 102
planes, Russian, 65, 66
Poleshajev, 51
Ponyri, 29
Popov, M. M., 2, 5, 6, 7
Pravorot, 68
Priess, Hermann, 193, 195, 237, 429
Pripet River, 463
Prochorovka, 34, 35, 36, 37, 65, 66, 67, 68, 69, 70, 73, 74, 80, 81, 82, 132, 174, 175, 176, 182, 235, 300, 301, 333
 analysis of battle, 77–80
 battle as microcosm of Eastern Front, 87–88
 battle of, x, xi, 37–63, 172, 179, 182, 184, 259, 475, 476, 477, 478–88, 492, 494, 496, 503
 course of battle, 85–87
 destroyed tanks at, 85
 misunderstandings about battle, 37–38, 46
 Tigers and Panthers at, 82–85
Psel River, 32, 33, 34, 35, 36, 37, 39, 41, 42, 43, 51, 58, 64, 65, 70, 71, 72,

74, 75, 85, 86, 88, 90, 91, 132, 175,
176, 182, 234, 333, 390, 442, 479,
480, 482, 483, 493, 495

rasputitsa, xv
Ratsch-bumm, 203, 410
Raus, Erhard, 459
reconnaissance, 101, 139, 264, 287,
290, 359, 376, 379, 393, 406, 422,
428, 442
regiments, German
Regiment *Der Führer*, 59, 60, 67, 68,
191, 216, 218, 224, 233, 246, 248,
260, 261, 262, 264, 270, 271, 272,
273, 274, 275, 276, 277, 278, 279,
280, 284, 289, 322, 324, 331, 332,
353, 354, 355, 363, 364, 365, 380,
386, 401, 491
Regiment *Deutschland*, 59, 212, 216,
217, 218, 219, 229, 232, 233, 245,
246, 248, 253, 264, 268–71,
278–79, 280, 335, 378, 396, 404,
408, 409, 417, 423, 429
Regiment *Eicke*, 34, 41, 42, 51, 66,
188, 191, 201, 202, 209, 212, 233,
235, 243–45, 268, 286, 322, 324,
359, 366, 380, 385, 391, 392, 393,
396, 402, 404, 412, 418, 428, 495
Regiment *Germania*, 380, 387, 401
Regiment *Totenkopf*, 34, 35, 188, 233,
286, 287, 322, 366, 378, 379, 392,
402, 404
Regiment *Westland*, 380, 389, 401
SS-Panzer-Regiment 3, 201–16, 326
Reichenau, Walter von, xiii
Removka, 123
Rhzev, xxi
rifle divisions, Soviet
3rd Guards, 257
13th Guards, 345, 346
33rd Guards, 257
46th Guards, 257
49th Guards, 137
52nd Guards, 391, 397, 407
87th Guards, 137
92nd Guards, 57
97th Guards, 345
118th, 100, 133
127th, 100
151st, 100

271st, 100
315th, 257
320th, 100, 137
347th, 100
387th, 100, 133
Rokossovsky, K. K., 29
Rommel, Erwin, xix
Roosevelt, Franklin, xv
Rotmistrov, P. A., 22, 34, 35, 36, 37, 38,
39, 41, 42, 45, 46, 48, 52, 54, 57,
58, 60, 62, 63, 64, 65, 72, 78, 82,
85, 86, 176, 178, 179, 297, 337,
353, 362, 370, 377, 382, 383, 389,
390, 394, 413, 414, 430, 433, 434,
438, 475, 477, 479, 480, 483, 484,
485, 494, 496
Rublievka, 419, 420
Rudel, Hans, 458
Rundstedt, Gerd von, xiii

Scharovka, 396
Schmidt, Gustav, 346
Schmundt, Rudolf, xx
Schwerin, Gerhard von, 281–82
Sea of Azov, 2
Seela, Max, 380
Semenovsky, 449, 451
Sicily, campaign on, 71, 491
Simon, Max, 111
Smolensk, xiii, 469
Sozh River, 470
Stadler, Sylvester, 60, 216, 233, 260,
261, 262, 263, 270, 271, 272, 273,
274, 275, 276–77, 281, 284, 291,
324, 330, 347, 491
Stalin, Joseph, xv, xvii, xix, 1, 34, 85,
175, 176, 177, 180, 181, 437, 476,
480, 484, 493, 501
Stalingrad campaign, xxi, xxii–xxiii, 1,
4, 7, 10, 53, 169, 172, 173, 438, 473
Stalino, 122, 136, 444, 453
Stalinorgel rockets, 51, 112–13
Stavka, xvii, 1, 177
Steiner, Felix, 335, 347
Stepanovka, 119, 121, 127, 129, 130,
133, 189, 198, 205, 207, 212, 213,
216, 217, 218, 225, 228, 233, 262,
264, 264, 245–49, 267, 268–71,
272, 277, 278, 279, 285, 292, 296

Stuka dive-bomber, 25, 35, 50, 51, 107, 115, 125, 134, 143, 185, 207, 210, 211, 230, 238, 249, 253, 256, 285, 286, 289, 290, 293, 322, 323, 341, 358, 359, 392, 402, 407, 411, 458
Sturmovik. *See* Ilyushin-2
summer offensive campaigns, German, ix

Taganrog, 8, 9
tank battalions, German
   schwere-Panzer-Abteilung 503, 27, 378, 387, 392, 402, 407
tanks, German, 40, 61, 120, 126, 127, 129, 182
   captured T-34s in German service, 41
   conduct of operations, 177–79
   good communications in, 47–48
   losses, 29, 79, 291, 486, 487
   Panther, 20, 26, 78, 82–85, 86, 257, 464
   Panzer I, 137
   Panzer II, 25
   Panzer III, xvi, 25, 26, 27, 28, 35, 43, 46, 47, 81, 84, 112, 188, 195, 203, 205, 224, 245, 248, 258, 259, 286, 299, 325, 360, 396, 423, 490
   Panzer IV, xvi, 25, 26, 27, 28, 35, 43, 46, 47, 78, 81, 112, 137, 188, 195, 203, 205, 224, 245, 248, 258, 259, 286, 299, 325, 360, 396, 423, 490
   rate of production, 20
   strength at Prochorovka, 41, 46–47, 58, 80–82
   Tiger, 20, 26, 27, 35, 41, 43, 44, 45, 46, 47, 48, 62, 67, 80, 81, 82–85, 86, 201, 202, 203, 214, 248, 257, 259, 286, 299, 325, 340, 378, 387, 396, 401, 402, 410, 414, 418, 423, 436, 479, 485, 486, 487, 495
tanks, Soviet, xix, 6, 29, 40, 61, 120, 122, 124, 127, 132, 137, 142, 147–48, 218, 275, 338, 340, 361, 406, 438
   British Churchill in Soviet service, 39
   KV-1, xvi, 105, 410
   losses, 66, 67, 77, 86, 134, 366, 381, 434, 479
   poor communications in, 48
   rate of production, 20

   strength at Prochorovka, 42, 43, 45–46
   strength in June 1941, 52
   SU-152, 56
   T-34, xvi, 20, 41, 42, 43, 45, 48, 49, 50, 51, 56, 60, 62, 81, 84–85, 105, 112, 115, 123, 127, 134, 141, 142, 143, 145, 175, 204, 205, 211, 214, 233, 249, 256, 274, 275, 276, 291, 293, 346, 348, 357, 360, 364, 367, 379, 396, 407, 410, 427, 442, 471, 479, 485, 489
   T-60, 105, 357
   T-70, 39, 41, 42, 48, 62, 100, 104, 105, 123, 134
   tactical development, 54, 134–36
   training of crews, 52–53
Terploye, 29
Tolbukhin, Fedor, 92, 104, 105, 106, 108, 109, 110, 112, 118, 124, 132, 136, 138, 139, 144, 172, 174, 183, 295, 296, 297, 332, 333, 334, 347, 435, 443, 445, 446, 447, 449, 450, 464, 453, 489, 491, 493, 494
Tomarovka, 338, 339, 342, 343, 344, 345, 347, 350, 352, 375
"Tortoise Line," 453, 463, 464, 465, 466
Turovo, 412
Tychsen, Christian, 324, 409

Udy River, 430, 434
Ullrich, Karl, 66, 191, 289, 427

Vatutin, N. F., 2, 6, 7, 32, 36, 175, 299, 300, 370, 375, 383, 383, 389–90, 394, 414, 417
Volga River, xvii
Volksdeutsch recruits, xii
Vyazma, xiv

Waffen SS divisions, 337–38, 348, 350, 496–500
   quality of, xii, 92
   receive more supplies, xvi
   See also individual units
weather conditions, 35, 68
Witt, Fritz, 497
Wittmann, Michael, 43–45, 46
Wohler, Otto, 431, 433
World War I, 330

Index   551

Yak-1, 394
Yelizavetinsky, 119, 137, 141, 143, 147,
    253, 254, 279, 280, 321

Zapovka, 356, 357, 363
Zeitzler, Kurt, 24

Zhukov, Georgi, xiv, xvii, xviii,
    176, 377, 378, 390, 391, 413,
    414
Zolochev, 353, 353, 354, 355, 356,
    358, 364, 370, 378, 382, 389, 413,
    496

Stackpole Military History Series

Real battles. Real soldiers. Real stories.

Stackpole Military History Series

Real battles. Real soldiers. Real stories.

Stackpole Military History Series

Real battles. Real soldiers. Real stories.

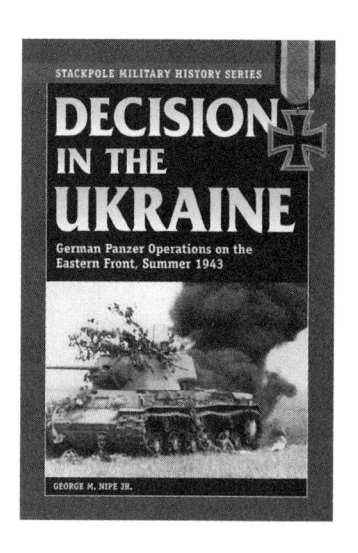

DECISION IN THE UKRAINE
German Panzer Operations on the Eastern Front, Summer 1943

GEORGE M. NIPE JR.

PANZER WEDGE
The 3rd Panzer Division's Drive on Moscow, 1941

LT. FRITZ LUCKE WITH ROBERT J. EDWARDS AND MIKE OLIVE

NEW for Fall 2012

MISSION 376
Battle over the Reich, May 28, 1944

IVO DE JONG

JG 26 LUFTWAFFE FIGHTER WING WAR DIARY
Volume Two: 1943–45

DONALD CALDWELL

Stackpole Military History Series

TIGERS IN THE MUD
THE COMBAT CAREER OF GERMAN PANZER COMMANDER OTTO CARIUS

*Otto Carius,
translated by Robert J. Edwards*

World War II began with a metallic roar as the German Blitzkrieg raced across Europe, spearheaded by the most dreadful weapon of the twentieth century: the Panzer. Tank commander Otto Carius thrusts the reader into the thick of battle, replete with the blood, smoke, mud, and gunpowder so common to the elite German fighting units.

*$21.95 • Paperback • 6 x 9 • 368 pages
51 photos • 48 illustrations • 3 maps*

**WWW.STACKPOLEBOOKS.COM
1-800-732-3669**

Stackpole Military History Series

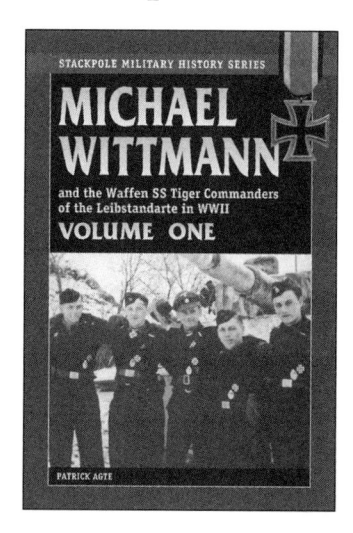

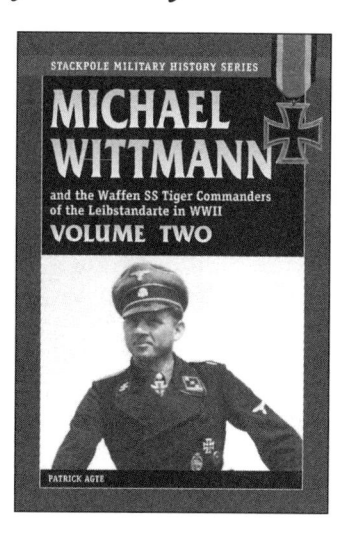

MICHAEL WITTMANN AND THE WAFFEN SS TIGER COMMANDERS OF THE LEIBSTANDARTE IN WORLD WAR II

Patrick Agte

By far the most famous tank commander on any side in World War II, German Tiger ace Michael Wittmann destroyed 138 enemy tanks and 132 anti-tank guns in a career that embodies the panzer legend: meticulous in planning, lethal in execution, and always cool under fire. Volume One covers Wittmann's armored battles against the Soviets in 1943–44 at places like Kharkov, Kursk, and the Cherkassy Pocket. Volume Two picks up with the epic campaign in Normandy, where Wittmann achieved his greatest successes before being killed in action. The Leibstandarte went on to fight at the Battle of the Bulge and in Austria and Hungary before surrendering in May 1945.

*Volume One: $19.95 • Paperback • 6 x 9 • 432 pages
383 photos • 19 maps • 10 charts
Volume Two: $19.95 • Paperback • 6 x 9 • 400 pages
287 photos • 15 maps • 7 charts*

WWW.STACKPOLEBOOKS.COM
1-800-732-3669

Stackpole Military History Series

PANZER ACES
GERMAN TANK COMMANDERS OF WORLD WAR II
Franz Kurowski

With the order "Panzers forward!" German tanks rolled into battle, smashing into the enemy with engines roaring and muzzles flashing. From Poland and the Eastern Front to the Ardennes, Italy, and northern Africa, panzers stunned their opponents—and the world—with their lightning speed and raw power, and the soldiers, like Michael, who manned these lethal machines were among the boldest and most feared of World War II.

$21.95 • Paperback • 6 x 9 • 480 pages • 60 b/w photos

WWW.STACKPOLEBOOKS.COM
1-800-732-3669

Stackpole Military History Series

INFANTRY ACES
THE GERMAN SOLDIER IN COMBAT IN WORLD WAR II
Franz Kurowski

This is an authentic account of German infantry aces—one paratrooper, two members of the Waffen-SS, and five Wehrmacht soldiers—who were thrust into the maelstrom of death and destruction that was World War II. Enduring countless horrors on the icy Eastern Front, in the deserts of Africa, and on other bloody fields, these rank-and-file soldiers took on enemy units alone, battled giant tanks, stormed hills, and rescued wounded comrades.

$19.95 • Paperback • 6 x 9 • 512 pages
43 b/w photos, 11 maps

WWW.STACKPOLEBOOKS.COM
1-800-732-3669

Stackpole Military History Series

GRENADIERS
THE STORY OF WAFFEN SS GENERAL KURT "PANZER" MEYER

Kurt Meyer

Known for his bold and aggressive leadership, Kurt Meyer was one of the most highly decorated German soldiers of World War II. As commander of various units, from a motorcycle company to the Hitler Youth Panzer Division, he saw intense combat across Europe, from the invasion of Poland in 1939 to the 1944 campaign for Normandy, where he fell into Allied hands and was charged with war crimes.

$21.95 • Paperback • 6 x 9 • 448 pages • 93 b/w photos

WWW.STACKPOLEBOOKS.COM
1-800-732-3669

Stackpole Military History Series

KURSK
HITLER'S GAMBLE
Walter S. Dunn, Jr.

During the summer of 1943, Germany unleashed its last major offensive on the Eastern Front and sparked the epic battle of Kursk, which included the largest tank engagement in history. Marked by fiery clashes between German Tigers and Soviet T-34s in the mud and dust of western Russia, the campaign began well enough for the Germans, but the Soviets counterattacked and eventually forced Hitler to end the operation. When it was over, thousands lay dead or wounded on both sides, but the victorious Red Army had turned the tide of World War II in the East.

$16.95 • Paperback • 6 x 9 • 240 pages • 9 photos, 1 map

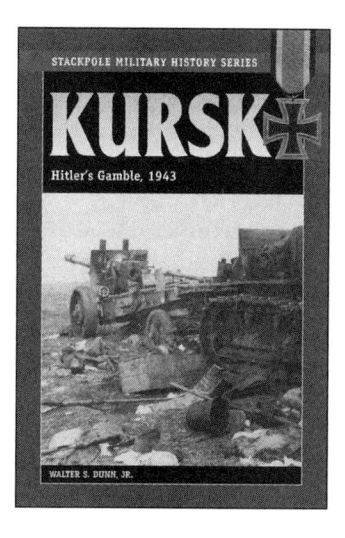

WWW.STACKPOLEBOOKS.COM
1-800-732-3669

Stackpole Military History Series

T-34 IN ACTION
SOVIET TANK TROOPS IN WORLD WAR II
Artem Drabkin and Oleg Sheremet

Regarded by many as the best tank of World War II, the Soviet T-34 was fast, well-armored, and heavily gunned—more than a match for the German panzers. From Moscow to Kiev, Leningrad to Stalingrad, Kursk to Berlin, T-34s rumbled through the dust, mud, and snow of the Eastern Front and propelled the Red Army to victory. These firsthand accounts from Soviet tankmen evoke the harrowing conditions they faced: the dirt and grime of battlefield life, the claustrophobia inside a tank, the thick smoke and deafening blasts of combat, and the bloody aftermath.

$16.95 • Paperback • 6 x 9 • 208 pages • 40 photos, 5 maps

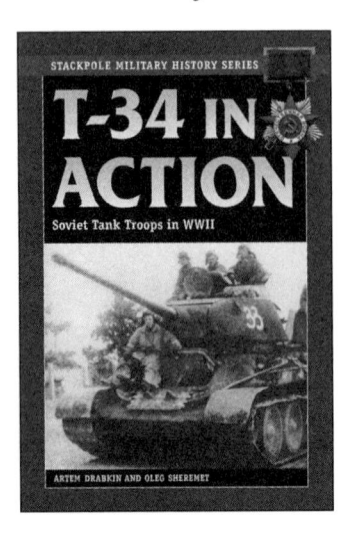

WWW.STACKPOLEBOOKS.COM
1-800-732-3669

Stackpole Military History Series

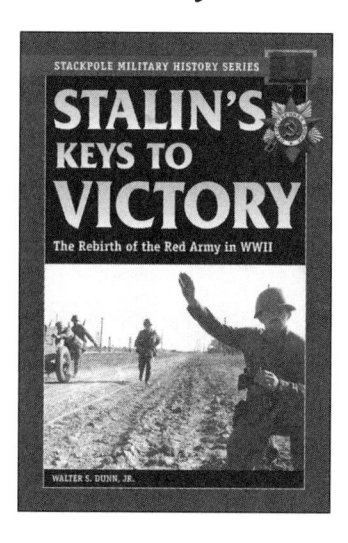

STALIN'S KEYS TO VICTORY
THE REBIRTH OF THE RED ARMY IN WWII
Walter S. Dunn, Jr.

When Hitler invaded the Soviet Union in June 1941, the German Army annihilated a substantial part of the Red Army. Yet the Soviets rebounded to successfully defend Moscow in late 1941, defeat the Germans at Stalingrad in 1942 and Kursk in 1943, and deliver the deathblow in Belarus in 1944. Eastern Front expert Walter Dunn examines these four pivotal battles and explains how the Red Army lost a third of its prewar strength, regrouped, and beat one of the most highly trained and experienced armies in the world.

$16.95 • Paperback • 6 x 9 • 208 pages • 12 photos

WWW.STACKPOLEBOOKS.COM
1-800-732-3669

Also available from Stackpole Books

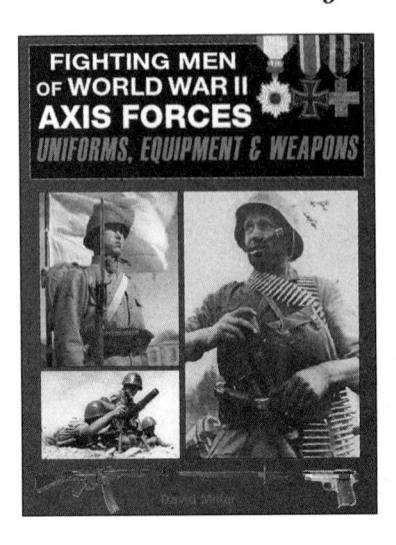

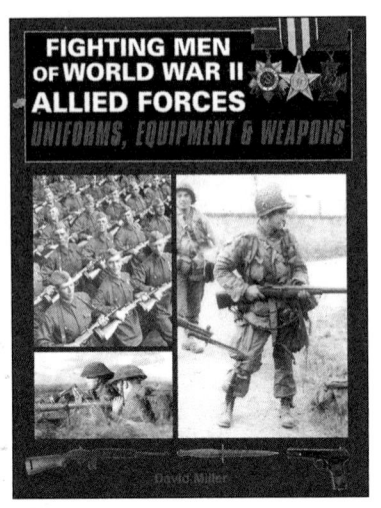

FIGHTING MEN OF WORLD WAR II
VOLUME 1: AXIS FORCES
VOLUME 2: ALLIED FORCES
David Miller

These comprehensive volumes present a full-color look at Axis and Allied soldiers in World War II, covering their weapons, equipment, clothing, rations, and more. The Axis volume includes Germany, Italy, and Japan while the Allied volume presents troops from the United States, Great Britain, and the Soviet Union. These books create a vivid picture of the daily life and battle conditions of the fighting men of the Second World War.

$49.95 • Hardcover • 9 x 12 • 384 pages • 600 color illustrations

WWW.STACKPOLEBOOKS.COM
1-800-732-3669